OUR MAGNIFICENT EARTH

OUR MAGNIFICENT EARTH

A Rand McNally
Atlas of Earth Resources

Rand McNally & Company
New York   Chicago   San Francisco
in association with Mitchell Beazley Publishers Limited, London

MITCHELL BEAZLEY PUBLISHERS LTD

Executive Editor/Art Editor Pat Gilliland
Associate Editor Frank Wallis
Assistant Editor Judy Garlick
Assistant Art Editor Mike Brown
Picture Researcher Elizabeth Ogilvie
Sub-Editors Maria Mosby
 Paulette Pratt
Researchers Lesley Ellis
 Ken Hewis
 Pam Taaffe
 Barbara Westmore
Political/Economic Advisor Arthur Kilgore
Cartographic designer George Glaze
Designers Pauline Faulks
 Ayala Kingsley
 Michelle Stamp
Editorial Assistant Atalanta Grant-Suttie
Production Controller Barry Baker

Editorial Advisor Brian Haynes

CONSULTANTS

GENERAL CONSULTANT Professor Michael Wise, MC, BA, PhD, D.Univ, Professor of Geography, London School of Economics and Political Science.

POPULATION The late **Professor David Glass,** FRS, Emeritus Professor of Sociology, London School of Economics and Political Science, and **Bernard Stonehouse,** DPhil, MA, BSc, Chairman, Post-Graduate School of Environmental Science, University of Bradford.

ENERGY Sir Peter Kent, FRS, formerly Chairman of the Natural Environment Research Council.

MINERALS Sir Kingsley Dunham, FRS, lately Director of the Institute of Geological Sciences.

AGRICULTURE Professor C. R. W. Spedding, DSc, FIBiol, Professor of Agricultural Systems and Head of the Department of Agriculture and Horticulture, University of Reading.

CONTRIBUTORS to *Our Magnificent Earth* include: **Professor Robert Z. Aliber,** Professor of International Economics and Finance, Graduate School of Business, University of Chicago; **A. Archer,** Head, Minerals Strategy and Museum Division, Geological Museum; **H. Christopher H. Armstead,** BSc, CEng, FICE, FIMechE, FIEE, ACGI; **C. G. Askew,** BSc, MSc(Soton), PhD (CNAA); **Anthony Baker,** Head of Economic Assessment Service, IEA Coal Research; **Professor Peter Beaumont,** BA, PhD, Department of Geography, Saint David's University College, University of Wales; **David Betts,** Department of Agriculture and Horticulture, University of Reading; **A. Blair Rains,** Principal Scientific Officer, Land Resources Development Centre, Overseas Development Ministry; **Dr Gerald Blake,** University of Durham; **John R. Blunden,** BA(SocSc), PhD, FRGS, Open University; **Dr Christopher Board,** London School of Economics and Political Science; **Professor John C. Bowman,** FIBiol, University of Reading; **C. N. Brown,** Science Museum; **R. A. Buchanan,** MA, PhD, University of Bath; **C. M. Buckley,** BSc(Econ), MA, Fellow of the Science Policy Research Unit, University of Sussex; **F. W. Carter,** MA, DNatSci, Joint Hayter Lecturer on the Geography of Eastern Europe, School of Slavonic and East European Studies and University College, University of London; **Czech Conroy,** BA(Hons), University of London; **Raymond Day,** BSc, PhD, Fellow of the Science Policy Research Unit, University of Sussex; **Professor A. N. Duckham,** Emeritus Professor, University of Reading; **M. R. Dunn,** BSc(Econ)(Soton), MInstR; **B. H. Farmer,** Fellow of St. John's College, Cambridge, Reader in South Asian Geography and Director of the Centre of South Asian Studies, University of

Cambridge; **Gerald Foley,** Director of the Energy Programme, Architectural Association Graduate School, London, Fellow of the International Institute for Environment and Development; **R. A. French,** MA, PhD, Senior Lecturer in the Geography of the USSR, University College London and School of Slavonic and East European Studies; **J. A. Gartner,** BAgriSci, University of Reading; **Dr John Gribbin,** Science Policy Research Unit, University of Sussex; **Angela M. Hoxey,** NDD, University of Reading; **Dr Robert J. Hyde,** Institute of Science and Technology, University of Wales; **D. C. Ion,** Energy Resources Consultant; **Brian Johnson,** MA, MIA, Senior Fellow, International Institute for Environment and Development; **Frank Leeming,** Senior Lecturer in Geography, University of Leeds; **Colin M. Lewis,** BASS, PhD, Lecturer in Latin American Economic History, London School of Economics and Political Science and Institute of Latin American Studies, University of London; **David F. MacInnes,** BSc, Dipl. Reg. Planning Research Fellow, Centre for Human Ecology, University of Edinburgh, UK Director, Firbank Fell, a Center for the Study of Alternative Societies, Meadowbrook, Pa, USA; **Andrew MacKillop,** BSc(London), Senior Lecturer, Hull School of Architecture; **J. D. McGee,** OBE, ScD, FRS, Emeritus Professor of Applied Physics, Imperial College, University of London; **Ian Miles,** Research Fellow of the Science Policy Research Unit, University of Sussex; **Professor J. D. B. Miller,** Australian National University, Canberra, Australia; **Dr R. M. Morris,** Senior Lecturer in Systems, Open University; **William Page,** Science Policy Research Unit, University of Sussex; **Professor J. H. Paterson,** Professor of Geography, University of Leicester; **Lynnette J. Peel,** MAgrSc, PhD, University of Reading; **S. Pizzey,** Science Museum; **R. S. V. Pullin,** BSc, PhD, ARCS, MIBiol, University of Liverpool; **Dr Judith A. Rees,** BSc(Econ), MPhil, Lecturer in Geography, London School of Economics; **Professor L. Roche,** MA, MF, PhD, University of North Wales; **John Rowley,** Editor of *People,* the International Planned Parenthood Federation journal; **Howard Rush,** Science Policy Research Unit, University of Sussex; **John Sargent,** BA, Reader in Geography, School of Oriental and African Studies, University of London; **John Stopford,** Professor of International Business, London Business School; **Roger S. Tayler,** BSc, NDA, Senior Lecturer in Crop Production, University of Reading; **Ruth B. Weiss,** BSc, NDD, University of Reading; **Michael West,** ARSM, BSc, FIMM, Editorial Director, Mining Journal Ltd., London; **Tom Williamson,** BA, MSc, Science Museum; **Andrew Wilson,** Mining Editor, *The Daily Telegraph,* London; **J. T. Worgan,** MSc, PhD, National College of Food Technology, University of Reading.

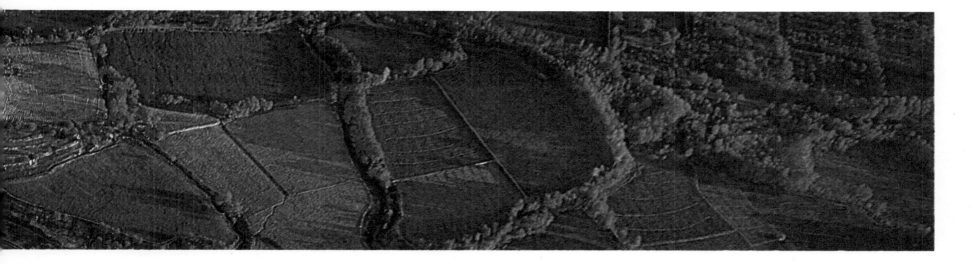

CONTENTS

FOREWORD

It is striking to reflect that although Man has inhabited the planet now for a million years or more, it is only in our own era that we have at last begun to have at hand detailed and comprehensive data about the global interrelationships that affect our lives.

This present volume suggests both the range and complexity of such considerations.

There is today a growing and welcome awareness of such worldwide phenomena as the precariousness of nature's balance; the implications of resource depletion; the penalties of environmental neglect; and most important of all, the human degradation of absolute poverty.

Though poverty is in itself an ancient affliction, it has become an intolerable injustice and an unacceptable anachronism in an age of technological sophistication and affluence in which the strictly technical and economic means are available to reduce it, and ultimately to end it.

It is evident that throughout the world today there is a growing desire for a greater degree of equity—for a more just and reasonable equality of opportunity among individuals, both within nations and between nations. This is becoming a major concern of our time.

It is a trend that has gradually been gathering momentum. The rise of the labor union movement, the drive against racial discrimination, the expansion of civil rights, the enhancement of the status of women—these and similar movements have all had one ingredient in common: the surge toward greater social justice and more equitable economic opportunity.

This broad thrust is growing more insistent nearly everywhere today. There is an accelerated search for new solutions to the increasingly unacceptable problems of poverty.

We speak glibly of "the poor" in the developing countries, but it is difficult for those of us in the developed world to begin to grasp what that really means.

"Absolute poverty"—which is what some 800 million individuals are suffering from in these countries—is life at the very margin of physical existence.

Malnutrition saps their energy, stunts their bodies, and shortens their lives. Illiteracy darkens their minds, and forecloses their futures. Preventable diseases maim and kill their children. Squalor and ugliness pollute and poison their surroundings.

The gift of life itself, and all its intrinsic potential—so promising and rewarding for us in the affluent world—is eroded and reduced for them to a desperate effort to survive.

Compared to those of us who by an accident of birth enjoy life in a developed nation, individuals in the poorest countries have an infant mortality rate eight times higher; a life expectancy rate one-third lower; an adult literacy rate 60 percent less; a nutritional level, for one out of every two in the population, below the minimum acceptable standards; and for millions of infants, less protein than is sufficient to permit the optimum development of the brain.

Now, what can be done to reduce this level of poverty?

The responsibility for such an effort lies first, of course, with the governments of the developing countries themselves. By and large they are making that effort—on the whole far more so than most people in the developed world realize.

Over the past decade the developing nations have financed 80 to 85 percent of their development investments out of their own limited incomes. But it is true that they must make even greater efforts. They have invested too little in population planning, too little in agriculture, and too little in essential public services. And too much of what they have invested has benefited only a privileged few.

Yet whatever the degree of neglect the governments in the poorest countries may have been responsible for, it has been more than matched by the failure of the international community to assist them adequately in the development task.

As this volume makes evident, individuals are not poor because the planet's endowment of natural and human resources is too meager. Individuals are poor because they lack the opportunity to fully utilize those resources, and share more fully in their benefits.

One thing is certain. Absolute poverty can never be eliminated simply by traditional welfare. The reason is obvious: no feasible redistribution of already inadequate national income in a developing society is, by itself, going to be enough to end poverty. There must be growth in that income, and the poor must be enabled both to contribute more to that growth and to participate more equitably in its results.

The tragedy of the absolute poor in most developing societies is that they remain largely outside the development effort. Such economic progress as there is often simply passes them by.

The only feasible hope, then, of reducing poverty is to assist the poor to become more productive, and to bring them more fully into the development process. Each developing society must formulate specific antipoverty objectives at national, regional and local levels; prepare operational programs to attain those objectives over a reasonable time; and determine the level of resources required to meet the minimum goals.

Such programs will, of course, cut across many entrenched interests in the developing countries, and will require sustained political courage to implement. And if such actions are to succeed, the developed nations, and the international community, must exercise comparable political courage in commiting generous assistance to support them.

The experience of the World Bank over the last few years demonstrates that all of this can work. The progress of its projects, designed specifically to enhance the productivity of the poor, is extremely encouraging.

The demonstrable fact is that the overall development effort—with its twin objectives of accelerating economic growth, and reducing absolute poverty—is of critical significance.

The character of international life in the 21st century will inevitably be shaped by the outcome of that effort.

Robert S. McNamara
President of the World Bank

WHAT IS A RESOURCE?

A dictionary defines the term "resource," as "a means of aid or support," implying anything that lends support to life or activity. But it is not enough, in this context, to think only in terms of human life, since plants, animals and fish also depend on a constant supply of resources to answer their physical needs. All life as we know it, whether in plant or animal form, can only be sustained by the consumption of natural resources, and of these the most essential is an extraterrestrial one: the Sun. Without the Sun, which is the principal source of energy for all living matter, man would not be on Earth. Nor is it enough to think of resources purely in terms of life support, for the richness and diversity of the Earth's substance can be harnessed to all human activity—from crude survival to the creation of great works of art. What separates man from other species is that he can choose what resources he makes use of, and in what quantities.

Uneven distribution

The problem is that the distribution of these resources (and so potentially their value) is wildly uneven across the globe. Some regions are richly endowed; others—the North Polar ice cover, for example—while having a part to play in the Earth's climatic system, lack anything remotely usable. There is no natural law of compensation, no guarantee that territory barren of soil will be rich in minerals, or that a hot region will have enough moisture to sustain plant life. Variations of latitude and the interrelationship of land and sea strongly influence the supply of basic resources of sunlight and moisture, while the distribution of minerals is the outcome of events far distant in geological time. The quantity of soil may depend on the nature of the underlying rocks, on past geological events, on climatic regimes, on the vegetation cover, or even on the ways in which men and their animals have used (or all too frequently abused) the land. Moreover this scenario is not a static one, fixed for all time. Climates change; ice caps advance and retreat; volcanic activity and earthquakes indicate immense subterranean forces at work; rivers and winds erode and deposit soil. But in terms of the human life span most of these changes are slow, barely perceptible and difficult to evaluate. Also, man's capacity to modify these natural conditions is strictly limited. We can, of course, create artificial microclimates by constructing greenhouses and centrally heated buildings; we can seed clouds to provide rain where it would not normally fall; we can move soil from one field to another; and (probably the single most important modification to natural conditions) we can sometimes irrigate land which would otherwise remain parched. But we cannot fundamentally change the climate or create mineral deposits where they do not exist.

Man is continually surveying and assessing the natural scene with an eye to his own needs, and a particular feature of the environment only becomes a resource when a use can be found for it. It is in the needs or capabilities of men which endow resources with their utility, and the history of their exploitation is in effect a continuing story of discovery, right from the use of the first primitive tools—made of hard, brittle rock such as flint or obsidian—to the present-day applications of the laser beam. Fire was an important discovery leading to the controlled use of heat energy from wood, fossil fuels and now from nuclear fission. More decisive still was the emergence of settled patterns of agriculture

12–13 Discovery of resources
14–15 Keeping track
16–17 Awareness of crisis
20–1 Sun and Earth
26–7 Mapping the living resource
94–5 Climate and man
102–3 Forests at risk
144–5 The substance of Earth
166–7 Conservation
172–3 Energy—the long term
174–5 Energy—non-nuclear options
178–9 Food—defining the problems
180–1 Are green revolutions the answer?
182–3 Minerals—are we running out?
184–5 Minerals—assessing future supplies
CONNECTIONS

—the domestication of animals and tilling of the land—which were eventually to result in the control of biological processes almost everywhere on land, and to no small intervention in the biology of the seas and oceans. From the beginning it has been the application of human intelligence, curiosity, skills and inventiveness which has brought into service previously unused materials or physical circumstances. There have been cultural considerations, too. Different societies and civilizations have developed in distinctive ways, and this means that, rather than moving in a way which has been universally consistent, the recognition and harnessing of resources have taken the form of a series of cultural appraisals. Certainly not every society has made the same kind or degree of technical progress. There have been times of no progress, even of regression. Since man first stood upright, he has in turn made much or little of his environment. His response to its riches has been bewilderingly erratic.

Today, natural or Earth resources can be bracketed into two categories: biological resources, which are the various organisms and levels of plant and animal life which sustain human beings; and physical resources, which are the inorganic materials present at or near the surface of the Earth. These two types of natural resource form a cover of variable thickness and quality across the world. Admittedly there are a few places where this cover is nonexistent, but generally there is something everywhere, even in the deserts and oceans, which is (or could be) a resource.

A second familiar classification of Earth resources is into the two categories *renewable* and *nonrenewable*. The difference between the two is essentially that of the time scales over which they develop. A grass or fodder crop, for instance, can often be cut several times a year, but it is still replenished year by year. However, a resource which has taken millions of years to form—and this applies to all minerals, including coal and oil—is, from the practical standpoint, nonrenewable. Here there is an important distinction to be made between the fossil fuels on the one hand and the metallic ores, nonmetallics and radioactive minerals on the other. When coal, oil or gas are burnt, combustion converts the hydrocarbon and other content into water, carbon dioxide and ash, and these cannot be reconverted into fuel. With the fossil fuels we are living on the capital of 325 million years of geological history. Once used, they are utterly destroyed. However, other concentrations of useful elements—though often recombined, or purified as metals—can be partially recovered by recycling, and their products are regarded as part of the overall resource. This is the case with iron, most nonferrous and all precious metals. Nevertheless, once a particular mineral deposit is exhausted, we cannot wait for it to regenerate; we can only seek a replacement.

Midway between the two extremes of renewable and nonrenewable resources are some environmental features which are capable of replenishment over a reasonable time span. Those currently receiving most attention include soils, forests and fish stocks. Each of these have differing life cycles: that of a coniferous forest is shorter than that of an oak wood; soil formation is more rapid in warm climates than in cold. But a resource remains renewable only so long as its regenerative period is taken into account. Otherwise it is lost—the fish disappear, the forest degenerates into useless scrub. Fortunately, the biological resources—plant and animal life—are for the most part fully renewable.

The need for reappraisal

Before World War II there had been very little thought of coal, oil, gas and mineral supplies ever being exhausted, but raised levels of demand during the war years sowed the first seeds of concern. Today there is a greater than ever concern with the need for reappraisal. We can think first in terms of the total *stock* of resources—the sum of all the material components of the environment, including both mass and energy, physical and biological substances. Yet the vast proportion of the Earth's total stock is of little relevance to human life at the present time. Much of it is no use; much remains inaccessible. A further complication is the fact that resource values may not remain constant: what is valuable today may, as technology advances, be worthless tomorrow.

What is important to economic life, and for planning in relation to key industries, is an estimate of *reserves*, which may be defined as those parts of the usable constituents of the total stock which we know with reasonable accuracy. In the case of food, reserves are those quantities of the stock already grown, harvested and in store. A prime example of the value of food reserves was the grain sold by the USA to the Soviet Union in the early 1970s to offset disastrous crop failures. This had been stored in grain elevators for as much as 20 years. The energy reserves provided by hydroelectric development (actual and potential) are equally capable of precise estimation, as will be those generated by solar, wave and tidal sources if these are ever successfully harnessed on a large scale. But reserves of fossil fuels, of radioactive and nonfuel minerals can only be accurately known where they have been opened up in mines or penetrated by boreholes. Here, then, reserves are defined as masses of solid fossil fuels, reservoirs of petroleum or concentrations of useful minerals whose extent and grade are known and whose nature is such that they can be extracted within certain economic limits.

Estimation of reserves

Reserves are categorized in a manner to indicate the level of confidence with which the estimate has been made. *Proven* reserves include those in bedded formations such as coal, dolomite, anhydrite, gypsum, brick clay and many others, where sufficient boring has been done to indicate fully the variations in overburden or roof conditions, the depth, thickness, grade, inclination and substrata. In the case of petroleum, proven reserves are those where the size, shape, permeability and depth have been defined by boring and there has been adequate testing as to quality. With steep mineral veins, underground drives linked by rises are required to define the ore bodies. The commoner, more irregular ore deposits are usually defined as to extent and grade by a network of boreholes, often on a grid, or by drilling from underground tunnels. Where exploratory work is less complete, mineral reserves are described as being *probable* or *possible*. It is standard practice in the mining and petroleum industries to keep reserves equivalent in tonnage to 10 to 15 years' production at current rates. This is often the period, or lead time, needed to bring a new deposit into production. Where development of a particular deposit fails to reveal reserves of this order, its end is probably already in sight. Consequently the fact that the total proven reserves of many fuel and mineral deposits have increased substantially during the past 20 years merely reflects increased production resulting from rising demand. It is not an indication that the total resource is increasing. On the contrary, fossil fuel and mineral deposits are being exhausted at an ever-increasing rate. However, there is some reassurance to be had from the fact that the work of proving up reserves generally reveals deposits which may be quite sizable but which cannot be worked economically at present-day prices. These are categorized as *subeconomic* resources, to be borne in mind for the future, when, given changed economic conditions, they may well become workable. The term *identified*, or *indicated*, resources represents known reserves as well as subeconomic resources.

Much more difficult to quantify are two further categories of resources: *speculative* and *hypothetical*. A cautious figure can be ascribed to speculative resources—those which can reasonably be expected in areas where deposits have already been proved. When the Romans began to work lead veins in North Yorkshire, England, they might well have concluded that similar rocks were widely exposed in the Pennines, and indeed later generations of miners uncovered at least 500 more deposits over a wide area of similar geology. Also geological mapping shows areas of promise where no workable deposits have yet been found, and these are known as hypothetical resources. However, it has to be said that, with many minerals, estimation of speculative and hypothetical resources is a complex business and it is difficult to arrive at reliable figures.

Earth resources, therefore, include the sum of vegetable matter already grown, harvested and put away in store (plus future generations of plant and animal life still to be reared or grown), along with proven resources of fuels and minerals in the ground and deposits still to be discovered in the future—hopefully in quantities far exceeding today's actual or estimated reserves. Above ground, it is perhaps too easy to forget that landscape, together with the remnants of ancient civilizations, the landmarks of recorded history and great works of art, are in themselves resources of a kind. What is not yet known is the extent to which human skill and ingenuity can enlarge the total stock, creating new resources from features of the environment which we are at present unable to exploit.

OUR MAGNIFICENT EARTH

This book has been planned and organized on the basis of self-contained, two-page spreads. However, a reading of the general introductory sections of the book as well as the introductory spreads in each individual section is recommended because of the distinctly interdisciplinary nature of the subject matter. By the same token, "connections" boxes on each spread suggest complementary reading to be found in other parts of the book.

A glossary (pp. 192–4) explains economic, scientific and political terms used throughout the book.

A bibliography (p. 205) recommends further reading on each subject and does not necessarily include works used by the authors in the presentation of their material.

The terms "developed," "developing" and "centrally planned," as used by the United Nations to describe national economies, have been followed throughout this work. This has influenced the arrangement of some material, particularly in The Living Resource section (pp. 90–141), where it has meant a necessarily close discussion of the geographically disparate developed market economies of Israel, Japan and South Africa. Where the book divides the world into two camps, the centrally planned economies of Europe and the USSR have been classified as "developed" and those of Asia associated with the "developing" or "less-developed" nations. Cambodia is referred to as Kampuchea, the name the country adopted in 1976.

Statistical material used in *Our Magnificent Continent* has been drawn wherever possible from the latest available compilations issued by the United Nations and similarly reputable international bodies. These works include the *UN Statistical Yearbook*, *the UN Demographic Yearbook*, the *FAO Production Yearbook*, the *International Monetary Fund Directory of Trade Statistics*, the *UNCTAD Handbook of International Trade and Development Statistics* and the *World Bank Atlas*.

Metric units such as the kilometer have been used throughout and converted to Imperial units in most cases. In the case of crop yields, however, where it has not always proved possible to provide such conversions, the following factors should be used in order to translate differing Imperial bushels to their metric equivalents:

wheat:	27.2 kilograms (60 pounds)
soybeans:	27.2 kilograms (60 pounds)
oats:	15.4 kilograms (34 pounds)
barley:	21.8 kilograms (48 pounds)
corn:	25.4 kilograms (56 pounds).

Throughout the book, a billion refers to a thousand million, that is 10^9, or 1,000,000,000, and a trillion to a million million, that is 10^{12} or 1,000,000,000,000. Units of energy are defined and converted on the spread entitled *What is Energy?* (pp. 58–59).

RICHES OF THE EARTH

The discovery and exploitation of Earth resources is closely bound up with the evolution of man himself. As human skills and technology have developed, so, too, has come growing recognition of (and capitalization upon) the great riches of the Earth. But it is impossible to make a single evaluation of these vast natural resources that holds true for all periods of history and for all parts of the world. Some materials, valued in the past, have been discarded and have lost their merit: flint, once precious, is now of largely archaeological interest: the chemical industry no longer relies on seaweed as a basic raw material; we no longer do battle over a cargo of spices. In our time, resources such as coal, oil, rubber, uranium and the various non-ferrous metals are essential, and the size of known reserves of many of these is a matter of some concern. Still other materials are only now beginning to acquire value as science and technology advance. There is a need, however, to establish how the Earth's resources can be used more effectively to benefit the whole of mankind, to determine to what extent constraints on the use of natural resources are scientific and technical (rather than political or economic) and to insure that the exploitation of natural resources throughout the world goes ahead without damage to the environment.

A range of resources

When considering the distribution and deployment of resources, what has to be borne in mind is the fact that the Earth is far from being the flat and uniform plain assumed in many economic models. It is characterized by highly diverse conditions, ranging from the uninhabitable ice cap of Antarctica to the humid tropical forests of western Africa and Amazonia. Oceans and enclosed seas occupy no less than 71 percent of the Earth's surface, and the distribution of the land as such is very uneven, with most of it lying in the Northern Hemisphere. In some areas, such as western Europe, natural conditions—climate, soil and vegetation—allow us to raise livestock and to grow a wide range of temperate foodstuffs, whereas the deserts of Africa and Asia imply far stricter limits on the use we make of the land.

But it is not just a question of physical considerations, for the use made of the environment depends also upon the traditions, culture, social organization, dietary habits and technical skills of the user society. In some parts of the world life styles are closely allied to the environment, as in southeastern Asia, where the rhythm of agricultural life is governed by the monsoon. In other areas environmental controls are less evident. In Europe and much of North America the environment has been transformed by human intervention and apparently natural landscapes are in fact contrived. Through his engineering man can reverse the flow of major rivers to create new habitable zones, or reclaim land below sea level to provide rich agricultural land as the Dutch have done. He has, too, great ability to pluck riches from seemingly unpromising sites—by substituting introduced grass for the original tussock, as in New Zealand, or by damming streams to afford vast irrigated areas such as the Nile valley.

Unfortunately, though, in commanding the Earth's riches man has often taken the shortsighted view. He is not only a creator and inventor but also a destroyer. The use of resources with short-run needs in mind has led to disastrous problems—the 1930s dust bowl in the USA, for instance, or the soil erosion which followed overgrazing on the ridges of Mediterranean lands. A distinction is sometimes made between true agriculture, in which man plays a constructive role in conserving or even improving upon the basic assets of nature, and spurious agriculture, which destroys soil and seriously pollutes the environment. In many industrial regions we are at present reclaiming land laid waste during the Industrial Revolution, but the problem of present-day industrial pollution of rivers, lakes and (in some cases) seas still begs solution.

In evaluating the riches of the Earth it is important to resist the tendency to think only of tangible substances, things like coal, oil, copper, textile fibers or rubber, which we actually use. Equally vital are the abstract factors—knowledge, skill, sane policies, social harmony—the human factors which mediate the quality of resource utilization. It is important, too, to remember that the pattern of supply and demand is an intricate one, and it is therefore often more useful to think in terms of a complex of competing resources. In the case of fuel and energy sources, for example, there are wood, coal, oil, natural gas, waterpower, geothermal energy and nuclear fission (not to mention the possible development of solar and tidal power and other energy sources). A change in the availability of one, due to price fluctuation or government policy, affects the value of and demand for all the other energy sources.

The question of how the Earth's riches are controlled—and it is a topical one given the widening gap between rich and poor countries—leads on to the wider issue of the relationship between the possession of natural resources and the state of economic development. Historical accounts of the industrialization of Western Europe and the United States illustrate the ways in which the application of capital and of new techniques to the extraction and processing of coal, iron and nonferrous metals (coupled with the arrival of new forms of transport) accelerated the development of the great urban-industrial complexes of the Western world. As these cities grew and prospered, their furnaces, forges and factories drew in more and more raw materials from the less-developed countries of Asia, Africa and South America—regions which, in turn, became markets for manufactured goods. Important influences have also been wielded by the multinational companies which produce and distribute commodities such as oil and nonferrous metals. However, in recent years the power of resource-producing nations has been seen to increase as many have banded together to fight for better prices and terms of trade. Most conspicuous has been the effect on the developed economies of the 1973/74 oil price rises forced through by OPEC.

It was increasing pressure from developing countries, especially those supplying raw materials to industrialized countries, which led to the UN lending its voice to the cries from less-developed nations for a new economic order: the Lima Declaration of 1975 proposed that the developing nations' share of world industrial production should increase from seven percent "to the maximum possible extent," and to at least 25 percent by the turn of the century. The intention here is a substantially higher degree of utilization of the resources and know-how of the developed world and the curtailment of a situation in which the interests of raw material-producing nations are regarded as subservient to those of manufacturing countries. The Lima Declaration implies that the problems of resource development are not simply technical in character, nor even economic, but that they also raise key moral questions regarding the rights of nations to the riches of the Earth and to a more equal share in the accruing benefits.

Man's use of resources

An examination of some of the ways in which man uses the resources of the Earth must begin with agriculture, one of the oldest of human enterprises and one which is primarily dependent on nature. Agricultural output does not simply involve making use of climate, soil and animal and plant life. The modern farmer works with nature—by selection of strains, scientific breeding and the fertilizing of soils—to achieve the best possible yields. In many parts of the world farming has become highly mechanized, a well-organized industry using, in

combination, resources of capital, skill, energy, technology and science to achieve maximum output of field and tree crops and livestock products. But just as agriculture has come to depend on industry to facilitate the production of food, so, too, have some major manufacturing industries drawn on agricultural produce—vegetable oils, cotton and wool—for their raw materials.

Also relevant to the whole question of land use is the future of forestry, in both its commercial and amenity aspects. Forests are multipurpose resources, yielding lumber for fuel, building and construction work and the pulp and paper industries, besides giving sanctuary to wildlife and serving as valued recreational areas. Sometimes care is taken to reafforest areas where lumber has been harvested and to limit felling to the rate of regeneration. In many parts of the world, however, wholesale deforestation has destroyed the ecological balance, leading to rapid and devastating erosion of soils and to the disappearance of human and animal communities adapted to forest conditions. In exploiting the world's forest resources it is important to remember the long-term cost likely to be incurred by a policy of short-term gains.

While animal and vegetable products remain

essential riches, over the past two centuries our civilization has switched from vegetable- to mineral-based production. This gradual shift from muscle-power to mechanical energy is now largely complete, and the application of the Earth's minerals to a wide range of productive enterprises has made possible the emergence of the vast urban-industrial complexes of the present age. The chain linking cities like Los Angeles, Tokyo or London to nature may be invisible, but it is a very real one nevertheless. Without heat and light, motive power and building materials, these great cities simply could not exist. At the other end of this chain lie the oil wells and coal mines, the iron ore, copper, mercury, tin and bauxite workings and the stone, clay and limestone quarries which have enabled us to build our civilization. It is in fact in this whole area of urban and industrial development that the question of resource-depletion assumes so much relevance.

A new significance

In the past 200 years or so, the mineral resources of the Earth have undergone marked changes in significance—and therefore in value. New ways of using one resource have tended to provoke fresh demands for others. Coal, for example—one re-source at least for which we have very large known reserves—fueled the Industrial Revolution. Nevertheless, the situation changed dramatically earlier this century with the substitution of oil—at first to provide light and heat, then for transport, for the generation of electricity and as a major source of raw materials for industry. The introduction of petrol-based road transport brought greater mobility, stimulated the demand for further materials, gave rise to new industries and changed the form of cities, enabling their spread. Today our universal dependence on oil gives growing cause for concern. True, we do now have the possibility of using energy derived from radioactive materials, but when and at what cost? What possibilities exist for converting the Sun's rays into usable energy on a large scale, for harnessing wave and tidal power, or for releasing sources of heat, as yet inaccessible, in the depths of the Earth? Currently perhaps the biggest dilemma of all, against our measure of the practical possibilities of developing such new resources, is determining the rate at which we should continue to utilize those substances which are finite, limited in their occurrence across the world, and some of which are already known to be nearing exhaustion. The resolution of this dilemma is central to the whole future of civilization. In sum, the riches of the Earth offer great potential. It is up to us to make decisions as to consumption—whether to squander these riches today or make some kind of provision for tomorrow—and as to the kind of society we require. Is it material wealth that we are seeking or freedom from poverty, hunger and disease?

The exploitation and deployment of naturally occurring resources calls for the application of a wide range of skills and expertise. The geographer lays bare for us the variety of natural conditions and of man's use of nature; the geologist comprehends the formation of mineral deposits and plays a key role in the discovery of new sources and the measurement of reserves; the chemist opens up fresh possibilities for the processing and application of new substances (as his predecessors did with coal and oil); the physicist advances our knowledge of nuclear power; the historian provides the record of experience. In effect the study of the conditions and materials found in nature is a study of human life in many of its aspects—its attitudes and beliefs, economies, political institutions and technological progress—for all of these factors have a bearing on the use we make of our environment and the decisions we take regarding its future.

DISCOVERY OF RESOURCES

Historically man's ability to exploit the Earth's vast natural resources—from its mineral wealth to the very atoms of which all matter is composed—has only grown along with his native skill and the development of increasingly sophisticated technology. These Earth resources, the raw materials of progress, have been there all along, but man has had painstakingly to learn how to exploit them, to find out in effect how to make the environment work for him. The discovery of resources is, then, a very ancient process, but it is nonetheless a continuing one, spanning all the way from the first crude stone tool to the complex and often baffling technologies which surround us today. In fact for the first million years or more after the appearance of humanoid beings, there was little to distinguish man from the other higher apes. But as he began to master primitive skills—to shape wood, stone and bone into weapons and other artifacts—man began to emerge as the dominant species. Here was the conscious toolmaker, and it was the development of skills such as these which began to mark him out as a superior being, a resource gatherer able to exploit the natural environment to suit his own ends. True, throughout the many thousands of years of the Paleolithic, or Old Stone Age, the development was very slow, although this period did produce innovations such as the harnessing of fire. Mostly, however, in the Paleolithic Age human beings survived only in small communities, widely dispersed, living at subsistence level and hunting for food.

The first step

It was not until the retreat of the ice cover in the Northern Hemisphere after the last ice age that man took his first great step forward in the discovery of resources. In the years between 10,000 and 5000 BC some Middle Eastern communities began to till the soil and raise their own herds. By increasing food production, these early attempts at agriculture paved the way for population growth and social organization. This transformation of primitive food gatherers into skilled farmers has since been judged significant enough to be known as the Neolithic Revolution. Still most of the tools were of wood or stone (although Neolithic groups pioneered the baking of clay for pottery and various other processes such as fermentation), but now there was a movement to exploit natural resources in place of the former random dependence on whatever was at hand from day to day.

As Neolithic communities grew in size, opportunities for specialization increased and some craftsmen, experimenting with new materials, began to acquire the skills of metalworking. It was the combination of community size, superior social organization, the emergence of specialist craftsmen and the introduction of a metal-based technology which marked the appearance of the first definitive civilizations in Sumeria, Egypt and China. Clearly, too, these same factors forged the transition from the Stone Ages to the ages of metal.

The first metals to be worked successfully were those which were soft and visually attractive, especially copper and gold. By the second millennium BC the discovery of bronze had yielded a metal serviceable for weapons and tools as well as for currency and ornamentation; and the succeeding millennium saw the dawn of the Iron Age once workmen had learned to use high temperatures to reduce the common oxides of iron to metallic iron. Other metals such as silver, mercury and lead were increasingly exploited as craftsmen turned their attention to a widening range of raw materials.

Growth of specialization

In its turn, the emergence of a metal technology —made possible by population growth leading to specialization of labor—generated further specialization in a number of fields. For example, there arose a demand for raw materials which could only be satisfied by the establishment of complex trading

For more than a million years man's impact upon the natural environment was virtually negligible. Little different from the other higher apes, he survived in nature as the animals did—seeking shelter from the elements and foraging for food from day to day. As yet unsullied, the primeval treescape must have appeared much as the few remaining pockets of virgin forest—the remote territory above is in northern Canada—which have survived to modern times.

Just as, in the wake of the retreating ice, Neolithic man hacked down the primeval forest to make way for crops, so today land clearance continues in the less-developed countries like Ethiopia (above) to extend the croplands vital for food. Labor is a basic attribute employed by man to shape the environment to his needs.

Skill, represented here by a boy shaping earthenware pots in Afghanistan, is another attribute which has assisted man in his role as a resource gatherer. It is human skill in all its diverse forms (dating back to the creation of the first crude tools) which has made possible the discovery and exploitation of resources.

arrangements. In particular the quest for sources of tin ores in the Bronze Age prompted the growth of elaborate mercantile communities, with a network of trade routes springing up all over the known world of the Middle East and Mediterranean.

This resource-based expansion (closely followed by an enhanced degree of social and political organization) reached its peak in the Roman Empire. In the utilization of natural resources this great civilization embodied, and was to some extent synonymous with, the highest achievements of man. Systematic agriculture was practiced throughout the Empire; building (in stone, brick and cement) reached a scale and magnificence hitherto unknown in the Ancient World; metals were in widespread use; and progress was made harnessing natural sources of power such as wind and water.

It is all the more extraordinary, therefore, to recall that such advances ground almost to a halt with the disintegration of the Western Roman Empire in the fifth century AD. The slowing-down in the discovery of resources was to last five centuries. (Events in China may be regarded as being too remote at this time to exert much influence on the Western world.) It was not until the rise of a new civilization in Western Europe, about AD 1000, that the wheels of progress began to turn again.

At first the revival was characterized by a return to and improvement upon techniques known to the Ancient World. However, the new Western civilization soon produced some striking innovations in

It is technological knowledge which has enabled the development and harnessing of resources which are perpetual: solar energy, for example, can now be stored, used direct or converted into other energy forms such as electricity; and great power is to be gained from intervening in natural waterways and the hydrological cycle. Irrigation of crops (shown above left, in Kenya) is an example of the contribution of technology to the many

power technology. Lacking the ready supply of captive slave labor, which had been a feature of the early civilizations, eleventh-century engineers began to seek more effective ways of exploiting natural energy sources. First there were improvements to the Roman waterwheel, which became an efficient power unit performing a number of tasks in addition to its original function of grinding corn. The windmill, hitherto unknown in Europe (there had been precedents in China and the Middle East), was introduced in the twelfth century. However, of impending global significance were the

8–9	What is a resource?	60–1	Electricity
10–11	Riches of the Earth	62–3	Coal—formation and use
38–9	Capital as a resource	86–7	Power from wind, waves and tides
44–5	The mathematics of growth	148–9	Iron and steel
50–1	Energy for the millions		

CONNECTIONS

improvements to the sailing ship, which ventured forth as a robust and versatile vessel capable of undertaking long voyages of discovery.

These voyages, pioneered by the great Portuguese navigators of the fifteenth century and continued by Spanish, English, Dutch, French and other Western explorers, were to change the course of history in a number of important ways. First, they established the near-global dominance of Western civilization: with fleets equipped with bronze and cast-iron cannon (cast-iron and gunpowder were both products of medieval technology, although here again there were Chinese precursors), the Western nations were able to impose their will on much of the rest of the world. Second, exploration led to the discovery of many new resource banks, most notably, perhaps, the deposits of gold and other precious metals which beckoned the rape of the New World. Third, the voyages of discovery (and the extensive colonization which followed in their wake) brought a much wider range of resources to Europe's doorstep. The West in fact positively blossomed on the wealth of resources which came with the expansion of mercantile and political power. This was the time of the emergence in Western Europe of a moneyed middle class—merchants who amassed vast private fortunes by shipping in exotic cargoes from the Indies and the East. Progress was being made also in the less obviously spectacular spheres of agricultural and industrial development. Throughout Western Europe, capital was being accumulated and certain manufacturing industries—woollen textiles, iron and the refinement of nonferrous metals—were already going ahead. Gradually the scene was being set for the process of rapid industrialization, which was set in motion in Britain in the eighteenth century and has since spread throughout the world.

The coal and iron technology of the eighteenth and nineteenth centuries relied on the exploitation of the coalfields first of Britain and Western Europe, later of North America. The discovery in 1709 of the method of smelting iron ore using coke instead of charcoal was a key one, and the development of the steam engine for pumping water from mines enabled minerals to be won from greater depths. Indeed the steam engine itself came to symbolize the achievements of the new technology—achievements which included the availability of cheap iron for building and construction, for ships, railways, weapons and household utensils. Raw materials were carried from mine to market along canals and wagonways, both later superseded by railroads. In the second half of the eighteenth century, the introduction of the factory system enabled manufacturers to improve the productivity of capital and labor, to standardize product quality and to install machines driven first by water and later by steam. This machine age became a time of increasing specialization, with the development of localities concentrating production in particular areas such as cotton or woollen textiles, metal products or ship-building. Now came a strong influx from the countryside of men and women drawn to the new industrial centers by the prospect of work.

Clamor for raw materials

The expansion of world mining, output of which rose in value from an estimated US$67 million a year for the first two decades of the nineteenth century to $3 billion a year by 1900, reflected the growing clamor for raw materials. The chemical revolution, for example, not only boosted demand for salt and coal (and later oil) but also yielded processes which made new metals, such as aluminum, available at lower cost. After 1840 agricultural chemists demonstrated the value of fertilizer and, besides potash, phosphorus, nitrogen and lime, sodium nitrate deposits from as far away as Chile and Peru suddenly took on new value. New processes, developed after 1856, yielded cheap steel to replace iron for many applications, and the by-product coke oven was perfected in the 1890s to become the backbone of the coal tar industry. Besides causing a massive rise in demand for copper, commercially generated electricity began to usurp the influence of coal.

The opening of the world's first power plant (at Holborn Viaduct, London, in 1882) marked the transition from a coal and iron economy to an even more technologically dynamic era powered by push-button fuel. In addition to electricity—distributed widely by grid systems from the 1930s onward—the newly industrialized nations soon had cheap, plentiful supplies of oil. In fact the world's first deep oil well (in Pennsylvania, USA) had already gushed forth its contents in 1859—at a time when oil was thought only to be useful for lighting and lubrication. But the invention of the internal combustion engine predetermined the role of oil as the one resource which above all would lubricate the economy of the twentieth century. Today the clamor for "black gold" remains so vociferous that it seems certain that oil will be the first of the fossil fuels to be depleted.

Scientists of today, following in the tradition of men like J. J. Thompson (whose discovery of electrons in 1897 prefaced the development of nuclear power), are providing a new perspective on the nature of resources. The modern quest for new resources is one which lays bare the Earth's crust and the ocean beds, which leads men to seek power from the Sun, wind and tides and which probes the very atoms of life itself. Moreover it is a quest which has been carried beyond our planet, to extraterrestrial sources such as the Moon. The discovery of resources is indeed a limitless enterprise and one which man must always pursue.

Modern education takes many guises: besides academic teaching, there is increasingly, too, a need for practical instruction at a level which will be of assistance to people in gaining a livelihood. Here Kenyan herdsmen are shown ways of feeding cattle to improve yields. Education is perhaps the West's most vital export.

From the invention of the wheel (some time during the Neolithic Age), human inventiveness has proved a vital concomitant to the discovery and application of resources. In a computer age it is salutary to realize that the simplest invention—such as a fish trap rigged up at Stanley Falls in Zaire—may still be best for the job.

uses which can be made of the land. Equally important is the application of technology to the discovery of new potentials: it was not, after all, until the smelting process was developed that metals took on the status of a resource. The same can be said of the role of nuclear physics in transforming uranium into a resource, or of the contribution of the microprocessing industry in making purified chips of silicon (center). Technological

knowledge is a fund to which man is always adding, and improvements may radically alter the significance of a particular resource. Iron, for instance, was for centuries one of the most important materials known to man, but the nineteenth-century discovery of a method of producing cheap, good quality steel (the steel mill seen top right is in Alabama) meant that iron was soon superseded by its alloy.

The interrelationships between various Earth resources are complex ones, often affected by the dynamics of availability, substitution and fresh discovery. The quest for new resources may sometimes be prompted by necessity—by shortages of existing materials. This was the case when supplies of wood for charcoal used in the manufacture of iron grew costly in the seventeenth century: coke, the chosen substitute, assumed what is still its most important role. Sometimes the substitution may only be partial, as with synthetics (such as the rayon fibers shown right) replacing natural fibers. Or the availability of one resource can suffer from the discovery, winning or application of another; the world's dwindling forests are felled to make way for road building (as shown in Brazil, far right) or croplands; agricultural land is taken for quarries; and the air we breathe is polluted by harmful dust and fumes.

KEEPING TRACK

Any estimates of future resource availability must contain assumptions about such key factors as future patterns of demand, investment needed to produce and process the resource, price levels and technological change. Clearly, it is extremely difficult to forecast how these factors will change, and this makes the task of keeping track of our resources extremely problematical.

The changing definition of what constitutes a resource must also be taken into account. Just as technological innovations may give previously unutilized substances value as resources, so demand changes or the development of substitutes may cause others to revert to "neutral" stock.

Even with perfect knowledge about Earth's physical substances, estimates of future resource levels would inevitably be subject to large degrees of error. Knowledge of Earth's total stock of coal, for example, would not in itself enable us to determine the level available as a resource in the future. To assess how much of the coal would have a resource value, we would also need to know the future costs of extracting coal, the total demand for energy and the price of substitute energy forms. It is even conceivable that the development of cheap solar energy or fuel cells could leave coal with no resource value.

A further critical problem arises from our incomplete knowledge of the availability of the various physical substances. Some attempts to estimate the life of resources have been made using "proven reserves"—that proportion of the total stock already discovered and known to be economically extractable under current economic and technological conditions. These assume no new discoveries, no changes in demand or price and no technological change. Given these assumptions, most resources will have a relatively short future life, particularly if it is assumed that the consumption of the resources will remain at current levels or will continue to increase in the future as they have done in the past.

On this basis, it has been estimated that oil reserves would last 31 years at 1970 consumption levels, but would be exhausted in 20 years if demand continued to increase as rapidly as it has in the past. Similar calculations also give relatively short lives for most of our commonly used metals. But it is easy to show how inaccurate this method of estimation can be. To take just one example, in 1950 the United States Bureau of Mines showed that world iron ore reserves would be exhausted by 1970. In 1970, however, enough proven reserves existed to last 240 years at the then current level of use.

Because it is expensive to search for and accurately prove the size of a reserve, mining companies, whether government owned or private, find it uneconomic to spend funds on exploration when they hold enough reserves to last about 15 years. For many resources, proven reserves simply reflect current consumption levels and say little about the potential size of the total resource stock. In fact, there is no evidence that the ratio of proven reserves to annual consumption has been falling. If it is assumed that consumption will continue to grow, on past evidence it should also be assumed that proven reserves will also increase.

Assessment of growth

Some forecasters attempt to add more realism to their estimates by assuming that proven reserves will continue to be developed, either by new discoveries or by technological improvements that will allow a greater yield from existing sources. In the computer model developed at the Massachusetts Institute of Technology in the early 1970s, on which the book *The Limits to Growth* is based, it was assumed that a fivefold increase in reserves would occur. But this means that many resources will still have relatively short lives, if it is also assumed that world consumption will continue to grow exponentially (at an ever-increasing rate) as it has done recently. It must be stressed that this fivefold increase is hypothetical and implicitly assumes that new discoveries and technological change will not act as they have done in the past to increase proven reserves in line with consumption.

For nonrenewable individual resources such as coal, oil or iron ore, it would clearly be absurd to assume that reserves are indefinitely expendable. There must be some absolute limit to the supply available on Earth, but we do not yet have the knowledge to say with any accuracy what this limit is. Several attempts have been made to estimate ultimate stocks of recoverable resources. This involves estimating the likelihood and size of discoveries in hitherto unexplored areas and at as yet untapped depths; assessing the extent to which reserves at existing sites will be revalued as knowledge and extraction methods improve; and estimating changes in technology which will allow us to use hitherto uneconomic sources of supply.

Given the complexity of the task, it is not surprising that widely different estimates have been made. Much depends on how optimistic the estimator is about the capability of technological innovation to redefine resource stocks at a fast enough rate to keep pace with increases in consumption. We do not know, in fact, if it matters whether we reach the ultimate physical limit for individual resources. One school of thought argues that the economic system will react to prevent absolute scarcity of resources occurring in the foreseeable future. When one resource becomes physically scarce, extraction costs will inevitably rise and this cost increase, plus the fact of greater scarcity, will drive up the resource price. This in turn will decrease demand and lead to the development of substitutes, greater economy in use and, in the case of metals, allow a higher level of recycling. In other words, it is argued that although individual resources may be exhausted, this will be compensated for by a re-evaluation of the total resource base. Shortages of traditional energy resources, for example, such as coal or oil, need not have serious effects if such renewable energy sources as solar, wind or tidal power can be exploited economically.

Ultimately, different views on resource scarcity come down to different beliefs about the pace of technological change. Pessimistic forecasters doubt whether change can occur on the scale and at the speed necessary to prevent acute shortages. In-

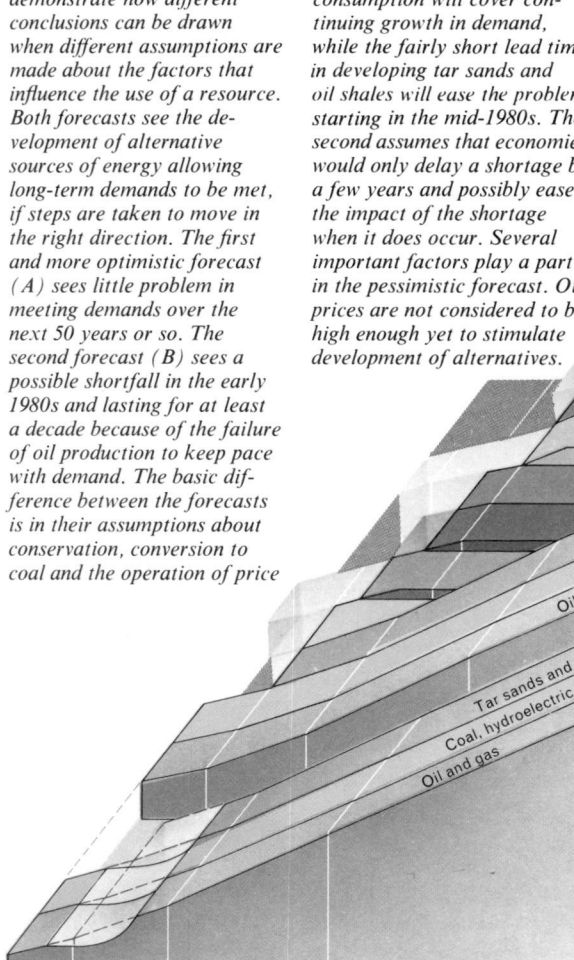

The two forecasts about future energy supplies shown here demonstrate how different conclusions can be drawn when different assumptions are made about the factors that influence the use of a resource. Both forecasts see the development of alternative sources of energy allowing long-term demands to be met, if steps are taken to move in the right direction. The first and more optimistic forecast (A) sees little problem in meeting demands over the next 50 years or so. The second forecast (B) sees a possible shortfall in the early 1980s and lasting for at least a decade because of the failure of oil production to keep pace with demand. The basic difference between the forecasts is in their assumptions about conservation, conversion to coal and the operation of price

mechanisms. The first forecast assumes that economies in consumption will cover continuing growth in demand, while the fairly short lead time in developing tar sands and oil shales will ease the problem starting in the mid-1980s. The second assumes that economies would only delay a shortage by a few years and possibly ease the impact of the shortage when it does occur. Several important factors play a part in the pessimistic forecast. Oil prices are not considered to be high enough yet to stimulate development of alternatives.

And, while it is agreed that development of tar and shale oil will begin in the mid-1980s, the lead times needed for complete development (or conversion in the case of coal) are too long to have much impact on short-term supplies, Such factors, though not readily calculable, must be taken into account.

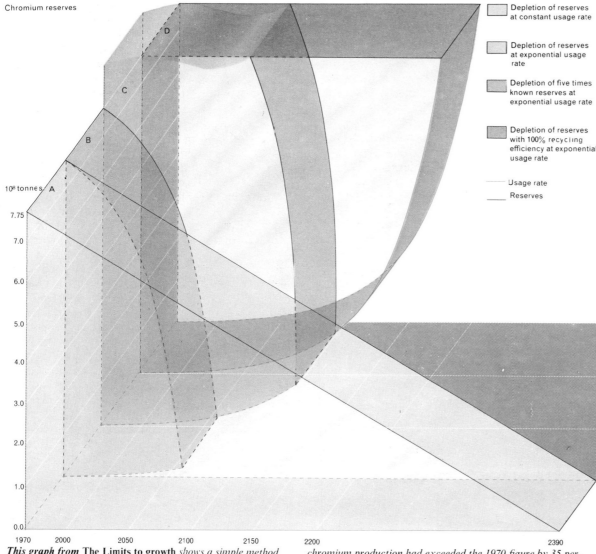

Chromium reserves

Depletion of reserves at constant usage rate

Depletion of reserves at exponential usage rate

Depletion of five times known reserves at exponential usage rate

Depletion of reserves with 100% recycling efficiency at exponential usage rate

Usage rate

Reserves

This graph from The Limits to growth *shows a simple method of calculating the life of a nonrenewable resource, assuming different patterns of demand. Line A shows the decrease in chromium reserves if annual use remained constant at the 1970 level, while line B assumes a continued growth in demand. In the first calculation, known reserves would last for about 400 years; in the second, only about 95 years. The second calculation is closer to the true pattern of use: by 1975 annual* chromium production had exceeded the 1970 figure by 35 percent. Line C assumes the discovery of five times the known chromium reserves, but, assuming exponential increases in use, this only increases the life of the resource by approximately 60 years. Line D shows how long it would take for exponential increase in demand to exceed the reserves, even if the known amount of reserves was perfectly recycled so that no part of the reserve was lost in processing.

evitably, governments will increasingly want to be involved in resource development to ensure that national security and national economic growth objectives are taken into account. In the field of energy resources, government involvement is already great, either in the form of direct ownership of resource industries or through controls on production levels and trade. Metallic mineral development is still largely in the hands of private companies, but we can expect that these, too, will be subject to increasing government control.

Feast or famine?

Another vital resource, food, cannot be ignored. Agricultural land is a fixed resource, one that is in fact declining as more space is taken for housing, industry, transport and mining. Furthermore, misuse of farmland has led to problems such as soil erosion and the development of salt flats, which reduce the stock still more.

In theory, it has been estimated that the total biological resources of the land and sea could produce about 40 tons of food per person per year at the present level of world population, some 100 times what is needed. But this is an unrealistic figure. Man is unable to "run" the Earth at more than a fraction of its theoretical efficiency. In the developed countries food production has increased at a faster rate than population growth. In the less-developed countries, however, increasing output has barely kept ahead of population growth. If the adequate diets of approximately two-thirds of the current population are to be improved and the growing population fed, great changes will be needed in the organization of farming, the capital and energy used in agriculture and in the distribution of food over the world. Many commentators doubt whether the necessary social, organizational and economic changes can—or will—be made.

Yet the potential is enormous. As man's demands and technology change, so too will our appraisal of what constitutes a resource, and our assumptions about the resources available to us in the future will continually be revised.

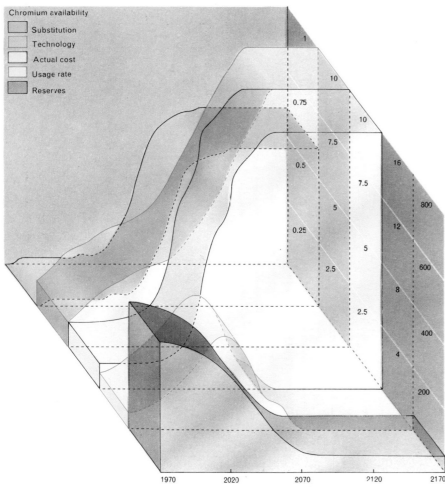

Chromium availability

Substitution
Technology
Actual cost
Usage rate
Reserves

A more accurate calculation of the availability of chromium, also from The Limits to Growth, *reveals that, at first, despite rapid depletion of reserves, improving technology keeps prices low. Eventually, technology is insufficient to* depress the price as reserves are depleted even further, and this stimulates the use of substitutes. By the time usage levels off, reserves are so depleted that chromium is only available at a very high price.

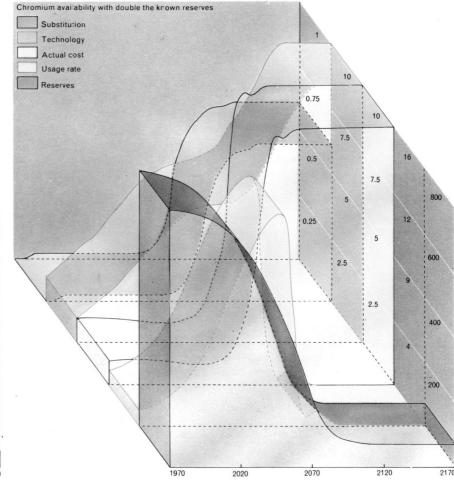

Chromium availability with double the known reserves

Substitution
Technology
Actual cost
Usage rate
Reserves

This computer run assumes double the chromium reserves. The interaction of the various factors—level of reserves, costs of extraction, technological innovation, substitution and rate of usage—follows a similar pattern. But while costs remain lower for longer, the life of the resource is only extended from 125 to 145 years because of the ability of exponential growth to deplete any additional reserves that might be discovered.

AWARENESS OF CRISIS

Fears for the future of resources are not new. History reflects man's recurring bouts of pessimism over supplies—his constant quest for new materials to maintain and improve his standard of living. From cattle raids between primitive villages to today's confrontations between superpowers, one society after another has secured resources for its population at the expense of its neighbors.

Man's predicament was analyzed in the late eighteenth century by the economist Thomas Malthus. In contrast to the Panglossian optimism of his time —that everything is for the best in this best of all possible worlds—Malthus was frankly pessimistic. Societies, he argued, contain the seeds of their own misery, for they inevitably outgrow their resources. Populations grow geometrically, by compound interest. Means of production grow arithmetically, by simple addition. To achieve prosperity, nations must balance "the power to produce and the will to consume"—a phrase any twentieth-century conservationist would be proud to have coined.

Although his insight stimulated the thinking of many nineteenth-century economists and scientists (Charles Darwin included), Malthus's fears for his own society proved groundless. Population grew apace, but so did prosperity. Better methods of farming improved yields from the land. The fuel crisis that had threatened the already depleted forests disappeared as deep mining techniques for coal developed. Surplus population emigrated overseas, and the prosperity of the industrial revolution brought raw materials and food flooding in from the developing colonial territories.

What chiefly defeated the Malthusian predictions was the discovery of new uses of coal. The development of energy-based industry and improved agriculture prevented the trap from closing in the countries we now think of as developed. But in Ireland, the great hunger of the 1840s showed the underlying truth of Malthus's thesis—a truth that is restated every time there is famine in a poor, less-developed country today. And by the end of the nineteenth century, ideas of conservation had already taken root, both in Europe and in the United States, where concern at the "passing of the frontier" created an awareness of crisis.

The emergence of oil

In the early twentieth century, when official circles were already expressing anxiety about diminishing coal reserves, oil began to take over as the major source of industrial energy. Richer in energy than coal, oil is easier to store and transport, and far more versatile in its end uses. In the period after World War II, the apparently limitless oil resources of the Middle East began to flow into Europe and Japan, which were reconstructing their economies. The oil-based community that dominates the world today is as far ahead of the smoke-blackened society of the industrial revolution as that society was of the mainly agrarian world which Malthus

Media coverage of Vietnam heightened the consciousness of millions of young people, such as these anti-war demonstrators in Washington DC, of the ultimate futility of warfare.

Continuing deaths from famine, despite the aid programs of the 1960s, led to a greater awareness of the problems, particularly an ever-increasing birthrate of less-developed countries.

The suffering seen in the victims of mercury poisoning in Minimata, Japan, forced a new awareness of the consequences of uncontrolled industrial pollution.

By the early 1970s, a fuller global awareness had emerged of the pitfalls man had created for himself in building an industrialized society. The bright prospects of the preceding decade were now dimmed. As knowledge about the scale of the problems grew, the considerable dangers arising from the unregulated pursuit of prosperity began to be studied more carefully, in an effort to avert the disaster that appeared to be imminent.

knew. As the economic miracles became manifest few, if any, questions were raised about the future.

The late 1950s and early 1960s saw a sudden resurgence of pessimism about the ability of industrial societies to solve the problems they had created, and about the ability of the world as a whole to cope with the twin problems of burgeoning population and diminishing resources.

One of the first publications to awaken modern awareness of crisis was *Silent Spring*, Rachael Carson's brilliant polemic against the widespread misuse of pesticides in the United States. Published in 1962, it contained little that was specific about the depletion of resources. Its author concentrated on the ability of the biosphere to absorb the abuses heaped on it by an overconfident industrial society. This was the first major questioning, by a qualified and respected scientific writer, of the progress of science and technology in the postwar years.

Silent Spring turned many minds toward a critical examination of what man was doing on Earth, including his use of resources on a massive and accelerating scale. Human achievements were great. They were bringing undreamed-of prosperity to the developed countries of the world. But had they disposed of the Malthusian argument, or merely fended it off for a few more generations?

Through the 1960s the doubts grew stronger, passing for many into bitter disillusionment with the whole of technical progress. The Vietnam war conjured up for millions of young people, in the United States and round the world, an image of science as malevolent, destructive and, finally, incompetent. Awareness of the dangers of pollution of all kinds began to become widespread. Testing of nuclear weapons had spread radioactivity over the whole globe; pesticide residues were found in birds even in Antarctica; hideous suffering was seen in victims of mercury poisoning in Minimata, Japan.

Certainly, by the early 1970s the bright prospects were dimmed. The so-called "green revolution," which had promised so much to the hungry, hit unforeseen economic and human problems. Nuclear power as an alternative energy, launched with such optimism in Eisenhower's "Atoms for Peace" program, appeared in the new guise of a dangerous monster. Antibiotic drugs, which were to have cleared disease from the Earth, lost some of their potency against new genetic strains. Material prosperity, which was to have eliminated poverty, remained in the hands of the few. Every solution created more problems than it solved.

Many were prepared to accept—even to welcome with a strange, puritanic relish—the view that industrial society was incapable of solving the problems it had created. Ecologists who questioned the invincibility of industrialism were fêted as prophets of doom; the bookstores carried ominous tracts foretelling how the end would finally come about.

Serious attempts were made to quantify trends, using newly developed computer-modelling techniques. The book *The Limits to Growth*, a computer-based study by a US team that extrapolated current trends of population, resource exploitation and pollution to the end of the century and beyond, was dubbed by one critic "Malthus with a computer." Its message—that current trends could not continue indefinitely—was misread by millions as a further portent of doom, and embraced with gloomy enthusiasm by a society that seemed to have accepted the inevitability of its own collapse.

Although the pessimism was exaggerated, the message was not lost on governments and industrialists responsible for the welfare of man. Collapse was inevitable only if current trends continued, and there were already indications—especially in rising prices of raw materials—that trends could not continue unmodified for long. Man has the advantage of foresight, and can alter the course of events once the problems have been seen and assessed.

A new wave of optimism

In resource management on a world scale there were problems indeed. They have not gone away, but there is a new wave of restrained optimism as to man's ability to deal with them. No problem of resources is so grave that it cannot be tackled. Warfare is no longer the answer. We may still have time to explore alternative possibilities.

There are certainly limits to resource development. One of the most immediate is availability of fuel oil. The supply has been able to grow with demand for so long that limitless oil seemed to be assumed. But we can no longer rely on it as a cheap source of energy. We may even have reached or passed the peak usage, and we should certainly be looking for alternatives. Our descendants may wonder that our age could use so much of this remarkable raw material simply for burning when there are so many ways of using it for man's benefit.

Nuclear power, which 20 years ago promised a solution to the problems of energy supply, has run into problems of economics and technology. Once

hailed as a panacea, it is now an expensive bogey. Some governments dedicated to it have lost credibility as doubts over reactor design and disposal of wastes continue. Few people now believe that it can be deployed with the rapidity that was believed feasible in the 1960s. Even by the turn of the century, unless there is a quite remarkable change in its fortunes, nuclear power seems incapable of taking up the energy load now sustained by oil.

The past two decades have thus seen large swings of opinion: from unwarranted optimism to black pessimism about the prospects for humanity. Neither is justified. The world is far from immediate exhaustion of the resources upon which it depends. It has enough arable land to feed many more than its present population. The webs of life in the biosphere have been damaged, but they are still strong.

But the nature of the problems we face, and their size, still require urgent and informed consideration. There are difficulties in the distribution and utilization of resources. Many people are short of energy and food, despite surpluses elsewhere; millions suffer from debilitating diseases. The harsh economics of world trade bear most heavily on those least able to look after themselves. The progress gained by the profligate use of resources has bypassed much of mankind, and this vast differential is a cause of growing resentment and hostility. The rate of growth to which the developed nations have become accustomed is no longer as easily achieved as it was. Adapting industrialized societies to the newly defined limits must not take place at the expense of the developing world. The struggle to improve the living standards of the poorest portion of mankind must remain a priority.

The task for the coming decades is to learn to recognize and live within the limits imposed on us by our resources. The more we raise expectations that cannot be fulfilled, the harder it will be to come to terms with the finiteness of the Earth. This is the immense gain that has been obtained from the pessimism of recent times: an awareness that we cannot expect to continue past trends of runaway consumption when planning for the future.

Chinese Vice-Premier Teng Hsiao-Ping and Japanese Prime Minister Fukuda *toast the signing of the Sino–Japanese Treaty of Peace and Friendship in Tokyo in October 1978. The détente acknowledges that some problems must be solved collectively between states. Transcending historical and ideological barriers, it sets a framework within which the two nations can cooperate more easily. On a broader scale, a more concentrated response to world problems at international levels will be made easier by a lessening of tensions between states. The hostile reaction of the Soviet Union to the Sino–Japanese Treaty shows that bilateral cooperation will not always be greeted warmly unless the traditional fears of states are allayed. But while the volume of information about the problems to be faced increases daily, this knowledge cannot be applied properly without appropriate frameworks for solving the problems. Erecting such frameworks must eventually involve social and political adjustments on both a regional and a global level. Because problems often have an impact beyond national borders, states can no longer afford to pursue their own values at the expense of others, though purely national goals are unlikely to be lightly sacrificed by anyone.*

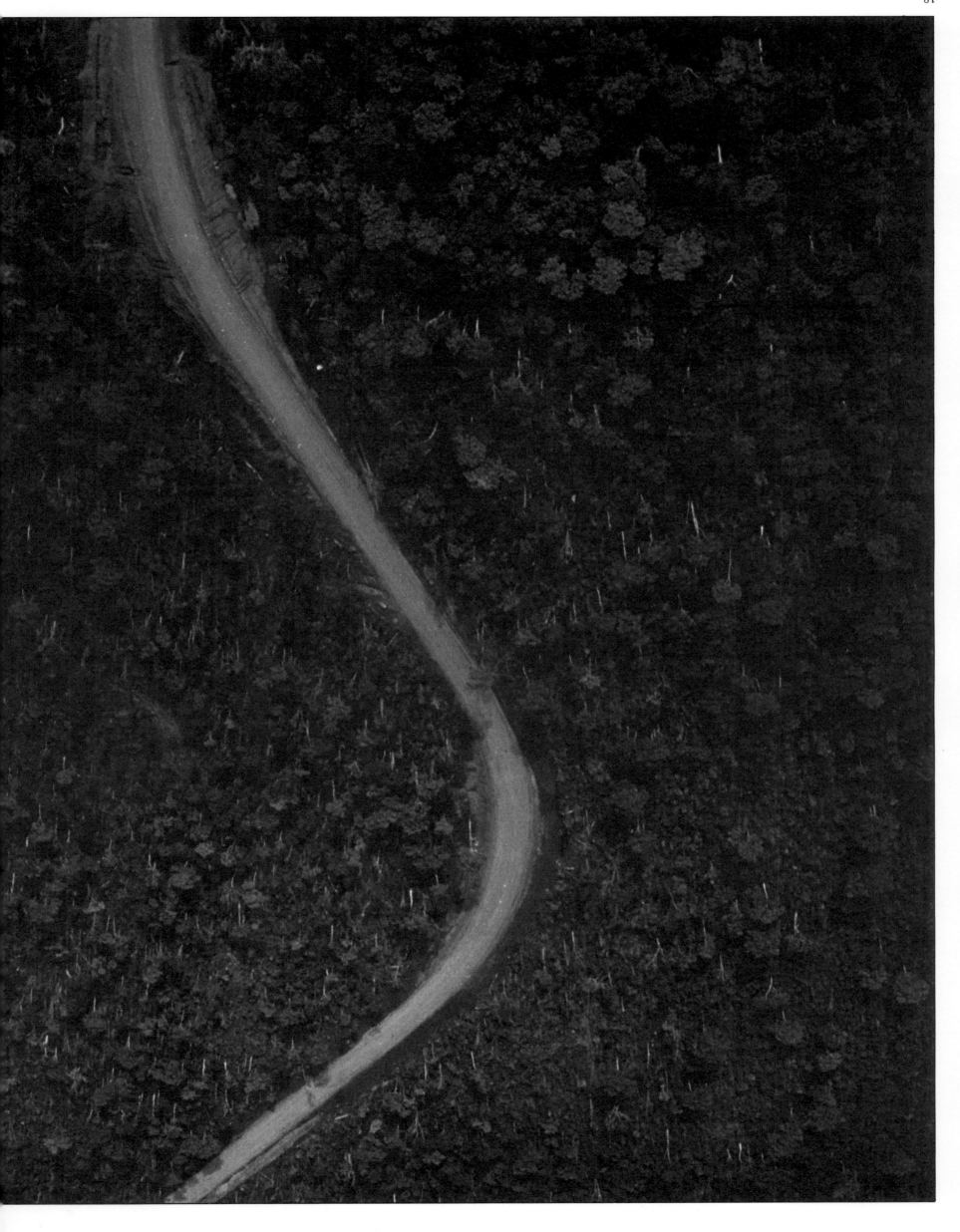

THE
NATURE
OF
RESOURCES

SUN & EARTH

The creation and continuance of life on Earth is powered by the energy of the Sun. Of all the energy on Earth, more than 99.9 percent comes from solar radiation; the tiny remainder comes from geothermal heat stored within the Earth's core, from the radioactive decay of rocks within the Earth's interior, and from the power of the tides created by the gravitational pull of the Moon and Sun. Solar energy reaches Earth at an average rate of a million kilowatts per square kilometer and the total amount reaching Earth each year far exceeds mankind's consumption of energy.

At the heart of the Sun a mass of hydrogen atoms at intense heat undergoes a nuclear reaction, fusing to form helium and radiating energy. This nuclear process will continue until all the hydrogen is consumed some billions of years hence: in terms of human existence on Earth, virtually for ever.

This then is the basis of the energy from the Sun, the Earth's primary resource. Half this energy is radiated in the form of visible light; most of the rest is in the form of infrared rays, which are not visible to man but are felt as heat; and a small proportion is ultraviolet radiation, which is also invisible to man and would be dangerous to all forms of life if it were not almost entirely filtered out by the Earth's atmosphere.

Some of the solar energy reaching Earth is reflected away by the atmosphere, clouds or the Earth's surface. About half of the total energy reaches the land or ocean and is absorbed as heat; the distribution of the absorbed energy depends on the varying properties of the Earth's surface. Dark areas, such as oceans and forests, absorb almost all the energy falling on them, while the light-colored polar areas reflect nearly all of it. Over a period of time, the Earth neither gains nor loses energy, since all surface warmth eventually returns into space. The crucial property of the Earth is its ability to store and distribute a small proportion of radiated energy and use it in various forms to sustain life. A key role is played by the waters of the oceans, covering 71 percent of the globe's surface.

Water is an efficient heat store—once warmed its temperature falls more slowly than that of land. This explains why, shortly after nightfall, an offshore breeze arises as the land and the air above it cool while the air above the sea is kept warm by the water. Warm air above the sea rises and is replaced by the cooler air from the shore, creating the breeze. Another important effect of the Sun on the oceans is the creation of oceanic currents which, to a large degree, determine the world's climates. As the Sun heats the surface water of equatorial seas the warm water expands to the extent that it is actually a few centimeters higher than the cooler water of the surrounding oceans. The warmed water tends to run down the gradient created toward the Poles, while the cold (and heavier) water sinks beneath it and travels back along the seabed to the Equator. This constant movement, deflected by the rotation of the Earth, sets the basic pattern of the ocean currents. Differential heating between the Equator and Poles produces atmospheric circulations, which are complicated by factors such as the Earth's rotation and distribution of land and sea.

The hydrological cycle

The hydrological cycle is a Sun-powered system that ensures the constant redistribution of water around the world. Fresh water is taken up by plants and evaporated back into the atmosphere in the process of transpiration. The Sun also evaporates water from the oceans, forming water vapor, sometimes manifested as clouds, in the atmosphere. The vapor is cooled as it is driven by winds across the landmasses and is precipitated as rain or snow. Water on the land eventually runs off in rivers to the sea. In this way the land is kept constantly supplied with the water necessary for the growth of plants and animals.

Photosynthesis

Photosynthesis is a crucial chemical process by which energy from the Sun is stored as chemical energy in plants and made available to animals when they eat the plants.

In the early history of the Earth, about 3.5 billion years ago, the atmosphere consisted of a mixture of gases unsuitable for the support of any form of life known today. There emerged very simple life forms that are capable of harnessing the Sun's energy to produce oxygen from carbon dioxide and water. The resulting oxygen, subjected to electrical charges by lightning, formed ozone. The important property of ozone in the atmosphere is that it absorbs dangerous ultraviolet radiation from the Sun. With this protection the primitive life forms on Earth evolved into sophisticated structures that could use water and minerals from the soil.

How the life process began, and why life took the forms it did, are questions yet to be answered: but it is clear that the present character of the Earth's atmosphere is a consequence of the action of chlorophyll (a green pigment) in plants, and that within this atmosphere plants can continue to live and to utilize the energy of sunlight.

The carbon and oxygen cycle

The carbon and oxygen cycle, which is fueled by the Sun, may be summarized as follows. Sunlight, in the process of photosynthesis, activates the chlorophyll of plants and the energy is used to convert carbon dioxide from the atmosphere and water from the soil into oxygen, carbohydrates and other complex organic compounds. When plants die the organic matter left behind is broken down

The biosphere (2) is that part of the Earth and its atmosphere (1) in which living things exist. Extending some 16 km (10 miles) above and below sea level the biosphere overlaps the hydrosphere (3) and the lithosphere (4).

Of the solar energy reaching Earth approximately 30 percent (5) is reflected back into space as light; about 47 percent (6) is absorbed but eventually leaves the Earth as waste heat; roughly 20 percent (7) drives the hydrological cycle; 0.02 percent (8) is used in photosynthesis and between 1 and 3 percent (9) is absorbed by the ozone layer. A small fraction (10) drives winds and waves.

The hydrological cycle basically involves evaporation of water from the oceans, transportation as water vapor in the atmosphere, precipitation as rain or snow, and runoff via rivers back to the oceans.

Plants take up groundwater for photosynthesis and intake of nutrients. By means of transpiration water vapor is returned to the atmosphere.

by microorganisms, a process called decay. Alternatively, living plants may be directly ingested by some animals and the carbohydrates in this food used to provide energy. Decayed matter from plants and animals provides nutrients for successive plants, which may in their turn be consumed to provide energy for more complex forms of life.

Animals obtain their energy by burning their food in the presence of oxygen, both ultimately derived from plants. In this process of animal respiration, carbon dioxide is released into the atmosphere, and this may be used again by plants in photosynthesis.

Bodies of organisms may be deposited in litter, soils and ocean sediments that become buried and eventually form deposits of organic carbon and fossil fuels. Coal was formed mainly about 300 million years ago, when much of the land was covered by swamp forest. The swamp water, deficient in oxygen, inhibited the action of the bacteria which normally break down vegetation,

which was converted into peat and eventually compressed into coal. Similarly, oil was formed from the remains of single-celled plants, plankton and other ocean organisms. They were eventually deposited on the seabed, forming a sediment which, after much compression by other sedimentary deposits, was transformed into hydrocarbons. As man burns the fossil fuels, oxygen is consumed and carbon dioxide released into the atmosphere, returning carbon once again to its global cycle.

Other cycles
The minerals used by plants to produce complex carbohydrates and proteins, and ingested by animals, are returned to the soil by excretion or by decomposition of the animals after death. River runoff from the land carries some of these minerals to the sea, where they circulate within aquatic organisms or lie as sediment on the ocean floor.

Nitrogen is an essential element of amino acids, the building blocks of proteins, which are present

in all living cells, and which must be present in the food intake of animals for growth and tissue repair. Nitrogen makes up four-fifths of the atmosphere, but it cannot be used direct by higher plants and animals; it must first be combined with oxygen or hydrogen, a process called fixation. Nitrogen is returned to the soil in plant and animal wastes in the form of nitrates, or, broken down by denitrifying bacteria, is returned to the atmosphere.

Phosphorus is present in adenosine triphosphate (ATP) and adenosine diphosphate (ADP). Conversion between ATP and ADP is the basis of biochemical reactions involved in respiration within living cells, providing the energy essential for life processes.

Sulfur is another essential element in proteins; it is responsible for the structure of protein molecules. Sulfur is present in the atmosphere in the form of sulfur dioxide and hydrogen sulfide. It is precipitated in rainwater as sulfate, and returned to the air in volcanic gases and by burning fossil fuels, and enters the ocean as runoff from the land.

The biosphere receives 99.8 percent of its energy from the Sun. Tidal energy (11), derived from the kinetic and potential energy of the Earth, Moon and Sun, and thermal energy (12), conducted to the surface from the Earth's interior, account for the rest.

Nitrogen, phosphorus and sulfur are involved, to varying degrees, in the processes of plant growth, grazing, predation and decay. Nitrogen in the atmosphere and soil is absorbed by nitrogen-fixing plants or bacteria, and returned to the air by denitrification. Some may be fixed in the air by cosmic radiation and lightning. Phosphorus is recycled between land and sea by means of phosphatizing bacteria on land and algae and diatoms in the sea. Sulfur too has a land-sea cycle: it is reduced on land by anaerobic bacteria in swamps and bogs and collects in the sea from decomposition of calcareous deposits.

Photosynthesis is the process by which plants absorb solar energy and produce oxygen and carbohydrates (compounds of carbon, hydrogen and oxygen) from carbon dioxide and water. The process operates only in the daytime, with sunlight available. Some energy is stored and used by the plants for growth. In the reverse process, respiration, the carbohydrates are broken down to release energy and carbon dioxide is given off.

The carbon and oxygen cycle is another aspect of the circulation of energy between atmosphere, land and oceans, and life forms on Earth. Carbon dioxide in the atmosphere is taken up by plants in photosynthesis and oxygen is released; the stored carbon is used for food by animals. Animal and plant respiration return carbon dioxide to the air, using up oxygen. Dead plants and animals decay, releasing carbon dioxide to the air.

MAPPING TECHNIQUES

Mapping techniques

1 Landsat satellite with multispectral scanners and return beam vidicons
2 Meteorological satellite providing cloud and temperature data
3 Aircraft equipped for conventional, multiband and infrared photography and thermal line-scan survey
4 "Bird" containing magnetometer or gravity meter
5 Side-looking airborne radar survey
6 Experimental autogiro with multiband camera equipment
7 Landsat receiving station and data center
8 Experimental ground station providing meteorological and hydrological data
9 Geophysics ground survey team providing magnetic, gravitational, electromagnetic, radiometric and seismic information
10 Borehole probe
11 Marine seismic survey
12 Side-scan sonar "fish"

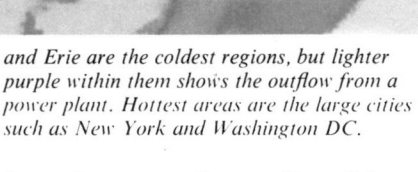

On a thermal satellite map of the east coast of the United States temperature values are color coded from purple, the coldest areas, through to white, the hottest. Lakes Ontario and Erie are the coldest regions, but lighter purple within them shows the outflow from a power plant. Hottest areas are the large cities such as New York and Washington DC.

Our knowledge of Earth's resources depends on the quality of environmental surveys. In such surveys there are three main phases: first, a descriptive, or exploratory, phase in which the physical environment is described and mapped; second, an appraisal phase concerned with evaluation of the resources; and third, a development phase in which plans for using the resource are constructed.

Resource mapping uses a great variety of methods. Some of them, like topographical mapping, have a long history, though they now employ modern technologies; others, like the use of satellites, are of recent development. However, we cannot yet be satisfied with the state of availability of the basic information provided by large-scale topographical maps for, in addition to the fact that large-scale maps are not available for wide areas of the Earth's surface, some countries restrict their availability on grounds of security.

The types of information which need to be surveyed and mapped include the relief and land forms, geology, climate, hydrology, soils, vegetation, fauna and the existing land use. For the planning of land use, especially for agriculture, it is important to have land classification and land capability maps based on surveys of soils, slopes and water conditions. Surveys of vegetation, for example of areas where forest resources are declining, are also of importance. So that besides topographical maps we look for thematic maps of land use, geology, geomorphology, climate, hydrological conditions, soils, vegetation, pests and diseases. In all these surveys, ground survey, remote sensing data and experimental enquiry need to be closely related.

The principal scientific basis for the mapping of mineral and fuel resources comes from a detailed understanding of the nature and spatial distribution of varied rocks that make up the accessible part of the Earth's crust. The lithology, or internal make-up, is investigated by means of the optical and electron microscopes, the mineralogy and chemistry by X-ray diffraction, spectrometry and the electron microprobe. The fossil contents of sedimentary rocks are important for the time data they supply and paleontology nowadays can be supported by radiometric dating. Time relations are essential in order to build up the structural picture upon which all resource assessments must depend.

A national archive
The construction of accurate geological maps was begun by Sir Henry de la Beche when he founded in Britain, in 1832, the first national geological survey. Over the years virtually all other governments have recognized their need of geological surveying; the federal United States Geological Survey was begun, for example, in 1882. Some of the emerging countries receive aid from the Special Fund of the United Nations for this purpose. A national archive to conserve and correlate all the data obtained from exploratory borings, which in an industrial country may number thousands in a year, is one important aspect of a continuing geological survey.

No method is effective without the ground control which surface geological mapping and boring provides, so there is still no real substitute for foot-slogging over the ground. Many useful aids, however, have been devised, including geophysics, geochemistry, aerial surveying and satellite imagery.

Taking a comparatively new method first, applied geochemistry, the determination of trace elements in soils, stream sediments, water and plants, has proved to be effective in uncontaminated areas leading, where anomalous concentrations have been found, to a good rate of discovery of new resources, especially of nonferrous metal ores.

The indirect methods of applied geophysics are valuable in providing data on the third dimension of geological structure. Gravity surveys use what is, in effect, a delicate spring balance to measure the small variations in gravity. After correcting for latitude, altitude and topography, the results indicate the variations in density of the underlying rocks, which can then be modeled. They are particularly useful for identifying deep sedimentary basins; the first step in the exploration for North Sea petroleum was a shipborne gravity survey. Mounted gyroscopically, the gravimeter works well on board ship, but it is less satisfactory in aircraft.

A powerful surveying tool
Seismic surveying is carried out by artificially generated shock waves which are reflected through, or reflected off, layers in the crust and are recorded on multichannel instruments in such a way as to produce a running profile of the layers, in effect making a geological map in a vertical plane. Under good conditions, penetrations to five kilometers (three miles) by reflection can be achieved. This is the most powerful surveying tool at the disposal of the petroleum geologist; the lines on the profiles are time lines, but given control borings they are readily converted to accurate geological lines. It is at its best offshore and in the North Sea investigations more than 160,000 kilometers (100,000 miles) of seismic shooting were done.

Magnetic surveys are carried out using sensitive magnetometers which enable localized variations

in the Earth's magnetic field to be plotted as a map. Although these instruments may be used by ground survey teams, they are generally incorporated in an aerial survey. Magnetic maps from aerial surveys show anomalies which resemble the contour lines on a conventional map and reveal the presence of magnetized rock structures. A skilled interpreter searching for oil deposits, for example, will select an area *without* strong local magnetic gradients as a likely site. Magnetic methods have been used systematically by the Canadian Geological Survey and the Australian Bureau of Mines and Mineral Resources ahead of ground survey to bring out the positions of belts of "greenstones" (old lavas) and thus to indicate some elements of structure.

Electromagnetic, self-potential and induced potential are all procedures designed to search specifically for sulfide deposits. Airborne scintill-ometers and lithium fluoride detectors show the varying level of radioactive concentration.

The objective of all these methods, as applied to the search for mineral and fuel resources, must be to choose good targets for drilling, for virtually all such deposits have to be assessed and proved by the drill. At costs in the range $5 to $50 a foot, drilling is an expensive operation and the geologist must narrow the target as best he can.

Besides providing a quick method of extending ground survey, aerial survey can also be used, though less satisfactorily, as a direct short-cut to target choice. Similar claims are made for satellite imagery. It has to be realized, however, that although some geological structures have sufficient effect on surface topography to enable them to be detected from the air, most structures do not. This is especially so in the great area where we know

least about mineral resources—the humid tropics —where thick laterite conceals the rocks and dense forests grow on the laterite. Aerial geological surveying involves a greater degree of guesswork than ground survey. The greatest contribution aircraft or satellites can make to the search for mineral resources is to indicate the nature of the terrain, and to provide good base maps on which to work.

The need rapidly to survey and to map large tracts of inaccessible territory has lent attraction to remote sensing methods to supplement the large-scale ground surveys which by their nature are slow and expensive. Stereoscopic and color photography, and the technique of image enhancement (very much a part of remote sensing) have greatly assisted interpretation. A black and white photograph may contain subtle differences in gray tones which, though not readily apparent, may be significant.

Revealing hidden information

A technique known as density slicing is often used to extract this hidden information. By printing all the areas of the same tone in a bold color a particular feature is emphasized. By printing different tones in strikingly different colors the photograph takes on an almost maplike appearance, greatly aiding interpretation. Another technique is known as multiband photography. Photographs are taken simultaneously in different bands of the spectrum on black and white film by a set of cameras each with a different colored filter over the lens. The choice of filter depends on the type of information needed: where one filter would clearly reveal an oil slick, for instance, another would not. An added advantage of this technique is that each band can be printed in a color best suited to emphasize certain features, for example subtle differences in soil types could be printed in sharply contrasting colors.

Of great interest in new mapping techniques is a region of the spectrum known as the near-infrared —just outside the region of the spectrum to which the human eye is sensitive. Specialized film emulsions which are sensitive to near-infrared are used in vegetation studies since plants reflect the near-infrared light in sunlight. The amount they reflect

is an indication of their vigor: even though diseased plants may look green and healthy to the eye, the camera reveals if they are diseased.

Thermal imaging from aircraft produces "heat maps" and can distinguish temperature differences to a fraction of a degree. The cameras are electronic devices which, in effect, see the infrared emitted by any warm object. The wavelengths detected are far beyond those to which photographic emulsions are sensitive.

A recent development in topographical mapping is side-looking airborne radar (SLAR), carried in fast-flying aircraft. The picture produced shows the terrain in startling relief. The technique is now widely used by oil and mineral companies in their exploration programs and has already paid dividends, for example the discovery of a previously unknown river in Brazil lined with millions of pounds worth of exportable timber.

SLAR and heat mapping have both been used to advantage in the search for minerals in a project undertaken jointly by Goodyear Aerospace and Lasa, a South American geophysical company. The radar images obtained for Brazil enabled detailed studies of hydrology, geology, soil and vegetation to be made for an area of more than 8,420,500 square kilometers (3,250,000 square miles). The flights were often carried out at night and in cloudy conditions. Study of the geological structures led subsequently to the identification of target areas for bauxite, uranium, tin and other valuable minerals.

The most inaccessible surface of all to survey is the seabed, large areas of which have never been surveyed at all. Geological maps of the seabed on the continental shelf are now beginning to appear in Britain and France. They depend on seismic profiling, the use of submersibles, manned and re-motely controlled, dredge sampling and boring from self-positioning ships, and even upon SCUBA diving. Submersible TV cameras play a valuable part and these are also used successfully in the deep oceans. In seas and oceans, side-scan sonar, collecting sound rather than light waves, is proving an excellent bathymetric tool. The waves are electronically analyzed and presented as a trace-out.

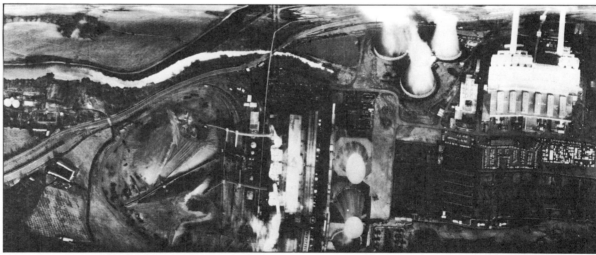

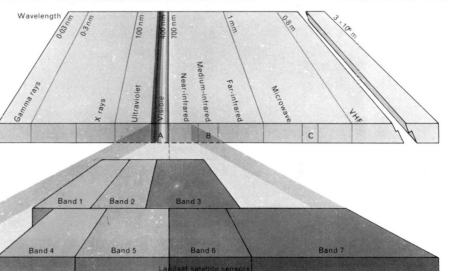

Waste discharged into a river (above) shows on a thermal image because its temperature is different from the river water. Methods of remote sensing different parts of the spectrum are numerous. Among them (left) are conventional photography using the visible part of the spectrum (A), thermal mapping using infrared (B) and radar, which uses microwaves (C). Landsat satellites carry sensors which respond to different sections or bands of the spectrum. Return beam vidicons (devices similar to TV cameras) detect bands 1 (green), 2 (red) and 3 (near-infrared). Bands 4, 5, 6 and 7, are picked up by multi-spectral scanners.

MAPPING MINERALS & ENERGY

The launch of the first Earth Resources Technology Satellite (later renamed Landsat-1) on July 23, 1973, heralded a significant advance in aiding the mapping of the Earth's resources. Satellites can provide a viewing platform from which to scan landmasses and the oceans in a way not possible by more conventional survey methods. From a height of 912 kilometers (566 miles) above the Earth's surface scanners on board Landsat view the scene below in two bands of the visible spectrum and two near-infrared bands. The satellite, joined in 1975 by Landsat-2, orbits the Earth every 103 minutes and scans a strip 185 kilometers (115 miles) wide. The same strip is scanned 18 days later and by 1976 more than 80 percent of the land surface of the globe had been scanned. Until then less than 40 percent of the world's landmass had been surveyed.

The basic data from the satellites is not in the form of a picture but is stored as digital data on magnetic tape from which a picture may be processed as hard copy on photographic paper or film. So far, more than 1,500,000 Landsat-generated photographs have been distributed throughout the world. Landsat's orbit was selected to supply complete coverage under constant lighting conditions, a feature not easily achieved by aerial photography. One of Landsat's first revelations was that many maps of remote areas were grossly inaccurate—even the Trans-Amazon Highway had been mislocated by 35 kilometers (22 miles).

The potential of Landsat is enormous. In agriculture, for example, the information gathered may enable crop yields to be predicted. Irrigation planning has benefited and as an aid to hydrology lakes have been located, reservoir levels monitored and water runoff predicted and monitored. Water—because it interacts with the Earth's atmosphere, soil and vegetation—is not easy to map. However, it does have a characteristic low reflectance of sunlight in the near-infrared portion of the spectrum which enables water/land boundaries to be delineated on aerial photographs using infrared-

sensitive film or on Landsat satellite imagery. Flooding can also be assessed and plotted from satellite imagery, as was done in the United States in 1973 when the Missouri and Mississippi valleys were inundated and 35,000 people had to abandon their homes.

A third Landsat satellite was launched in 1978. It carries a high-resolution TV camera sensor and a scanner which images in two bands of the visible spectrum, two bands of the near-infrared spectrum and in the thermal infrared band. This thermal band will be used for studies of heat losses associated with industrial development. Ground receiving stations are now operating in the United States, Canada, Italy and Brazil with others under construction or being planned in Iran, Argentina, Chile, India and Zaire. Australia, Japan and Sweden are also considering their own stations.

A saving in time

Landsat images have revolutionized the work of geologists who wish to study major geological structures stretching across a continent without the tedium and expense of piecing together thousands of individual overlapping aerial photographs. A geological map of Egypt which was to have been prepared using conventional aerial photographs and was to have taken 10 years to complete is now nearing completion in less than half that time using satellite imagery.

Nevertheless, few mineral deposits will be found by looking at continent-wide structures: they are small, highly specialized features of the Earth's crust. One notable exception, however, was where the special coloration of copper deposits at outcrop was detected. On the basis of a rock-type classification map prepared from Landsat data, 30 target sites were selected in Pakistan. Of the 20 sites visited by ground survey teams, five showed evidence which indicated enriched zones of copper deposits.

Knowledge of the terrain is important in resource evaluation. The location of a mineral influences

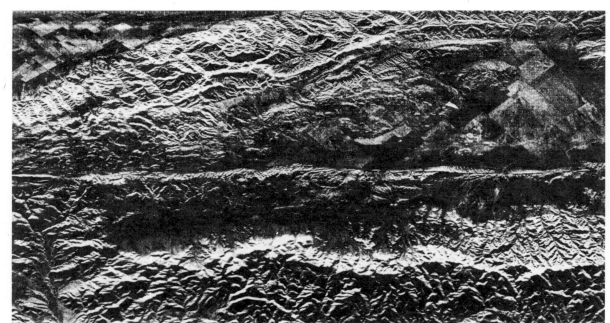

A Landsat image of the San Andreas fault in southern California emphasizes physical features and helps the geologist in his mapping of areas prone to earthquakes.

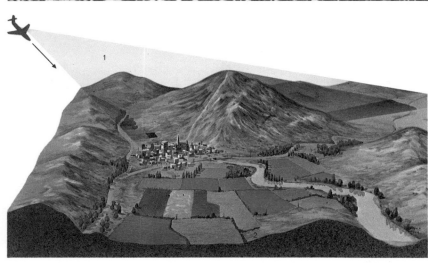

Surface features of terrain are shown clearly on SLAR images (above). From these, geologists can deduce underlying structure. An antenna on the belly of a plane surveying a mountainous region (left) directs pulses of microwave energy in a narrow beam (1) at right angles to the flight-path (2). As a pulse hits the ground it is scattered and some of it is reflected back to a receiver in the aircraft. The stronger the return of microwave energy, the lighter the area appears on the image but, as microwaves travel in straight lines, shielded areas, such as the far side of a mountain (3) appear dark.

Landsat images can be processed to emphasize different features. In the Arabian desert, eroded limestone gravels (left) are in white areas, gravel with little limestone in red (right).

CONNECTIONS

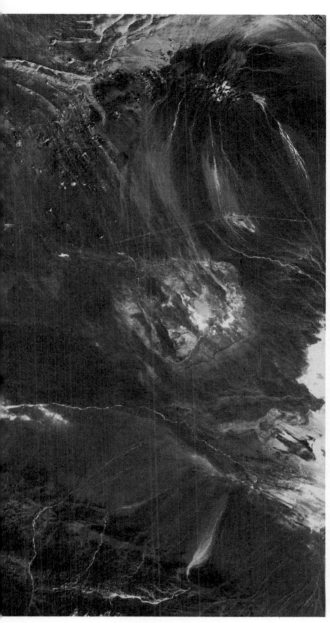

The US Geological Survey used this known site of porphyry copper deposits (1) in Pakistan's Baluchistan desert as a training site for further identification of deposits which were found at (2). As these surface copper deposits have a distinct coloration, the original picture was image-processed by computer to enhance certain color and tonal differences, so distinguishing for the trained eye those colors likely to be associated with copper deposits.

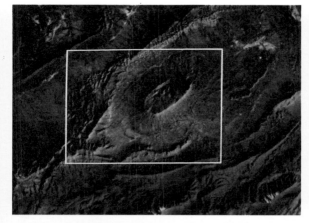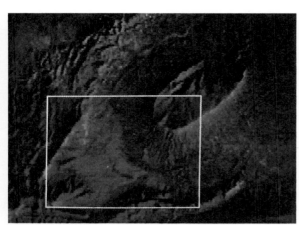

Once a particular area of interest has been geologically identified in a Landsat scene it may be progressively enlarged so that the local detail can be examined. In the enlarged sub-scenes, the rectangular elements, or pixels, from which the scene is constructed, are revealed as blocks of color from which the interpreter can deduce the type of rock.

transportation costs, the nature of the terrain may influence extraction costs and the availability of other resources such as water, fuel and power have a bearing also on the processing costs. Place value and unit value are vital statistics in the consideration of mineral deposits. They determine how the materials enter trade. Sand and gravel are examples of deposits which have a high place value since much of their value depends on their location. It is important that they are close to a developing urban area or to a proposed site of a construction project. An example of this was the discovery of substantial gravel deposits, from interpretation of satellite images, near a proposed highway scheme in Saudi Arabia. As a result, millions of pounds were saved on the estimated cost of the scheme not because of the export value of this newly mapped resource (which is nil) but because the transportation costs were greatly reduced.

At the other extreme, a commodity such as diamonds has a high unit value and as a result enters into international trade. Most minerals fall between these two extremes and the possibilities of future commercial exploitation have to be examined in great detail.

The arguments continue

The Landsat program has so far cost $251 million and yet some estimates indicate that its data have played a prominent role in exploration which has led to the discovery of billions of dollars worth of mineral resources; others take a more sceptical

view. There is no question, however, that beautiful pictures of the topography, valuable for the overview of crops, forests and similar resources, have been produced, capable of enlargement to almost any desired extent.

Mapping can also play an important part in research being done into finding alternative sources of energy such as wind, wave and solar power. Based on meteorological information collected over a number of years from a number of locations, suitable sites for wind-powered generators and solar devices can be mapped. Another promising source of energy is geothermal. The temperature of rocks increases by somewhat less than 30°C (86°F) for every kilometer (0.62 mile) depth and some sedimentary rocks are permeated by hot water which can be drawn off to provide domestic heat. Sources, such as those found in volcanic regions, are readily located by satellite or airborne thermal sensors. A large volume of careful observations made in boreholes is available for geothermal maps. Monitoring by satellite of temperature data automatically transmitted by ground stations on icebergs, in volcanic craters and elsewhere is being used, having been collected from a large number of sites in the United States. Thermal gradients within the oceans are also a promising source of energy. Oceanographic information already exists which will enable favorable sites at which that energy can be extracted to be mapped. Finally, thermal imaging highlights a great negative resource—wasted energy in the heat loss from factories and homes.

In seismic surveying an explosive shot (1) generates shock waves, the speed of which depends on rock elasticity. They are either reflected back (2) through the upper layer or refracted (3) through the lower rock before returning to detectors.

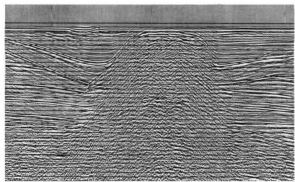

Seismic waves provide information to a computer which produces a trace. This one shows the distinct lines of a salt dome.

MAPPING THE LIVING RESOURCE

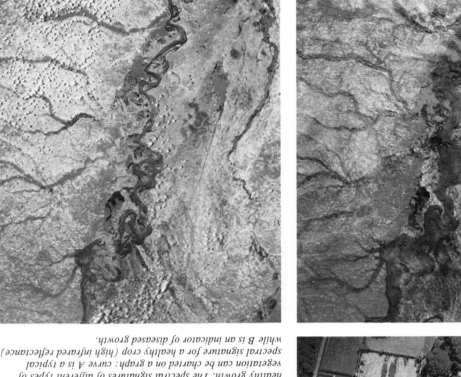

In many parts of the world water supplies are drawn from rivers. Problems arise with inconstancy of supply—floods one season, drought the next—and it is here that remote sensing by satellite can help, by monitoring flow patterns throughout the seasons. Infrared and visible light composites, taken during the Mississippi floods of 1973, show the effects on vegetation and indicate areas vulnerable to future flooding. Healthy growth shows up as bright red; cities are green or dark gray; suburban areas light pink; and clear water is black.

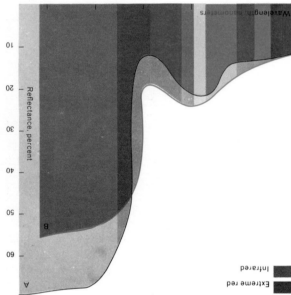

Color infrared film adds a new dimension to the use of aerial photography in mapping resources, and is of particular value in agricultural and forestry surveys. Healthy vegetation strongly reflects infrared, whereas areas with impoverished growth the reflectance is much weaker. Stricken areas of an English wheat-field, seen here as dark gray, are easily distinguished from healthy growth. The spectral signatures of different types of vegetation can be charted on a graph: curve A is a typical spectral signature for a healthy crop (high infrared reflectance), while B is an indicator of diseased growth.

Wavelength, nanometers — 400 500 600 700 800 900
Reflectance, percent — 10 20 30 40 50 60
Extreme red — Infrared

Although many countries, for example Japan, now produce large-scale land use maps, many others have no systematic records of the use that is being made of their land. It is thus difficult to make even a rough inventory of crops and their likely yields. It is also important to obtain more exact information on how much land remains unplanted and how land can be more efficiently used. With world population expanding—and with it the demand for food and other produce of the land—it is vital that there should be some overall form of surveillance and control. Monitoring of agriculture would be helpful both to governments—in drawing up their planning priorities—and to individual farmers faced with decisions as to what crops to plant and how best to manage their land.

Help for agricultural experts

There are already projects in hand yielding information as to terrain and soil types, plant vigor, rainfall and the like. In the arid regions of Arizona, for example (where dense growth may appear shortly after rainfall), satellite scanning has been useful in evaluating seasonal changes in the pattern of plant growth. This information, backed up with meteorological data and detail gleaned on the ground, is an aid to agricultural experts in advising on cropland use policies.

Satellites, too, have been put to work to help map forested areas and to estimate timber volume as an aid to forestry management. The forested regions of the Amazon in Brazil are among the many places where good management is essential not only to exploit timber resources but also to preserve the ecological balance. When satellite images were first used in this context in Brazil, it was discovered that one company had been illegally cutting down vast tracts of forest.

The concept of mapping crop potential is not a new one: the first documented instance of the use of aerial photography as an aid came with an attempt in 1927 to assess crop disease. In this case—a cotton crop attacked by a fungus disease—healthy growth showed up in a dark tone in contrast to the lighter tones of the soil exposed by stricken plants. Despite the success of this exercise, it was many years before aerial photography was put to this use again. It is only recently that there have been renewed efforts to adapt the technique, using aircraft and satellites, to map out an inventory of agricultural resources.

Vegetation reflects 80 percent of the near-infrared energy it receives from sunlight. Consequently it is easily recognized on infrared-sensitive film or sensors responsive to that part of the spectrum. It is the reflectance factor which the film exploits, and characteristic spectral signatures provide a means of distinguishing crop types. Because of the complexity of factors influencing spectral signatures, ''ground truth sites''—areas of known crops growing under various known conditions—are used as an aid to interpretation.

Health of crops

Aerial photography and satellite imagery yield information, too, as to the condition and vigor of crops. Leaf maturity can be gauged from infrared film, with young plants showing up pink and mature growth seen as bright red. Also detectable from the air are crops whose spectral signature is modified by disease, lack of moisture, wind damage and pollution. In the case of disease, the focus of the outbreak can be located and its nature and progress closely monitored.

Today, with satellites providing continuous coverage almost worldwide, there is a real possi-

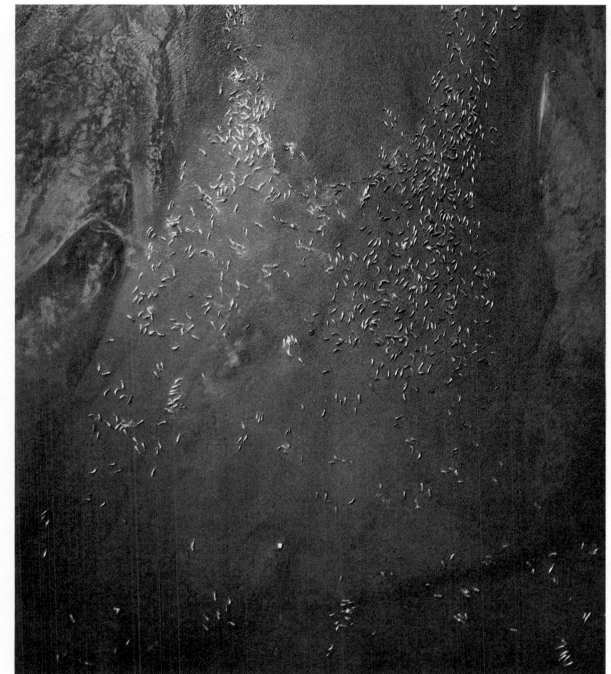

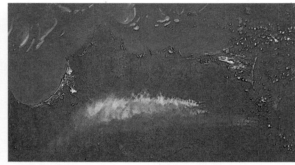

An Apollo 7 shot *of forest fires in Australia illustrates one use of satellite monitoring in forestry management. Other data include tree types, growth patterns, density and disease.*

Manned space missions—*this view of the Earth is from Apollo 17—paved the way to a better understanding of cloud formations. Today unmanned satellites transmit meteorological data.*

Aerial photography, the most important remote-sensing technique for mapping, is further improved by special-purpose film: water-penetration film catches whales off the Canadian coast.

Thermal mapping of estuaries, *as on the Merrimack River, Massachusetts, defines the boundary between fresh and salt water. Aerial photography using a thermal infrared scanner distinguishes warm river water—seen here in light tones—from cooler ocean water. Monitoring of tide cycles provides information valuable to local shell fisheries and water authorities.*

Satellite survey *reveals effects of irrigation on the southern California/New Mexico border. The tract of water at top left is the legacy of a 1905 dam burst on the Colorado River.*

bility of obtaining a global assessment of agricultural resources. Already in progress is a feasibility study of the use of Landsat data to provide an inventory and crop forecast for wheat production in Canada and the United States. The viability of Project LACIE (Large Area Crop Inventory Experiment) hinges on whether satellite data—as to crop type, condition and acreage—can be usefully combined with meteorological information, soil condition and history to give a final production estimate. If it is a success, LACIE will be extended to encompass wheat production worldwide. Ultimately it could become the instrument for mapping and predicting yields of all major crops.

Weather forecasting

There have been many efforts to plot weather conditions in relation to crop yield. Recently, in addition to conventional meteorological forecasting, there have been successful attempts at mapping temperature variations from satellites. Temperature and water vapor profiles are obtained using infrared sensors, which scan a vertical column of air beneath the satellite. Particularly valuable are time-lapse films, made up of a series of satellite images showing cloud cover, to provide a dynamic record of the buildup of severe storm systems. Here again the advantage of satellite scanning is continuous global coverage.

Watching water levels

Monitoring of the water reserves essential to agriculture is highly complex: there are more than 15,000 instrumented data collection stations in the United States alone. Ground mapping—measuring water levels—is a time-consuming business providing only point data. However, ground data, combined with information from maps derived from satellite imagery, insures a high level of accuracy in the estimation of water volumes. The boundaries between water and land can be delineated using aerial photography or satellite imagery. Satellites can be used to plot inundation by flooding and to forestall drought.

An important aid to water resource management is the way in which satellites can be used to map reserves of water in the form of ice or snow. At any given time three-quarters of all fresh water is contained in this form, and in the United States, for instance, seasonal runoff from melting snow represents an important contribution to the overall water budget. Snow cover shows up clearly on satellite images, and, by mapping seasonal movement of the snow line over vast areas, the accuracy of runoff forecasting is greatly enhanced.

The range of remote sensing methods to detect the presence of water includes radar mapping of soils. The radar energy reflected back from the land depends largely on the electrical properties of the soil—properties which are modified by the presence of water. Another technique, which relies on slight variations in temperature, involves the use of airborne thermal sensors to map the interface between fresh and salt water in estuaries.

Sophisticated resource mapping techniques extend, also, to the oceans—still largely untapped and as yet not overexploited by man. Here the fishing prospects can be monitored just as crop potentials are surveyed on land. Already fisheries throughout the world rely on aerial detection of schools of fish. By night, shoals can be located by the bioluminescence of plankton in the water disturbed by the fish. The whereabouts of the fish can also be determined by means of the thermal wake which results from the mixing of water from different depths. Other techniques of use in fisheries management include thermal mapping of coastal currents by infrared scanners.

27

RESOURCES, POLITICS & POWER

Resources can be transformed into ideological and military power, as in this parade of Soviet-made arms in Havana, Cuba.

guarantee that they can be used, as a country may possess resources it cannot afford to exploit. Zambia, for example, might have to leave its copper in the ground if British and American technology and capital were not available to extract it. Free trade economists argue that it is better to let international trade provide for resources to be developed in the interests of all than for each country to try to be self-sufficient, either by conquest or by impoverishing itself by trying to make things that its resources do not encourage. They point to the prosperity of Sweden and Switzerland, whose natural resources are few but which profit from trade and from the exploitation of technology. The ability of a skilled and well-organized population to make optimum use of available resources may be almost as important as possession.

Nearly every country goes some way toward free trade since only a few, such as the United States, the USSR and China, have enough resources to maintain largely self-contained economies. But it is still true that basic urges seem to drive governments toward the possession of as many resources as they can manage. The reasons are numerous: fear of war and of being cut off from external supplies; distrust of other countries, which may refuse to

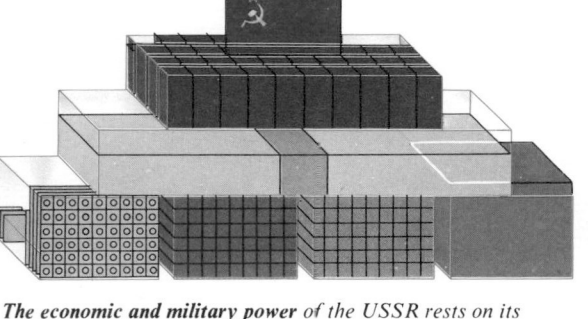

The economic and military power of the USSR rests on its possession of formidable strength in all four of the basic resources and on a political policy of maximum self-reliance.

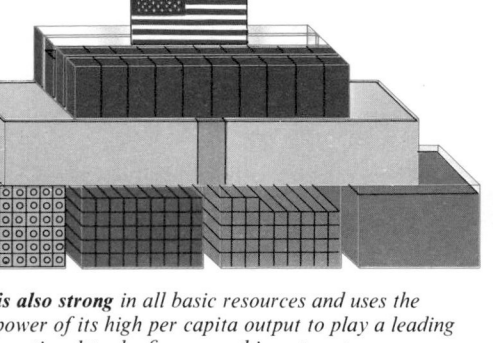

The USA is also strong in all basic resources and uses the economic power of its high per capita output to play a leading role in international trade, finance and investment.

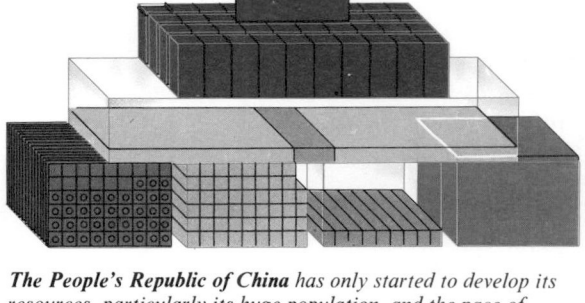

The People's Republic of China has only started to develop its resources, particularly its huge population, and the pace of development is geared to policies of self-sufficiency.

Throughout history, people have thought it obvious that the possession of resources leads to strength and plenty. The use of armed force has often been prompted by the desire to seize a neighbor's territory and acquire the resources contained in it. European colonization of America, Africa and much of Asia enabled countries such as Spain, Portugal, Holland, Britain, France and Belgium to enrich themselves by exploiting the food and mineral resources of vast territories. In the years leading up to World War II, Japan's desire for the resources of China and Southeast Asia, and Germany's for those of Eastern Europe, were significant factors in their decision to use force. Both wanted oil, industrial resources and command of populations.

The idea that a country will necessarily be better off if it is able to acquire the resources of other countries has been traditionally disputed by economists of the free trade school, who maintain that what counts is not the possession of resources but their use; it does not matter where the resources are so long as they can be traded. For example, Britain uses copper from Zambia and eats meat from Ireland and New Zealand; it does not need to possess the copper mines or grasslands within its own territory. Since World War II, the process of decolonization has, in general, reversed the tendency for powerful countries to acquire the possessions of others. Relieved of the burden of administration and the expense of maintaining military garrisons, some ex-colonial powers have found it more profitable to trade with their former possessions than to try to regain control of them.

Technology and capital

Complex patterns of dependency often remain between a newly independent nation and the previous imperial power, and these may leave considerable economic power in the hands of the former owners. Mere possession of resources is no

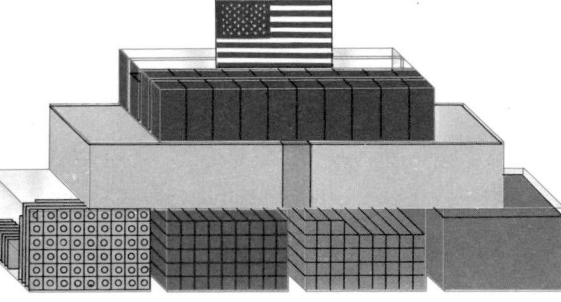

Sweden's power derives mainly from the high quality of its comparatively small population. This has led to optimal use of resources and efficient institutional frameworks.

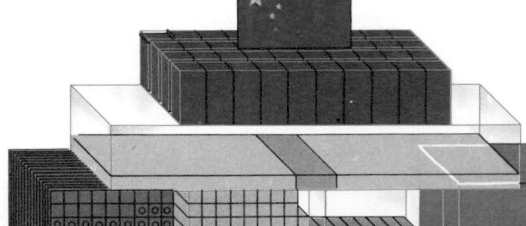

France has a relatively large, well-trained population, a sound agricultural base and the capacity to import much of the energy and minerals needed to maintain its power.

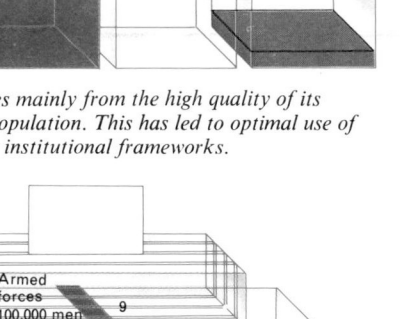

Armament levels

Nuclear arsenal
Nuclear capacity
Sophisticated weapons
Production of above

Armed forces
100,000 men   9

7   8   7

1M people
1M literate people

3   1   4   5   6

Population density   Nutritional levels

<10	<2,000
10–30	2,000–2,500
30–100	2,500–3,000
100–550 people per sq km	>3,000 Calories per day

The resource structure of certain selected countries is represented here in a series of building blocks showing how economic and military power rests on four basic resource categories. The population resource (1) is measured not only by size and density but also by quality, as indicated by literacy rates and the percentage (2) of eligible population (3) following a course of higher education. Agricultural production (4) is blocked in where countries rank among the top few nations in total output of certain foods. But output must be measured against population density, and nutritional levels more accurately represent the power of each state to feed itself well. Mineral strength (5) is shown only where a state is a leading producer of some important mineral. A nation's energy resource (6) involves a ratio of production to consumption and is indicated by whether countries have a deficit or surplus. These four fundamental resources are a major source of economic and

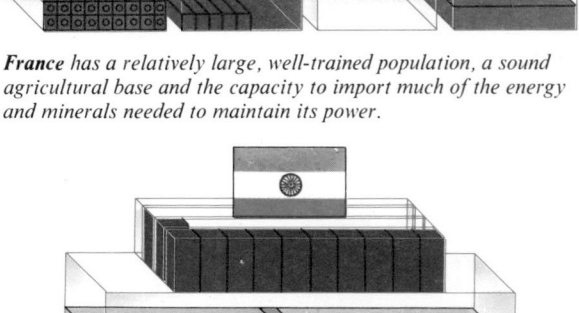

India's unskilled population, disproportionately large compared to its other basic resources, has hindered its emergence as a major world power economically and militarily.

military strength, indicated by per capita GNP (7), percentage of military expenditure (8) and force and armament levels (9). A number of other factors, difficult to show diagrammatically, also contribute to the power of a state. The ability of a well-organized country to make the best use of its resources is important, for instance. National will to exert influence over other states may account for some perceived differences in the relative power of states with similar resource bases. And while the most powerful states usually possess a broad spectrum of resources, some can exert influence through being strong in a single resource on which other countries are heavily dependent. Finally, the structure of the international system of trade and investment can be a source of power when some states, former colonial powers, are historically linked to countries that have retained trading relationships and are still economically dependent on them.

trade; inability to earn the foreign currency needed to buy resources from elsewhere; suspicion of foreign investors, who may develop resources solely in their own interests, and so on. There is a sense of security and independence in being able to say that your country is strong in the possession of the four basic natural resources—people, food, energy and minerals.

The ability to achieve such a sense of security is one of the ways in which a country's relative power can be measured. Powerful countries can either rely on their own resources to safeguard their standards of living or can exert sufficient influence to make sure that they are able to use the resources of others on favorable terms. Their influence may be military, political, economic or cultural. By possessing capital or technology, some countries are able to exert more power than others with large but undeveloped resources. Access to natural resources nevertheless remains crucial. Their acquisition by overt military force is today rare. But military force may be used to protect access. The rich copper resources of Shaba province have been a key factor in French and Belgian military involvement in Zaire, in 1978 for instance.

Internal conflicts

Resources thus provide the occasion for a good deal of international conflict, which sometimes leads to war. They also cause domestic conflict. The oldest form of politics is probably that which arises over land. In Europe, up to the industrial revolution of the eighteenth and nineteenth centuries (and afterward too), the possession of land was the main source of wealth, and control of land meant power within the state. Peasant societies have been characterized by land hunger and sometimes by riots over land tenure. Apart from the land itself, the products of the land—in particular, food and minerals—have also led to controversy. When

people in a city find that the food supply is failing they protest: "bread riots" are among the oldest forms of disturbances.

Conflicts arising from exploitation of minerals are equally deep-seated; in European history, coal and metal miners have been among the most militant of workers. Demands for public ownership have been strongest in the field of resources, so that coal mines have been a target for such demands in Europe, and energy resources in the United States. Most developing countries, whatever their ideological outlooks, believe that minerals should be under public ownership. Today there are conflicts over the rights of Eskimos and Native Indians in Canada and Aborigines in Australia, whose traditional lands contain minerals such as uranium, which provide great profits but the exploitation of which will disturb the future lives of the peoples on whose lands they are found. In every democratic country, farmers and miners are among the most politically minded groups. Everywhere, too, there is argument over which energy resources (coal, water, nuclear power) should be developed. The lesson seems to be that resources cannot be divorced from politics. Because economic activity cannot proceed without them, the people who own or control them, or can affect the way they are used, are likely to demand the right to say how they are to be used and what price must be paid, whether in money, in privileges, or in control over the economy.

Important political issues affect each of the four main kinds of natural resources. People are a basic resource prized by ambitious countries until recently when it became clear that too many mouths to feed could impede development and the achievement of higher living standards. It is now recognized that manpower is an advantage when skilled, a disadvantage when unskilled and unemployed (as in India). A government may seek a larger population so as to increase the range of skills or a smaller one to maximize the living standards of those left. There are social difficulties in either case. The zealous application of extreme birth-control measures by Mrs Gandhi's government in India was one of the reasons for its downfall in 1977. In other countries, such as Australia and Canada, positive efforts by governments to increase the flow of migrants in order to widen the range of skills are often opposed by trade unions.

Food is a resource that every country wants to maximize so as to reduce imports. Britain has continually done so since its dependency on others was exposed in World War II. However, self-sufficiency

in foodstuffs may mean paying high prices for local food, especially if land is poorly suited to food production and farmers lack special skills. The cost may be high in government expenditure on irrigation, roads, railways, storage facilities and agricultural education, and there may be high capital costs for machinery, stock, fencing and the like. People in cities may object to paying high prices for food simply because it is locally produced; there may be conflict over the size of farms and whether farmers with large properties on good land should be allowed to become rich.

Political aspects of development

The main sources of energy are in public hands in most countries, especially dams, power plants and electricity supply systems. Fundamental political issues are involved. The aim is cheap power for industry and private use, spread over as wide an area as possible; but costs of the basic facilities are high, consumers want cheap gas or electricity, rural users complain if they have to pay more than city dwellers, workers at power plants are likely to demand high wages, and there are arguments over where dams and power plants should be sited.

Minerals are a potent source of disagreement too. Orderly and sensible programs of exploitation are what everyone wants, with high return for the countries in which minerals are found and cheap raw materials for those that use them. This involves the age-old dispute between consumer and producer about what is a fair price. The oil, copper, aluminum and other companies getting minerals from the ground and marketing them are often worldwide in their activities, with no necessary concern about the welfare of the countries in which they operate. They are interested in keeping costs down and ensuring a free flow of products to the consuming countries, whereas countries for which the product is a prime source of prosperity, such as Jamaica with bauxite and Zambia with copper, want to get as much out of it as they can. At the same time some governments are uncomfortably aware that the pursuit of production and export profits for their own sake make them economically dependent on their customers and creates social problems within the country.

Internally, there are bound to be strains when a traditional society is suddenly exposed to technology, the wage system and the typical attitudes of large-scale modern industry. In a country such as Papua New Guinea, for example, the development of copper on the island of Bougainville has caused considerable disruption. Externally the country may find itself bound to particular buyers, without much power to affect prices. At the same time, it may find that the benefits of exporting minerals are confined to a relatively small number of its own people, while the rest are disaffected because the benefits are not spread to them.

There is concern about the harm done by the winning of resources—even the growing of more food—on ecological as well as social grounds. Environmental considerations have become more prominent in all the Western countries in recent years. These are real difficulties; but most governments in developing countries would rather risk them than leave resources undeveloped.

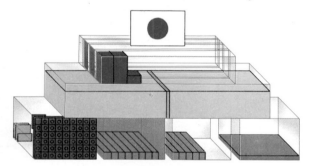

Japan's skilled, hard-working population is the basis of its large GNP, little of which is absorbed by military spending. A weakness is reliance on imported oil and raw materials.

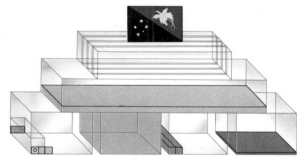

Papua New Guinea, one of the newest and least developed nations, has important mineral resources but lacks the broader base needed to convert this into significant power.

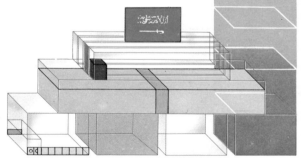

Saudi Arabia wields power through the possession of a single resource, oil. But its expanding economic and military strength will be limited by the narrowness of this base.

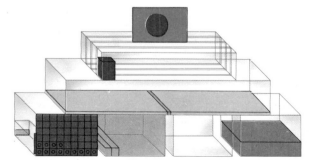

Bangladesh has difficulty in feeding and educating its large population and its energy deficit is serious because it cannot afford to pay for imports to fill the gap.

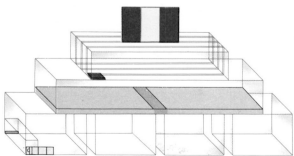

Chad, one of the least developed African nations, has not developed its resources to any extent and is thus dependent on outside help in its struggle to improve its economy.

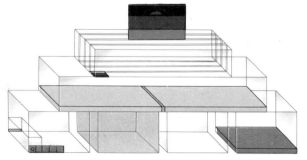

Malawi is similarly weak in basic resources, but has a better basis for development than Chad because of its higher levels of education, nutrition and energy output.

PATTERNS OF POSSESSION

The desire for the power and prestige that often accompanies wealth created from possession of a broad spectrum of resources was exemplified by the coronation of Emperor Bokassa in the Central African Empire on December 4, 1977. While Bokassa was crowned with all the trappings of wealth, similar to his idol, Napoleon, the coronation did not accurately reflect his position as head of a weak state in the international system. The Central African Empire is one of the poorest countries in the world, with virtually no developed resources and a per capita GNP of about $220. Even the coronation itself was largely financed by France. The desire of the developing countries for security, power and prestige, coupled with the uneven pattern of distribution and development of resources throughout the world, has led them to call for a redistribution of resources—they are no longer resigned to the mere imitation of well-being, expressed in Bokassa's coronation. Developed countries, on the other hand, often feel that the meager wealth of the developing countries is mismanaged or misspent. The United States was so displeased by the lavish spending on Bokassa's coronation that it discontinued all aid to the Central African Empire. The occasion illustrated the fact that in many developing countries it is the rich who have access to resource based wealth. The poor remain at subsistence level.

The uneven distribution of natural resources throughout the world leads to political problems, both within countries and internationally. In domestic politics, the argument is often one of who should own the resources and how wealth from them should be shared. Countries of the Western bloc usually favor a mixture of public and private ownership, relying on the profit motive to provide efficient use of some resources and on wage bargaining and some regulation of prices to redistribute the profits. The extent to which wealth is actually shared depends largely on how effective are the demands of the lower income earners. Centrally planned economies, on the other hand, rely almost wholly on public ownership and on state direction of resource development.

Internationally, imbalances in the pattern of resource possession have to be overcome mainly by countries selling what they have in return for what they need. Of the four basic resources—population, food, minerals and energy—population is the most difficult to redistribute. Although groupings such as the European Economic Community make possible limited migration of labor forces it is much more difficult for workers from overpopulated countries such as India to move to countries with the industrial capacity to employ them. Social and economic factors make it impossible for countries that have a large growth potential, such as Canada, to absorb labor in the way that the United States was able to in the nineteenth century. It is the quality of population—especially its capacity to operate the sophisticated techniques of modern industrial processes—rather than its size that now makes population a desirable resource. Population size alone can no longer be equated even with military power. It is true that countries with nuclear weapons (the United States, the USSR, China, Britain and France) all have large populations and that their capacities to produce these weapons arise partly from the effect of large populations in the

Redistribution of resources through international trade or aid is influenced by the economic organization and political alignments of the countries possessing or needing the resources. This diagram separates 46 countries according to the political poles to which they gravitate, with socialist, centrally planned economies to the left and market economies to the right. States with market economies are further grouped into those with traditional democratic institutions and those that do not have full working democracy or that are subject to periodic military or military backed rule. Members of military alliances are usually located close to each other on the political scale. Trade in other kinds of resources, however, can often cross political boundaries, although most of it takes place between states with similar economic organization. Countries with a degree of political or economic flexibility can trade more readily anywhere in the world. Tanzania and Yugoslavia, for instance, both conduct major resource-based relationships with countries that are politically dissimilar. Traditional socialist states (the nontraditional follow a pattern similar to that of nontraditional democratic states) are more limited in the number of states with which they exchange resources. Often a source of conflict, resources also enable political differences to be transcended.

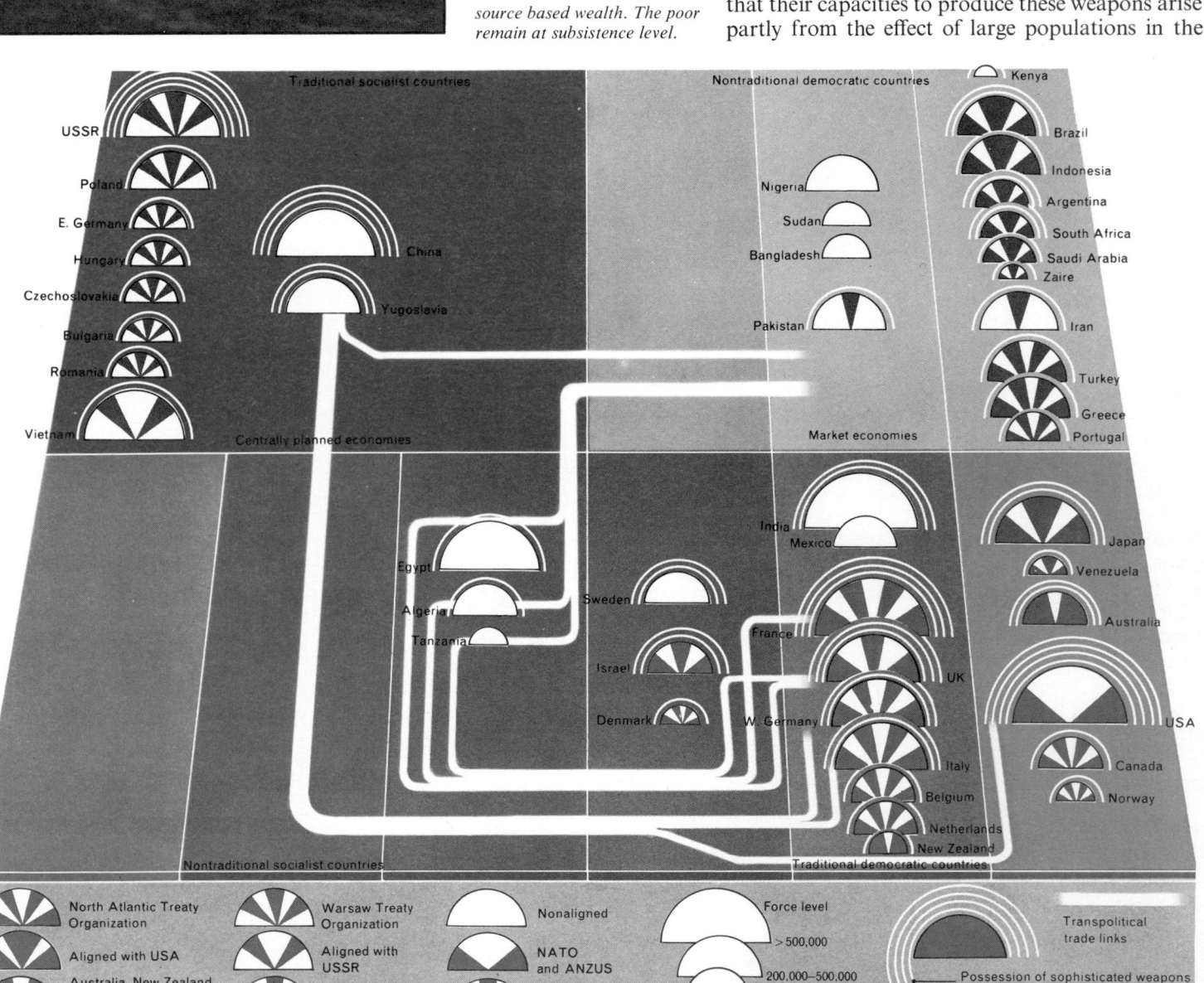

past helping them to build up productive and military capacity. But other countries with quite small populations and high technology, such as Israel, South Africa and Sweden, are also capable of producing nuclear weapons.

While there is relatively little scope for international cooperation in adjusting imbalances of population, it is easy for countries to exchange food, energy and minerals. But trade in all these resources is fraught with political problems, and complex patterns of dependency emerge. Japan, for instance, with few energy and mineral resources of its own, is placed in a potentially difficult position because its suppliers may combine against it to raise prices. Yet its financial strength is such that suppliers may find it attractive to offer it long-term contracts at favorable prices because there is no comparable alternative market. Brazil, on the other hand, has large potential resources of minerals and energy, but is heavily dependent on foreign investment and technology to develop them. Its military ruled political system and low wage level economy reflect its dependency on the goodwill of external investors and its need to show evidence of stability. A strong dependency pattern can also be seen in the trading and investment relationship between many newly independent countries and the former colonial powers.

Oil as a political weapon
In general, the less widely distributed an important resource is, the more valuable it is and the more power it confers on those who possess it. Oil, produced in relatively few places and needed by all, is the outstanding example of a resource becoming a political weapon. In international sanctions against unpopular countries such as Rhodesia (or Italy in the 1930s), oil is the commodity thought most essential, the denial of which might bring a country to its knees. Attempts by the UN Security Council to deny oil to Rhodesia show how hard it is to cut off all possible sources of supply, especially when, like Rhodesia, the boycotted country has other resources that people want to buy. Members of the Organization of Petroleum Exporting Countries (OPEC), however, have effectively used their near monopoly of supply to force the industrialized countries to pay much more for oil and to take more notice of their political wishes.

Middle East oil states, which produced 90 percent of the oil traded in 1972, were in a position to achieve a fivefold increase in the oil price in 1973–74, causing tremors throughout the economies of both the industrialized countries and the developing world. Through production cutbacks, a selective embargo and the threat of further price rises, the Arab states achieved more support for their position against Israel, a greater say in monetary decision making and gains in technical and economic cooperation. Nations such as Iran are using their oil wealth to become significant regional military powers and the same revenues are placing in the hands of some developing countries formidable investment resources.

Broadly speaking, the major powers are self-sufficient in energy at low levels of production and consumption; but to sustain economic growth they have to import. Countries that lack major energy resources and also (unlike Japan) lack the industrial power to pay high prices for the raw materials, find themselves in grave difficulties when prices for oil and other fuels rise.

In essential food resources, most countries are largely self-sufficient. But in some countries, where normal production is subject to drought, flood, pests and other scourges, famine remains a real threat. The conscience of the Western world is stirred from time to time by reports of famine in India or Africa. The solution of the problem of underproduction is, however, often hard to find, because it is bound up with climatic factors and also with the traditional social organization (including the ownership and

The economic dependence of five former UK colonies is shown by their export patterns. First, exports make up a large proportion of GNP, which demonstrates their im- portance to the overall welfare of each nation. Second, the exports are mainly raw materials, which are subject to price fluctuations and hence deny the exporter sustained *earnings on which to base economic diversification. Third, the bulk of the exports goes to a single country, the UK. In contrast, the UK is not reliant on any particular* country or group of commodities and can easily adapt to market changes. The significance of dependency is that it provides the metropolitan power with a political lever.

cultivation of land). In India and the USSR there is also argument over the competing claims of agriculture and industry for capital.

In terms of living standards, countries that export food are in some ways more vulnerable than those that import it, for many of them are largely or wholly dependent on these exports for their foreign exchange earnings. The Caribbean countries, for example, are heavily dependent on sugar exports, Mauritius even more so. Latin American countries such as Brazil and Colombia still depend heavily on sales of coffee, as does Sri Lanka on tea. Of the developed countries, New Zealand has based its high standard of living largely on exports of meat, wool and dairy products.

Such dependence on exports of food, or of fibers such as wool and cotton, can cause bitter argument when consumer countries reduce imports or prices. Food exports, like mineral exports, are much at the mercy of market forces, being subject to gluts or shortages. Efforts have been made to remedy this by international commodity agreements, whereby producer and consumer countries would settle price ranges and production quotas. Such agreements are hard to keep up: consumer countries are tempted to go beyond them when supplies can be obtained more cheaply outside the agreement, while producers are similarly tempted when demand is high. A further complication is that many countries are both producers and importers of food. Prices paid to local farmers are influenced by political factors and can have major effects in discouraging or encouraging production.

Commodity agreements are also sought for minerals, especially by developing countries such

as Zambia that are almost wholly dependent on mineral exports for their foreign exchange earnings. But commodity agreements for minerals are even more difficult to achieve than those for foodstuffs. The example of OPEC has encouraged hopes of similar price-fixing schemes for minerals such as bauxite, tin, copper and iron ore. But mineral resources tend to be widespread and producer countries lack the common interests shared by the Middle East oil-producing states. The industrialized countries, many of which are themselves rich in minerals, can sometimes turn to alternatives.

In exploiting minerals, technology and capital is often more important than the possession of a resource. The technological lead established by the industrialized countries puts them in a strong position to exploit new mineral resources, including those on the seabed. Developing countries depend largely on multinational companies located in the consumer countries for the capital as well as the technology required to mine and transport their mineral resources.

The political problems inherent in the pattern of international possession of food, mineral and to some extent energy resources can thus be simplified by saying that poor countries that have them face rich countries that need them—but which also control the markets, the capital and the technology that enables them to be sold. It is no wonder that so much political discussion between the rich and poor countries has centered on the terms and conditions under which the poor will supply the rich. Those that possess resources are increasingly aware that they need to use their combined strength to obtain adequate rewards.

THE DIPLOMACY OF RESOURCES

Cooperation between the governments of China, Zambia and Tanzania led to the construction of the Tan-Zam railway—an event celebrated by these children holding aloft photographs of the national leaders Kenneth Kaunda (Zambia), Julius Nyerere (Tanzania) and Mao Tse-tung (China), at a ceremony held to mark the border crossing in 1974. A vital part of the transport system of Tanzania and Zambia, the railway carries commodities to urban areas for consumption and to the port of Dar es Salaam for export to other countries. Skilled personnel, a resource in short supply locally, was provided by China in this instance of international liaison in resource development. The need for international pooling of effort is widely recognized, but because of political problems the sharing of resources has remained largely a bilateral affair. Most important multilateral institutions are at present used to promote the interests of particular groups of nations, and states are usually unwilling to surrender to multilateral organizations the right to determine who shall receive resources they allot to aid. A less competitive atmosphere is needed before resource development can be put on a multilateral footing.

Since World War II, and especially since the establishment in 1964 of the United Nations Conference on Trade and Development (UNCTAD), the number of organizations dealing with international management of resources has expanded steadily. Governments as well as traders in particular commodities can now exchange information and negotiate about resources through a wide range of organizations, many of them staffed by civil servants whose task it is to encourage rich and poor countries to cooperate.

The diplomacy of resources is not confined to the multilateral level of the UN and its agencies. More significant, at least in the short run, are the negotiations between groups of countries with related interests. A notable example was the series of negotiations leading up to the Lomé Agreement between the European Economic Community and the former colonies of EEC members. This agreement safeguards access to traditional markets in Europe and guarantees minimum earnings in spite of fluctuating world prices. Bilateral negotiations are equally important. These may be between a government and a multinational company seeking to exploit mineral resources. Or they may involve barter agreements—particularly between communist governments, which themselves own resources and products and can trade in food, raw materials and energy as well as processed goods without the need for foreign exchange.

Market uncertainties

Fully bilateral trade under market conditions is more difficult to achieve. The ideal situation is one in which the one possible buyer of a resource is negotiating with the one possible seller. Instead, a number of producers of a resource are usually trying to sell to a number of markets. As a result, both buyers and sellers find it hard to agree. A commodity agreement may break down if a higher price or supplies from outside are obtainable; a barter agreement may not survive if a new customer appears in the offing; a cartel's members may disagree about policy; and the free market may not provide a price high enough to encourage pro-

duction. The fallibility of these alternatives, and the uncertainties that result, are amongst the reasons why the developing countries have increasingly demanded that international economics be seen as a whole and operated to improve their positions permanently. This is what underlies the debates at UNCTAD, at the UN General Assembly, and in such specialized conferences as those on the law of the sea: the poorer states have been demanding a new international economic order.

The pattern of dependency

Basically, these discussions have arisen from the conviction of many people in less-developed nations and of those in the developed countries who are interested in their future that the processes of international trade, finance and transport—in fact the international economy at large—are unfair to the developing countries and prevent their achieving higher living standards. Those who support this view point to the frequent swings up and down in world commodity prices in contrast with the relatively stable or rising prices of manufactured goods. It is true that some industrialized countries are themselves leading exporters of commodities—notably of wheat, rice, zinc, lead, tungsten and copper. But developing countries are more dependent on a narrow range of exports, and therefore more vulnerable to falls in commodity prices. Developed countries protect their own food producers but are reluctant to enter into commodity agreements to stabilize the prices of foodstuffs from less-developed nations. Within UNCTAD, the Group of 77 (virtually all the developing countries) has been trying to stabilize supply and demand for 10 core products—cocoa, coffee, cotton, copper, jute, rubber, sisal, sugar, tea and tin—but attempts so far have met with limited success.

UNCTAD has nevertheless been an important means of dramatizing the needs of the developing world. Apart from commodity price fluctuations, critics of the existing economic order have drawn attention to the difficulties faced by developing countries when they seek capital investment in a wide range of economic activities, in contrast to

the ease with which capital can be raised for such exploitative pursuits as mining. They point to what amounts to a Western monopoly of international insurance and shipping. They argue that the dependence of developing countries on the training facilities, patents and expertise of the developed countries puts them in a permanently inferior position. They emphasize the difficulty most developing countries have in catching up to the economic development of the West; and they seek not only economic aid of the conventional kind but a fundamental readjustment of the international economy—a new kind of relationship between states with spare resources and those that wish to use the resources.

Essentially, such a readjustment would mean the Western countries paying more for the things they buy from the Third World, contributing much more to their development capital (80 percent of investment in the developing countries now comes from local sources), opening up trade secrets and subsidizing the growth of services such as shipping and insurance in the less developed countries. Developed nations would also be expected to lower the high tariffs they have imposed in order to protect certain industries from low-cost goods from abroad. There would need to be much more processing of resources in the country of origin, together with a greater ownership of equipment by that country, and a scheme for avoiding fluctuations in prices on the world market so that a developing country could plan for further investment and greater proceeds in the future.

Political problems

In the most basic sense, the demand for a new international economic order is for a massive transfer of the means to create goods and services from the rich to the poorer countries. It is not surprising that there has been resistance in the major developed countries to this sort of thinking. Massive transfers of the kind envisaged would go well beyond the aid programs of the past, under which the average contribution made by major Western nations has been about 0.33 percent of their GNP. Direct aid as such has not proved a particularly fruitful way of encouraging development, being often misapplied or manipulated by a donor government for political ends. The kind of assistance now sought is likely to be more effective —but also raises more political problems in the countries that are expected to contribute.

Since Europe, North America and Japan are being asked to bear the burden of the change, and since their economies are geared to profit making, the major companies engaged in the international economy must be assured of their profits before any change could work. (Although they operate some aid programs, the USSR and other communist states in general stand clear of the debate on a new economic order, arguing that the deplorable condition of poorer countries is due to their exploitation by capitalists in the past and that the capitalists should pay.) Another difficulty is that the developing countries differ considerably in their possession of resources, so that commodity agreements might benefit some without helping others.

To sum up, there is an abstract argument for continual transfers from the haves to the have-nots, but it is difficult to decide who are the most deserving have-nots and how they should be helped. The political instability of some developing countries is a discouragement. At the same time, there is difficulty in persuading the governments and electors in democratic developed countries to improve the living standards of others at the expense of their own. Meanwhile, the possession of resources remains an advantage in itself, but an advantage much modified by the fact that the resources often have to be exploited in cooperation with others, and the further fact that those who eventually use them do not want to pay much for them.

Aid-giving countries listed below provide the bulk of world development assistance. The blue-coded countries are members of the Development Assistance Committee, the red are centrally planned economies and the gray are OPEC states. Bars on the graph represent total aid for 1975, expressed as a percentage of GNP, while darker colors show how much of this was concessional aid rather than investment and non-concessional loans. The dramatic scale of assistance from OPEC states reflects the oil revenues of 1974. Much of it went to Islamic developing countries of the Middle East and Africa, a notable example of the way in which aid is usually linked to the cultural or political interests of the aid-giving states. This is brought out more fully in the three maps on the right, which show the comparative levels of per capita aid received by Latin American,

African and Asian developing countries for 1973–75, segmented according to the contribution made by each category of donor states. Political changes since 1975, especially in Southeast Asia, have in turn altered the aid-giving partners of such countries as Angola, Laos and Kampuchea. Another indicator of the political nature of aid is the way it has resulted to a large extent from bilateral agreements.

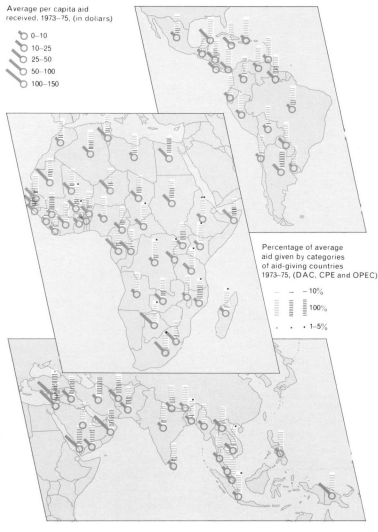

Average per capita aid received, 1973–75, (in dollars)
0–10
10–25
25–50
50–100
100–150

Percentage of average aid given by categories of aid-giving countries 1973–75, (DAC, CPE and OPEC)
– – 10%
100%
1–5%

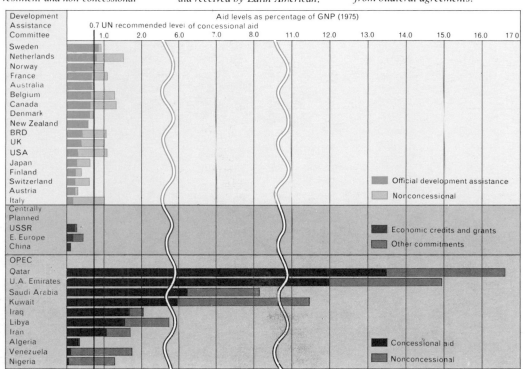

Development Assistance Committee	Aid levels as percentage of GNP (1975)														
0.7 UN recommended level of concessional aid	1.0	2.0	6.0	7.0	8.0	11.0	12.0	13.0	14.0	15.0	16.0	17.0			
Sweden															
Netherlands															
Norway															
France															
Australia															
Belgium															
Canada															
Denmark															
New Zealand															
BRD															
UK															
USA															
Japan															
Finland															
Switzerland															
Austria															
Italy															

Official development assistance
Nonconcessional

Centrally Planned															
USSR															
E. Europe															
China															

Economic credits and grants
Other commitments

OPEC															
Qatar															
U.A. Emirates															
Saudi Arabia															
Kuwait															
Iraq															
Libya															
Iran															
Algeria															
Venezuela															
Nigeria															

Concessional aid
Nonconcessional

International organizations play a prominent role in the diplomacy of resources because of the collective political power that can be expressed through them. In those with the widest membership—the UN and UNCTAD—conflicts of interest appear between developed and less-developed countries. For the less-developed UNCTAD is a particularly useful forum.

Membership is broad in both the International Monetary Fund (IMF) and the General Agreement on Tariffs and Trade (GATT). But the IMF uses a voting structure that is weighted heavily in favor of developed countries, while GATT's efforts to promote free trade in manufactures have tended to reinforce the status quo internationally.

Regional organizations link strong and weaker states and usually reflect the interests of the majority, although policy may be swayed by a single powerful member such as the US in the OAS. For developing countries, the Conference of Nonaligned Nations provides a wider forum for pressure on decolonization and development issues.

Military and general economic groupings need a degree of political cohesiveness if they are to be effective. NATO and WTO, whose members have close common interests, are more effective, for instance, than CENTO. In the economic field, CMEA and OECD unite nations with common interests in coordinating resource management.

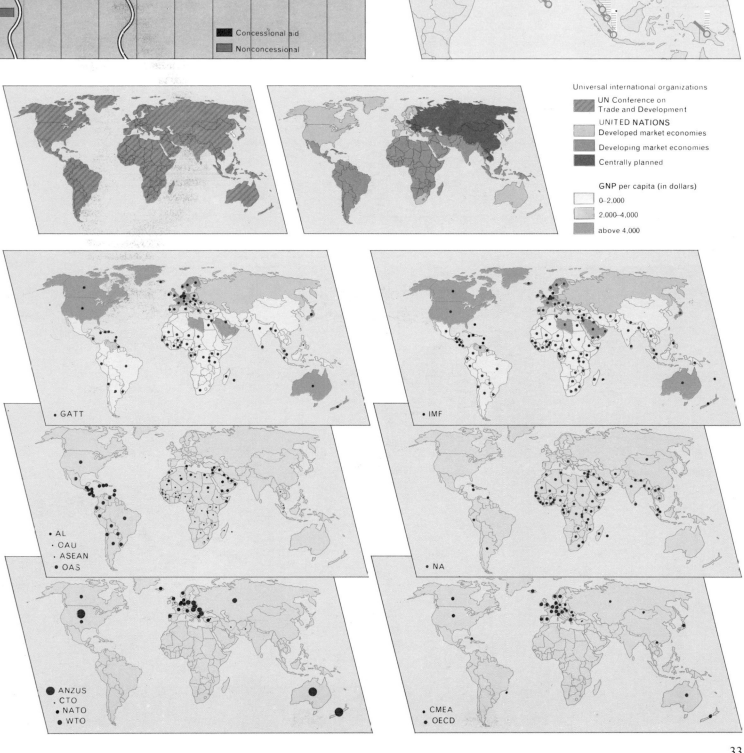

Universal international organizations
UN Conference on Trade and Development
UNITED NATIONS
Developed market economies
Developing market economies
Centrally planned

GNP per capita (in dollars)
0–2,000
2,000–4,000
above 4,000

• GATT

• IMF

• AL
• CAU
• ASEAN
• OAS

• NA

• ANZUS
• CTO
• NATO
• WTO

• CMEA
• OECD

33

PATTERNS OF TRADE

Sacks of Brazilian coffee are here being loaded into a ship's hold at the port of Santos. Brazil is the world's largest producer of coffee and the foreign exchange earned from its export plays a vital role in the country's development. With capital earned from coffee Brazil is erecting an industrial sector to process many of its vast resources.

In the earliest days of international trade the most sought-after trade goods were the luxuries of the wealthy, from the gold, silver, precious stones and ivory mentioned in ancient Egyptian records to the spices, tea, coffee and tobacco which were highly valued in seventeenth-century Europe.

With large-scale industrialization, however, the nature of world trade changed dramatically. Industry generated demands for large quantities of fuel and raw materials, and the growth of urban populations, which provided the industrial labor force, created demands for food far beyond what could ever be produced locally. Thus, the industrialized regions of the world came to rely on increasing imports of industrial raw materials and foodstuffs, while, in turn, deriving much of their own prosperity from the export of manufactured goods.

The deployment of resources in the modern world accordingly became based on specialization and exchange; just as individuals specialize in certain kinds of work, so countries, or regions within countries, specialize in the production of certain types of goods, which are then distributed to other countries by means of trade.

One classic economic justification for this specialization of production is found in the principle of comparative advantage. Suppose that two countries, A and B, both produce only two commodities, wheat and cloth. Country A is the more efficient producer of both commodities, producing twice the output of wheat as B for the same cost; while, of cloth, A is able to produce three times as much as B for the same cost. It does not follow that A should produce both these commodities and B

neither, since the most efficient use of the total resources of both countries is achieved if each specializes in producing the commodity in which it has a comparative advantage. Otherwise the resources of B would be underutilized. Thus, country A, which produces cloth three times as efficiently as B, but wheat only twice as efficiently, should concentrate on producing cloth, while B should concentrate on producing wheat. According to this principle, there is always an incentive toward specialization and trade, even when one country is better endowed in all sectors of production than another.

The principle of comparative advantage suggests that a free trade, or *laissez faire*, policy should prevail, to the mutual benefit of all countries. In practice, nations often attempt to control trade by imposing tariffs, or other nontariff barriers, on imports, which may make some goods so costly as to effectively bar their entry.

An era of free trade

Two periods have had great influence on the evolution of the present international trade system. The first was the mid- to late-nineteenth century, which is generally accepted as an era of free trade. During this period there were few international conflicts; great advances in industrialization were made and, at least for Europe and the Americas, it was a period of rapidly increasing prosperity.

In contrast, the inter-war period between 1919 and 1939 was neither economically nor politically stable. It was a period of depression, and the need for resources on which to build national economies is considered to be one of the foremost causes of World War II. Armed with these two examples negotiators attempted to erect an international system of trade after World War II that was based on free trade and flow of capital.

The General Agreement on Tariffs and Trade (GATT) was set up in 1947 by 23, mainly industrialized, countries with the intention of dismantling protectionist mechanisms within international trade, while the International Monetary Fund (IMF) is the organization intended to stabilize international currencies. The existence of GATT has facilitated the emergence of customs unions, and these have had a fair degree of success in lowering

The import–export balance of various groups of countries, and the destination of exports from each, is shown on the diagram. All the groups, except one, registered trade deficits in 1975. The location of the major oil exporting nations in the Middle East, coupled with oil price rises, has caused the Middle East as a whole to register a significant surplus, which, in turn, has added greatly to the deficits suffered by the other groups of countries. It can be seen that the developed nations dominate the pattern of world trade and that the greatest percentage of their trade is among themselves.

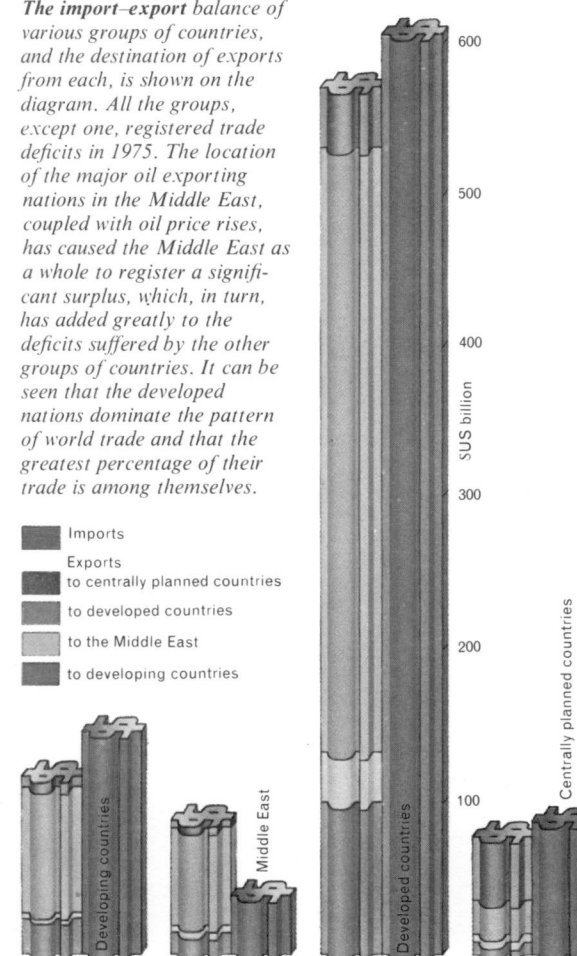

- ■ Imports
- Exports
- ■ to centrally planned countries
- ■ to developed countries
- ■ to the Middle East
- ■ to developing countries

High tariffs are levied against manufactured goods to protect domestic industries, usually at the behest of pressure groups.

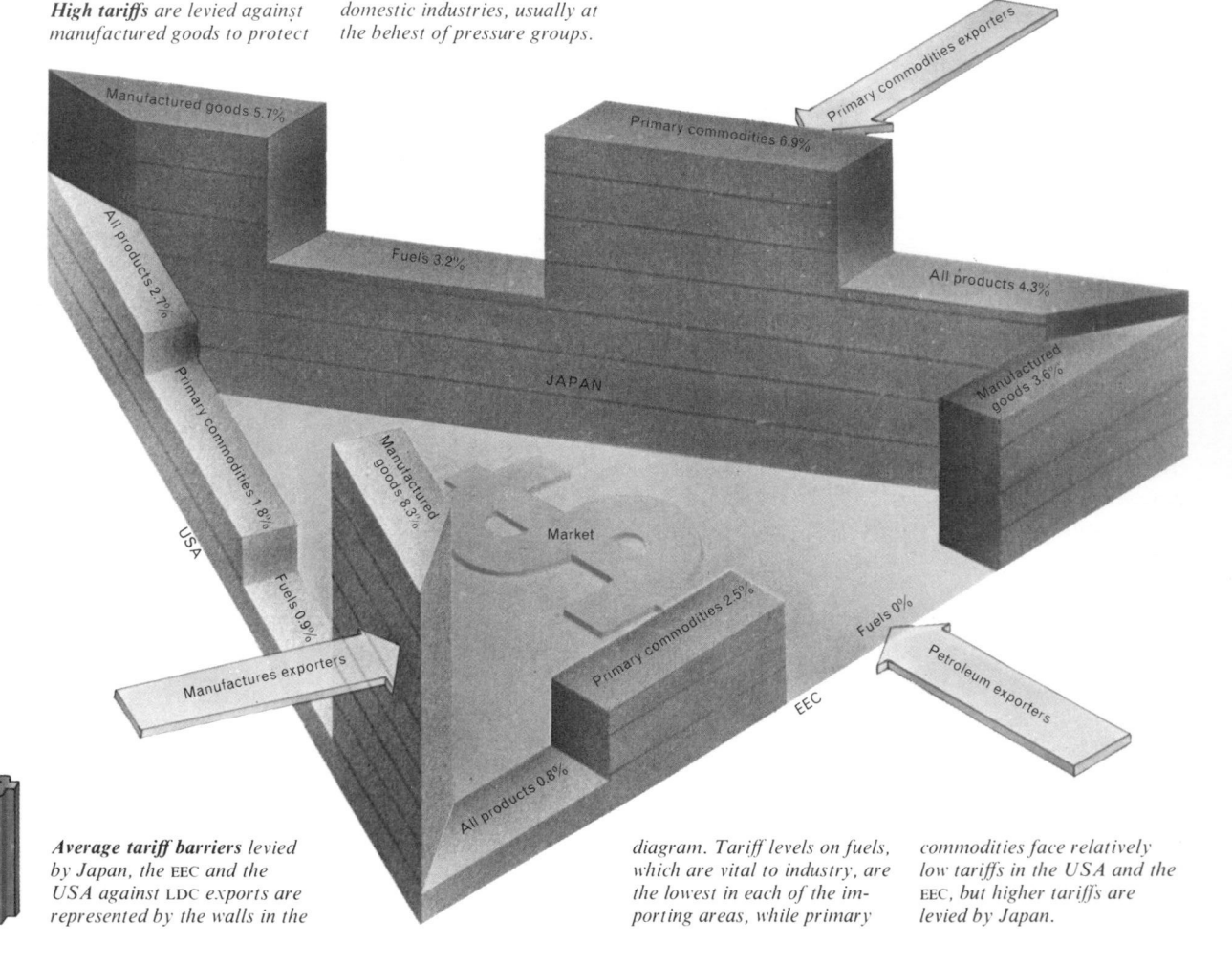

Average tariff barriers levied by Japan, the EEC and the USA against LDC exports are represented by the walls in the diagram. Tariff levels on fuels, which are vital to industry, are the lowest in each of the importing areas, while primary commodities face relatively low tariffs in the USA and the EEC, but higher tariffs are levied by Japan.

trade barriers between the participating countries. Next the European Coal and Steel Community (ECSC), established in 1952, provided for the free movement of coal and steel products between six countries of Western Europe, leading the way to fuller economic union under the now-enlarged European Economic Community (EEC). The success of the EEC in stimulating trade can be gauged from the fact that during its first decade the Community's exports and imports to and from external partners more than doubled, while trade between the member countries increased fourfold.

The Council for Mutual Economic Assistance (COMECON) allows wide-ranging free trade and barter between the USSR and its allies in Eastern Europe. Other customs unions exist in varying stages of development in Latin America, Africa and the Middle East.

While the greatest volume of trade takes place between industrially developed countries, the relative importance of foreign trade tends to be less in those countries which have very large areas and populations, the technical capacity to produce a wide range of goods and a viable internal market. Among developing nations, a few, such as India, are large enough to support a wide range of industries and rely little on trade, but most have smaller economies and have to import manufactured goods for which they must pay by exporting primary products. For them, trade becomes vitally important as a foreign exchange earner.

The USSR, with its vast area and resources and a self-contained, centrally planned economy, has not generally been a major participant in world trade; but in its massive grain purchases from the USA at lower prices than demand dictated it has demonstrated a shrewd ability to operate in the international trading market.

While much of the prosperity of the industrialized nations has been based on trade, those countries which are dependent on the export of primary products, such as Zambia with copper and Sri Lanka with tea, remain to an uncomfortable degree dependent on the more powerful economies.

Changing situations

Increasing cooperation among primary producer countries, however, means that they can exercise a degree of power over market conditions much greater than was once considered possible. The best example of this is the case of the Organization of Petroleum Exporting Countries (OPEC) which, through concerted action and the control of a sufficiently large share of world production, has been able to stabilize oil prices at a high level. Petroleum is today the largest single commodity in world trade, a situation which has changed dramatically since the earlier years of the century when the leading commodities were coal and wheat.

The developing countries want to change the present system of international trade. Their aim is to eliminate the biases of the system against primary-commodity exporters and low-income countries. In 1964 the United Nations Conference on Trade and Development (UNCTAD) was established in recognition of the deficiencies of international trade under the GATT regime.

Principles and plans to eliminate the bias in the international system of trade include access to markets of developed countries for LDC goods on the basis of non-reciprocity (that is LDCs need not lower their trade barriers in order to obtain the same from developed countries), and, more recently, the notion of an integrated commodity scheme under which a common fund would provide for the financing of buffer stocks to maintain stable prices on important primary commodities. It is notable, however, that those who are calling for the reform of the international system of trade do not wish to renounce the free market system altogether, as some socialist countries have done, but merely to correct the deficiencies that exist.

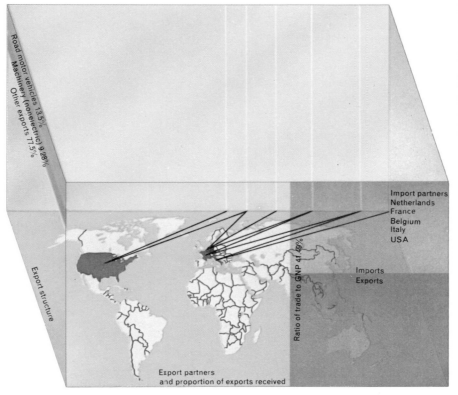

West Germany
Trade structure (1976)

	$ US million
Exports	102,032
Imports	87,782
Total trade	189,814
Trade balance	14,250
Export growth 1970–76	15.1%
Import growth 1970–76	13.6%
Primary commodities as a percentage of merchandise exports	11%

West Germany has a healthy trading sector, and with a trade surplus that is now approaching the level of Saudi Arabia and a significant growth of exports the country's moderate reliance on trade has proved profitable. Furthermore, West Germany is neither dependent on primary commodities nor on a small group of products for export earnings, so fluctuating prices are less likely to affect earnings. Germany is not reliant on imports because its industry can supply much of what is needed to run the economy. Some primary commodities are imported.

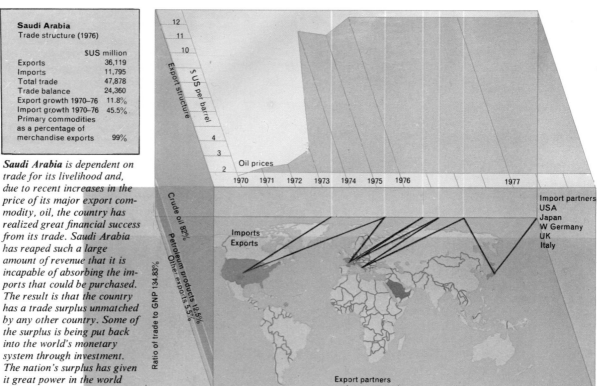

Saudi Arabia
Trade structure (1976)

	$US million
Exports	36,119
Imports	11,795
Total trade	47,878
Trade balance	24,360
Export growth 1970–76	11.8%
Import growth 1970–76	45.5%
Primary commodities as a percentage of merchandise exports	99%

Saudi Arabia is dependent on trade for its livelihood and, due to recent increases in the price of its major export commodity, oil, the country has realized great financial success from its trade. Saudi Arabia has reaped such a large amount of revenue that it is incapable of absorbing the imports that could be purchased. The result is that the country has a trade surplus unmatched by any other country. Some of the surplus is being put back into the world's monetary system through investment. The nation's surplus has given it great power in the world monetary system.

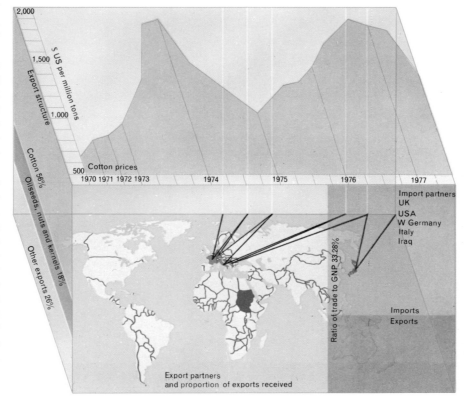

Sudan
Trade structure (1976)

	$ US million
Exports	554
Imports	980
Total trade	1,534
Trade balance	426
Export growth 1970–76	9%
Import growth 1970–76	7.8%
Primary commodities as a percentage of merchandise exports	99%

Sudan is a developing nation which has not had much success in financing its development through trade. The country is heavily dependent on primary commodities for export earnings and throughout the 1970s Sudan has consistently registered a trade deficit. The price of its major export, cotton, has fluctuated during the same period. The trade situation in Sudan has left the country with a shortage of foreign exchange with which to finance vital imports. Loans, particularly from Middle Eastern countries, help to fill the gap in foreign exchange earnings.

TRANSPORT & RESOURCES

Movement over any distance, whether passenger travel or the transshipment of raw materials or manufactured goods, depends on the availability of suitable means of transport. Historically, since the invention of the wheel the development of transport technologies has proved a vital concomitant to the discovery and exploitation of the Earth's resources. Still today, advanced nations and developing countries alike are preoccupied with the need to secure the effective (and cost-efficient) transport systems which are essential to social and economic growth.

During the second millennium BC, China had a highly developed, centrally administered road network. In the West, the demands of commerce and military control in the Roman Empire resulted in the creation of the network of wide, straight highways which was to form the basis of much of Europe's present-day road system. In later centuries, improvement of roads was at best piecemeal, stimulated less by the demands of trade than by military requirements.

The railroad revolution

There was no major innovation in land transport until the Industrial Revolution gave birth to the railroad. Even before then, difficulties of hauling coal and limestone to the iron furnaces in bulk had given rise to the use of iron tracks for horse-drawn wagons. By 1801 the development of the steam engine had progressed to the stage where it could be applied to traction, and experiments were made in steam locomotion. It was Stephenson's Rocket which, in 1829, proved the feasibility of the steam railroad by pulling a 13-ton load over 48 kilometers (30 miles) of track in just over two hours. From the 1830s on, railroad construction spread rapidly to many parts of the world. During this pioneering age, the main role of road transport was in supplementing the rail network. Road transport was nowhere as efficient, and was only used where necessary—to destinations not served by rail. It was not to become competitive with rail until paved roads, suitable for high-speed motor traffic, were built following the development of the internal combustion engine a century ago.

Water transport

Historically, water transport has proved as important as movement on land. Rivers provide natural routeways along which movement is often easier than it is on land. From the sixteenth century onward, expanding trade in Europe led to the construction of extensive canal networks, linking navigable rivers, for the bulk transport of raw materials and goods. Slow and inflexible, however, canal transport was largely eclipsed in Britain by the coming of the railway.

Trading incentives, too, prompted the development of seagoing vessels. Although the Phoenicians are credited with having circumnavigated Africa in the sixth century BC, the trouble with the early trade routes was that they were often circuitous, relying on prevailing winds to assist navigation by sail. So, the introduction of steam power in the mid-nineteenth century not only led to faster ships carrying more cargo but also paved the way for more direct trade routes. The opening of the Suez and Panama canals (in 1869 and 1914 respectively) further altered the patterns of use of ocean routes. Although many of the main shipping routes have changed little over the past century, new routes—notably the oil tanker routes from the Middle East to Europe and North America—have assumed major significance as a result of changing patterns of world trade.

While, in principle, shipping routes in international waters offer free passage to ships of all nations, movement is often influenced by political and strategic factors. For example, the closure of the Suez Canal due to hostilities in 1956 and 1967 caused cargoes to be diverted to much longer routes

Containerization, the carriage of goods in standardized steel crates, is a time- and cost-saving solution to the problem of cargoes which require transfer between road or rail and ships. Massively expensive to build, special container ports, such as this one at Norfolk on the east coast of America, feature deep-berthing facilities and are equipped with high-speed lifting gear to guarantee container vessels a quick turnaround.

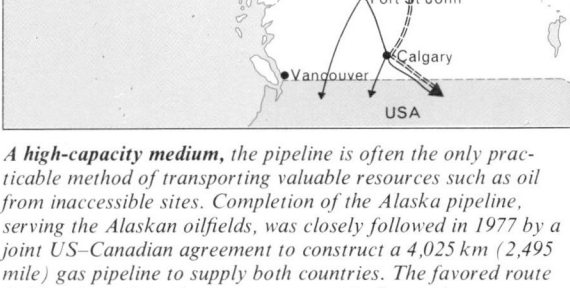

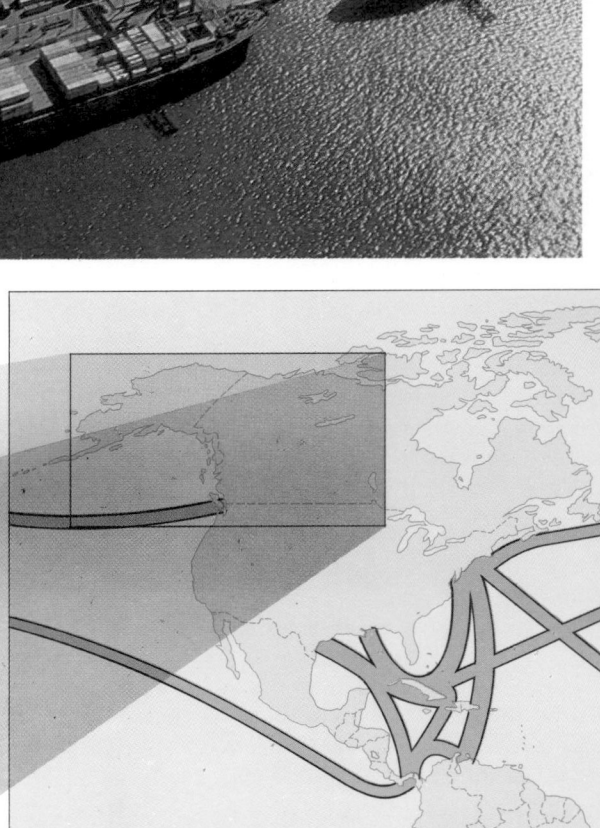

A high-capacity medium, the pipeline is often the only practicable method of transporting valuable resources such as oil from inaccessible sites. Completion of the Alaska pipeline, serving the Alaskan oilfields, was closely followed in 1977 by a joint US–Canadian agreement to construct a 4,025 km (2,495 mile) gas pipeline to supply both countries. The favored route (of four investigated over some years) is shown above.

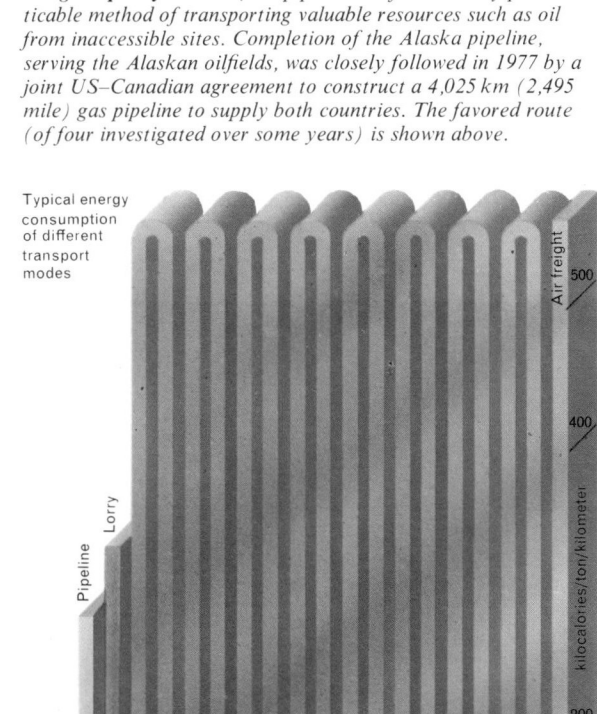

Typical energy consumption of different transport modes

Energy—a principal determinant of cost—is an increasingly important factor in the movement of the raw materials and manufactured goods which are the substance of trade. Other variables include time, labor and distance. At either extreme are inland waterways, slow but fairly cheap, and air freight, which is expensive and extravagant in energy, but may be the only feasible option in the case, say, of perishable goods.

Landlocked Zambia's main lifeline, the rail link south through Rhodesia, was severed following UDI in 1965. Two main alternatives were tried: the rail line through Angola and the new Tan-Zam railway running northeast. However, both sides' ports are inadequate for the copper which is Zambia's principal export and for the imported fertilizer vital to its corn. To forestall famine, Zambia has had to reopen the southern link.

Guardian of the world's largest proven oil reserves, Saudi Arabia is using its revenue to tackle underdevelopment. Much of the country is uninhabited, with the area known as the Empty Quarter extending to more than 647,500 sq km (250,000 sq miles). The government has earmarked $43 billion—almost a quarter of its budget—under the current five-year plan for the development of transport and communications.

around the Cape of Good Hope. There are important strategic implications, too, to the control of the Panama Canal.

Although the world shipping industry has, through UNCTAD conferences, achieved a considerable degree of cooperation, national fleets are often in competition for trade. This sometimes prompts protectionist measures by governments anxious to safeguard the interests of their own national fleets. Many developing countries, in particular, benefit little from the growth of the world shipping industry. In 1975 developing countries accounted for 61 percent of all goods loaded and 19 percent of all goods unloaded, yet their national fleets comprised less than seven percent of the world total deadweight tonnage.

A major breakthrough

The invention of powered flight—and ultimately the development of commercial aviation—was arguably the single most important breakthrough in the history of transport. For the first time movement was no longer confined to the Earth's surface, and it became possible, therefore, to traverse physical obstacles of land and sea with equal ease. Since 1910, air transport has expanded throughout the

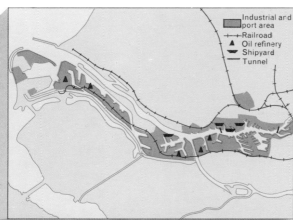

Many traditional ports, unable to take bulk carriers, have responded by developing deep-water facilities downstream. Rotterdam's "outport," Europoort, was built along with associated industrial areas after World War II; a container port, the Rijnpoort project, is newly completed. The world's largest port, Rotterdam handled 280 million tons of cargo in 1977.

Though eclipsed in some places by rail and air, inland waterways remain competitive. The Netherlands, a focal point of European and world trade, has an elaborate canal network based on its own and neighboring river systems (left) broad enough for large vessels. More extensive than the rail network, Dutch waterways carry more than a third of goods in transit.

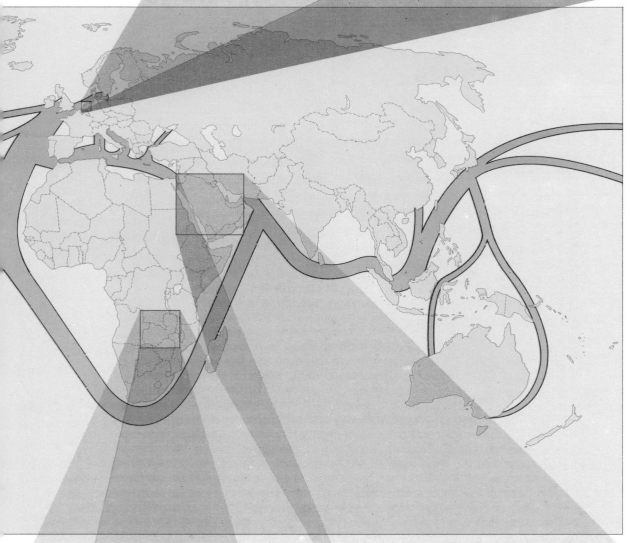

world. Today, besides speeding movement over established routes, it provides a link with places inaccessible to surface transport.

Different transport modes may be both complementary and competitive. Most often the fundamental factor governing choice is cost, but, while rates increase with distance for all methods of carriage, the relationship is rarely a simple linear one. In addition to operating costs, the movement of goods involves certain "terminal" charges—including port or airport facilities, loading and unloading—and these are essentially the same for a given mode, irrespective of distance. Water transport generally has the lowest operating cost per ton-kilometer, but it is the slowest and terminal costs are high. Rail transport also has a relatively high terminal cost, and is similarly confined to a fixed track. Road vehicles, though, can be moved at will along any desired combination of routes, offering a door-to-door service. But, while the terminal costs are low, overall cost rises more sharply as bulk and distance increase.

In international trade often the only possible choice is between sea and air (though traffic is increasing on overland routes such as the Trans-Siberian Railway and the long road haul from Europe to the Persian Gulf). Sea transport is ideally suited to the carriage of bulk raw materials over long distances. Bulk carriers, each carrying up to half a million tons of a single homogeneous product—oil, iron ore, grain—reduce costs per ton-kilometer to a minimum. However, as ships have become larger the number of ports with adequate depth of water and handling facilities has declined. This has had a profound effect on the location of some industries, with oil refining, for example, becoming concentrated at a few port sites with deep-water berthing facilities. The overwhelming advantage of air transport is its speed, but it is expensive and imposes severe limitations of weight. On short hauls, savings in time may be cancelled out by delays on the ground. Like water transport, air comes into its own where long distances are involved. It is best suited to the carriage of passengers and of high-value or perishable goods.

Where there are various transport options competing for the same traffic—passenger or freight—carriers are likely to go in for price-cutting or incentive schemes. Or governments sometimes choose to influence transport habits, either by subsidizing a preferred mode or through differential taxes (on fuel, say, to shift freight from the roads over to rail). For the commercial shipper and individual traveler alike, the cost, time and distance equation is an increasingly complex one.

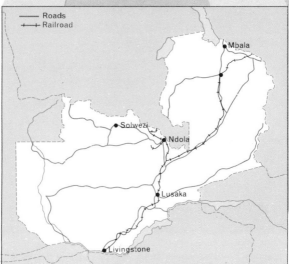

CAPITAL AS A RESOURCE

A group of farmers in Mali receive training as a result of an $8 million credit from the International Development Association, a body affiliated to the World Bank. The use of multilateral institutions as a source of capital for development has increased in recent years, and is an important part of the proposals for reorganizing the international economic system. Developing countries prefer to borrow from such organizations as their terms are not as harsh as those of the banks, and there are no political strings attached. The Mali project shown here is intended to develop the country's agriculture, particularly the production of peanuts and cereals, by supplying farm equipment, seeds and other necessities. But even more important is the training program designed so that farmers will have the technical proficiency to make the project a success. The aim is to increase the farmers' per capita income threefold. The total cost of the project, begun in 1974, is estimated at about $19 million. The IDA credit is for 50 years and is interest free, apart from a small service charge.

All the Earth's productive activities involve the use of raw materials, singly or in combination. Our energy and power systems, from electric light and household appliances to automobiles and jet airplanes, rely on fossil fuels. Food production uses fertilizers from natural sources and those derived from petroleum, while the metal industries manufacture steel from iron ore, aluminum from bauxite and magnesium from sea water.

Few basic raw materials are readily available in a form appropriate for immediate consumption. Coconuts, bananas and some other agricultural raw materials can be consumed without much processing. Most other resources, however, need extensive development and processing before they become available to consumers; and years elapse from the initial stages of discovery and production to the time when the goods are commercially available.

Capital for development
Capital is required to discover the resources, to process them and to transport them to market. Labor must be paid, and an infrastructure created to develop and transport the resources. The provision of capital is affected by the international monetary system, which historically has been either directly or indirectly linked to gold. In 1870, the monetary system set up as a basis for international trade was the gold standard, which linked the value of trading currencies to gold. This broke down with World War I and in the interwar period there was no adherence to a particular monetary system, which was unhealthy for international trade. Toward the end of World War II, in 1944, the United Nations' Monetary and Financial Conference at Bretton Woods established a dollar standard.

This use of the dollar as the major international reserve currency has recently worked to the detriment of the international flow of capital. As the dollar has declined, the capital with which the less-developed countries are provided purchases less and less. This has prompted OPEC, for example, to consider asking for payment for oil in a "basket" of various international currencies. On the other hand, fluctuating exchange rates may be an advantage. In 1977, Rio Tinto Zinc was able to reduce its debt obligations by about £47 million simply as a result of the dollar declining against the pound.

In the 30 years following the meeting at Bretton Woods 90 nations achieved independence; their needs had not been considered at the Conference, yet these countries now make up a large part of the developing or less-developed world. Most capital is in the developed countries that created the postwar international monetary system. The LDCs, on the other hand, have been unable to generate sufficient capital on their own to develop their resources, and thus have to depend on developed countries for funds. This capital comes from three sources. First are the multinational companies, or transnational corporations (TNCs), concerned less with the development of countries where they operate than with profits. The capital generated by their projects may, however, be reinvested elsewhere.

The big banking corporations provide a second source of capital in the form of commercial loans, mainly to the richer LDCs, such as Brazil, Mexico and Peru. The borrowing country has to repay the original loan, and the high interest rates and other servicing charges from which the banks derive their profit. These is little risk to the banks in all this, since few LDCs are willing to risk alienating their source of capital and other borrowers by refusing to repay a loan. Commercial loans have not been readily available to the least-developed countries that constitute a greater risk to lenders because of their inability to make rapid returns on development projects. The total debt of developing countries to the banks is now about $250 billion.

The third source of capital intended to help correct the capital deficiency of the developing

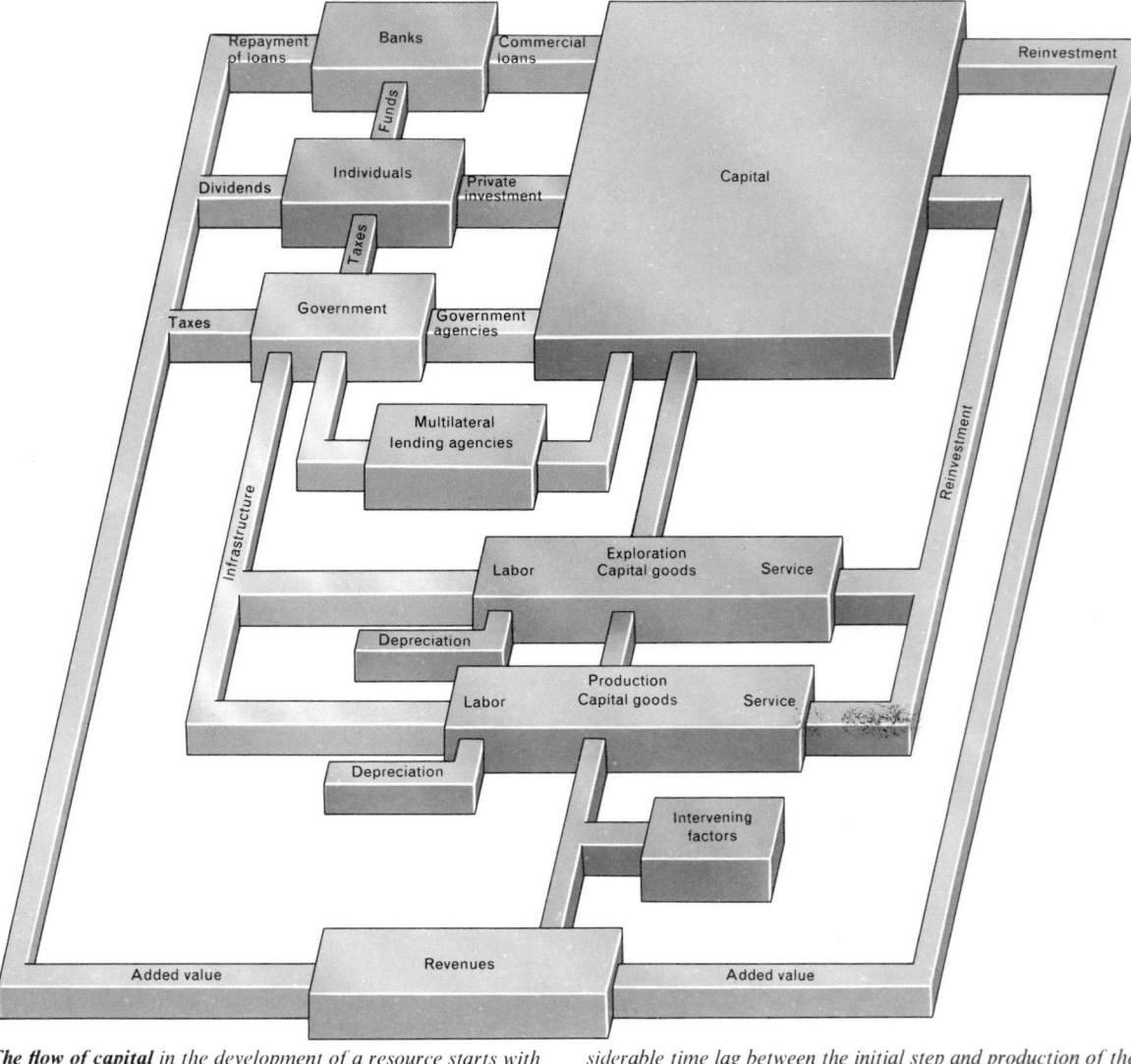

The flow of capital in the development of a resource starts with the original sources of the capital, which include banks, private investors, governments and multilateral lending agencies. Once capital has been obtained, investment can be directed toward the initial steps in the development of the resource, such as exploring for a mineral or sowing a crop. There is often a considerable time lag between the initial step and production of the resource. From production come revenues, which are affected by factors such as exchange rates and prices. From revenues, production costs are defrayed; added value (the difference between costs of production and revenues) is used to repay the providers of capital and for fresh investment.

countries comes in the form of bilateral and multilateral grants and loans. In 1976 the developed countries devoted about 0·33 percent of their GNP to assistance of this nature. By comparison, Marshall Aid to Europe at the end of World War II constituted 2–3 percent of the GNP of the United States—a proportion about eight times higher than the grants now going to the LDCs from the USA. Also, Marshall Aid was going to an already developed region, with a complex infrastructure and capital goods industries.

In market economies, the financial capital for the production of resources is obtained by borrowing from the public, the banks and other financial intermediaries, and from profits on current production. In nonmarket economies, initial investment is financed by the state, which obtains the funds mainly from taxes. Of all the initial investment costs, by far the most important is the cost of discovering a new resource, as there may be many false leads. In the case of a major oil company, the productive oil wells must pay for the dry holes; the bigger the company, the more risks it can afford to take in its exploration. Shell Oil provides a revealing example. In 1977 the company's total revenues after tax were nearly $46 billion; costs were something more than $43 billion, while net profits were $2·5 billion. Out of the total costs, exploration amounted to $760 million, or less than one-fiftieth of the costs for the year.

There is always a danger that the quality of life may decline as the readily available materials become depleted, while the availability of resources may decline if there is not enough capital for exploration and development. Moreover, the amount of capital investment required before natural resources can be economically produced increases as the more accessible materials are reduced. Finally, the rarer they become, the greater the risks involved in exploring for them. A basic question for all economies is whether there is enough capital available both for the exploration and the production of resources, and for other productive activities such as investment in industry, housing and services. Related to this is the question of how the capital available is to be allocated.

The answers to both these questions are summed up by the common economic principle: an activity should be pursued as long as its benefits exceed its costs. Thus the allocation of capital to the discovery, exploitation and development of resources is economically attractive as long as the market value of the resources produced exceeds the costs incurred in obtaining the material. Economic welfare is also enhanced by investing in any activity, until the revenues no longer exceed the costs. However, when this principle is applied, the difficulty arises that many of the costs of investments are incurred well before the revenue starts to come in. For example, a liquefied natural gas project at present under construction in Malaysia will have cost £2 billion by the time full production capacity is reached in 1987. In projects of this nature present costs and future revenues are related by the use of interest rates. It is economic (cost-efficient) to invest only if the anticipated returns exceed the costs (including the interest rate) of financing the investment. This cost-benefit principle also applies in the allocation of capital for fuel production, metal production and agriculture, as well as in distribution of investment between production of materials and other activities such as housing.

Those engaged in the development of resources must project both their future prices and revenues, which are highly uncertain, and their future costs, which, though variable, are not quite so uncertain. Because of the financial risks inherent in the discovery and production of such materials, investors need to be attracted by the hope of greater profits than are associated with less risky investments.

From time to time, most recently after the price of oil increased fourfold in 1973–74, fears about the growing scarcity of resources show a sharp increase, usually triggered by large price increases in the context of a world economic boom. Producers no longer believe that their own interests will be served by investing in new plants to cope with infrequent, sharp booms, since the presence of such productive capacity would depress prices and returns in other, nonboom years.

Application of the cost-benefit principle has meant the cost of a unit of any natural resource has not increased relative to unit cost of manufacture. Although more readily available supplies of that resource may have become depleted, the improvement in productivity per man-hour has meant that relative costs have not increased.

Growth of nationalism

In recent years the growth of nationalism in the LDCs has had its effect on the availability of raw materials. Because investors are afraid that their sources of revenue may be nationalized, they will require a higher return on their capital to compensate for the additional risk. If these fears persist, companies will seek fresh resources in the more stable countries. Ideally, the LDCs should produce their own raw materials for sale in the international market, and there have been various suggestions for setting up a special financial institution to achieve this. The World Bank and the various regional development banks are beginning to extend loans, which are especially useful when private investors are reluctant to risk their money, or when the country's borrowing ability has been exhausted. Part of the "New International Economic Order," at present under discussion in the UN and elsewhere, would reform the monetary system and give developing countries greater access to capital for long-term development.

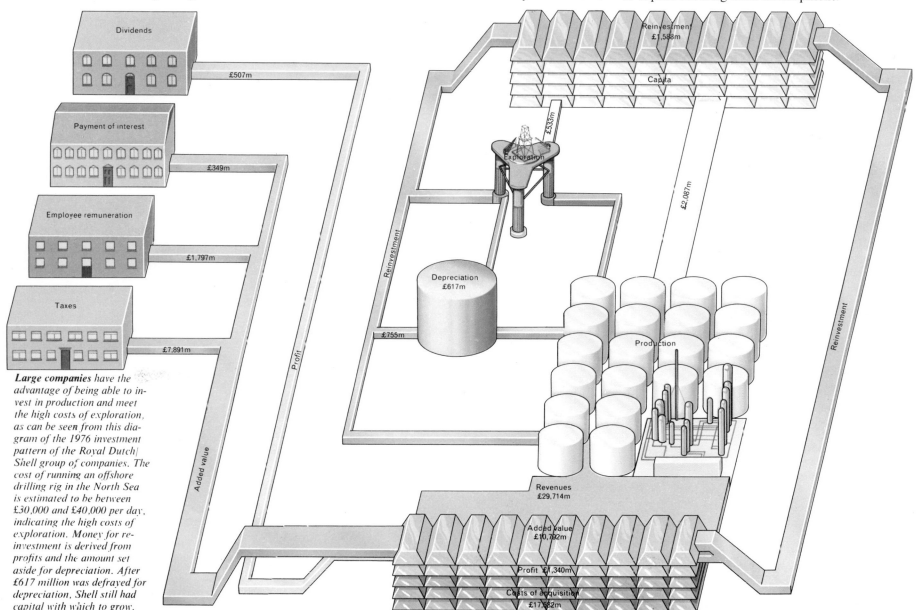

Large companies have the advantage of being able to invest in production and meet the high costs of exploration, as can be seen from this diagram of the 1976 investment pattern of the Royal Dutch/Shell group of companies. The cost of running an offshore drilling rig in the North Sea is estimated to be between £30,000 and £40,000 per day, indicating the high costs of exploration. Money for reinvestment is derived from profits and the amount set aside for depreciation. After £617 million was defrayed for depreciation, Shell still had capital with which to grow.

Dividends £507m
Payment of interest £349m
Employee remuneration £1,797m
Taxes £7,891m
Added value
Profit
Reinvestment £1,588m
Capital
Exploration £533m
Reinvestment
Depreciation £617m
£755m
Production
Reinvestment £2,087m
Revenues £29,714m
Added Value £10,792m
Profit £1,340m
Costs of acquisition £17,682m

THE ROLE OF BIG BUSINESS

Percentage of foreign sales and assets of TNCs by sales				
Company	Home country	Total sales in millions of dollars	Foreign sales as % of total	Foreign assets as % of total
Exxon	USA	48,631	72	54
General Motors	USA	47,181	24	12
Shell	ND/UK	36,087	62	50
Ford	USA	28,840	31	40
Texaco	USA	26,452		54
Mobil	USA	26,063		49
National Iran Oil	Iran	19,671		
Standard Oil	USA	19,434	59	43
BP	UK	19,103	83	
Gulf Oil	USA	16,451	55	43
IBM	USA	16,304	50	36
Unilever	ND/UK	15,762	48	36
General Electric	USA	15,697	38	27
Chrysler	USA	15,538	28	33
ITT	USA	11,764	49	36
Standard Oil (Ind)	USA	11,532	25	34
Philips	ND	11,522	37	26
ENI	Italy	9,983		
Francaise des Petroles	France	9,928	54	65
Renault	France	9,353	45	

Of the largest transnational corporations in the world, a great proportion are oil companies, and many are based in the USA. The TNCs are a great source of wealth and influence to their country. An idea of the size of this wealth can be gained from the fact that the sales of these 20 TNCs are larger than the GNPs of many developing countries.

Very large firms dominate the world's natural resource industries. Most of these firms are transnationals because resources are unevenly distributed throughout the world and commercially attractive resources are typically far from the markets they supply. This dominance by large transnational corporations (TNCS) is a twentieth-century phenomenon, especially in the decades following the end of World War II. More recently, state-owned corporations have emerged to provide a powerful challenge to the TNCs.

With the increase in technological developments in the nineteenth century, TNCs began to appear in the raw materials industry to cope with the larger scale of production and the increased demand in consumer markets. They could also supply the increased capital needed to finance each stage of the activity. In the early 1900s many small firms, each specializing in one activity, were displaced by fewer large firms controlling all activities from exploration to selling in the consumer markets. In oil, Standard Oil (now divided up into Exxon and numerous other companies) and Royal Dutch/Shell were early leaders to form powerful combines. In copper, ASARCO, Kennecott and Phelps Dodge were active. Some of today's major mining companies, such as RTZ, span many of the basic materials. The same is true of most mineral industries and, to a lesser extent, of products such as rubber and tea.

These new companies wanted to bring all stages of production and marketing under their control to reduce the risks of high capital investment in production. Firms needed market outlets and reliable sources of supply to ensure full-capacity production. Without such outlets and supply, the firms were at a disadvantage, particularly for products subject to rapid price changes in volatile commodity markets.

Trying to integrate various stages of production led many firms abroad, particularly to less-developed countries. Remote mines, oil fields and plantations created a need for transport. Specialized transport was often pioneered by the TNCs; refrigeration in ships brought beef from Argentina, bananas from Guatemala and lamb from New Zealand; supertankers keep oil transport costs down; natural gas is now transported by LNG carriers. Today, investment in transport is a major expense for large firms. At the end of 1977 British Petroleum had over £150 million invested in its own tankers and an even larger fleet on charter.

Increasing complexity
At the same time as firms were integrating their systems of production and transport, they had to invest a large amount of money in the development of new and highly specialized systems of manage-ment to deal with the increasing complexities of their operations. Management in itself becomes a competitive resource, which, combined with the advantages of large-scale operation, gives the TNC a seemingly unassailable edge over purely local competition.

It is these factors that account for the relatively few giant firms involved in such a high proportion of all the activity. The world aluminum industry, for example, is dominated by only six firms, who between them accounted for 65 percent of bauxite production, 80 percent of alumina production and 72 percent of aluminum output in 1974. The extent of such an oligopolistic structure varies enormously from one industry to another, depending on the technical difficulties to be overcome, the scale of financing involved and the entrepreneurial skills likely to be necessary.

Financing most extractive ventures is extremely costly. In 1978 it was estimated that a new copper mine would cost $2,500 for every ton of yearly output, at a time when copper prices were about $1,400 a ton. These investment figures are double those for 1970, and such new projects need annual outputs of thousands of tons to be economic and competitive. Because of the immense cost (sometimes thousands of millions of dollars) it is only the largest of firms that have or can borrow this kind of money. World capital requirements for the non-ferrous mining industry alone are expected to come to more than $50 billion (in 1975 dollars) during the period from 1977 to 1981. Since the top 20 mining firms earned post-tax profits of only $2 billion in 1977, clearly alternative sources of finance will have to be found.

Entrepreneurial skills are as important today as they were in the days of Patiño in tin or Rockefeller in oil. Most entrepreneurs have come from the USA or Europe, where the parent companies of most TNCs are based. Even developed countries such as Canada and Australia have not always had sufficient indigenous entrepreneurs to exploit local resources. During the 1960s in Australia the major part of an investment of more than US$7 billion was developed by foreign firms. Recently governments in developing countries have sought local participation. Occasionally the state itself has become the entrepreneur in creating new resource industries.

Seeking a larger cut
The large TNCs have contributed greatly to the development of the world's resource industries and have supplied industrialized countries for decades with the low-cost energy and raw materials that were the basis of their economic policies. But many countries now feel that they can and should get a larger cut of the rewards and wealth of their own resources. The hard minerals industries illustrate how many developing countries see this imbalance in the creation of resources. Relatively few processing facilities are at present located near the mines. But processed ores are worth far more in export revenue than raw materials. Building and operating processing plants near mines could mean more local industry and could provide a base for further industrialization. The TNCs have on occasion been harmful to developing countries when they have used local resources inefficiently in terms of their contribution to local development.

Yet, as the firms are in business to make money, their investment reflects calculations of transport costs, difficulties of training a skilled local workforce, difficulties of processing far from the market and many other factors. These economic considerations are not always seen to be in the best interests of the resource-exporting country. In addition to the imbalance in the location of investment, the firms control export prices and rates of output, often to the disadvantage of the exporting country. In bauxite, for example, there is no free international market in operation, as almost all trans-fers take place among the affiliates of TNCs at prices and volumes set by head office. Developing countries are also greatly concerned that exclusive reliance on the transnationals reinforces conditions of economic and, to some extent, political dependence. Economic dependence comes in the form of having parts of the economy managed in response to forces acting in other countries. For example, there is evidence that when recession strikes at the parent company it is the foreign subsidiaries that are cut back first. Technology transferred by the TNC may not be entirely appropriate to local needs. With technological resources concentrated in the parent company, the prospects for creating more appropriate processes are constrained. Wider problems of industrialization, such as mass urbanization and pollution, are also related to the decisions of the TNCs. In addition, when a country depends upon foreign capital it is vulnerable to external political influence that transcends the operations of individual firms.

Whether free-market conditions would substantially alter the status quo is open to speculation. But governments want to increase their control over the transfer of resources to increase their share of the wealth. Some governments have done this by forming producer associations (of which OPEC is the most successful), have renegotiated existing concession agreements, have insisted upon a degree of local ownership and have nationalized some of the local affiliates of the TNCs.

All these actions have been possible because of political and economic changes that have shifted the advantage away from the firm and toward governments since the 1950s. First, many developing countries have become politically independent and have thus wished to become economically self-reliant, especially in exploiting their natural resources. Second, as their political and economic infrastructure has improved, so has their capacity to manage the activities involved. Third, the large firms are no longer the sole suppliers of risk capital. More and more developing countries can borrow in the international capital market or from such agencies as the World Bank or the OPEC Special Fund. Fourth, the availability of technology for sale in the form of licenses has been increasing. Much of the basic technology used in mineral or agricultural processes is now widely available. Occasionally, whole processing plants complete with managers can be purchased, although this is rare where the firm has developed a specialized process to deal with particular minerals or metallurgical conditions. The pressure that can be exerted by a group of countries was demonstrated in the early 1970s by OPEC. Together the OPEC nations controlled enough of the world's crude oil to dictate terms and supply to the consuming countries and the oil companies. At a time when demand for crude oil had outstripped short-term supply, OPEC forced through a fourfold price increase and took over ownership and control of the oil fields. Because of the strategic importance of oil and the vast sums of money involved, their actions caused widespread inflation and recession in the major industrialized countries. It also transferred wealth on an unprecedented scale from rich companies to OPEC members, which has completely altered the assumptions on which governments and firms base their negotiations.

Contractors to government
Many governments have long wanted permanent sovereignty over their natural resources. This has not been easy, especially over ownership of assets and division of profits. After selling a concession, the governments' role was traditionally a passive one. With the bargaining power of groups like OPEC, governments can now dictate the terms and conditions of starting or continuing ventures. The firm's role is increasingly that of contractor to the government. Although this establishes a more

satisfactory relationship for the government, the risk to many firms is greatly increased and many firms have yet fully to implement these changes. Many producer associations have been formed in an attempt to emulate the actions of OPEC, though none have achieved the same changes in supply conditions. Even though the 11 members of the International Bauxite Association controlled over 90 percent of the world's exports in 1975, they have not yet managed to control rates of output or prices, or agree on the objectives necessary for political cohesion. Few commodities are as easily controlled by collective action as oil, and, for most, substitutes can easily be found, making a restrictive supply more harmful to the suppliers in the long run.

A tax on profits

Producer associations seem unlikely to become a major political force in the future: unilateral government action seems more likely. Although nationalization will undoubtedly continue, possibly at a slower rate, governments now favor negotiating the terms of the contract and allowing the TNCs to operate with a minority equity participation. This is part of a general preference among developing countries to tax the affiliates directly on profits rather than relying solely on output royalties. A TNC's relationship with government is now becoming characterized by the TNC's heavily taxed minority equity combined with a management or sales contract. As governments have increasingly entered the natural resource industries, the TNCs no longer enjoy the power or very high share of output that they used to. The dominance by the giant firms is breaking up, most noticeably in the oil industry, where changes can be seen not only in the production of crude oil but also in refining and marketing. Some of the state-owned corporations, like Petrolbras in Brazil, are themselves becoming transnational: incentives to invest abroad are not restricted to private enterprise.

Further pressure for fragmentation is coming in the form of investment from countries such as Japan. Japanese direct investments in iron ore, coal and oil are expanding rapidly and provide a major challenge to the previous dominance of Europe and the USA. More pressure is coming from smaller firms entering one or two stages of production. Some of these firms are a result of diversification by very large firms. Oil companies especially are entering many other natural-resource industries, largely because of changes in the petroleum industry since 1973. The Royal Dutch/Shell group has major investments in coal, bauxite, uranium and other non-ferrous minerals; Exxon has bought copper and coal. Because of their financial backing, this latter group of new competitors could be as important in shaping the structure of the nonferrous mining industry as government.

These developments pose a substantial threat to the continuing profitability of the established firms. Despite publicity suggesting that the large natural-resource firms make excessive profits, a recent World Bank study concluded that high profits were obtained over only a short period. A long-term view shows that such firms showed no more profit than the average manufacturing industry.

Increased threat means increased risk to the investor. Added to the general economic risk is the perceived political risk of operating in developing countries. Accordingly, firms have redirected their exploration efforts to politically safer areas, principally the developed world. In 1961, for example, European mining firms allocated 57 percent of their exploration budgets to developing countries and 43 percent to developed ones. By 1975 these proportions were 15 percent and 85 percent. This swing would have been even greater had some European countries not given subsidies for exploration in developing countries. Naturally, smaller firms are much more politically sensitive than larger firms, which tend to accept a certain amount of political risk. Large firms, however, are slower to move into new areas. If the large firms cut back on exploration and investment, this is to the disadvantage of the smaller, poorer developing countries who still need the TNCs to help them reach their targets for development.

Controversial role

Controversy about the role of TNCs has marked all stages of their transition into virtually all countries. It is only now that the developing countries are becoming able to harness the useful components of the TNCs so that they are responsive to the needs of the developing countries.

It is now apparent that the economic and political institutions have not kept pace with the great innovations of the TNCs. Only now are people coming to realize the full impact of the philosophy of the TNCs and to reconcile that to the international political system. The future role of the larger firms will depend crucially on their capacity to adapt to new political and social conditions. As finite resources become more costly and difficult to produce, a fine balance will have to be struck between the legitimate ambitions of government and the maintenance of a level of investment and the companies' ability to deal with increasingly difficult operations to which they can apply their sophisticated technology, research and human skills.

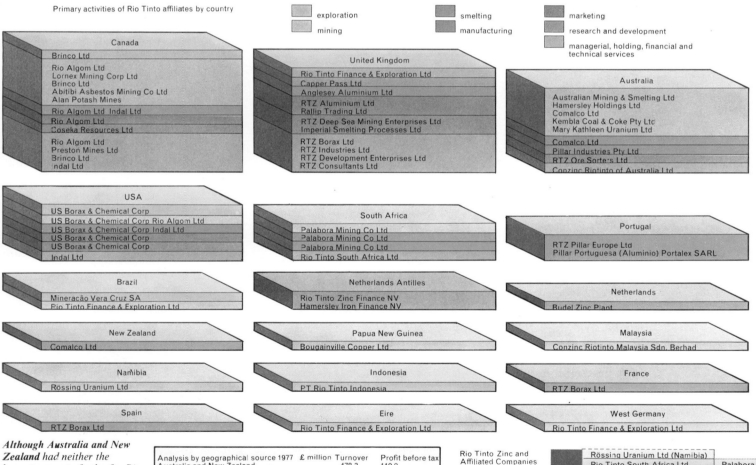

Primary activities of Rio Tinto affiliates by country

exploration · mining · smelting · manufacturing · marketing · research and development · managerial, holding, financial and technical services

With affiliates in several countries, Rio Tinto Zinc's operations span the complete range of activities from extraction of a resource to the manufacture, sale and distribution of the finished product. The central coordination by the parent company and the ability to transcend national borders has made the TNC the success it is. RTZ carries out no extractions in the UK, its home country, but in countries such as Papua New Guinea and Malaysia mining is the only activity. Recently, pressure has been mounting from the developing countries for TNCs to do more processing and manufacturing in the host country. This is because processed goods are worth far more in export revenue than raw materials and processing in the host country would provide more local industry and a possible base for further industrialization. TNCs that are responsible for operations in several different countries are under increasing pressure to take into account the social and political factors present in each country concerned.

Although Australia and New Zealand had neither the largest amount of sales for Rio Tinto Zinc nor constituted the largest market in 1977, the figures (right) show that affiliated companies in that area were the most profitable for the year. A possible explanation is the sizeable sales to Japan, the second largest market for RTZ products despite having no major affiliates. The corporate structure of RTZ (far right) shows that it is a largely decentralized organization that operates through major affiliates.

Analysis by geographical source 1977	£ million Turnover	Profit before tax
Australia and New Zealand	478.3	119.2
United Kingdom	520.8	84.8
Canada	315.0	49.4
United States of America	314.6	17.4
Papua New Guinea	138.9	29.6
South Africa	90.8	18.8
Other countries	10.4	0.1
Mainland Europe	48.8	2.4
Total	1,917.6	271.5

Sales analysis by destination	
United Kingdom	491.3
Other EEC countries	236.7
Rest of Western Europe	61.2
United States of America	299.8
Canada	180.6
Australia and New Zealand	142.9
Japan	369.4
South Africa	39.1
Middle East and North Africa	11.9
Latin America	12.7
Other Developing countries	50.6
Centrally Planned Economies	21.4
Total	1,917.6

Rio Tinto Zinc and Affiliated Companies

RIO TINTO ZINC (UK):
RTZ Oil and Gas Ltd (UK)
RTZ Development Enterprises Ltd (UK)
RTZ Consultants Ltd (UK)
Rio Tinto Finance & Exploration Ltd
RTZ Deep Sea Mining Enterprises Ltd (UK)
RTZ Aluminium Holdings Ltd (UK)
Anglesey Aluminium Ltd (UK)
RTZ Aluminium Ltd (UK)
Rallip Trading Ltd (UK)
Mineração Vera Cruz SA (Brazil)
Imperial Smelting Processes Ltd (UK)
RTZ Ore Sorters Ltd (UK)
PT Rio Tinto Indonesia

Rössing Uranium Ltd (Namibia)
Rio Tinto South Africa Ltd — Palabora Mining Co Ltd (South Africa)
RTZ Borax Ltd (UK) — US Borax & Chemical Corp
Allan Potash Mines (Canada)
Rio Algom Ltd (Canada) — Lornex Mining Corp Ltd (Canada)
Preston Mines Ltd (Canada)
Brinco Ltd (Canada) — Abitibi Asbestos Mining Co Ltd (Canada)
Coseka Resources Ltd (Canada)
RTZ Industries Ltd (UK) — Pillar Aluminium Ltd (UK)
Capper Pass Ltd (UK)
RTZ Pillar Europe Ltd (UK)
Indal Ltd (Canada)
Pillar Industries Pty Ltd (Australia)
Conzinc Riotinto of Australia Ltd — Bougainville Copper Ltd (Papua New Guinea)
Hamersley Holdings Ltd (Australia)
Comalco Ltd (Australia)
Kembla Coal & Coke Pty Ltd (Australia)
Mary Kathleen Uranium Ltd (Australia)
Conzinc Riotinto Malaysia Sdn. Berhad
Australian Mining & Smelting Ltd

Canada
Brinco Ltd
Rio Algom Ltd
Lornex Mining Corp Ltd
Brinco Ltd
Abitibi Asbestos Mining Co Ltd
Alan Potash Mines
Rio Algom Ltd Indal Ltd
Rio Algom Ltd
Coseka Resources Ltd
Rio Algom Ltd
Preston Mines Ltd
Brinco Ltd
Indal Ltd

United Kingdom
Rio Tinto Finance & Exploration Ltd
Capper Pass Ltd
Anglesey Aluminium Ltd
RTZ Aluminium Ltd
Rallip Trading Ltd
RTZ Deep Sea Mining Enterprises Ltd
Imperial Smelting Processes Ltd
RTZ Borax Ltd
RTZ Industries Ltd
RTZ Development Enterprises Ltd
RTZ Consultants Ltd

Australia
Australian Mining & Smelting Ltd
Hamersley Holdings Ltd
Comalco Ltd
Kembla Coal & Coke Pty Ltd
Mary Kathleen Uranium Ltd
Comalco Ltd
Pillar Industries Pty Ltd
RTZ Ore Sorters Ltd
Conzinc Riotinto of Australia Ltd

USA
US Borax & Chemical Corp
US Borax & Chemical Corp Rio Algom Ltd
US Borax & Chemical Corp Indal Ltd
US Borax & Chemical Corp
US Borax & Chemical Corp
Indal Ltd

South Africa
Palabora Mining Co Ltd
Palabora Mining Co Ltd
Palabora Mining Co Ltd
Rio Tinto South Africa Ltd

Portugal
RTZ Pillar Europe Ltd
Pillar Portuguesa (Aluminio) Portalex SARL

Brazil
Mineração Vera Cruz SA
Rio Tinto Finance & Exploration Ltd

Netherlands Antilles
Rio Tinto Zinc Finance NV
Hamersley Iron Finance NV

Netherlands
Budel Zinc Plant

New Zealand
Comalco Ltd

Papua New Guinea
Bougainville Copper Ltd

Malaysia
Conzinc Riotinto Malaysia Sdn. Berhad

Namibia
Rössing Uranium Ltd

Indonesia
PT Rio Tinto Indonesia

France
RTZ Borax Ltd

Spain
RTZ Borax Ltd

Eire
Rio Tinto Finance & Exploration Ltd

West Germany
Rio Tinto Finance & Exploration Ltd

RESOURCES AND PEOPLE

THE MATHEMATICS OF GROWTH

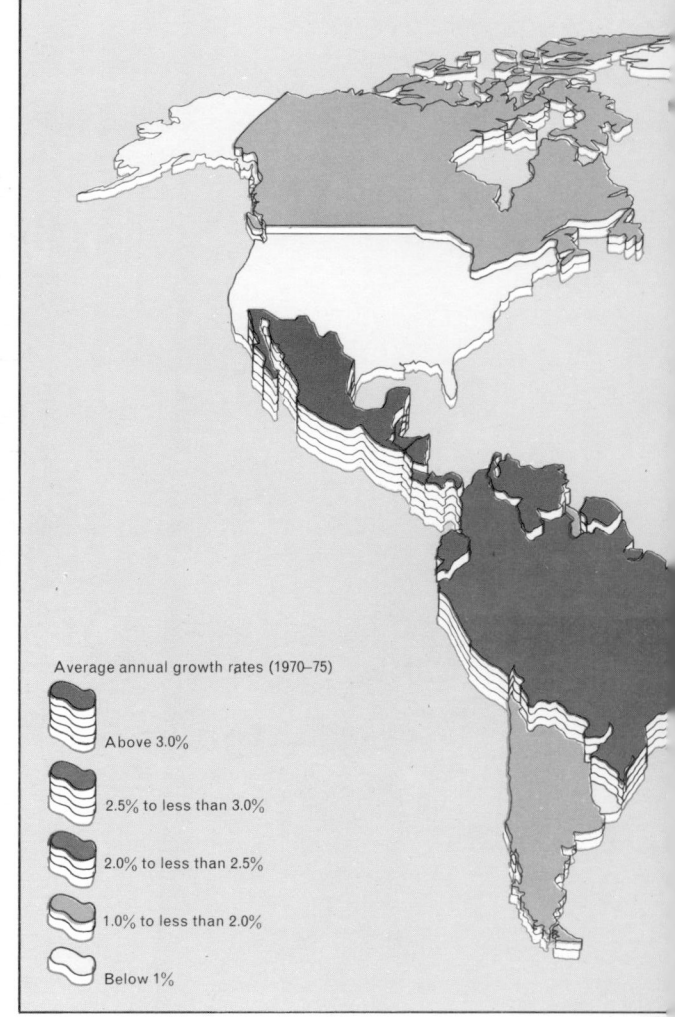

Youth dominates the populations of most less-developed countries. The Tutsi children (above) live in Rwanda, where 44 percent of the population is under 15. Rwanda has no population control and has doubled in size from 2 million people in 1950 to 4.5 million in 1978. Tribal and religious ethics tend to encourage procreation. The Tigre babies at a welfare clinic in Ethiopia (right) were born into a country at war, with a 2.4 percent population growth rate and limited resources.

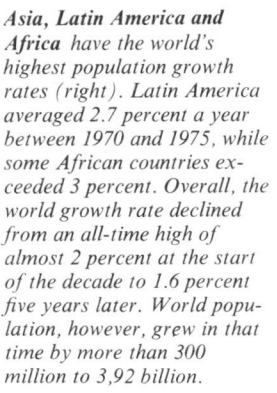

Asia, Latin America and Africa have the world's highest population growth rates (right). Latin America averaged 2.7 percent a year between 1970 and 1975, while some African countries exceeded 3 percent. Overall, the world growth rate declined from an all-time high of almost 2 percent at the start of the decade to 1.6 percent five years later. World population, however, grew in that time by more than 300 million to 3,92 billion.

Average annual growth rates (1970–75)

Above 3.0%

2.5% to less than 3.0%

2.0% to less than 2.5%

1.0% to less than 2.0%

Below 1%

The arithmetic of recent population growth is startling: babies are being born into the world at the rate of about four every second, 335,000 a day, 1.22 million a year. For most of his 500,000 years, man's numbers have increased fairly moderately. When the agricultural age first began to dawn somewhere between 10,000 and 8,000 years ago, there were probably not more than about five million people on the planet. Today there are just over 4.2 billion—the net result of a birthrate of 30 a thousand and a death rate of 12 a thousand.

The great expansion of the human race began with the Industrial Revolution. Until then the world population had been doubling about once every 1,500 years, and in 1650 had reached 500 million. But it took only 200 years for the next doubling to 1 billion. In another 80 years it had doubled again to 2 billion. Between 1930 and 1975 it doubled again. If the present rate of increase continues, the next doubling will take only 39 years.

The effect of this geometric rate of population growth has been likened to a pond where the lily leaves double in number each day. On the 29th day the pond is half-full. On the 30th day it is completely covered.

The Earth is not yet in danger of reaching standing room only, and the recent unprecedented rate of increase has started to slow down, but the strain of

exponential population growth on the Earth's space and resources is already becoming uncomfortably apparent. Pollution, overcrowding, unemployment and the inflationary scramble for scarce raw materials are all symptoms of the relentless pressure of more and more people and a lack of adequate social and economic action.

History of growth

Human population, as with other animal species, has always been closely related to the food supply. The growth rate reflected its first significant leap after the introduction of agriculture. The great surge at the time of the Industrial Revolution was also due in large part to increased food supplies through the opening up of new areas, especially in the Americas, and improved transport. The period saw changes in personal behavior, especially in relation to infant care, and two important contributions to health, variolation and, later, vaccination against smallpox. Still later, came better sanitation and drinking water and the application of scientific methods in medicine and agriculture.

From World War II onward, the death rates in less-developed countries dropped sharply as independence resulted in mortality control; new developments in pesticides, antibiotics and immunization were introduced; and international

action was spread wider and more effectively. The result has been annual population growth rates in Asia, Latin America and Africa sometimes exceeding three percent—equivalent to a nineteenfold increase in population in one century.

In theory, Mexico's population, growing at 3.5 percent, could exceed the present population of China and the USSR put together within a century. Indonesia's 2.4 percent growth rate, if not checked, could result in a population of more than 1 billion in 2078. But no one seriously supposes that such abnormally high rates will be sustained.

The most recent indications are that the trend of accelerating population growth which began with the introduction of agriculture 10,000 years ago has finally been reversed. After reaching an all-time high of about two percent a year at the start of this decade, the rate of the world's population increase has slowed to around 1.6 percent. Most of the slowing has been concentrated in Western Europe, North America and eastern Asia. The expected upturn of birthrates in the United States as children of the post-war baby boom reached their prime reproductive period failed to materialize. Instead, birthrates dropped by a third between 1970 and 1975. New social attitudes, including fewer marriages and a steady growth in female employment, contributed to this trend.

Falling birthrates

In Western Europe, birthrates are falling in virtually every country. Six countries now have virtually stable or declining populations. Though no reliable figures have been published, China's tremendous efforts to curb births are estimated to have brought the growth rate of one-fifth of mankind down from 1.9 to 1.2 percent in five years—if so, the most dramatic reduction ever recorded.

In the rest of mainland Asia, in much of Latin America and in Africa, however, birthrates remain alarmingly high. India alone, with a growth rate of

The staggering acceleration in the growth of the world's population is shown by the graph below. Numbers increased quite slowly until the 18th century, when new food supplies played a major part in reducing death rates. By 1830 the population had reached 1 billion. It had doubled by 1930 and again by 1975. In 1977, more than 122 million babies were born. In mid-1978 world population was estimated at 4.2 billion.

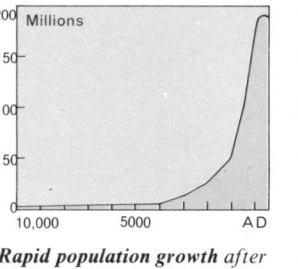

Rapid population growth after 5000 BC levelled off about AD 190 as population outstripped technology. The Han and Roman empires fell soon after.

Feudal societies steadily increased their populations until they were cut back by famines and bubonic plague (the Black Death) in the 14th century.

The expansion of population that began with the Industrial Revolution was boosted by a reduced death rate in poorer countries from the 1940s.

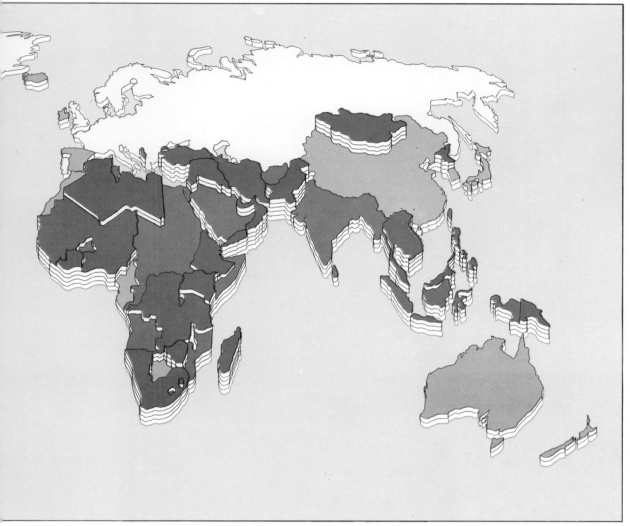

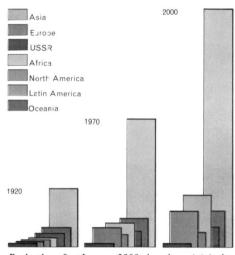

Projections for the year 2000 show how Asia's dominance will continue, its total population reaching 3.58 billion. At that time it will equal the 1970 world population. Even now, cities like Calcutta (top) cannot house all their citizens.

1.9 percent, adds 13 million people to the world's total each year, and, along with China, Mexico and Bangladesh, is now seeking to promote policies that will lead to zero population growth.

Though the last, and most spectacular, spurt in the world's population has eased, the consequences are still with us in the high proportion of young people alive today. In many of the poorer countries, more than 40 percent of the population is under 15 years of age. In Nigeria and Peru the figure is nearer 45 percent. In the developing countries as a whole, more than half the population is under 19. These young people present a formidable challenge in terms of providing basic human needs.

The specter of an Earth overrun by starving billions was first raised by the English political economist and mathematician Thomas Malthus toward the end of the eighteenth century. At a time when the rising age of science and reason seemed to hold out the prospect of plenty for all, he suggested that "the power of population is indefinitely greater than the power of Earth to produce subsistence." He even put his forebodings in mathematical terms: "Population, when unchecked, increases in geometrical ratio. Subsistence increases only in mathematical ratio."

Two hundred years later, the debate about just how many people the Earth can support is still fiercely controversial. Current UN projections show the world's population increasing to between 10 and 15 billion before stabilizing in the second half of the next century. Some scientists, such as Soviet academician Yevgeny Fyodorov, believe that enough food can be grown in seas and on unused land to sustain 15 billion people.

Others disagree. Part of the problem is the scale of consumption in advanced countries such as the United States, where the average person requires a million Calories of food and the power equivalent of 13 tons of coal a year—500 times more than his fellow man in India.

Wealth is said to be the best contraceptive. The plight of the Brazilian widow with 10 of her 13 children (above) contrasts with that of the West German family (right), who are typical of "Der Pillenknick" (the Pill Pinch). It has been estimated that a third of West German women use the Pill.

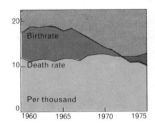

By 1972, West Germany had reached zero population growth, at 61,670,000. It thus became the second country (after East Germany) to do so.

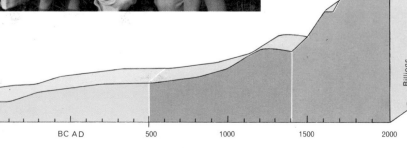

SEARCHING FOR LIVING SPACE

At present two trends are altering the pattern of human settlement: the rapid increase in numbers in many countries of Asia, Africa and Latin America, and the continuing movement of people from the countryside into the cities.

Following the population surge that began in Europe 200 years ago, this remains the most densely populated area of the globe, with 96 inhabitants to every square kilometer (248 per square mile). But not far behind are the vast territories of southern and eastern Asia, where there are now more than 80 people to each square kilometer of land.

Asia, with nearly one-third of the Earth's land area, contains over half the world's population. By the end of the century the numbers living there will almost certainly have increased from 2 billion to about 3.6 billion—equal to the entire world population in 1970. By 2000 the UN estimates that the population density of southern Asia will be 150 per square kilometer (397 per square mile), or more than one and a half times Europe's present density.

Africa and Latin America

The second largest addition to world population will come from Africa, which now contains one-tenth of the people of the world and is likely to add another 400 million by the year 2000. Few of the countries of that vast and relatively lightly populated continent view this increase in numbers with alarm, though the density of population in relation to productive land in some African countries such as Rwanda and Lesotho is already high.

Latin America's population is growing equally fast—2.7 percent a year—but even assuming that this slows down in the later years of this century it is still likely to add 262 million to its present population of 344 million by the year 2000. One result of such trends is that Europe's proportion of the world's population, which stood at 18 percent in 1920, will drop to nine percent by 2000.

Population densities vary widely within indi-

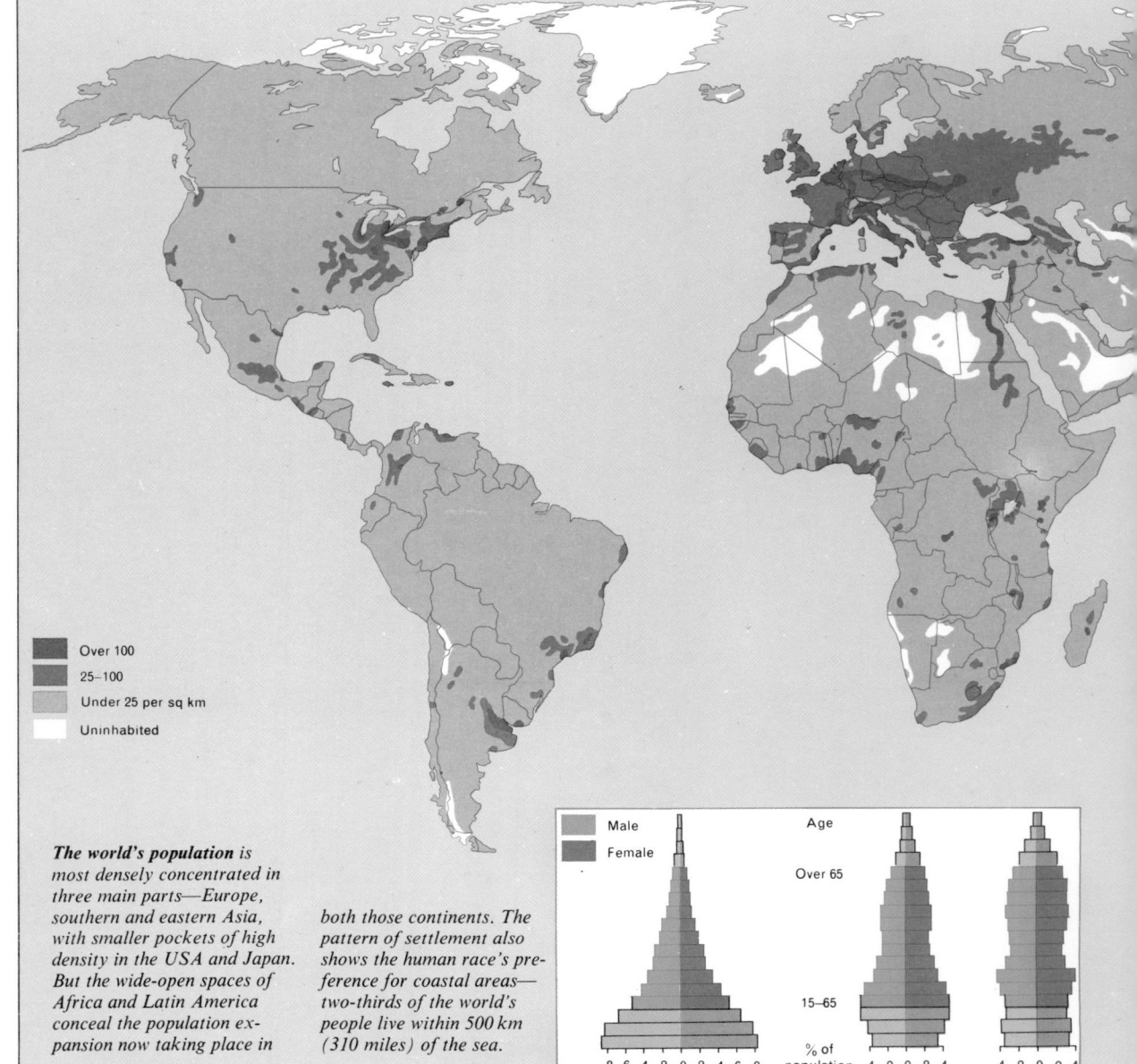

Over 100

25–100

Under 25 per sq km

Uninhabited

The world's population is most densely concentrated in three main parts—Europe, southern and eastern Asia, with smaller pockets of high density in the USA and Japan. But the wide-open spaces of Africa and Latin America conceal the population expansion now taking place in both those continents. The pattern of settlement also shows the human race's preference for coastal areas—two-thirds of the world's people live within 500 km (310 miles) of the sea.

Male

Female

Age

Over 65

15–65

% of population

São Paulo, Brazil, had a population of eight million in 1970, bolstered by an influx of rural migrants which forced officials to permit the growth of shanty towns like this. By 2000 the city is likely to be the world's second-largest, with 26 million people.

Jakarta's population is expected to reach 17 million by 2000. Many of its present inhabitants live between the railway lines.

Hong Kong has built workers' flats alongside shacks that, if primitive, are sometimes more spacious than the new flats.

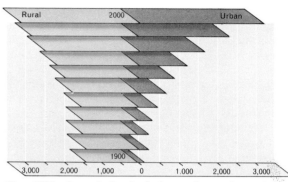

Since 1900, when only London had a population of more than one million, the rush from the land to the cities has accelerated. By 2000, most of the world's people will be urban dwellers.

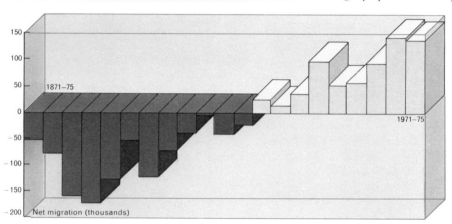

The Netherlands, with 396 people per square kilometer, is one of the world's most densely populated countries. The distribution of its people, however, is very uneven. More than two-thirds of the country consists of intensely cultivated farmland (left) with about 46 percent out of a total population of 13 million compressed into the horseshoe-shaped West Holland conurbation, formed by the joining up of the cities of Amsterdam, The Hague, Rotterdam and Utrecht. The pressures on this region are acute. Housing is in short supply, there is a lack of open spaces for recreation, air pollution blowing in from industrial areas is a serious problem, and Rotterdam has to make do with purifying the heavily contaminated waters of the Rhine for drinking supplies. In recent years the government have encouraged people to move away from congested urban areas.

Population pyramids illustrate the contrast in age distribution between the developed and developing countries. Mexico is typical of the latter in having high birth and declining death rates, leading to a preponderance of young people, represented by the broad base of the pyramid. In the USA, and more so in Sweden, a much larger proportion of the population is middle-aged or elderly. Because the age structure of a country has a direct bearing on its future birthrate, diagrams like this are useful in estimating future population growth trends.

Reversal of the tide of migration in the case of a typical European country is seen in this bar chart, which records the movement of people in and out of Sweden since the middle of the 19th century. Before 1914 shortage of farm land led to mass emigration to the New World. From the 1930s onward, Sweden's growing standard of living led to an influx of people. A similar pattern in Britain saw emigration to America and the colonies, later followed by a period of immigration.

vidual countries. In some regions, such as southern Brazil, a high proportion of the population may be packed into a few large cities; in others, such as Morocco or Egypt, settlement may be limited to a relatively small part of the country owing to inhospitable deserts or mountain ranges.

Some idea of the scale of these variations may be gathered from the fact that while the Earth's land surface averages 28 people per square kilometer (73 per square mile) a city such as Tokyo has a density of 8,000 (20,700) and Manhattan Island, New York, 26,000 (67,340). Australia, by contrast, has only 1.5 people per square kilometer (4 per square mile).

Historically, migration has been an important factor in altering population distribution. Many of the great migrations of the past, such as the barbarian invasions of Europe, may have been influenced by population pressure. The promise of golden opportunities in the New World, and the growth of British and other colonies, certainly helped to export Europe's population explosion. From 1840 to 1930 more than 50 million people left Europe to settle in North America and other territories. In more recent times migration from the Caribbean has helped to ease the rapid growth of population in those islands.

Such movements of people across national borders are likely to have a diminishing effect on population distribution in future as more and more countries strengthen barriers to immigration. In Europe the Iron Curtain has effectively put a stop to movement of population between the Communist bloc countries and their neighbors to the west. For countries like the United States, with long land frontiers, or Britain, with traditional links with former colonies, immigration controls are a difficult and politically sensitive task.

Apart from population growth, the most dramatic change in the distribution of the human race has been the massive migration from the land to the cities. On a world scale, this is essentially a twentieth-century phenomenon. At the end of the nineteenth century, after 100 years or so of industrialization, there were still only 250 million city dwellers out of a world population of 1,650 million. Today 1,500 million of the world's 4,000 million people are urban dwellers and by the end of the century, for the first time in history, most people will make their homes in cities.

In what sort of cities they will live, and how, is one of the most daunting prospects facing the human race. The number of cities with one million-plus inhabitants has grown from 75 in 1950 to more than 200 today. By 1985 there are likely to be no less than 17 cities with more than 10 million people. By then the population of Mexico City will have grown to 18 million—almost as big as New York's, but still some way behind Tokyo's projected population of 25 million.

Problems of the cities

Three out of every five of the two to three billion additions to the human race during the next three decades can be expected to join just those Asian, African and Latin American cities which will have the most difficulty in supporting them. Almost half the world's 20 fastest-growing cities are in Asia, led by Karachi, Bandung, Baghdad, New Delhi, Tehran, Bangkok, Seoul, Jakarta and Manila—all of which are expected to increase in size by well over 50 percent in the next decade. The rest of these mushrooming cities are in Africa and Latin America. Only four cities of the developed world—New York, Tokyo, London and Paris—are likely to be among the 20 largest urban areas by 2000.

Already a third of the people living in the cities of the developing countries are slum-dwellers or squatters, living in makeshift shelters or waterless, insanitary shacks. The ratio of slum-dwellers in such cities is growing by 15 percent a year.

The cities of the developed countries are impressive monuments to affluence and sophistication, but even they have problems. Expansion outward—there is now, for example, an almost continuous urban area stretching 960 kilometers (595 miles) along the eastern seaboard of the USA from Boston to Washington DC—has left the hearts of many cities, particularly in the United States, filled with poor housing, high unemployment and inadequate social services. People who suffer from discrimination tend to be forced into such areas: in Atlanta, Georgia, where half the population is black, a black child's chances of surviving to the age of one in the worst parts of the city are no better than those of a child in Colombia and Guatemala. Outward expansion also creates financial problems: New York is facing bankruptcy because its most affluent citizens live outside the city's taxation net.

The French geographer Jean Gottman coined the word "megalopolis" to describe the northeast coast of the USA: another megalopolis is centered on the 2,141 square kilometer (827 square mile) area of Tokyo, Yokohama and Kawasaki with a population of more than 22 million.

There are signs that one of the major problems of both developed and less developed countries—but particularly of the latter—may diminish. In 1970 the dependency ratios (that is, the ratios of adults aged 15–64 years to children and old persons) for developed and less developed countries were 1.75 and 1.24 respectively. Projections for the year 2000, made by the Harvard Center for Population Studies, put the ratios at 1.93 and 1.75 respectively. The Harvard figures assume a substantial fall in the net reproduction rate, but even projections which assume a lesser fall show improvement.

FEAST OR FAMINE?

The world potential for food production is more than adequate for the population, for the present and well into the future. According to the United Nations Food and Agriculture Organization (FAO), the population grew during the 1950s and 1960s at an annual rate of two percent—the greatest growth rate so far recorded—while food production was increasing annually at 2.8 percent. These figures indicate that "Malthusian" arguments that the world is in imminent danger of widespread famine are not justified.

Obviously, population growth on this planet will one day have to stop; but what is the real "carrying capacity" and how much breathing space do we have before we reach a genuine Malthusian limit to growth? And why do some people starve while others throw food away?

Human food needs and consumption
Estimates of food requirements made by the FAO suggest that each person needs the equivalent of 250 kilograms (550 pounds) of grain a year to remain healthy. Over the past few years an average of 1.3 billion tons of grain have been produced annually, enough to feed 5.2 billion, this may be compared with the present world population of about 4.2 billion. The poor who starve do not do so because food is unavailable but because they can neither afford to buy it nor obtain the means of producing their own. This is illustrated by the 1978 record harvest in India, with an estimated production of 125 million tons of grain; this ought to be more than enough to feed India's population of 630 million, but the government estimates that nearly 40 percent of the people will go hungry.

In fact, estimates of food requirements have often been too high. The intake of protein and calories needed by individuals to maintain good health varies according to age, sex, amount of physical activity and even the climate. Early FAO estimates of food needs were 3,000 Calories of food, including 90 grams (3 ounces) of protein per day. These figures were based on the requirements of a North American manual worker. To allow for people who obtained less than this average, this figure was, illogically, increased by 20 percent. The result was that food needs were overestimated by as much as four times the true requirement of the population of particular countries. The figures quoted above for requirement in terms of grain

Ethiopia, the United Nations estimates, has only 93 percent of its dietary requirements at the best of times, and its population is growing so rapidly that when disasters strike, famine is not far away. Relief operations include distributing wheat meal fortified with protein-rich soybean flour (above) and giving the country's children top food priority (right).

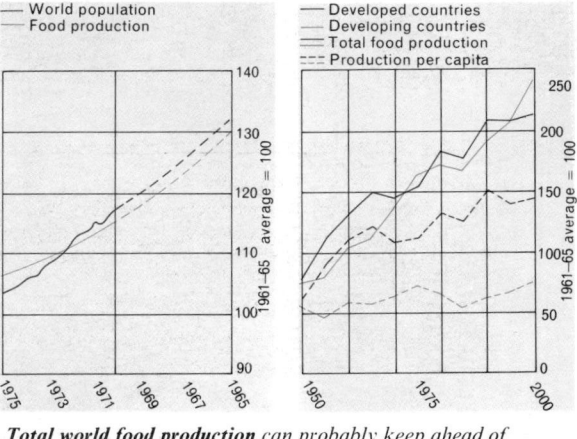

— World population
— Food production
--- Developed countries
--- Developing countries
— Total food production
--- Production per capita

Total world food production can probably keep ahead of population growth (right), but plotting per capita production against population growth (left) reveals that the developing world's production is not keeping pace with its growth.

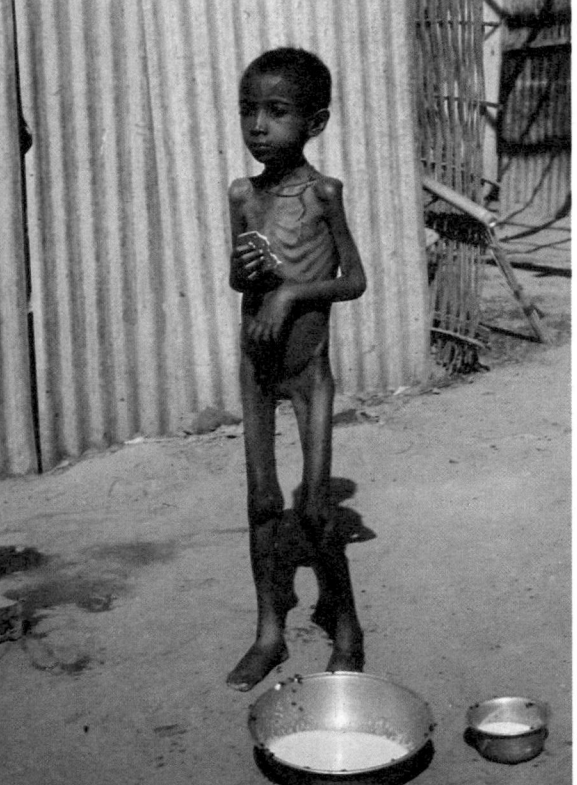

Malnutrition includes overconsumption, about which there is much concern in the developed world (left), as well as undernourishment. Unfortunately, extreme malnutrition resulting from famine still occurs in parts of the world today (above).

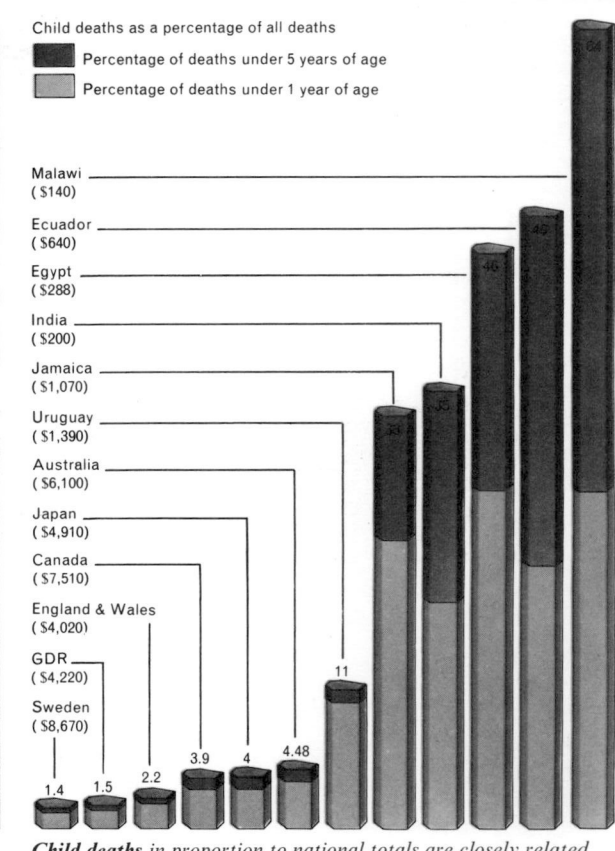

Child deaths as a percentage of all deaths
■ Percentage of deaths under 5 years of age
▨ Percentage of deaths under 1 year of age

Malawi ($140)
Ecuador ($640)
Egypt ($288)
India ($200)
Jamaica ($1,070)
Uruguay ($1,390)
Australia ($6,100)
Japan ($4,910)
Canada ($7,510)
England & Wales ($4,020)
GDR ($4,220)
Sweden ($8,670)

1.4 1.5 2.2 3.9 4 4.48 11

Child deaths in proportion to national totals are closely related to per capita GNPs and malnutrition is the major factor, as it increases vulnerability to disease. Malnutrition in pregnant women severely affects the development of the child.

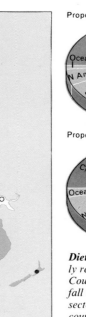

Proportion world population

Proportion world food supplies

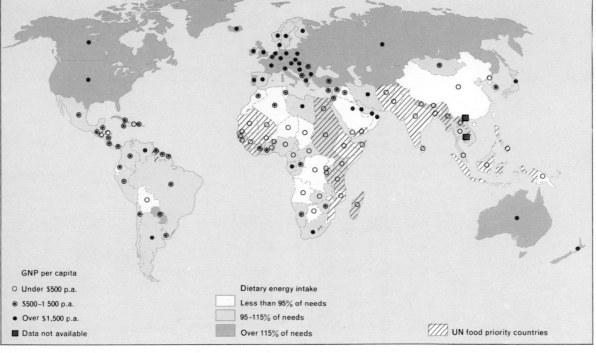

Dietary energy intake is closely related to national income. Countries with adequate diets fall in the 95–115 percent sector—alone of the developed countries, Norway, Sweden and Finland are not overeating. The countries with the most people (above) do not always produce the most food.

GNP per capita
○ Under $500 p.a.
⊙ $500–1 500 p.a.
● Over $1,500 p.a.
■ Data not available

Dietary energy intake
☐ Less than 95% of needs
▨ 95–115% of needs
▨ Over 115% of needs

▨ UN food priority countries

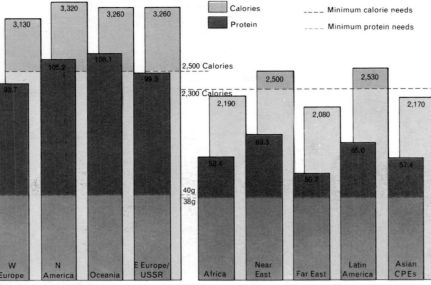

Calorie and protein requirements recommended by the UN FAO vary with age, body size, weight and geographical location. The actual intakes in the developed world greatly exceed these, while in contrast the developing countries' energy intakes are well below recommended needs. However, it is worth remembering that even in the wealthier nations there are those who go hungry: more than 10 million Americans are today reported to be undernourished, and in 1936 half the population of the UK was reported to be subsisting on an inadequate diet.

Subsidized school meals are provided by many governments throughout the world. In Colombia they are fortified by supplies from the World Food Program, and in Britain dietary intake is regulated by the Department of Education and Science.

equivalent are based on a downward revision of 2,354 Calories per day, averaged over a range from 820 for a female baby to 3,500 for a male aged 16. Our picture of food needs is improving but is still far from perfect, as demonstrated by the recent confusion over the role of protein in the diet. Throughout the 1960s the "protein gap" was thought to be a major problem, and the cause of the protein-deficiency diseases often found in poor regions. More recent studies show that when calorie intake drops too low the body starts to use up its own protein to provide energy, resulting in the symptoms of protein deficiency. When energy intake was increased the symptoms disappeared, without the need for extra protein.

It is true that there are nations in which population has grown more rapidly than food supply, but even so, with existing techniques of agriculture but with a more efficient and equitable distribution of the produce, the world could support 25 percent more people than are alive today.

Potential for production
Far from being close to the limits of the Earth's ability to provide food, the full potential has scarcely begun to be exploited. One of the first serious attempts to estimate global agricultural resources was made by the United States President's Science Advisory Committee (PSAC), whose report was published in 1967. This gave an estimated maximum possible area of land available for cropping of 6.6 billion hectares (16 billion acres), of which about half has been cultivated at some time in history and only 1.4 billion hectares (3.5 billion acres), or less than a quarter, is in use in any one year now. Even these figures indicated that food production could be doubled if all the land ever used for agriculture were put back into use, but by the late 1970s it was clear that the estimates were far too low.

With improved techniques, including satellite monitoring, we have a much better picture of land availability. For example, the PSAC estimated that in southeastern Asia 93 percent of available land was already under cultivation in 1967; but in 1978 more accurate studies showed that only 73 percent of land was being used for production. Globally, if all accessible land were cultivated by traditional methods, some 8 to 10 billion people could be fed.

In 1973 and 1974 a team at Wageningen Agricultural University in the Netherlands made studies to determine the "absolute maximum food production of the world," based on best yields already achieved, and assuming no improved technology—not even desalination, nor farming the sea or production of "artificial food." They arrived at a theoretical total of 50 billion tons of grain equivalent per year; about 40 times present world production. With only two-thirds of the land used for grain, the world could feed 25 times the present population. Obviously, this maximum could never be achieved in practice, but it does suggest that we are far from any absolute agricultural limit to growth: until well into the next century the world has the capacity to support even an exponentially increasing population. The most urgent problems are human ones: not just producing the food but sharing it; controlling population, not for lack of food but to improve the quality of life.

Once it is realized that poverty—inability to buy food—rather than scarcity—inability to grow food—is at the heart of the world food problem, the picture of the next few decades changes. Estimates of needs have been too high: estimates of potential too low. But potential is just that—before it can be fulfilled there are many problems to overcome. Can those countries now on the edge of starvation increase productivity without wrecking the environment? And can this successfully be done so that, for once, the poorest people benefit and get enough to eat? If these questions can be answered satisfactorily for the most vulnerable regions, it follows that the world as a whole can get over the present crisis. Ironically, in view of recent concerns, it now seems that growth—but not undirected growth—far from being harmful, is in fact necessary in order to fulfill this potential.

RESOURCES AND PEOPLE
ENERGY FOR THE MILLIONS

From 1950 to 1975—a quarter of a century free from major pestilence and global war—the world population increased by 60 percent, from 2.5 billion to 4 billion. Suddenly, following these years during which birthrates and life expectancy increased, there were 1.5 billion extra people to be fed, clothed, housed, transported and employed. It was hardly surprising that this population boom, coupled with improved standards of living, placed a phenomenal strain on resources, creating an unprecedented demand for energy in all its forms. During this period world consumption of commercial energy—energy which is bought or sold in the market—rose by 330 percent.

Disparities in consumption

Energy use is not, however, evenly distributed across the globe. There are wide disparities in per capita consumption from country to country, ranging from almost profligate use in the affluent nations through to very modest consumption in the poorer countries, where the burden of population is greatest. With less than a fifth of India's population, highly industrialized Japan, for instance, uses more than three times more fuel. North America more than five times. Unlike the Communist bloc, which is virtually self-sufficient in energy, none of the Western nations produce anywhere near as much as they consume.

United Nations figures on energy consumption for 1975 are split into three broad groupings: with only 19 percent of the world population, developed market economies burned up 58 percent of all commercial fuels; centrally planned economies such as China and the Eastern European bloc had 31.6 percent of the population and used 32.4 percent of world fuel; and less-developed countries, representing 49 percent of the world population, used a mere 9.7 percent. However, energy consumption is increasing at a faster rate in the developing nations than it is in the West.

What is not precisely quantifiable is the extent to which many less-developed countries still rely on noncommercial sources—traditional fuels and human and animal power for agriculture—for a

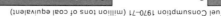

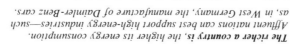

A developed country, the United States uses nearly four times as much energy—all in commercial form—as India, where almost half the fuel consumed comes from traditional sources.

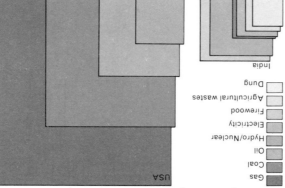

The richer a country is, the higher its energy consumption. Affluent nations can best support high-energy industries—such as, in West Germany, the manufacture of Daimler-Benz cars.

Fuel Consumption 1970–71 (million tons of coal equivalent)

Gas	
Coal	
Oil	
Hydro/Nuclear	
Electricity	
Firewood	
Agricultural wastes	
Dung	

USA

India

Energy-saving industrialists can make use of infrared imagery (above), taken from the air, to detect heat loss from factory premises. Light patches indicate greatest heat loss, dark areas least. A similar technique reveals heat wasted arising from a poorly insulated house (left). The color scale ranges from black, showing coolest areas, through greens and yellows to white where the heat loss is greatest. An encounter with rush-hour traffic (right) in Tokyo—43 percent of Japanese own a car—indicates why transportation accounts for nearly a quarter of Japan's petroleum use. Worldwide, the combustion of fossil fuels is beginning to cause measurable changes in the composition of the Earth's atmosphere.

great proportion of their energy requirements. In a number of these countries, particularly those where the pressure of population is high, growing demands for energy are having detrimental effects on the environment. Tree clearance is leading to soil erosion and, ultimately, desertification; and the burning of animal and vegetable wastes eliminates valuable sources of soil nutrient.

Elsewhere, rapid growth in energy demand throughout the 1960s and early 1970s led to widespread fears of an "energy gap" which would have serious economic and social consequences. The basis of this concern was a somewhat overdue recognition of the fact that oil in particular, but also coal and natural gas, are nonrenewable resources. Now (although the economic recession which buffeted the West in the mid-1970s led to slowing of spiralling energy growth rates) demand is once again on the increase, and these earlier fears are being revived. The view taken by the World Energy Conference is that, if future economic growth is similar to that of the past 40 to 50 years, by the year 2000 world demand for energy will be three to four times present consumption.

Energy prices will almost certainly rise as a result. For instance, the United Kingdom Department of Energy's forecast is that, by the end of the century, oil prices will probably be double or treble what they are at present. This could result in considerable difficulties in adjustment for consumer nations, especially if there is a series of big price rises rather than a progressive increase over a period of time. Most vulnerable are the less-developed countries, many of which were seriously hit by the oil price rises of 1973–74. The problem is

that the process of economic development in itself involves increasing reliance on petroleum products as a country's basic transport infrastructure is established and expanded as industrial requirements grow. Food production, too, relies on petroleum-based fertilizers and on irrigation systems which often require pumping capacity. Cutbacks in energy imports as a result of higher costs would seriously affect the progress of less-developed countries toward economic and social objectives. Or, increasing payments for oil imports could take funds away from other priority sectors of their economies, proving a further deterrent to growth. Recent World Bank estimates imply that a 25 percent cut in oil prices would nearly double the poorer nations' per capita growth of GNP.

All countries facing the energy threat share the same need to make more of the available resources by seeking greater efficiency of use and by eliminating waste. Priority measures include the introduction of energy-efficient processes in industry and, indeed, a reappraisal of industry which would call into question the future of some high-energy products which are for the most part nonessential —for example, the more frivolous output of the packaging industry. Similarly, some aspects of food production—intensive rearing of livestock and greenhouse growing of fruit and vegetables out of season—are questionable in terms of energy use.

The need for conservation

The scope for conservation in our energy-rapacious cities is by definition relatively limited: the energy-ideal city would offer no transport, public buildings or services of any sort. Crammed with buildings which are totally unsuited to an era of scarcity, the modern city is a monument to affluence and the easy availability of low-priced fuel. There can, for instance, be nothing more inappropriate than the modern, glass-walled office block—cold in winter, sweltering in summer—requiring a heavy expenditure of energy on both heating and cooling equipment. It is the same with residential development: with some 30 percent of their energy spent on nonproductive domestic consumption—most of it heating empty space—the highly urbanized countries of the Northern Hemisphere are badly disadvantaged in comparison with the warmer territories of the south. There is room, too, for a rationalization of transport, where savings could be had by a reduction in use of the private car, or at least by a move toward more efficient cars.

It is in the developing countries that the likely contribution of renewable energy resources looks promising. Here it is not costly production methods designed for laborsaving and job elimination which are required but the initiation of techniques appropriate to labor-surplus societies. The development of solar, wind and ocean power and other so-called alternative technologies would go some way to relieving the pressure on scarcer fossil fuels. Meanwhile nuclear power and coal will substitute in particular applications for fossil hydrocarbons, which will increasingly be restricted for use where there are no obvious substitutes.

Certainly the rising curve on the demand graph points to some sort of impending energy crisis provoked by such factors as population increase, the bustle on the part of the less-developed countries to catch up with the West, and the universal clamor for improved standards of living. But the crisis is not likely to take the spectacular form often predicted, scuttling economies and lifestyles overnight. There is, after all, enough oil left for at least a century of judicious use, besides an endowment of coal rich enough to last a couple of thousand more years. The outlook, therefore, is one of continuing reliance on—but more frugal use of—the fossil fuels for some generations. The challenge now is to gather the research and development needed to establish the defensive planning and technologies with which to support a lower-energy way of life.

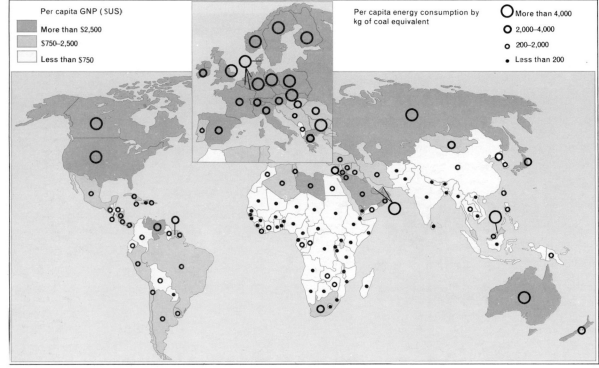

World comparison of national incomes and energy use shows vast differences between the West and less-developed countries.

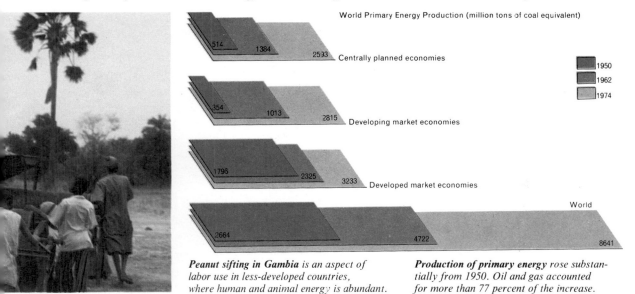

Peanut sifting in Gambia is an aspect of labor use in less-developed countries, where human and animal energy is abundant.

Production of primary energy rose substantially from 1950. Oil and gas accounted for more than 77 percent of the increase.

THE WORLDS WE LIVE IN

The growing scale and complexity of the man-made environment is typified by Gravelly Hill motorway interchange (nicknamed "Spaghetti Junction") near Birmingham, England. Pollution hazards for the people in the nearby houses include noise and the possibly harmful effects of lead from exhaust fumes.

In developing countries such as India, pressure on land is so great that agriculture has to compete with industry —here, Indian women winnow corn in the traditional way against the backdrop of Calcutta's steelworks. In all countries, agriculture is losing ground to industry as industry seeks "green field" sites which are cheaper than the cost of reclaiming old sites.

A vicious circle is created as growing populations force communities to overuse poor land, thus lowering its productivity even further. These Senegal villagers, herding goats on the fringes of the semi-arid Sahel region, are contributing to the Sahara's southward expansion at a rate of about 100 m (328 ft) a year.

Man has been modifying his environment ever since he first started clearing forests and growing food. But only recently has a sudden acceleration in population growth begun to threaten the natural systems of the entire planet.

Population has been growing at about two percent a year since the middle of this century. At the same time, civilization's demands on the Earth's air, oceans, grasslands, croplands and forests are increasing at an even faster rate.

Man's exploitation of the world's forests has a long history. For centuries the trees have receded before increasing numbers of people who have cleared the land for agriculture and gathered wood for fuel. By the mid-twentieth century the Earth's original forested area had been reduced by a third.

In most industrial countries today ecologically important forests are reasonably well protected, but in almost every country with a rapidly growing population woodlands are being decimated by expanding village communities that have no alternative fuel. One exception is China, where a major tree-planting program is under way. Attempts at reforestation in North Africa, however, are failing to prevent a net loss of trees.

Countries such as Morocco, Tunisia and Algeria have lost nine-tenths of their forest cover. The Ivory Coast has lost 30 percent of its rain forests in 10 years, while Java retains only 12 percent of its original trees. Commercial interests and conservation are also in conflict over the tropical forests of southeast Asia, central Africa and the Amazon.

Creation of dust-bowls

Some of today's most serious deforestation is occurring in the Himalayas as farmers and wood-gatherers clear the hills, aggravating erosion and flooding in the plains below. More hillside deforestation and flooding has been reported from eastern India, Pakistan, Thailand, the Philippines, Malaysia and Tanzania.

As with deforestation, overgrazing of the world's grasslands, which supply most of man's meat and milk, is not new. But the pressure of population growth is, in some places, compressing the deterioration of centuries into years. The Sahara is steadily creeping south, partly because of overgrazing and deforestation due to a doubling of population over the past 35 years.

Alongside overgrazing is the problem of over-ploughing, with the extension of agriculture into marginal lands where topsoil is easily destroyed. Colombia, Mexico, Pakistan, Nepal and Nigeria have all suffered severe losses through soil erosion due to the use of marginal lands.

Though population growth inevitably puts pres-

sure on land, it does not necessarily reduce the supply of food. The Food and Agriculture Organization index (with 1961–65 as a base of 100) shows a per capita world food production increase from 103 in 1966 to 110 in 1976. Some countries actually increased land in production: China, for example, is estimated to have raised its arable and permanent cropland from 118,940,000 hectares (293,781,000 acres) in 1961–65 to 129,000,000 hectares (318,630,000 acres) in 1975.

Another sign of environmental stress is the fall of the fish catch in 1972 to 66 million tons, following its rapid increase from 20 to 70 million tons in the previous 20 years. Several key species, including anchovies, cod and herring, were overfished.

The oceans, which cover two-thirds of the world's surface, are also suffering from being used for too long as the Earth's dustbin. Among the thousands of waste products polluting the oceans are oil, radioactive waste, metal, trace elements, organic and inorganic wastes, pesticides and detergents. An estimated two million tons of oil seep into the seas each year from ships and drilling rigs. When the explorer Thor Heyerdahl sailed a papyrus raft across the Atlantic in 1970 he reported: "Clots of oil are polluting the mid-stream current of the Atlantic from horizon to horizon."

Oil is organic in origin and can be broken down in time by marine organisms. Heavy metals such as lead, cadmium and mercury discharged by factories remain toxic indefinitely and may even become more toxic. Mercury dumped in Minimata Bay, Japan, in the 1950s and 1960s was converted by marine organisms into highly poisonous methyl mercury. This accumulated in fish which were

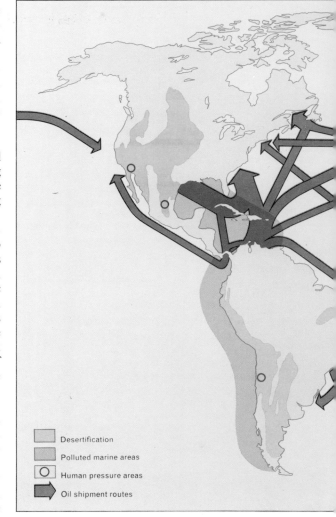

Desertification

Polluted marine areas

Human pressure areas

Oil shipment routes

CONNECTIONS

In cities thronged with motor vehicles like New York, more than half the air pollution is caused by exhaust fumes. Carbon monoxide content of the air may, when traffic is held up, approach 400 parts per million—exposure for eight hours to a concentration of only 80 ppm has about the same effect as losing a pint of blood. Symptoms of acute carbon monoxide poisoning include headache, loss of vision, decreased muscular coordination, and abdominal pain.

River blindness—onchocerciasis—affects 300 million people in tropical Africa. The disease, which leads to whole areas becoming deserted as communities move in an endeavor to escape it, is carried by the black fly. Control measures include spraying rivers with DDT—an insecticide banned in many countries.

eaten by the local population leading to illness, malformed children and death. Fishing there will probably never be safe again.

Many once fertile coastal waters and estuaries are now "dead seas." Parts of the Baltic, Mediterranean and Caspian are also heavily polluted, while the Great Lakes of America—the largest freshwater lakes in the world—have been devastated by industrial and domestic pollution.

Increasing urbanization creates its own dilemma: progress is equated with cities, and the most sophisticated industries and talents gravitate to them; but as they expand the older, central areas tend to become slums, inhabited—particularly in the United States—by unskilled, poorly educated ethnic minorities. In such conditions, crime, alcoholism and drug addiction flourish. Those people who have the will to move find that they cannot because suburban communities frequently set minimum sizes on land or houses, which cost more than the ghetto residents can afford.

Atmospheric pollutants

Air pollution is caused mainly by the burning of fossil fuels. Smog from coal fires contributed to the deaths of about 4,000 Londoners in 1952, leading to the Clean Air Act, which reduced this type of pollution. Cities such as Tokyo and Los Angeles are now afflicted by photochemical smogs caused by the reaction of sunlight on exhaust fumes. It has been suggested that the effect of lead from exhausts on the human nervous system may be a factor in behavioral problems among urban children.

Other atmospheric pollutants could be creating hazards on a much larger scale. Chemicals, such as freon gas, used as aerosol propellants, may be interfering with the protective ozone of the upper atmosphere, allowing dangerous concentrations of ultraviolet light to reach the Earth's surface. Increased quantities of carbon dioxide released by the burning of fossil fuels could upset the heat balance of the Earth.

Air pollution is also responsible for considerable agricultural damage, amounting in California to an estimated $25 million a year. In some industrial areas, sulfur so overwhelms the natural cleansing processes of the air that acid rain falls thousands of kilometers downwind.

Alongside all this evidence of the strains on the Earth's resources must be put the threat to other life forms by man's impact on the environment. The thoughtless use of chemicals and destruction of animal habitats is reducing wildlife populations. Many wild plant species are also under pressure, while the enormous expansion of monoculture has increased the possibility of epidemic crop failure.

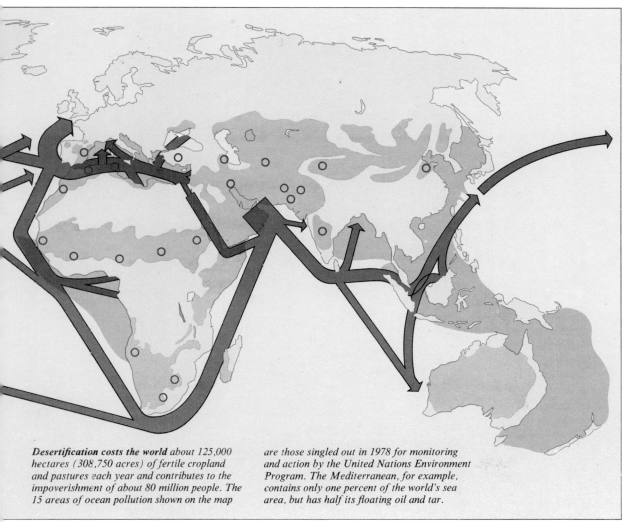

Desertification costs the world about 125,000 hectares (308,750 acres) of fertile cropland and pastures each year and contributes to the impoverishment of about 80 million people. The 15 areas of ocean pollution shown on the map are those singled out in 1978 for monitoring and action by the United Nations Environment Program. The Mediterranean, for example, contains only one percent of the world's sea area, but has half its floating oil and tar.

POPULATION POLICIES

Sophisticated advertising promotes the Pill as part of "the good life" in the United States. While material produced in developing countries emphasizes the need for planned families, the message here seems to be that it is better to rear houseplants.

Population policies in West Africa encourage the spacing of children rather than reducing their numbers. This village chief in Ghana, with some of his four wives and 10 children, is a recent convert to his country's family planning program.

Most generations before our own regarded the growth of population as a source of strength and a sign that the battle with disease and famine was being won. Only in the last 25 years or so have positive steps been taken to prevent the sheer weight of numbers overwhelming the natural resources needed to sustain them.

In fact the first clear population policies were in the opposite direction—an attempt by a few European countries in the years before World War II to encourage larger families because of the fear of a future decline in population.

An awareness that population control policies required high priority did not surface until the 1950s, when some Asian countries with rapidly growing populations began to perceive rapid growth as a liability rather than as an asset. By 1974, when the UN World Population Conference was held, 80 countries had policies to reduce fertility or were supporting family planning programs.

The message from the Bucharest conference was that family planning should be promoted as a human right and countries should "give priority to implementing development programs and educational and health strategies which, while contributing to economic growth and higher standards of living, have a decisive impact upon demographic trends, including fertility."

Among the 46 countries now actively committed to reducing their birthrates are the two with the largest populations—China and India. Overall 82 percent of the developing world's people now live in countries with government population programs. International funding for population policies has gone up from $2 million in 1960 to some $300 million in 1977, about a third of it coming from the United States. This funding now totals about two percent of all international development aid.

World attitudes to family planning

In general, since the Bucharest conference, there has not been any great shift in attitudes among governments to population planning, which still vary from continent to continent.

In Africa there has been greater resistance to family planning in countries that were formerly colonies of Catholic France and Portugal than those that once belonged to Britain. Countries such as Cameroon, Malawi and Upper Volta believe that more people are needed if they are to grow in importance. Others, such as Mali, Senegal and Zaire, have changed their stance and are now supporting

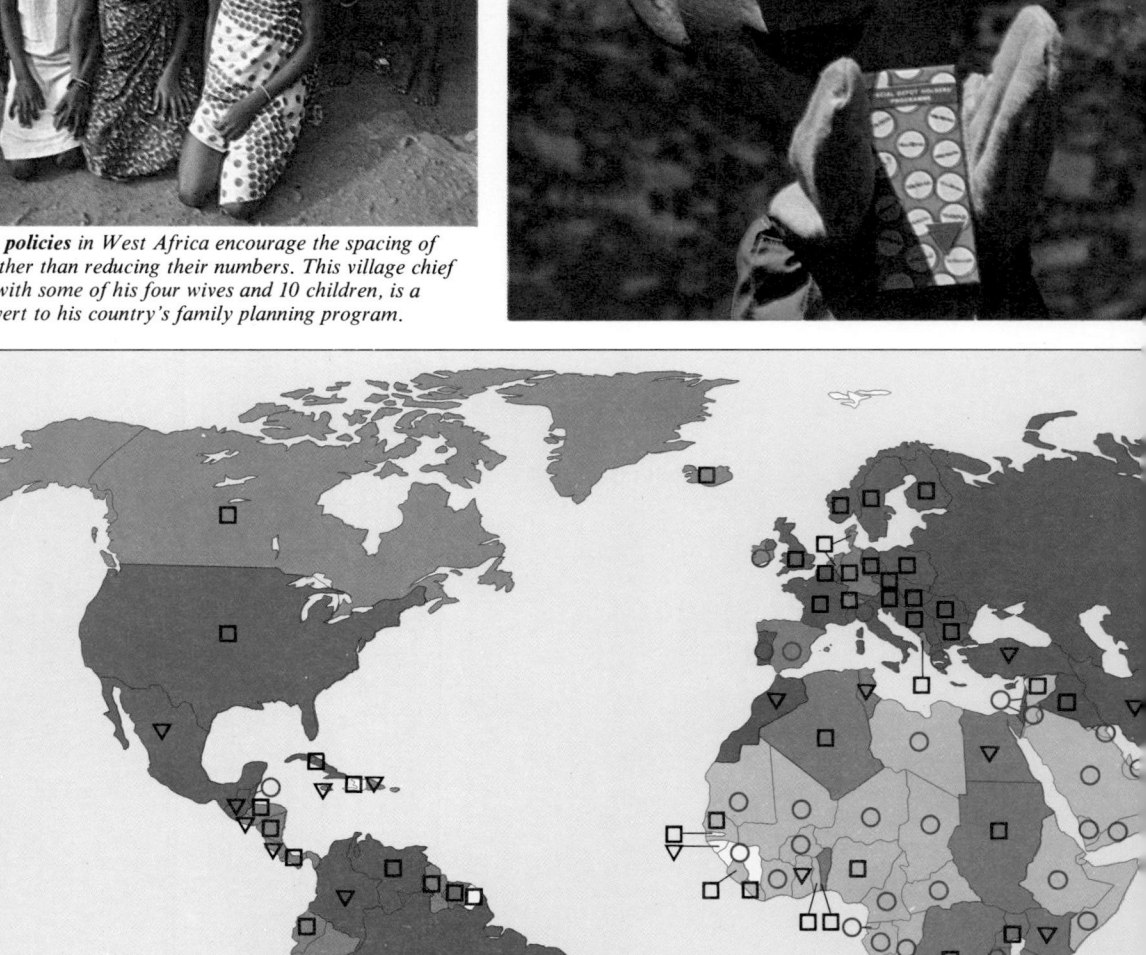

▽ Official policy to reduce population

□ Official support of family planning

○ No policies or support

All abortions per 1,000 live births

Over 500

201–500

50–200

Less than 50

Unknown

Official and semiofficial family planning programs have been supported by many countries since the mid-1960s to give 95 percent of the world's population some access to contraception. Roughly two-thirds of the world now lives in some 30 countries which have liberal abortion laws or policies.

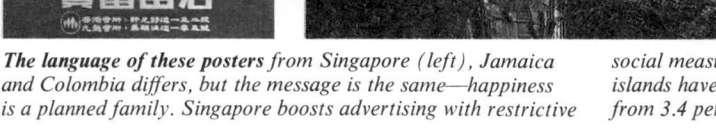

The language of these posters from Singapore (left), Jamaica and Colombia differs, but the message is the same—happiness is a planned family. Singapore boosts advertising with restrictive social measures to encourage small families. Several Caribbean islands have curbed their growth rates, while Colombia's fell from 3.4 percent in the 1960s to 2.4 percent in 1978.

CONNECTIONS

A wide variety of approaches is employed to encourage the use of contraceptives in developing countries. Puppet plays in Maharastra, India, feature the Pill and the coil, while supplies are available out of normal shopping hours in Sri Lankan stores.

most widely used method of contraception in the world, with about 80 million couples so far having opted for this means of limiting their families.

The country which today holds out the greatest hope for the success of population control policies is China, which is estimated to have reduced its birthrate from 32 per 1,000 in 1970 to 19 per 1,000 in 1975. In some cities in China low birthrates have been so enthusiastically adopted as a goal that neighborhoods collectively decide how many births will be allowed each year and award the privilege of having babies to "deserving couples."

Although birth control in some form is almost universally practiced in the developed countries of the world very few have any specific policies on population growth other than restrictions on immigration. In the United States and most European countries the trend has been toward the gradual liberalization of abortion laws and the provision of family planning advice and services. The change has naturally been slower in Catholic countries, though even Italy has relaxed its strict religious stance. It has now legalized abortion.

Fears of future labor shortage

In the USSR and East European countries extremely low birthrates since World War II have caused a reversion to more pronatalist policies because of fears of future labor shortages. The Soviet government, which is also concerned with the different rates of growth of its various national groups, periodically exhorts its people to have more children, while East Germany offers inducements such as pregnancy leave on full pay and generous financial support during a baby's first year.

Japan, the only fully developed country in Asia, legalized abortion and launched a massive family planning campaign in the 1950s, which sharply reduced the birthrate. But in 1970, alarmed by an apparent labor shortage, industry began clamoring for more births. However, a recession in 1974, concern for the environment and the growth of the women's liberation movement in Japan have largely silenced the campaign for higher fertility.

With a few exceptions the overall view is that policies so far pursued to slow the world's population growth have had only limited success. According to Robert McNamara, President of the World Bank, the misery of an impoverished world of 11 billion people cannot be avoided unless these policies are intensified.

There is a growing understanding that people are themselves a resource, and that family planning is only part of an essential package of basic needs which people require if they are to fulfill their physical and mental potential and plan for smaller families. Such needs include education, health, maternity and child care, nutrition, opportunities for employment and equal rights for women.

Despite all the efforts the fact remains that today only about one woman in three is practicing any form of contraception, leaving some 361 million at risk of an unwanted pregnancy. Until this situation is altered the prospect of a stationary world population remains distant.

family planning for health and welfare reasons. Many Latin American countries have also been reluctant to accept the need to slow down population growth, often taking the view that they need more and more people to exploit the vast resources of land and minerals. The exceptions are Chile, Colombia, all of the Central American countries, and several in the Caribbean. Brazil has begun a tentative family planning program, but Argentina, with a relatively low birthrate, and feeling threatened by the growth of Brazil, banned the spread of birth control information and closed family planning clinics in 1974.

In Asia, with more than half the world's population, both birth and death rates have generally been declining, with the biggest falls in fertility in countries with strong family planning programs: China, Thailand, Indonesia, Sri Lanka, Hong Kong, Singapore, Taiwan and South Korea. The impact of programs in Pakistan, Bangladesh and Malaysia has been less encouraging.

India's family planning program began as far back as 1952, when the population was about 360 million and growing at two percent a year. But the program was not very effective and by 1975 the population had grown to almost 600 million. In early 1976, under Indira Gandhi's emergency regime, population policy took a radical turn. A sterilization campaign aimed at couples with two or more children was waged with excessive zeal, particularly in the north. These drastic measures were a major factor in Mrs Gandhi's electoral defeat in 1977. The new government not unnaturally announced a return to more orthodox policies.

Apart from abortion, sterilization, in fact, is the

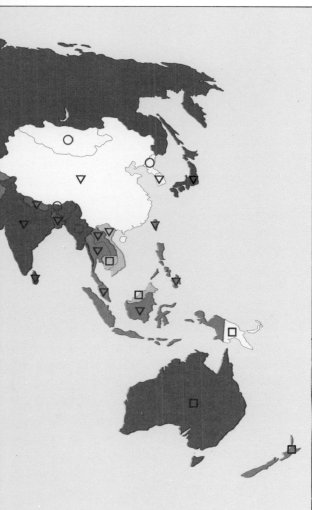

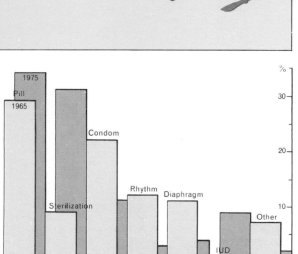

Though few developed countries have population policies, birth control trends are constantly changing. In the United States sterilization is rapidly approaching the Pill in popularity.

CHINA

The birthrate revolution in China is the most encouraging sign for the future of the world's population policies. Family planning, an integral part of the overall development program, has spread from the cities to the farthest reaches of the country, partly through the efforts of "barefoot doctors." These part-timers are given basic medical training and then assigned to local clinics (right). China is estimated to have reduced its birthrate faster than any other large developing country without birth control laws. The results have been achieved almost entirely by a discipline that insists on late marriage (27 for men, 25 for women, in urban areas) and well-spaced families of two or three children. Family planning methods range from abortion and sterilization to "morning after" or "visiting husband" pills. China also recognizes the role family planning programs play in increasing the part played by women in Chinese society: most women of childbearing age now work.

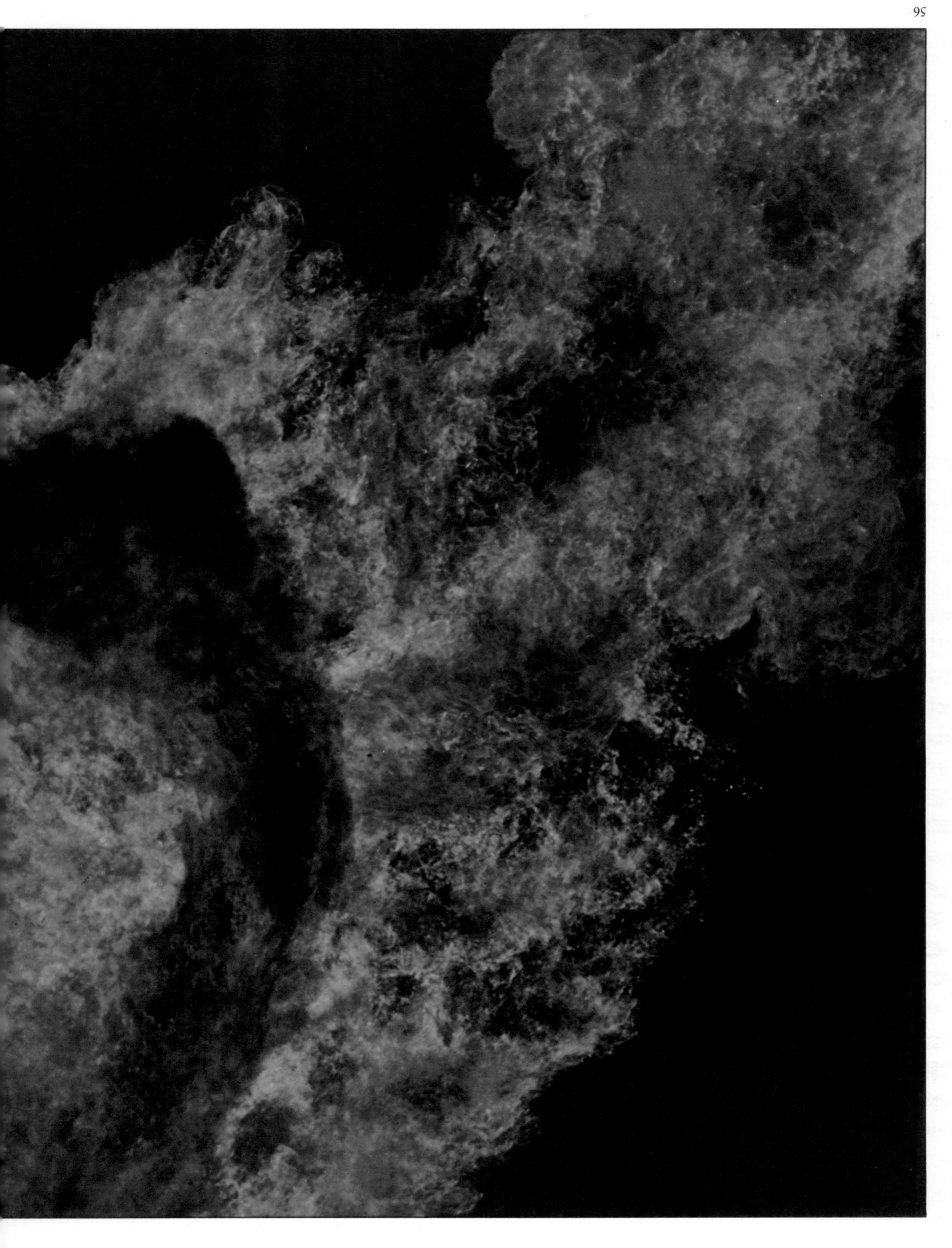

ENERGY

ENERGY
WHAT IS ENERGY?

Energy is one of the most fundamental but at the same time most mysterious of natural phenomena. We tend to think about it and then we comes to thinking closely about it until it can be specific about its effects but not about the nature of the thing itself. No better definition of energy can be given than that in any school textbook: ''Energy is the capacity to do work.''

Energy can take many different forms, and an important fact is that it can be transformed from one guise to another. For example, nuclear energy from the Sun reaches Earth as radiation energy; this can be absorbed by plants to form chemical compounds, which may then be used as food for animals and man. The chemical energy of the food is stored as chemical energy in the body tissues.

It was only after scientists had come to realize all the forms in which energy can manifest itself that they were able to reach one of the most profound conclusions of natural science: that although energy may take many forms—kinetic, potential, electric, heat, light, nuclear, chemical—the sum total in a closed system always remains unchanged. This principle of ''the conservation of energy'' is a fundamental law of physical science.

The principle is based on a mass of experimental evidence and no departure from the law has ever been detected. The branch of science that deals with the phenomenon of energy is thermodynamics and the principle of conservation of energy is expressed in the first law of that discipline. The second law of thermodynamics deals with the limitations of the process of conversion from one form of energy to another and is concerned particularly with heat. It is concerned with the operation of engines by heat, but, more importantly, with many other problems in physics which can be solved by the application of this law without consideration of the details of the processes involved.

Understanding energy

The phenomenon of energy was little understood until the nineteenth century, when physicists such as Count Rumford, Davy, Mayer and Joule were among those who showed experimentally that when a measurable amount of mechanical ''work,'' as represented by the lifting of a known weight through a measured distance, was dissipated by allowing the weight to fall and the energy so released was used in some heat-producing action, they were able to measure the rise in temperature of a certain mass of matter and hence deduce that the heat generated by the action was proportional to the mechanical work done.

In due course the quantitative relationships between the units of measurement of different forms of energy were established. Finally came the prediction by Einstein from his theory of relativity that kinetic energy (the energy of a moving body) can be transformed into mass, and that mass may be transformed into energy according to the relationship $E = mc^2$, where E is the energy resulting from the transformation of mass m, and c is the velocity of light. This relationship, which was soon shown to be essential to the understanding of nuclear physics, destroyed the older concept of the conservation of mass and is the basis of much of the fundamental physics of nuclear energy. What is more, it is now one of the basic concepts in the theory of the origin and evolution of the physical universe, as envisaged in the ''big bang'' theory.

The weight of evidence at present seems to point to the creation, about 18 billion years ago, of a vast amount of photon energy, mainly in the form of radiation, at an extremely high temperature (about 10^{12} degrees Centigrade). To start with, possibly for about the first second of its existence, there was practically no ''material'' in this ball of energy, but it was expanding with the speed of light and cooling, so that the radiation became cooler and of longer wavelength, changing sequentially from photon to gamma radiation, X rays, ultraviolet, visible, infra-

A brilliant display of energy in the form of electricity can be seen as a high voltage is applied across an insulator in what is known as a

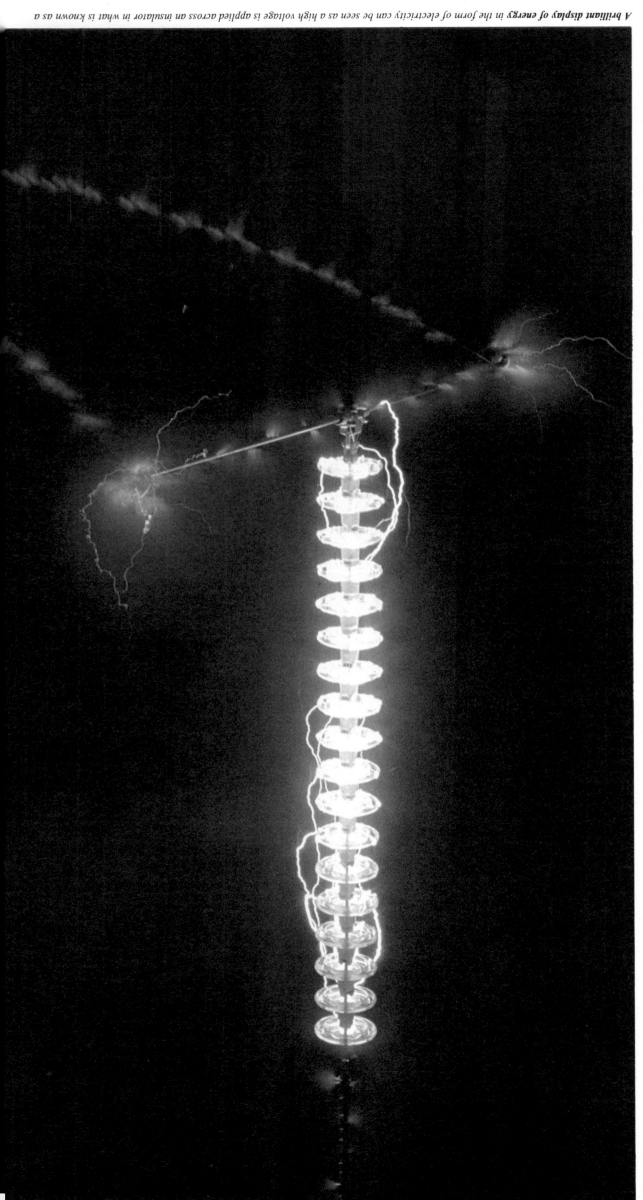

red and microwave radiation, over many eons, until now almost all (about 99 percent) of the energy in the universe pervades space as very short-wavelength isotrophic radio waves. During this cooling process, various stages were reached where the photons (fundamental particles of radiation energy) could be transformed into pairs (positive and negative) of particles: the negative electron and its positive antiparticle the positron; the positive proton and its antiparticle the negative proton; and many others. This was the first massive transformation of radiation to mass in the evolution of the universe.

There followed over millions of years a complex process of evolution wherein, at one stage, vast quantities of negative electrons combined with equal numbers of positive positrons to form hydrogen and helium atoms. These were slowly pulled together by the force of gravitational attraction to form the vast clouds of gases, that we call galaxies, and, still later, to produce local condensations within these gas clouds to form stars.

The detailed process by which this happens is not well understood, but the end result is readily visible with the techniques of modern astronomy. We see the universe populated with a large number of galaxies and vast groups of stars, sometimes embedded in clouds containing hydrogen and helium gas and cosmic dust.

Star formation

The creation of a typical star can be followed in outline. A very large cloud of hydrogen and some helium gas, with a certain amount of cosmic dust from previous reactions, begins to be pulled together by the force of gravity. As it contracts, the force increases according to the inverse-square law by which gravitation acts. Thus if the distance between the atoms decreases by a factor of ten, the gravitational pull between them increases by a factor of a hundred. In this way the gas pressure at the center of the cloud increases and its temperature rises. Quite soon (in a million years or so) the temperature and pressure at the center of this cluster of gases become so great that the hydrogen atoms move with sufficient kinetic energy that, when they collide, their nuclei fuse together to form helium atoms. During this process a fraction of their mass is transformed into radiant energy. The process is called nuclear fusion and is the source of energy of most of the stars, including our Sun.

This energy, first as "hard" gamma radiation, further heats the gas of the star, increases the pressure and so sustains the fusion process, with the outward pressure of the radiation balancing the contraction force of gravity on the gas. The

radiation gradually penetrates outward through the ball of glowing hydrogen that is now a star, and eventually, very much cooler, reaches the white-hot surface and is radiated into space. A minute fraction of it reaches the outer regions of the atmosphere of our planet and an even smaller fraction of this penetrates the atmosphere and reaches the Earth's surface. Much of the radiation reaching Earth is filtered out by the atmosphere. This is mostly gamma, X and ultraviolet radiation, which would otherwise be injurious to living beings.

However, this radiation by its direct and indirect effects is an essential factor in the support of life on this planet, both by its warming of our environment by radiant heat energy, and by the building up of organic materials by plant photosynthesis. Radiation interacts with the chemical elements of the Earth—carbon, oxygen, hydrogen, nitrogen and so on—to produce living and growing organisms. Much of this has been preserved as coal, oil and natural gas, now our most important sources of energy; in burning these fuels with the oxygen in the atmosphere, chemical energy is released as heat, which can then be converted to mechanical energy, electricity, light, heat or many other energy forms.

Nevertheless, a significant part of our energy store comes by a very different route. Most of the heavier elements of the Earth were not synthesized in the early days of the universe, when hydrogen and helium were formed. These had to wait for the second generation of synthesis, when giant stars were formed. These stars were so large that they burned up their hydrogen and helium very rapidly and their cores reached very high temperatures—high enough to cause the fusion process to continue to such an extent as to synthesize the heavier elements.

Eventually, after a relatively short life, such a massive star reached an unstable state and finally exploded with enormous violence as a nova or supernova, ejecting its material out into the surrounding gas clouds of its galaxy. This is the raw material from which the Earth and solar system is built, and quite clearly it contains a great deal of energy—kinetic, gravitational and nuclear. The building process is not understood in detail, but it is likely that heat was generated in great quantity by the dissipation of the kinetic and gravitational energy of the material as it accumulated and was pulled together by gravitation. It also contained a great deal of radioactive material which has been generating heat as it has decayed over a period of about 4.5 billion years. These were the sources of heat energy that produced the hot molten metal interior of the Earth.

"flashover" test to determine electrical characteristics.

ENERGY UNITS

The basic unit of energy in the widely adopted International System (SI) is the joule (symbol J), or, alternatively, the kilojoule (kJ) or megajoule (MJ).

Heat is often measured in terms of the calorie (cal), defined as the amount of heat required to raise the temperature of one gram of water by one degree Centigrade (at 15°C). The corresponding imperial measurement is the British

Electrical energy is expressed by the kilowatt hour (kWh), the amount of

Chemical energy is expressed in a number of ways. Nutritionists measure energy content of food and man's energy requirements in kilocalories (kcal), which are also called Calories (with a capital "C"). In the case of fuels, it is convenient when comparing global reserves to give values as tons of coal or oil. The equivalent energy content can then be found using the

Nuclear energy is commonly expressed as the amount of energy released in the nuclear fission of the fuel (generally uranium), which again allows an

Although different forms of energy are interconvertible and they can all be expressed in terms of the joule, a variety of units is used. **Power** is defined as the rate of doing work (or equivalently the rate of transferring energy) and is measured in watts (symbol W), which are joules per second, or megawatts (MW). MWe (electrical) are distinguished from MWt (thermal).

thermal unit (Btu). One therm is equal to 10,000 Btus. The work of nineteenth-century scientists established the "mechanical equivalent of heat," giving a quantitative relationship between heat and work.

energy transferred in one hour by one kilowatt, or the megawatt hour (MWh).

calorific value, which is the amount of heat liberated when a fuel is completely burnt. Units for this are megawatts per kilogram (MW/kg), kilocalories per kilogram (kcal/kg) or British thermal units per pound (Btu/lb). Calorific values vary according to the quality of the fuel, so an average figure is used in order to give the overall energy equivalent.

energy equivalent to be given. The power density of a nuclear reactor gives the energy released per second in a given volume, usually kilowatts per liter.

Energy conversion factors

1 calorie	4.184	J
1 British thermal unit	1.055	kJ
1 therm	105.5	MJ
1 kilowatt-hour	3.6	MJ
1 Calorie (kcal)	4.184	kJ
1 ton coal	25,000	MJ
1 ton oil	43,000	MJ
1 gram uranium in thermal reactor	300	MJ

ELECTRICITY

ENERGY

Electricity cannot be stored in large quantity, but it is a highly convenient means of transmitting and using energy available from other sources; and it is the only practicable method of harnessing nuclear, wind and wave power. The advantages of electricity are its instant availability, ease of control and lack of pollution at the point of use.

Apart from hydroelectricity, the bulk of the world's electric power is produced in generators driven by steam turbines. The steam may be pro-duced by burning oil, coal or natural gas as in gigantic boilers, or by nuclear reactors. The Longannet power plant in Scotland, which has four 600 MW generators, uses five million tons of coal a year and requires millions of liters of cooling water every day. Some power plants are even larger—a 1,200 MW generator has been installed in the USA.

Of the total energy contained in the primary fuel, about 35 percent is converted into electricity; the rest appears as heat in the cooling water. This apparently low efficiency is in fact very close to the theoretical limit and cannot be much improved until some alternative to the steam turbine is found.

Power plants inevitably produce some pollution. Nuclear power plants have their own particular problems, but conventional power plants generally burn low-quality fuels which are difficult to use in other ways. In coal-fired power plants solid particles can be removed in giant precipitators, but the only economic remedy for such pollutants as sulfur dioxide is to build high chimneys to disperse them over a wide area. Cooling water, which is returned a few degrees above its original temperature, can cause changes in the local ecology.

The very presence of a power plant is a visual intrusion, especially if it has the vast cooling towers needed to recycle water. Power plants need exten-sive areas of land and large supplies of water, and are often built on coastal sites or clustered on major rivers in rural areas.

Uses

Electricity is the one form of energy without which modern society could not exist: so much so that many organizations install their own emergency generators to maintain emergency supplies should there be a power cut. Lighting, for all purposes, is one of the major uses of electricity. Electric motors are ex-tremely versatile and robust, so that it is worthwhile to install a diesel generator unit and electric motors in a railway locomotive, rather than using the diesel engine to drive the wheels more directly. Electric motors of all sizes have an enormous variety of

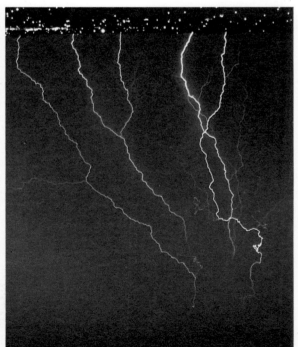

A violent storm triggered a 24-hour electrical blackout on America's east coast in July 1977 and resulted in millions of dollars' worth of damage. The hot summer had resulted in record summer consumption of electricity for air-conditioning.

uses, from domestic appliances and light commer-cial machinery to the giant industrial motors used in steel-works. There is no realistic alternative to electric motors for most of the smaller applications.

A number of applications are inherently electric: broadcast radio and television and effective long-range communication, by electrical or radio. Mechanical calculating machines do exist, but it is the electronic computer that has produced the vast growth of data processing on which society in-creasingly relies. Similarly, the control of auto-mated machinery is beyond the capability of mech-anical instruments, but electrical systems can moni-tor and control such devices accurately and safely.

Transmission

All electricity generating systems produce alter-nating current because transformers can be used to step it up to high voltage for transmission to distant load centers; and at these higher voltages the power losses are reduced.

A transmission system forms a network (known in Britain as the National Grid) linking all power plants and main substations: at these the electricity is stepped down to a lower voltage and distributed to small substations, and finally to the consumers. Wherever possible, transmission is by overhead lines. Underground cables are used at lower vol-tages, but at high voltage the insulation and cooling requirements make them 15 times as expensive, so their use is restricted to places where preservation of the environment is all-important, and to built-up areas where there is insufficient overhead clearance.

Significant amounts of power are lost in trans-formers and transmission lines, and power is used to keep the boilers fed and the cooling water circu-lating, so the final power delivered is considerably less than that generated. Of course, similar losses occur with all other energy sources.

Batteries can be used to store electricity, but they are too bulky and expensive except for supplying

small amounts of power in cases where continuous connection to a main supply is not possible, or as an emergency supply in case the main supply fails. Pumped-storage hydroelectric plants consume electricity when there is a surplus and regenerate it when there is a shortage, usually on a 24-hour cycle to meet regular peaks in demand.

Problems of meeting peak demand can some-times be eased by exchange of power between dif-ferent supply systems, perhaps in adjacent coun-tries, but it is difficult to maintain stability in such large linked systems. There is also a small chance that a single fault will cause a chain reaction and black out a large part of a supply network, as hap-pened on the east coast of North America in 1965. An alternative method is to use a direct-current link such as the cable under the English Channel be-tween England and France. Problems of this method include the expense and power loss in-volved in conversion to and from direct current.

Costs

In some respects electricity is an expensive form of energy, because the cost of generation has to be added to the cost of the primary fuel. However, the fuels used are relatively cheap, and such is the effi-ciency of generation and transmission, and the con-venience in use, that electricity is the most econ-omical form of energy for many purposes.

The capital costs of power plants and trans-mission lines are extremely high, so they must be used as much as possible to recoup these costs. One of the factors pushing up these costs is the need to maintain capacity to meet variation in demand. A proportion of a generating plant has to be kept run-ning as a "spinning reserve" in case of a sudden rise in demand or failure of a generator. Some genera-tors are run for a few hours a day only, to meet peaks in demand, and this starting and stopping of steam-driven generators is wasteful of fuel. Another way of meeting peak demands is to use plant that is

19

ELECTRICITY GENERATING COSTS

Nuclear power plants cost less to run than coal- or oil-fired plants, but are much more expensive to build. Both generating and building costs for alternative sources of electricity, such as tidal plants or windmills, can only be estimated as they are still in the experimental stage. It is also difficult to provide figures which can be fairly compared; proponents of each source give figures that best suit them.

Electricity Generation Cost 1976-77

	Nuclear plants pence/kWh	Coal and oil fired plants pence/kWh
Fuel for generation (including transport)	0.1746	0.3290
Fuel handling cost (excluding operation repairs and maintenance)	0.0369	0.9027
Operating cost (excluding fuel handling)	0.1186	0.1449
Total works cost*	0.6222	1.0845

Estimated construction costs
Coal £290   Tidal £355   Wind £200
Nuclear (thermal) £470   Geothermal £300   Wave £600

U.K. Department of Energy Statistics (excluding interest)
*U.K. Central Electricity Generating Boards Statistical Yearbook

A large proportion of the electricity generated is used by domestic consumers, and demand for such purposes undergoes rapid fluctuations. A popular television program, for example, can lead to a marked peak in demand. Supply authorities may charge lower rates to encourage the use of electricity at off-peak times. Similarly, charges to industrial customers may be based on the maximum demand during any period of perhaps half an hour. The main commercial load occurs during working hours and the main domestic load in the evening, which helps even out demand. Large industrial concerns operating 24 hours a day cause different problems, for the starting and stopping of large machines create surges which strain transmission systems and switchgear to the limit.

cheap to build and easy to start and stop, but expensive to operate. Small gas-turbine plants are suitable for this, and several have been built in Britain in recent years.

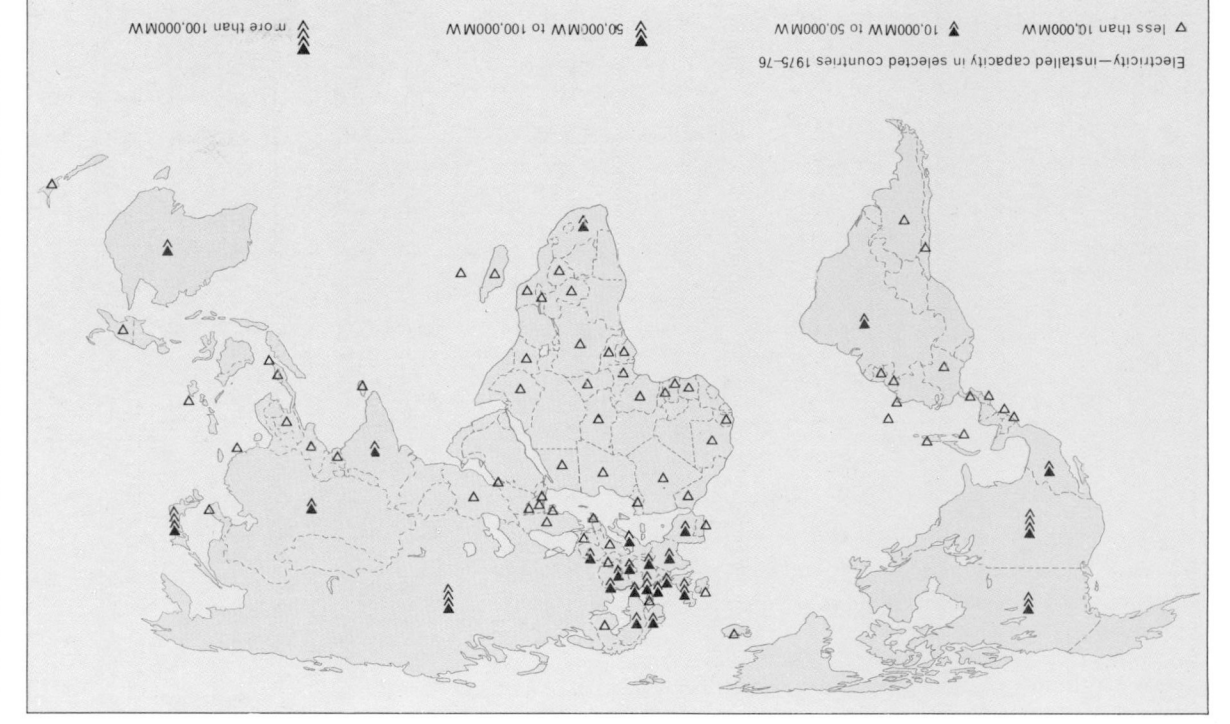

World electricity production in 1975-76 was 6,438,900 million kilowatt-hours—1,533 kWh for every man, woman and child alive. Annual consumption growth rate in 1976, at five percent, was more than double that for 1973, proving that attempts to conserve electricity had failed. The map shows the installed capacity of selected countries: the figure for China is estimated.

Electricity—installed capacity in selected countries 1975-76
△ less than 10,000MW
▲ 10,000MW to 50,000MW
▲ 50,000MW to 100,000MW
▲ more than 100,000MW

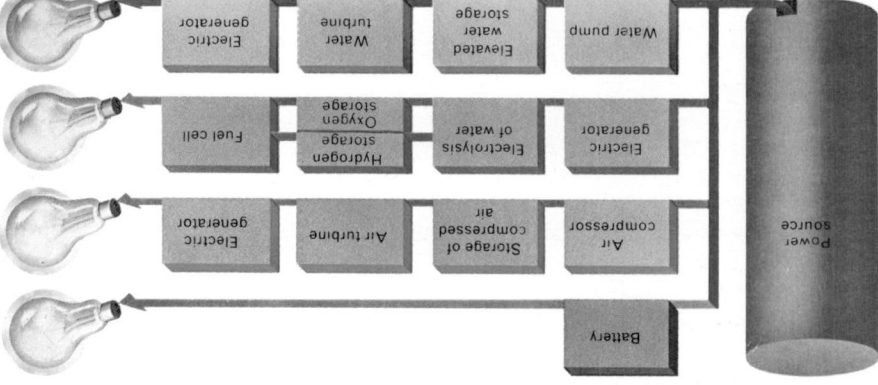

The battery, the most common form of electrical storage, converts chemical energy into direct current. **The air compressor** is used in a proposed form of storage; air at high pressure is stored underground and then used to drive a turbine. **The fuel cell** uses the energy of the reaction between hydrogen and oxygen to produce electricity. It has been used in space programs. **The water pump** may store energy by raising water to an upper reservoir.

Battery

Air compressor — Storage of compressed air — Air turbine — Electric generator

Electrolysis of water — Hydrogen storage / Oxygen storage — Fuel cell

Water pump — Elevated water storage — Water turbine — Electric generator

Power source

The Severn cable tunnel is part of a 3.5 km (2 mile) tunnel under the rivers Severn and Wye to establish a 100 km (62 mile) electric power link between England and Wales. Underwater cables are usually used for telegraphic applications.

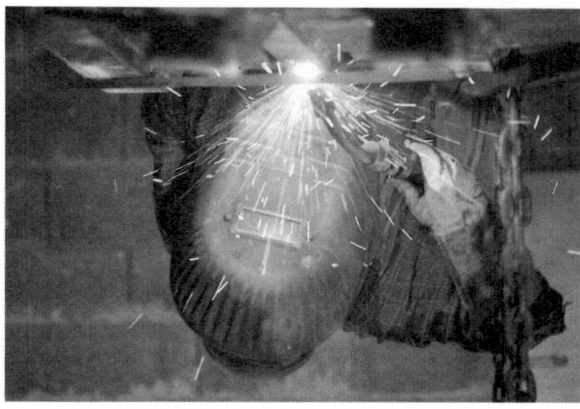

Arc welding is an important industrial application of electricity that can use alternating or direct current. In this process two pieces of metal are joined together by creating an electric arc between an electrode and the metal. The result is that the temperature is raised sufficiently to melt some of the metal, thus fusing together the two parts of the joint.

Overhead transmission lines are unsightly but cheaper than underground cables; air provides the insulation and there is no need for special cooling. Their disadvantages are that they can be damaged by severe weather conditions and can sometimes cause radio interference.

Hydroelectric plants, such as the one at Niagara Falls in the USA, can generate up to four million kW of electricity. Much of this is used by nearby electrochemical industries. The normal maximum distance for transmission is about 560 km (350 miles).

CONNECTIONS

COAL—FORMATION & USE

Coal in the Earth's continental crust represents a vast and comparatively unexploited store of energy. Coal seams began to form soon after the first land plants had evolved, about 320 million years ago. During the later part of the Carboniferous era, known as the Pennsylvanian in North America and the Westphalian in Europe, 80 percent of the world's coal was laid down in peat beds. Those destined to become workable coal seams, 0.6 to 2.5 meters (2 to 8 feet) in thickness, varied from 12 to 50 meters (40 to 164 feet) or more deep. A major belt included what is now central and eastern North America, Scotland south of the Highlands, England, Wales, France, the Low Countries, Germany and Poland, and continued across the USSR to China.

As the beds were buried under an increasing load of sediment, water and other volatiles were expelled to leave the coal, which, essentially, is a compact concentrate of carbon, hydrogen and oxygen. The change from plant material, here loosely called cellulose, to high-rank coal proceeds via peat, lignite and bituminous coal. In the evolution toward coal, or coalification, the physical characteristics also change. Peat is still plainly a mass of vegetable material, lignite is incoherent, while coal is hard and brittle, and anthracite more so. The transition to anthracite probably requires very deep burial, perhaps aided by Earth pressures or heat from a nearby mass of molten rock. There is a still further stage, when graphite, virtually pure carbon, is produced. This certainly requires heat or Earth pressures of a type found only at a deeper level in the crust than can usually be reached by mining.

The world's coalfields

The Carboniferous era terminated with the Earth's crust being flexured or bent into basins and domal uplifts throughout much of the coal-bearing area. Subsequent erosion removed much of the upfolded strata, leaving the great coalfields of the world as a series of separated basins, some of which were later covered with newer formations ("concealed coalfields"). The northward migration and drifting apart of the continents also occurred, producing the present configuration with the principal coalfield basins strung out around the northern temperate belt. There have been later episodes of coal formation, the most important embracing what is now eastern Australia, India, South Africa, Antarctica and South America, which 250–200 million years ago were still part of a single continent. The most recent episodes, in such places as the foothills of the Canadian Rockies, in New Mexico, along the Rhine Valley and in southeast Europe, belong to the last 50 million years, and most of the deposits are not yet high-rank coals but lignites or brown coals. Of still more recent origin is the peat, formed in the last 10,000 years, that has long served as a traditional fuel in East Anglia and northern England, and today in Ireland is cut with modern machinery to supply power plants.

Up to the sixteenth century wood was everywhere

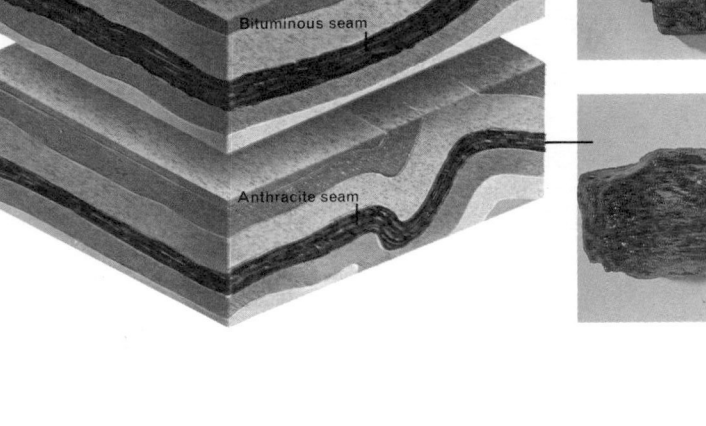

Iron and steel industries are the world's largest industrial users of energy, much of it supplied by bituminous coal that has been processed to make coke. Coke-fed blast furnaces consume 1.57 tons of coke for every ton of steel that is produced, and there are fears that the world resource of coking coal will not match industrial demand in the future.

			Calorific value kJ/kg
Wood	0.92%		
49.66%	6.23%	43.20%	19,770
Peat	1.72%		
55.44%	6.28%	36.56%	18,663
Lignite	1.31%		
72.95%	5.24%	20.50%	27,200
Bituminous coal	1.52%		
84.24%	5.55%	8.69%	32,100
Anthracite	0.97%		
93.50%	2.81%	2.72%	32,560

■ Carbon ■ Hydrogen ■ Nitrogen □ Oxygen

Coal-forming forest swamp

Peat layer

Lignite seam

Bituminous seam

Anthracite seam

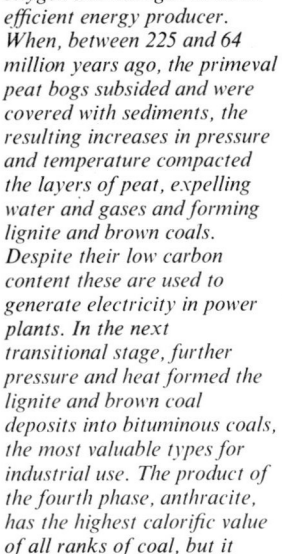

The main constituents of wood, peat, lignite, bituminous coal and anthracite, and the calorific value of each are shown above. On the left is a sectional view of how coal is gradually formed from plant materials. In suitable boggy conditions the plants decompose to form peat, a fibrous mass that can provide a cheap source of fuel but contains too much hydrogen, oxygen and nitrogen to be an efficient energy producer. When, between 225 and 64 million years ago, the primeval peat bogs subsided and were covered with sediments, the resulting increases in pressure and temperature compacted the layers of peat, expelling water and gases and forming lignite and brown coals. Despite their low carbon content these are used to generate electricity in power plants. In the next transitional stage, further pressure and heat formed the lignite and brown coal deposits into bituminous coals, the most valuable types for industrial use. The product of the fourth phase, anthracite, has the highest calorific value of all ranks of coal, but it is expensive to extract. Formerly in demand as a steam-producing agent, anthracite is needed less in present-day industry.

The most important function of coal is to provide coke for smelting iron and steel. Coke is formed by heating good-quality bituminous coal to between 700° and 1,200°C (1,292°–2,192°F), thereby driving out unwanted volatiles. Small coal of lesser ranks can be mixed with a bituminous coking variety and processed to make coke.

At the present rate of extraction, Pakistan's coal

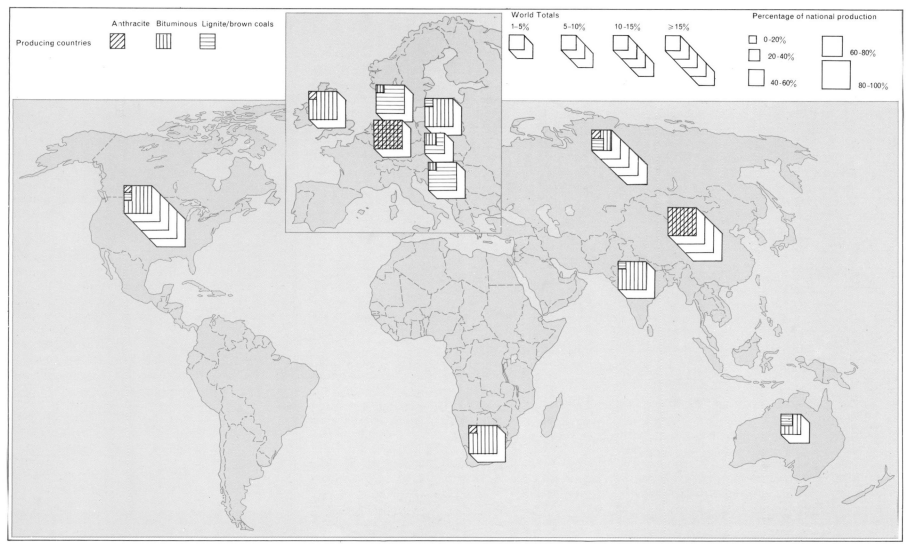

the chief fuel, and from it was made charcoal, the essential reducing agent for the smelting of iron and other metals. The only sources of mechanical energy for industry were water wheels, windmills and horses. London at the time of Elizabeth I (reigned 1558–1603) was probably the first major city to adopt coal for heating; it was brought by sea from the Tyne, around which developed the first of England's great coalfields. In the early eighteenth century came the discovery that must be regarded as fundamental to the Industrial Revolution: how to make coke from coal and use it not only as an energy source but also as a reducing agent for smelting iron. For the first time, iron could be made in quantity. There followed the steam engine, originally developed for pumping water from mines, the factory engine and the railway engine. These provided the basis of modern industry.

In 1913 United Kingdom coal production reached its all-time high of 289 million tons. Other Western countries, notably the United States and Germany, eventually exceeded Britain's output. Until the 1930s, coal remained the world's chief source of industrial energy. It was not surpassed until the 1960s when another fossil fuel, petroleum,

took the lead. Petroleum is preferred today because it is easier to recover, cheaper to transport, cleaner to use and contains approximately 1.7 times the calorific value per ton of coal.

Coal production in Britain and most other western European countries had already begun to slip back before the impact of cheap petroleum was felt. Although the present total figure for Britain is little more than 100 million tons per year, there are hopes that output can be increased to help offset dwindling oil resources. The USA is steadily increasing its coal production, the USSR has rapidly enlarged its to nearly 500 million tons annually, and total world production is currently estimated at 2,600 million tons.

Reserves and resources

Because coal seams have a wide lateral continuity, often forming layers hundreds of square kilometers in extent, estimation of reserves is easier than for many other natural resources. Even so, the state of development of the coal basins varies considerably from one to another, and estimates of the total global resource cannot be made with great accuracy. Figures produced since the mid-1960s vary in their total amounts between 7.6 and 12 trillion tons. Of the 12 nations listed, those richest in coal are the USSR (5.7 trillion tons), USA (1.5), and China (1.0). These are followed by a middle group that includes West Germany (287 billion), the UK and Poland (both 165 billion) and Australia (108 billion).

Such total estimates, coupled with the present annual production rate of 2,600 million tons, might seem to suggest that there is enough coal to last for 3,000 years at the present rate, or 1,000 years at an exponential rate allowing for population increases. These are not safe figures, however, given all the geological, technological, economic and social uncertainties that must also be allowed for. All that can safely be said is that there are very large resources of coal, in particular in the USSR, USA and China, which are far greater in their energy equivalent than those of petroleum.

Of the nations producing, consuming and trading in iron ore, iron and steel, the USA is the largest coal producer and has the largest reserves. The USSR has fewer coal reserves but double the resources, though the West might regard much of it as unrecoverable economically at present prices. World trading is most active in high-ranking coking coal needed to service the metal industries. Nations such as West Germany, with a large supply of poor-quality indigenous coal, maximize this resource by using it to generate electricity in power plants, and also hold it in reserve for emergency use, as in a fuel crisis.

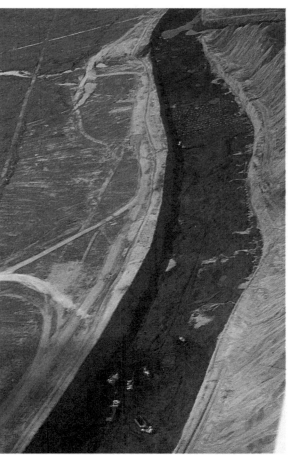

One-third of Australia's coal is located in the Bowen Basin, Queensland, where open-pit mining is practiced. Since nearly 80 percent is of coking quality, world demand for Australian coal is high, and exports account for 16 percent of world coal trade; Japan is the chief customer. Australia consumes only half its coal (USA uses 90 percent, and USSR 95 percent).

supplies will run out in 12 years. The country's lack of
indigenous energy resources is stunting its industrial growth.

COAL—NEW DEVELOPMENTS

The exploitation of massive quantities of cheap oil from the Middle East in the 1950s and the discovery of natural gas fields in other areas diminished the importance of coal. Actual coal production increased by 56 percent from 1950 to 1972, reaching 2.4 billion tons a year, but, as oil and gas met much of the increased demand for energy, coal's share of the market fell from 60 percent to 30 percent in the same period.

The era of cheap oil and gas is now seen to be past. The OPEC group showed in 1973 how oil prices could be increased sharply. Also, the relatively limited resources of fluid hydrocarbons suggest that, as has already happened in the USA, the underlying costs of extracting oil and gas will generally increase compared with coal costs.

Coal in the future

In some areas, though, coal has never lost its importance. Coke, produced from coal, has continued in its major role in metallurgical reduction and refining. Also, coal has long been a major fuel for raising steam in bulk and producing electricity. In the future, as gas and fuel oil are reserved for special uses, coal, like nuclear power, must continue to be a main source of electricity generation. More industrial use is also expected and for this, and for electricity generation, new techniques are being developed.

Fluidized combustion of coal (but also of heavy fuel oil and solid waste) is being widely developed, especially in Britain, the USA and West Germany, to offer more efficient and clean combustion in boilers comparable in size to oil-fired boilers. Coal in small lumps is fed onto a heated bed of sand, or ash, through which air is kept bubbling. By adjustment of the bed height and the air velocity, optimum conditions of heating can be obtained. The process is relatively tolerant of varying quality of coal feed, and sophisticated engineering design secures the same amount of steam from a smaller plant.

Substitutes for oil and gas

Heat for homes and offices in the modern city is now largely provided by oil and gas and modern transport depends heavily on oil. While coal could provide energy for these markets via electricity production, clean gas and liquid fuels can, in fact, be produced more cheaply from coal. Already this has happened in some special situations, such as in Germany during World War II and currently in South Africa, where gasoline and chemicals are produced from coal. Widespread use of such synthetic fuels cannot be expected for some decades.

Conversion of coal into gas and liquid fuels is not new. Byproducts have been produced for 100 years in coke-making, and "town gas" has been produced for a similar period. Compared with oil or gas, coal not only has an extraneous mineral content, it also contains much less hydrogen. Therefore, in conversion, hydrogen has either to be provided as an extra or has to be made available by the internal reorganization in the coal molecule that takes place during distillation of coal when volatiles are driven off.

Modern conversion technology is aimed at controlling the basic chemical reactions through process design and use of catalysts. Thus a more accurate range of desired products can be produced cleanly, with higher efficiency of conversion, from a wide range of coal types.

Gasification and liquefaction of coal

The basic reaction in coal gasification is to combine carbon and water to give carbon monoxide plus hydrogen. In practice, more complicated reactions take place to produce methane (CH_4) and carbon dioxide. Also, the above reaction requires external heat and this is usually provided by the combustion of some of the coal in the same gasifier reactor.

Depending on coal type, the design and pressure of the gasifier, and whether air or oxygen are used together with steam, different types of gas can be produced at greater or less efficiency. A weak gas, basically carbon dioxide, hydrogen and nitrogen, is produced by using air in the gasifier. This gas has only local heating uses or, if produced under pressure, it can generate electricity. If oxygen is used in the gasifier a carbon monoxide/hydrogen mixture is produced. This is a valuable medium-heat fuel and is (as "synthesis" gas) a chemical raw material. Further refinement in gasification processes yields a gas which is largely methane and

Mechanized mining has expanded rapidly since World War II. At a drift mine in South Wales an automatic cutting machine works backward and forward across the seam, breaking off the coal, which is taken away by a conveyor. Self-advancing hydraulic roof supports, introduced in the 1950s, reduced the number of men working in dangerous parts of the mine. While mining is still one of the most hazardous occupations, accident rates have been reduced across the world.

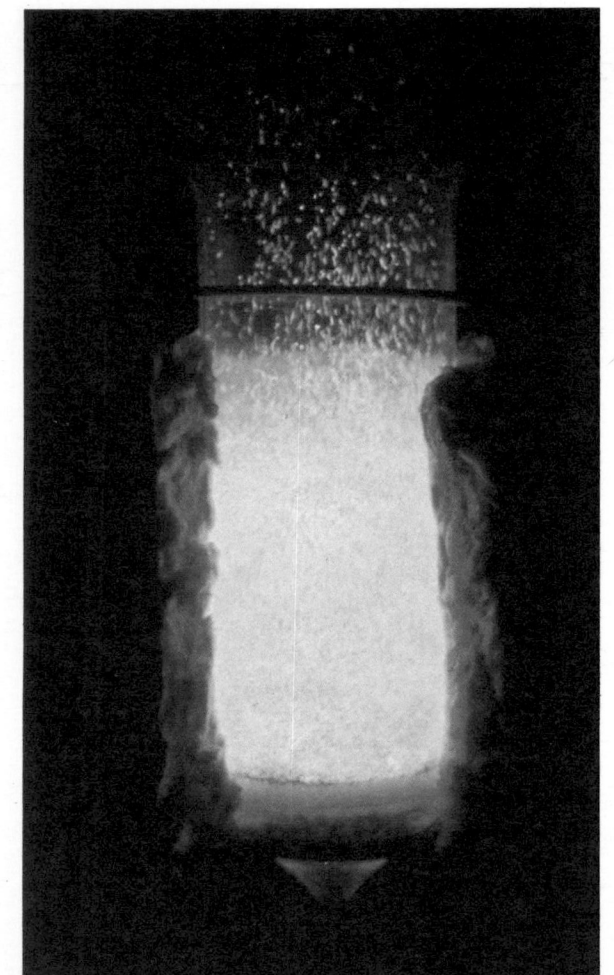

Accident rate per 100,000 manshifts in British coal mines

	Fatal	Serious
1960		
1965		
1970		
1975		
1977		

0   0.2   0.4   0.6   0.8   1   1.2   1.4

Research into fluidized bed combustion has been carried out, particularly in the UK, the USA and West Germany. Fluidized bed boilers are now near to commercial production. One advantage of the process is that if limestone is fed into the bed, sulfur oxides can be kept out of the flue gas and atmospheric pollution reduced, an important factor when sulfur emission laws are becoming stricter. The burners can also use a lower quality of coal in an unwashed state.

Coal can be converted into many usable forms by the solvent extraction process. Fuel oils and gasoline are the most important products, but by products could supply feedstock for the plastics and chemical industries.

Products derived from coal via solvent extraction

Process		Solvent recycle		
solvent → coal →	Digestion	Separation	Solvent recovery	Coking

Primary product				
Digest	Residue	Coal solution	Coal extract	High-purity coke

Potential uses				
Crude plastics	Filter aid	**Hydrocarbon products**	Carbon fibers	Graphite and carbon electrodes
Bitumen-like materials	Active char		Coal derived plastics	Nuclear graphite
Briquetting pitch	Loose-fill insulant		Porous carbon and graphite bodies	Metal oxide reduction
Coking additives			Fiber-reinforced composites	
Mastics and jointing compounds			Electrode binder and impregnant	

Negative effects of coal mining include land subsidence and despoliation of landscape by strip mining and by slag-heaps such as this (left) in West Virginia, although in many countries land reclamation is now obligatory. The dying forest (above), skirting an open-pit mine in British Columbia, is a stark reminder of another serious environmental problem: escaping coal-dust, which is carried in the mine-waste water leaking out from tailings ponds. Also a threat to plant and animal life is the release of sulfur dioxide into the atmosphere when coal (or oil) is burned; this mixes with rain to form a weak sulfuric acid.

Railways, still the most important way of transporting coal, are expensive. The industry is now evaluating other methods, such as inland waterways and pipelines carrying slurry.

therefore suitable as a substitute for natural gas. Perhaps the simplest approach to producing liquids from coal is pyrolysis, or controlled heating in the absence of air, to drive off a volatile fraction which can be further refined to give commercial gases, liquid fuels and chemicals. The carbon residue is then suitable for gasification or combustion. A difficulty with pyrolysis is that the yield of liquid products is relatively low, and their quality is poor.

The yield of liquids can be increased by dissolving the coal in a solvent and then distilling off and refining the product. Suitable solvents are anthracenes and other aromatic liquids obtained as part of the liquid product. A new British process is developing the extraction of liquids from coal using compressed gas as the solvent. Processes such as liquefaction are being developed. No one process has a clear advantage, since the products and yields obtained vary considerably with coal used and the engineering features of the process. In this sense liquefaction technology is much less well developed than is gasification. The exception is in the use of catalytic synthesis of carbon monoxide/hydrogen gases from coal to produce liquids ranging from methanol to gasoline.

Competitiveness of coal-based energy

Even with these technical developments coal will again become the dominant fossil fuel only if low extraction costs can be maintained. Historically, coal mining is labor-intensive (perhaps 50 percent of US and British coal costs are for labor) but this position is changing. For one thing, much modern mining outside Europe is large-scale surface mining

where both investment and labor costs are low. In deep mining, remote control and other automated methods are being developed to cut manpower requirements and increase productivity to perhaps five times that of an average old mine. The use of full mechanization is limited to areas where geological conditions are simple: severe folding or faulting of the strata prohibits its use.

Many of the easily mined deposits of coal are sited well away from energy-consuming centers. Handling has therefore become an important consideration. There have been three developments in coal transport during the last two decades. Large ocean-going vessels (carrying up to 100,000 tons) have reduced costs by 25 percent. For long-distance rail distribution, "unit trains," carrying up to 10,000 tons, have reduced rail costs by 50 percent. Piping of wet coal (slurry) over long distances is even cheaper than movement by rail.

Historically coal has been dangerous to mine and dirty to use. This is becoming much less true today. Increasing mechanization and automation in mines has greatly reduced accident rates. The trend to surface mines may be expected to reduce accidents still further.

Fortunately the modern developments in coal have tended to fit in with increasingly strict land and air pollution requirements. Thus fluidized bed combustion cuts down sulfur and nitrogen oxide emission during combustion and the gasification techniques can provide clean fuel for local use. Land reclamation in surface mining is now seen as essential, and ash wastes, after combustion, can be widely used in building, or for land-fill material.

OIL & GAS—FORMATION & USE

Oil and gas provide the modern world with nearly three-quarters of all the primary energy it uses. They constitute a resource of overwhelming economic and political significance. Yet the resource is finite and there is increasing debate about the way it should be exploited.

Known as hydrocarbons, oil and gas are combinations of carbon and hydrogen, ranging from simple methane (the main constituent of natural gas) to complex molecular compounds. Crude oils were produced over millions of years by the decay of organisms that sank to the bottom of seas and were buried as sediments under later formations of rock. Natural gas has a similar origin but is sometimes produced more simply by decaying vegetable matter in marshy areas. Where not found in separate reservoirs, it may be associated with light crude oils in solution or separated into a gas cap.

Because of the infinite variety of nature, hydrocarbon deposits differ greatly in composition. They range from light and liquid crude oils, and gases that condense into liquids at the surface, through heavy viscous oils that have to be warmed to flow, to the solid kerogen in oil shale, which has to be heated or "cracked." Deposits differ also in the impurities they contain. Sulfur is one undesirable impurity because it makes the crude oil or gas "sour" and has to be removed to avoid atmospheric pollution. Natural gas can contain nonflammable gases such as carbon dioxide (up to 50 percent in some Mexican fields) or nitrogen (up to 90 percent in some deposits near the west coast of Denmark). Growing awareness of the variability of hydrocarbons is improving resource evaluation and maximum use.

How oil and gas are used

Oils from seepages and hand-dug shallow pits were used from ancient times—to caulk boats with pitch for instance. But wood was still the world's primary fuel in 1859 when the opening of the Drake well in Pennsylvania really began the oil industry, and it was coal that first supplanted wood. The initial uses of oil were for lighting and lubrication. But as more oil was produced its advantages over coal became obvious: as a liquid it could be handled more easily; as a chemical compound it could be refined into many products. Even in the USA, coal still provided 90 percent of locomotive fuel in 1925, but the fuel oils gradually became competitive with coal in furnaces and under boilers, in plants, locomotives and ships. Meanwhile the lighter range of oils led to new uses in the new automobile, aviation and petrochemical industries where end products now range from plastics and synthetic fibers to pesticides and drugs. These developments caused world demand for oil to soar after World War II.

Total consumption of petroleum products in the world excluding the USSR, Eastern Europe and

OPEC state Venezuela, with its rich Maracaibo field, bars outside participation.

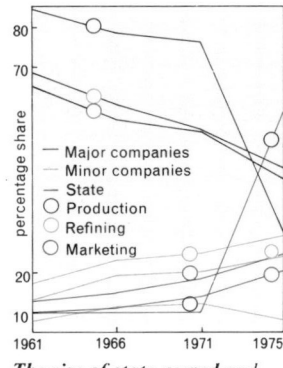

Oil use in industrialized USA, Canada, Western Europe, Japan and Australia was four times that of other non-Communist states in 1977.

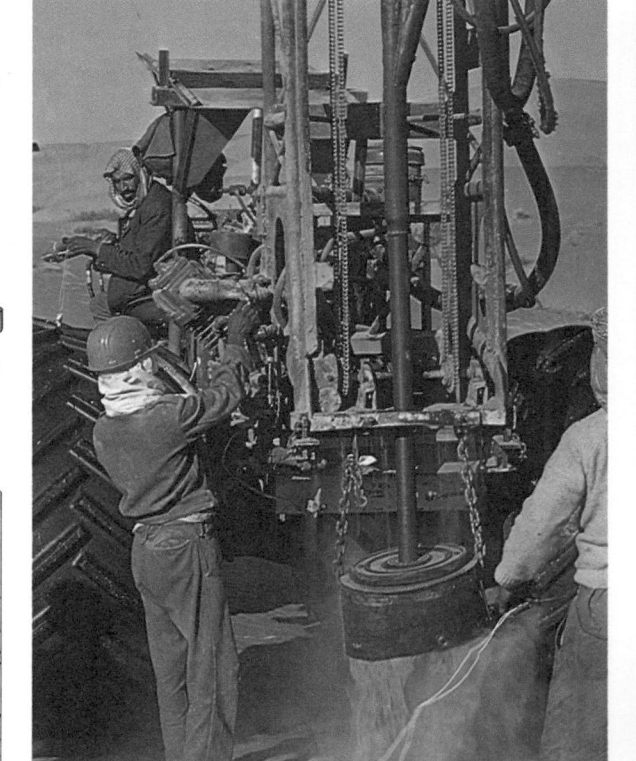

The rise of state-owned and small oil companies at the expense of the "big seven" is shown, excluding Communist states and North America.

Geological structures, either onshore or offshore, that would make suitable oil and gas traps are detected by seismic profiling. Here, an explosive charge is being set up for release underground in Saudi Arabia. Reflected shock waves picked up by geophones will show the underlying rock structure.

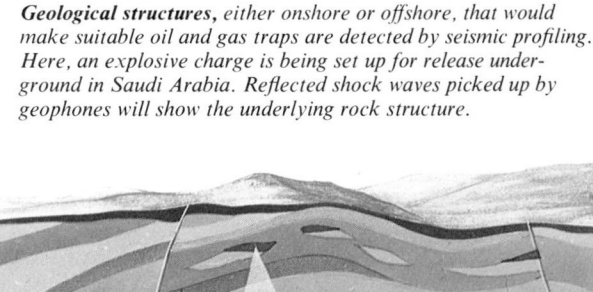

Petroleum formed by the slow decomposition of marine organic material in sedimentary rock basins usually migrates under pressure until *it is trapped by a layer of impermeable rock, where it accumulates to form a reservoir. Such reservoirs, often formed in the pore spaces of* *permeable rocks commonly have layers of water, oil and gas superimposed in order of density. Among geological structures containing* *petroleum the most important are anticlines (1), which contain 80–90 percent of proven oil and gas reserves. Less common are faults (2), salt* *domes (3) and unconformities (4). Oil may form without water in hollows of basement rock (5) or be trapped in a sand lens (6) or reef (7).*

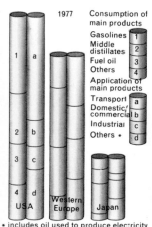

1977 Consumption of main products
Gasolines 1
Middle distillates 2
Fuel oil 3
Others 4
Application of main products
Transport a
Domestic/commercial b
Industrial c
Others • d

• includes oil used to produce electricity

Consumption and application of different oil products varies even between industrial countries, with gasoline being the product used most in the USA, the middle distillates in Europe and fuel oil in Japan.

Offshore rigs increased from 70 in 1965 to 371 in 1978. Output is at present a fifth of total world production of oil.

Refineries vary in size from those with outputs of 2,000 tons of crude oil a day to big ones such as the oil and gas refinery at Ras Tanura in Saudi Arabia (above), handling more than 75,000 tons. Crude oil is broken down by a series of different processes into usable products ranging from gases, gasolines, diesel and heavy fuels to kerosines (paraffins), liquefied gases (butane and propane), lubricating oils, waxes and bitumens and feedstocks for the petrochemical industries.

China rose from 488 million tons in 1960 to 2.34 billion tons in 1973. After a brief drop in 1975, it began rising again to reach 2.4 billion tons in 1977. Demand for oil in the industrialized countries rose only eight percent between 1972 and 1977 compared with a 48 percent rise in the rest of the non-Communist world. Including the Communist world, where consumption figures are less reliable, global consumption of oil is put at about 3 billion tons in 1977. Consumption patterns vary from country to country. In the USA, 50 percent of oil is used in transport and only 10 percent in industry, whereas in Western Europe 28 percent of oil use is industrial and 30 percent goes into transport. In broad terms, gasoline is the world's main oil product (27.5 percent in 1977) just ahead of fuel oil (26.5 percent).

Natural gas is used mainly for domestic heating and cooking and in the petrochemical industry. It is also a preferred clean fuel for industrial plant and even for power plants. The extent and nature of its use depends both on its availability and on how industrialized the consuming country is. In 1974, for instance, the Netherlands, with a large indigenous supply, exceeded even the USA in per capita consumption (1,000 therms), whereas Japan, with little local gas and no big source nearby, had almost the lowest per capita consumption (50 therms). Natural gas provides about a quarter of global consumption of all hydrocarbons. Important changes have taken place in the structure of the oil and gas industry during the past 20 years. In 1952 seven large groups of companies—British Petroleum, Gulf Oil, Royal Dutch Shell, Mobil, Exxon (Esso), Standard Oil of California (Chevron) and Texaco—accounted for more than 90 percent of production, 72 percent of refining output and 75 percent of product sales outside North America and the Communist countries. Since 1960, smaller companies have taken a growing share of the production industry, seeking cheaper oil outside the USA. There was a dramatic growth of state oil companies in the 1970s and both state and non-major companies have expanded their refining and marketing operations as well as their involvement in production.

The search for oil and gas

As hydrocarbons are formed in sediments, can migrate through porous rocks and are trapped by impervious rocks, the search for oil has been concentrated on basins of sedimentary rocks that have been deformed only moderately by earth movements. The first searches were at or near known indications of oil or gas on land. The industry was a worldwide one from the start with drilling in Romania and elsewhere closely following discoveries in the USA. Production in Baku, USSR, started in 1873 and in Java in 1888 (Royal Dutch Shell was founded in 1890). Oil was discovered in Iran in 1908 after about eight years' search. In 1912, when the Anglo-Persian Oil Company (later British Petroleum) shipped its first cargo of oil from Iran, it had to compete with oil from the USA, the USSR and the East Indies.

Since those early days the footslogging geologist has acquired new tools such as aerial photography, satellite imagery and rock dating by radioactivity measurement. He can reach difficult sites by helicopter and is backed up by an increasingly versatile team of scientific and technical specialists ranging from geochemicals to computer operators.

The extent of potential oil and gas fields has expanded erratically with new geological concepts or exploration techniques, including improvements in drilling—the final test of any petroleum prospect. The latest surge forward followed the development of deep-sea drilling capability and the synoptic view of large areas from satellite imagery, coinciding with revived interest in the theory of continental drift. The tectonic plate concept of the Earth's crust as a series of large plates on a fluid mantle brought new ideas about the formation of the sedimentary basins in which petroleum is found. There is no reason to think that current knowledge is final.

Exploration restrictions

During the first 60 years of the oil industry explorers were free to look for petroleum anywhere. In 1918 the USSR withdrew its territory from the common pool. Mexico withdrew in 1938. With these exceptions, knowledge gained in one area was applied, often by the same people, in other areas. Today the increasing involvement of governments in the oil industry is reducing the freedom of action of explorers and the free, firsthand application of new knowledge and techniques.

Politics have, of course, always affected exploration and production, as investment is encouraged by political stability. Outside OPEC and the Communist world only Mexico is handling its own industry without significant foreign help. Otherwise, exploration rights can be secured in return for input of foreign capital, labor or technology. The conditions attached to such permits and the subsequent rights to exploitation after discovery are very diverse, however. As a result, it is very difficult to predict how future exploration effort will be directed or whether the changing industry will be more successful than in the past in finding petroleum in the large land and offshore areas that remain to be explored thoroughly.

OIL & GAS—RESOURCES & RESERVES

Estimates of world reserves of oil and gas can provide no more than a rough guide to possible future production capacity. In round terms, the world is using about 3 billion tons of oil a year now and has proved reserves of about 88.1 billion tons. The real recoverable reserve of crude oil could be at least four times as great, however. Reserve estimates for natural gas are even more liable to error. Annual world use of natural gas is the equivalent of about 1.2 billion tons of oil and there are proved reserves of 72,359 billion cubic meters—equivalent to 62 billion tons of oil. But each day development drilling is converting into proved reserves some deposits that were only probable reserves, while the constant refinement of geological knowledge and recovery techniques is bringing to light further probable resources of both gas and oil.

Problems of estimating reserves

There are no accepted worldwide standards for estimating resources and reserves. Rarely can the reserves of an oil field be estimated on the results of a discovery well and prior survey. Yet in many circumstances, and for different reasons, estimates are made long before there are adequate data. In the Middle East, with relatively simple geology and single ownership, prospects can be interpreted generously at an early stage. In the USA estimates tend to be more conservative, with considerable annual revisions and additions to reserves. Revisions are the rule in offshore fields, where the high cost of drilling limits the amount of testing that can be carried out before a decision is made whether or not to develop a field.

In 1970 it was estimated that some 187 giant fields out of the world total of about 30,000 fields had provided 75 percent of world oil production to date and that 82 percent of their original reserves still remained. Giant gas fields play an equally

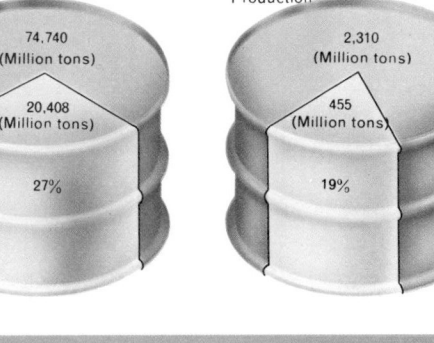
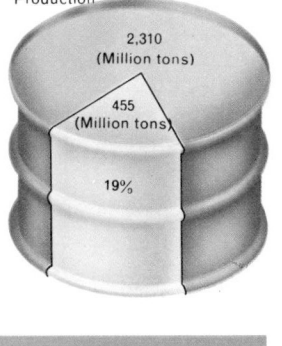
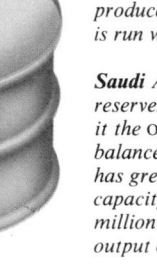
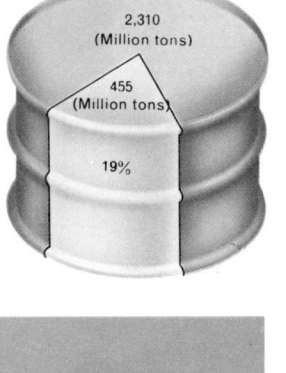

Saudi Arabian dominance within the non-Communist world and OPEC

■ Non-Communist world
□ Saudi Arabia

Reserves
74,740 (Million tons)
20,408 (Million tons)
27%

Production
2,310 (Million tons)
455 (Million tons)
19%

New drilling in Mexico, both onshore and offshore, has recently opened up discoveries in the southeast and northwest that have returned this country to the forefront of oil and gas producers. Mexico's industry is run without foreign help.

Saudi Arabia's share of both reserves and production makes it the OPEC price leader and balance wheel, especially as it has great excess production capacity (estimated at 11.8 million barrels a day over output of 8.25 mbd in 1976).

important role in hydrocarbon resources, especially offshore, where it is often the discovery of an "elephant" that justifies the high cost of a safari into surrounding territory.

The fluidity of natural gas makes easier an early assessment of gas fields that are not associated with an oil reservoir. Estimates of the value in an oil field are more difficult when the gas is associated with oil and may not become available until most, if not all, of the oil has been recovered. The quality of gas in a field and the presence of nonflammable constituents has to be taken into account also. Still more important is the question of whether the gas can be economically marketed.

Gas not associated with oil may have to be shut in if the field is so distant from a market that transport is not feasible. Where it occurs in solution in oil it may have to be flared if it cannot be used locally as a fuel or to maintain reservoir pressure in the field. Flaring may be a resource waste but not an economic waste. For instance, if the associated gas had not been flared, the development of Middle East oil might have been inhibited for 30 years. Only since the development of large pipelines and, in some cases, ocean gas tankers have distant gas reserves really moved from being a potential to a usable resource. Development is still constrained by the need for long-term contracts of 20–30 years to justify the funding of transport facilities.

Just as the inert gas content of one natural gas field makes it different from another, so do the different characteristics of crude oil deposits affect the value of an oil reserve, because it is these characteristics that determine not only the ease and cost of production but also the optimal use and so the cost of refining the crude oil. Political aspects also have to be borne in mind in assessing resources and reserves. Politics can affect price and market demand as well as the transfer from resource to market. There may also be technical constraints.

The pattern of resource development is affected in each area of the world by economic factors and the

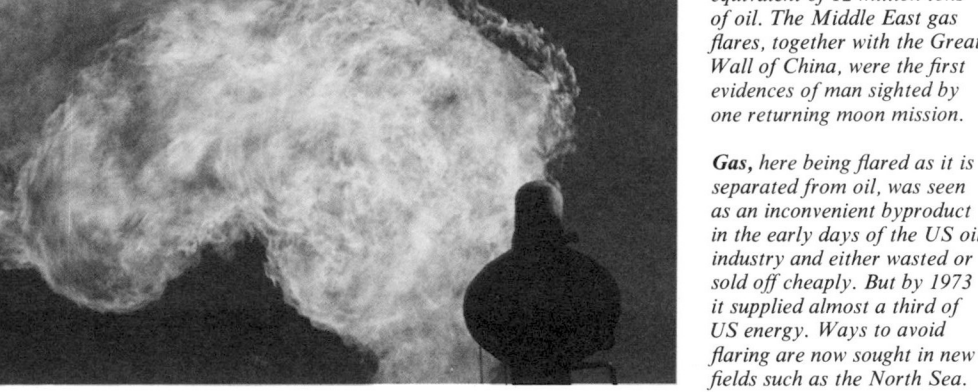

Gas storage tanks in Saudi Arabia store only a fraction of the gas associated with oil production there, and in 1973 14 billion m³ was flared—the equivalent of 12 million tons of oil. The Middle East gas flares, together with the Great Wall of China, were the first evidences of man sighted by one returning moon mission.

Gas, here being flared as it is separated from oil, was seen as an inconvenient byproduct in the early days of the US oil industry and either wasted or sold off cheaply. But by 1973 it supplied almost a third of US energy. Ways to avoid flaring are now sought in new fields such as the North Sea.

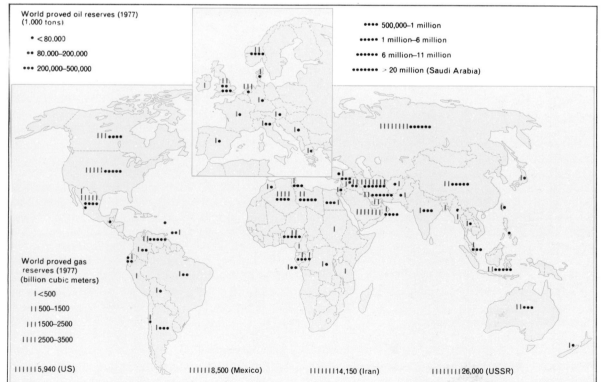

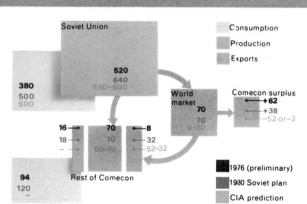

Oil from the vast reserves of the Middle East (60 percent of proved global reserves) gave the world an era of cheap energy until 1973, when OPEC used its supply dominance to lift prices.

Comecon has a favorable oil and gas balance with the rest of the world through Soviet surpluses, but there is disagreement about whether this will continue after 1980.

The steep rise in oil prices initiated by OPEC producers in 1973 slowed the rate at which consumption was rising in industrialized nations.

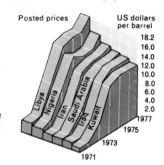

Estimates of world proved reserves of oil and gas are based on known deposits recoverable with today's technology and at current prices, using Soviet figures for "explored" reserves, which include some possible as well as probable deposits. The global reserves total 150 billion tons of oil equivalent compared with annual consumption of about 4.2 billion tons.

availability of other energy sources. In Western Europe, oil outstripped coal as the dominant energy source only in 1966. The discovery in 1959 of the giant Groningen gas field in the Netherlands not only changed consumption patterns there, and opened up an export market in Europe but also turned exploration attention to the North Sea. Fortunately the first effort was in the British sector, where "elephants" were soon found. The rapid exploitation of the Groningen field and the southern basin of the North Sea was possible because a local pattern of both pipelines and appliances already existed, based on manufactured coal gas. Norway, in contrast, had based its industry on hydroelectricity and the large gas reserves found in the Norwegian North Sea basin beyond the deep Norwegian Trench have only export value. Again, fortunately, the northern basin has proved to be "elephant" country, justifying the high cost of work in ever deeper waters. Without the combination of these circumstances, encouraged by high oil prices, the North Sea resources would not have been exploited as rapidly as they were.

Middle Eastern production

In the Middle East, oil production was linked historically to meeting market demand, with little attempt to assess reserves. The Organization of Petroleum Exporting Countries (OPEC), formed in 1960, considered controlling production according to reserves, but could not reconcile its members' conflicting definitions. Kuwait, a small country with one giant field, followed the example of another OPEC state, Venezuela, in restricting production to conserve a wasting asset. And Libya used conservation reasons for curtailing production in 1971. But there was ample Middle Eastern oil to satisfy the market until 1973, when Arab producers restricted supplies as a weapon in their quarrel with Israel and OPEC unilaterally raised oil prices.

OPEC had 70 percent of the proved oil reserves of the non-Communist world in 1977. Although OPEC may often seem to act as a cartel, using price to control production, the organization has not yet agreed production totals for its members based on reserves or other criteria. Its oil prices are determined mainly by the leadership dominance of Saudi Arabia with its huge reserves. The price for Saudi Arabian light crude is fixed by OPEC agreement as the "market" price.

Soviet resources

The USSR has large reserves of oil and gas, but data on the crude oil reserves are subject to State Secrets Laws. Information pieced together from several sources gave 1977–78 estimates of oil reserves varying between 4.1 and 50 billion tons. The part the USSR will play in the world oil industry is hard to predict. Some think its consumption of oil and gas will be controlled by development of coal, nuclear and hydroelectric power. The aim would be an export surplus of oil and gas to maintain Soviet balance of trade in the Council for Mutual Economic Aid (Comecon) and to pay for imports of equipment and technology from elsewhere. Figures for Soviet gas resources are more public, showing rapid development since 1957 and massive reserves estimated at 27,000 billion cubic meters (6,000 billion gallons)—more than a third of the world's proved reserves.

Recent discoveries of oil in southeastern Mexico have meant that this long-established oil-producing country can now be ranked with the world's leading producers of oil and gas. Government figures estimate that Mexico's total potential reserves of oil amount to 5.1 billion tons. This does not compare with Saudi Arabia with reserves totalling 20.4 billion tons, but it does rival other OPEC countries. These new discoveries may provide the Western World with an alternative to Middle Eastern oil and help to "buy" time in which alternative energy sources can be developed.

OIL & GAS–PRODUCTION & PROCESSING

Oil refineries such as this one at Dhahran are being altered continually to keep pace with new technology and changing market demands. Since 1973, efforts have been made to reduce energy losses, which can be up to 15 percent of throughput. Many refineries are located alongside petrochemical plants with a full interchange of product streams to maximize the *value of each fraction used or discarded in either plant. The biggest refineries have up to 1,600 km (1,000 miles) of pipework, with pipes varying in diameter from 5 to 60 cm (2 to 24 in).*

Crude oils and natural gases make up the bulk of hydrocarbon production. The heavy viscous oils, merging to the very viscous "tar sand" oils and the solid kerogen in oil shales, still await exploitation on a scale of global significance, as do the gases frozen as hydrates, first found in northern USSR, or dissolved in deep, high-pressure aquifers.

The existence of commercial crude oil and natural gas can only be proved by drilling into a reservoir. The depth to which the drill can reach has increased along with drilling skill and technology. Early drillers gauged the depth of a hole by tying string on the line, the hardness of the rock by the feel of the shaking derrick, and the efficiency of the drilling mud (used to plug the hole and carry up debris) by testing it between thumb and forefinger. Sometimes they hit a reservoir without warning and had a blowout or gusher. Gradually, in the 1930s, engineering standards improved with the help of scientists. Geologists determined the age of the rock by microscopic examination, identified marker beds and forecast the formations ahead of the drill; chemists improved the efficiency of the drilling fluids; then log interpreters added other markers and correlated with geophysical surveys. Developments in automatic continuous monitoring added to control and safety and equipment improved in both design and materials.

By 1975 there were more than 600,000 wells in production and in 1978 some 48,000 wells were drilled in the USA alone. In the most dramatic technological advance of all, drilling was taking place off the shores of 100 countries. It is now possible to drill in more than 1,000 meters (3,280 feet) of water.

Production of oil by the inherent energy of a reservoir, whether by an effective drive from water below the oil, by expansion of gas, or by a combination of these forces, is known as primary recovery. The introduction of supplementary energy by injection of water, gas or other liquids, or by heat, can give secondary recovery oil. The distinction between primary and secondary recovery oil becomes blurred when a supplementary technique is introduced early in the life of a field, as in the USSR, where water flooding has been common practice. "Tertiary oil" can be recovered by subsequent application of different extraction methods.

Recovery of the heavy oils and the oil locked in shales and oil sands requires the input of additional energy. Such oil comes into the category of oil won by "enhanced recovery" and is often called nonconventional oil. Heavy oils are being exploited in some areas of the USA, but large deposits in western Canada, in the Orinoco basin of Venezuela, in Iraq and elsewhere await significant exploitation, although plans are most advanced in Canada. The only oil sands in commercial production are in Canada, which has some 3.5 billion tons of proved recoverable synthetic oil. It is thought that by the end of the century these sands could be producing one million barrels of oil a day.

Although oil shale ventures have a long history throughout the world, the only significant production is now in Soviet Estonia (mostly used as power plant fuel), in China, particularly in Fushun, where the shales overlie shallow bituminous coals making extraction of both economic, and in Brazil (to a much lesser extent). In spite of considerable work in the USA, the rich deposits in the Piceance basin of the northern Rocky Mountain states still await exploitation, mainly owing to waste disposal problems and lack of water.

Pipeline and ocean transport
As the demand for oil increased, petroleum product pipelines became economic, whether from coastal or inland refineries or from major distribution centers in North America and later in Europe and the USSR. Recent years have seen improvements in increasing the diameter and length of pipe, in methods of laying and protecting lines at sea and

on land, in the variety and safety of pipe materials and in the automation and control of flow. Crude oil lines up to 1.25 meters (4 feet) in diameter are commonplace on land, and lines one meter (3.28 feet) in diameter are laid in water at depths of 160 meters (525 feet).

Pipelines sometimes provide transshipment of oil. The Suez–Mediterranean line, for instance, allows Very Large Crude Carriers (VLCCs), which could not use the Suez Canal, to discharge at the southern end and smaller tankers to offtake at the northern end and serve southern European ports. Pipelines also carry natural gas over land and under the sea. The most notable are the lines in the Gulf of Mexico, in the North Sea, the Algeria–Italy line under construction and involving traversing the deep straits to and from Sicily, the line under consideration between Algeria and Spain/France and the lines planned to cross the deep Norwegian Trough from the North Sea fields to Norway. A major problem is stress imposed on the pipelines by the weight of deep water.

Ocean transport, in special tankers, of liquefied natural gas at very low temperatures is a growing sector. In 1975 there were 20 of these tankers in service with a total capacity of one million cubic meters (220 million gallons) and 48 vessels under construction with a total capacity of 5,558,000 cubic meters (12,227,600 gallons). The heaviest traffic is from Algeria to Britain, France, Spain and the USA, from Libya to Spain and Italy and from Abu Dhabi, Brunei and Alaska to Japan. One probable development is the carrying of methanol in ordinary tankers after conversion from natural gas. Advocates claim significant cost savings over liquefied natural gas.

Crude oil tankers have grown in size since 1950 in line with the growth of international trade in oil. As VLCCs can enter few ports, entrepot oil ports and methods of discharging at sea into smaller ships have been developed. The size of tankers has added

CONNECTIONS

The world's largest tarsands deposit is on the Athabasca River in the Canadian province of Alberta (above). It covers an area approximately the size of Belgium.

The 542,400-ton **Batilus,** *here discharging into a smaller oil ship to land its cargo, is the world's largest tanker, with a length of 400 m (1,312 ft) and a draft of 28.3 m (93 ft).*

Energy transportation costs 1976 Cents per million BTU per 100 miles	
Oil by tanker	0.3–0.6
Oil by pipeline	0.6–1.5
Natural gas by pipeline	2.0–4.5
Oil by rail	3.5–6.0
Coal by rail	5.0–7.5
Extra high-voltage electricity	15.0–25.0

The Trans-Alaskan pipeline (right), completed in 1977 at a cost of $8 billion, can carry 60 million tons of oil a year. Although the table (left) shows that tankers are the cheapest means of transporting oil, pipelines can be more economical where they cut a corner, as in the Trans-Arabian pipeline from Saudi Arabia to the Mediterranean.

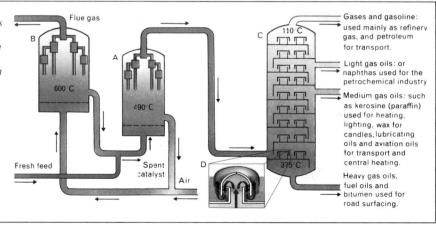

World oil totals: 1977

	0–5%	5–10%	10–15%	15–20%	20–25%	25–30%	30–35%	35–40%
Production	O	OO	OOO	OOOO	OOOOO	OOOOOO	OOOOOOO	OOOOOOOO
Consumption	O	OO	OOO	OOOO	OOOOO	OOOOOO	OOOOOOO	OOOOOOOO

Processing of crude oil to extract more valuable products begins with distillation in a furnace. Vapors then pass to a reactor (A) for cracking. A catalyst speeds up the reaction and is blown by an air current back to a regenerator (B), where it is cleaned ready for reuse. Cracked vapors are separated in a fractionating column (C) by condensing at various temperatures into horizontal trays. Bubble caps (D) allow lighter vapors to rise but prevent condensed liquids running back down.

Flue gas

Fresh feed

Spent catalyst

Air

Gases and gasoline: used mainly as refinery gas, and petroleum for transport.

Light gas oils: or naphthas used for the petrochemical industry

Medium gas oils: such as kerosine (paraffin) used for heating, lighting, wax for candles, lubricating oils and aviation oils for transport and central heating.

Heavy gas oils, fuel oils and bitumen used for road surfacing.

to the risk of large-scale pollution after accidents. Since the first major spillage in 1967 the oil and tanker companies have sought improvements in safety and repair measures. Advances have been made in tanker design, cargo handling (the Load-on-Top system), insurance and indemnity schemes, oil dispersal and collection at sea and beach cleaning. International cooperation is being extended through the Intergovernmental Maritime Consultative Organization (IMCO).

Storage and processing

The best storage for oil and gas is in their original reservoirs. Artificial storage is expensive and may involve deterioration in quality. But although the commercial aim is an unimpeded flow from well to consumer, crude oil terminals and distribution centers often need considerable storage facilities. Recent developments include underground storage in old salt mines, in specially leached caverns in salt deposits, in old coal mines and in specially excavated caverns in hard rock. An advantage of such storage is that it is out of sight. Offshore there are massive tanks sunk in the seabed, as off Abu Dhabi, tankers moored close to production platforms, or tanks built into the structure of the platforms.

Storage tanks are also needed at refineries. A simple refinery distills crude oil into gases (some burned for refinery fuel), light gasoline, naphtha, diesel fuel and heavy fuel. When sweetened by a simple chemical process the light gasoline could be used in a car, but would have low antiknock properties. The naphtha can be re-formed to increase its octane number from, say, 40 to between 95 and 105 and then mixed with the light gasoline to meet the automotive market demand of about 90 octane. A plant in addition to these three simple units of distillation, sweetening and re-forming can widen the range of crude oils that can be handled and the refinement to more precise specifications of an increasing number of products.

OIL & GAS—SUPPLY & DEMAND

The most striking aspect of the resource pattern of oil and gas is the dependence of major consuming areas of the world on exports from the Middle East, Africa and southeastern Asia. Until now supply has been able to grow with demand, but a turning point appears to be near when demand will have to be matched to available supply. There is a need for adequate finance in all sectors of the oil industry, which was historically run by private enterprise but is now increasingly subject to government intervention.

Availability of oil

The availability of crude oil depends in the first instance on reserves and the ease or difficulty of exploiting them. Although there are abundant known reserves in the Middle East (45 times as great as present annual production) and Africa (26 times present annual production) the position elsewhere is not so satisfactory. In the Middle East, oil recovery has not so far been a problem; the reservoirs are large with high initial permeability, porosity and pressure. But production from the older fields is declining and increasing effort will have to be put into enhanced recovery methods. Elsewhere, some reserves can be readily exploited but others will involve higher production costs.

The maximum productive capacity of any system is that of the lowest capacity of any link in the chain from the reservoir to the delivery point. The ideal is for men, effort and investment to be aimed at a demand target five to 10 years ahead but scheduled to keep pace with annual targets. It is an ideal that is seldom achieved and there are considerable and changing differences between the capacities of the various links.

Transport and refining

The continually expanding market to 1973 encouraged continual investment in transport facilities. But the drop in demand between 1973 and 1975 immediately threw up a massive tanker surplus which, despite cancellations of orders, may take several years to eradicate unless demand rises faster than most expect. In the 10 years to December 1977 the world tanker fleet not only trebled in size from 103.5 million deadweight long tons (dwt) to 332.5 million dwt, but the Very Large Crude Carriers (VLCCs) of more than 200,000 dwt now constitute more than half the tonnage. The pattern of voyages has also changed. Shipments from the Middle East to the USA have become more important and the Cape of Good Hope has become the normal route for tankers carrying Middle East oil to Europe and America.

Major pipelines take a long time to build and their flexibility is limited. They are also more vulnerable to political action than tankers, although these are not immune. More major as well as minor pipelines will be built in the next 15 years for both gas and oil. Construction has begun on a new oil line costing $400 million from the eastern Saudi Arabian fields to a new port, Yanbu, on the Red Sea, while a gas line south from the Canadian Arctic is among several other major lines being planned. But unless the 1980s bring a radical change in supply prospects, there will be greater caution in planning new lines for the 1990s.

The refining side of the oil industry is becoming progressively larger, more complicated and more expensive. Provision of plant to cope with demand variations is costly. The 1973–75 check in oil consumption hit refineries almost as hard as it hit shipping and in 1977 the refining capacity of Western Europe actually fell. Yet world refining capacity was still about 900 million tons in surplus in 1977. There is increasing government intervention in refinery building to save foreign currency by importing crude rather than higher-priced products. This has encouraged a shift of refining centers from the producing to the consuming end. Refineries are also shifting inland with the laying of crude oil pipe-

Crude oil tankers, such as these docked at Genoa, made up a world fleet totalling 332.5 million dwt in 1977. The oil companies owned a third of this tonnage and private charter companies nearly two-thirds. But with the trend toward nationalization, shipping owned by producer governments (11.8 million dwt in 1977) is increasing. Although inhibited by a tanker surplus in the mid-1970s this trend could have a marked effect on transport of oil and gas if producers insisted on their oil being carried in their own ships. (The USA allows only its flag ships to carry its coastal oil trade.)

lines. The future may see renewed development of refineries in the oil exporting countries as they build up their industrial bases. In all countries there will be emphasis on reducing energy losses in refineries.

Marketing and demand

The demand for heavy crudes is likely to decrease with trends against sulfurous crudes (because of pollution) and against wastage of the chemical value of oil used as primary fuel under boilers. But overall, the incentive of increasing demand will continue to encourage increases in total oil supply. Since 1973 the industrialized countries have sought more oil, preferably indigenous, outside of OPEC. This has spurred exploration into new areas, often involving higher costs in hostile environments. Large investments are necessary. A 1978 American survey predicted that the US industry would lift its investment rate by two or three times in the 1980s to an annual average of $25–30 billion. The UK Government estimated in 1978 that total industry investment in the British sector of the North Sea from 1965 to 1977 inclusive had been £7 billion and that a further £6 billion might be invested by the end of 1980. These sums cannot be provided from company profits, making finance market funds and government involvement increasingly necessary. In

World hydrocarbon supply and demand

Natural gas · Total hydrocarbons

Crude oil · Disputed

World supply and consumption of oil and gas is expected to peak in the late 1990s with a decline as the world accustoms itself to doing without oil. The upper of the two oil decline curves is based on a reasonably optimistic estimate of the total recoverable crude oil reserve at 360 billion tons, the lower curve on the less optimistic figure of 300 billion tons.

The difficult environments faced by oil explorers range from intense cold to searing heat. Technology has not yet obviated the need for on-site inspection by geologists. Here, a drill takes rock samples from a Saudi Arabian field.

The scale and cost of the world effort to recover oil in increasingly hostile environments is shown by this BP sea lift of equipment and prefabricated houses to an oil township of some 550 people serving the Prudhoe Bay oil field in Alaska.

This newly opened field is the biggest in North America, yielding some 1.2 million barrels a day. The sea lift is feasible only during a six-week period in the summer when enough ice has melted to allow the convoy to pass through.

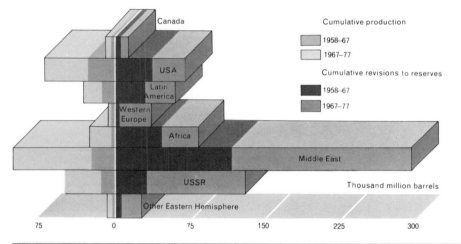

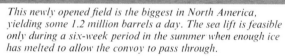

Cumulative production
1958–67
1967–77

Cumulative revisions to reserves
1958–67
1967–77

Canada
USA
Latin America
Western Europe
Africa
Middle East
USSR
Other Eastern Hemisphere

Thousand million barrels

75   0   75   150   225   300

Cumulative revisions to oil reserves have been greater than cumulative production during the 20 years from 1958 to 1977 in all the major oil-producing areas with the single exception of the USA. There, oil production has moved ahead of additions to proved reserves only since 1967. The level of proved reserves is dynamic, with constant revisions depending on the relative rates at which oil is extracted and probable reserves are converted to proved reserves through new development and technology.

1975 the major oil companies still controlled 44 percent of marketing. Sophisticated supply planning, covering the whole chain of operations from exploration to retail sales, gives them both economies of scale and great flexibility in meeting the requirements of different customers. Their future role will depend on the extent to which their technological and managerial skills keep ahead of growing governmental knowledge.

Looking 15 to 20 years ahead, one can expect evolution but not complete revolution in the pattern of petroleum consumption. Rapid change is inhibited partly through the inertia caused by habit and by vast accumulated investment in facilities and appliances. The world recovered more quickly than many expected from the fourfold price rise initiated in 1973 and the trauma of oil becoming a political weapon. This was due mainly to energy conservation, a recession induced fall in demand and the increase outside OPEC of actual or potential supplies from the North Sea, Alaska and Mexico, which brought a change from a seller's toward a buyer's market.

The future

The situation could still change quite rapidly. Demand may rise more quickly than the increase in non-OPEC oil, particularly if the USA does not restrict its expanding imports. OPEC might drastically cut production to reassert its control and to raise prices. In either case, countries without oil in the developing world would suffer severely as their growth is dependent on access to petroleum. Greater international cooperation in the field of hydrocarbon resources seems urgently needed.

Many different scenarios were put forward in reports on the future conceived after the oil crisis of 1973. The relatively slow recovery of demand for petroleum products since then has caused surpluses that have increased the complacency of the optimists and made them eager to listen to the superoptimists. Yet although more oil—and certainly much more gas—will be found, new conversion processes developed and more efficient end-uses evolved, the hydrocarbon resources of the world are finite. Perhaps, as was said at the World Energy Conference in 1977, the biggest problem is to make governments and people appreciate that there is a future supply problem and that it must be tackled immediately because of the long lead-times for effecting changes in both supply and demand patterns within the oil industry.

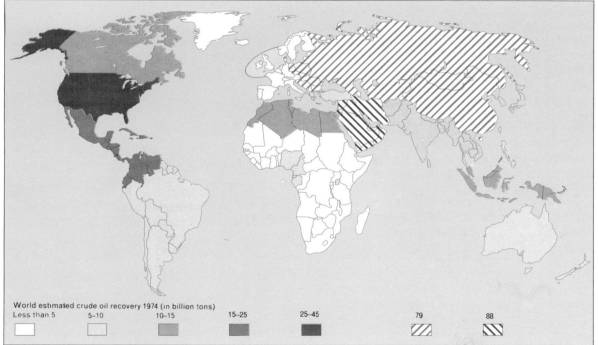

World estimated crude oil recovery 1974 (in billion tons)
Less than 5   5–10   10–15   15–25   25–45   79   88

Estimation of total recoverable crude oil resources is necessarily tentative. Geological knowledge of some prospects is incomplete. Future technology, prices, demand and competition from alternative energy sources could all affect production, as

could political circumstances. Classification of reserves is inconsistent and some figures are not published. Finally, political and geological boundaries seldom coincide and allocations of deeper ocean floors are not yet internationally agreed.

HYDROELECTRICITY

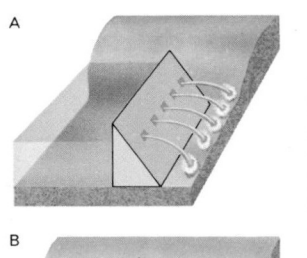
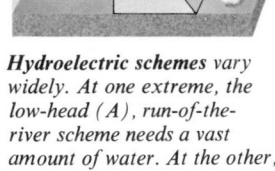
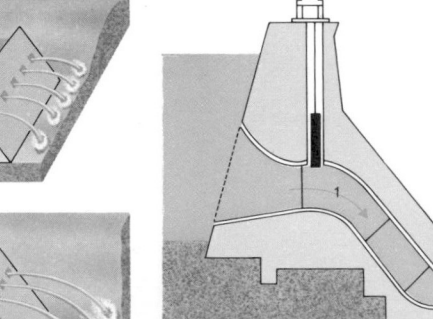
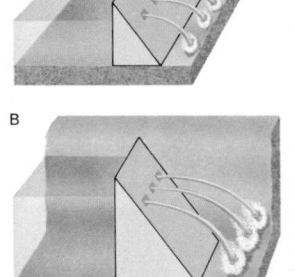

Hydroelectric schemes vary widely. At one extreme, the low-head (A), run-of-the-river scheme needs a vast amount of water. At the other, the very-high-head scheme (B) can use a much smaller quantity of water from high in the mountains fed to generators in a valley.

A spillway at Mangla dam, Pakistan, acts as a safety valve on a reservoir with a planned generating capacity of 3,000 MW.

The total amount of energy dissipated by the world's flowing water is enormous. Even the United States has exploited only about a third of its hydroelectricity potential, the USSR only a ninth. Africa, Latin America and Asia have still greater unused resources, amounting to 60 percent of the world's potential, but produce only about 20 percent of world hydroelectric output.

Whereas the generators of most thermal plants are powered by the steam produced from irreplaceable fossil fuels, hydroelectric generators are driven by water that is both free and constantly renewed. From some points of view, hydroelectricity is therefore among the most desirable forms of power generation—one that has derived naturally from man's early use of water wheels to drive corn mills. In terms of land conservation, however, the construction of hydroelectric schemes has far-reaching consequences. Environmental factors, together with high capital costs, will limit the contribution that hydroelectricity can make to world energy output.

Systems and costs

Any body of moving water can provide energy if it is practicable and economic to extract it. While water power resources are found mainly in mountainous country, schemes can also be established on flatter land if river flows are adequate—there is a trade-off between the amount of water and the height or "head" of water. Schemes with large reservoirs may produce large amounts of power almost continuously. But many have a maximum power output that can be met for only a short period from the water resources available. Their purpose is to meet the peaks in demand that are typical of most electricity supply systems. A hydroelectric plant is particularly useful for this purpose because it can be easily stopped and started. Pumped storage schemes, even quite small ones, can make valuable contributions to supply systems by smoothing out peaks in demand.

The capital cost of a hydroelectric plant in relation to power output can vary over a huge range, according to the topography and geology of different sites. Each scheme has to be evaluated individually. Some are among the largest engineering projects ever undertaken. Egypt's Aswan high dam, with a generating capacity of 2,100 megawatts, created a lake 500 kilometers (310 miles) long—to cope with a year-long drought. Uganda's Owen Falls dam holds back 205 billion cubic meters of water.

Apart from a massive capital investment in dam construction, major schemes usually involve large compensation payments for land and other rights affected by reservoirs. Building and running hydroelectric plants is made more expensive by remote and difficult sites. Allowance also has to be made for the cost of transmitting electricity from the generating plant to the load center. On the other hand, such projects must be considered over a longer time scale than most, for a reservoir or dam may remain useable for centuries if there is not an undue buildup of silt. Even the machinery in hydroelectric plants tends to last longer than that in thermal plants, being slower moving.

Environmental effects

The engineering of schemes can present risks on more difficult sites, in seismic areas or where valley walls are too steep. The failure of the Malpasset dam near Fréjus in the south of France (1959) and a landslip behind the Vaiont dam in the Alps (1963) caused many deaths. Although such disasters are rare, the construction of any large dam, with all its associated works, amounts to a massive interference with the environment, often involving loss of agricultural land or scenic reserves, cutting of roads and communications and perhaps the drowning of whole villages. Development of hydroelectric resources therefore raises unusually complex political and economic issues. In the developed world, where many of the best sites have already been exploited and where environmental factors now strongly influence government policy, hydroelectric plant construction is slowing down. Countries such as Switzerland and New Zealand, once almost wholly dependent on hydroelectricity, are increasing their reliance on other power sources.

In the developing world, hydroelectric plant expansion is likely to be rapid, however, especially where dams can be made the basis of multipurpose schemes in which the other objectives may be to store water for irrigation, to control flood waters and to improve fishing or navigation. An early example of a hydroelectric scheme becoming a catalyst for major economic change was the establishment of the Tennessee Valley Authority in

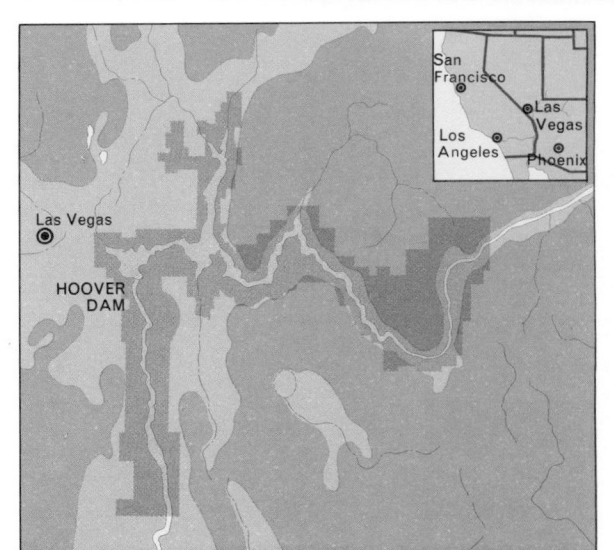

Lake Mead and the scenic areas shown on this map were created in the 1930s by the damming of the Colorado River at the Arizona–Nevada border. The arch gravity Hoover dam, seen above, not only changed the map's physical features but also stimulated the economic development of the whole surrounding area, providing cheap power (1,253 MW), irrigation, water supply and flood control.

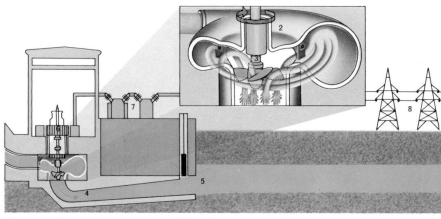

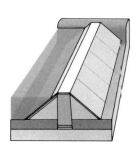
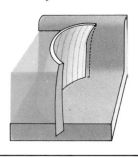

Water reaching the turbine house via penstock tubes (1) enters a spiral turbine casing (2) and travels past turbine blades—a Kaplan type (3) is shown here—making it rotate. A draft tube (4) expels water to the tailrace (5). The generator rotor (6) turns with the turbine, producing electricity, which is transformed to a high-voltage and passed through switchgear (7) to the transmission network (8).

Pumped storage schemes transfer water to an upper reservoir at off-peak times for release when demand for electricity is greatest.

DAM SYSTEMS

Dams are key factors in hydroelectric schemes, in terms both of the capital costs of construction and land purchase and of the environmental changes they cause. Larger reservoirs are able to store more water to cope with peak demand and to provide for periods of low rainfall.

Embankment dams, which use the weight of earth or rock filling to resist the water, are often the simplest and cheapest. An example is the Aswan high dam in Egypt, completed in 1970 at a cost of £2 billion, which stores 164 billion cubic meters of water.

Concrete gravity dams, above, are massive and costly structures, usually running straight across a broad valley. Steeper valleys with strong walls can support a thin arch dam, right, which curves upstream so that the force of the water is transferred sideways and downward.

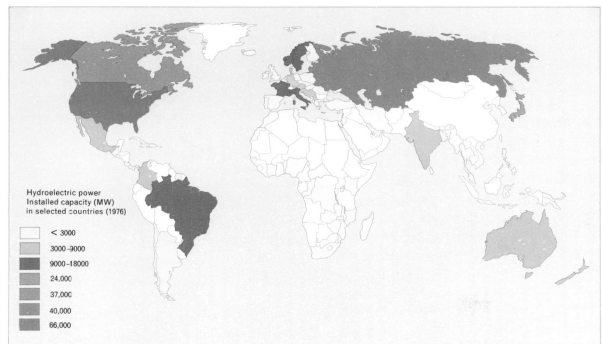

Hydroelectric power
Installed capacity (MW)
in selected countries (1976)

< 3000
3000-9000
9000-18000
24,000
37,000
40,000
66,000

Hydroelectric installed capacity in selected countries of the world totalled 349,028 MW in 1976. USA led with 66,825 MW.

the 1930s. In addition to power generation, some 20 dams within a watershed of 104,000 square kilometers (40,000 square miles) provided the means of controlling floods and drought and of revitalizing agriculture, shipping and recreation.

The potential rewards of such development-linked schemes have encouraged many developing countries to invest scarce resources in hydroelectric plants in spite of capital cost. For instance, the annual output in crops and energy from the system associated with the Bhakra dam in India is reckoned to equal in value the whole capital cost. The benefits of increased water for irrigation that followed the building of the Aswan high dam, together with the benefits of its cheap power, outweigh such ill effects as the blocking off of fertilizing silt and the loss of the sardine fishing grounds at the mouth of the Nile.

The availability of huge resources of cheap power can attract industry to new areas—aluminum smelting in Canada and New Zealand is a notable example. This has obvious attractions for developing nations in Africa, Asia and South America. If power cannot be absorbed locally, it may be exported. The 2,040 MW Cabora Bassa plant on the Zambesi in Mozambique transmits power more than 1,400 kilometers (900 miles) to South Africa.

Output and potential

Hydroelectricity provided some six percent of world energy production in 1974—equivalent to the energy from 360 million tons of oil. It contributes about 20 percent of the global output of electricity, ranging from 98 percent in Norway to 50 percent in France and Italy, 30 percent in Japan, 20 percent in West Germany, the United States and the USSR, and only two percent in the UK. Development of all potential water resources could provide much more energy, but at the expense of putting scenic waterfalls into tunnels and drowning trees, houses and farmland.

In practical terms, installed hydroelectric generating capacity is expected to increase four- or five-fold by the year 2020 from a base of 350,000 MW in 1976. An example of the things to come is the Itaipu scheme being developed jointly by Brazil and Paraguay, which has a planned capacity of 12,600 MW, double the size of the world's largest existing hydroelectric plant.

GEOTHERMAL ENERGY

Only a fraction of the Earth's gigantic store of heat is at present commercially accessible, and then only in a few favored places. Within the seismic belt, boiling water or steam can be brought to the surface in "hyperthermal fields." Several countries elsewhere have "semithermal fields" where subterranean hot water at 100°C (212°F) or less can be tapped; but by far the greatest part of the Earth's crust is "nonthermal" at shallow depths. Geothermal exploitation for electricity production has hitherto been virtually confined to the hyperthermal fields, where easily tappable steam is available to drive turbines, as at Larderello in Italy, Wairakei in New Zealand, the Geysers field in California, Cerro Prieto in Mexico, and several other places. Both hyper- and semithermal fields have been used for district heating, industrial and farming purposes in Iceland, Hungary, Japan, New Zealand, the USA and the USSR. Near Paris even an area with no surface manifestations is being exploited for space heating by deep drilling. In the future, Earth heat may be used to heat water supplied from the surface: the key to this lies in the technique of rock fracturing, which has yet to be perfected. Governments have been sufficiently encouraged by the prospects for geothermal energy to allocate funds for exploration and research—in 1973 the United States voted to spend $16 million over six years, while about £1,750,000 has been granted for the United Kingdom over a decade. In addition, the United Nations Development Program Special Fund has helped finance exploration in countries whose governments have not been able to risk capital for such schemes.

Hyperthermal fields
Hyperthermal fields are often, though not always, accompanied by surface manifestations—geysers, fumaroles, hot springs and boiling mud pools—which are evidence of tectonic disturbance at depth: that is why such fields are to be found mainly in the seismic belt. Fluid losses from the field, through surface manifestations or through man-made bore holes, are normally made good by rainwater entering the aquifer from a replenishment area, but this may sometimes be supplemented by small amounts of magmatic vapors, associated with various gases, rising from the mantle through faults in the bedrock. Convection currents in the aquifer bring very hot water up from greater to shallower depths. Owing to its pressure, boiling water at the base of the aquifer may be at 250°C/350°C (482/662°F), or even more. As it rises from

great depth in the middle of the field, a fraction will flash into steam as the pressure falls with reduced head. In most fields this steam will migrate upward and condense on meeting cooler surface waters. Such fields will be "water dominated" or "wet" (as at Wairakei and Cerro Prieto). If the base of the caprock is domed, steam may be trapped beneath it: in this case the field is "steam dominated" or "dry" (for example, Larderello or the Geysers). Drilling through the caprock into the aquifer will allow either flashing hot water (in a wet field) or steam (in a dry field) to rise to the surface. Dry fields are the most valuable economically and the least common.

Semithermal fields
Semithermal fields probably have a similar structure, except that instead of the heat source being due to a magmatic intrusion, it is likely to be due to one or more of three local features—an abnormally thin crust, a hot spot in the magma, or exceptionally high radioactivity.

Geopressurized fields occur in a few places, notably in the southern USA and Hungary. These may even be in nonthermal areas, their high fluid temperatures (up to about 150°C/302°F) being due to their great depth. They have been formed by the trapping of "connate waters" (that is, of crystalline origin or relict from early seas) beneath an overburden of rocks so dense that the pressure of water in the rock pores greatly exceeds the hydrostatic value for their depth. Such waters contain energy by virtue of their heat content, hydraulic pressure, and sometimes also because of the presence of natural gas in solution.

Even tepid waters can be used for fish hatcheries, soil-warming, deicing of roads, facilitating mining in permafrost areas, medicinal purposes, and so on. Geothermal steam, even at 100°C (212°F)—though preferably at 160°C/320°F or more—can drive turbines, while water at between about 55°C (131°F) and 100°C (212°F) can be used for district heating and domestic hot water—well over half the population of Iceland gets its hot water from geothermal sources and within a decade or so it is probable that all but the remotest dwellings will be served in this way. The original fields in Reykjavik are still producing at undiminished capacity after 50 years.

Several industries are already using Earth heat, including a paper factory in New Zealand, which consumes about 200 tons/hour of natural steam, and an Icelandic diatomite plant that uses about 50 t/h of steam.

Kisiliojan at the western edge of Iceland's Namafjall steamfield produces steam that is used industrially to dry diatomite (a clay used in filters) and to generate 2.5 MW of electricity. It is estimated that Iceland's geothermal areas have a production potential of 3,200 MW thermal for 50 years, but most of Iceland's power at present comes from hydroelectricity.

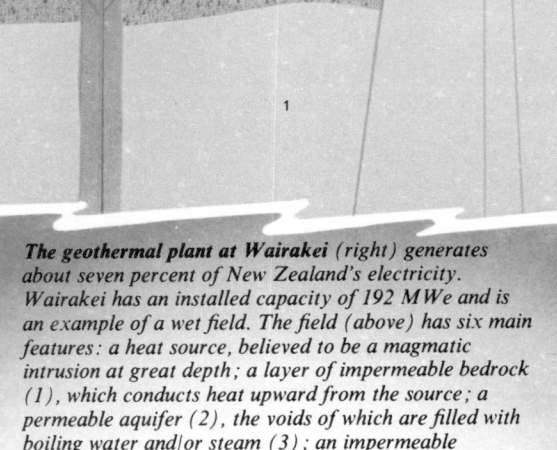

The geothermal plant at Wairakei (right) generates about seven percent of New Zealand's electricity. Wairakei has an installed capacity of 192 MWe and is an example of a wet field. The field (above) has six main features: a heat source, believed to be a magmatic intrusion at great depth; a layer of impermeable bedrock (1), which conducts heat upward from the source; a permeable aquifer (2), the voids of which are filled with boiling water and/or steam (3); an impermeable caprock (4), to hinder the escape of heat from the aquifer to the surface; and a source of water replenishment (5), usually a surface outcrop of the aquifer at some distance from the field. The illustration has been exaggerated to reveal the faulting (6).

At present, geothermal power contributes only about 0.25 percent of the world's electrical needs. In the 1960s a good thermal field could produce bulk heat at perhaps 20 percent, and bulk power at perhaps 50–60 percent, of the equivalent cost of oil; the fact that fuel prices have risen in recent years more rapidly than labor and material costs has placed geothermal energy in a still more favorable position. In California, the contribution that geothermal energy is making to a mixed electricity supply system (with hydro, nuclear and fossil-fueled plants) is the cheapest. In Reykjavik the cost to the consumer of geothermal domestic heat, inclusive of charges on the urban reticulation system, was in 1974 only 25–30 percent of individual oil heating. In the suburbs of Paris, geothermal district heating in a nonthermal area is costing only 80–84 percent of oil heating.

New developments

Immense and widespread heat reserves are contained in hot, dry rocks at various depths within the practical range of the drill. These rocks, lacking any permeability, are unable to contain a working fluid (water and/or steam) without which their heat content cannot be exploited. The only obstacle that now prevents exploitation of this heat, which lies up to three to five kilometers deep (two to three miles), is mastery of the art of rock fracturing. Experiments are already under way in the USA and have had fairly promising results. By applying hydraulic pressure at the base of a cased well, it is possible to create in the rock a vertical lenticular crack some hundreds of meters in diameter though only a few millimeters wide at the center. A closed water circulation circuit can be formed by sinking a second bore to intersect the crack and pick up heat by conduction. This technique has the disadvantage of being virtually two-dimensional; for since rocks are poor thermal conductors, heat extraction is confined to a thin disk of rock. Attempts are being made to produce a three-dimensional labyrinth by means of explosives at the bottoms of wells. When these techniques have proved successful, and are married with deeper penetration of the crust, man will hold the key to intense deep-heat mining. Present experiments include an Italian attempt to drill to 5,000 meters (16,400 feet).

With rising fuel prices and the attainment of higher temperatures and efficiencies, geothermal power generation will become increasingly attractive: every kilowatt of geothermal base load saves about two tons a year of oil fuel.

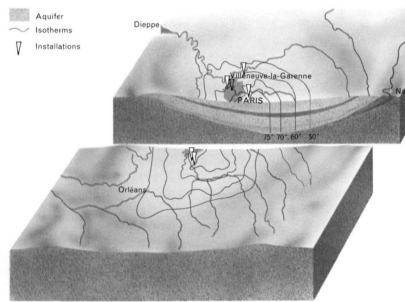

Aquifer

Isotherms

Installations

At Larderello in Tuscany the Italians have been extracting boric acid from steam jets since the 18th century and it was there that geothermal power was first successfully generated in 1904. Now a group of stations in the district is collectively generating 421 MWe. Net geothermal power production in 1974 amounted to 2.29×10^9 kWh.

Notable among attempts to exploit the heat in a nonthermal region is that begun in 1975 at Villeneuve-la-Garenne, near Paris. Deep drilling into the Paris basin tapped thermal water at 63°C (145°F) and 1,700 dwellings are supplied with underfloor heating and hot water. Five other major sites in the basin are being developed.

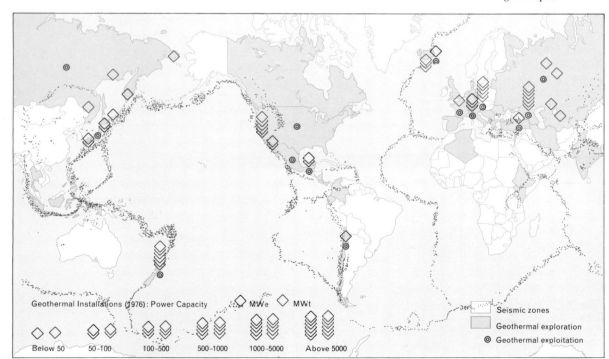

Geothermal Installations (1976): Power Capacity ◇ MWe ◇ MWt

Below 50   50–100   100–500   500–1000   1000–5000   Above 5000

Seismic zones

Geothermal exploration

Geothermal exploitation

Total installed capacity of geothermal power in the world is about 1,500 MWe and it is estimated that this will increase to between 12,500 and 14,500 MWe by 1985. The map above shows existing electrical capacity (MWe) and also the existing thermal capacity (MWt)—the direct use of geothermal energy for heating homes, factories and offices, and in agriculture—of individual countries. Exploration sites are also shown, with the exception of five islands—Azores, French Antilles, Montserrat, Santa Lucia and the Canaries—difficult to locate at this scale. World seismic belts are also shown.

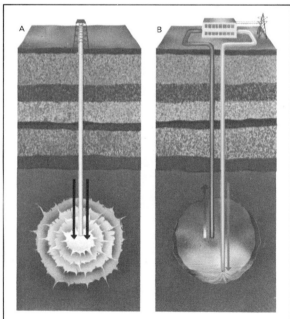

Rock-fracturing experiments, designed to tap the heat in impermeable rock, are being carried out at Los Alamos in New Mexico. The rock is shattered by hydraulic pressure (A), forming a lenticular fracture that will accept water. A second, deeper bore (B) is then sunk. Water passed down this bore is heated by the rock and then, because it is less dense, rises to the surface.

NUCLEAR REACTOR TYPES

At a Canadian mill in Uranium City drums of uranium concentrate are loaded for shipment—operators wear special protective clothing and dust masks. It takes one ton of uranium ore to make 1.58 kg (3½ lb) of concentrate.

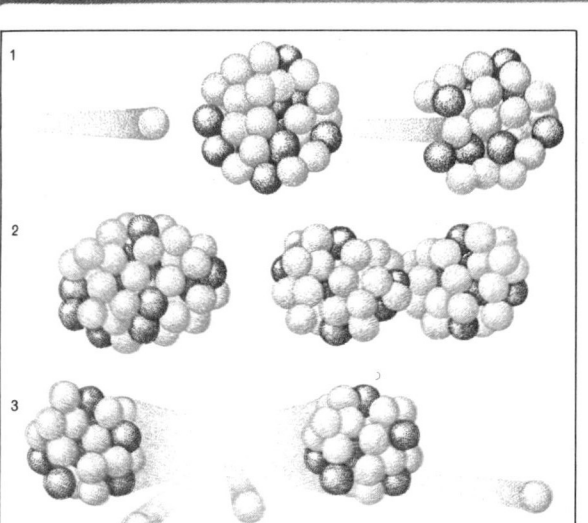

Uranium ore is extracted by surface or underground mining. The crude ore is fed into a series of crushing mills, which grind it to the consistency of fine sand. Chemical solvents then dissolve out the uranium, which emerges from the process in this form, a mixture of uranium oxides usually called "yellow cake."

In nuclear fission an atom of uranium (1), which contains a large number of protons and neutrons in its nucleus, is induced to split into two atoms (2) of lighter elements. The spare neutrons then stimulate another atom to divide (3) and criticality—a self-sustaining chain reaction—is built up.

The sub-assembly shown above contains a mixture of plutonium and uranium oxide pellets clad in stainless steel cans. About 100 sub-assemblies are needed to charge the prototype fast breeder reactor at Dounreay, Scotland, shown right, where a dummy assembly is being lowered into position manually—normally refueling would be done by remote control to guard against the extreme radioactivity of spent fuel. The surrounding rods are reflectors designed to economize on neutrons by reflecting escaping neutrons back into the core and adding to the higher neutron density required in fast breeders.

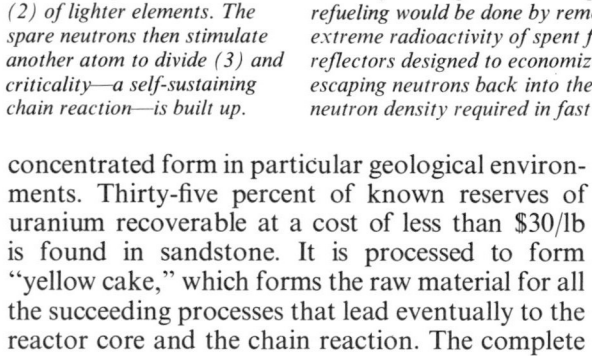

By 1980 30 countries are scheduled to be operating a total of 471 nuclear reactors. Dwindling supplies of fossil fuels, and rising prices, have encouraged pursuit of an energy program that is at once economically attractive—one ton of uranium can produce as much energy as 10,000 tons of oil or 20,000 tons of coal—and potentially hazardous: nuclear plants contain enormous quantities of lethal radioactive material.

During World War II research was concentrated on military aspects of fission with American, British and Canadian physicists cooperating to produce the first atom bomb in 1945. In 1951 a reactor in Idaho in the United States was used to generate electricity on a small scale and in 1956 the world's first commercial reactor came into operation at Calder Hall in England. Since then the USSR, France, West Germany and Canada have joined Britain and the United States at the forefront of nuclear power research and development. Many different reactor designs have been produced—but at the heart of them all is uranium, an element that has virtually no use except—because it is particularly fissile—as a nuclear fuel.

Uranium is found in the Earth's crust and in seawater in small amounts, and it is found in more concentrated form in particular geological environments. Thirty-five percent of known reserves of uranium recoverable at a cost of less than $30/lb is found in sandstone. It is processed to form "yellow cake," which forms the raw material for all the succeeding processes that lead eventually to the reactor core and the chain reaction. The complete sequence of processes is called the nuclear fuel cycle, described in more detail on page 80.

In a nuclear reactor, the speed and intensity of the chain reaction is controlled so that the enormous energy released can be harnessed to generate electricity. At present there are two types of reactors: the thermal reactor and the liquid metal fast breeder. Only the thermal, however, has been technologically proved on a commercial scale. Fast breeders, still at the prototype stage, "breed" more fissile material and potentially could extract up to 60 times more energy from their fuel than thermal reactors.

There are several different designs of thermal reactors but they all are fueled by rods either of natural uranium (which consists of two main isotopes, the highly fissile uranium-235, utilizing slow neutrons, and the more stable uranium-238, fissioned only by fast neutrons) or of uranium enriched with a higher than usual proportion of U-235. These rods are surrounded by a "moderator," usually water or graphite, which is used to slow down the neutrons released by fission until they reach optimal speed for bombarding another U-235 nucleus to stimulate further fission. Some of the U-238 may, on bombardment, turn into plutonium 239, which is itself fissile. Heat is given off by fission and is carried away from the reactor core by a coolant. The heat contained in the coolant is then used to produce steam which powers a turbine to generate electricity, in exactly the same way as in a coal- or oil-fired electricity plant. Rods of a material such as boron, which absorbs neutrons, can be lowered into the reactor core to control the speed of the reaction or to shut it down altogether. The reactor core is usually contained in a steel vessel and/or a thick shielding of prestressed concrete to protect its operators from radiation.

Various designs have been developed in an attempt to improve safety, to reduce costs or to improve the efficiency with which the heat of fission is converted into electricity. Light water-cooled reactors (LWR) have become the most widely preferred type. By 1980 there will be about 205,000 megawatts (MW) of both light and heavy water-cooled types (HWR) in operation as compared to

about 21,000 MW capacity of gas-cooled reactors. Scientists are now looking at the possibility of using thorium to extend the use of U-235 in HWRs, modified LWRs, and possibly high-temperature reactors. Like uranium, thorium is a naturally occurring element, but it is more plentiful. It can produce much higher temperatures and can be used to fire steel furnaces as well as to generate electricity. If thorium was to be used, however, the whole nuclear cycle would have to be adapted.

The "fast" breeder is so named because it has no moderator to slow down the neutrons. The first nuclear reactor ever to generate electricity was a fast breeder, but following two serious accidents its development in the United States was restricted and has mainly been pursued in Britain, France, West Germany and the USSR. Fast neutrons are much less efficient than slow ones at inducing fission in U-235, but the fission they do induce involves a much greater number of neutrons being given off than with slow neutrons.

Fast breeder technology

To make use of a high proportion of these neutrons, fast breeders have a compact core of fissile plutonium mixed with highly enriched U-235. The core is surrounded by a blanket of U-238. The U-238 may be converted into plutonium 239 on being bombarded with neutrons that have escaped the core. Heat produced in the reactor core is carried away by a fluid, usually molten sodium. This primary sodium circuit is intensely radioactive and must be confined entirely within the metal and concrete shielding so that a second sodium circuit with a heat exchanger inside the shielding—but itself protected from the primary sodium—is required to pick up the heat from the primary circuit and carry it out through the shielding to a second heat exchanger, where steam is generated. In early reactors sodium circuits and heat exchangers were outside the main reactor vessel and this was known as the loop system. This has now been superseded by the pool system, where the whole of the circuit assemblage is housed inside the reactor.

Though fast breeders create more fissile material than they consume as fuel, it takes a minimum of 10 years to create enough plutonium to fuel a new reactor. The time required for a breeder reactor to produce enough plutonium to fuel another reactor is called the reactor's doubling time. The most recent development in fast breeders, the 1,200 MW Superphénix power plant at Creys-Malville in France, is the prototype for the commercial breeder plant of the future, and construction has begun. It is described on pages 80–1.

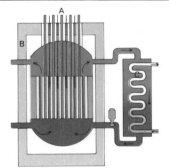

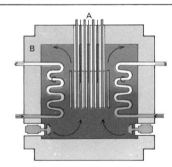

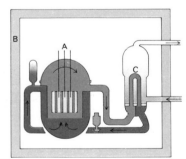

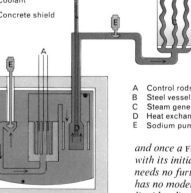

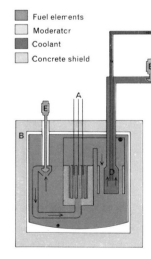

■	Fuel elements
☐	Moderator
■	Coolant
☐	Concrete shield

A Control rods
B Steel vessel
C Steam generator
D Heat exchanger
E Sodium pump

The Magnox gas-cooled reactor uses natural uranium clad in a special magnesium alloy called Magnox. The moderator is graphite and the coolant carbon dioxide. The reactor core is contained by a steel pressure vessel, which is surrounded by a thick concrete shield. Refueling can be carried out while the reactor is supplying power. The power density is 1.1 kW per liter and is by nuclear standards low. The life span of the fuel is 3,000 to 4,000 MW days per ton of uranium and this is one of the limitations that encouraged development of the advanced gas-cooled reactor.

The Advanced Gas-cooled Reactor (AGR) uses enriched uranium oxide clad in stainless steel. The moderator is graphite and the coolant carbon dioxide gas. The pressure vessel is made of prestressed concrete 5 meters (16 ft) thick, which also acts as the shield. AGRs are refueled while in operation and their fuel life span is 18,000 MW days per ton of uranium. The power density is 4.5 kW per liter. An AGR's fuel load is considerably less than that of a Magnox reactor of comparable output, while the fuel rating is considerably higher.

There are two types of light water reactor, the Boiling Water and Pressurized Water Reactor. The latter, shown here, is the most popular. Both use enriched uranium clad in zirconium, which is more expensive than stainless steel but less inclined to absorb neutrons Both moderator and coolant are light water and the pressure vessel is welded steel. PWRs shut down to refuel. The life span of the fuel is 21,800 MW days per ton of uranium and the power density is 102 kW per liter. The development of this type of reactor began originally in submarine research.

The Liquid Metal Fast Breeder Reactor (LMFBR) uses a mixture of uranium and plutonium oxides clad in stainless steel. There are four tons of fuel in the core, which is more compact than those of thermal reactors,

and once a FBR is provided with its initial fuel load it needs no further supply. It has no moderator and uses liquid sodium as a coolant. Power density is 646 kW per liter: 10–100 times that of thermal reactors. Main drawbacks of sodium are its violent reaction with water and its opacity. Also the temperature of the sodium must not fall below its melting point anywhere in the circuit, or it solidifies.

NUCLEAR SAFETY & WASTES

Much of the criticism leveled against the nuclear industry by its opponents concerns radiation limits, operational safety and disposal of wastes.

Experts remain at variance on radiation effects on health. The OECD Nuclear Energy Agency estimates that levels in a society relying heavily on electricity generated solely by nuclear power present little danger and that in a population of 50 million people there would eventually be about 100 deaths and non-fatal malignancies each year. Against this an American group has estimated that exposure to the maximum permissible level of 170 millirems a year would result in 32,000 deaths in the USA.

Figures on radiation dose levels to bone marrow and reproductive cells issued by the OECD Nuclear Energy Agency in 1976 show, in bone marrow, a level of 53 millirems from man-made sources of radiation compared to 101 millirems from naturally occurring sources; and levels of 24 millirems and 105 millirems respectively in reproductive cells. Man has always been exposed to a certain amount of naturally occurring radiation—there are several radioactive elements in the human body and these account for a quarter of the two figures given above. Radioactive materials in rocks and cosmic rays account for the rest. Of man-made sources, which include X-rays, radiation therapy and the nuclear power industry, diagnostic X-rays accounted for 32 millirems in bone marrow; the nuclear industry for 0.25 millirems. In reproductive cells X-rays accounted for 14 millirems as opposed to 0.2 millirems from the nuclear industry.

Operational safety

The safety record in the industry is based to date on about 1,000 reactor years of commercial experience (only a fraction of which has been obtained with the new generation of large-size reactor) and does give cause for some concern. There have been a number of disturbing incidents. In 1957 a fire at Windscale in England released radioactivity amounting to 33,000 curies. Milk was contaminated in the area and thousands of gallons were dumped. There is evidence, too, of a large nuclear explosion in the southern Urals, USSR, in 1958, where it is claimed a nuclear waste disposal dump exploded, and in 1966 a portion of the core of a fast breeder reactor in Michigan melted. The situation was so serious that it has been suggested that contingency plans were laid for the evacuation of Detroit 48 km (30 miles) away. In 1975 a fire was started at the Browns Ferry plant in the United States by a worker using a candle to determine whether air was leaking into an area under the control room. The accident was particularly disturbing because many automatic safeguards failed, and the emergency was controlled only by operator initiative in switching off. If cooling had not been restored in time there would have been a serious release of radiation. In March 1979, safeguard mechanisms failed to prevent a serious increase in temperature and pressure in the thermal reactor at Three Mile Island, near Harrisburg in Pennsylvania, and radioactive materials leaked out. The reactor developed a gas "bubble" in its core, increasing the danger of a further rise in temperature and, ultimately, a "meltdown". An area housing nearly 900,000 people was alerted for possible evacuation.

Disposal

In 1977, Windscale discharged one and a half million cubic meters (330 million gallons) of low-level liquid wastes by pipeline into the Irish Sea. Such discharges are authorized by the Department of the Environment and the Ministry of Agriculture, Fisheries and Food in accordance with maximum permissible levels laid down by the International Commission on Radiological Protection. Before the first discharge from Windscale a seaweed was identified as the critical radiation exposure pathway. It has been closely monitored ever since for increases in radioactivity. Expert opinion is by no means unanimous on effects of discharges of this kind. It has been suggested that plutonium in bottom sediments could be mobilized more quickly than was thought as a result of chemical reactions and plutonium particles might be resuspended and transported ashore.

Low-level solid wastes are packed in bitumen, concrete or metal drums and disposed of in the Atlantic by European nations in a 65 kilometer (35 nautical mile) radius (centered on 46° 15′N 17° 25′W) where the ocean is about 4.5 kilometers ($2\frac{3}{4}$ miles) deep. Such operations are monitored by the Nuclear Energy Agency of the Organization for Economic Cooperation and Development.

High-level liquid wastes are stored in stainless steel tanks fitted with cooling systems. About five cubic meters (1,100 gallons) of high-level liquid waste is produced per ton of fuel processed. Such wastes would boil for decades if not cooled in this way. At Windscale it is estimated that 1,800,000 liters (396,000 gallons) will be stored there in 1985. There have been no reported leaks from British tanks, but in 1973 in the United States 435,000 liters (95,700 gallons) leaked from tanks in Washington State – due to lack of surveillance by the operators in a six-week period.

With the expansion of the nuclear industry, storage problems will become more difficult. The radioactivity decay of the fission-product solutions to harmless levels will take hundreds of years, while those of plutonium will remain radioactive for hundreds of thousands of years. Research has been done into the possibility of putting waste into glass blocks for disposal and the search for suitable sites is being pursued by several nations. Some favor permanent disposal while others, for example scientists in West Germany, are examining the possibility of later retrieval.

Several problems remain to be resolved. It is not certain that it will be possible to incorporate liquid waste into a solid mixture immediately after reprocessing, which would thus eliminate storage as a liquid at the most crucial time, when the waste is most active. With a large nuclear program in Britain it is anticipated that by the year 2000 solidification plants would have produced about 2,000 cubic meters (70,600 cubic feet) of waste and 4,500 cubic meters (990,000 gallons) of liquid waste would be stored in tanks. The total land area occupied would be about 7,000 square meters ($1\frac{3}{4}$ acres).

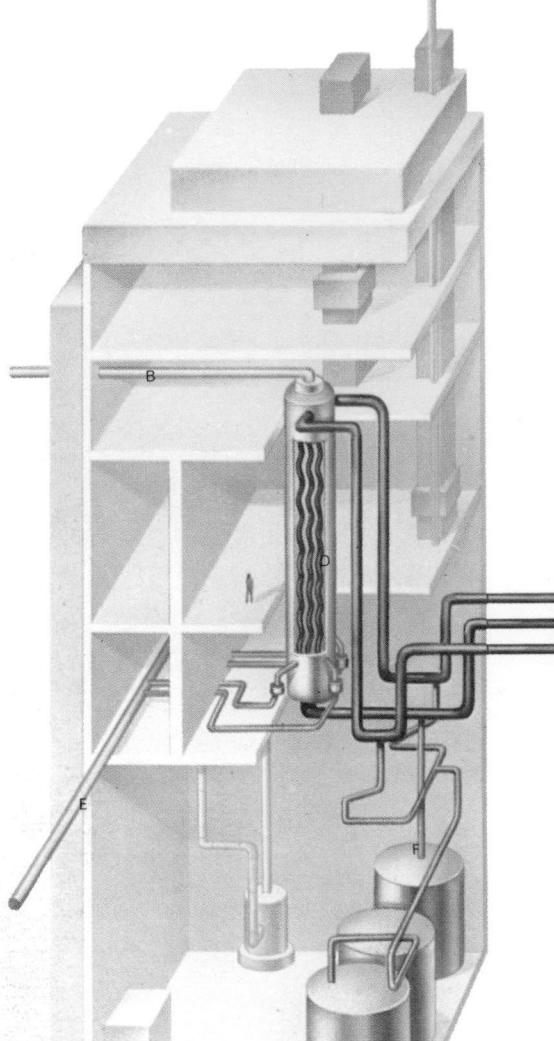

Superphénix, the world's first commercial fast breeder reactor, should be ready for operation in the early 1980s. It will have a power capacity of 1,200 MW and the potential to convert low-grade fertile uranium into fissionable plutonium. The Superphénix is situated in the Rhône Valley, equidistant from Lyons, Geneva and Grenoble and therefore in a convenient position for international power networks.

(A) Automatic fuel-handling flask
(B) Steam carried to turbines
(C) Secondary sodium pump
(D) Steam generator
(E) Water supply
(F) Sodium discharge circuit
(G) Argon tanks

The nuclear fuel cycle is the stages through which the fissile fuel passes from the mining of uranium to the reprocessing and management of spent fuel. The mined ore (1) is milled and processed to form "yellow cake" (2) and the uranium begins its cycle (A). If it is for use in a reactor using enriched uranium, it is converted (3) into uranium hexafluoride—UF$_6$. The enrichment process (4) increases the concentration of the isotope U-235 in the fuel. In the future the use of lasers will permit much higher levels of enrichment to be easily achieved. At present the two most common of a number of processes—diffusion through membranes or by centrifuges—separate the isotopes according to their different masses. Fuel fabrication (5) is a major and complex industry in its own right in which the uranium is prepared for use in different types of reactors. Keeping the materials free of neutron-absorbing impurities is essential. After generating electricity for three to five years in the reactor (6) the fuel elements are removed and stored in cooling ponds to allow the short-lived fission and activation products to decay. The spent fuel may then be transported to a reprocessing plant (7) for separation by chemical processes involving the use of nitric acid. Fissile uranium and plutonium, much too valuable to discard, can be recycled (B, C) with a recovery rate of about 99 percent. Further processing separates high-level and low-level wastes which are placed in storage or disposed of (8) into the environment, depending on their form and activity. Windscale in Britain and La Hague in France are the only two commercial reprocessing plants presently operating in the world. But pilot plants have been built in such countries as Italy, West Germany, India and Japan.

Before transportation to the reprocessing plant most of the radioactive waste in the spent fuel is stored in tanks of water, called cooling ponds, at the power plant to allow shorter-lived fission products to decay to low levels.

Spent fuel is transferred to the reprocessing plant under water into the first of a series of "caves," the walls of which are concrete 2 m (6½ ft) thick to intercept radiation. Operators watch on closed circuit television.

Irradiated fuel for disposal is transported in flasks that have been designed to recognized international standards to give maximum protection. They weigh 75 tons, including the weight of up to ¾ ton of fuel, and are constructed in steel 7.5 cm (3 in) thick with a 19 cm (7½ in) lead lining.

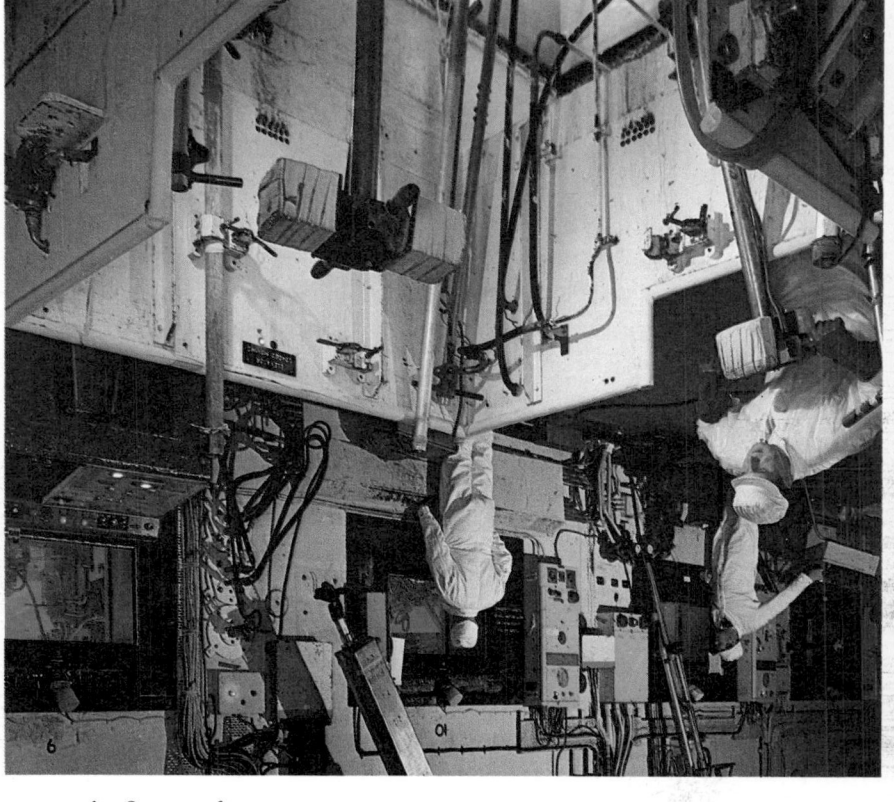
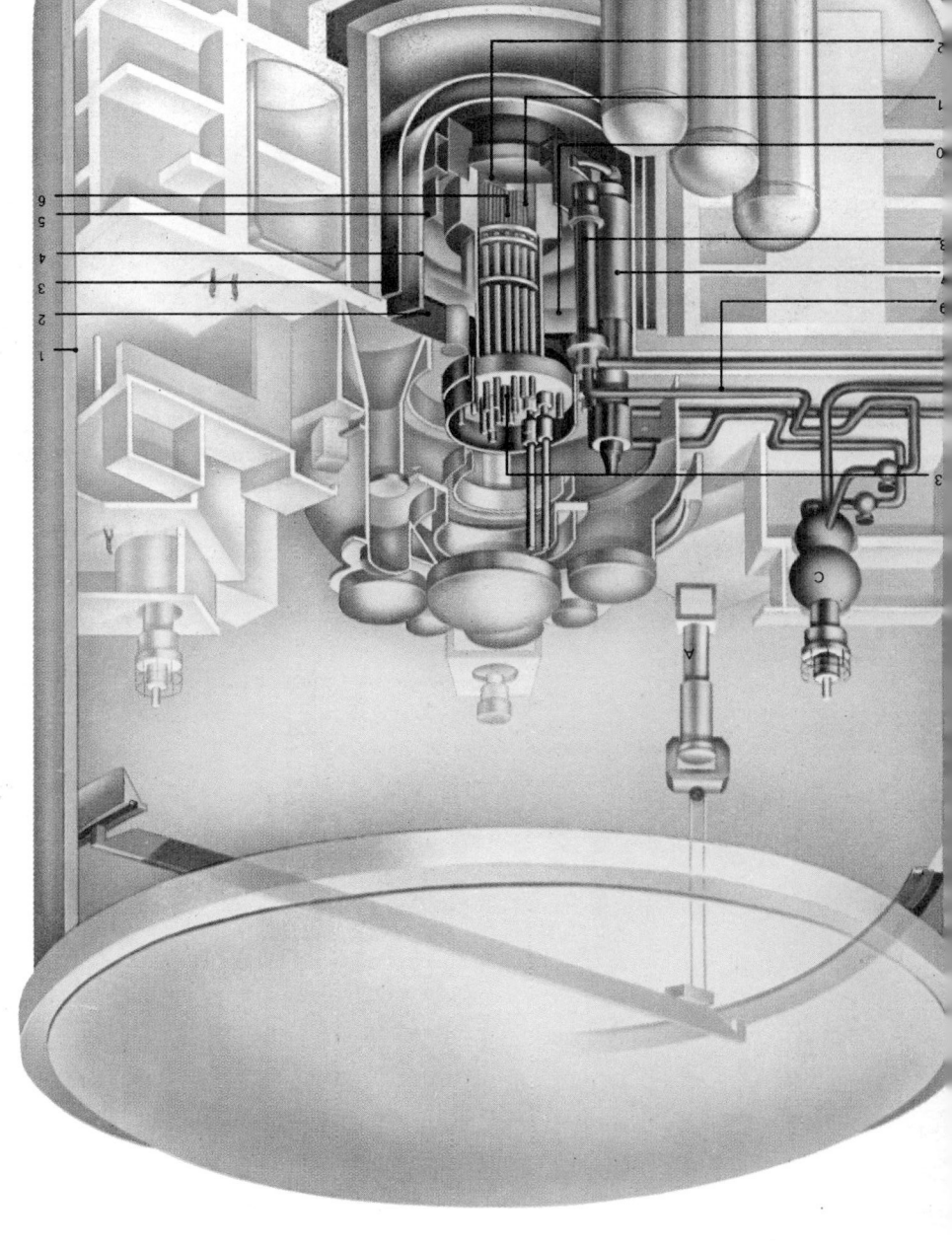

Attention to safety has played an important role in the development of Superphénix. The reactor is sited in a sparsely populated area that is little subject to seismic activity and it has a number of safety features in its advanced design. Protection from explosions, fire and radiation is given by four enclosures—(1) reinforced concrete 1 m (3¼ ft) thick around the reactor building; (2) steel and concrete slab from which a second safety vessel (3) is hung; and (4) the main steel vessel. The main pool-type reactor vessel (5) houses the active core (6), primary sodium pumps (7) and intermediate heat exchangers (8), where the integrity of the primary sodium circuit can be better maintained than if distributed in an intricate piping system. The vessels and circuits do not need to be pressurized because of the high boiling point (882°C [1,620°F]) of the sodium coolant. Reaction between the radioactive sodium and water is prevented by the insertion of a secondary sodium circuit (9), while a buffer layer of argon gas (10) prevents reaction with air. The nuclear fuel is divided into long pins, less than 1 cm (⅜ in) in diameter, to rapidly disperse the heat generated by the fission reaction (450 watts per centimeter of pin in the center of the core). 271 pins of both fissile and fertile material make up a fuel subassembly (11), and within the active core and breeder blanket (12) there is a total of 596 subassemblies. These are manipulated by automatic ultrasonic devices that ensure correct positioning at any point in the core and blanket. Three independent groups of control rods (13) housed in a rotating plate are designed to penetrate the core in the case of an emergency.

It has been proposed that canisters of glassified waste could be buried in disused salt mines. Salt, which is usually embedded in different layers of impermeable rock, has high conductivity, which would help dissipate the intense heat radiated by the canisters. On the surface a carrier (1) would transport the spent fuel to a hoist and work platform at the mouth of the shaft (2). In the mine, a carrier (3) operated by remote control from the work platform would take the spent fuel to designated areas (4) for disposal.

Old mine shaft 315 m (1,024 ft)

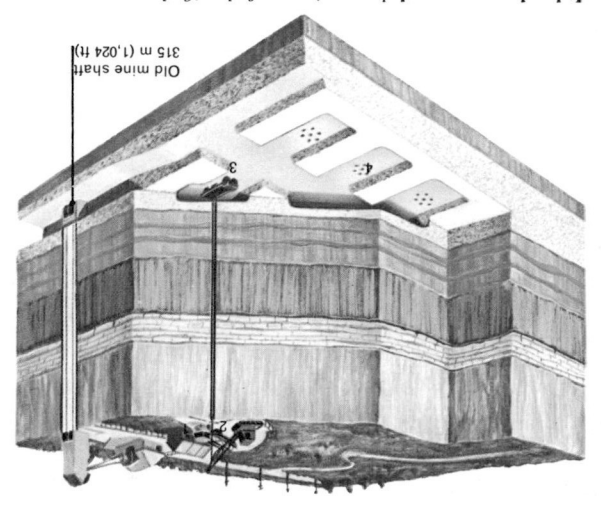

Several nations are considering the idea of putting high-level wastes into glass blocks and disposing of these in the ocean. Three methods are suggested: free-fall containers (1) dropped on the surface of the deep ocean floor; free-fall projectiles (2) to penetrate the sediment of the ocean; and a more complicated technique that would entail a drilling platform from which waste would be disposed of in shafts (3) drilled in the consolidated sediment above bedrock (4). Likely sites would need to be free of any geological activity.

4,000–5,000 m (13,000–16,250 ft)

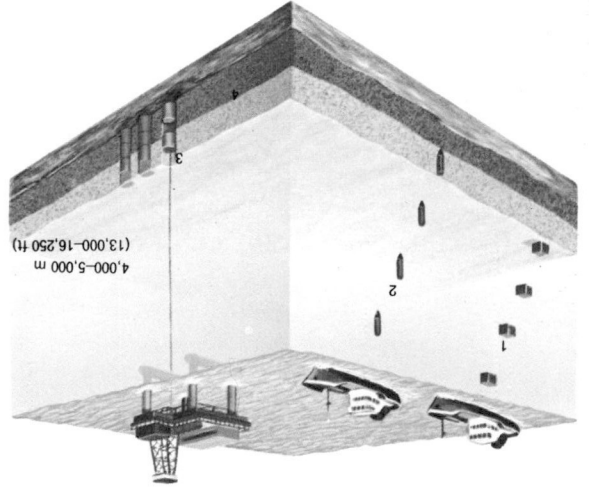

NUCLEAR COSTS & RESERVES

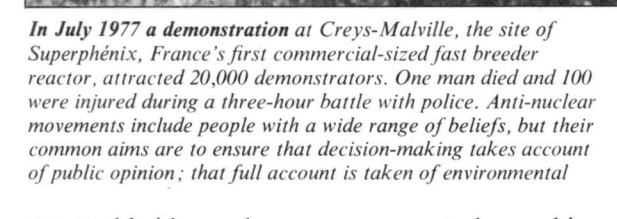

In July 1977 a demonstration at Creys-Malville, the site of Superphénix, France's first commercial-sized fast breeder reactor, attracted 20,000 demonstrators. One man died and 100 were injured during a three-hour battle with police. Anti-nuclear movements include people with a wide range of beliefs, but their common aims are to ensure that decision-making takes account of public opinion; that full account is taken of environmental risks, the risk of nuclear terrorism and the potential for nuclear weapons proliferation; and that civil liberties are not infringed by the controls needed to ensure security. In some countries, such as Britain and Australia, commissions of inquiry have been established to investigate particular areas of concern with the further development of nuclear power and these have helped to expose many of the important issues to public debate.

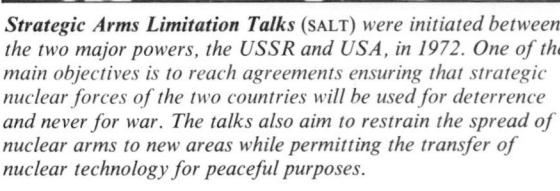

Strategic Arms Limitation Talks (SALT) *were initiated between the two major powers, the USSR and USA, in 1972. One of the main objectives is to reach agreements ensuring that strategic nuclear forces of the two countries will be used for deterrence and never for war. The talks also aim to restrain the spread of nuclear arms to new areas while permitting the transfer of nuclear technology for peaceful purposes.*

Worldwide, nuclear power seems to be marking time. In the United Kingdom, decisions on which technology to choose have been postponed to 1982. Environmental issues and the extensive Windscale inquiry into the expansion of reprocessing facilities have affected the progress of the nuclear program. Development has slowed also in the United States, West Germany, Sweden and France.

Increasingly, opposition movements in a number of countries are becoming an important consideration in the formulation of national energy policies. In Sweden, for instance, the downfall of the Socialist Government in 1976 is attributed in large part to the government's support of a nuclear power development program. Besides environmental issues, the most intractable problems remain the possibility of technology falling into the hands of unscrupulous groups and the risk of weapon proliferation resulting from civil nuclear programs. Various safeguards have been established through the International Atomic Energy Agency (IAEA) and embodied in the Nonproliferation Treaty (NPT). They include the international inspection of nuclear installations and the controlled reprocessing of irradiated fuel elements. The problem is that not all countries have signed the NPT and the IAEA admits that the system is inadequate—that it would not necessarily be able to detect any diversion of nuclear fuel within the "critical time period." This is the time it would take a government to turn nuclear fuel into a bomb —between 10 days and six months.

The limitations of the NPT safeguards were demonstrated when India developed a nuclear bomb in 1974—a direct result of its peaceful nuclear technology. In 1977 this led the nuclear suppliers to formulate an agreement insisting that safeguards apply to any future use of materials derived from the fuels and equipment originally supplied. This, in turn, was followed by much criticism from the countries of the European Economic Community (EEC), which import more than half their enriched uranium from the United States. By the terms of the NPT, members were required to agree to let the United States authorize the production, movement and use of reprocessed nuclear fuel that originally came from America. Eight of the nine were reluctant to agree and the French were firmly against the idea. So the Americans imposed an embargo. In 1977, however, on the initiative of the USA and in line with its non-proliferation policy, the International Nuclear Fuel Cycle Evaluation (INFCE) was established. INFCE is basically a 40-nations' study designed to find a nuclear technology that will make it less easy to produce material directly usable in bombs. The French have accepted INFCE, but the USA has agreed to postpone the question of reprocessing until the group meets in 1979.

Security remains a major headache, particularly in the light of incidents such as the alleged "hijacking" by Israel of 200 tons of uranium oxide in 1968 from stockpiles in Belgium. Against a background of rumor and counter-rumor it has never been established what happened to the uranium.

Costs of nuclear power

Cost comparisons between nuclear and coal- or oil-fired stations are difficult to make accurately. They may be distorted by inadequate allowances for research and development and capital expenditure, and their assumptions of the load factor (the amount of time that the reactor will be operating) may be unrealistic. Hoped-for factors of 70–75 percent have in practice turned out to be 55–60 percent. Construction and licensing delays, partly caused by more stringent safety and environmental regulations, have caused capital costs of new plants to soar. In the United States costs per kilowatt have risen almost eight times since the first light water reactors were built in the early 1960s and, contrary to original hopes, building larger installations has not yet reduced the cost of the electricity produced. Partly as a result of these high capital costs the nuclear program in many countries has been curtailed or delayed, especially as expected increases in electricity demand have failed to materialize following the oil price rise of 1973. Even in the countries most committed to nuclear power, only about 15–20 percent of their electricity comes from nuclear power.

Reserves and resources

The radioactive elements uranium, thorium and potassium are naturally concentrated by movements of molten rock in the upper part of the Earth's crust, where the heat generated by their disintegration keeps the Earth from cooling down. Potassium is the most widespread, but no means of using it for generating usable energy has been found; thorium may become important if the fast breeder reactor is developed. Additional natural concentration of the ores is necessary before they are workable. There are three ways in which this may happen. First, uraninite (uranium oxide) and monazite (the chief thorium mineral) may be weathered out, transported by streams, and collected in placers: the Witwatersrand (South Africa) and Eliot Lake (Canada) are important examples of uranium ores while the monazite-bearing beach sands of eastern and western Australia, South Africa, India and Florida may be rich future resources. Second, groundwaters may dissolve uranium from volcanic rocks and concentrate it where appropriate reducing conditions exist: the

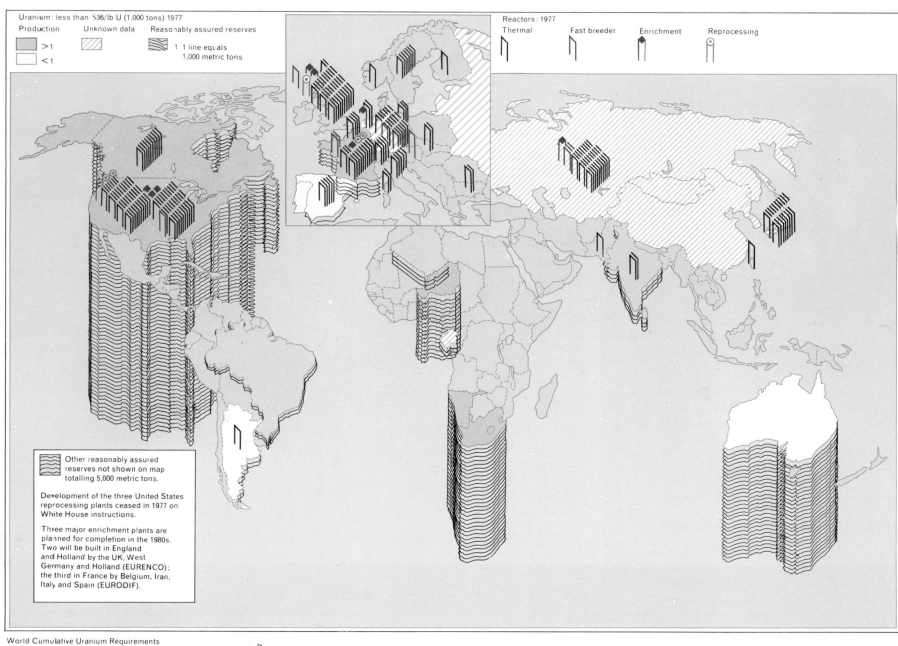

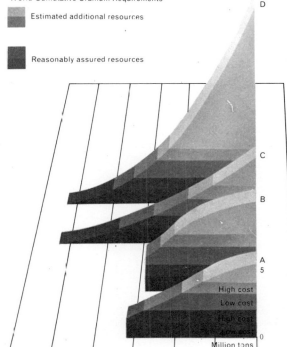

World Cumulative Uranium Requirements

Estimated additional resources

Reasonably assured resources

Reasonably assured resources and estimated additional resources are shown divided into high- and low-cost categories (the costs at which they can be extracted). The rate at which this uranium is used depends on the program of nuclear power that is chosen. The four possible programs shown use the recycling process and would be the most efficient users of uranium. Fast breeder reactors, whether following present trend (A) or accelerated development (B), produce substantial savings compared to thermal reactors following present trend (C) or accelerated trend (D). The introduction of FBRs toward the end of the century prolongs the sufficiency of known uranium resources by only a few more years, but FBRs do substantially reduce the amount of new uranium that must be found to maintain nuclear power growth in the next century. Uranium of higher cost categories may be considered if the rise in fossil fuels continues.

Colorado Plateau sandstones, the chief United States resource, illustrate this. Third, uranium may become dissolved in ocean water and enriched where black mud is being deposited under reducing conditions; the black shale that results may some day become a large-scale but low-grade source of the metal. The Kolm Shale of southern Sweden is an example of this.

Because of the worldwide decline in the building of nuclear power stations there is less immediate concern in the short term (until 2000) about the reserves of uranium. Reserves at up to $36 a lb were estimated in 1977 at 1,650,000 tons. Reasonably assured resources, at up to $59 a lb, amounted to another 540,000 tons, with an additional estimated resource at the same price of 2,100,000 tons. There are fears that uranium reserves are insufficient to maintain a nuclear energy program beyond 2000. Thorium is plentiful, but to use it the whole nuclear fuel cycle would have to be adapted.

As a result of the military origins of nuclear power, uranium exploration was mounted in limited areas in the 1940s and 1950s. This is reflected in the location of the known reserves—80 percent of them are in four countries: Australia, South Africa, the United States and Canada. Australia, which has one-quarter of them, has experienced opposition to production. In South Australia the state government is strongly against the mining of uranium. In Western Australia uranium mining has been postponed because of pressure by environmental groups and in the Northern Territory problems of Aboriginal rights remain to be resolved. Finally, the Labor Party has threatened that should it be returned to power in Australia, it will not recognize uranium contracts negotiated by the present government.

A past history of fluctuating prices has not given the uranium mining companies incentive to look for new reserves. During the 1950s, when many of the known reserves were developed, prices were about $11/lb. Demand for uranium for commercial purposes did not develop until the mid-1960s and prices then ranged from $6 to $8/lb. Although commercial demand grew in the late 1960s consumers were slow to plan for future needs. Because of large stocks prices fell to below $5/lb by 1972. After the 1973–74 oil crisis prices adjusted to $12–$13/lb then rose to $20/lb by the mid-1970s.

Demand for uranium
Excluding the centrally planned economies, the requirements for uranium were 23,000 tons in 1977. The 1977 OECD NEA/IAEA report on uranium placed production at 29,000 tons a year (in 1977) from an industry with a production capacity of 33,000 tons. Possible further developments could raise world annual requirements to 43,000 tons in 1980 and perhaps 88,000 in 1985.

The report estimated installed nuclear generating capacity based on high growth and low growth, and on assumptions of present trend power growth and accelerated power growth, and concluded that in 1985 the lower assumption would mean that 278 GW were required and the higher that 368 GW were required. In 1990 these figures would rise to 504 and 700 respectively and in 2000 to 1,000 and 1,890. Based on these projections prediction for future demand for uranium (in kilotons) would be between 71 kt and 88 kt in 1985; between 102 and 156 in 1990; and between 178 and 338 in 2000. These figures do not account for the recycling of plutonium, which would mean demand for uranium would be lowered. Without recycle, the cumulative needs of uranium would be between 423 and 477 kt by 1985; and 2,276 to 3,591 by 2000.

POWER FROM THE SUN

The world's largest untapped resource is one that is universal: the Sun. The sum of its output reaching Earth—and this is only one-billionth of the total—amounts to about 10 million times current world energy consumption. Every single square centimeter of the Sun's surface gives out a constant seven kilowatts—more than double the output of the average household electric heater.

Here is a vast energy source—free, noiseless, non-polluting, exempt from political controls and unlikely to run out—which, as yet, has not realized its full potential. The problems are technological ones, ranging from how to store sunlight, to the highly sophisticated—and costly—challenge of putting the Sun to work to power industry.

There are four broad applications of solar energy: heating water; heating space; creating electricity; and generating mechanical power. Of these the first two, involving only relatively low-key heat-transfer technology, are by far the cheaper and more immediately viable. The use of solar power in industry —though already in existence in various prototype forms—is as yet a far-off reality, demanding ultra-high technology and still reckoned to be about five times more costly than, say, a nuclear plant.

Solar collection devices

At present, then, it is primarily as a source of heat that the Sun is becoming more productively involved in our daily lives. Already there is a small but lively market in the various solar collecting devices, which bring warmth and hot-water systems to millions of homes, shops, offices, schools and factories and, also, provide a pre-heating capacity for certain industries, such as food processing, which are dependent on heat-intensive techniques. In addition, in hot, dry regions—parts of the United States, Australia, Israel and several less-developed nations—heat from the Sun is being used for evaporation, to obtain salt or other minerals from solution, and for desalination plants where the salt is a reject product. Among the biggest evaporation systems under development is an experimental one in Jordan (funded by the World Bank) for producing potash fertilizer.

Still the most common type of collector is the "active" flat plate type. At its cheapest and simplest this consists of a black surface (exposed to the Sun) with water running over it. Generally, however, flat plate collectors are built to include a number of refinements, such as insulation. A flat plate collector with a surface area of three square meters (32 square feet), yielding up to 227 liters (50 gallons) of heated water per day, costs between $510 and $1,280 complete. Flat plate models heating air—in use in the United States, Australia and Japan, for instance, for curing and drying timber—are slightly cheaper. Mostly equipped with pumps, controls and sensors (unlike the "passive" type), active collectors work well, and at low cost, in hot countries, where they

are used mainly for steam-cooking, baking and hot-water systems. At present Japan leads the world in solar water heaters, with an estimated two million in use. Active collectors are not, however, suitable for cold climates, which call for more complicated (and costly) collectors with one or more layers of glazing and some form of protection against freeze-expansion damage.

Climatically the countries best situated for optimum, year-round conversion of solar energy are those lying between 15° and 30° latitude north or south of the equator. In more temperate zones there is the problem of seasonality, with winter solar input in Britain or Sweden, for example, dropping to perhaps only one-tenth of the summertime level. Also in northern latitudes, the Sun is often blanked out by cloud or fog. This is in dismal

contrast to the more stable conditions on the plains and prairies of the United States or Canada, where there are many clear winter days. Snow, on the other hand, can be a bonus: snow banks sited conveniently in relation to solar collectors act as reflectors, dramatically improving the heat-conversion rate.

In general, however, it is obvious that the less sunlight there is available the greater are the limitations on the development of solar power. In temperate zones in particular the worst of many technological problems is storage—how to retain solar heat for the sunless days (and nights) ahead.

Research is being done by several nations on four main methods of "passive" collector systems for providing indoor heat: phase-change heat stores, water tanks, rock stores and building fabrics.

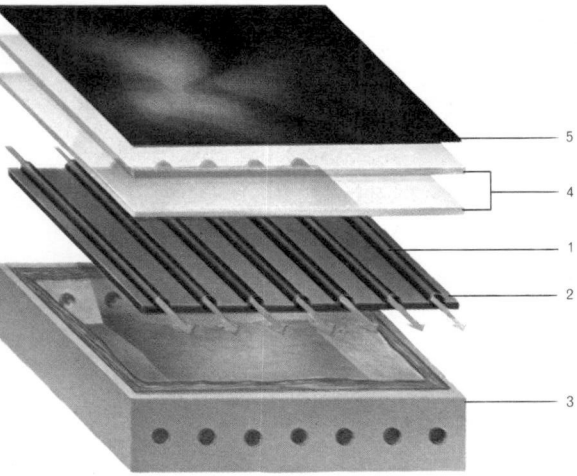

The basic plate collector may have several refinements. Here the water runs through pipes (1) in an absorbent surface (2), which cuts evaporation. An insulation box (3) reduces heat loss. Re-radiation is cut by glass (4), which takes in heat from the absorbent, radiating some back. A selective absorber (5), a polished black metal plate, helps absorb and emit heat.

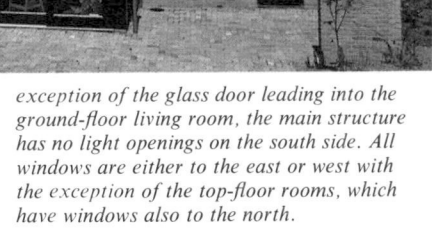

This prototype solar house is in Eindhoven, Holland. Part of a project to show solar energy can help cut costs even in temperate climates, it is a true solar house built round the collector —unlike most models, which are conventional houses with collectors added. With the

exception of the glass door leading into the ground-floor living room, the main structure has no light openings on the south side. All windows are either to the east or west with the exception of the top-floor rooms, which have windows also to the north.

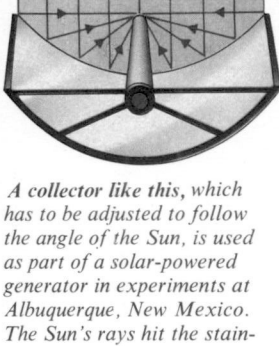

A collector like this, which has to be adjusted to follow the angle of the Sun, is used as part of a solar-powered generator in experiments at Albuquerque, New Mexico. The Sun's rays hit the stainless steel surface and the reflected light then converges onto the pipe in the middle. The pipe is filled with water, which draws off the heat to be used for hot water.

Sun reflected from a New York skyscraper emphasizes a source of power largely ignored—indeed, Americans use 50 percent of their electricity in summer to run air-conditioning plants. Properly utilized direct sunlight can both heat and cool buildings. The heating principle was proved by St George's School in Wallasey, England—built of insulated concrete walls and one glass wall, facing south, the school uses solar heat, the heat from light bulbs and the heat produced by its occupants to supply all its needs even in winter. The cooling principle is demonstrated in the Trombe house. With the bottom flap closed and the top one open (A) the hot air is dispersed upward drawing cool air in from the shaded rear of the building. To heat the house (B) the top flap is closed and the bottom flap is opened.

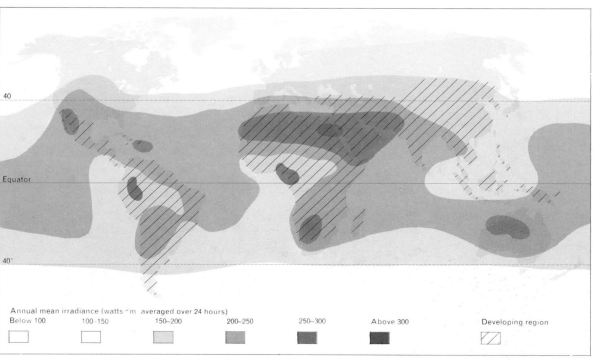

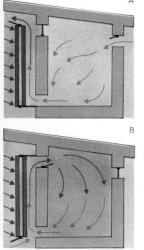

Countries best suited to utilizing solar energy are on the equatorial side of the world's arid deserts with very little annual rainfall. One of the best locations is the Atacama Desert of north Chile. The area has 1mm of rain a year, 364 days of bright sunshine and no dust. Theoretically this region (at present largely undeveloped) receives annual solar heat greater than all the heat produced in the world in a year by the burning of coal, oil, gas and wood.

Phase-change heat stores—where chemical salts release the heat stored in them—are at present very expensive and therefore little used. Water tanks, rock stores and building fabrics are all extremely bulky but have the advantage of cheapness. In each case the solar heat must be transferred to the store and then retrieved as efficiently as possible.

A rock store typically consists of one to five tons of rock, stored in an insulated bin beneath the building. The rock is usually crushed into fist-sized lumps, allowing air to pass freely, in both the heat delivery and retrieval operations. Cooling through 20°C (68°F) will release about 10kWh of heat per ton of store compared with about 22kWh for a one-ton water store cooled through the same temperature. Efficiency increases with the surface area of heat-exchange material, which favors rock.

The building fabric method has been most adopted in temperate countries and attention has been focused on the "solar house," which is a unit for trapping sunlight for conversion to interior heat. Typically (in the Northern Hemisphere) a building drawing on solar energy for its heating is constructed with extra large windows on the southern aspect (and on the west wall of a southeast-facing unit, to make the most of the afternoon Sun); the remaining walls, especially any which face north, are fitted with very small windows to minimize heat loss. Insulating shutters are operated by timing devices or photo-cells. At its best, with high-quality insulation, the solar house built on the large-window principle can approach total heating self-sufficiency. However, a difficulty with many of the units now in use is overheating in the summer.

Solar furnace
A novel variation on the solar house theme is one developed by staff at the world's largest solar furnace, at Odeileo in the French Pyrenees. This scheme (known as the Trombe solar wall after its designer, Professor Felix Trombe) calls for a sheet of glass to be fixed in front of a wall facing the Sun. Air caught in the space between the glass and the wall is heated by the Sun and rises to enter the building through inlets in the top of the wall. Airflow is controlled by flaps in the glass sheet. An attractive feature of the Trombe solar wall is that it doubles as a partial cooling system. The drawback with the Trombe design, as with all building fabric designs, is that the south-facing wall cannot usually supply heat for more than one cloudy day.

Meanwhile, obstacles in the path of commercial exploitation of the Sun are both practical and economic. Many buildings are not well placed to utilize sunlight, but even for those which are the cost of conversion to solar power (which is still relatively expensive compared to oil, gas or coal) would prove prohibitive. To date only a handful of nations—led by the United States, Australia, Israel and Japan—are committed to solar development, but the construction and demonstration of 100 percent solar heated buildings has led to an improving understanding of the potentials for solar heat. In the United States the Housing and Urban Development agency has been cooperating with government agencies interested in solar energy. In order to assess the individual merits of different types of solar heating systems 450 fully monitored buildings had been completed in a four-year period to 1978. Other countries, however, including some of the less-developed countries, which could stand to profit most from the Sun, argue that industrialized countries are subsidizing the exploitation of solar energy in developing nations to conserve the primary energy reserves—coal and oil—for themselves. Even so, some solar enthusiasts claim that by the turn of the century 15 percent or more of all domestic heating worldwide will come directly from the Sun.

Another true solar house—this one in Malters, Switzerland—was finished in 1975. Special attention was given to insulation and wood was chosen as the building material rather than brick or stone, which are more common there. In its first 12 months, 70 percent of total heat load was supplied by solar energy. An open fireplace in the living room supplies auxiliary heating.

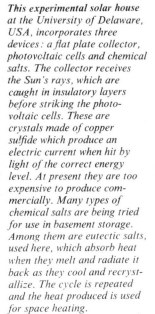

This experimental solar house at the University of Delaware, USA, incorporates three devices: a flat plate collector, photovoltaic cells and chemical salts. The collector receives the Sun's rays, which are caught in insulatory layers before striking the photovoltaic cells. These are crystals made of copper sulfide which produce an electric current when hit by light of the correct energy level. At present they are too expensive to produce commercially. Many types of chemical salts are being tried for use in basement storage. Among them are eutectic salts, used here, which absorb heat when they melt and radiate it back as they cool and recrystallize. The cycle is repeated and the heat produced is used for space heating.

POWER FROM WIND, WAVES & TIDES

Waves, wind and tides possess enormous energy, too often expressed in the destructive forces of hurricanes, typhoons *and tsunamis. If that energy could be tapped and turned to man's advantage, there would be no need to worry about* *dwindling fossil fuels. Between the dream and the reality lie complex technical, economic and environmental problems.*

Swirling around in the world's oceans is enough power to meet all foreseeable energy needs—if only it could be cheaply harnessed and brought ashore. Because of the sheer volume of water involved, the energy density of a single, slow-moving current such as the Kurile around Japan, for instance, is estimated at more than one billion kilowatts—20 times as great as present global electricity generating capacity.

The two forms of ocean power most likely to provide significant energy sources are the visible ones: waves, formed by the wind whipping large "cells" of water into continuous rotary motion, and tides—the result of the gravitational pull of the Moon and Sun—which are sometimes greatly reinforced by the wind. It is the enormous but diffuse energy of these two endless forms of movement that scientists are seeking to capture in some way that will be economically viable.

Tidal power
Tidal power turbines are driven by the oscillatory flow of coastal waters rising and falling. The natural feature best suited to this form of energy is a narrow estuary with a difference of at least 10 meters (33 feet) between high and low water. Promising regions include the Bay of Fundy in eastern Canada, the Pacific coast of Alaska, the Severn and Solway estuaries in Britain, the Barents Sea and Okhotsk Sea in the USSR, northwestern Australia, northeastern Brazil, southern Argentina, western Africa, the eastern fringe of the West Indies and western France. Fully developed, tidal power plants at favorable sites in these regions could contribute perhaps 1,750 billion kilowatt hours a year—eight times the current annual electricity consumption of the UK or France.

A fundamental difficulty with tidal energy, however, is that the action and power of tides vary greatly according to the relative positions of the Earth, Moon and Sun. Without considerable storage capacity, a tidal power plant cannot provide the kind of dependable output needed in most electricity supply systems. In addition to the cost of building turbine halls, massive civil engineering works may be needed to impound water unless natural features are exceptionally suitable, as at La Rance, Brittany, where the world's first tidal power plant opened in 1966. La Rance and the Kislaya Guba scheme on the Barents Sea (USSR), completed in 1968, generate 300 megawatts and 400 MW respectively under optimum conditions. The USSR is considering much more ambitious schemes for a 2,000 MW plant on the White Sea

and a 20,000 MW one on the Okhotsk Sea. Projects of this magnitude would have a profound environmental impact, producing changes in water temperatures, evaporation rates, salinity and even local weather. Leaving aside these considerations, the economic cost, together with the difficulty of finding suitable sites near major consumption areas, has severely restricted programs for tidal energy.

Wave and thermal potential
The energy potential of ocean waves is 10 times as great as from tides and the costs involved in harnessing it seem likely to be much lower. Waves in the Atlantic, Pacific and Indian Ocean coastal zones contain energy densities of 40–70 kW per meter of wave front. The realization that enough power could be extracted from north Atlantic waves on a 500 kilometer (300 mile) front to meet a substantial proportion of Britain's energy needs has prompted the UK to fund a large-scale research program. In economic terms, the problem is not so much the cost of trapping wave energy as the cost of bringing it ashore. The four wave power devices now at the experimental stage in Britain are all for electricity production but could be used to power offshore electrolysis of seawater, producing hydrogen gas that could then be shipped to onshore fuel cells. Tests on scale models are encouraging.

On any major scale, however, offshore wave power plants would raise formidable environmental problems, as each would have to be several kilometers long to produce 100 MW of power. If a British prototype plant is to operate in the 1990s it will have to be cleared as safe for shipping.

A less obvious form of ocean power derives from heat differentials rather than movement. In the clear waters of the tropics where light penetrates to a depth of 30 meters (98 feet) or more there are vast reserves of energy in the form of heat from the Sun. Using cold water pumped from about 250 meters (820 feet), a French team off the coast of Dakar in the 1960s was able to use the heat differential to operate special low-temperature turbines. Thermal energy extracted by evaporating a fluid such as ammonia with "hot" surface water and condensing it again with cold water in an electric power turbine can be used to produce hydrogen gas through electrolysis. There have been proposals for Ocean Thermal Energy Conversion (OTEC) plants to be built in giant offshore complexes. Energy produced in this way, however, is likely to cost 20 times as much as coal-fired electricity.

Alongside ocean power research and development there is a revival of interest in wind, one of the

The world's largest windmill is a horizontal-axis model at Tvind in Denmark, a country which has a good wind blowing 300 days of the year. Standing a colossal 52.5 m (175 ft) high it has three 27 m (90 ft) glass fiber blades weighing five tons each. It began working in May 1978 and should produce 4 million kWh a year —enough power to light 120 homes. The vertical-axis windmill (left) is the Darrieus rotor version, which was developed in Canada.

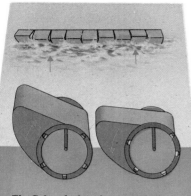

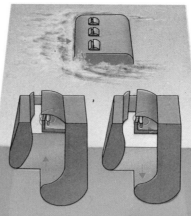
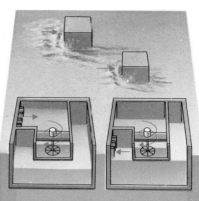

The Salter duck is the most advanced of four wave power devices being tested in Britain, the only country so far to show keen interest in this form of energy. Strings of ducks or vanes (top), each 10m (33ft) in diameter, would rock to and fro and this motion, capturing 90 percent of the power potential in waves, would pump oil under high pressure to drive generators in the central spine.

The contouring raft, proposed by Sir Christopher Cockerell, inventor of the hovercraft, envisages rafts at least 10m (33ft) long and 20–40km (66–130ft) wide, built in modular fashion, floating with their axes at right angles to the wave front. The relative movement of each raft would operate hydraulic motors or pumps situated between them. This energy would then be converted to high pressure in a fluid.

The oscillating water column, based on a Japanese navigation warning light, uses an air pressure buoy to drive an air turbine. The height of a wave can be increased inside a floating break-water in the form of an inverted box with air holes in the top. Water inside the breakwater displaces air with the rocking motion of the sea.

The Russell wave rectifier consists of a single structure containing two reservoirs, one higher than the other. As a wave flows into the device, water is allowed to enter the upper reservoir through a nonreturn valve and then allowed to fall through a water turbine into the lower reservoir, which has been emptied by the wave. A continuous energy supply to the turbine is provided by the artificial head of water.

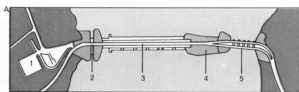
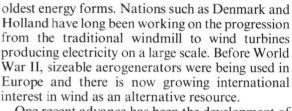

Chalibert Rock

The tidal power plant spanning La Rance estuary in north-western France (left) exploits an ideal site. With a tidal range averaging 12 m (40 ft) there is ample flow on both the ebb and flood tide to drive the turbines, and beyond the dam the estuary widens into a large basin where water can be stored at high tide for release at low tide. This goes some way toward overcoming irregularity of output. The layout (A) shows the substation (1), shipping lock (2), main dam with underwater turbines and generators (3), fixed dike (4) and movable dam containing six great sluice gates (5). As seen in the cross section of the estuary bed (B), there is a rocky base with adequate depth for the main plant and a protuberance (Chalibert Rock) that helps to minimize the structure needed to span the 750 m (2,460 ft) gap. Sited 4 km (2.5 miles) from the estuary mouth discharging into the Bay of Dinard, the dam is also well protected from wave damage.

oldest energy forms. Nations such as Denmark and Holland have long been working on the progression from the traditional windmill to wind turbines producing electricity on a large scale. Before World War II, sizeable aerogenerators were being used in Europe and there is now growing international interest in wind as an alternative resource.

One recent advance has been the development of a high-speed vertical-axis wind turbine, a concept patented by the French pioneer Georges Darrieus in the 1920s. This design, which works best in strong winds, has two major advantages: it does not have to be turned into the wind and the electrical generator can be located at ground level. Being simpler in design than the traditional horizontal-axis mill, its weight and cost are lower. Developed in Canada, vertical-axis mills provide power in remote locations such as Herschel Island in the Northwest Territories and the Magdalen Islands in Quebec Province.

Offshore Wind Energy Clusters
In supplying a national system, the governing principle is that large mills in regions of high wind speeds give the most economic power. It is for this reason that some scientists advocate Offshore Wind Energy Clusters (OWECS)—squadrons of windmills in coastal waters to receive the full force of offshore winds. The estimate is that a 100 square kilometer (39 square mile) block of sea, allowing for 400 1 MW mills, would power a city of 420,000 inhabitants. A notorious difficulty is storage of energy to cover windless days and the best solution could again be large-scale electrolysis of water.

For remote areas with no electricity and for developing nations struggling with rising fuel prices, low-cost windmills are often the most practical form of energy. Among the simplest versions is one on the Finnish Savonius pattern, built from oil drums and mounted on a vertical rotation axis. Functioning even at low wind speeds, this mill is being used for irrigation in the Caribbean.

Although wind is a capricious resource (a handicap that can be overcome only by the development of low-cost storage systems), wind power is beginning to look increasingly competitive as the price of other fuels rises. Already windmills are economical for traditional uses, and the forecast is that within the next 20 years large-scale aerogenerator systems will be producing electricity at competitive rates. In the United States, one of the countries backing development, some estimates suggest that wind power systems could meet 10 percent of national electricity needs in the year 2000.

A more traditional use of wind power is the pumping of water for irrigation or stock watering in isolated areas. This

Australian windmill has metal fan-blades on a horizontal shaft with a tail vane to keep the rotor facing the wind.

THE LIVING RESOURCE

FEEDING THE WORLD

Although sufficient food is produced to feed the world, the stark fact is that every day 10,000 people die of starvation and hunger-related disease. The problem is not shortage of food but unequal distribution. The developed countries consume far more food than the developing nations even though world population is concentrated in the latter.

In the early 1970s, world food production ran at about the equivalent of 1,250 million tons of grain a year (a person needs an average of 250 kilograms (550 pounds a year). With only a quarter of the world population, the developed countries consumed half this production total. The animals alone in developed countries eat as much grain as all the people of China and India combined. It takes about 4.5 kilograms (10 pounds) of grain to "produce" 454 grams (1 pound) of beef, though the grain is perfectly nutritious for man. Meat eating is a "custom" rather than a biological necessity.

World markets are dominated by the richer nations. In the late 1960s the food production system of the United States had built up large surpluses, reducing the price of grain on world markets. So millions of acres were taken out of production and farmers paid a government subsidy to reduce stockpiles and increase prices—at the expense of the poor. In the 1970s, production was increased in response to a publicized "world food crisis," but prices have again fallen and the cycle is being repeated. Canada has claimed that its food production could be increased by 50 percent in five years given the incentive. But who will pay?

Improving farming standards
The alternative is for the poor to produce their own food. Food produced now in the world is sufficient to feed 5.5 billion people—one and a quarter times the present population. If the standards of current "best" farming practice were applied worldwide, on only 60 percent of available cultivatable land, 30 times the present population could be fed. Improvements based on studies of soil fertility and local climates, applied through labor-intensive small farming units, seem likely to be most productive. For, almost invariably, wherever inefficient small farm units have been merged into large, mechanized units the gain has been financial. Large, mechanized farms give a better return on capital invested—but they almost always result in a reduction in the amount of food produced per hectare. Small farmers working their own plots produce the best yields per hectare.

Most developing countries rely heavily on agriculture for their export earnings—totalling between 50 and 90 percent of their foreign exchange. For many, this has meant a dependence on one or two cash crops such as bananas or rubber—whose values depend on a highly fluctuating market. In addition to uncertain prices in the past two decades (the price that growers receive for bananas has fallen by more than 25 percent) many of these products—jute and rubber particularly—have been replaced by synthetic substitutes which cut heavily into the export earnings required to purchase machines and manufactured goods—and indeed food itself. As less-developed countries have tried to expand their agricultural exports their food import bills have grown steadily, from $996 million in the mid-1950s to more than $11 billion in the mid-1970s.

There has been much criticism of the giant multinational companies and the advertising campaigns they use to glamorize products which then disrupt traditional diets and cost developing countries money they can ill afford. In some countries mothers have been convinced that imported fruits and juices are good for health and simply do not realize the vitamin C content of their own local produce. Also critics claim that multinationals have had a major influence in the decline of breastfeeding in areas where bottle feeding is neither economically nor hygienically feasible. The waste of the natural

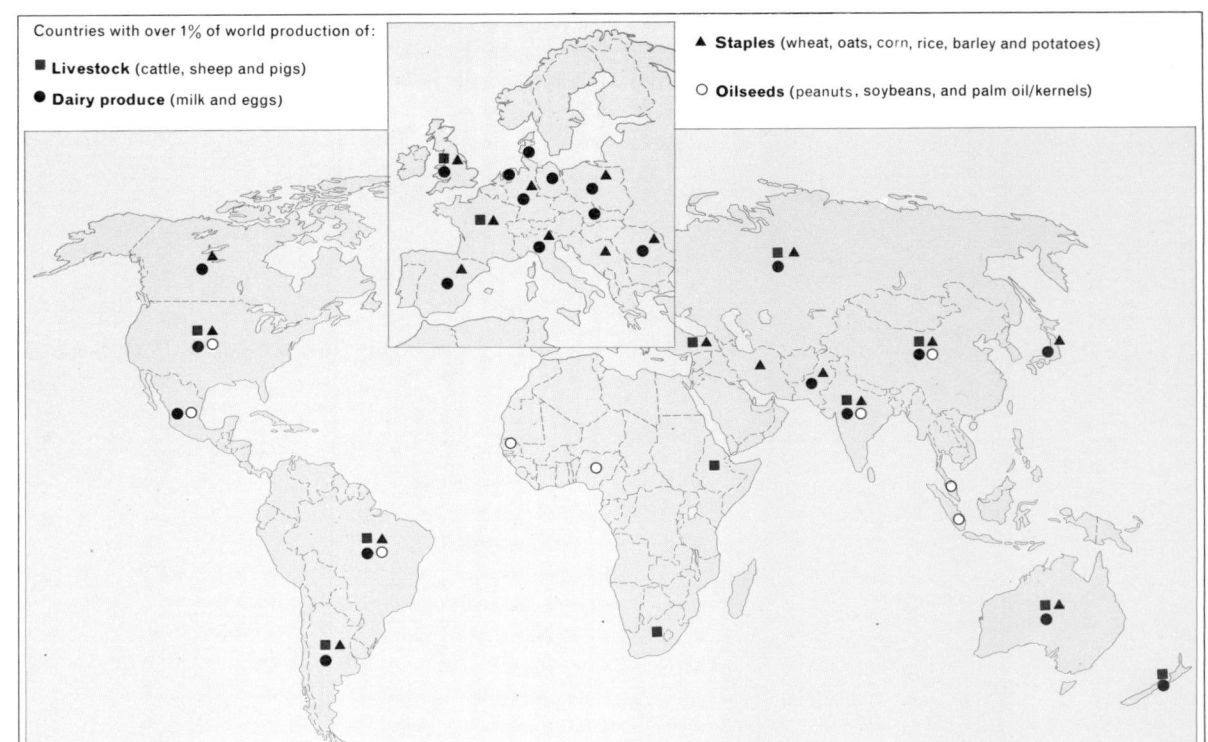

Countries with over 1% of world production of:

■ **Livestock** (cattle, sheep and pigs)

● **Dairy produce** (milk and eggs)

▲ **Staples** (wheat, oats, corn, rice, barley and potatoes)

○ **Oilseeds** (peanuts, soybeans, and palm oil/kernels)

*Although the USA produces nearly **48%** of the world's oilseed, 16% of the staples, 12% of the dairy produce and 5% of the livestock, it has only a little more than 5% of the world's* *population. In contrast India, which has 15% of the world's population, produces 7% of the world's oilseed, 7.5% of its staples, 5.7% of its dairy produce and 5.5% of its livestock.*

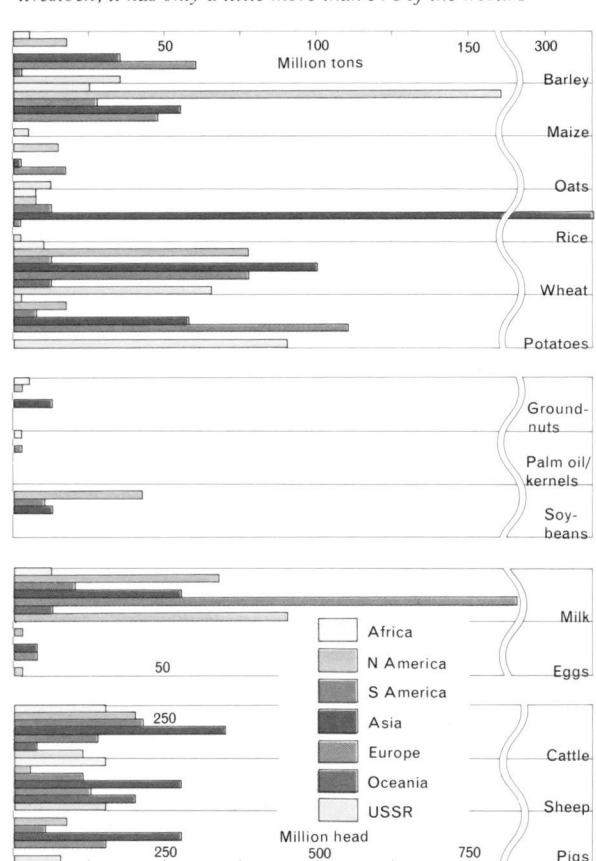

Africa
N America
S America
Asia
Europe
Oceania
USSR

Barley
Maize
Oats
Rice
Wheat
Potatoes
Ground-nuts
Palm oil/kernels
Soy-beans
Milk
Eggs
Cattle
Sheep
Pigs

Asia is the largest grain-producing continent and China the largest national producer. Cereals are an important part of the Chinese diet and emphasis is put on efficient production. China has less cropland than India and nearly twice as many people but produces 50 per cent more cereals per capita.

Cash crops—bananas, cocoa and coffee—make up 82 percent of Ecuador's exports, but crops for national consumption, such as potatoes, maize and, increasingly, wheat, are also produced.

Imports of little nutritive value—such as soft drinks— have a prestige in developing nations above that of cheaper, more nutritious local produce.

With independence in 1960 Senegal introduced a policy to boost peanut production —it is now the world's third-largest producer. Earnings are used to import rice and other food, but the world price of peanuts has plummeted and the gap between the value of Senegal's exports and the cost of imports is growing.

resource of breastmilk is dramatic. In Chile alone 95 percent of mothers breastfed 20 years ago: by 1969 only six percent did. Moreover many mothers —through hardship—dilute powdered milk so much that it is no longer nutritious. Some food is provided free or cheap to developing countries, but often on a strings-attached basis. While the public in most developed countries would unhesitatingly favor such aid as humanitarian, recent analysis shows that humanitarianism is not always the motive. Too often the aid is merely a means of keeping surplus production in the developed countries from depressing their internal markets, or is given to support a particular regime, and is independent of actual food needs. It is rarely checked to see if it suits local diets and the effects on local agricultural production are not known. There is even doubt about the effects of "emergency" food aid such as the 27,000 tons of grain donated to Guatemala after an earthquake there in 1976. Adequate supplies already existed in the country and local markets were disrupted by the aid for nearly a year after the disaster. Although a strong case can still be made for food aid on a short-term basis in genuine emergencies, close scrutiny should be made first. Ideally a shift away from export of cash crops to growing food intended for local consumption would reduce the number of cases in which food aid need be considered at all.

Miracle crops

The "green revolution" of the 1960s was initially hailed as the answer to hunger. Genetic breeding of high-yield varieties of wheat, corn and rice seemed to offer a chance for everyone to grow more on the same land, ending famine. But there were many early failures when the "miracle" crops proved unequal to local conditions. Shorter stems, bred to allow a plant to hold up a larger head of grain, proved a boon to rats; many of the early high-yield strains produced their high yields only under ideal conditions of weather, soil and so on. So the pendulum swung the other way and for a time it was fashionable to dismiss the green revolution as a terrible mistake which had encouraged peasant farmers to give up traditional methods for a system that had proved all too fallible. Now it seems that the truth lies somewhere in between. There have been, and will be, not one but many green revolutions as lessons are learned and crops further improved. Plant breeders now concentrate more on rugged dependability of a reasonable yield in all conditions than on super yields only available in perfect conditions.

Hybrid plants developed in research laboratories have a major part to play in feeding the world— but at a price. The real problems with such a change in traditional methods are now seen as social. Hybrid wheat has dramatically increased the food production of India, but only by introducing not just the seed itself but also fertilizers, pesticides, and new irrigation and harvesting methods. The result is a completely different way of life: the farmer must now grow not just to eat but to earn money to pay for his investments. Perhaps society must change if the specter of famine is to be removed; but as that change occurs as much care and attention will have to be given to social problems as to the biological puzzles of breeding better crops.

Large shiploads of cheap grain from developed nations can destroy national grain markets when small local producers cannot compete. In this way a country becomes dependent on imports which, with no guarantee of price stability when world production is low, it may not be able to afford when prices are high. The UN's World Food Program is trying to ensure a guaranteed food commitment from donating countries. The UN directs about $250 million worth of food each year to developing nations.

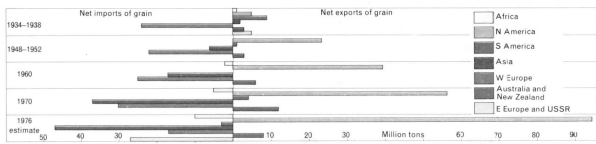

	Net imports of grain			Net exports of grain		
1934–1938						
1948–1952						
1960						
1970						
1976 estimate	50 40 30	10	20 30	Million tons	60 70	80 90

- Africa
- N America
- S America
- Asia
- W Europe
- Australia and New Zealand
- E Europe and USSR

North American dominance as a world grain supplier began in the 1940s and exports grew until, in the 1970s, they had nearly doubled. In Asia, Africa and Latin America grain production has grown steadily, though in many cases failing to keep pace with population increase. Japan is by far the largest grain importer, buying more than any other two nations combined.

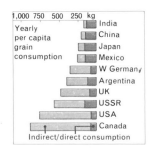

1,000 750 500 250 kg	
Yearly per capita grain consumption	India
	China
	Japan
	Mexico
	W Germany
	Argentina
	UK
	USSR
	USA
	Canada
Indirect/direct consumption	

Animals reared for meat in developed countries eat a quarter of all the world's grain.

ENERGY & FOOD PRODUCTION

Solar energy is the basic source of energy for food production. Energy from the Sun's rays is fixed by green plants through the process of photosynthesis, and this energy is then utilized by the plants for growth.

During the twentieth century increasing amounts of nonsolar energy have been used in the course of improving plant yields per hectare and in mechanizing the processes of food production. This nonsolar energy (that is, energy not directly derived from the Sun) is known as "support energy," and the greatest use of support energy on farms is in the form of fertilizers, and fuel for tractors and other agricultural machinery.

Fertilizers

For many centuries crops have been fertilized with organic matter gathered on or near farms. In the nineteenth century this organic matter was supplemented by materials such as Chilean nitrates and German potassium salts which were mined and then transported over long distances. As time went by a fertilizer industry gradually grew up, fostered by the growth of the general chemical industry. The specific elements required for plant growth were supplied to farmers by the fertilizer industry in an increasingly pure form as inorganic salts. Of these elements nitrogen, phosphorus and potassium (NPK) are applied in the greatest amounts. Today, phosphatic and potassic fertilizers are derived from mined ores and, although energy is required to mine and treat these ores, the energy cost is low compared with that of nitrogenous fertilizers.

Nitrogen is a major constituent of protein and is essential for plant and animal growth. Dry air consists of about 79 percent nitrogen, but this nitrogen gas has to be "fixed" or combined with

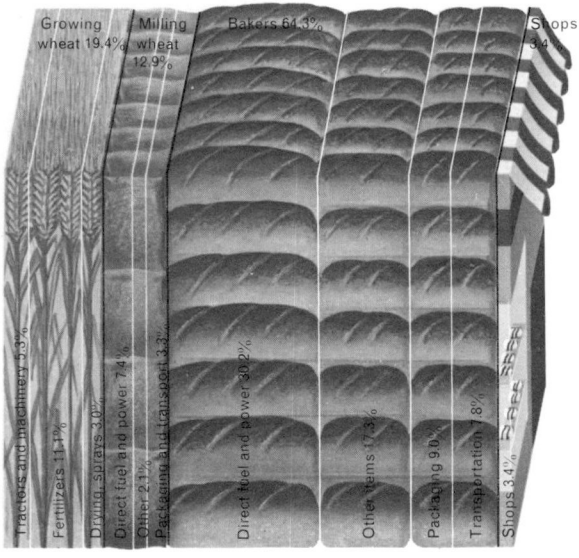

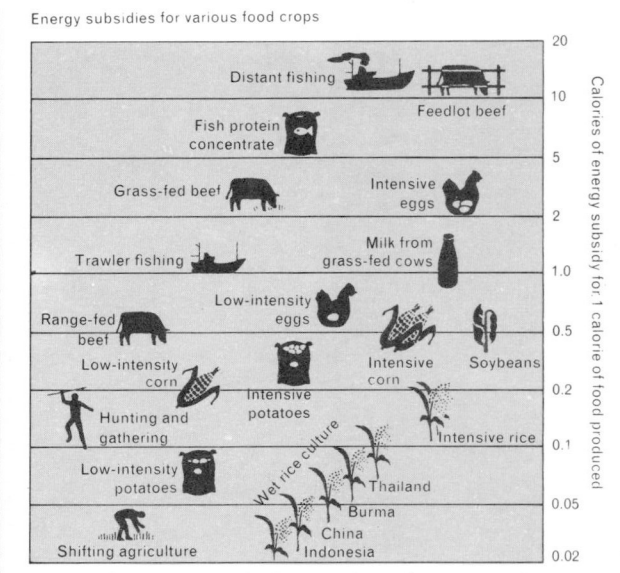

Energy subsidies for various food crops

Distant fishing · Feedlot beef
Fish protein concentrate
Grass-fed beef · Intensive eggs
Trawler fishing · Milk from grass-fed cows
Range-fed beef · Low-intensity eggs
Low-intensity corn · Intensive corn · Soybeans
Hunting and gathering · Intensive potatoes · Intensive rice
Low-intensity potatoes · Wet rice culture · Thailand
Shifting agriculture · Burma · China · Indonesia

Calories of energy subsidy for 1 calorie of food produced

The energy subsidy for food production—the amount of energy support input per unit of food output—varies enormously. Shifting agriculture, for instance, is a very low energy support system, whereas deep-sea fishing utilizes 10 to 20 times the energy value of the food produced.

Energy required to produce 1 kg white loaf: 20.7 MJ (0.48 kg oil equivalent)

Growing wheat 19.4% | Milling wheat 12.9% | Bakers 54.4% | Shops 3%

Tractors and machinery | Fertilizers | Direct fuel and power | Other | Packaging and transport | Direct fuel and power | Other items | Packaging | Transportation | Shops

Indian women farming the land with primitive hand tools (above) and Solomon Islanders harvesting by means of relatively sophisticated machinery (right) illustrate a labor-intensive system on the one hand and more energy-intensive agriculture on the other. Some experts believe that less-developed countries are best helped if they are supplied with simple mechanical devices that ease the burden of farm laborers.

A breakdown of energy inputs to a 1 kg (2.2 lb) white, sliced and wrapped loaf shows some surprising hidden costs. Just under 20 percent of energy consumed is in growing the wheat; all but three percent of the rest is in processing, packaging and transport.

other elements before it can be utilized by plants and animals. This fixing process demands energy. In biological systems where, for example, fixation is carried out by bacteria in the nodules of legumes, the products of photosynthesis provide the requisite energy. In the manufacture of nitrogenous fertilizers the energy is usually provided by fossil fuels, particularly petroleum and natural gas.

It can be safely assumed that whenever inorganic fertilizer is applied to a crop a certain amount of support energy must have been used to produce that crop. Since the 1950s, rapidly increasing quantities of inorganic fertilizer, and thus of support energy, have been used in crop production in various parts of the world. Nitrogen fertilization particularly has been used in conjunction with plant breeding, to produce greatly increased yields per unit of land.

In parallel with the change in fertilizer practice, there has been a change in working methods on farms. Tractors have replaced horses and men as the power units and this too has meant a transfer from dependence on plants, and made available as plant foods for animals and men, to dependence on petroleum products to drive the tractors and other machines.

Dependence of support energy

Agricultural systems vary greatly throughout the world, but they can be grouped according to their dependence on inorganic fertilizers and mechanization. This in turn yields a classification in terms of the system's dependence on support energy. Group I systems have a low dependence on support energy. Little or no inorganic fertilizer is used and there is little mechanization. An example is a traditional double cropping system practiced in China in the late 1930s. Humans and animals provided the labor and animal excreta was used for fertilizer. The energy output in the form of rice and beans has been calculated at 41 times the energy input.

Group II systems use little inorganic fertilizer but they are highly mechanized. They have a medium dependence on support energy. Wheat cropping and livestock grazing in Australia are examples. These enterprises are mechanized but soil fertility is maintained by the use of legumes to fix nitrogen, together with an extensive use of superphosphate fertilizer. From 1965 to 1969 direct fuel use on farms represented 63 percent and fertilizer 22 percent of all energy inputs to Australian agriculture. The total energy output from all farms of crop and livestock production (including those employing the most intensive systems) was about three times the energy input.

Group III systems also have a medium dependence on support energy. They are highly dependent on inorganic fertilizer but mechanization is low. In Mexico dwarf wheats were developed to give high yields under irrigation when high levels of NPK fertilizer were applied. The total energy input for a crop of this wheat would depend on the system of cultivation used. On some farms mules, horses and oxen still provide the draft power and thus fuel requirements for machinery are low. Increasingly, however, oil-powered tractors are being used, thus producing a shift toward a Group IV type system. Calculations in 1975 for sugarcane production in more humid climates, using high levels of fertilizer, suggest an energy output of nearly five and one-half times the energy input when cultivation is performed by hand and animal power, and nearly two and three-quarter times the input when tractors are employed.

Finally, Group IV is made up of those systems that use large amounts of inorganic fertilizer together with a high degree of mechanization. This results in high dependence on support energy, as seen, for example, in England and Wales. From 1970 to 1971 heavy use of nitrogenous fertilizer and highly mechanized production gave an energy output put in cereal production of almost twice the energy input, while for "mainly dairy" farms the energy output was slightly more than half the input.

These groupings refer primarily to plant production. If the plants are then consumed by animals before human food is produced, further support energy will probably be used depending on how extensive (ranching, for example) or intensive (feedlot cattle, for example) the system is. In any event, part of the energy content of the plants will be used up in the biological processes of the animal, so that the food energy yield in terms of meat, or other products, will be less than if the plants were consumed directly as food.

This picture is further complicated as food production becomes increasingly specialized or dependent on changing or modifying the environment. Purchased feed used in intensive pig, poultry and dairy production represents a very high support energy cost because of the energy that is used in processing, compounding and transporting the feed, in addition to producing the raw materials for it. Energy expended in pumping water for irrigation or in producing heat to warm greenhouses can represent a use of support energy that is far in excess of the energy content of food produced. One estimate for the energy output of winter lettuce produced in a heated greenhouse in the UK is about 0.002 times the energy input.

The way to economy

In recent years there has been much concern expressed about the amount of support energy used on farms in food production, and methods are now being sought which will require less support energy per unit of food produced. For instance, systems of cultivation are being developed which will require fewer transits of a tractor across a field for the production of a crop at a noticeable saving in fuel. And more attention is now being given to enriching the soil with nitrogen by growing legumes rather than relying on nitrogenous fertilizers.

In the food production system, however, the greatest use of support energy is to be found not on farms but in the food processing industry and in the commercial and home treatment of food. Thus if the energy cost of food is to be substantially reduced many changes will be needed throughout the whole food system right from the farmer to the consumer at the end of the line.

China has developed one of the most efficient systems in the world for utilizing human and animal waste and crop residues. Such a system produces high crop yields and involves an intensive use of human labor (left). China's consumption of inorganic fertilizers, however, has increased since 1950, as shown in the diagram (above). This reflects a desire to maintain or increase crop production while releasing some rural labor for industry. It is a trend which follows that already well established in, for instance, Western Europe and North America.

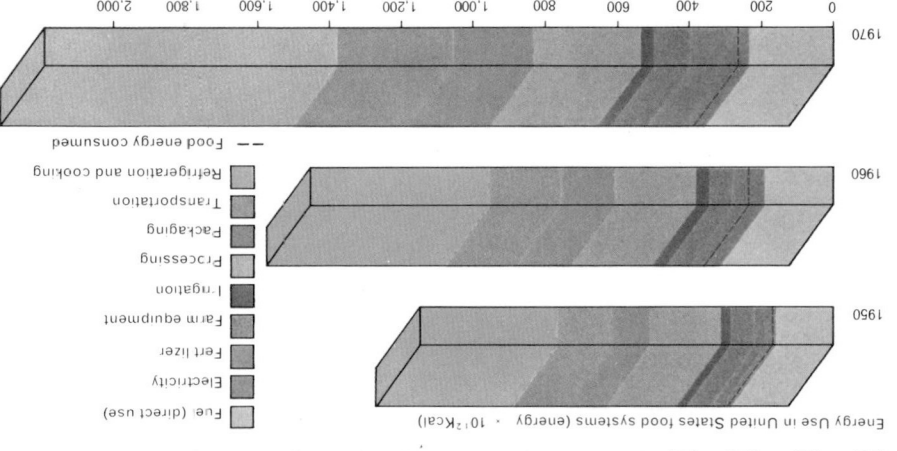

Energy Use in United States food systems (energy) · 10^12 Kcal — 1950, 1960, 1970. Fuel (direct use), Electricity, Fertilizer, Farm equipment, Irrigation, Processing, Packaging, Transportation, Refrigeration and cooking. -- Food energy consumed

A breakdown of energy inputs to US food production reveals that the USA is a good example of a system which uses a high level of support energy, not only in primary food production but also in the processing and packaging of food, compared with food consumed.

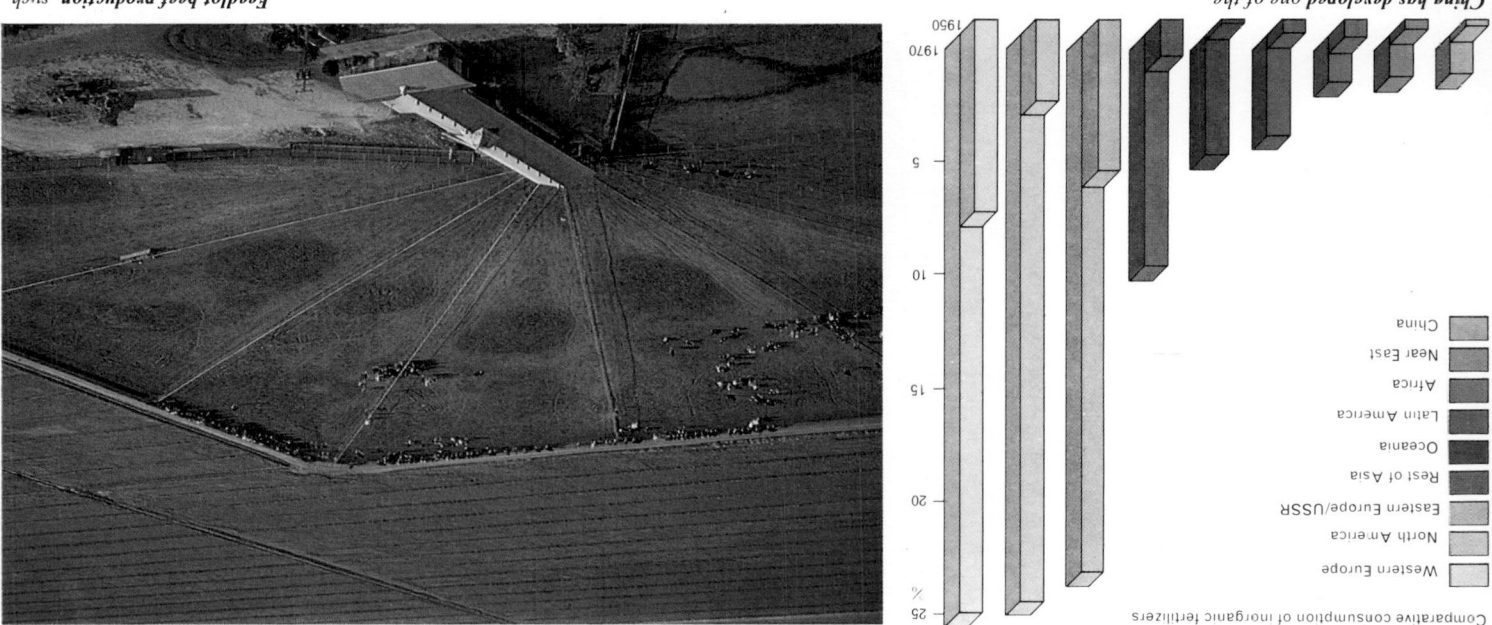

Comparative consumption of inorganic fertilizers — Western Europe, North America, Eastern Europe/USSR, Rest of Asia, Oceania, Latin America, Africa, Near East, China.

Feedlot beef production, such as that practiced in the USA, is a system that requires a high energy subsidy. Energy is needed to grow, process, transport and handle the grain and other feedstuffs; to transport the cattle and to dispose of waste materials.

CLIMATE & MAN

Features of the Earth's climate are determined by the interaction of atmosphere and oceans which, powered by the Sun, act like a vast heat engine. The Sun's heating is greater at the Earth's surface than in the upper atmosphere, setting up local convection cells, and more effective at the equator than at the poles, driving immense, global circulatory systems. The most important of these are the circumpolar vortices. Polar air forms a relatively thin, dense layer close to the surface and at a height of five kilometers (three miles) pressures are lower over the poles than over tropical regions. The polar "lows" suck in tropical air, which is deflected by the Earth's rotation to flow in a westerly direction around the Earth at middle latitudes. These broad rivers of air meander far to the north and south as they girdle the Earth and are responsible for the wet, changeable weather that characterizes the temperate zones of both hemispheres. Equatorward of the circumpolar vortices, between 20 and 30 degrees latitude, lie two zones of high surface pressure and dry, descending air, where most of the world's great deserts are found. The equatorial region itself is a zone where moist, rising air gives rise to more cloudy, rainy climates.

The Earth's broadly latitudinal climatic belts are modified by geographical features such as mountains and the distribution of land and sea to give rise to the innumerable local climates and microclimates that determine the kinds of crops man grows for food and the kind of life he leads.

Climatic change

Ever since the Earth was formed approximately 4,600 million years ago, the climate has been changing. Fifty million years ago the Earth enjoyed a warm, equable climate, while only 18,000 years ago it was in the grip of a full ice age with average temperatures perhaps 5°C (9°F) below those of today. Between 8,000 and 4,000 years ago temperatures seem to have been about 1°C above their

Gases and dust particles, released into the atmosphere by man's industrial activities, are known to affect local weather. Dust-sized particles may increase local rainfall, but gases like carbon dioxide and chlorofluoromethanes absorb long-wavelength radiation emitted by the Earth and this could result in an increase in temperature on a global scale. The precise extent

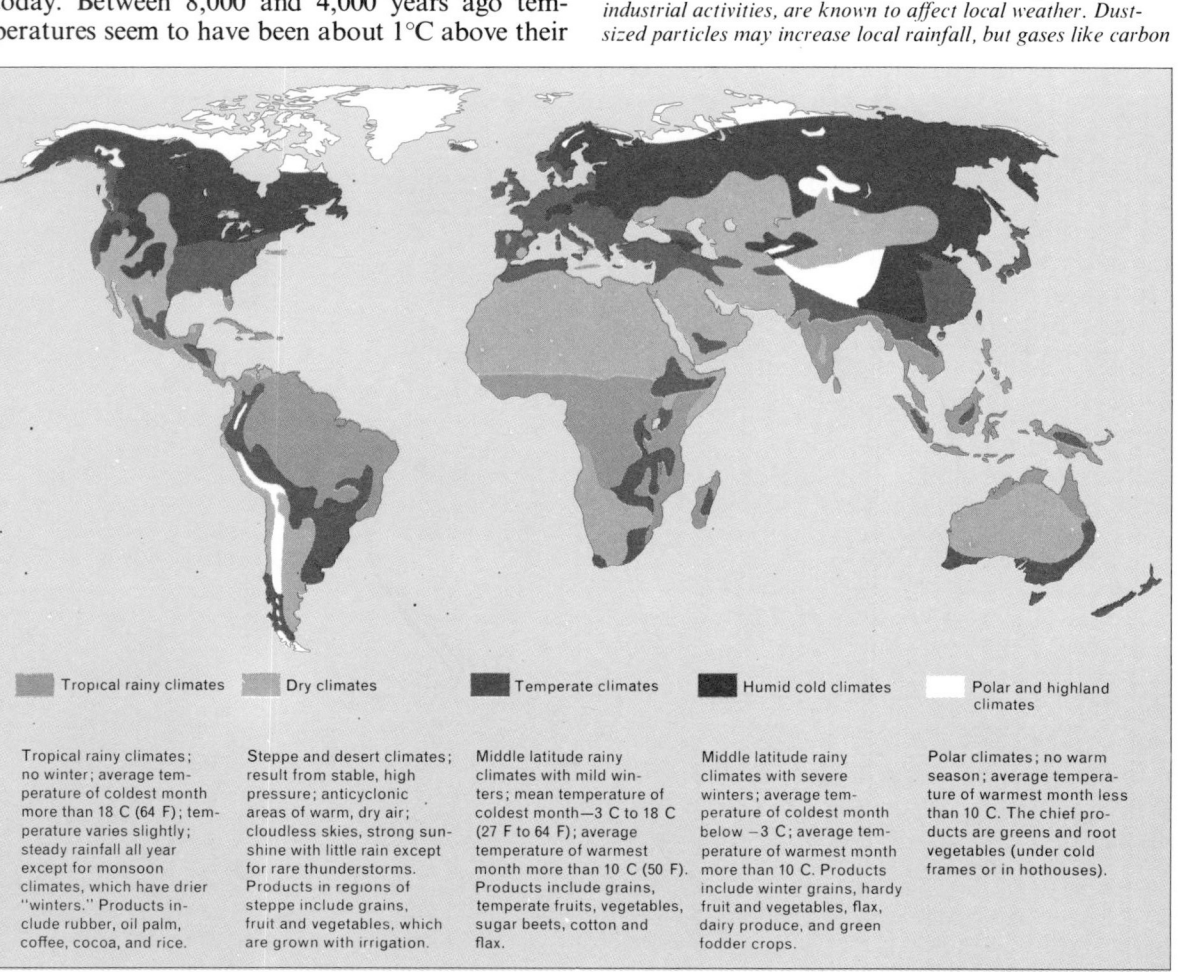

Tropical rainy climates | Dry climates | Temperate climates | Humid cold climates | Polar and highland climates

Tropical rainy climates; no winter; average temperature of coldest month more than 18 C (64 F); temperature varies slightly; steady rainfall all year except for monsoon climates, which have drier "winters." Products include rubber, oil palm, coffee, cocoa, and rice.

Steppe and desert climates; result from stable, high pressure; anticyclonic areas of warm, dry air; cloudless skies, strong sunshine with little rain except for rare thunderstorms. Products in regions of steppe include grains, fruit and vegetables, which are grown with irrigation.

Middle latitude rainy climates with mild winters; mean temperature of coldest month—3 C to 18 C (27 F to 64 F); average temperature of warmest month more than 10 C (50 F). Products include grains, temperate fruits, vegetables, sugar beets, cotton and flax.

Middle latitude rainy climates with severe winters; average temperature of coldest month below –3 C; average temperature of warmest month more than 10 C. Products include winter grains, hardy fruit and vegetables, flax, dairy produce, and green fodder crops.

Polar climates; no warm season; average temperature of warmest month less than 10 C. The chief products are greens and root vegetables (under cold frames or in hothouses).

The range of climates on Earth results from the interaction of the broad features of atmospheric circulation with local geography. At the beginning of the 20th century, a German meteorologist and climatologist, Wladimir Köppen, evolved a classification of climates that is still widely used today. Köppen devoted much of his life to studying climate, and he modified his system many times. He divided the world into five major climatic zones: equatorial and tropical rainy climates; dry climates; temperate climates of the broad-leaf forest zone; humid, cold climates; and polar and highland (dissimilar but with common features) climates. The climates are defined in terms of temperature and rainfall. (There are additional symbols for times of the year in which most rain falls and other climatic qualities that affect vegetation growth.) A climatic classification of this kind reflects the close link between vegetation and climate. The rain forests of South America, Africa and the Far East correspond to the regions of tropical rainy climates. Similarly, the world's major deserts straddle the subtropical latitudes, as do Köppen's dry climate zones. Humid, cold climates, with their typical vast areas of coniferous forest, are found mainly in the Northern Hemisphere, where the continental landmasses provide suitable conditions.

The principle of cloud-seeding has been applied in an attempt to reduce the destruction caused by tropical cyclones. The storm clouds are seeded with silver iodide smoke on the outer edge of the wall of the "eye," building clouds and releasing heat in the region of high winds, thus weakening them.

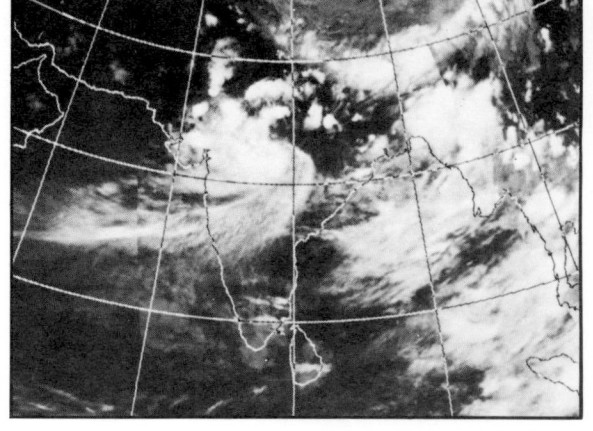

The monsoon helps to support the world's largest populations— in India and China. It results from the summer heating of the great Asian landmass which distorts the global pattern of air circulation so that moist trade winds sweep over Southeast Asia from the Indian Ocean, bringing vital rain to the region.

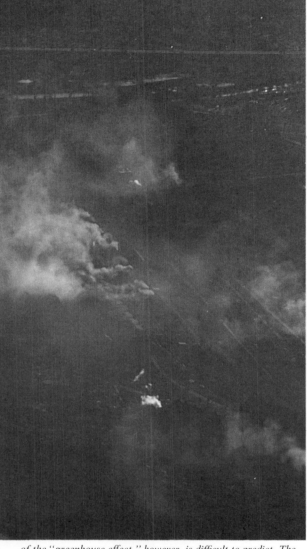

Droughts were an alarming feature of the Earth's climate in the early 1970s. *In several countries along the southern fringe of the Sahara Desert, an area of scanty rainfall and subsistence agriculture, there was widespread crop failure and herdsmen lost more than half their animals.*

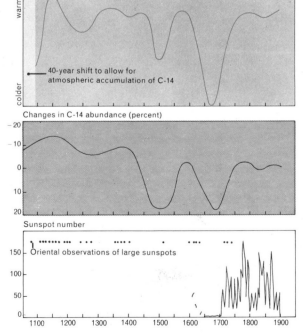

Great volcanic explosions, such as Tambora, Sumbawa, in 1816 and Krakatoa in 1883, seem to affect the climate. Following such eruptions, large quantities of dust remain in the upper atmosphere for months or years. The dust particles reflect solar radiation away from the Earth, producing a cooling effect.

of the "greenhouse effect," however, is difficult to predict. The warming of the atmosphere could result in increased cloudiness which would keep further warming in check.

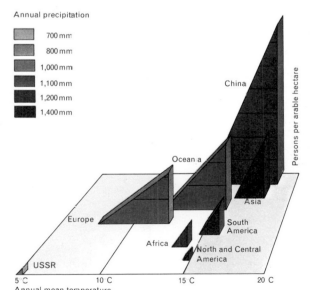

Westerly wind belt
■ normal range
■ possible variability

Northern penetration of monsoon rains
— average
— possible variation

Annual precipitation
700 mm
800 mm
1,000 mm
1,100 mm
1,200 mm
1,400 mm

China
Oceania
Asia
Europe
South America
Africa
North and Central America
USSR

Persons per arable hectare

5 C   10 C   15 C   20 C
Annual mean temperature

A University of Wisconsin study in the early 1970s showed how even a small climatic change could have enormous impact. A dramatic example is China, which currently supports more than seven people per hectare (17 per acre) of arable land. A drop in temperature of only 1°C could reduce this number to four.

Winter severity in western Europe
warmer
colder
← 40-year shift to allow for atmospheric accumulation of C-14

Changes in C-14 abundance (percent)
−20
−10
0
10
20

Sunspot number
150
100
50
0
Oriental observations of large sunspots

1100   1200   1300   1400   1500   1600   1700   1800   1900

The apparent increased variability of climate in the Northern Hemisphere and variations in the northern limit of summer monsoon rainfall could result in decreased yields in major food-producing areas.

Climatic changes over the last 1,000 years correlate with variations in the Sun's activity. The degree of solar activity is reflected by the amount of carbon-14 in the atmosphere, inferred from tree-ring measurements; more C-14 is produced when the Sun is quiet. The Sun was quietest in the late 17th century—the peak of the Little Ice Age.

present levels, while during the coldest period of the Little Ice Age, in the late seventeenth century, temperatures may have been 0.5°C lower than today.

There is little doubt that natural fluctuations of this kind will continue in the future, and it is therefore important to understand why they occur. One of the most significant scientific achievements of recent years has been a breakthrough in our understanding of ice ages. Analyses of climate records contained in layers of shells on the ocean floor have supported the suggestion, made by the Yugoslav geophysicist Milutin Milankovich in the 1930s, that the orbital motions of the Earth have been the principal factors responsible for the repeated comings and goings of the ice. The precession of the Earth's axis (which takes about 26,000 years), changes in the tilt of the axis to the orbital plane (about 40,000 years) and variations in the Earth's orbit (90,000–100,000 years) all produce changes in the intensity of seasonal solar heating at different latitudes. Although small, these changes appear to be critical for the growth or decay of ice sheets.

The Milankovich effect is only one of the external factors that may influence the Earth's climate. The Sun itself may vary in output over the centuries; a solar "flicker" between 1645 and 1715 seems to have been one reason why these years were among the coldest of the Little Ice Age.

As far as current climatic changes are concerned, the Milankovich effect predicts a long-term cooling trend, but it will be many thousands of years before another ice age is likely. In the short term, the Northern Hemisphere has cooled about 0.2°C from a peak of warmth reached in the 1940s. Whatever natural fluctuations occur, however, the future course of the Earth's climate may well depend on man's own activities. Heat from houses, factories and power plants, for instance, makes urban areas warmer than the surrounding countryside. By the next century, direct thermal pollution could raise world temperatures by several degrees. Clearance of land for agriculture and overgrazing of marginal land both tend to increase the surface reflectivity and, by reducing the proportion of solar energy absorbed, may cause decreases in local temperature and rainfall. The most important way in which man's activities are affecting the global climate is by the addition of carbon dioxide to the atmosphere, where it is already about 14 percent above its preindustrial level. Carbon dioxide, released primarily by the burning of fossil fuels, absorbs much of the long-wavelength radiation emitted by the Earth's surface, keeping the lower atmosphere warmer than it would otherwise be. According to one calculation, this "greenhouse effect" could raise global temperatures by 1.5°C to 3°C by the year 2050.

Effects on agriculture

Two developments over the last decade have made the world's agriculture increasingly vulnerable to changes in climate. The failure of agricultural production in many countries to keep pace with expanding populations has led to an increasing dependence on North American grain exports; at the same time, world grain reserves have fallen steadily, standing in 1976 at only 31 days' supply.

If the cooling trend continues, a shorter growing season will result, adversely affecting wheat production in Canada, the USSR and other countries in high northern latitudes. The current trend toward greater climatic variability in the zone of the westerly wind belt, if it continues, will mean lower grain yields in lower latitudes—the USA, Europe and southern USSR—which will make grain-importing countries even more dependent on the grain surplus of the United States. At the same time, a reduction in the northward penetration of summer monsoon rainfall in Asia and Africa could bring famine to the vast populations dependent on the rains for irrigation. The implications for world food production in the next decades need to be considered by all concerned with planning for the future.

About 97 percent of the world's water is contained in the major oceans. Almost three-quarters of the rest, which represents the planet's fresh water resource, is locked up in the ice sheets of Antarctica, Greenland and the Arctic Ocean. It is on the tiny fraction remaining in the rivers and lakes of the continents that the human race depends for almost all its water needs.

Each year about 420,000 cubic kilometers (9.26 × 10^{16} gallons) of water is evaporated from the Earth, mostly from the oceans, and approximately the same amount falls back on the surface. This hydrological cycle is powered by solar radiation and as this varies little from year to year so the total volume of water involved in the cycle is more or less constant.

The importance of runoff

For man the most important part of the hydrological cycle is the evapotranspiration and precipitation of water on the continental masses. This varies greatly from region to region. In planning water resources one of the most important variables is the total amount of runoff in a given area (runoff being defined as precipitation minus evapotranspiration). A world map of runoff reveals maximum values occurring over the northern parts of South America, the equatorial regions of west and central Africa and over most of southeastern Asia. In contrast extensive belts of low runoff are found in southwest North America, and in an area stretching from northern Africa through the Middle East and into central Asia.

Generally it is in the areas of high runoff that the world's great rivers are found. The exception is southeastern Asia, where, though runoff totals are large, the absence of extensive land areas means that no major river system has a chance to be formed. At the opposite extreme, throughout the vast area of the Sahara Desert the only major river system is the Nile and it owes its existence to the monsoon rainfall of Ethiopia and runoff from the highlands of eastern Africa.

The amount of water needed to sustain the essen-

The valley of the Indus River in Pakistan is one of the world's largest irrigation systems. Begun in 1860 it now comprises a network of 60,000 km (37,000 miles) of canals covering more than 10 million hectares (25 million acres). The sheer scale of man's works has unwittingly added a new dimension to the hydrological cycle. The Indus Valley system has grown above an enormous natural underground reservoir extending to a depth of 350 m (1,148 ft). Water diverted from rivers into the canals seeped into the reservoir, raising the water table to create a vast and unexpected new water store. The system has brought an extra four million hectares (10 million acres) under cultivation.

Irrigation system of the Indus River basin

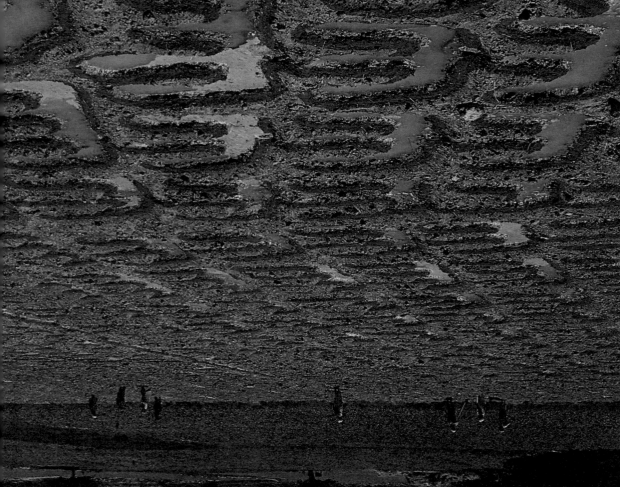

The need to boost food production in a country where a tenth of the land is desert has made China the most highly irrigated nation on Earth. More than 84 million hectares (207 million acres) are cultivated in this way. Shrubs and trees are planted to stabilize the desert before channels are dug and water piped in. Communes often make their own pipes from clay or cement.

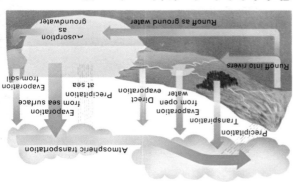
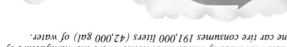

The hydrological cycle, which keeps the world's water resources in a constant state of dynamic change, is the largest single user of the energy that reaches the Earth from the Sun.

Traditional water mazes irrigate rice and potatoes in Afghanistan, which relies on agriculture for most of its export income.

The simple needs of Tuareg tribesmen at a well in Niger contrasts with those of industrial societies where the manufacture of one car tire consumes 191,000 liters (42,000 gal) of water.

CONNECTIONS

Small windmills which raise water from the Omo River in Ethiopia illustrate how technology can profoundly affect traditional living patterns. The local people were nomadic cattle herders, but their movements were restricted by changing political boundaries and the tsetse fly. The windmills, introduced by the American Mission in the early 1970s, enabled the people to settle by the river and grow irrigated crops all the year round.

At a Zambian copper plant molten metal cast automatically in molds located round the rim of a large wheel is cooled by a constant fine spray of water. Cooling processes take most water used by industry, power plants being the largest consumers.

The industrial use of water at its simplest may involve no more than directing a high-pressure jet to break down soft rock covering rich tin deposits on Thailand's Phuket Island.

tial bodily functions in man is surprisingly small, amounting to about two liters (four pints) per day, though this varies with climate. Besides these minimum physiological requirements, however, man in modern society has developed many extra water needs as living standards have risen. Domestic consumption began to surge from the middle of the nineteenth century with the advent first of water sewage systems and later of piped household supplies. Since World War II the use of washing machines has again rapidly increased demand for water (an automatic washing machine uses up to 180 liters/40 gallons for a single wash).

In the United States domestic water consumption averages about 454.6 liters (100 gallons) per person per day. About 41 percent of this is used for toilet flushing and 37 percent for washing and bathing. In drier regions lawn watering is also a significant factor. Water consumption in Britain is lower, at around 195 liters (43 gallons) a day, but this is expected to increase to about 300 liters (66 gallons) by the end of the century. The industrial use of water falls into three main categories: water for cooling, water for processing and water to supply the needs of employees. In the United States about 45 percent of all water used goes for cooling in power plants.

In many of the developed countries of the world water supply problems revolve round regional deficiencies in urban areas rather than absolute shortages. In many cases this has led to large-scale schemes for the transfer of water from one area to another. One of the biggest is the California State Water Project, devised to transport water surpluses by aqueducts from the northern part of the state to the major urban complexes around Los Angeles. En route a large proportion of the water will be used for irrigating the fertile soils of the Central Valley. When fully commissioned in the mid-1980s the California aqueduct is expected to transport 4,936 million cubic meters (1,085 billion gallons) of water each year.

In Britain severe water shortages seem likely to develop in the Midlands and the London area

before the end of the century. There are plans to transfer water to these areas from Wales and northern England by means of a complex distribution system.

Dams and reservoirs

Since the beginning of the nineteenth century the most common method of water conservation has been the construction of dams in upland areas behind which flood waters could be impounded, with pipelines to transport the water to urban regions. Recently, this direct supply system has tended to be replaced by the practice of river regulation, in which the water is released from the dam into the river and then abstracted where needed.

Throughout the world dam construction accelerated rapidly after World War II to a peak during the late 1960s. Some of these dams have produced serious environmental problems, while many have failed to yield the results that were hoped for, and the growth of dam building has diminished.

Countries in the sub-tropical arid zone, with limited natural supplies of fresh water, must turn to new methods of increasing water resources as their populations grow. In the Middle East the state of Kuwait is almost completely dependent on desalination for water supplies, while Saudi Arabia plans a series of desalination plants on the Red Sea and Gulf coasts producing more than 1.2 billion liters (264 million gallons) of fresh water a day. Costs are high, however, amounting in 1975 to about $6 for each 4,546 liters (1,000 gallons).

Irrigation

Of the water tapped by man, more is used for irrigation than for any other purpose. Six countries account for over 70 percent of all the irrigated land in the world: China, India, the USA, Pakistan, the USSR and Iran. China, with about 84 million hectares (208 million acres), has more than 37 percent of the world's irrigated land.

Traditional irrigation techniques usually involve either the basin method, in which a low bank is built around a field to form a pond with the water

gradually sinking into the soil, or the furrow method, where water is led along trenches dug between the growing crops. One problem with such methods is that much of the water evaporates, leaving little for downstream users. A number of new irrigation techniques have been devised to make more efficient use of available supplies. Among these are sprinklers and drip feed systems.

Alternative sources

A number of optimistic forecasts have been made about the feasibility of towing icebergs from the Antarctic to the coastal deserts of Australia, southern Africa and South America, but the technical problems, including the possibility of the ice breaking up during the tow, the rate of melt, and cost, remain to be quantified. Until a pilot project is successfully carried out this method cannot be considered as a viable solution to water shortages.

Cloud seeding has been used for some years as a means of increasing rainfall in arid areas. In some cases the injection of crystals of silver iodide into cloud formations has increased local precipitation by up to 10 percent. However, such techniques cannot be used to produce rain from a cloudless sky and their value to the really arid zones of the world is therefore limited.

In future it seems likely that man will have to rely on the more efficient use of conventional water supplies, with recycling becoming increasingly important. For this reason the problems of pollution will be a major preoccupation. Most large urban areas in the developed countries now have efficient sewage treatment plants to recycle domestic waste water, but these are not able to cope with pollutants from industrial processes. In some cases, such as the Rhine in Europe and the Ohio River in the United States, industrial pollution has reached critical levels.

If it does not prove possible to prevent the entry of toxic materials into water bodies reuse will involve the construction of very expensive treatment systems with a consequent rise in the cost of this most basic of man's resources.

97

THE LIVING RESOURCE
LAND & THE FARMER

Even with the potential for novel sources of food, such as microbial protein or an extended reliance on the oceans for meeting our dietary needs, farming the land is certain to remain both our major source of food and the principal means of employment for a majority of the world's population in the foreseeable future.

A changing relationship
While the actual number of those remaining on the land continues to be high, the changing methods of agriculture have drastically altered the traditional relationship between the farmer and the land. This changed scene has perhaps been most obvious in the developed countries. The increased involvement of large corporations in the production of grains, fruits and vegetables has resulted in larger concentrations of land in fewer hands, in the use of bulkier and more complicated farm machinery and in planting to a strict timetable with assured standards of quality. Farming in the developed countries has been backed by intensive scientific research and extensive government policies in recognition of that sector's importance to the economy.

In the less-developed countries the changes have not been as comprehensive because of the number of farmers involved. But increasingly the changes being experienced are even more dramatic because of their comparative suddenness. With the onset of the "green revolution" in the 1960s and its requirements for a carefully controlled pattern of watering, weeding and so on, the farmer's job has become more and more that of the businessman. The need to enter the market, both to purchase fertilizers, pesticides and other inputs, as well as to sell surplus produce, has reinforced this change in roles—a change that requires different skills from those traditionally associated with farming.

The farmer and the green revolution
Although the green revolution has in some regions resulted in significant increases in food production (notably in India), not all farmers have had equal access to the inputs and services needed to reap the rewards offered by this new technology. The same is true of agencies offering credit facilities and extension services which, often overburdened and understaffed, look to the larger landowners as offering the best means of spreading new technologies over the widest area and as being the most reliable credit risk. This has in many instances widened the gap between rich and poor. With the higher profits to be made from increased production, landlords and wealthier farmers have used their privileged positions to enlarge and consolidate their holdings. The introduction of new, high-yield varieties of seed has been reflected in the higher rents now charged to tenant farmers, with payments of well over half the crop going to the city-dwelling absentee landlords.

It has already been seen that larger holdings do not necessarily mean larger yields and, because of the profits to be made, the new pattern often favors the growing of crops for export. This changing relationship between the farmer and the land bodes ill for the need to feed a growing local population from local resources.

Risks and rewards of innovation
The failure of many of the world's poor farmers to adopt new agricultural technologies and to acquire modern farming skills has sometimes been attributed to laziness or stupidity. But for most of the world's farmers growing food is a matter of survival. A successful year for the farmer is measured by his ability to feed the family and to pay off his debts, which will allow him to keep his land for another year. For such a farmer, innovation is not simply a matter of education. Ironically it often happens that a farmer who is aware of modern inputs dare not innovate because of the risk to his subsistence. He may have to settle for traditional

Plowing in Tigre Province, Ethiopia, is done by ox-drawn plows. Seed is sown by hand and manure is used for fuel instead of fertilizer. Said to be one of the 10 poorest countries in the world, Ethiopia's potentially fertile land remains therefore largely unexploited and, as a result, 45 percent of the population exists at subsistence level.

Contour cultivation in the state of Paraná, Brazil, helps to counteract soil erosion. Paraná is the country's principal coffee producing area. Government policies of land reform have encouraged the breakup of the latifundia (large estates) in order to create a more balanced pattern of land ownership.

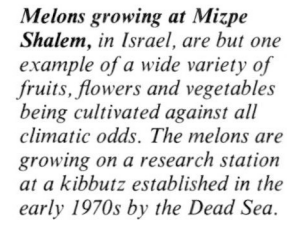

Terraced wheatfields in Kehu Lungpa Valley, Nepal, are essential where 75 percent of the land is mountainous, 30 percent is forested and most people rely on agriculture.

A Chinese experimental farm in Tanzania is part of a system of cooperative village communities under the country's policy of African socialism. China has provided much aid.

Melons growing at Mizpe Shalem, in Israel, are but one example of a wide variety of fruits, flowers and vegetables being cultivated against all climatic odds. The melons are growing on a research station at a kibbutz established in the early 1970s by the Dead Sea.

methods and varieties. Much, however, can be done to reduce the small farmer's risks to a more acceptable level. But it will require social and economic change to ensure access to the inputs he requires, from credit facilities to information extension services. The most obvious and important physical inputs to farming are land and water, but agrarian reform in many areas is also an essential requirement. The value of small, carefully tended plots is well known both for the possibilities of increased employment and high yield potential. Land reform, if maintained despite the pressure of those seeking to increase their holdings, is therefore an efficient means of increasing food production and at the same time reducing poverty.

Hand in hand with land reform goes access to water supply. Unfortunately, in most parts of the world access to water is also easier for the wealthy because water pumps and the power to run and maintain them are beyond the means of most subsistence farmers.

The role of women
With the emphasis on new technologies and their effect on food production, the highly important role played by women in agriculture is often overlooked in the relationship between land and the farmer. Most farm labor in small-scale production in the less-developed countries is carried out by women. The amount of time spent in planting, collecting water, weeding, harvesting and tending vegetables for home consumption—all done by women—is enormous and growing with the emigration of men to urban areas in search of better-paid work. It has been estimated that more than a quarter of rural households in the less-developed countries are now headed by women, and their farm work has increased to include nontraditional jobs such as tending livestock and clearing the land. For many women, farming is the only employment available, yet development programs—even those that focus on agriculture—fail to understand the

role of women and the abundant skills they bring to food production, nor do they provide a decision-making role for those who are ultimately affected by innovation. Given the knowledge and the means to help themselves, women could play a far more significant role in increasing productivity on a local basis than they have done so far.

Making the most of the land
Best practice must therefore imply social change, whether this results from more "scientific" application of agricultural techniques, the introduction of hybrid strains, improved irrigation or any other factor. How is society likely to change in response to the pressure to produce more food in the future? Land "reform," combined with the proven value of small, carefully tended plots in giving high yields, indicates a possible future path. In terms of food rather than cash profits, small, labor-intensive farms have a better track record than large, machine-intensive agricultural units.

"Best practice" in the short term can mean the introduction of such simple good farming habits as maintaining plant cover throughout the year by growing different crops to ensure minimum erosion; covering bare soil with mulches of leaves, rubbish or even plastic sheeting in order to trap moisture; and making the most of nutrients in the form of waste material, sewage and manure. All of this good farming practice can be greatly aided by the provision of inexpensive and rudimentary machines such as "mini" tractors, simple water pumps for irrigation purposes and so on.

But if the less-developed nations are to achieve real progress along these lines, more unconditional aid, as opposed to that motivated by self-interest, will be needed from the wealthier nations, and this raises political issues. The one overriding lesson we can learn from a look at the physical carrying capacity of the Earth is that the world food problem facing us is one of poverty and politics, and not of any immediate limit to growth.

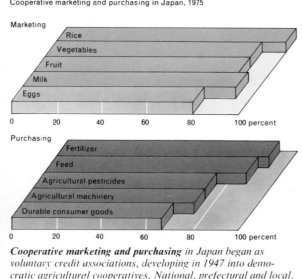

Cooperative marketing and purchasing in Japan, 1975

Marketing

Rice
Vegetables
Fruit
Milk
Eggs

0   20   40   60   80   100 percent

Purchasing

Fertilizer
Feed
Agricultural pesticides
Agricultural machinery
Durable consumer goods

0   20   40   60   80   100 percent

Cooperative marketing and purchasing in Japan began as voluntary credit associations, developing in 1947 into democratic agricultural cooperatives. National, prefectural and local, they also include insurance, processing and farm guidance.

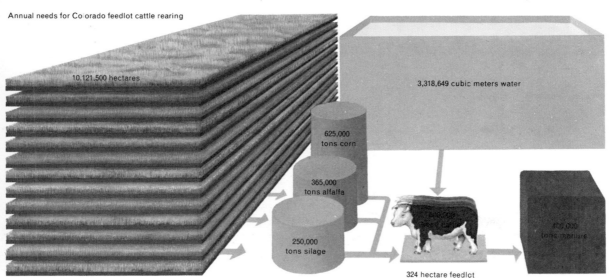

Annual needs for Colorado feedlot cattle rearing

10,121,500 hectares

3,318,649 cubic meters water

625,000 tons corn

365,000 tons alfalfa

250,000 tons silage

324 hectare feedlot

A rice cooperative, north of Tokyo, is heavily subsidized by the government. Such subsidies, which include a fixed price, ensure adequate supplies of staple crops such as wheat and rice in a country where only 16 percent of the land is cultivatable.

Agribusiness in Colorado illustrates the level of agriculture in some parts of the USA, where agriculture and industry have become highly interdependent. Huge amounts of feed and water are consumed by large numbers of beef cattle. The original investment in such a venture is large, so capital is likely to come from corporate companies.

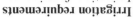

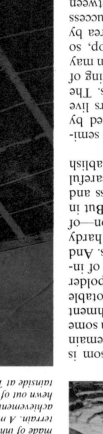

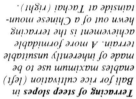

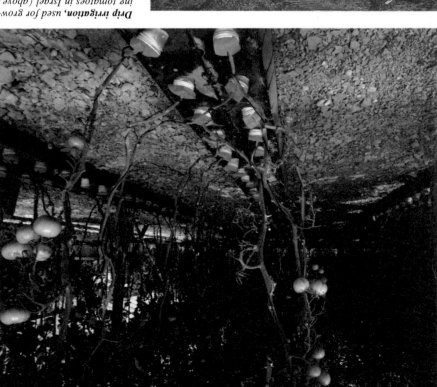

THE LIVING RESOURCE

MAKING BETTER USE OF THE LAND

Man's dream of making the desert blossom is elusive. Huge regions of the world remain barren and the extension of cultivated areas in some countries is offset in others by the impoverishment of soils that once produced food. There are notable reclamations in temperate regions, as in the polder farms of the Netherlands or in the recovery of industrial wastelands around some urban areas. And in cold climates the recent development of hardy crop varieties has allowed wider cultivation—of corn, for instance, in Europe and America. But in semiarid regions the balance sheet of success and failure has brought home the fact that careful methods of land control are needed to establish stable systems of farming.

In the absence of irrigation, farming in the semi-arid tropics is of two types, often conducted by different tribal groups. The nomadic graziers live off the milk, blood and meat of their herds. The other form of rainfed agriculture is the growing of short-term crops such as millet. One rainstorm may have to suffice for the production of a crop, so farmers add to the supply in a cultivated area by guiding runoff from a higher catchment. Success depends on calculating the correct ratio between these two areas. In the Negev desert in Israel, where ancient runoff farming is being revived, the ratio of catchment to cultivated area is 20 or 30 to one, enabling effective use of rainfall as low as 50–80 mm (2–3 in) annually.

Irrigation requirements

Irrigation farming requires a reliable water supply from rivers, reservoirs or underground sources. The problems of inadequate rainfall in semiarid regions is increased by high evaporation rates. Although evaporation in a temperate summer rarely exceeds 3 mm (0.1 in) a day, the rate may be as

Cultivation of crops in the Negev desert, southern Israel, has been extended by a water transfer project that integrates water distribution from all sources. The population of this semiarid region was increased from 14,000 in 1948 to 300,000 by 1971. Half of Israel's cultivable soils are in the south while 85 percent of water resources are in the north.

Drip irrigation, used for growing tomatoes in Israel (above), applies precise amounts of saltier water than would be suitable for surface or spray irrigation. Such ingenuity allows Israel to exploit 95 percent of its scanty water resources. In 1975, 10,121 hectares (25,000 acres) of Israeli crops were grown by means of drip irrigation.

Terracing of steep slopes in Bali for rice cultivation (left) enables maximum use to be made of inherently unsuitable terrain. A more formidable achievement is the terracing hewn out of a Chinese mountainside at Tachai (right).

26–7 Mapping the living resource
46–7 Searching for living space
52–3 The worlds we live in
94–5 Climate and man
96–7 Water—the basic resource
98–9 Land and the farmer
102–3 Forests at risk
108–9 Improving yields—plants
126–7 Israel, Japan and South Africa
128–9 Africa—development in diversity
132–3 The Near East—problems of aridity
134–5 Southern and southeastern Asia
136–7 China—planning with people
178–9 Food—defining the problems
180–1 Are green revolutions the ans
CONNECTIONS

15th century
16th c
17th c
19th c
20th c
Fresh water
Dam
IJsselmeer

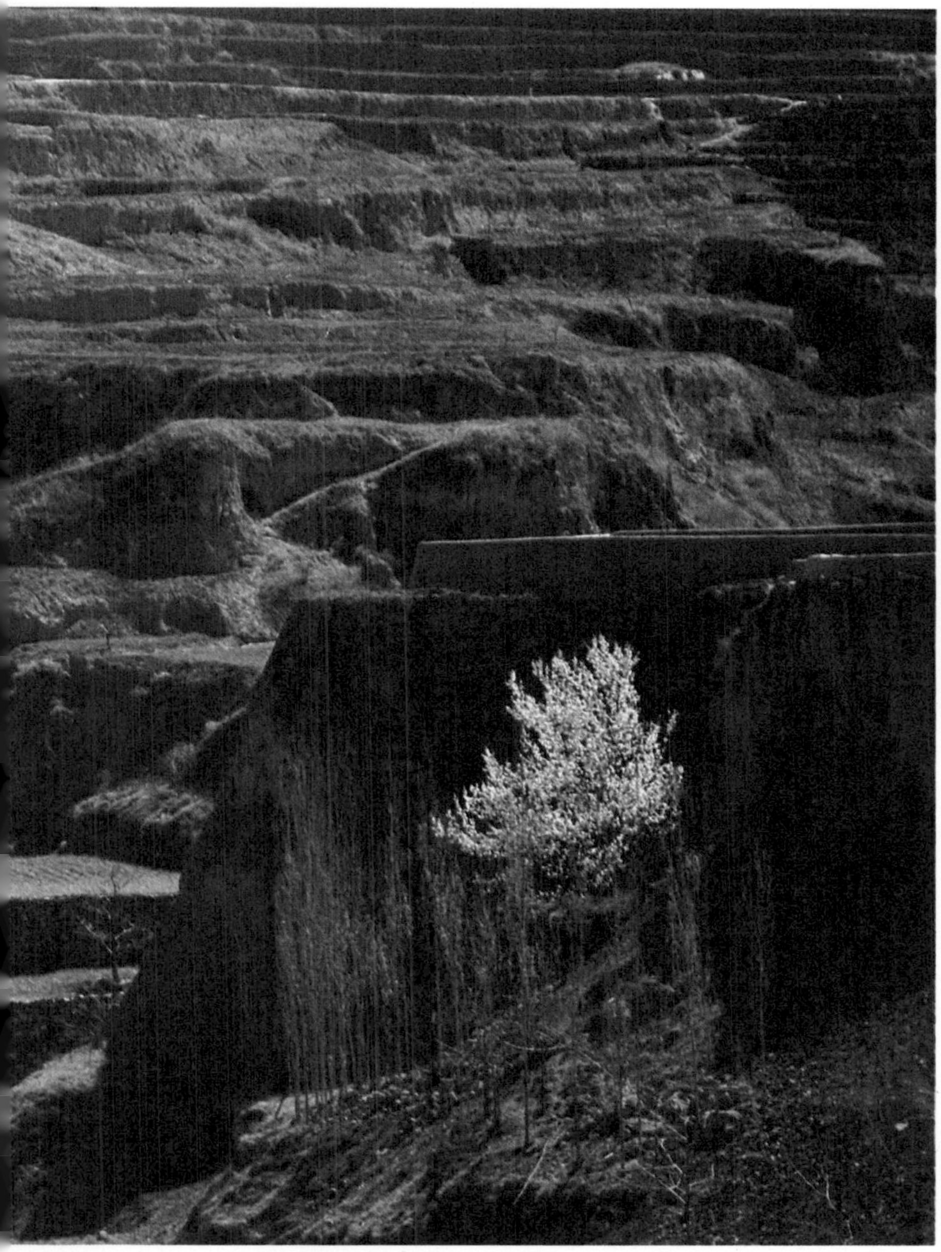

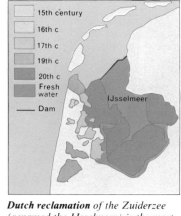

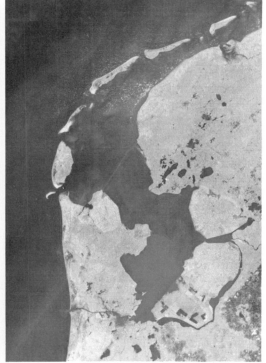

Dutch reclamation *of the Zuiderzee (renamed the IJsselmeer) is the most dramatic example of farm land being won from the sea. A barrier completed in 1932 led to the draining and planting of an area now approaching 230,000 hectares (568,000 acres), with a freshwater lake of half this area. The diagram traces a long history of reclamation in the area. Differences in soil composition show in the satellite picture (left). Newer polders appear a lighter blue.*

Rehabilitation *of industrial wasteland can be achieved through schemes such as the Lower Swansea Valley Project in Wales. Wastes dumped in the area since the 1730s have been cleared for parks and recreational areas.*

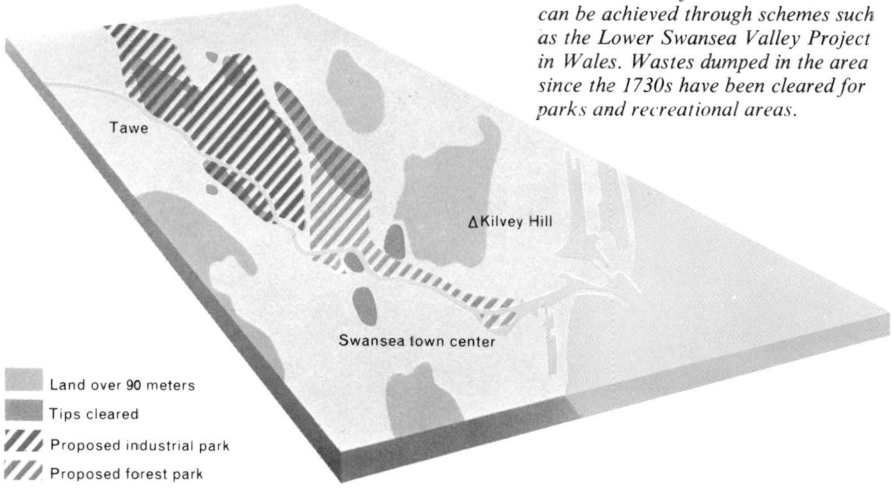

Tawe
Kilvey Hill
Swansea town center
Land over 90 meters
Tips cleared
Proposed industrial park
Proposed forest park

high as 8 mm (0.3 in) in hot, dry and windy climates. Enormous quantities of water are required for effective irrigation. The 10,000 cubic meters (2,200,000 gallons) needed to irrigate a three-month crop on 1.2 hectares (3 acres) would alternatively supply 100 nomads and all their stock for three years or 100 consumers in a modern industrial city for two years. The quality of water must also be considered. Some ground water contains dissolved salts, which will gradually accumulate in the irrigated soil and make it useless for cropping. About 200,000 hectares (495,000 acres) or 0.1 percent of the world's irrigated land goes out of production each year for this reason. Irrigation with slightly saline water is possible if the accumulating salts can be flushed out of the soil by occasionally over-irrigating the land.

Irrigation methods

Irrigation schemes vary greatly in size from large-scale state- or company-run schemes to farming activities that make an important contribution to local food and wealth. Water may be applied by surface or overhead methods. Surface methods are usually labor intensive and need little mechanization, but careful planning is required if water is to be used efficiently. The topography must be suitable or the soil deep enough to allow terracing.

In overhead irrigation, water is pumped to sprinklers or rainguns. These differ only in size. One hectare (2.5 acres) can be irrigated by about 50 sprinklers or five to 10 rainguns. Except in windy conditions the water is distributed more evenly and accurately than by surface methods and there are no supply ditches to interfere with cropping. With greater degrees of automation, less labor is needed to operate the equipment.

Trickle irrigation is a recent development in which water is distributed at low pressure through plastic tubes. It is most commonly used for crops in greenhouses, but can also irrigate perennial orchard crops such as citrus fruits and peaches. Evaporation losses during application are avoided and less energy is needed than with overhead methods. Crops can be continuously supplied with water and need never suffer water stress.

The problem of erosion

In many dry parts of the world, desert areas are increasing. A landscape of shifting sands and little or no vegetation is extending into areas that did not previously have these characteristics. The southern border of the Sahara, for example, moved south 100 km (60 miles) in some areas between 1958 and 1975. This appears to be due not to any long-term climatic change but to the effects of increasing population on the ecological balance. Erosion has been caused by overgrazing as cattle numbers increased, loss of woody vegetation taken for fuel, uncontrolled burning of vegetation, unsuitable crop production methods and poor irrigation practice leading to salt accumulation.

Once the process of erosion has started it may be almost irreversible on younger and thinner soils, but other areas can be restored by restricting their use for a number of years. Both reclamation and prevention of erosion depend on appropriate and planned land use. Exposure to erosion can be minimized by simple terracing, avoidance of bare tillage, use of crop residues for mulching, or the maintenance of a cover of natural vegetation. This means reducing pressure on fuel gathering and limiting the number and movement of livestock. Neither is an easy task. Fossil fuels are costly and not readily available, but controlled use of plantations may be possible. The nomadic grazier measures his wealth by the number of cattle he owns rather than their condition. If he loses half of them in a run of drought years his reaction is to increase his original holding when circumstances allow. He has no incentive to assist in the conservation of commonly owned land by limiting his herd size.

Other measures of land management include some form of rotational grazing, local improvement to forage production by simple water-harvesting schemes, assistance with breeding programs and better marketing methods. All these need a degree of organization that is often lacking.

Rainfall intensities make erosion a constant threat in the tropics, particularly where population pressure is forcing a change from shifting cultivation to continuous cropping with annual crops. Recent studies suggest that mulch tillage may hold the best prospect yet for a stable system. The residue of the previous crop is left on the land (this may pose pest and disease control problems) and weeds, controlled with herbicides, can add to the soil-protecting mulch. The new crop is sown through the mulch by hand or machinery without cultivation.

As a result, the uncultivated soil has more organic matter and a more stable structure, while the soil fauna and the undisturbed root holes of previous crops allow rainfall to soak in. Erosion is controlled, nutrient losses are reduced and the cooling effect of the mulch avoids the problem of impaired or delayed germination that can accompany high temperatures in unprotected surface soil. This is a good example of research leading to a farming system that suits the physical, social and economic environment so that yield can be sustained or improved without reducing the land's long-term productivity. In farming systems such as this lies the key to better management, improved output and a more optimistic outlook for the future.

THE LIVING RESOURCE
FORESTS AT RISK

At one time almost two-thirds of the Earth's surface was covered by forests. The area covered now—3.9 billion hectares (9.63 billion acres)—has diminished to less than a third of that surface area. It is a reduction which is the result of the depletion by man of the world's natural forests.

Most of the remaining natural forests (those native to a region and which regenerate themselves without the intervention of man) occur only in the tropics and the boreal regions of Scandinavia, the USSR and Canada. Almost all of the seven major zones have been and in some cases continue to be massively disturbed by man. Some, such as the temperate mixed forest and warm temperate moist forest, were affected many centuries ago, while parts of the tropical zones have been devastated in recent times. The regression of tropical moist forest ecosystems has, in fact, greatly accelerated since World War II. The natural forest ecosystems of eastern and western Africa, for example, have been reduced to 72 percent of their former area. Similarly in northern forests man's presence is continually felt. In Canada it is estimated that there is a yearly accumulation of 151,470 hectares (374,000 acres) of inadequately regenerated land following forest harvesting. Yet another enemy of the world's forests is the natural catastrophe. Each year 121,000 hectares (300,000 acres) of forests are adversely affected by natural disasters.

Man-made forests

Because of this shrinkage of natural forests and the growing needs of industry, the area under man-made forests is actually growing. The industrialized nations of Europe are slowly increasing their forests while the nations of the tropics also are becoming increasingly aware of the need to conserve forests and to create new ones by planting. Yet despite this extension the area of man-made forests still represents only a small fraction of that covered by natural forests, whether in the temperate zone or tropics, the species being planted are light demanding, fast-growing and short-lived. Such species give maximum volume production when grown as monocultures. The choice of species depends on the environment of the area to be planted. For example, in the maritime environments of western Europe species such as Sitka spruce (*Picea sitchensis*), indigenous to western North America, do well. *Pinus radiata*, indigenous to California, is planted extensively in New Zealand, Australia and Chile. Eucalyptus species, several species of tropical pines, for example *Pinus caribaea*, *P. kesyia*, and the broadleaved species of *Gmelina* and *Cedrela*, are planted throughout the tropics.

Throughout the developing world wood is by far

Forestry supports thousands of sawmills and to a lesser extent pulp mills in Canada's northwest. In the early 1970s British Columbia's contribution to national production was 70 percent

of sawn lumber, most of the plywood and more than 25 percent of chemical pulp. Plants vary from one-man operations to massive concerns including byproduct industries.

Half the world's population still uses firewood for cooking and heating, but deforestation has thinned the supply. In some areas the time taken to gather wood has increased eightfold.

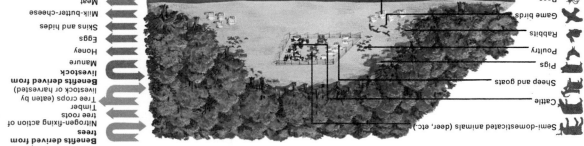

Farmers and foresters are increasingly pooling efforts to gain maximum production of food and wood from the same land. The chief aspects are: tree planting to maintain the nitrate supply in the soil; use of tree products for food and manufacture; and grazing of animals among the trees to fertilize the soil.

Benefits derived from trees
Nitrogen-fixing action of tree roots
Tree crops (eaten by livestock or harvested)
Timber

Benefits derived from livestock
Manure
Honey
Eggs
Skins and hides
Milk-butter-cheese
Meat

Semi-domesticated animals (deer, etc.)
Cattle
Sheep and goats
Pigs
Poultry
Rabbits
Game birds
Bees

CONNECTIONS

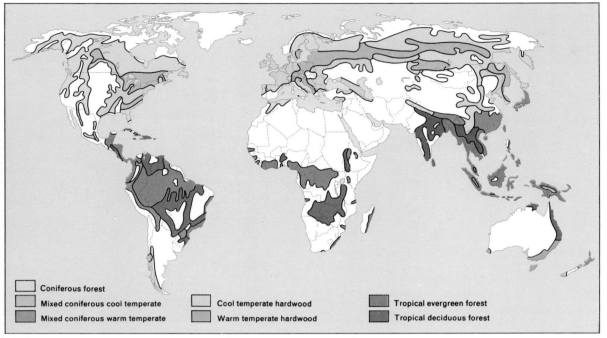

Coniferous forest

Mixed coniferous cool temperate

Mixed coniferous warm temperate

Cool temperate hardwood

Warm temperate hardwood

Tropical evergreen forest

Tropical deciduous forest

Commercial timber is from three major forest types: softwoods, from coniferous forests, and temperate and tropical hardwoods. Softwoods are used for building, packaging and paper pulp, while *temperate hardwoods are often cut for specialized uses such as furniture making. Tropical hardwoods are mainly used locally, but there is some export of teak, rosewood and mahogany.*

In Brazil much of the tropical rain forest is being cleared for farming. This could seriously affect the global ecological balance as large forest areas are a major source of oxygen.

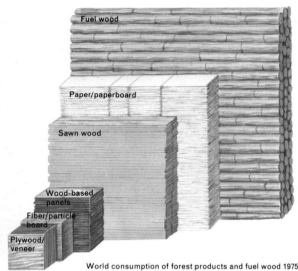

World consumption of forest products and fuel wood 1975

Firewood is by far the main forest produce: 1.2 billion cu m (1.57 billion cu yd) were used in 1975. Paper and paperboard accounted for 450 million cu m (588 million cu yd).

In countries such as Ethiopia where firewood is scarce UN forestry schemes are now in progress. Often they begin with an introduction to planting: many countries have no such tradition.

the most important source of fuel and in some regions of the seasonal tropics it has become a scarce and expensive commodity. As countries become more prosperous there is a gradual fall in firewood consumption as other sources of energy are used. A gradual decline was, for example, apparent between 1960 and 1975. However, this decline now appears to be coming to an end and there is every indication that total and per capita consumption of fuel wood will increase in developing countries. Since more than 70 percent of the world's population lives in these countries the total consumption of fuel wood for the world will increase.

It is believed that the world's forest resource is theoretically large enough to cater for human energy needs without affecting the supply of wood for industrial purposes, provided that silvicultural systems are adapted to the production of fuel wood together with the production of timber.

Because of the abundance of oil, a relatively cheap source of energy until recent times, cellulose as a chemical and energy resource has not attracted the research funds necessary to develop its full potential. This has now changed following the massive increases in the cost of oil and an increased awareness that oil is a wasting resource. Already some authorities believe that methanol liquid fuel produced from forests could become competitive with petroleum based fuels in the next 10 years, and in certain countries pulverized wood is being added in substantial quantities to ruminant feeds. There are a number of chemical processes involved in converting wood to animal feed and food for human consumption. In the USSR commercial develop-

ment of feedstuff based on wood has reached a higher level than anywhere else and is estimated to be about three percent of the total high-protein feed concentrate used there. Because of increased research on wood as a renewable raw material there should be a more rapid increase in the range of products, including foods produced from it.

For centuries forest management has been largely devoted to the production of cellulose. In recent years, however, there has been a remarkable change in society's understanding of the role of forestry; a change which has paralleled the enhanced public awareness of the quality of life in industrial society as a whole. There is now a greater appreciation of the potential of forestry as an instrument for rural development, the rehabilitation of degraded lands, water catchment, provision of shelter and above all in industrial societies as a means of enhancing the beauty of the environment.

Trees serving the community

European forests are increasingly providing recreation facilities for millions of people, and urban forestry is now recognized as a discipline in its own right. In the great arid zones of northern Africa foresters are engaged in reestablishing tree crops in areas degraded by excessive grazing and by burning. Trees such as *Acacia albida* provide fodder for cattle in the dry season as well as enhancing the fertility of the soil and ensuring a supply of fuel. In the humid forest zone, tree plantations are being established by means of agrisilvicultural systems, which ensure the sustained yield of food, fodder and wood from the same land. Areas of natural forests are being set aside so that faunal habitats are conserved and centers of genetic diversity of plants and animals are maintained for future study, enjoyment and use. Local food-producing trees are being domesticated and propagated on a large scale for local consumption and it is being increasingly recognized that forests, woodlands and trees can serve the community in a multitude of ways as well as producing cellulose.

The world's natural forest resources will continue to shrink under exploitation and agricultural development, particularly in Latin America and southeastern Asia, until eventually most countries will reach the stage of western Europe, where only a relatively small percentage of each country's land mass is retained under natural forest. Simultaneously with this reduction in the natural forest, the area of man-made forest will increase and many tree species, most of them now wild, will be brought under cultivation. As a result much greater yields will be obtained from a smaller area of forest.

W hile the growing of food represents the most important use of the world's resources of fertile land, many valuable crops are cultivated to meet other industrial and domestic needs. These include cotton and other sources of fiber, rubber, tobacco, plants that yield oil, and a range of nonfood byproducts from agricultural activities, particularly animal hides and skins.

Worldwide some 63 million hectares (156 million acres) of land are given over to nonfood crops, of which about half is used for cotton production. Cotton is easily the most important of all fibers, natural or man-made, accounting for about 42 percent of total fiber output.

Cotton fiber is made from hairs attached to the seed of the plant. Consumption reached a record 13,600,000 tons in 1975-76 with estimated consumption for 1977-78 slightly lower. Other leading vegetable fibers include jute, hemp, sisal and flax, which go into the making of a variety of products ranging from rope and matting to linen fabric.

These natural fibers face competition from synthetic substitutes, which fall into two main groups—those made from reconstituted cellulose (rayon and acetate) and those derived from petrochemicals (polyamide, polyesters and acrylic fibers). In the 10 years up to 1971 man-made fibers increased their share of world markets from 17 percent to 32 percent. During the same period, while natural-fiber production increased by 10 percent, that of synthetics rose by 150 percent. However, the oil crisis of 1973 gave natural fibers a price advantage and they have at least maintained their share of the market since then.

Rubber and oils
Rubber is produced from latex collected by making spiral incisions in the *Hevea brasiliensis* tree. The latex is solidified and exported as sheets of raw rubber, which is strengthened and given elasticity by a process known as vulcanization, in which sulfur is added. Natural rubber is comparatively expensive to produce and from the mid-1960s lost ground to synthetic rubber, most of which is petroleum-based. The world consumption of all types of rubber during 1978 was estimated at 12 million tons, 68.2 percent of it synthetic. It is estimated that consumption will reach 18,800,000 tons by 1988 with synthetic rubber increasing its share of the market to 71.8 percent.

The major industrial oils of vegetable origin are linseed, castor and tung. In 1976 world production

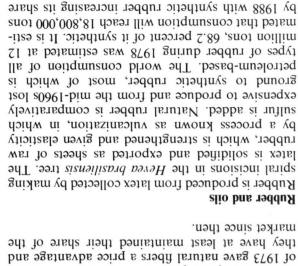

Most of Mozambique's sisal harvest goes into the manufacture of binder twine for agriculture, but production declined in 1977-78 due to increasing competition from polypropylene.

World tobacco consumption continues to rise, despite increased taxation and health warnings. In India, where tobacco is grown in most parts of the country, output in 1975 was 363,100 tons.

Man-made substitutes often bear a striking resemblance to the natural product. Real silk being prepared by a worker in China looks very similar to reels of synthetic silk in a factory in Germany. The art of rearing silkworms is said to have been discovered in China by the empress Hsi-ling Shih over 4,000 years ago. Today China, along with Japan, is still the world's leading producer of natural silk. The chemically made substitute was named rayon in 1924.

Wool is one of the products now benefiting from a recent trend back toward natural fabrics. In Marrakech, which often undercut the market. For many developing countries this has meant that while exports of crops such as cotton and rubber have increased, their real value has hardly changed at all.

About four percent of the world's arable and permanent cropland is used for nonfood crops, half of it for cotton. Almost all natural fibers face competition from synthetic substitutes.

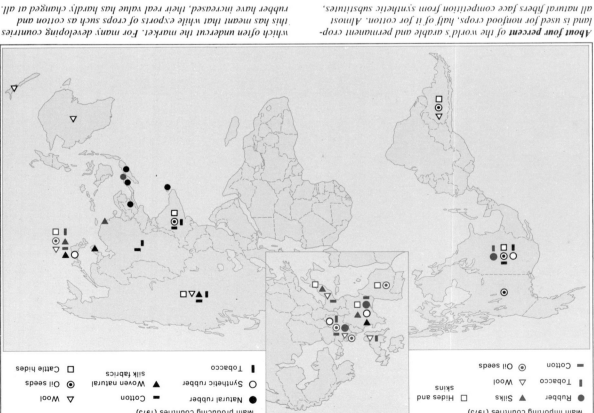

Main producing countries (1975)
- ▽ Wool
- — Cotton
- ● Natural rubber
- ◉ Oil seeds
- ○ Synthetic rubber
- ▲ Woven natural silk fabrics
- ▮ Tobacco
- □ Cattle hides

Main importing countries (1975)
- ● Rubber
- ▲ Silks
- □ Hides and skins
- ▽ Tobacco
- ▽ Wool
- ◉ Cotton
- ◉ Oil seeds

CONNECTIONS

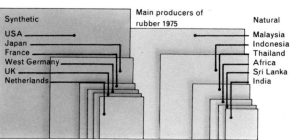

Main producers of rubber 1975

Synthetic
USA
Japan
France
West Germany
UK
Netherlands

Natural
Malaysia
Indonesia
Thailand
Africa
Sri Lanka
India

The rubber tree is a native of South America, but seeds grown in Malaya last century were the start of what remains the world's largest source of natural rubber. Synthetic rubber, developed in the USA during World War II, is increasing its share of the market. Most rubber products, such as tires, are a mixture of synthetic and natural rubber.

Morocco, freshly dyed wool is often dried in the streets.

Nigeria's cotton output (69,000 tons in 1976) is growing, but its value as an export has been

declining as more and more of the crop goes directly into the country's rising textile industry.

The paint industry makes extensive use of the drying properties of certain vegetable oils, particularly linseed, castor and tung.

of linseed oil was around 860,000 tons, of castor 308,000 tons, and of tung 104,000 tons. These oils are used mainly in the manufacture of paints and varnishes, to which they add valuable drying properties. In addition some edible oils, such as palm and coconut, are used to make soap and candles. Industrial vegetable oils are facing increasing competition from synthetic substitutes, derived largely from petroleum.

Of the remaining nonfood crops one of the most valuable is tobacco. Production (5,400,000 tons in 1975) continues to increase despite widely publicized warnings about the risk to health involved in smoking. The chief impact of such warnings has been a trend toward lighter tobacco leaf. Synthetic smoking materials, which have recently been put on the market, are not likely to provide important competition in the near future.

Other nonfood plant products in wide-scale use include cork, tannins, pharmaceuticals such as opium and quinine, and dyes and insecticides.

Wool, silk and skins
The main nonfood material produced by animals is wool. In 1976 production stood at 1,500,000 tons. Most wool comes from sheep, but the cashmere goat supplies a small percentage of the market.

Wool is under fierce competition from man-made fibers, but its texture and warmth ensure continuing demand, especially in the luxury market, and it is also widely used in combination with synthetics. Other principal animal fibers are mohair from Angora goats, camel hair and Angora rabbit hair.

More than 50,000 tons of silk were produced in 1976, most of it by Japan and China. Despite competition from synthetic fibers—nylon, for example, has ousted silk in the hosiery market—production, principally for luxury textiles, is expanding.

Hides and skins in world trade are chiefly from cattle, buffalo, sheep and goats. There has been a long-term upward trend in production, particularly in cattle hides and calfskins. In 1975 production from these two sources stood at 273,600,000 pieces, with 386,400,000 sheepskins and 145,800,000 goat-skins. Consumption is likely to continue to rise, with increasing sales of fashion footwear and other leather luxury goods. A wide range of synthetic substitutes for leather exists, particularly for consumer goods in the lower price bracket, but these do not form a major threat to leather at present.

India and Pakistan have a tradition of tanning and leather manufacturing, but countries in Latin America and the Far East are processing more and more of their own skins themselves.

Speciality hides, skins and furs account for a small but valuable world trade. Many of those produced from wild animals have recently been subject to conservation restrictions, but there remains a wide range derived from domestic and commercially reared animals, including pigskins, alligator hides, ostrich skin and feathers, mink and silver fox furs, and Persian lamb wool. Furs account for about 30 percent of the value of all hides and skins entering world trade in the raw state.

Land use
It is unlikely that land at present used for nonfood crops could usefully be turned over to food production. It is more likely that the revenue from such crops could be used to pay for improved methods of production to give increased yields from existing food-producing land.

Synthetic substitutes exist for virtually all the nonfood materials derived from agriculture. Not all of them, however, have the same aesthetic appeal as natural materials and many are byproducts of fossil fuels, which may become less plentiful and more expensive. Other synthetics cannot be produced without high inputs of energy. These factors indicate that natural products are likely to maintain their competitiveness.

FISHING—A QUESTION OF QUOTAS

World fish catches within the last decade have been reasonably stable, averaging around the 67 million tons mark. Yet this apparently stable situation conceals a number of important changes that the fishing industry has been faced with in that time. A revolution in fishing equipment and methods; the exploitation of unfamiliar species; and a worldwide change in fishery limits have seen some countries significantly improve catches while in others harvests have slumped dramatically.

In 1976 the total harvest figure reached a new record total of more than 72 million tons. Forecasts of demand, based on population and income increases, indicate that the annual demand for fish by the year 2000 will be 110 million tons. This target will be reached only with sensible management of the existing heavily exploited stocks and rational exploitation of underdeveloped fisheries. It is possible that less than 50 percent of this catch will be eaten directly by man.

Utilizing the catch

At present, fish provides only four percent of the world's total protein and less than one percent of its calories. Annual fish consumption a head is only 12 kilograms (28 pounds). However, fish supplies for human consumption have increased much faster than agricultural supplies, growing at some four percent a year for more than 20 years—twice as fast as world population growth. The proportion of the total catch that has gone to produce fishmeal has, however, risen from nearly 20 percent in the 1950s to 50 percent in the 1970s. Although Peru took the largest fish catch in the world in 1970 of 12 million tons, only three percent was consumed locally—the rest was used by the developed world, much of it for pig and poultry feed. Though the world's developed countries comprise only 28 percent of the world's population, they use 50 percent of the catch. They also maintain the busiest of fleets. Only a few developing nations such as Peru, Korea and Thailand have built up deep-sea fishing operations and Thailand and Korea have done so encouraged by aid programs and technical advice. A fishing school set up in Korea by the United Nations Food

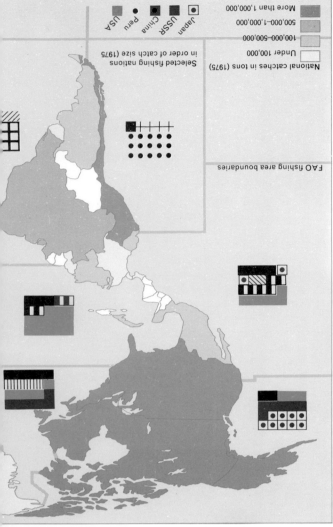

106

In 1975 70 percent of the world's catch of fish (left) was used for human consumption and the rest mainly for fishmeal. Though figures indicate that the proportion made available for human consumption is increasing steadily, it is estimated that half of that 70 percent is made up of inedible waste. Countries which reduce a large percentage of their catches to fishmeal are Peru (79), Denmark (79), and Norway (69). In Hammerfest, Norway (right), frozen slabs of fish waste wait for transportation to Finland.

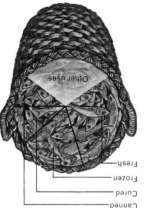
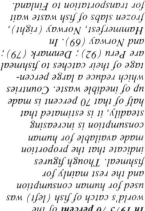
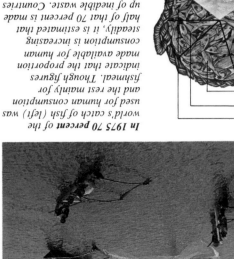

A Russian flotilla of trawlers centered round a factory ship (above) illustrates the modern technique of canning at sea to maximize yield from catches. Sri Lankan fishing by net casting (left) employs unsophisticated equipment but is important to the economy of a developing country that does not have the resources to develop a large offshore fleet. Catches are only sufficient to cater for the needs of Sri Lanka's population—93 percent of its fish is marketed fresh.

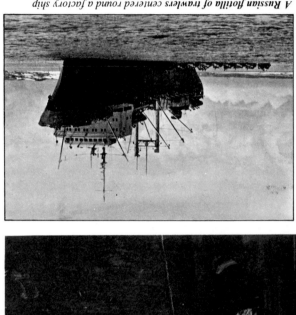

In a traditional cod trawler operating in the Atlantic the fish is gutted by hand and packed in ice for transportation to the home port, where it may be further processed. Lack of investment as well as competition from nations with more sophisticated fishing equipment, such as Japan and the USSR, have influenced many countries in unilaterally declaring EEZs.

National catches in tons (1975)

Selected fishing nations in order of catch size (1975)

Under 100,000
100,000–500,000
500,000–1,000,000
More than 1,000,000

Japan, China, USSR, Peru, USA

FAO fishing area boundaries

and Agriculture Organization provided the crews for deep-sea ships that have raised the Korean catch to more than two million tons a year.

Economic considerations

The economic and political complications of sharing out the global fisheries' wealth are many. Advances in fishing vessel and gear design have evolved so quickly that regulations such as quotas, which are designed to avoid overexploitation, come under pressure. A modern Soviet factory trawler with a crew of 70 can land 10,000 tons of fish annually and some of the factory mother ships serving catching fleets approach 15,000 tons. The vessels have satellite navigation and are equipped with electronic aids for fish finding and position fixing. Increases in raw material, labor and fuel costs have increased construction and running costs for fishing fleets, resulting in a need for larger catches.

Open-sea fishing has become, to a large extent, a battle of wits between the fishermen, seeking to improve efficiency, and the international bodies formulating regulations restricting catches, mesh size, vessel length, and so on. These measures usually achieve too little too late and there are few examples of successfully controlled fisheries. An expanding fishing industry provides employment not just for the fishing fleet but for boat builders and a host of service industries, so while fisheries scientists can advise catch restrictions for stock replenishing, political and economic considerations often prevent this advice being taken. It is now hoped that the establishment by more than 60 countries of exclusive economic zones (EEZs) of 200 nautical miles (370 km) will help to correct overfishing problems. The North Sea herring fisheries serve as a classic example of what can go wrong when quotas are ignored. In 1974 the North East Atlantic Fisheries Commission reduced the annual quota from 550,000 to 488,000 tons while its fisheries scientists were advising a low 390,000 tons quota. The total catch in 1976 fell to 169,000 tons. History has proved that resistance to restricted catch quotas usually results in a total collapse such as this. In its 1977 annual report the United

A LIFELINE FOR WHALES

Whales, although they make no major contribution to world resources, have nevertheless been the focus of a wide-scale dispute in recent years. On the one hand are those concerned about the endangering of species, on the other are those engaged in the industry and concerned with protecting their livelihood. Some members of the International Whaling Commission (IWC) have taken up the rallying cry of conservation with, however, limited success.

Over the years suggested 10-year moratoriums have never been accepted because it is argued by those still engaged in whaling that the industry would not survive such an interval. The central weakness of the IWC, established in 1946 as a commercial management body but whose role has changed as member nations have dropped out of the whaling industry, is simply that it has no binding powers. Members, who account for 90 percent of the world catch, can simply ignore international agreements if they wish.

On the credit side, quotas have been reduced—Southern Hemisphere catches fell to 23,000 in 1977–78, half the 1964–65 total—and attention is now focused on the sperm whale where there is some prospect for the rational management of existing stocks. In addition blue whales, reduced to approximately five percent of their original numbers, are now protected, as are the small fin whales.

Most whaling is done in South Polar regions and the USSR, an IWC member, takes about 40 percent of the world catch. Products are used in pet foods and for oil and margarine.

Kingdom Herring Industry Board pressed for a three- to four-year ban on fishing to allow stocks to recover and the United Kingdom banned fishing by other nations within its EEZ limit.

Political outlook

Free-swimming fish do not recognize national boundaries and the EEZs, and their various migrations to feeding, spawning and nursery grounds complicate the issue enormously. It is hard to imagine that the exploitation of new species such as krill, now being fished by some countries, will enjoy a climate of international cooperation sufficient to avoid the feast and famine cycles of the traditional fisheries. The 1977 Norwegian catch of capelin for fishmeal of two million tons is already recognized as dangerously high and reduced quotas have been proposed. In theory, however, the establishment of well-managed and adequately policed EEZs should enable more effective conservation of coastal stocks and it is certain that open-

sea fisheries will continue to supply the bulk of the world's fish protein in the future, whatever the fate of individual stocks.

As fisheries do not exist in isolation, and since the use of the sea involves more than just fishing, the problem of resolving management objectives and dividing the benefits is a difficult one. In declaring EEZs, countries are thereby establishing sole ownership rights over resources and allowing in only traditional users or other favored nations. The problems of the International Law of the Sea Conferences in reaching any other agreed conclusions about limit extensions and other issues reflects the continuing conflict. One problem is that in developed economies fishing tends to rank rather low in relation to other maritime activities—the exploitation of oil or natural gas fields, for instance, or the improvement of maritime trading facilities—and often the interests of the fishing industry are ignored or sacrificed in the face of development in these other areas.

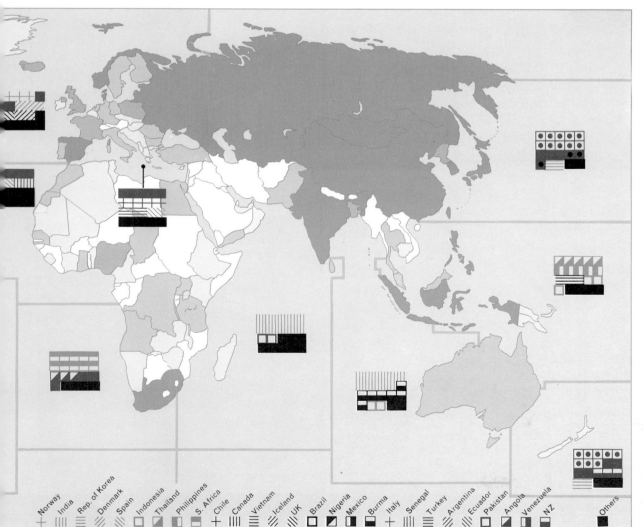

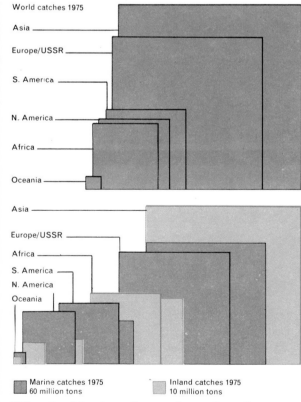

World catches 1975

Asia
Europe/USSR
S. America
N. America
Africa
Oceania

Asia
Europe/USSR
Africa
S. America
N. America
Oceania

■ Marine catches 1975
60 million tons

Inland catches 1975
10 million tons

Fish catches (above) are often out of proportion to the populations of the nations landing them: Japan has three percent of the world's population but harvests 15 percent of its fish. On the other hand fish consumption in the Far East is greater than that in any other region. Japan consumes 32 kg (70 lb) a head each year compared to 8 kg (17½ lb) a head in the USA. The disposition of the sea's harvest by national catches and by proportionate catches (left) within each Food and Agriculture Organization fishing area shows how five countries dominate world fishing. Each repeated symbol represents five percent of that area's catch: Japan makes catches in each area.

Norway India Rep. of Korea Denmark Spain Indonesia Thailand Philippines S. Africa Chile Canada Vietnam Iceland UK Brazil Nigeria Mexico Burma Italy Senegal Turkey Argentina Ecuador Pakistan Angola Venezuela NZ Others

IMPROVING YIELDS–PLANTS

Improving crop production, which means either improving yields or reducing the cost of production, depends on two major factors: increasing control of the crop environment and the successful breeding of cultivated varieties better suited to different environments. Significant features are breeding and selection, fertilizers, time and method of planting, weed and pest control.

Breeding and selection to suit the conditions of cultivation are very important: many developments in this area have been the basis of the "green revolution." Both crops and varieties within crops vary in their suitability for different climates, different lengths of growing season and soil conditions. There is an increasing demand for wheat in Africa, for instance, but in many areas temperatures are too high. African countries seeking to grow wheat as an import saver must look to their cooler highlands or grow it as a winter crop. Some rice varieties are daylength sensitive; they must therefore be planted at an appropriate season so that the stage of "ripeness to flower" coincides with shortening days.

The farmer must choose varieties which are suited to his market and his system of production. The development of prepacked vegetables has led to a demand for smaller and more uniform components. At the same time, once-over mechanical harvesting requires that a high proportion of the yield must reach the correct stage at the same time. Both these factors have led to the development of F_1 hybrid brussels sprouts and more compact varieties of peas. Mechanical harvesting of peas can sometimes be difficult because of the amount of leaf present and because the crop does not stand well. Varieties are being developed without leaves and with many tendrils to help support the crop.

Building up resistance

Another part of the plant breeder's work is the development of varieties showing greater resistance to pests and diseases. This is an unending battle. When pathogen, an organism or substance that causes disease, and plant are closely adapted to each other it is often possible to select new crop types which show resistance to the pathogen because of some small structural or biochemical change. But the pathogen may be equally capable of genetic change and new races can develop which break down the resistance of the crop.

The major contribution of the plant breeder is the development of higher-yielding varieties. In many cereal varieties, about 25–30 percent of the total dry matter accumulated is in the grain. The rest is stem, leaf and root. Newer varieties have been developed with shorter stems and a 40 percent harvest index. Yields have thus been increased, but by altering the partition of dry matter within the crop rather than by increasing total growth.

Much of the increase in world food production in the last 25 years has come from increased use of fertilizers. They are essential for large yields because the natural supply of plant nutrients from weathering and recycling is inadequate for intensive farming. Phosphorus, potassium and nitrogen are the major nutrients required from fertilizers. Of these, nitrogen (used as urea, ammonia or nitrate) is the most important because of the quantities needed and because of its high energy cost in manufacture. It alone accounts for 30 percent of all the support energy used in farming, yet no more than 50–70 percent of the nitrogen fertilizer is taken up by crops; the rest is lost. Because of declining fossil fuel reserves, efficient farming in the future may depend on reducing these losses and on greater use of leguminous plants.

Legumes such as peas, beans, clover and alfalfa live in symbiosis with bacteria which inhabit root nodules and use carbohydrate from the host plant as the source of energy to fix gaseous nitrogen to supply themselves and their host. Grain legumes therefore require little or no nitrogen fertilizer and

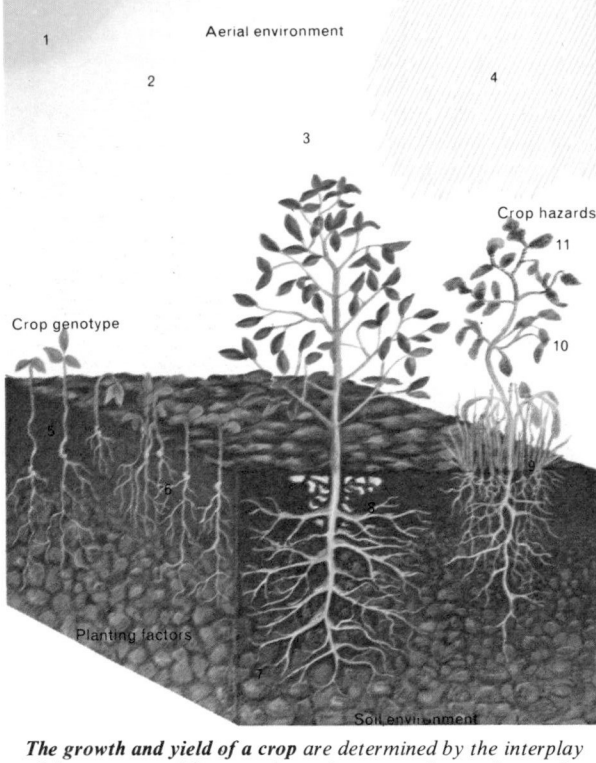

The growth and yield of a crop are determined by the interplay of three groups of factors: the environment, the crop's genetic characteristics and conditions of planting. The aerial environment cannot usually be altered for field crops so the farmer must work with the existing daylength (1), light intensity (2) and temperature patterns (3). Rainfall (4) can also be a limiting factor in dry areas when irrigation is not possible. Planting factors include method and depth (5), and seedrate and spacing (6). The soil environment provides anchorage (7), nutrients and water (8). Features such as soil texture and depth are not easily altered; a shallow, stony soil can impose a low upper limit on crop yield. Crop hazards include weeds (9), diseases (10) and pests (11). The phytotron, right, aids manipulation of the environment by producing artificially any climatic conditions for the study of plant growth.

Soviet scientists at the Cotton-Farming Research Institute in Tashkent, as well as successfully increasing cotton yields, have been working on new varieties which would resist disease and lend themselves to mechanical picking. Shown here are experiments in growing cotton by hydroponics: plants are artificially provided for within totally soilless conditions.

There is now an international network of agricultural research centers which, it is hoped, will extend the green revolution to all the principal crops of the developing world. This vast center in the Ukraine for experimental seed selection and breeding includes laboratories and test fields.

While the use of newer farming techniques is encouraged in developing countries it is equally important that the policy of "appropriate technology"—based on available resources—is followed. The method of insecticide spraying used in Kenya (above) is practical for this particular region.

The use of biological pest control limits the need for chemicals, keeping environmental damage to a minimum. The male pea moth (left) is lured into a sticky trap by synthetic female sex attractant. The "catch" of moths indicates whether the crop needs to be sprayed.

Once a new crop variety has been developed it can be reproduced exactly by grafting, giving a genetically homogenous group called a clone. Shown here is clone propagation of Kenyan tea bushes. This brings quick results, but extensive monocultures are more prone to disease.

Primitive Japanese farming relied on rainfall. Irrigated cultivation more than doubled rice yields from AD 600 to 1850 and scientifically researched techniques were introduced in the 1870s. Postwar transformation of the country's rural sector has made high yields commonplace. Current farming practice in other Asian countries is here compared with Japan's four-stage progression.

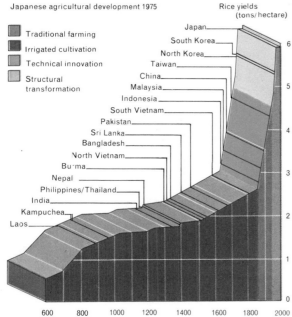

Japanese agricultural development 1975

Rice yields (tons/hectare)

- Traditional farming
- Irrigated cultivation
- Technical innovation
- Structural transformation

Japan
South Korea
North Korea
Taiwan
China
Malaysia
Indonesia
South Vietnam
Pakistan
Sri Lanka
Bangladesh
North Vietnam
Burma
Nepal
Philippines/Thailand
India
Kampuchea
Laos

600 800 1000 1200 1400 1600 1800 2000

forage legumes have the additional benefit of leaving appreciable residues in the soil. Future techniques of genetic manipulation may allow this facility to be incorporated in the cereal crops, which are major users of nitrogen fertilizer.

Seedrate (the number of seeds or plants per unit area), spacing, time and depth of planting can greatly influence crop performance, often with little effect on the costs of production. In temperate areas, time of autumn sowing can affect the winter hardiness of a crop, and late sowing in the spring can reduce yields. It can be equally critical in the tropics. Sown too early, crops may germinate and then die because the rainy season is not fully established. Sown too late, they may miss the flush of nitrates released from soil organic matter when moist conditions follow a hot, dry spell.

One of the disadvantages of annual crops is that the growth rate per unit area is slow until they develop a sufficient leaf area. Various measures have been used to overcome this. Selection of plump seed and the avoidance of overdeep sowing can help. Transplanting enables crop plants to be started in a glasshouse or nursery bed and so speed up growth rates in the field. A new process begins germination before sowing. The seed is imbibed to the point of germination and then sown in a gel strip, a process known as "fluid drilling." It is particularly useful for slow-germinating species and also makes for more uniform crops because all seedlings emerge together.

The control of weeds, pests and diseases is a major part of the task of maintaining and increasing yields. In less-developed areas, cultivations remain the usual means of weed control and hand-hoeing is the most common technique. It is laborious work, often inadequately done, limiting crop yield and restricting the total area farmed. Despite the cost and possible hazards of herbicides, their introduction will do much to increase timeliness and reduce the toil of the subsistence farmer. Pest and disease control is of importance in all

farming systems, but can be critical in hot, humid parts of the world. Some control can be achieved by varying the sequence of crops or by growing a mixture of crop plants so that susceptible host plants are separated in time or space. Pesticides need careful handling to avoid risk to wealth, but we can dispense with them only at the expense of a smaller and more costly food supply.

Exploiting the potential
On a world basis there is the need to feed a population which is increasing by nearly three percent a year. Advancing technology can be expected to keep pace with this increase at least for the foreseeable future. Average national grain yields (wheat, corn, rice) vary around the world from 0.6 to 5 tons per hectare, but individual farmers' yields of 10 tons have been recorded in favorable environments and in some areas triple cropping produces 20 tons per hectare per year. Yet even these yields do not fully exploit the potential. Increasing control over the processes of crop production will gradually raise average yields. In addition, it has been calculated that the total potential agricultural land of the world is 3.4 billion hectares (8.4 billion acres)—one-quarter of the land surface—of which 470 million hectares (1,160 million acres) could be irrigated. At present 1.4 billion hectares (3.4 billion acres) are cultivated and 201 million hectares (496 million acres) of these are irrigated. The question of whether world food production is sufficient to meet world needs is, however, complicated by political factors.

While improving yields requires the selection of appropriate crops and varieties and the use of management suited to their needs, it is also essential to consider the farming system as a whole. It must be stable and, in particular, must avoid deterioration of the land resources. It must also suit the prevailing economic and social conditions, including the availability of purchased inputs and the availability of labor and equipment.

IMPROVING YIELDS—ANIMALS

About 18,000 years ago man hunted animals as a source of food, hides, bones and fuel for cooking and lighting. He relied entirely on the luck of the chase for the quality and quantity of the animals he caught. Since then, man has tamed and domesticated a number of species and he has gained some control over their rate of reproduction and over their physical and physiological characteristics to suit his own purpose.

Not only did man learn to control and breed animals in captivity, he learned to provide sufficient food for them all the year round. He had to develop a method of harnessing the animals for pulling vehicles and implements. In other words, man had to develop the techniques of animal husbandry.

Only when a species had been domesticated to the stage of being bred in captivity could man set out to change such traits as milk yield and carcass composition. This probably happened some 3,000 to 5,000 years ago. At that stage, man selected sheep that retained their fleece so that he could collect it when he wished. Some sheep, however, particularly primitive breeds like the Soay, still shed their fleece over a period of months each year. Man also selectively bred cows that release their milk in the absence of the calf. Primitive cattle and even some tropical cattle will only release their milk when they are suckled by a calf.

Selective domestication
For many species, such as horses and cattle, the descendants of the original wild ancestors became extinct as man multiplied his improved domesticated populations. Only in the last 300 years have the distinct breeds been developed from the landraces that formally existed. Man has selected animals which not only have recognizable color patterns, horn shapes and sizes, but which also differ in more important productive traits, such as milk yield and composition, wool yield and fiber quality, growth rate and body composition, efficiency of converting feed into meat, milk, eggs and fiber, and reproductive rate.

The gradual process of domestication, which has taken several thousand years, can now be successfully repeated with chosen objectives in a matter of decades. The wild stocks of some species and domesticated breeds of other species are exploited by man in three definable situations. These are, first, hunting and trapping of wild animals, which requires some understanding of population conservation if a sustained yield is to be obtained. Second is extensive animal husbandry, in which there are relatively few animals per unit of land and there is little expenditure on labor, buildings and equipment. Third is intensive animal husbandry, in which there are many animals per unit of land and there is more expenditure on labor, buildings and equipment. The output per animal is invariably seen to increase from hunting through extensive to intensive husbandry.

In the last 100 years the rate of improvement in livestock performance has increased. Yields per animal—such as eggs per hen per year, milk yield per cow per year and body weight gain per unit weight feed—have been increasing by between two and three percent a year. Accumulatively, this is a very substantial improvement. For example, in 1920 an average yield per hen was 120 eggs per year, but by 1970 it had increased to 250. Similarly, in 1950, it took 10 weeks and 6 kilograms (13 pounds) of feed for a chicken to reach 1.5 kilograms (3¼ pounds) bodyweight. Today, chickens take less than eight weeks and 3 kilograms (6½ pounds) of feed to reach the same weight.

Controlled circumstances
These changes in animal performance have been achieved by a combination of genetic improvement in the animals, better diets with more appropriate mixes of nutrients, better accommodation, including control of temperature, lighting and air com-

The yak is ideally suited to the mountainous terrain of Nepal, where it is used as a pack and saddle animal. Domestic yaks, which are often kept and bred with domestic cattle, are reared for milk and beef. Their hides provide leather and the hair is used for making rope.

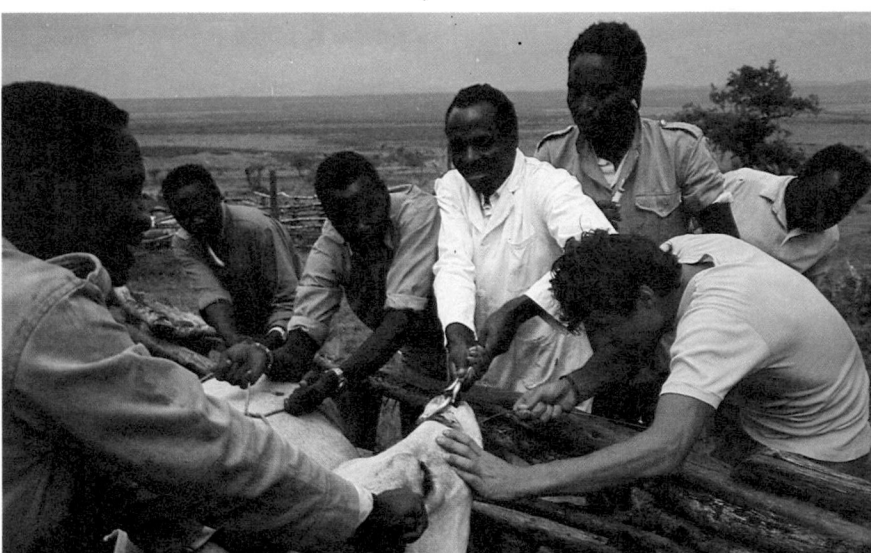
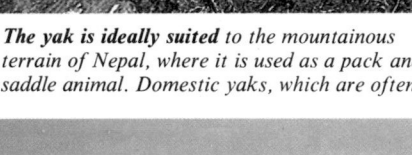

Inspection of animals, seen here in Kenya, helps to prevent the spread of foot-and-mouth disease. Eradicated in many areas, this remains the most contagious disease in livestock.

position, the eradication of some diseases and the control of many others, and much greater attention to intelligent management, particularly of the grazing animal.

The genetic improvement in livestock has happened in three main ways. First, livestock breeders have compared the performance of different landraces and breeds and have multiplied those found to be most suitable for man's purposes. The performance of breeds can differ by 500 percent to 1,000 percent. Today, Merino and Leicester sheep, Hereford and Friesian cattle, Large White and Landrace pigs and White Leghorn hens are found on many farms throughout the world. As man's requirements and economic circumstances change, so those breeds in greatest favor change. Second, livestock breeders have exploited hybrid vigor. When two or more breeds are cross-mated their offspring are often found to have better reproduction, growth rate and yield than the average of the parents; sometimes they are even better than the better parent. Continued production of hybrids depends on continued maintenance of the parent breeds for crossing. Hybrids are widely used for beef, pig and poultry production. They are also used to combine special characteristics from different parents. Thus, in the tropics, the heat tolerance of Zebu cattle, such as the Sahiwal, is combined with the higher milk yield of temperate cattle, such as the Ayrshire, by cross-breeding. Third, selection within favored breeds to improve

The Corriedale sheep, above, was developed in New Zealand to thrive on farms and ranges as a dual-purpose animal, suitable for wool and meat production.

The Charolais breed originated in France, where the cattle were fed on grass to produce lean and tender meat. Now, because of their rapid growth rate, they are established worldwide.

CONNECTIONS

their special characteristics is giving yield improvements of about one-half to one percent per year.

The understanding of the nutritional requirements of animals has improved both in terms of the quantity and quality of food required by the animal at different stages of its life cycle. Knowledge of the physiology and biochemistry of digestion and metabolism in the animal has also increased. Not only is it possible to match the feeds available to the animals' requirements to maximize yield but it is also possible to alter the quality of the animals' yield (such as milk) by altering the feed. The use of computers has enabled the animal feed industry to formulate rations for livestock to a nutritional standard to suit the animal, but at the same time using the least expensive ingredients.

A reduction in mortality

The environment provided for animals on farms has improved during the last 25 years with a simultaneous reduction in mortality and disease. The introduction of insulated buildings, reducing temperature extremes, has not only reduced the amount of feed required by animals in cold weather and heat stress in hot weather but has also improved yield characteristics. The control of lighting patterns for poultry and sheep has enabled egg and lamb production to become aseasonal, so increasing animal performance. Some aspects of animal housing, such as battery cages for hens, and darkened, restricted pens for calves are widely criticized and may be discontinued. Nevertheless, as far as hygiene and length of life are concerned, prospects are better in well-managed animal housing than in free-range circumstances.

Some diseases in animals, such as rinderpest, tuberculosis and brucellosis, are being eradicated by disease-control programs. Other diseases are being controlled by vaccines, medicines and by slaughter policies. Restrictions and records on the movement of animals, together with worldwide coordinated observation of diseases, is helping to control and reduce their incidence and effect.

The main emphasis now is on hygiene and management practices, linked to production records, which lead to disease prevention and control, rather than cure, and there is no reason to doubt that research and the continued application of existing knowledge will give still higher levels of animal performance in the future.

Open-air methods of pig raising can be profitable in temperate climates, as on this hog farm in Indiana, but pork production can easily be adapted to intensive housing.

Comparison of egg production efficiency—New Hampshire (1938) White Leghorn (1964)

- New Hampshire
- White Leghorn

number of birds
body weight
feed per day
egg mass per day
percent of energy efficiency
percent of egg production
percent of protein efficiency

Egg-laying was the first aspect of livestock farming to be subjected to intensive methods of production (left). The life cycle of poultry is comparatively short and results of selection are seen more quickly. The diagram (above) shows the improvement in egg-laying birds resulting from better management.

Reindeer have been domesticated in arctic Europe and Asia and are, to the Lapps for instance, what cattle are to farmers in temperate regions. Reindeer are kept as pack and draft animals and provide milk, cheese and flesh. Their hides are used for tents and clothing.

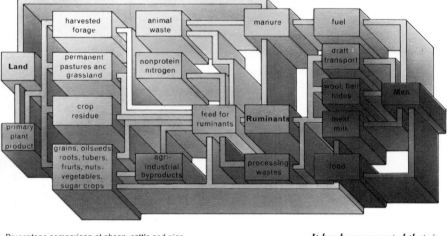

Percentage comparison of sheep, cattle and pigs

- edible meat
- edible fat
- intestines
- bones
- skin/waste
- blood
- wool

sheep
cattle
pigs

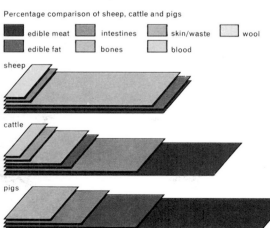

It has been suggested that, in order to combat world food shortages, livestock farming should cease and the agricultural sector should concentrate on crop production, allowing grain to be consumed by man. The chart, above, shows how animals fulfill other important functions, forming part of the human diet, but, more importantly, converting crop residues and cellulose into an edible form.

Although man uses most of the principal food animals, geneticists are constantly striving for improvements.

111

IMPROVING YIELDS—FISH

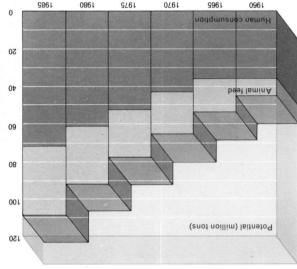

It is expected that by 1985 the developing countries will contribute 63 percent of the world's annual fishmeal production (above) and 29.4 percent of the live fish catch. Inland fishing (including natural and aquaculture) will make up 20 million tons of the expected total world yield of about 110 million tons. Potential yields (right) can be affected by national mismanagement—the most dramatic example has been Peru's anchovy harvest. The 6 million tons drop in catch in 1972 was due partly to changing oceanic conditions and partly to overfishing which exceeded maximum sustainable yields.

Fish farming adds significantly to the world's supply of fish. In China (left), where it has been practiced for thousands of years it contributes 40 percent of the fish eaten. In a typical European trout farm (above) fertilized eggs are incubated (1) to produce larval fish (2), which are then transferred to a fry tank (3). When they can feed on their own (at about three months) the fry (4) are moved to an outdoor pond (5) and then, a year later, at marketing age, to a second pond (6). Those used for breeding are transferred to a third pond (7).

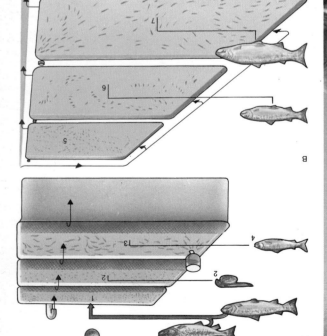

As the fishing industry looks to the future for new sources and ways of maximizing present yields, the net is being cast wider and the hunt plunges deeper. Future potential can be considered in two categories: existing stocks (unfamiliar and conventional species); and aquaculture (products of both controlled and natural environments). The total minimum potential each year is perhaps 170 million tons of fish and the realistic maximum is of the order of 320 million tons. Such estimates are vulnerable due to the lack of knowledge of unfamiliar species. The yield of krill, the large shrimp-like species of zooplankton found in the Antarctic (which the USSR and Japan have already started fishing), could be more than 100 million tons—more than the 1976 total world fish catch of 72 million tons. If smaller zooplankton are included, the yield could be two billion tons or more. The drawback is that many of these unfamiliar species, some grotesque in appearance, have not been accepted at marketing level and processing and palatability tests have yet to be done. One which has made a considerable impact, however, is the blue whiting and stocks of this could yield one million tons annually. Though difficult to process, it has passed initial palatability tests.

As far as conventional species are concerned there is a potential of 90–120 million tons—most of it coming from marine rather than freshwater fisheries—but overfishing is always a problem. There are still some gaps in man's knowledge of the population dynamics of exploited fish stocks (egg and larval mortality rates for example), but the signs of overfishing can be clearly seen by analysis of the age structure of samples. The proportion of new "recruits" to the fishery can be measured and those recruitment levels used to calculate the maximum sustainable yield of the fishery and to provide catch quotas for new regulations. Fish that swim in dense shoals are particularly vulnerable to overfishing and stocks can collapse suddenly. Overfishing contributed largely to the collapse of Peruvian anchovy stocks in 1972.

One area of the industry where yields may be improved is in the cutting down of waste when fish is being processed. Improved filleting techniques alone can raise yields by five percent and recovery of residual flesh after filleting can provide usable morsels to produce fish fingers and so on. Better cold storage alone could increase food supplies of fish by five million tons a year.

Aquaculture
The yearly contribution of aquaculture to the total world fish catch is five to six million tons—about eight percent. Again the potential estimate is wide, between 25 and 100 million tons. The most important marine operations involve shellfish, particularly oysters and mussels, and the leading proponent is Japan. The world production of oysters is around 770,000 tons annually and a rise to around two million tons is forecast by the year 2000. Aquaculture also includes a wide variety of high-value/low-tonnage operations in-

volving many species of finfish and shellfish. In Japan, the leading nation in marine aquaculture, annual production of Kuruma shrimp in tank and pond culture rose from 200 tons in 1965 to 1,300 tons in 1974. This is an example of "intensive" aquaculture which produces luxury foods and involves feeding low-grade fish protein to produce high-grade fish. The term "semi-intensive" is applied to operations in which fertilizers are added to increase plant growth but no direct feeding is given. There are also many important "extensive" operations in which fish are released into and harvested from large bodies of water with no supplementary feeding. Ocean ranching is one of these and is arguably the most exciting development in aquaculture. It is most widely practiced in Japan, North America and the USSR using mainly species of Pacific salmon. The principle is to raise juvenile fish in land-based freshwater hatcheries, to release these to the sea, and then to trap the returning adults. About 1.9 million juveniles of Pacific salmon species are released each year. Ocean ranching avoids the high capital cost of feeding fish and the construction costs of large farms.

Aquaculture is currently entering a growth phase and is likely to become an increasingly important contributor to world fish supply. Success will depend upon increased knowledge. Japan currently invests about 100,000 million yen ($520 million) in support of an aquaculture industry which produced about 800,000 tons of fish (equivalent to about 44 percent of her coastal fisheries' landings) in 1973.

Algae cultured at an oyster farm in Kent, England (above), provide food for 50 million oysters produced annually. In Brittany (left) trays attached to posts sunk in the seabed are filled with oyster larvae, which feed on phytoplankton.

Shrimp are raised indoors at a Japanese shrimp farm at Takamatsu (right) before being transferred to outdoor ponds. Phytoplankton culture is often used for first feeding.

CONFLICTS AND CONCESSIONS
The declaration of Exclusive Economic Zones (EEZs) by most maritime nations since 1977 has brought a welter of change to the fishing industry. With the loss of fishing rights and potential conflicts providing a gloomy backdrop, many of the large fishing fleets are already looking beyond these 200-nautical-mile (370 km) offshore limits. Investment in exploratory expeditions has been stepped up and countries such as the USSR have turned to new grounds farther out and to the unfamiliar inhabitants of the deep oceans. Another effect of EEZs is the dramatic change in beneficiaries with nations agreeing on a series of concessions and trade-offs. The new EEZ owners often lack the technology to exploit their

fish stocks, but wish to encourage others to do so in order that they may, for instance, benefit from levies on the catches. Argentina has drawn up agreements with both the Japanese and the West Germans. As a result, Argentina is expected to expand its yearly fishing catch by three-fifths. In 1977 the catch was a record 340,000 tons. Japanese and West German groups will fish experimentally off Argentina's south coast for a one-year period. Both groups will provide an annual catch of up to 100,000 tons, and the agreements include a commitment from both Japan and West Germany to provide finance for building oceanographic vessels for Argentina. Also, New Zealand has carefully regulated the catches that Japan, the USSR and South Korea can make within its EEZ.

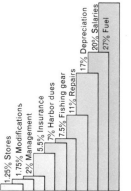

Fuel and salaries account for half the cost of a proposed £1 million survey to find new British fishing grounds. Catches could justify the cost. Unfamiliar species are likely to be exploited in the future.

An Icelandic gunboat squares up to British trawlers in the 1975–76 cod war when fishing zones were in dispute. Cost to Britain was heavy: the loss of 9,000 jobs and damage to Royal Navy frigates of £1 million.

The target for returning salmon in Japanese ocean ranching operations is set at 80,000 tons for the 1980s. A recent Aquaculture Plan prepared by the National Oceanic and Atmospheric Administration of the United States, proposing annual funding for aquaculture of about $18 million by 1979, is encouraging. The attraction of aquaculture is that it offers more direct management than open fisheries and therefore supply and demand can be much more stable.

Research needed
Much more research is also needed to help the growth of aquaculture. The diseases that can develop in cultured fish can be devastating and the techniques of prevention and treatment are not well known. More serious, however, is the legal vacuum in which aquaculture has to operate, particularly in new developments. The absence of adequate legal definitions for aquacultural operations and of ownership of cultured stocks are serious drawbacks which tend to dissuade investors. As with wild fisheries, it is certain that only a much greater degree of international cooperation will bring the stability necessary for efficient harvesting of the world's aquatic resources.

FOOD TECHNOLOGY

The role of agriculture is to insure that enough nutritious food is produced to feed the peoples of the world adequately. Food technology can help to eliminate waste and provide the population with agricultural produce in the most beneficial form. Selected aspects of food technology contribute to maintaining supplies by preserving perishable foods, reducing wastage during storage and preservation and, in some instances, improving the nutritional quality of harvested crops. Untreated food can sometimes prove harmful, and the pasteurization of milk is an example of a process that helps to reduce the risk of food-borne disease.

Methods of preservation
Most of the world's diet is based on cereal grains, grain legumes and some root crops, such as the potato. None of these foods requires extensive processing for its preservation. Grains that are adequately sundried after harvesting can be stored for long periods without deterioration provided they are protected from their surroundings. Proper storage facilities should include protection from damp and from infestation by insects or rodents.

During bad weather, natural drying processes may be speeded up by subjecting grains to a current of warm air. Air drying can also be used to preserve other foods, such as meat and fish. Dried foods are forming an increasing proportion of man's diet as technology in this sphere improves, reducing nutritional damage to a minimum. Driers with improved fuel efficiency are also currently being designed.

Salting and the so-called fermentation methods, which are used in various parts of the world to preserve milk, meat and fish, are not energy-intensive processes. Cold-storage facilities and refrigerated transport for perishable foods probably justify the

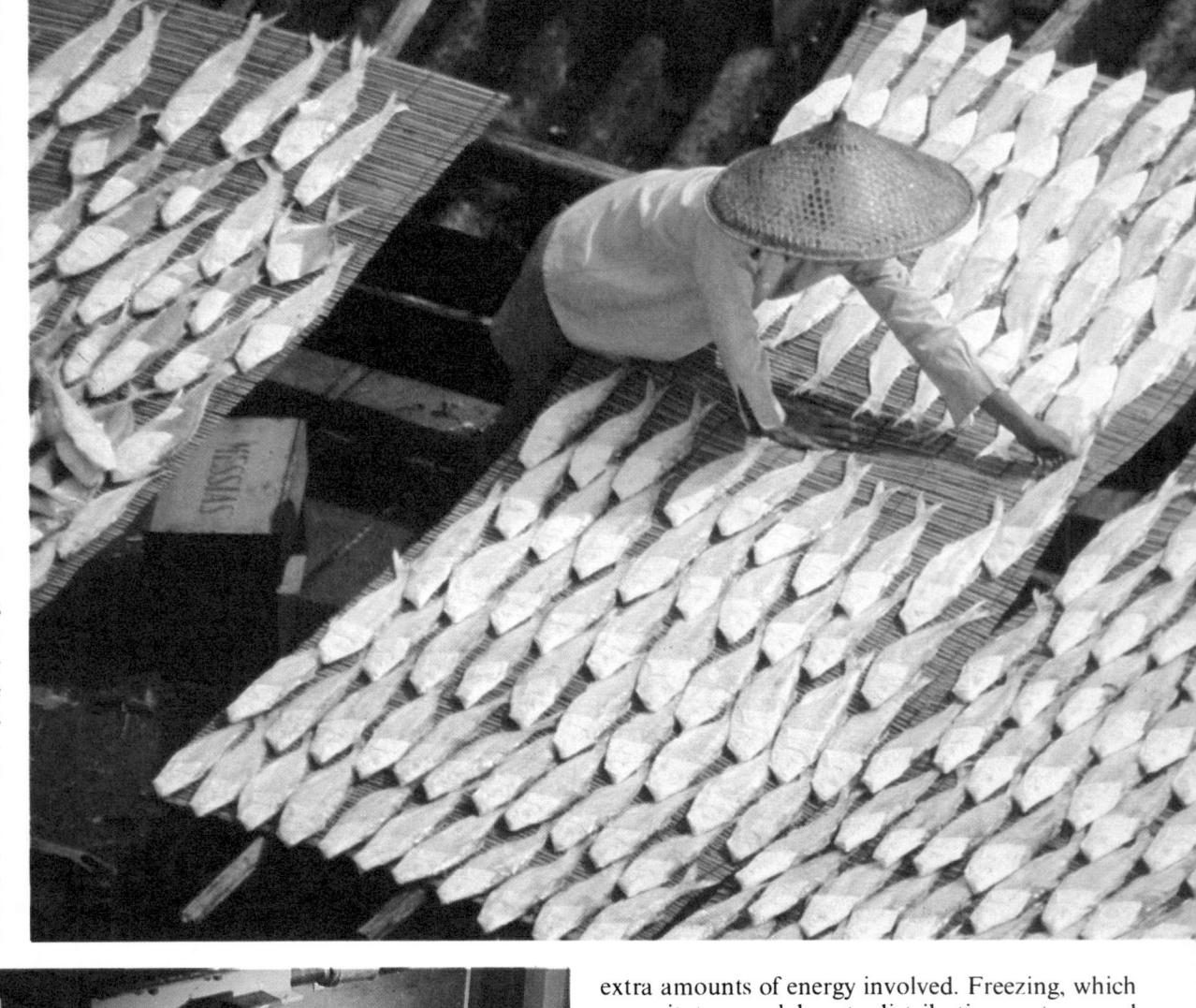

extra amounts of energy involved. Freezing, which necessitates an elaborate distribution system, and canning and bottling, are energy-intensive processes yielding products of low nutritional value that can usually be preserved by other methods. Pickling, smoking and the preparation of sugar preserves add taste and variety to the diet, but are of no nutritional value.

Other methods of preservation, old or new, may assume greater importance as they are applied on a wider scale. Marinating is a traditional method applied mainly to fish—the amount of heat needed is reduced by mixing the food with vinegar, thus increasing its acidity. Irradiation preserves food but at the cost of impaired flavor, and this disadvantage has still to be overcome.

Intermediate moisture foods are preserved by the osmotic effect of chemical compounds such as glycerol or polypropylene glycol. This method is widely used for pet foods, and some of the food for the Apollo space flights was prepared in this way, but so far no marketable food product for general human consumption has been developed.

There are a number of chemical compounds and antibiotics in use as food preservatives. Nisin, for example, reduces the amount of heat needed for preservation and as a result helps to reduce the energy input to the process. Hydrogen peroxide is used as a preservative in the cold sterilization of milk, and is removed completely before consumption by the addition of the enzyme catalase. A limiting factor to the more extensive use of chemical food preservatives is the unknown long-term effects they may have on health. If a harmless, tasteless substance, guaranteed to inhibit all microbial growth could be developed, it would revolutionize the food processing industry.

Eliminating storage losses
In the immediate future, the wider application of established methods of food preservation rather than new technologies is more likely to make the best use of the world's food resources. The storage losses that occur in the developed countries are

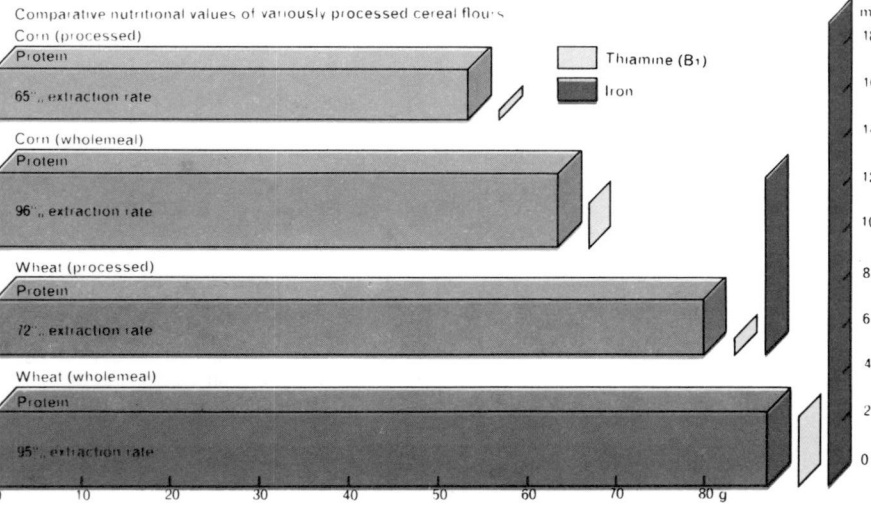

The processing of soybeans to supply a useful substitute for or complement to meat known as textured vegetable protein (TVP), above, is becoming increasingly acceptable in the developed world. The beans (right) are crushed to extract their protein-rich oil, which is mixed with water to form a slurry. This is heated and expanded by extrusion through a nozzle and flavoring and coloring are then added.

Comparative nutritional values of variously processed cereal flours

Corn (processed)
Protein
65% extraction rate

Corn (wholemeal)
Protein
96% extraction rate

Wheat (processed)
Protein
72% extraction rate

Wheat (wholemeal)
Protein
95% extraction rate

☐ Thiamine (B₁)
■ Iron

Processing cereals for flour reduces the nutrient content of the grain in proportion to the extraction rate. In the developing countries traditional methods of preparing cereals, using the whole of the grain, have been replaced to some extent by Western technology for large-scale milling of grain. This provides flour of 65 percent extraction in the case of corn, 72 percent if wheat is used. Both types of flour are prevalent in the affluent West, where the nutritional deficit is less significant. In the less-developed countries, where the dietary range is severely restricted, this loss in food values can be critical.

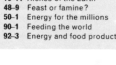

Freshly caught shrimps in French Guianese fishing boats (left) are preserved in ice until they can be processed. By far the most important aspect of food-freezing, however, is that it improves the storage life of foods so that they can be harvested at the peak of freshness and then stored and transported with much greater facility. Consumption of such convenience foods is largely restricted to those countries whose peoples can afford refrigerators and freezers. National consumption of frozen foods differs markedly. In both gross and per capita consumption the USA and Canada are way ahead of Japan or any European rival (below), and total consumption in France and Germany is far more than that in Scandinavian countries.

Fish-drying in Macao is an example of a simple and effective form of food technology in the developing countries. It usually consists of natural drying in the open air and results in an increased concentration of nutrients in the food concerned. The nutrient value of dried food is comparable to that of fresh food. In the developed countries, drying is usually more rapid and is carried out by controlled hot air. Other commercial methods of drying include vacuum-drying and accelerated freeze-drying techniques.

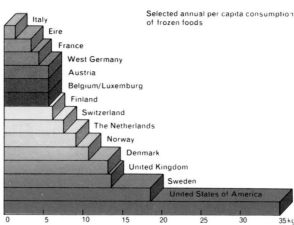

Selected annual per capita consumption of frozen foods

Italy
Eire
France
West Germany
Austria
Belgium/Luxemburg
Finland
Switzerland
The Netherlands
Norway
Denmark
United Kingdom
Sweden
United States of America

0   5   10   15   20   25   30   35 kg

insignificant compared with losses of 30 or 40 percent that take place in the less-developed regions, which are the areas of greatest shortage. The most helpful contribution to be made in the immediate future by developed nations to insure adequate food stocks could be advice on the prevention of losses during storage, the provision of materials for food-store construction and the supply of fuel-efficient drying equipment.

Food is a unique commodity since besides meeting nutritional needs it also has consumer appeal based on color, flavor and texture. In most cases price does not bear much relation to nutritional value. In the developed countries many aspects of food technology are counterproductive because some processes discard or destroy valuable nutrients. White wheat flour and polished rice are examples of foods that have suffered in this way.

New sources of food

World consumption of food is approximately 900 million tons per year. Clearly, adequate resources will have to be available for the large-scale production of any new source. The chemical synthesis of food from carbon dioxide, water and nitrogen is technically feasible but would require 30 times the energy of agricultural methods. Hardly more practical is the chemical conversion of the fossil fuels—coal, natural gas and petroleum—into nutrients. Although some vitamins, fats and amino acids are currently being manufactured on a limited scale using such processes (mainly for livestock feed), the energy cost of converting the fossil fuels by chemical means is reckoned at six times the agricultural energy input. Neither of these ventures into the realms of chemical synthesis is likely to be of much practical use.

However, the conversion of fossil fuels to foods by bacteria, fungi or yeasts is less demanding of energy and a few factories now operate these processes. Algal culture uses the same raw materials as chemical synthesis and may be operated with the same energy input as mechanized agriculture. Its advantage is that it does not compete with agriculture for fertile land.

The only other raw materials available are the wastes from agriculture and the processing of foods. More than half the biomass (the total quantity of living organisms per unit area) from agricultural production is discarded each year and this represents the Earth's most under-utilized bio-resource. There are nutrients that could be separated from some of this waste material.

Oils and fats are being extracted from inedible oilseeds such as cotton and rape seed to provide a substantial contribution to the supply of edible fats. Protein-containing residues from other oilseeds amount, after oil extraction, to 20 million tons a year; for various reasons, most are not currently available as food products. The isolation and texturing of soybean protein from defatted soybeans to form meatlike products is an example of the use of an oilseed residue for food.

Most plant leaves, in the untreated form, cannot be digested by human beings because of their high fiber content. But by means of leaf protein extraction processes a leaf protein concentrate is separated out from the fiber to yield a digestible, palatable and nutritious food which could become an abundant addition to man's diet in the future.

Most other wastes contain carbohydrates which, after the addition of a nitrogen source, can be converted to food by the action of fungi or yeasts. The first most extensive application of these processes is likely to be where the growth of the microorganism also reduces the pollution value of food factory effluents. Foods similar to textured soybean protein have been prepared from bacterial, fungal and yeast products. However, the future of these products as palatable, nutritious foods hinges not least on extensive testing to establish their safety as part of the human diet.

Australian silos in India (left) have successfully protected grain from the depredations of insects and rodents. Some of the food problems in the developing world could be resolved if more attention was given to careful storage. Cockroaches infesting soybean meal (above) are one result of failure to control pests, which often stems from cultural and religious beliefs.

Indian post-harvest losses

Field

Storage

Handling and processing

Other losses
Net harvest

Post-harvest losses in the Indian grain crop can amount to as much as 60 percent of the total crop each year, as the diagram (left) shows. Sacks of Mali grain infested with mold (right) have been spoiled as a result of incorrect storage. Even with proper facilities, yields in developed countries can be susceptible to mold and mildew during storage, but in nontemperate climates where there may be extremes of temperature and humidity, the problems of spoilage through incorrect storage can be even more damaging to crops.

UNITED STATES & CANADA

In North America land has always been plentiful: indeed this very abundance encouraged the early European settlers to be flagrantly wasteful with it, simply moving on when they needed to. Even today there is nothing resembling the pressure on land which has forced Asiatic cultivators, for example, to build staircases of terraces on their hillsides. In an area of 17.3 million square kilometers (6.7 million square miles) 240 million people are only now beginning, in a few areas, to feel short of land.

Most of Anglo-America was uncultivated before the Europeans arrived: it was the hunting ground of Indian tribes. Now agriculture has spread over much of southern Canada and the United States lowlands, but hunting is still a staple of life in the northlands among the Eskimo, and forest still covers nearly 40 percent of the continental surface. The pioneers brought their livestock and farming methods with them, but some of the regions were not suitable for their practices and they adapted from the Indians techniques such as dry-farming and the cultivation of native plants such as maize.

The time is far past when every community had to produce its own food or starve. With fertile farmland elsewhere providing surpluses, and excellent communications across the continent, no part of Anglo-America is required to be self-supporting. American agriculture and American fisheries can feed 240 million people and still have a large surplus left to export.

To achieve such a high level of productivity farming had to be made more intensive than before and yields, traditionally well below European standards, had to be raised. This process of intensification has been made possible in three ways: by increased use of fertilizer (in North America fertilizer consumption doubled between 1955 and 1975); by conservation; and by the development of new strains of heavier-yielding crops and new breeds of livestock, which depended on the establishment of research stations and experimental farms.

Conservation of soil and surface has become an important part of modern farming. The careless techniques of an earlier generation were highlighted in the desperate years of depression, drought and dustbowls in the 1930s. These have now been largely effaced, thanks to the education of the farmer (for example, by the United States Soil Conservation Service) and the work of government agencies like the Tennessee Valley Authority in the United States and Canada's Prairie Farms Rehabilitation Administration.

Some notable breakthroughs have also occurred in crop research. Corn, which in 1937 gave an average American yield of 1,572 kilograms/hectare (25 bushels/acre), yielded 6,098 kilograms (97 bushels) across the nation in 1972. A wheat has been developed yielding up to 13,203 kilograms (210 bushels), or more than five tons an acre, in commercial growth. The average yield of potatoes rose by nearly 40 percent in 20 years. So far, as population density in North America has increased, yields of leading crops have more than kept up.

Financial and social cost

There is, however, a cost to be paid for the high-yield farming of today. In part this cost is financial —that of additional inputs. But it is also a social cost—that of chemical pollution. Fertilizers, weed-killers and crop sprays introduce into the natural ecosystem foreign chemicals which disturb it. Streams become polluted, fish die, and drinking water is affected. There is also an energy cost of production. Farm machines and fertilizer manufacture consume huge quantities of petroleum. It has been estimated that if the whole world adopted the food-production methods of the United States, known reserves of petroleum would be exhausted in less than 30 years. In other words, food is being produced by the massive consumption of non-renewable fuel resources. On the other hand many nations have been grateful for North American food supplies in the past 40 years. For the future, it seems clear that there is enormous scope for further

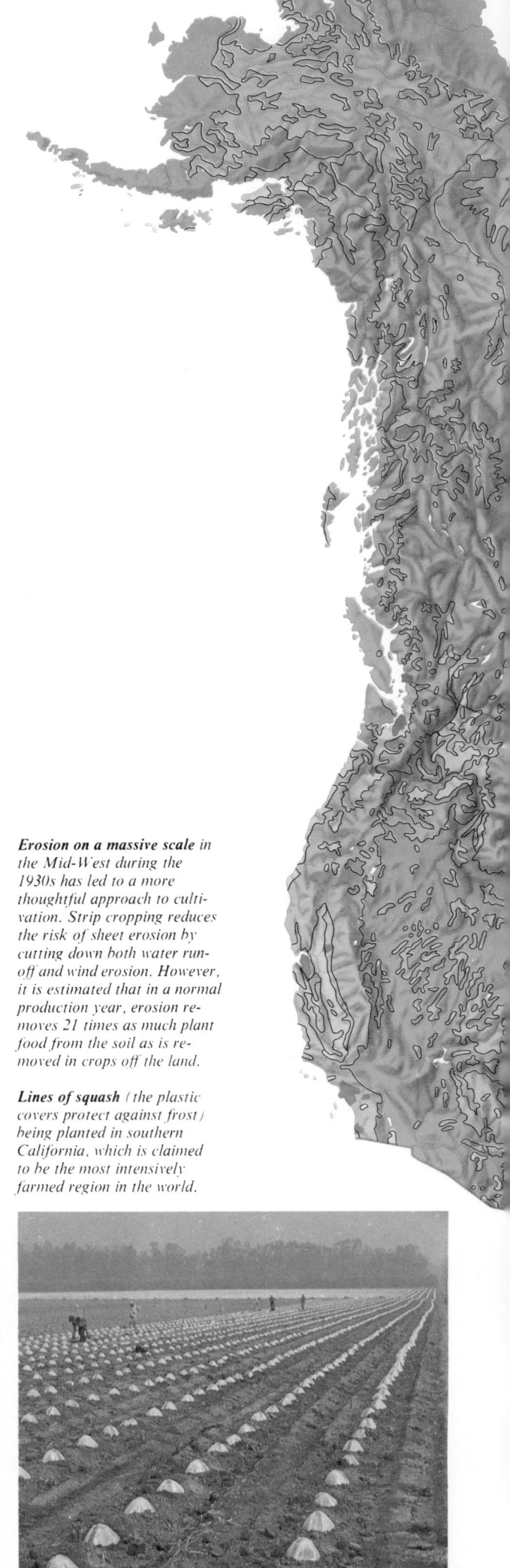

Erosion on a massive scale in the Mid-West during the 1930s has led to a more thoughtful approach to cultivation. Strip cropping reduces the risk of sheet erosion by cutting down both water run-off and wind erosion. However, it is estimated that in a normal production year, erosion removes 21 times as much plant food from the soil as is removed in crops off the land.

Lines of squash (the plastic covers protect against frost) being planted in southern California, which is claimed to be the most intensively farmed region in the world.

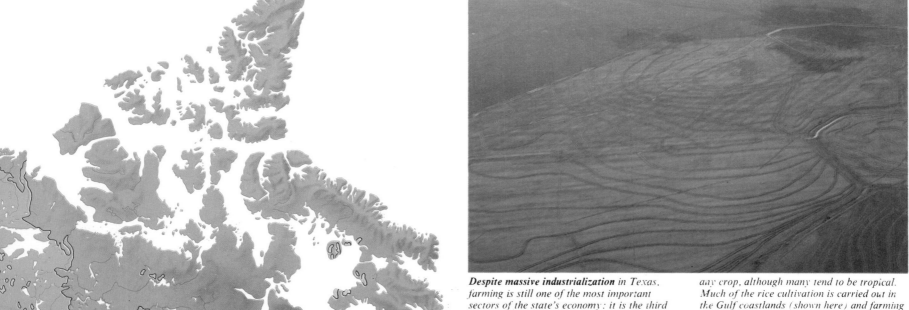

Despite massive industrialization in Texas, farming is still one of the most important sectors of the state's economy; it is the third largest agricultural producer in the USA. The state is so vast that climatic and soil conditions vary enough to permit the growing of almost any crop, although many tend to be tropical. Much of the rice cultivation is carried out in the Gulf coastlands (shown here) and farming of this type tends to be highly mechanized—a far cry from the labor-intensive rice production of the developing nations.

New dams have been built on the Colorado River to ease the water shortage—a result of increased irrigation for crops such as these citrus fruits.

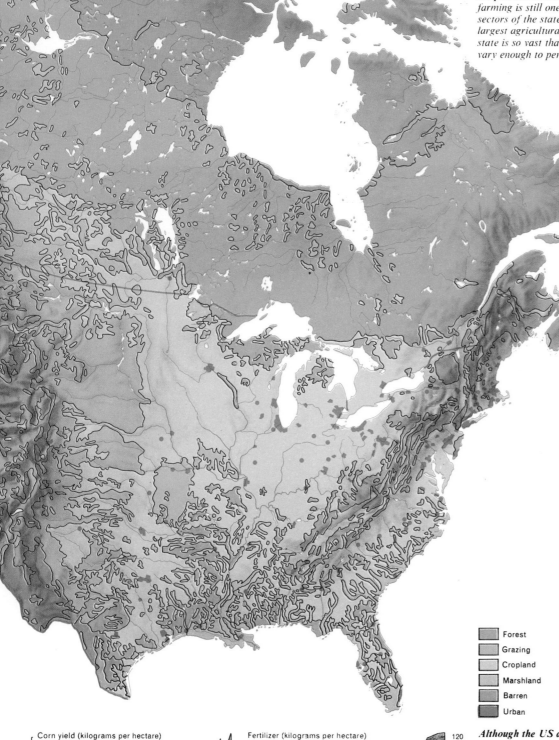

Forest
Grazing
Cropland
Marshland
Barren
Urban

Corn yield (kilograms per hectare)

Fertilizer (kilograms per hectare)

Nitrogen
Phosphorus
Potassium

Although the US acreage under corn has declined, yield per hectare has increased. The production of hybrid corn is one of the notable successes of modern agriculture: yields increased by 240 percent from 1945 to 1970. Fertilizer is the largest single input in corn production, but phosphorus and potassium reserves are limited and nitrogen processing requires large energy inputs, so substitutes are needed.

advances in methods of cultivation, especially using controlled (indoor) environments to raise yields still higher.

The farms of North America are large compared with the peasant holdings of Africa or Asia, but small considering the country's size. The great majority of them are operated by an individual farmer and his family: they are "family farms." The number of giant corporate farms, covering thousands of acres, is small although it is true that such farms play a disproportionately large part in total output. The family farm is a North American institution that has been cherished since the earliest days of settlement. Much of the land legislation in both countries has been couched in terms of a unit size of 64.8 hectares (160 acres), the so-called quarter section (one-quarter square mile), which in humid regions was a reasonable size for a mixed farm. In the dry west it represented the grazing for, perhaps, one cow, but still it symbolized the government's concern to encourage the family farm.

The coming of machines

That these nations of small farmers should have performed so spectacularly in the 20th century has been primarily due to the technical progress they have made. Hired labor has been replaced by machines for virtually all tasks, and the machines perform in minutes jobs which by hand took days or weeks. A whole class of agricultural laborer has disappeared (generally moving to the city to find work), leaving the owner-operator alone with his machines. These machines, however, are so costly that they must be fully employed if they are to pay for themselves. As a result, two points are generally true about the North American farm today: the operator must enlarge his acreage to remain in business, and because of the increasing size plus the machinery involved, the investment represented by a North American farm will be vast.

117

In 1974 it was estimated that in North America the optimum size for a one-man wheat farm was a barley farm in Montana of 793 hectares (1,960 acres). Few are fortunate enough to possess the optimum, but the idea that one man and his family can cultivate almost 800 hectares of prime American wheatland is as exciting as it is exceptional.

The optimum sizes for other one-man farms were 324 hectares (800 acres) for a corn/soybean farm in Indiana, 146 hectares (360 acres) for a rice/soybean farm in Louisiana, and 162 hectares (400 acres) for an irrigated cotton farm in California. The average-sized farm in the United States in 1930 was 61.1 hectares (151 acres) — that is close to the 160-acre ideal. By 1976 it had risen to 157.8 hectares (390 acres). In Canada at the same date the average was 223.8 hectares (553 acres). These farms represent investments of between $150,000 and $160,000. A Class 1 farm today can hardly cost less than $1 million. The chance of a young man buying into the farming world is therefore negligible; he must either inherit, or find one of the scarce jobs as manager, or leave the land. Meanwhile, the average age of the farmers who remain steadily increases.

While the farmers are recognizable descendants of the original settlers, the nature of their life and work has changed radically. Formerly, each farm was, as far as possible, self-contained, and the farmer carried out his own processing and some of his own marketing. Today, he is likely to be a producer, pure and simple. He buys in his supplies of seed or fertilizer, and ships his produce unprocessed, as merely the production link in a system of agribusiness dominated by food corporations.

The North American governments have been drawn into playing an increasing role in food production and marketing. This was due, back in the 1930s, to the obvious economic distress of millions of farmers; more recently, it has been due to wartime needs and, latterly, to the recognition that the continent has become the larder of the free world. The United States government has all along been able to intervene more directly on the farmers be-

half than the Canadian, because in Canada agriculture plays so important a part in the economy that the rest of that economy could not subsidize it on the scale of the United States. But both governments have had policies of supporting prices and regulating sales. As a result, and thanks to the productive efficiency of the farmers, there is no doubt that North America can feed itself. The two important questions are: how many other people can it feed and what sort of diet should be encouraged?

Markets for food

American exports before 1870 were mainly of raw materials and foodstuffs: for Canada this was true up to World War II and beyond. What is remarkable about both countries is that, although they developed as industrial powers, they have not stopped producing and exporting food; still less have they become net importers like Great Britain. Throughout the 1950s and 1960s, their main problem was precisely to find markets for these exports. The United States gave away huge amounts of grain and cotton by which it was embarrassed, but ran into difficulties since other countries. Canada among them, were trying to sell what the United States was giving away. In the 1970s, however, the market has been much tighter and the international value of surplus food crops has risen accordingly. In an emergency, both countries could quite quickly put back into service lands withdrawn to pasture in times of plenty.

The answer to the second question reflects the fact that society's consumption of particular foods varies through time. The average North American was eating 65.8 kilograms (145 pounds) of meat a year in 1950 but 81.7 kilograms (180 pounds) in 1975; he was eating 4.9 kilograms (11 pounds) of butter in 1950 but only 2.1 kilograms (4.7 pounds) in 1975 (margarine made up the difference). Partly this has reflected a rising standard of living but also a concern for a balanced diet and the belief that North Americans have usually eaten too much. In 1977 the United States government through the

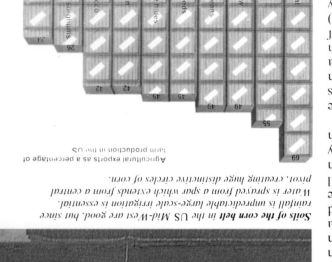

North America is still regarded as the bread basket of the world with exports of wheat in 1974 amounting to about half the grain available on the world market at that time.

Agricultural exports as a percentage of farm production in the US.

Corn	21
Grain sorghums	26
Tobacco	42
Cotton	42
Cattle hides	45
Almonds	49
Soybeans	49
Tallow	55
Rice	
Wheat	69

Soils of the corn belt in the US Mid-West are good, but since rainfall is unpredictable large-scale irrigation is essential. Water is sprayed from a spur which extends from a central pivot, creating huge distinctive circles of corn.

Agribusiness, the marriage of agriculture and industry, is now an established fact in North America. Investment in machinery is great: cattle rearing is mechanized, ensuring rapid animal growth and relatively quick turnover.

The average Canadian farm size has increased from 187 hectares (462 acres) in 1971 to more than 200 hectares (494 acres) in 1977, but it is unlikely any more land will go to farming despite its importance to the economy. Saskatchewan, the location of this mixed farm, is now the only province where more people are involved in agriculture than in industry.

Food and Agriculture Act committed itself to encouraging dietary improvement. Other food sources are being explored: for example, the long-existing coastal fisheries are being supplemented by freshwater fish farming and by attempts to increase fish growth in the shallow seas, where overfishing by foreign boats has threatened supplies.

Agriculture is only one of the uses to which land can be put and in North America agriculture faces more competition than anywhere else in the world. Between 1966 and 1976, the United States lost 19 million hectares (47 million acres) of farming land. In Canada over the same period there was a small gain (600,000 hectares/1.5 million acres), but it was all in a small area of the northwest (the Peace River Region) and the rest of the country witnessed the same sort of loss as the United States experienced. Some of the land lost reverted to forest; much of it disappeared under housing or airports.

Safeguarding farmlands
Forestry and built-up areas are not the only challengers; one of the largest claimants is recreational use. No one can dispute the need for public open space in a continent where more than three-quarters of the people live in urban areas, but in North America the amount of space devoted to parks of all kinds exceeds 162 million hectares (400 million acres). Agriculture, in fact, is usually at the bottom of land uses, in terms of income yield per hectare. Despite the obvious danger which this presents to the nation's food supply, however, only a few scattered attempts have been made to safeguard the farmlands. There exists no federal control with which to do so. The states and provinces have the powers, but few have used them (Wisconsin, one of the most forward-looking states, passed a Farmland Preservation Act only in 1977) and individual

counties and cities normally resist the idea of controls because of their effect on the tax revenue. So the past 30 years have seen the disappearance beneath suburbs and highways of some of the richest farmlands even in California, the leading farm state in the United States—which also happens to be the most populous. To arrest this takeover process some new attitudes would have to be developed.

Forests have also displaced agriculture along the frontiers of cultivation in eastern Canada and the northern United States and on the worn-out lands of the southeast. There is no reason to regret this, however, since these areas yield more; and yield it naturally, under trees than under poor farming. In Canada, their importance to the national economy is enormous. Wood products contribute more than a quarter of the nation's exports and their processing occupies the largest group of industrial workers—nearly 300,000. Most of the provinces exercise controls over cutting timber, especially on the Crown or public lands, so that even in the most accessible areas the cut is kept well below the annual growth rate. This makes Canada's forests an attractive target for United States companies short of reserves on their own side of the border, but the activity of such companies is carefully controlled by most provinces. The United States in fact relies heavily on imports from Canada of sawn timber and paper. To adjudicate between the claims of conflicting land users is, in most societies, one of the roles of government. In North America, it is a function which has, up to the present, largely gone by default. The states and provinces have the powers, but exercise them sparingly or not at all; the federal governments can only cajole, and meanwhile set a good example on their own lands. The idea of controlled land use is one to which the Anglo-Americans have yet to become reconciled.

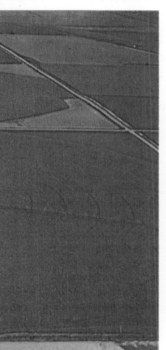

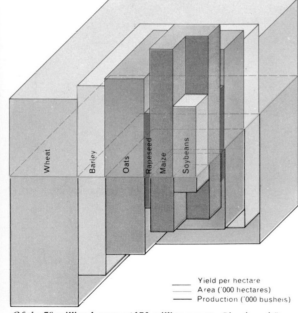

Yield per hectare
Area ('000 hectares)
Production ('000 bushels)

Of the 70 million hectares (173 million acres) of land used for agriculture in Canada, 42 million hectares (104 million acres) have been improved and used for intensive cultivation.

British Columbia *has approximately 60 percent of Canada's natural reserves of standing timber. Because Douglas fir is an all-round softwood with good rot resistance there has been a tendency to overexploit it in some areas and it has been saved from extinction only by good forest management. Though conservation is now the key word, the processing of wood continues—there are mills along the west coast of Vancouver Island, and at Nanaimo on the east coast of the island there are several sawmills and a large pulp-processing plant.*

In the past *the US established fish hatcheries for salmon and trout, but the fish raised were used primarily for sporting purposes. Now fish farms such as this one in Florida are increasing and the pond culture of catfish has reached small industry status. The Americans are also trying to establish fish farms in the open sea and have copied ideas originating in Japan. Reefs consisting of old car bodies and concrete pipes have been sunk offshore. In many cases this has turned a once-barren region into one which yields a sizable fish catch.*

WESTERN EUROPE–THE EEC

The EEC Nine (shown in green) cover a small area compared to, say, the USSR, but they are much more densely populated.

At first the European Economic Community was known as "The Six": Belgium, France, West Germany, Italy, Luxembourg and the Netherlands were founder members when the Community was formed in 1958 to promote economic and political cooperation between member states. In 1973, with the accession of Denmark, the Irish Republic and the United Kingdom, the Community enlarged to "The Nine." Now, with Portugal, Spain and Greece seeking admission, the EEC is likely to achieve the round dozen by the early 1980s. Population density of The Nine—110 persons per square kilometer (307 per square mile)—is greater than that of the United States (23/58) and far exceeds that of the USSR (11/30). It is hardly surprising, therefore, that food is a major preoccupation, and that a key area of cooperation within the Community is agriculture. Centerpiece of this cooperation is the Common Agricultural Policy, designed to boost farm production while at the same time ensuring stable markets, reasonable prices to farmers for their produce and a fair standard of living for those who work on the land.

About three-fifths of the EEC's land area is devoted to agriculture, a total of 93 million hectares (230 million acres). A further fifth is forest or woodland, which, in 1974, contributed about three percent of world roundwood production. Agriculture, forestry and fishing (EEC fleets land about four million tons of fish a year) employ less than nine percent of the Community's working population. Today, although there are less than half the number of people working on the land than there were in 1960, agricultural output is continuing to rise. Production began to climb with the postwar drive to modernize agriculture. The success of this effort can be judged not least by the improved yield of wheat, which, by the mid-1970s, was almost double what it had been in 1950. Yields of more than 10 tons per hectare have been recorded.

Major farm products

About 26 million hectares (64 million acres) of land produce wheat, barley, oats, rye and corn, but only a little rice is grown in the EEC. Each of The Nine is more than 90 percent self-sufficient in potatoes: an annual crop of some 40 million tons is grown on 1.3 million hectares (3.2 million acres). Less than two million hectares (5 million acres) of sugar beet provide the Community with 90 percent of its sugar needs, besides yielding byproducts for animal food. The present area of oilseed crops— rape, linseed, sunflowers—gives only 40 percent self-sufficiency in oils and fats. Vegetables are grown on about one million hectares, and a similar area is given over to a variety of fruits. Also, France and Italy each devote more than a million hectares to vineyards, and a further one million hectares, mostly in Italy, are taken up with olive groves.

More than half the EEC's cultivatable area is grassland, varying widely in productivity from intensively managed lowland sites (rich enough to

These giant straw bales are a common sight on the rolling plains of northern France. Made up of leaves, husks and dried stalks of grain crops, they are used for animal feed and bedding. France is Western Europe's largest agricultural producer, with 32 million hectares (79 million acres) under cultivation. Most of the land is given over to cereals.

- Forest
- Grazing
- Cropland
- Marshland
- Barren
- Urban

The agricultural trade of the European Economic Community

- 1964–66 (average figures)
- 1974

Imports

Exports

- EEC
- LDCs
- USA/Canada
- Other European countries
- Australia/New Zealand
- Eastern Europe
- Other countries

As agricultural production within the EEC has increased over recent years, food imports have fallen. However, the high level of price fixing for EEC produce is costly to maintain and has created many surpluses, besides necessitating high tariffs on food imports from outside.

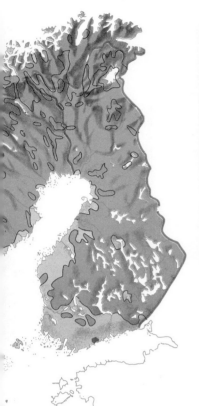

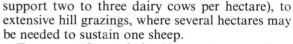

Denmark's milk yield, mostly produced on small family farms, is tested each week and graded according to quality (top left). Livestock markets (top right) are an important feature of the farming scene in Devon, where the rural economy relies largely on stock farming. Holland's bulbfields (left) provide tourist appeal and a key export commodity; millions of bulbs are auctioned off each year at Aalsmeer.

French vineyards and a brewery in Germany provide contrasting views both of land use and of national tastes within the EEC. Grapes are one of France's premier crops, and these vineyards—terraced on sunlit granite slopes above a bend in the River Rhône— produce one of the great Rhône wines: grapes have been cultivated here, at Tain l'Hermitage, since Roman times. In the mid-1970s, the West Germans were drinking more beer—150 liters (33 gallons) a head each year— than any other EEC country. The Italians had the highest wine consumption in Western Europe—103 liters (23 gallons) a head. Southern Ireland had least use for the grape, with wine intake at two liters (four pints) per head.

support two to three dairy cows per hectare), to extensive hill grazings, where several hectares may be needed to sustain one sheep.

For every 10 people in the EEC there are three head of cattle, three pigs and two sheep or goats. Though the number of dairy cows, currently about 25 million, is falling slightly, milk output is increasing at a steady rate because of the continued rise in average yields, which have reached 4,000 liters (1,065 gallons) per cow year in the Netherlands, Denmark and the United Kingdom. In addition, the Community has 7.8 million head of beef cattle (one-third in France), 43 million sheep (almost half in Britain) and 69 million pigs (a quarter of these in West Germany). The production of pigs and poultry for meat and eggs is tending to move indoors—to highly intensive factory farming systems, where animals are housed in large units with automatic control of temperature and ventilation. It is this trend toward intensification which accounts for a vastly reduced manpower requirement, but, at the same time, produces greater yields. Today in the EEC, animal products contribute 60 percent of the value of total farm output.

Prices in the EEC

Agricultural production in the EEC rose by 20 percent from 1965 to 1975, a decade during which the increase in population was only seven percent. This is how the Community has progressed from being a net importer of food to self-sufficiency. However, prices of farm produce within the EEC are substantially above world price levels, and this means that surpluses must either be sold into storage or heavily subsidized in order to compete on the world market. At present sugar exports are receiving a massive subsidy, and vast quantities of butter—world price £900 a ton, £1,630 in the EEC— skimmed milk and beef are coming off the market to be sold into intervention. The distribution of support between countries and commodities has not been equitable. A particular embarrassment, with milk output exceeding consumption by 10 percent, is the high level of support for dairying.

Relatively high EEC prices have also necessitated high tariffs on food bought in from outside, and this has changed the whole pattern of agricultural trade. In 1964 only 30 percent of imported food came from within the Community, compared with 45 percent a decade later: the value of imports from less-developed countries fell from 33 to 25 percent. Not surprisingly, outsiders view the Common Agricultural Policy as highly protectionist.

The long-term solution to the Community's problems lies in the reduction of price levels for agricultural products, but such suggestions provoke considerable political opposition. This is a resistance which, it is thought, will only disappear along with the vast number of very small farms in Europe. The restructuring of agriculture through the amalgamation of farms is considered to be of vital importance to the future of the EEC.

WESTERN EUROPE—NON-EEC COUNTRIES

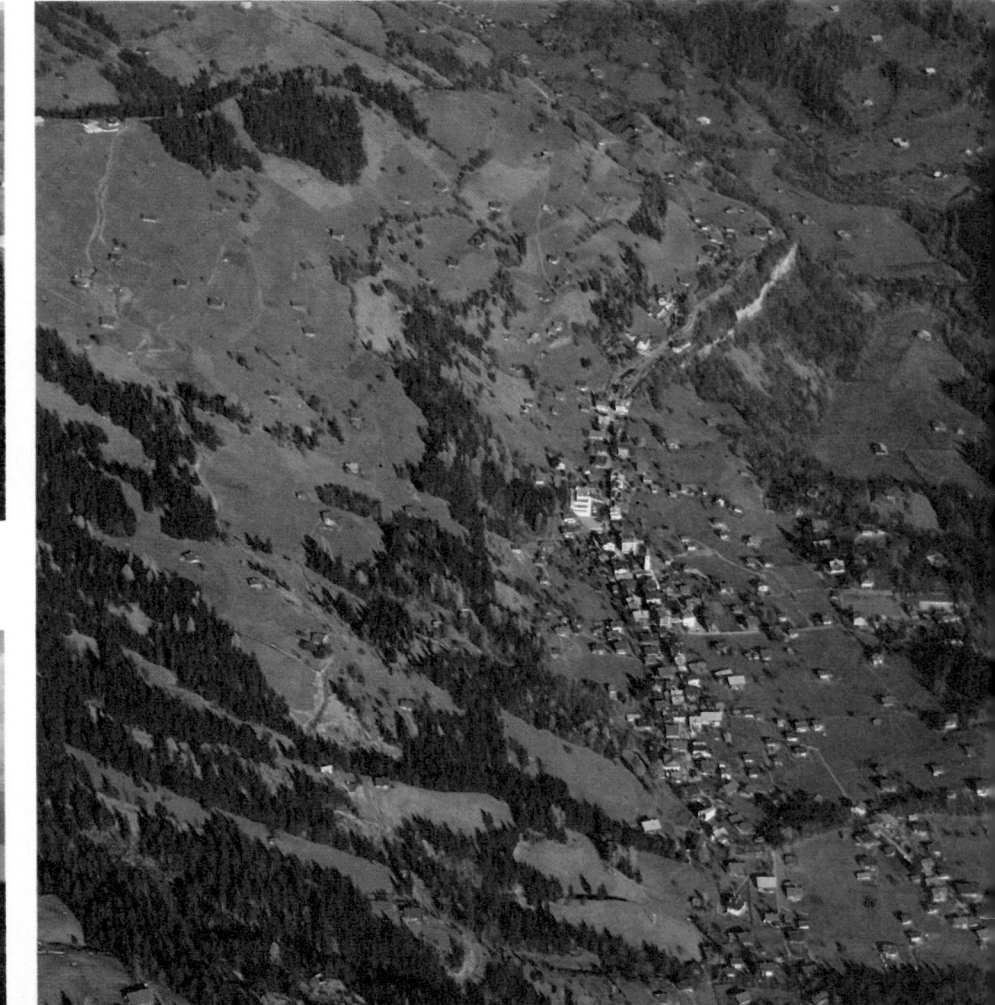

Sweden retains its traditional methods of land use. Half the land is wooded, and forestry and farming are inseparable: farmers turn to timber for extra winter income. Government plans include increased production of oilseeds, like the rapeseed shown here.

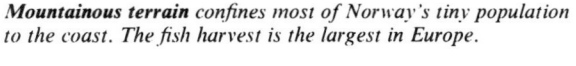

Green on this map, countries outside the EEC fall into three groups: Iceland, Norway and Sweden in the north; Switzerland and Austria; and Spain, Portugal and Greece.

Mountainous terrain confines most of Norway's tiny population to the coast. The fish harvest is the largest in Europe.

Despite Switzerland's extensive mountain ranges, agriculture is an important part of the economy. Three-quarters of the land is used for farming and forestry. Alpine pastures can only

The non-EEC countries of Western Europe can be bracketed together in three groups, each quite distinct from the point of view of climate, geographical location and economic status. The northern group consists of three countries—Iceland, Norway and Sweden—extending from the Arctic Circle southward to latitude 55°N. With long, hard winters limiting crop production, all three have capitalized on their long coastlines to develop flourishing sea-fishing industries. Standards of living are high, with annual Gross Domestic Products per head ranging from $5,700 in Iceland to almost $8,500 in Sweden. Also economically advanced are Austria (GDP $5,000) and Switzerland ($8,500), landlocked countries of the central group. Here the climate is less severe, but the amount of usable land is limited.

In contrast, the southern countries—Spain, Portugal and Greece—are characterized by economies which are far less developed. Their climates are more favorable to agriculture, although shortage of water presents some difficulties. The contribution of agriculture to meager GDPs—less than $3,000 per head in each case—is nine percent in Portugal, 14 percent in Spain and 17 percent in Greece. Land use figures are fairly similar to those for EEC member countries. Agriculture, forestry and fishing employ relatively far more people—well over a third of the population in Greece—than in countries of the central and northern groups.

Regional patterns

THE NORTHERN GROUP includes Iceland, which has a sizeable land area—103,000 square kilometers (39,770 square miles)—but one which is inhospitable and largely unusable for farming. Only one-quarter of the land surface carries any vegetation, and of this area only about five percent can be tilled. Rough pasture provides summer grazing for approximately 60,000 cattle and 900,000 sheep. But these animals have to be wintered indoors and fed on hay and imported concentrate feeds.

Iceland relies on its fishing industry—fish and

fish products—for 70 percent of its exports. More than five percent of the tiny population of 0.2 million is employed in fishing, with a further eight percent manning processing plants. The annual catch has been increasing in recent years, although catches of cod, the single most valuable species, have risen relatively more slowly. It is this economic dependence on the fishing industry which accounts for Iceland's firm stand during 30 years of controversy over national fishing rights. However, the 1975 extension of fishing limits to 200 nautical miles (370 kilometers), together with careful monitoring of the quality and composition of fish stocks, contributes to the authorities' confidence with regard to long-term prospects.

Norway, consisting largely of upland pasture and uninhabitable mountains, is another country short on cultivatable land. Here the cultivated area is only about 10,000 square kilometers (3,860 square miles), or 3.4 percent of the total land surface. However, the Gulf Stream brings relatively warm waters to Norway's western coast, where crops such as potatoes, cereals and fruit are grown. The general profile of farming in Norway, however, is of small upland units with the emphasis on livestock production, in particular dairying. The authorities are attempting to bolster self-sufficiency. Prices paid to farmers, most of whom also work part-time in forestry or fishing, are geared to production costs rather than retail food prices. Norway's timber estate is a profitable one, and forests cover almost one-quarter of the land surface. The country also enjoys a rich haul from the sea. Its catch—more than three million tons in 1976—is greater than that of any other country in Europe.

Sweden is largely mountainous in the north, but the south is generally low-lying and has less rainfall. Grain, grass and potatoes can be grown, although here again farmers rely on livestock rearing. Dairy produce accounts for about 30 percent of agricultural output. Approximately half the country is covered with forests—principally birch and fir—which sustain timber, pulp and paper-

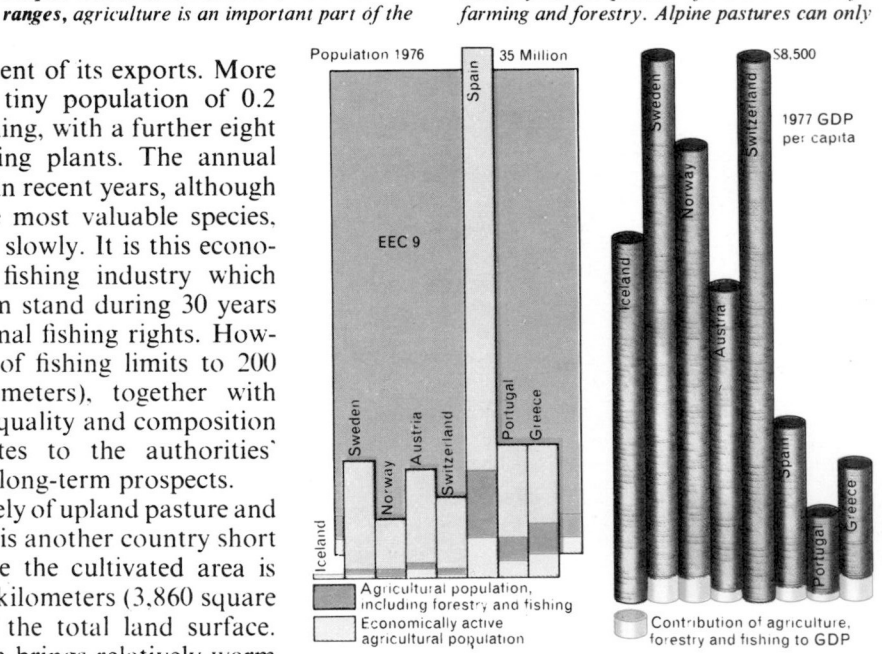

Population 1976 · 35 Million · 1977 GDP per capita · $8,500

EEC 9 · Spain · Iceland · Sweden · Norway · Austria · Switzerland · Portugal · Greece · Spain

Agricultural population, including forestry and fishing
Economically active agricultural population
Contribution of agriculture, forestry and fishing to GDP

While entry into the EEC of Spain, Portugal and Greece would mean an increase in consumers, the number of farmers would increase too, by up to 60 percent, bringing the total in the Community to about 14 million. The prospect of a surplus of Mediterranean produce will lead to tough political bargaining before these three nations can be admitted to the Community.

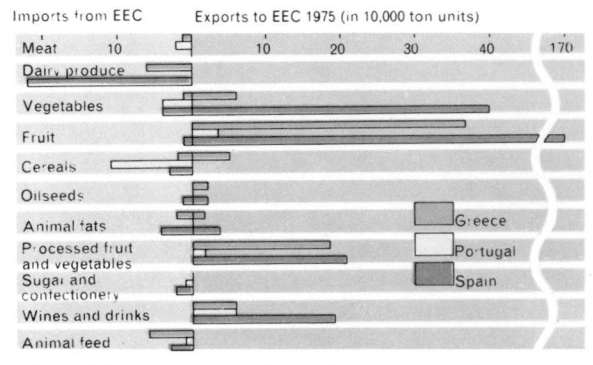

Imports from EEC · Exports to EEC 1975 (in 10,000 ton units)

Meat		
Dairy produce		
Vegetables		
Fruit		
Cereals		
Oilseeds		
Animal fats		
Processed fruit and vegetables		
Sugar and confectionery		
Wines and drinks		
Animal feed		

Greece · Portugal · Spain

Sharp differences in economic standing are revealed between non-EEC countries in northern and central Europe and the southern states. Within the EEC, price support mechanisms favor agricultural produce from northern countries. Entry of Spain, Portugal and Greece to the EEC would increase demands for the development of the agricultural economies of southern Europe.

be used in summer: cattle are taken to the mountains for summer grazing and brought back to winter in the valleys.

milling industries. Sweden is responsible for four percent of world softwood production and forestry products constitute half the value of exports.

THE CENTRAL GROUP of non-EEC countries also has the problems of a mountainous terrain. Alpine ranges in Switzerland cover about 60 percent of the total land surface, and, on slopes too steep for machinery, much of the farmwork is still done by hand. Compared with dynamic development in other areas of the Swiss economy, modernization of farming is slow. Nevertheless, agriculture is an important feature of the economy and well supported by government. Most farms are small and owner-occupied, with dairying as the major enterprise. However, due to a surfeit of dairy produce, there are moves now to increase beef production. Cheese is the only farm product exported in quantity. Arable farming is restricted chiefly to the valleys. Switzerland's forests—two-thirds publicly owned—serve as protection against avalanches and landslides, as well as yielding a timber crop.

Austria is Europe's most mountainous country, with roughly 64 percent of its territory lying within the alpine region. Agriculture is, however, an important part of the economy and Austria's self-sufficiency for foods has continued to rise, reaching 84 percent in 1975. Grassland alpine farms support livestock, and arable crops—chiefly cereals and potatoes—are grown on plains and hills outside the mountainous regions. Forests and woodland cover about 40 percent of the land surface.

THE SOUTHERN GROUP's largest country in terms of both area (512,000 square kilometers/197,632 square miles) and population (35 million) is Spain. Traditionally the Spanish economy has been an agricultural one, but the growth of industry has been so rapid over the past two decades that farming is now losing its predominance. From 1960 to

1970 the percentage of the population employed on the land fell from 41 to 28. Principal crops are cereals, citrus fruits, olives, almonds and vines. The fishing industry is also, traditionally, of importance.

In Portugal, too, the climate favors the growth of similar crops, including grapes for wine. Farm output fell, however, following "agrarian reform," including nationalization of more than half the land, in 1974–75. Some land was returned to the private sector in 1977, and the emphasis is now on the coexistence of private farms and collectives. Extensive forests of pine, cork, eucalyptus and chestnut cover 20 percent or so of the land surface.

Greece is another country with a strong agricultural tradition, meeting most of its own food requirements and exporting some products. But here, too, the growth of industry has reduced the contribution of agriculture to the export trade—from 90 percent in 1960 to 36 percent in 1974.

New applicants to the EEC

The future of agriculture throughout Western Europe could soon be influenced by the fact that all three southern states have applied for membership of the EEC. If Spain, Portugal and Greece were to be admitted, the effects would include a 49 percent increase in land being farmed, but the growth in agricultural output would only be 24 percent. Application of the Common Agricultural Policy mechanism of support prices and intervention buying would no doubt encourage the new entrants to step up production, and here the dilemma is that some of their principal products—wine, olive oil, fresh fruit and vegetables—are already in, or approaching, a situation of surplus in the Community. Admission of these three countries to the EEC would bring about increased pressure for changes in the Common Agricultural Policy.

On the island of Thera in the Aegean many varieties of vines flourish in the volcanic soils. Of an annual production of 500 million liters (110 million gallons) a fifth is exported.

Olive groves *such as this one, warmed by the Andalusian sun, are a major feature of Spain's economy. However, high yields of olive oil, along with other produce such as citrus fruits, could, by creating additional market surpluses, prove a major obstacle to the admission of Spain to the EEC.*

Portugal's climate *favors the growth of fruit and vegetables, and the country's tomato concentrate, produced at low cost, is an important export. Yet a run of bad harvests has forced the authorities to turn to US aid in order to buy foreign produce. The price of food rose by 52 percent in 1977.*

In Greece, with an economy hitherto grounded in agriculture, almonds are a traditional crop. But the growth of industry is well under way. Greece is already negotiating to join the EEC.

123

AUSTRALIA & NEW ZEALAND

Isolated deep in the Southern Hemisphere between two vast oceans, remote from early trade routes and centers of civilization, Australia and New Zealand were settled by Europeans only from the end of the eighteenth century. European settlement brought the successful introduction of new plants and animals capable of producing large quantities of food, so that both countries became exporters of surplus farm products. Australia's recent development of its great mineral resources is leading to a broad-based economy, while New Zealand has established manufacturing with some industry based on its water power, ironsands and forest resources. But with combined populations of only 17 million, both countries remain economically dependent on food exports and are major contributors to the world food basket. In spite of striking geographical differences they share a common heritage with similar political and social structures.

Australia's pastoral resource

With an area of almost 770 million hectares (1,901 million acres), Australia ranks with the large countries of the world such as Brazil and the United States. Yet a vast region in the center and west has an average rainfall of less than 200 mm (8 in), and rainfall is so variable that at times 400 mm (16 in) may fall in a few days, causing widespread flooding. At the outer fringe of its "dead heart," Australia's extensive pastoral resources begin, with beef cattle mainly in northern Australia and sheep in the southern states.

Australia's sunburnt rural image belies the fact that 70 percent of its 13.8 million people live in 10 cities with populations of more than 100,000, most of them clustered along the southeastern fringe of the continent. Yet Australia remains essentially a pastoral country. It has more sheep than any other country in the world—nearly 150

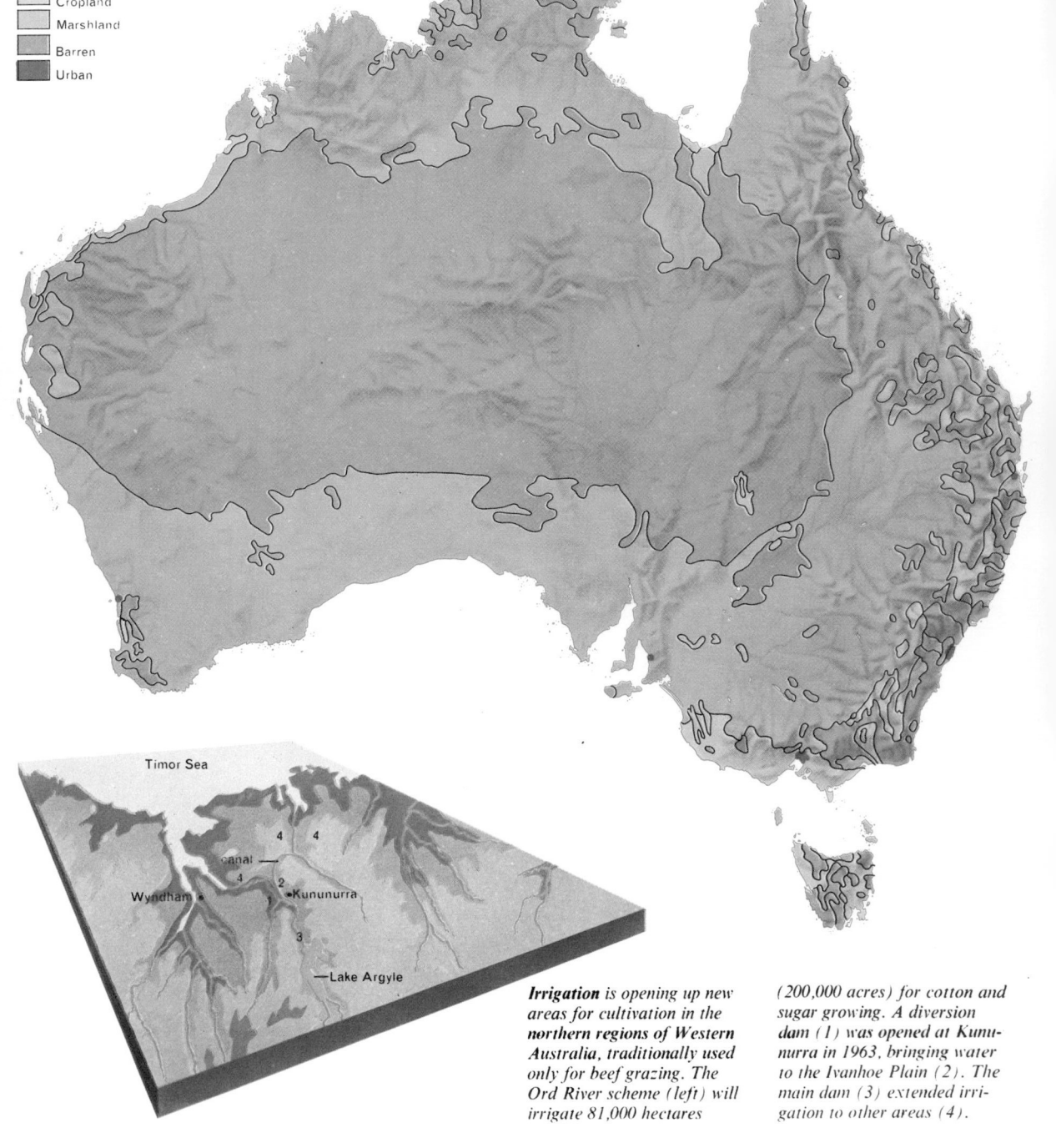

Forest
Grazing
Cropland
Marshland
Barren
Urban

Merino sheep, here shorn of their wool for assessment by farmers at a stock sale, were introduced to Australia in 1796 and remain the preeminent breed for their ability to withstand heat while producing a heavy, high-quality fleece. The diagrams show modifications in champion rams over a 70-year period. The fleece of the 1880s (1) became heavier in 1905 with a Vermont breeding strain (2) in a less robust animal. By 1916 the heavy folds were disappearing (3) and a 1955 champion (4) combines strength with a massive fleece.

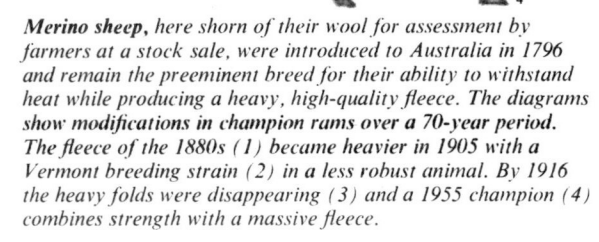

Irrigation *is opening up new areas for cultivation in the northern regions of Western Australia, traditionally used only for beef grazing. The Ord River scheme (left) will irrigate 81,000 hectares* *(200,000 acres) for cotton and sugar growing. A diversion dam (1) was opened at Kununurra in 1963, bringing water to the Ivanhoe Plain (2). The main dam (3) extended irrigation to other areas (4).*

The heat and aridity of much of Australia's pastoral land is summed up in this picture of a sheep station near Whyalla, South Australia. Most areas in this state, the driest in the country, receive an average of about 250 mm (10 in) of rain a year and falls are highly variable. To provide stored water for the merinos carried on such properties, reservoirs are bulldozed out of the flat, scrubby land so that any sudden downpour can be collected.

million. They yield about 800,000 tons of wool—one-third of world production—and in some years up to 90 percent of this is exported. With 30 million beef cattle, Australia is not a major producer of beef by world standards, but it is the largest beef trader, exporting nearly 50 percent of its production. Because of the importance of exports, the wool and meat industries are highly vulnerable to changes in the world economy and in market demand. Even so, both are admirably suited to the Australian environment. They have benefited from strong research and other services operated by Federal and State governments, resulting in the introduction of improved pasture species and the selection of animal breeds adapted to the wide range of environments encountered across the Australian continent.

The extensive pastoral areas merge with large-scale farming of cereal crops on better soils in regions of higher and more reliable rainfall (500–1,000 mm/20–40 in). There are almost 14 million hectares (35 million acres) under a wide variety of crops. Wheat is by far the most important of these, spreading over eight million hectares (20 million acres), mostly in New South Wales and Western Australia. About 75 percent of the total yield of more than 11 million tons is exported. Grain sorghum is the principal summer cereal crop and grows mainly in Queensland.

The other crop of considerable importance to the Australian economy and world food production is sugarcane. A strictly organized and efficient industry operates mainly in the high rainfall zone (more than 1,600 mm/63 in) along the northeastern coast of Queensland. Almost 300,000 hectares (741,000 acres) are under cultivation, yielding about 2.5 million tons of raw sugar. Up to 80 percent of this is exported in some years.

In other coastal areas, depending on climate and

soils, dairying and fruit farming are of most importance as exporters of surplus production to other parts of the world, but are of less significance in size and value of production.

Australia's former reliance on British and European markets for its farm exports has been greatly modified as new trading partners bordering the Pacific—particularly the United States and Japan —have become important customers. The old "Far East" of Europe has become the new "Near North" of Australia. New Zealand, which was traditionally even more dependent on the British market, has also successfully diversified its export outlets during the past 15 years.

New Zealand's primary industries
In contrast to the harshness of Australia, New Zealand's environment is sublime. The reliable and well-distributed rainfall, mild temperatures and relatively fertile soils were ideal for the introduction of European methods of agriculture. This sound physical base has been remarkably exploited by the selection and breeding of new varieties of grasses and clovers and the widespread application of superphosphate, particularly by aerial methods. An enlightened government applied the findings of agricultural researchers to large areas of hill country, often developing this resource before releasing it for private ownership. New Zealand's farmers have achieved the highest rate of agricultural productivity per man in the world.

A major dairy industry has been developed on the rich grasslands of the North Island. Carrying capacity can be as high as 2.5 cows a hectare (one an acre) and annual production as high as 400–500 kilograms of milkfat a hectare (356–400 lb an acre). Sheep and beef fattening farms are often associated with dairying, but generally fat lambs are raised as the major industry in specific areas of high-quality land on the coastal plains and river valleys of both islands. Annual carrying capacities range from 7–15 ewes on each hectare (3–6 an acre). The farmer's aim is to sell lambs fat off their mothers at carcass weights of 12–16 kilograms (26–35 lb) to overseas markets. The country has about 56 million sheep and wool is the principal product of the hill farms. Sheep and cattle are also reared in the hills to be fattened on excess pasture growth on the lowland farms in spring and summer for autumn slaughter.

It is this excellent system of animal production that provides more than 65 percent of New Zealand's export income. The country is one of the largest exporters of butter in the world, exporting about 290,000 tons of butter and cheese annually, and is a leading exporter of other milk products, of wool (272,000 tons), meat (more than 600,000 tons) and pasture seeds. Arable farming, chiefly on the plains of the South Island, meets only national needs. Apples, pears and other fruits are exported and the fishing industry could be expanded to provide a greater surplus for export.

Aerial top-dressing brought a breakthrough in New Zealand farming after World War II, when the fertility of hilly and inaccessible land was improved by the spreading of super- *phosphate and lime carried in the plane's hoppers and released in controlled amounts by the pilot. Higher-quality grasses and clover have helped to increase livestock numbers.*

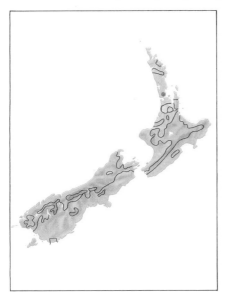

Fire-fighting by helicopter is among measures used to protect New Zealand's large and economically important forests of exotic conifers (left).

Kiwifruit (above) has recently become a New Zealand export worth $20 million a year.

Frozen lamb forms the most valuable part of New Zealand's large meat trade. Annual production of mutton and lamb is more than 500,000 tons, four-fifths of this exported. The UK and Europe remain important customers, but growth markets are in Japan, the USSR, the Middle East and the Pacific area.

ISRAEL, JAPAN & SOUTH AFRICA

Left to nature, Israel would be two-thirds desert, yet political factors make self-sufficiency in food essential. Kibbutzim like

this, Mizpe Shalem near the Dead Sea, are bringing some notoriously unpromising land into productive use.

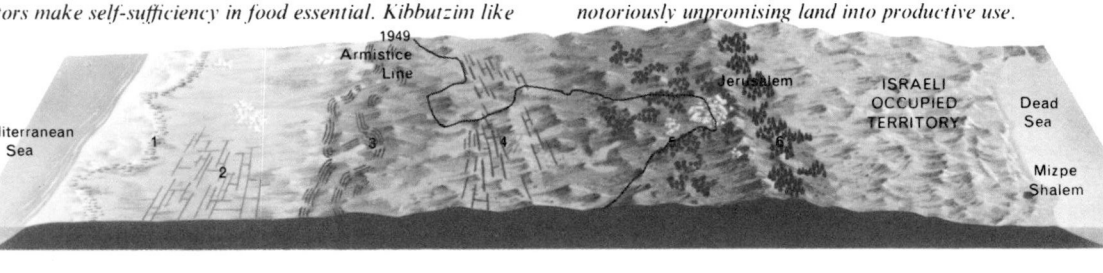

N ecessity has forced Israel to develop one of the world's most productive and efficient agricultural systems in a land that, left to itself, would be two-thirds desert. Although climate and soils permit a wide range of farming, cultivatable land and water are limited and intensive land use is essential. Political considerations and shortage of foreign exchange underlie the drive to achieve self-sufficiency in food production, while labor shortages encourage a high degree of mechanization.

Though small in area, Israel has a varied climate. About 85 percent of the rainfall is concentrated in the north, but half the cultivable land is in the south. As a result 42 percent of Israel's 430,000 hectares (1,062,000 acres) of cultivatable land is irrigated. The country already uses 95 percent of its estimated potential water resources, so while more land could be irrigated there are few reserves to draw on.

Jewish pioneers acquired practical experience of farming following the migrations to Palestine in the 1880s. With the birth of Israel in 1948 their hard-won knowledge combined with the various skills of large numbers of immigrants to achieve notable success in the scientific use of land. There is still great emphasis on research and development.

Before 1960 farming was largely mixed, with dairying the mainstay. The 1960s saw the spread of industrial crop production, notably sugar beet, cotton, peanuts, sisal and tobacco. In the past decade, production of winter vegetables and fruit for daily delivery by air to Europe has become important, particularly in the south. These exports include peppers, zucchini, eggplant, onions, avocados, celery, strawberries, melons and cut flowers grown in plastic greenhouses. Citrus fruits, however, still account for over 60 percent of Israel's agricultural export revenue.

Land and politics
Jewish agricultural colonization has often been closely associated with political and military objectives. In the decade following the 1967 war 85 rural settlements were established in occupied areas,

Since the founding of Israel in 1948 large sums of money have been spent to restore much-neglected land. Stabilization of coastal dunes (1), swamp drainage (2), terracing and prevention of soil erosion (3), irrigation (4), reclamation (5) and afforestation (6) have made new landscapes.

▨ Israeli occupied territory

▢ Forest/woodland
▢ Grazing
▢ Cropland
▢ Barren
▢ Urban

notably the Golan Heights and the West Bank. Some are agriculturally successful, but their future will depend on political arrangements in the region.

Perhaps surprisingly for such a new nation, less than 15 percent of Israel's population is rural. About four percent of rural dwellers are members of moshavim (smallholders' cooperative villages), three percent live in kibbutzim (collective farms) and about eight percent live in Arab villages.

S hortage of good agricultural land is one of the salient features of the geography of Japan. Mountains and rugged uplands are predominant and only 16 percent of the total area is cultivated. Yet the population, which in 1978 stood at more than 114 million, is the world's sixth largest. The result is that Japanese agriculture is characterized by high intensity of land use. South of latitude 38 N arable land usually carries two crops a year. Yields per hectare are among the highest in the world.

Japanese farm holdings are small, averaging only one hectare (2.47 acres). The farms are usually divided into five or six scattered parcels of land. This imposes severe constraints on the use of Western-style farm machinery so that labor productivity is low by international standards. The most important crop is rice, which accounts for 48 percent of the cultivated area.

With Japan's emergence as one of the world's leading industrial countries, the relative importance of agriculture has steadily declined. In 1974 it contributed only 4.9 percent of net domestic product and employed only 11.6 percent of the civilian labor force. Rural depopulation is particularly evident in remote prefectures.

Land reform and agricultural output
Since World War II living standards of Japanese farmers have improved greatly. The 1946 Land Reform transformed the rural community from tenant farmers into small proprietors. Improvement of irrigation systems and new farm technology, including specially designed hand tractors for use in small fields, have helped to raise farm output. In addition state policies aimed at winning rural electoral support have resulted in generous farm subsidies, especially for rice. During the 1960s high guaranteed prices resulted in a large rice surplus and the government has since attempted to persuade prefectures to limit rice production.

Despite the improvement in rural living standards most Japanese farmers supplement their incomes with jobs outside agriculture. In 1975 more

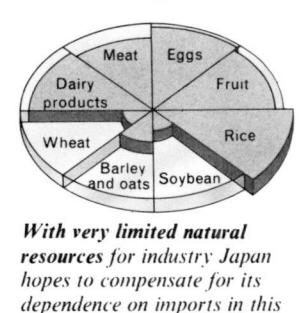

With very limited natural resources for industry Japan hopes to compensate for its dependence on imports in this sector by aiming for self-sufficiency in food. In 1975 Japan was producing 74 percent of its requirement for general agricultural foodstuffs.

Though small, Japan's farms are intensively cultivated, output per hectare being very high by international standards. Small

than 66 percent of the average farm income was derived from employment outside agriculture.

Changes in the Japanese diet have contributed to new patterns of land use. There has been a growth in livestock farming and in vegetable and fruit output. Domestic beef farmers and citrus growers are protected by import quotas. Japan now ranks as one of the world's leading importers of wheat, barley and soybeans, reflecting both the rising demand for bread and the country's growing dependence on imported animal feed. Current government policy aims to increase Japan's self-sufficiency in food and fodder production.

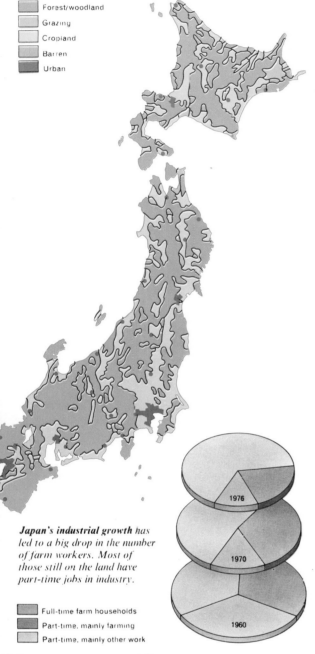

Forest/woodland
Grazing
Cropland
Barren
Urban

Japan's industrial growth has led to a big drop in the number of farm workers. Most of those still on the land have part-time jobs in industry.

Full-time farm households
Part-time, mainly farming
Part-time, mainly other work

machines and hand tools are used to cultivate every part of plots, while fertilizers and weedkillers insure good harvests.

Black laborers and modern machinery help to make South Africa's commercial farms relatively efficient and prosperous.

The other side of the country's classic dual economy is represented by the subsistence farmers of the Bantu homelands.

Owing to the aridity of large parts of South Africa, less than 10 percent of the agricultural land is cultivated. The use of the country's land resources is to some extent dominated by the politics of separate development. The noncommercial farming sector represented by the African reserves, or Bantu homelands, has a significantly higher proportion of cultivated land (14 percent) than the commercial, or white, sector (12 percent).

A notable distinction between the two sectors is the virtual absence of permanent crops and planted pasture in the homelands. In 1965 nearly 13 percent of the farmers in these areas had no agricultural land or grazing rights and only about 55 percent had rights to both arable and grazing lands. The reduction of woodland in the homelands in recent years reflects the pressure to clear land for agriculture.

Only about 10 percent of cropland in the homelands is irrigated, much of it in the wetter eastern half of the country. The potential for further development is not being exploited due to lack of capital and the absence of an established tradition of intensive farming practice under irrigation.

Climate and crops
The variations in South Africa's climate allow a wide range of crops to be grown, including corn, wheat, sugar cane, cotton, citrus fruits, tobacco and vegetables. In 1975 the commercial farming sector produced over 95 percent of South Africa's corn, while the homelands, for which it is the staple food crop, produced only about 3½ percent. Corn yields on Bantu farms are generally low, due to droughts, poor seed, rampant weeds and impoverished soil. In the 10 years up to 1975 South Africa's sugar, cotton and wheat production all increased considerably, perhaps reflecting an attempt to replace imports. On the other hand many traditional pastoral products, such as wool, mohair and karakul sheep pelts, did not increase as much.

Livestock rearing again reflects segregation policies. One-third of the country's cattle are in the homelands but the relatively higher proportion of cattle losses in these areas is attributed to overgrazing and the lack of fodder crops.

Government agricultural policy has been to maintain farm incomes for whites by stabilizing prices for the main products. Because of this only wool has suffered markedly from international price fluctuations. Homelands policy has concentrated on soil conservation and the improvement of grazing grounds.

Forest/woodland
Grazing
Cropland
Barren
Urban

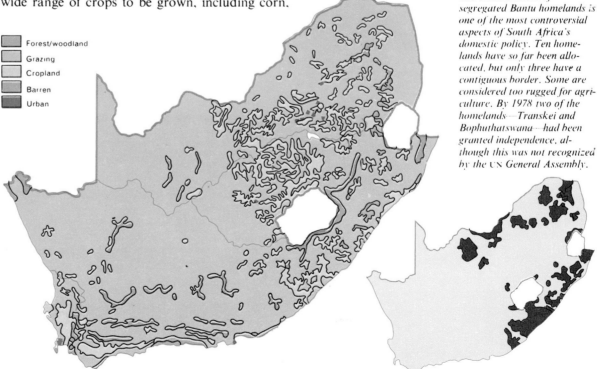

The establishment of segregated Bantu homelands is one of the most controversial aspects of South Africa's domestic policy. Ten homelands have so far been allocated, but only three have a contiguous border. Some are considered too rugged for agriculture. By 1978 two of the homelands—Transkei and Bophuthatswana—had been granted independence, although this was not recognized by the UN General Assembly.

127

AFRICA–DEVELOPMENT IN DIVERSITY

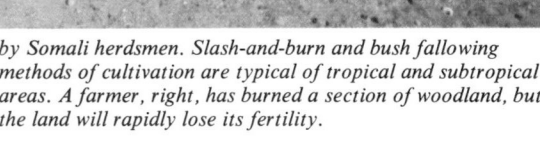

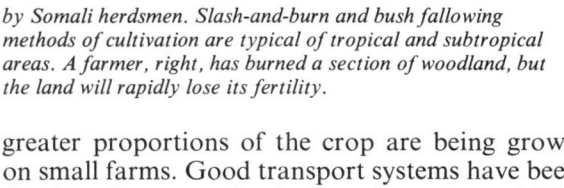

Subsistence farming is still the way of life for most Africans. In areas too dry for reliable cropping, extensive pastoralism is virtually the only agricultural pursuit. The Kenyan water hole, above, provides valuable supplies for cattle and camels owned

by Somali herdsmen. Slash-and-burn and bush fallowing methods of cultivation are typical of tropical and subtropical areas. A farmer, right, has burned a section of woodland, but the land will rapidly lose its fertility.

Africa is the second largest continent, after Asia, and its 30,311,680 square kilometers (11,703,404 square miles) encompass regions of great diversity and enormous resources. The nature of its vegetation cover ranges from barren desert to impenetrable rain forest. It supplies the world with timber, tea, coffee, rubber, cocoa, sugar and minerals, but most of its inhabitants are subsistence farmers. Long exploited by colonial powers, many countries are now grappling with the problems arising from independence.

Despite some of the highest population growth rates in the world, the people of Africa are, for the most part, spread very thinly across the continent. Arable areas are separated by vast stretches of territory unsuited to cultivation. Even within the arable belts soils are generally poor. Rainfall over large parts of the continent is low or erratic and is the primary constraint on the development of agricultural resources, though the widespread incidence of the tsetse fly has held back entire regions, particularly with regard to livestock potential.

Agriculture provides 60 percent of Africa's export earnings yet the 1970s witnessed a developing crisis in food production. It is the only area in the world where production is falling. Between 1971 and 1975 per capita food production was seven percent lower than 10 years previously. The "green revolution" has yet to reach much of Africa, there is little capital investment and deforestation has led to soil erosion. Migration to estates and mines has created labor shortages in many areas.

Regional patterns

EAST AFRICA, extending from the Zambezi River to the Horn of Africa and the Red Sea, is dominated by the Great Rift Valley and the drainage systems of the Blue and White Niles and the Zambezi itself. The main crops are tropical, though higher parts of the region can sustain agricultural systems based on small grains and dairying.

Most of the population are peasant farmers concerned with subsistence agriculture, cash crops being of increasing, but still of secondary, importance. Coffee is a major export in Ethiopia, Kenya, Uganda and Tanzania. It has been introduced with great success on small farms and is responsible for the present prosperity of the indigenous farmers of northern Tanzania and central Kenya. Tea is an important crop in areas with higher rainfall, particularly in Kenya and Malawi. Progressively

greater proportions of the crop are being grown on small farms. Good transport systems have been developed to get the leaf to factories quickly.

At lower altitudes, particularly in Kenya, Uganda, Tanzania, Zambia and southern Somalia, sugar cane is grown extensively and is likely to increase in importance. Cotton is prominent in the economies of Uganda, Kenya and Tanzania, but its companion fiber crop, sisal, formerly Tanzania's main export commodity, has declined rapidly with the advent of synthetic fibers.

A large proportion of eastern Africa is too dry to sustain any form of crop production and livestock rearing is the primary means of subsistence. Considerable progress has been made in improving cattle breeds. In some areas it has been shown that wild herbivores can produce greater yields of meat than domestic livestock.

WEST AFRICA, comprising the countries to the west of Cameroon, is dominated by the 75 million people of Nigeria. Unlike eastern and southern Africa, the region was traditionally considered too unhealthy for permanent settlement by Europeans, with the result that agriculture has remained largely in the hands of peasant farmers, although some plantations of tree crops, sugar and pineapples have been established by foreign companies.

As much as 90 percent of the population works on the land. The usual system of farming is the method known as bush fallowing, which means after three or four years' cropping the land is fallowed for five, 10 or even 20 years: immediately adjacent to the village there is a zone which is farmed continuously. Output includes tree and root crops, rice and corn in the moister southern areas, millets and peanuts in the drier north. Cultivation of rice has increased greatly since World War II, particularly in Sierra Leone, Guinea and Nigeria.

Chief exports from the south of the region are palm oil and kernels, coffee, cocoa, bananas and rubber, while the north markets peanuts and cotton. Tropical forest timber, often in the form of veneers and plywood, is exported from the Ivory Coast, Ghana, Guinea, Liberia and Cameroon.

CENTRAL AFRICA, which is defined as the interior of the southern limb of the continent, is drained by the Congo River and its tributaries and consists of a series of plateaus characterized by a total lack of relief. The central part of the region carries tall forest, while to the north and south are extensive woodlands merging into savanna. The forests are

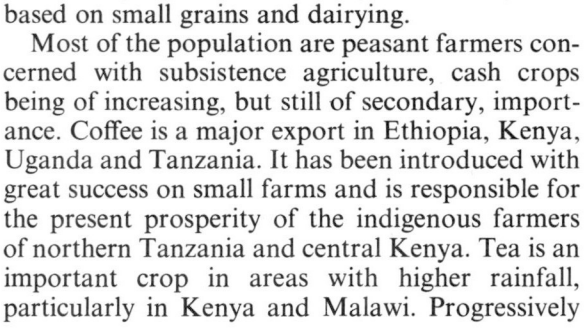

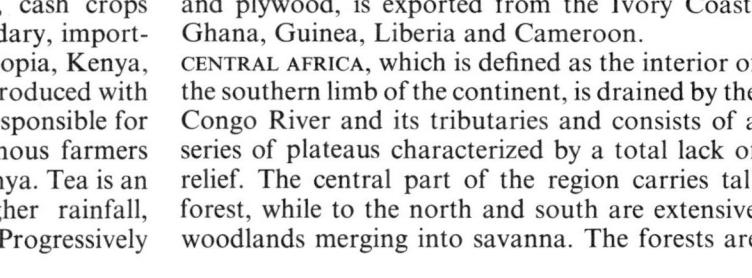

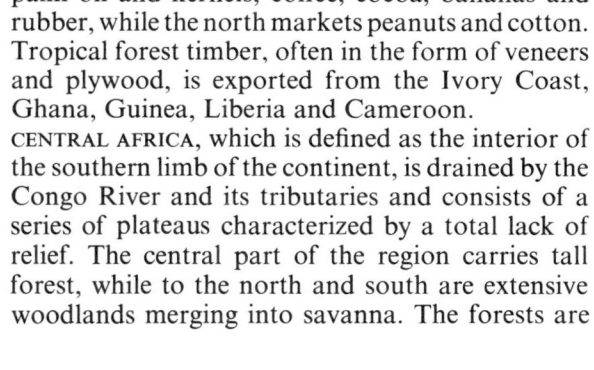

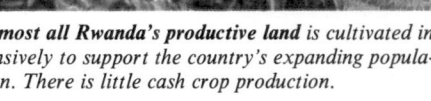

Almost all Rwanda's productive land is cultivated intensively to support the country's expanding population. There is little cash crop production.

CONNECTIONS

28–9	Resources, politics and power	90–1	Feeding the world	100–1	Making better use of the land
46–7	Searching for living space	92–3	Energy and food production	102–3	Forests at risk
48–9	Feast or famine?	94–5	Climate and man	178–9	Food—defining the problems
52–3	The worlds we live in	96–7	Water—the basic resource	180–1	Are green revolutions the answer?
		98–9	Land and the farmer		

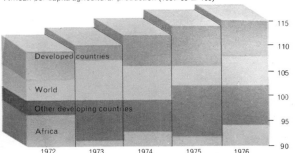

Grapes on sale at a market in Morocco typify the Mediterranean character of the countries of the Maghreb. Cereals and citrus fruits are also widely grown, but nomadic pastoralism is still the dominant way of life over large areas of the region.

African per capita agricultural production (1961–65 = 100)

Africa is the only area of the world where agricultural output is falling. Contributory factors include wars, political instability and the neglect of rural communities.

Forest
Grazing
Cropland
Marshland
Barren
Urban

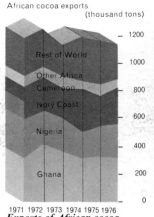

African cocoa exports (thousand tons)

Exports of African cocoa, *dominated by four major producing countries, account for 64 percent of total world consumption of cocoa.*

Tea from Kenya, *worth more than $110 million a year in export revenue, is a post-colonial crop produced mainly by highland farmers.*

exploited for timber, including such highly prized woods as okoume, mahogany and iroko. The production of plywood and veneers is important in all countries of the region. Crops grown on plantation scale include oil palm, rubber, coffee, cocoa, tea and sugar cane.

Food crops cultivated by peasant farmers within the forest zone are cassava, yams and banana tree, while in the savanna corn, peanuts, sorghum, millet and grain legumes are grown. The average size of a subsistence plot in Zaire is less than half a hectare and typifies a problem common to much of Africa in that output since 1958 has not kept pace with the increase in population.

Peasant farmers in Cameroon, the Central African Empire and Zaire also cultivate cotton, some of which is used locally in the manufacture of textiles. Rice is grown throughout the region. Livestock rearing is restricted by the tsetse fly.

SOUTHERN AFRICA, excluding the Republic of South Africa, embraces the countries surrounding the basin of the Zambezi and the Kalahari Desert—Angola, Namibia, Botswana and Rhodesia. The favorable climate encouraged European settlement, particularly in Rhodesia, but also in Angola and, to a limited extent, in the other countries. Although only a small proportion of settlers in Rhodesia and Angola are farmers, most of the marketed agricultural production comes from their plantations and farms. Angola's main products are coffee, cotton, sisal and sugar, while Rhodesia produces corn, tobacco, wheat and livestock. In Botswana and Namibia European farmers raise cattle and sheep. African farmers grow cassava in northern

Angola, and corn, millet and peanuts elsewhere in the country. Corn is the principal food crop of Rhodesia's African farmers. In Botswana the cultivation of corn, sorghum and peanuts is almost entirely restricted to the eastern part of the country. Corn and millet are also cultivated in Namibia, but more important both here and in Botswana is pastoralism. The Botswana government is attempting to improve the management of grazing land.

NORTHWEST AFRICA is isolated from the rest of the continent by the Sahara. Collectively known as the Maghreb, the territories of Morocco, Algeria and Tunisia are more Mediterranean in climate.

Wheat, barley and other cereals occupy the largest part of the cultivated land of the Maghreb; 51 percent in Morocco, 46 percent in Algeria and 45 percent in Tunisia. The region also produces a number of crops equipped to withstand the summer droughts. These include olives, figs, chestnuts and cork-oaks. Irrigated areas yield grapes, citrus and deciduous fruits, vegetables and flowers.

The future for food production in most African countries poses vast problems. Many rural areas are already supporting as many people as is possible at present levels of input. The provision of adequate transport facilities is also essential in some regions. A large number of countries are dependent for their export earnings on a very narrow range of crops and their economic survival depends upon the number of cash crops being increased. The FAO has predicted that, if present trends continue, although Africa was producing 90 percent of its food needs in the early 1970s, by 1985 this figure will have been reduced by 10 percent.

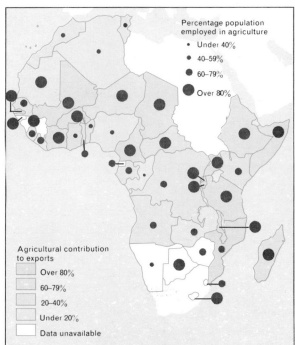

Percentage population employed in agriculture
- Under 40%
- 40–59%
- 60–79%
- Over 80%

Agricultural contribution to exports
- Over 80%
- 60–79%
- 20–40%
- Under 20%
- Data unavailable

A mechanized plow for the paddy fields of The Gambia, supplied by international aid, illustrates the efforts of foreign countries to assist Africa's rural development. More than half the World Bank's agricultural funding for 1977–78 went to Africa.

The high proportion of the population *employed on the land, coupled with the comparatively low contribution of agriculture to gross national product, reflects the low productivity of African farming. In only four out of 42 countries does agriculture contribute more than half the gross national product.*

129

LATIN AMERICA—THE COST OF GROWTH

Farming conditions in Latin America vary sharply between intensive cultivation of marginal land and open cattle ranching. Wooden plows are used to work tiny plots (left) in the Altiplano foothills of the Andes in Peru, where pressure on agricultural land forces terrace cultivation of subsistence crops such as maize, wheat, barley and potatoes. Yields are low and subject to frosts, unreliable rainfall and soil erosion. Only two percent of the land area is arable and agriculture contributes but 18 percent of GDP although employing 45 percent of the population. However, coastal farming of sugar and cotton produces export yields.

Cattle ranching predominates on the Argentinian pampas, which cover about half the total land area of the country. A third of exports are meat and its products, and the total contribution of agriculture to export income is 90 percent, although it accounts for only 10 percent of GDP. Despite its importance in the economy, Argentinian agriculture has often been criticized for being "complacent." Yields of wheat, for example, have dropped during the past 10 years.

Forest
Grazing
Cropland
Barren
Marshland
Urban

The term Latin America, although geographically convenient, implies a unity or similarity that does not exist within the vast region it designates. A number of contemporary problems are nevertheless common to many Latin American countries. Chief among them is a high rate of population growth (except in the southern cone of Argentina, Uruguay and Chile), together with urban expansion and efforts to industrialize previously agrarian-based economies. The cost of growth has tended to be high, both socially and economically, with foreign exchange bottlenecks and inflation often resulting from failures to implement balanced and flexible development programs.

Together with the Spanish- and French-speaking islands in the Caribbean, the 17 countries of the mainland that gained their independence from Spain and Portugal during the early decades of the nineteenth century cover an area of about 20.2 million square kilometers (7.8 million square miles). Ranging in latitude from 30°N to 50°S, mainland Latin America stretches for 10,800 kilometers (6,750 miles) between Mexico and Tierra del Fuego and is some 4,960 kilometers (3,100 miles) from coast to coast at its widest point.

Within the region there are significant variations in climatic and soil conditions. The main physical features are a series of mountain chains running virtually the whole length of the west coast, several major river basins (Magdalena, Orinoco, Amazon and Parana/Plate) draining to the Caribbean or Atlantic, and the llanos and the pampas.

The high, arid Atacama Desert of the west coast (one of the world's driest regions) contrasts with the fertile, well-watered *terra roxa* zone of Brazil and the tropical Amazonian rain forest in the north central region of the country.

Agricultural exports

Latin America has given the world several food items that are indigenous and were exclusive to it: for example, potatoes, maize, vanilla, chilies, cacao, tomatoes and avocado pears, as well as tobacco and rubber. Until the 1940s, the region was a major supplier of agricultural products; in 1938 it provided 85 percent of world coffee exports, 64 percent of maize, 44 percent of linseed, 39 percent of meat and about one-quarter to one-third of all the wheat and sugar traded internationally. A wide variety of temperate and tropical products was exported to Western Europe and a selection of tropical and subtropical commodities was sent to North America.

The region, now supporting eight percent of the world's population, and experiencing some of the Earth's highest rates of population growth, remains rich in both agricultural and mineral resources. But since World War II there has been a substantial reduction in Latin America's contribution to world food supply. In some countries there has even been a decline in output, either because production has been disrupted by agrarian reforms or because local resources have been transferred to industry.

In the postwar period industrial expansion was

seen as a means of lessening dependence on imports, of providing employment for the rising population and of reducing social disparities created by the agrarian structures established in the nineteenth century, which favored large landholders and plantation interests. These hopes have not generally been realized. Hence agrarian change is now considered essential if production, both for export and domestic consumption, is to be stimulated, thereby generating higher incomes and widening markets for manufactured goods. State-aided agriculture in Brazil, socialism in Cuba and co-operative ventures in Mexico are among the methods being applied, with varying degrees of success, to overcome the supply bottleneck and to move away from dependence upon single crops, a characteristic of many Latin American countries.

Regional patterns

THE SOUTHEAST has traditionally produced large quantities of meat, grains and wool for export as well as some fruit and dairy products. Highly urbanized, Argentina and Uruguay are now large consumers of rural products, and domestic consumption has increased along with real incomes. The agricultural sector was neglected during the officially sponsored drive toward industrialization and reacted slowly to changes in world demand. WEST-COAST COUNTRIES, with the exception of Bolivia, were until recently not only self-sufficient in food production but also food exporters. Chile supplied grain, Peru fish, sugar and cotton, and

CONNECTIONS

28–9	Resources, politics and power	36–7	Transport and resources
30–1	Patterns of possession	40–1	The role of big business
32–3	The diplomacy of resources	44–5	The mathematics of growth
34–5	Patterns of trade	54–5	Population policies
		90–1	Feeding the world

102–3	Forests at risk
106–7	Fishing—a question of quotas
168–9	Providing for people
178–9	Food—defining the problems
180–1	Are green revolutions the answer?

The Trans-Amazonian high-way stretches for 5,400 km (3,380 miles) in an attempt to give access to timber and mineral resources in Brazil.

Bananas in Honduras account for 70 percent of export income and typify the cash crop situation in much of Latin America. For historical and economic reasons, many countries where agricultural land is at a premium have concentrated on monopro-duction of staple crops, which earn them sufficient income to import other types of food that could possibly be produced locally. Brazil is a more im-portant banana producer (35 percent of Latin America's output) than Honduras, but is less dependent on a single crop. In 1974, following the success of OPEC, Honduras led a cartel of seven nations accounting for 66 percent of world banana exports in an attempt to force up banana prices. But lacking the lever-age of oil producers, the cartel failed to overcome resistance to this move by three US multinationals that control 70 percent of banana exports.

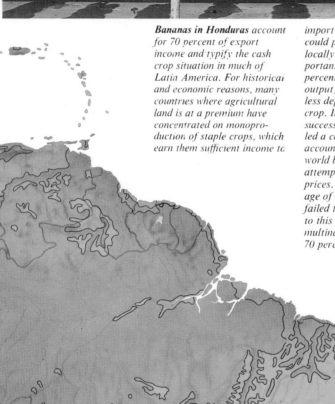

An extensive program of road building was undertaken in Brazil between 1964 and 1974 to open up the Amazon Basin, and to improve facilities in the rich farming regions of the south and encourage ex-ports. The Great Escarpment impeded railway construction and agriculture is largely dependent on road transport, which is costly and places a strain on foreign exchange, needed for gasoline, oil and spare parts. This has led to discussion of the need to over-haul the rail system.

Legend	
○	Major towns
═══	Federal roads
────	Paved highway (1964)
────	Paved highway (1974)
-----	Roads under construction
······	Gravel roads
────	Navigable rivers

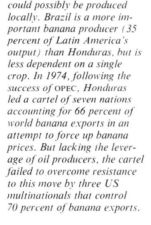

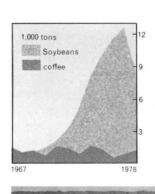

Coffee, here being raked to dry, has always been regarded as Brazil's principal crop, but a severe frost in 1975 and drought in 1978 have greatly reduced yields. Much attention has been paid in the last decade to soybeans as an alternative crop, also grown mainly in the fertile south. Soybeans (above right) ex-ceeded coffee in export value in 1974 and 1975 as pro-duction soared, while coffee harvests fluctuated as shown in the comparative production graph. A high-yield soybean strain has been developed. But yields may be affected by double cropping with wheat as Brazil attempts to reduce its large imports of grain.

Ecuador bananas. In the 1960s fishmeal and fish oil became a boom export of Peru, only to decline to almost nothing because of changes in the ocean currents and overfishing. In Chile, population growth, urban expansion and soil exhaustion through intensive cropping has made the country a net importer of food, spending 30 percent of its export earnings in this sector.

BRAZIL, covering half of the land surface of South America and with a fast-expanding population, has raised its agricultural output considerably, with government incentives for growth and diversifi-cation. Production of soybeans has risen dramati-cally. The benefit of diverting resources to open up vast new tracts of land in Amazonia has yet to emerge, while the northeast lags behind develop-ments in the south, where improved transport and storage facilities, together with access to easy credit, stimulate output.

THE CARIBBEAN AND CENTRAL AMERICA is the region most in need of agrarian change. A few major cash crops are produced on large, efficient estates while the provision of basic foodstuffs is often neglected and large populations live close to subsistence.

MEXICO has been more successful in land reform. The establishment of peasant cooperatives and state aid for the private sector has achieved a remarkable increase in productivity, turning a region of food deficit into one of export surplus. As throughout most of Latin America, the basic resources exist and the problem is largely one of finding the means of exploiting them.

131

THE NEAR EAST—PROBLEMS OF ARIDITY

Aridity, which affects about one-third of the world's total land surface, is nowhere more acute than in the Near East. Here it is the dominant climatic characteristic, and economic life throughout the region is considerably influenced by a shortage of water for agriculture. True, exceptional areas, such as the coastal belt and uplands of Turkey and Iran and parts of the southern Sudan, receive upward of 1,000 mm (40 in) of rainfall annually, but elsewhere the figure falls sharply—to less than 100 mm (4 in) a year in some places. Most rainfall is associated with the passage of eastward-moving winter cyclones, leaving a long, hot summer of almost unrelieved drought. It is for this reason that summer irrigation is widespread.

Productive land

A mere seven percent of the Near East is cultivated, though this figure may eventually be doubled with extensive land reclamation and irrigation schemes. Of this cultivated area about one-third is under irrigation; the remaining two-thirds is rain fed. Variability of rainfall is marked and is reflected in the wildly erratic statistics for agricultural production in the Near East. Aridity, however, is not the only limiting factor. There are also extensive mountainous areas and salt marshes that are unsuitable for cultivation, and vast tracts of the Arabian peninsula. Egypt, Libya and Afghanistan are covered by moving sand dunes or rocky deserts too inhospitable even for trees or rough pasture. Altogether more than two-thirds of the Near East is totally unproductive agriculturally.

A harsh environment, coupled with poor techniques and shortage of labor, means that in recent years agricultural production has not kept pace with the rapid growth of population (roughly 2.8 percent a year) to the present level of more than 200 million. Today there is growing concern over the long-term political and economic implications of heavy reliance on imported foodstuffs. Arab countries alone will need some 62 million tons of

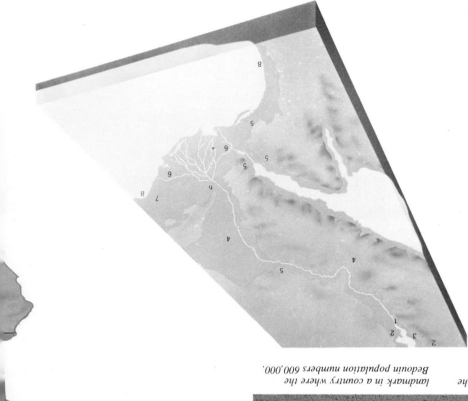

Completed in 1970, the $3.6 billion Aswan dam (1) gives an output of 10 billion kilowatt hours a year. *Together with the mighty Lake Nasser,* which it created, it will bring 550,000 hectares (1,358,000 acres) under irrigation and ensure in Upper Egypt two crops of rice a year (2). *Its construction* entailed an enormous displacement of people from the areas due to be flooded (3), including 100,000 Egyptian Nubians (half of whom have been resettled in the Sudan). *Today the problems are* mainly those to do with the ecological effects of restricting the rate of siltation in the Nile delta. There has been an increase in the prevalence of the tropical disease bilharzia (4), an enhanced rate of salinity (5), a loss of fertility in the soils of the delta zone (6), some increase in coastal erosion (7) and damage to offshore fisheries (8).

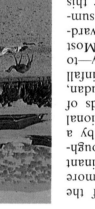

The black tents of the Bedouin in the Saudi desert remain a traditional landmark in a country where the Bedouin population numbers 600,000.

The aridity of the desert is relieved here and there by oases, pockets of lush vegetation fed by underground water sources. *Here the main crop,* as at this oasis in Saudi Arabia's eastern province, is the date palm, which also yields wood and fronds for thatching. Construction of roads to the oases has enabled the farmer to transport vegetables and fodder to market.

cereal annually by the year 2000, compared with present production of about 23 million tons. Throughout the Near East agricultural development is a vital issue.

By far the largest reserves of cultivatable land are in the Sudan, where only eight percent of an estimated 85 million cultivatable hectares (210 million acres) are in use. In 1975 the Arab Fund for Economic and Social Development (financed mainly from oil) announced a $6 billion investment plan for Sudan to produce most Arab food needs by 1985. Two great irrigation schemes have already been implemented in the Near East, both with Soviet technical aid: the Euphrates dam in Syria, completed in 1975, which will eventually lead to irrigation of 640,000 hectares (1,580,000 acres) of desert; and the Aswan high dam, which will extend Egypt's cultivated land by about 550,000 hectares (1,358,000 acres), much of it already in use. Both projects are controversial. The Euphrates dam has upset the Iraqis, who see it—jointly with Turkey's Keban dam farther upstream—as a threat to water levels in the lower Euphrates. Critics of the Aswan dam argue that its benefits are offset by adverse ecological effects.

Hundreds of smaller dams have been constructed throughout the Near East, notably in Turkey and Iran. In addition, there is a move to further exploit underground water resources—found sometimes at great depth. Both Egypt and Libya are tapping a vast reservoir of "fossil" water, discovered in the eastern Sahara, for extensive irrigation schemes around existing oases. At Kufra in Libya there is a remarkable scheme producing irrigated fodder for the large-scale rearing of sheep, though the products are expensive due to high transportation costs. Irrigation schemes are often costly and sometimes difficult to manage. Rates of evaporation from open canals and reservoirs are high—a problem which the Egyptians are solving partly by using underground pipes to carry irrigation water. Similarly, drip-feed irrigation equipment at ground level, now widely used in Israel, reduces evaporation.

Meanwhile there is increasing emphasis on more efficient use of existing water resources. Already in Egypt and Israel urban waste water is being purified and recycled for use in agriculture. In the Gulf states salad crops are grown in automated greenhouses using precise amounts of recycled water. For the future much more attention will be given to increasing the yield from rain-fed culti-

vation. This can be done by experimenting with new varieties; by the use of better dry-farming techniques; and by concentration on tree crops such as olives. Ultimately desalination of sea water may ensure a plentiful water supply for the Near East—if only the cost of the process can be reduced. Already the region possesses the largest concentration of desalination plants in the world, but their output is used to meet urban needs.

Results of overgrazing

Earlier civilizations seem to have been very successful in cultivating arid regions. In the first and second centuries AD the Romans dry-farmed grain crops in Libya: they built numerous terraces along wadi beds to prevent erosion and trap the run-off during winter storms. In the Negev desert (now in Israel), the Nabateans collected water from occasional flash floods to irrigate grain crops and orchards. It now seems clear that parts of the desert have become further impoverished over the past 1,000 years, chiefly by overgrazing. Vast tracts of desert pasture are now irreparably damaged, and the rest can only be improved by rigorous techniques to conserve soil and keep back the encroaching sand. Action is imperative if the desiccation is to be reversed: research has shown that when desert soils are stripped of vegetation, their increased reflectivity may further reduce rainfall.

It is these parched conditions that traditionally accounted for the high prevalence of nomadism in the Near East. The Bedouin of Arabia survive in regions where annual rainfall is less than 100 mm (4 in), relying for a livelihood on their camels. More numerous are tribal groups, specializing in sheep and goats, that inhabit the steppe regions between the true desert and the cultivated zone. Today, however, nomadism probably involves less than two percent of the population.

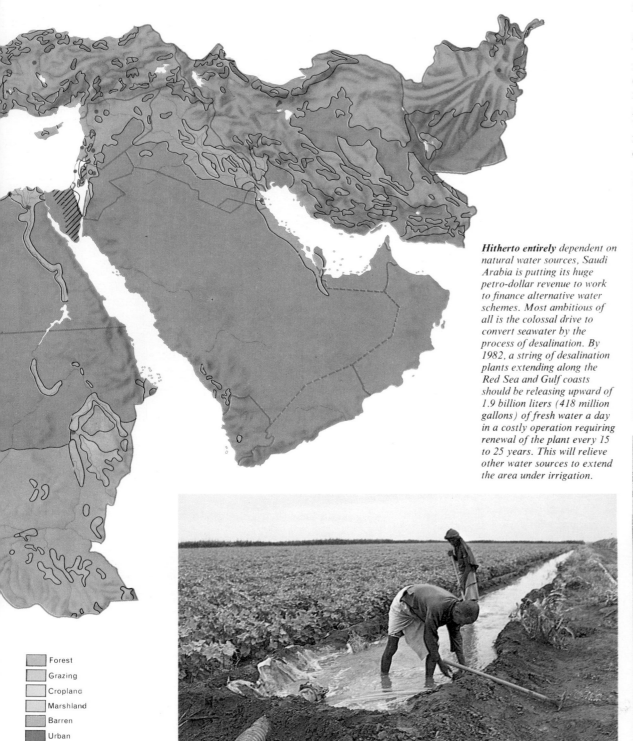

Forest
Grazing
Cropland
Marshland
Barren
Urban
Israeli occupied territory

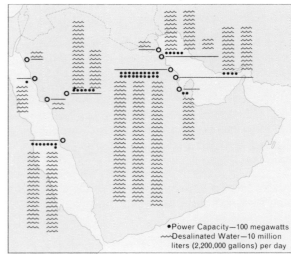

Hitherto entirely dependent on natural water sources, Saudi Arabia is putting its huge petro-dollar revenue to work to finance alternative water schemes. Most ambitious of all is the colossal drive to convert seawater by the process of desalination. By 1982, a string of desalination plants extending along the Red Sea and Gulf coasts should be releasing upward of 1.9 billion liters (418 million gallons) of fresh water a day in a costly operation requiring renewal of the plant every 15 to 25 years. This will relieve other water sources to extend the area under irrigation.

• Power Capacity—100 megawatts
∿ Desalinated Water—10 million liters (2,200,000 gallons) per day

Inevitably, furrow irrigation is labor-intensive. Two minor improvements, in use on Yemeni cotton and sorghum, are plastic sheeting and a piped system to help conserve water.

An oasis in the Najd, a fertile enclave in Saudi Arabia, shows how shrubs stabilize the dunes and keep the desert at bay.

SOUTHERN & SOUTHEASTERN ASIA

Southern and southeastern Asia together stretch over a vast area. Not surprisingly they contain a wide variety of natural environments: from the world's highest mountains, the Himalayas, to some of its largest plateaus, plains and deltas; from the burning sands of the Thar Desert, India, to the humid rainforests of southeastern Asia; from regions subject to the rigors of alternating wet and dry seasons (monsoonal southern Asia, Burma and Thailand) to those, like southwestern Sri Lanka and Malaysia, with little seasonal variation.

Some food crops reflect this diversity. Wheat, for instance, is confined largely to drier areas of Pakistan and northern India, where it is a winter crop, often irrigated. Millets of many kinds are a standby in the dry plateaus of peninsular India and in some southeastern Asian hill areas, while tea grows well in wetter tropical and subtropical regions, especially on hill slopes.

Other crops, notably corn, sugar cane and manioc (cassava) have a wider distribution. But none is as ubiquitous or as dominant as rice. Depending on availability of rainfall or irrigation it is grown everywhere except the most mountainous or arid areas, with the heaviest concentrations on plains and deltas. Asian farmers over the millennia have selected a vast number of rice varieties, each adapted to a particular environment or season. In well-watered regions more than one crop a year is taken. Rice, often supplemented with fish for protein, is in fact the staple food of most people in southern and southeastern Asia.

Land resources
Pressure of population on scarce land resources is much more marked in southern Asia than in the countries to the southeast. In Pakistan and Nepal, thinly populated regions of mountains, desert or semidesert bring the ratio of people to land down to about 90 per square kilometer (35 per square mile), but there is pressure on more cultivatable areas —plains and eroded foothills in Nepal, and the great Punjab and Sind plains in Pakistan. Elsewhere the population/land ratio rises to 186 per square kilometer (72 per square mile) in India, 204 (79) in Sri Lanka and no less than 547 (211) in Bangladesh, which has one of the highest rural population densities in the world. The average ratio in India is reduced by low populations in jungle, mountain and desert areas. But grave pressure of people on land resources has built up in the Indo-Gangetic Plain, the deltas and much of the southern peninsula. Sri Lanka has high population densities and scarce land resources in the wet zone (southwest) and hills but lower densities and spare land in the dry zone of the north and east.

In India, Pakistan, Sri Lanka and especially Bangladesh, the main efforts to keep food supply ahead of population growth have had to be directed toward the improvement of yields on land already cultivated. In spite of efforts since 1968 to increase rice production by means of the "green revolution," India has only just managed to keep rice production ahead of population growth. An important reason is the lack, so far, of sufficient varieties to cover the enormous range of environments. Success has been more evident with India's other basic foodgrain, wheat, although the surge of production that began in the late 1960s has not been sustained. Rice remains a more important crop than wheat, but the gap between the two has narrowed. Production fluctuates from year to year in both crops, due mainly to rainfall variations.

Pakistan parallels, though at a rather lower level, northern India's success with wheat. Bangladesh had its time of troubles in the early 1970s, but now its rice production gives a little more reason for hope. Sri Lanka has also been successful in increasing rice yields.

Excluding Singapore (essentially an island city state), most countries of southeastern Asia have land available for agricultural expansion. The

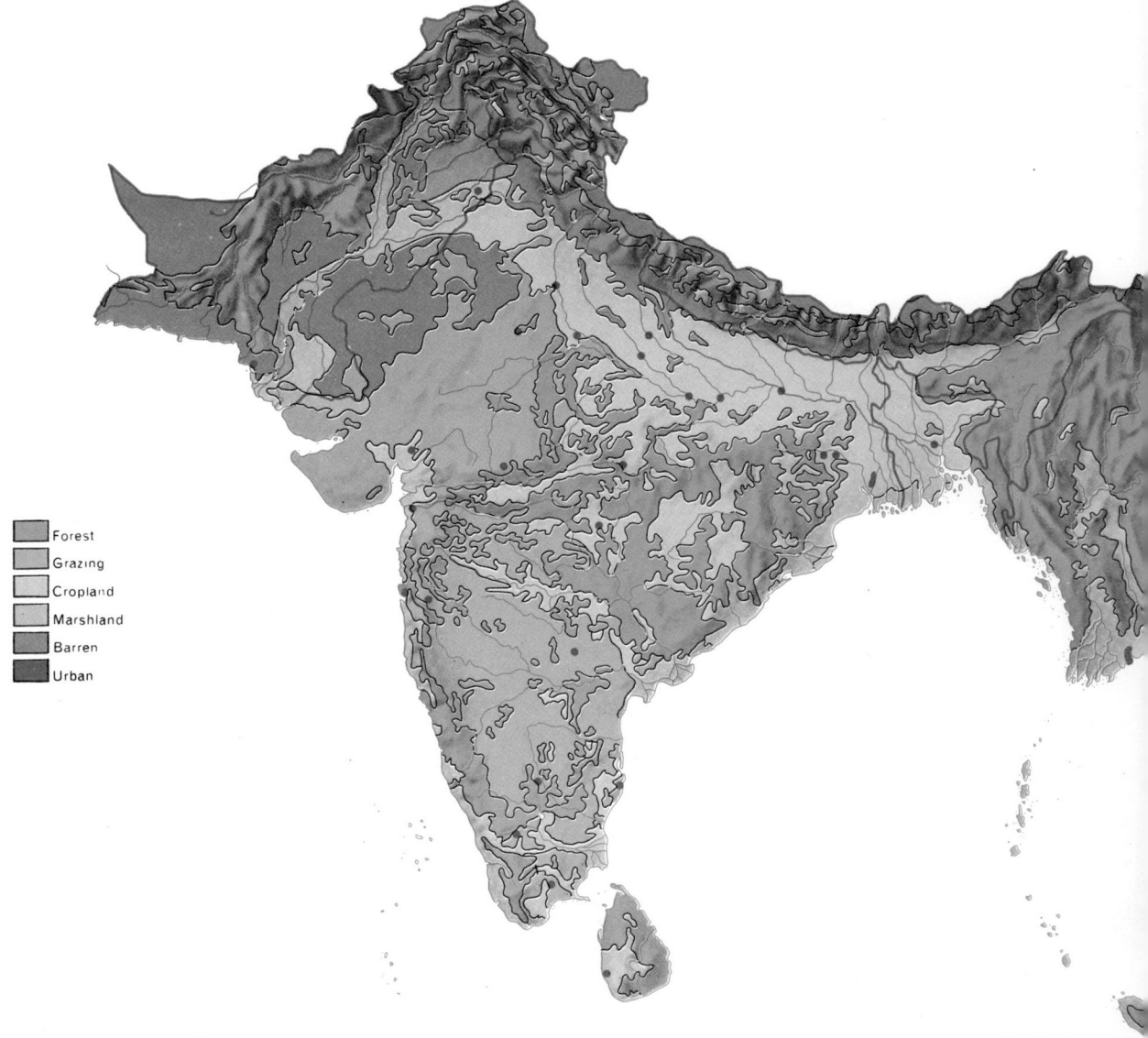

Forest
Grazing
Cropland
Marshland
Barren
Urban

Intensive use of available land is essential in Nepal, where 92 percent of the people are engaged in agriculture but 75 percent of the land is mountainous. Rice, corn, millet, potatoes and fruit are grown on these terraces.

Indonesia's population, now 140 million, is expected to rise to at least 224 million by the year 2000. As 80 million are crammed onto the fertile but small island of Java, resettlement in less populated areas is a government priority.

Population distribution in Indonesia (population/km²)

0–50 51–100 101–500 501–1,000 more than 1,000

Foodgrain production and availability in India (million tons)

Production   Net availability
Imports   Loss

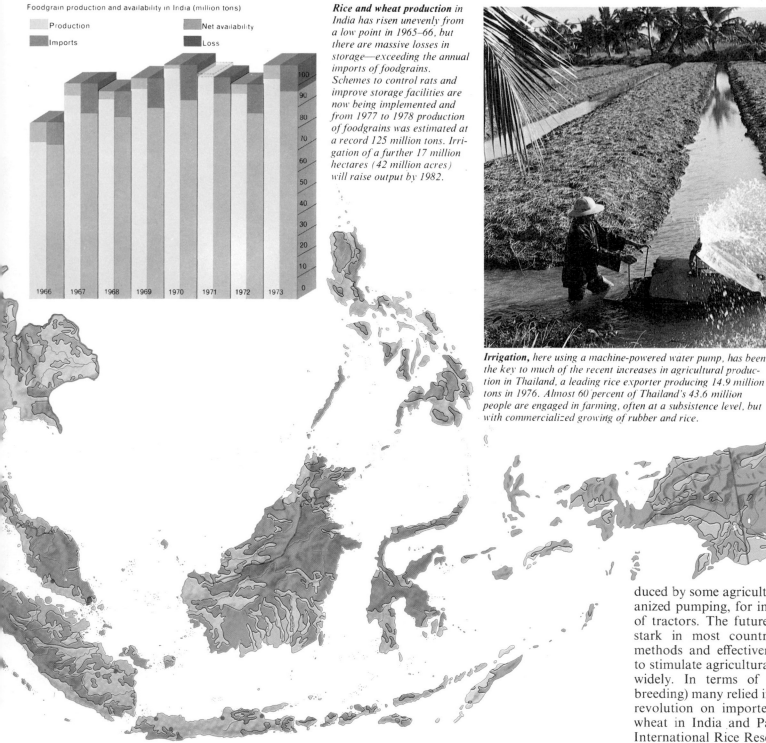

Rice and wheat production in India has risen unevenly from a low point in 1965–66, but there are massive losses in storage—exceeding the annual imports of foodgrains. Schemes to control rats and improve storage facilities are now being implemented and from 1977 to 1978 production of foodgrains was estimated at a record 125 million tons. Irrigation of a further 17 million hectares (42 million acres) will raise output by 1982.

Irrigation, here using a machine-powered water pump, has been the key to much of the recent increases in agricultural production in Thailand, a leading rice exporter producing 14.9 million tons in 1976. Almost 60 percent of Thailand's 43.6 million people are engaged in farming, often at a subsistence level, but with commercialized growing of rubber and rice.

Rice production in Java (above) cannot keep pace with the fast-growing population. Indonesia is the world's largest importer of rice. Tea (below) is the leading export crop in Sri Lanka's mainly agricultural economy. Output was 197,000 tons in 1976.

average population/land ratio varies from only 13 per square kilometer (5 per square mile) in Laos, through 35 (14) in Malaysia and 71 (27) in Indonesia to 144 (56) in the Philippines. The option of increasing agricultural production by moving to new land is being vigorously exercised in Malaysia and attempts are being made to settle Javanese peasants in the "outer islands" of Indonesia. Yet parts of some countries have dense and rapidly increasing populations with little, if any, spare land —the Tonkin delta in Vietnam, some of the Philippine islands and Java, for instance. At present, only Burma and Thailand have large exportable rice surpluses. But the green revolution has lifted rice yields in the Philippines and Java as well as in Thailand. By 1971 Javanese per capita rice production had increased by one-quarter, although there has been little improvement in production of corn and cassava, which together cover as much land as rice in Java.

The success of the green revolution

The distribution of benefits from the green revolution has been uneven, tending sometimes to increase disparities between different regions and between towns and villages (which hold 70 to 80 percent of the population in southern and southeastern Asia). Those who benefit least are the landless villagers whose numbers tend to increase while demand for the labor by which they subsist is re-

duced by some agricultural improvements—mechanized pumping, for instance, or the introduction of tractors. The future of the landless laborer is stark in most countries within the area. The methods and effectiveness of government efforts to stimulate agricultural improvement have varied widely. In terms of research (especially plant breeding) many relied in the early days of the green revolution on imported crop varieties: Mexican wheat in India and Pakistan, and rice from the International Rice Research Institute. Many more locally adapted varieties are needed, some of which are now being bred and tried out. Sri Lanka has benefited from its almost exclusive use of locally bred varieties. The failure of the wheat "revolution" to spread far from the two Punjabs is a matter less of plant breeding than of irrigation and agrarian structure.

At least in the more agriculturally advanced areas of southern and southeastern Asia, knowledge of new methods is widespread. But the essential feedback from farmers to research stations is often weak and government extension services vary in their effectiveness. Thus India has oscillated between a policy of universal coverage, with inevitable loss of impact, and concentration on favorable areas, with increases in regional disparities. Java has moved through a whole series of different programs, to the bewilderment of the cultivator.

Land reform is often urged as a precondition of desirable change, notably toward greater equity. The most revolutionary changes have taken place in Vietnam, Laos and Kampuchea. It remains to be seen whether postwar reconstruction will lead to food surpluses in their traditionally rich rice-growing areas. In Java successive reforms have been attempted but are now largely forgotten under an avalanche of "rice intensification" programs. Land reform has been effective in the export (tea and rubber) sector in Sri Lanka but has had little impact on food producers. In India and Pakistan, legislation and implementation have often been sluggish.

CHINA—PLANNING WITH PEOPLE

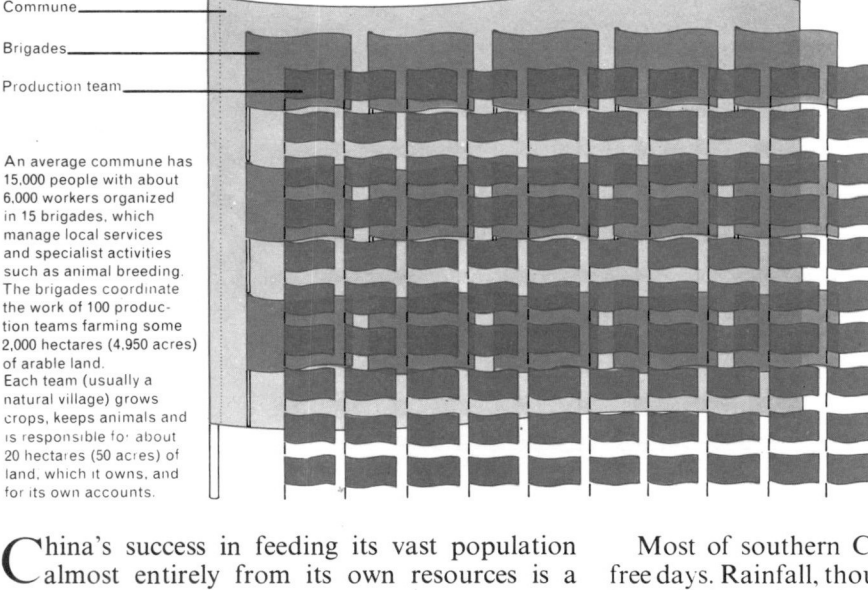

Commune_____
Brigades_____
Production team_____

An average commune has 15,000 people with about 6,000 workers organized in 15 brigades, which manage local services and specialist activities such as animal breeding. The brigades coordinate the work of 100 production teams farming some 2,000 hectares (4,950 acres) of arable land.
Each team (usually a natural village) grows crops, keeps animals and is responsible for about 20 hectares (50 acres) of land, which it owns, and for its own accounts.

Zeal and manpower trans-formed hillsides into pro-ductive terraces at Tachai, where thousands of tons of rock and earth were moved by hand after floods in 1963. Visitors now file past workers on a commune that has become a model of self-reliance, hard work and re-jection of profit motive. The communes with their sub-sidiary units (left) are the fundamental elements in the organization of rural China. Numbering about 70,000 they manage rural industries, clinics, schools and marketing and negotiate with country and state agencies in planning and commerce. They average about 3,300 households.

Political seminars for brigade workers enable the central government to maintain links even with isolated rural areas. Education, particularly political education, is regarded as crucial to the success of rural development—a process that is as much ideological as it is technological.

The contrast between a rice-planting machine and the bent backs of paddyfield workers illustrates how much manpower could be freed for industry if China mechanized its farms. In

China's success in feeding its vast population almost entirely from its own resources is a major achievement of a centrally planned economy instituted by the People's Republic after 1949. Although China has been exceptionally self-sufficient throughout its long history, under-nourishment was widespread before the 1950s and famine was a periodic threat. Communal control of food supplies and intensive agricultural practices now ensure an adequate, if frugal, diet for 900 million people.

The concentration of manpower and effort on a relatively small area of its total landmass is a key feature of China's agriculture. Out of a total of 970 million hectares (2,396 million acres) only about 120 million hectares (296 million acres) or 12 percent are cultivated. (As a comparison, the United States, with 25 percent less land, has 33 percent more land under cultivation.) More than 90 percent of China's population lives in the eastern fifth of the country. The rate of population increase—at least 10 million annually—appears to be slowing, but areas of new land coming under cultivation, together with in-creased yields from present cultivated areas, are barely sufficient to maintain the balance between population and food resources.

Land, crops and people
China has an equable climate only in the southern rice-growing lands. The north and west are affected by harsh seasonal variations. Dry, freezing winds sweep out of central Asia in winter, while in summer the warm winds that carry rain to coastal areas bring high temperatures and drought to the north-west. The southern, northern and western regions of China therefore form three sharply contrasting resource areas.

Most of southern China has at least 240 frost-free days. Rainfall, though concentrated in summer, is sufficient for double cropping—either two summer crops or a summer and a winter crop. Some areas are now growing three crops a year. The valleys and plains have deep, mixed soils, suited to rice. Tea and silk are grown on the poorer soil of hillsides, and fish, duck and water vegetables are farmed in delta and lake areas. As elsewhere, pigs, chickens and vegetables supplement the staple diet of rice or cereal.

Northern China has a less generous environment. The frost-free period drops to less than 90 days in northern Manchuria. Annual rainfall is only be-tween 500 and 1,000mm (20–40in), is unreliable, and falls only in summer. Soils are dry but fertile. The North China Plain carries 200 million people and is a major grain-growing area, together with the Manchurian Plain in the northeast. Manchuria has some 80 million people.

The western half of China, dominated by the bleak Tibetan plateau and the arid highlands and basin country of the northwest, has a population of only about 50 million. Many of China's 100 million sheep are grazed in the northwest, together with extensive goat herds. But apart from this pastoral resource, the agricultural potential of the west is limited. Although the government devotes energy and resources to the area in an attempt to settle it, poor transport and communications add to the difficulties of development.

Most of the land in China was redistributed to the people after 1949, to be owned communally rather than individually. Mutual aid teams soon gave way to producer cooperatives of an increasingly collective nature. In 1958–59, these were swept into communes—units managed by revolutionary com-

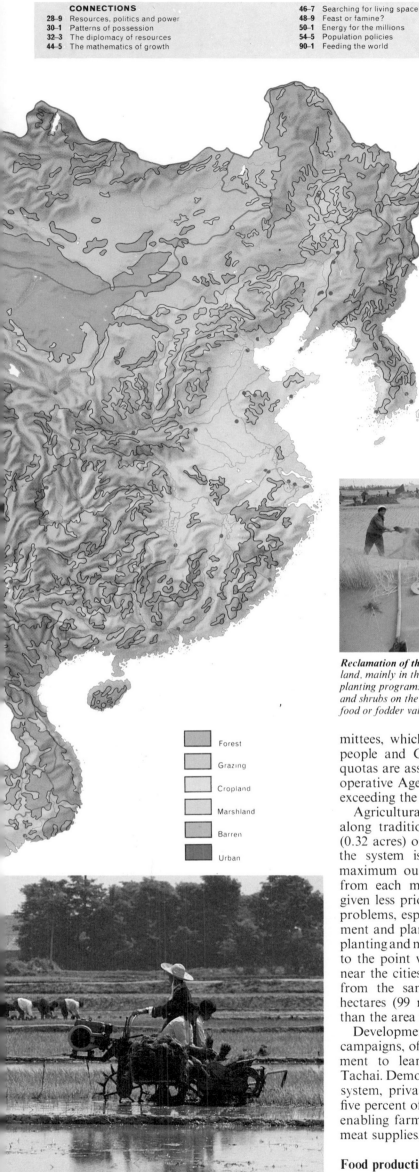

Forest
Grazing
Cropland
Marshland
Barren
Urban

Annual mean rainfall
Below 20 in
20 in–40 in
40 in–60 in
60 in–80 in
Above 80 in

Rainfall variability
Below 15%   15%–25%   25%–30%   Above 30%

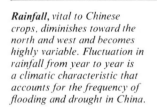

Rainfall, vital to Chinese crops, diminishes toward the north and west and becomes highly variable. Fluctuation in rainfall from year to year is a climatic characteristic that accounts for the frequency of flooding and drought in China.

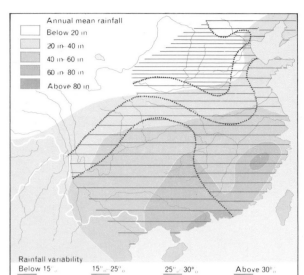

Home-made rockets, produced in Shashiyu (Sand Stone Hollow Brigade) to disperse hailstorms, are typical of the measures that have to be improvised to protect crops. The propellant is gunpowder.

Reclamation of the deserts that cover one-tenth of China's land, mainly in the northwest, has begun on a small scale with planting programs to stabilize dunes. Trees in the dune hollows and shrubs on the dune face are chosen for their medicinal, food or fodder value or for their timber.

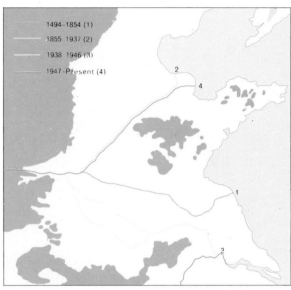

1494–1854 (1)
1855–1937 (2)
1938–1946 (3)
1947–Present (4)

The Hwang Ho (Yellow River), named after the fine loess soil it carries across a fertile and densely populated plain, has changed course radically during the country's history and caused such disastrous floods that it is also known as "China's sorrow." Measures are being extended to control it.

spite of campaigns for more machinery to provide spare capacity at planting and harvesting times, mechanization is still small-scale and labor-intensive methods are the rule.

mittees, which take decisions together with local people and Communist Party units. Production quotas are assigned, sales are made to a State Co-operative Agency, and income is based on output exceeding the quotas.

Agricultural practice since 1949 has been mainly along traditional lines. With only 0.13 hectares (0.32 acres) of cultivated land available per head, the system is highly labor-intensive—aimed at maximum output from each hectare rather than from each man-hour worked. Basic research is given less priority than the solution of immediate problems, especially improvement of soil management and planting densities. Close spacing, transplanting and multiple cropping have been developed to the point where some vegetable-growing areas near the cities can produce up to 12 crops a year from the same ground. More than 40 million hectares (99 million acres) are irrigated—greater than the area irrigated by any other country.

Development is closely linked with specific campaigns, of which the most famous is the movement to learn from the exemplary commune, Tachai. Demonstrating the flexibility of the Chinese system, private plots now occupy about three to five percent of the arable land held by most teams, enabling farmers to improve their diet, especially meat supplies, and to sell their own vegetables.

Food production, needs and prospects

China leads the world in production of rice (more than 100 million tons) and manages to export some. The country is also a leading producer of cotton, barley, wheat, soybeans, potatoes and other vegetables, as well as of pork, fish and chicken. Yet the ancient struggle for self-sufficiency continues and in most years three to four percent of grain needs are met by imports (mainly from Canada and Australia). In the big cities—30 of which have populations of more than one million—diets are monotonous, with frequent shortages of green vegetables and with some rationing of food and clothing.

In rural areas, where two-thirds of the population lives, the housing, health, security and self-respect of the people have been transformed, however. Some argue that China's model should be followed by the less-developed countries in general. Apart from the primary economic success in suppressing starvation and gross poverty, China's achievement includes the degree of social egalitarianism and working-class participation in decision making. Critics point out that a high political and social price is paid for the stability achieved, with wide-ranging economic and social restriction.

A major question facing China is whether its revolutionary momentum can be sustained to provide export surpluses, prosperity and shorter working hours. Potential for rapid expansion of new land development appears to be limited. The cultivated area is growing slowly—probably by about one million hectares (2.5 million acres) a year. Faster development depends on new dams and water delivery systems, roads and other capital investments. Immediate increases in food production are more likely to come from existing cultivations, especially through increased supplies of fertilizer. China makes intensive use of animal and human manure but is a large importer of nitrogenous fertilizers. New plant under construction will greatly expand fertilizer production. Special prominence is also being given to farm mechanization. Meanwhile, China's people continue to be the country's main resource but, at the same time, its main burden.

USSR—PLANNING FROM THE CENTER

The USSR is the world's leading producer of cotton despite the fact that its cultivation is confined only to irrigated areas in central Asia where temperatures are high. In 1976 2,800,000 tons of cotton were produced compared to a US production of 2,298,000 tons.

The USSR's largest trading partners are still other Communist countries, but these combines for cotton picking, manufactured near Tashkent, are destined for cotton-producing countries all over the world.

Mechanized complexes are being set up on state farms and collective farms in those areas where livestock breeding is a major occupation. Here sheep are feeding at mechanized pens— the feed is prepared, chopped and distributed to the animal, eliminating much of the supervision.

The Soviet Union, the major partner in the Comecon group of countries, is by far the largest country in the world, with an area of 22,403,600 square kilometers (8,650,000 square miles). It owes its superpower role primarily to this and to the fact that it possesses large reserves of raw materials (it claims to have more than half the world's potential of fossil fuels), plus a population of 257,800,000—the third largest manpower pool in the world.

With the establishment of Soviet power in 1917 the state assumed responsibility for all aspects of economic development. This responsibility is exercised through a command economy, where each enterprise operates to fulfill the planned directives of central authority. The central organs of power—the Presidium and Council of Ministers of the Supreme Soviet, with the parallel Politburo of the Central Committee of the Communist Party—decide the broad priorities and strategies for the development of the country. The execution of the policies is worked out by the central state planning agency, GOSPLAN, which allocates resources accordingly. The plans the agency issues have to cover every sector of the economy and are normally for a five-year period. Each is broken down, both regionally, to the Union Republics and to lesser administrative units, and sectorally, to the various ministries of the central government.

Such a highly centralized system of decision-making is capable of focusing capital investment, manpower and resources into those developments

In the USSR *any large-scale extension of land used for agriculture will depend on water supply. Schemes to divert northward-flowing rivers to the irrigated areas of the south and west have been discussed since the 1930s, but it is believed that they may now become a reality by the year 2000.*

Canal
Reservoir
Proposed river reversal
Irrigated areas

Moscow
Kiev
Tobolsk
Volgograd
Tashkent

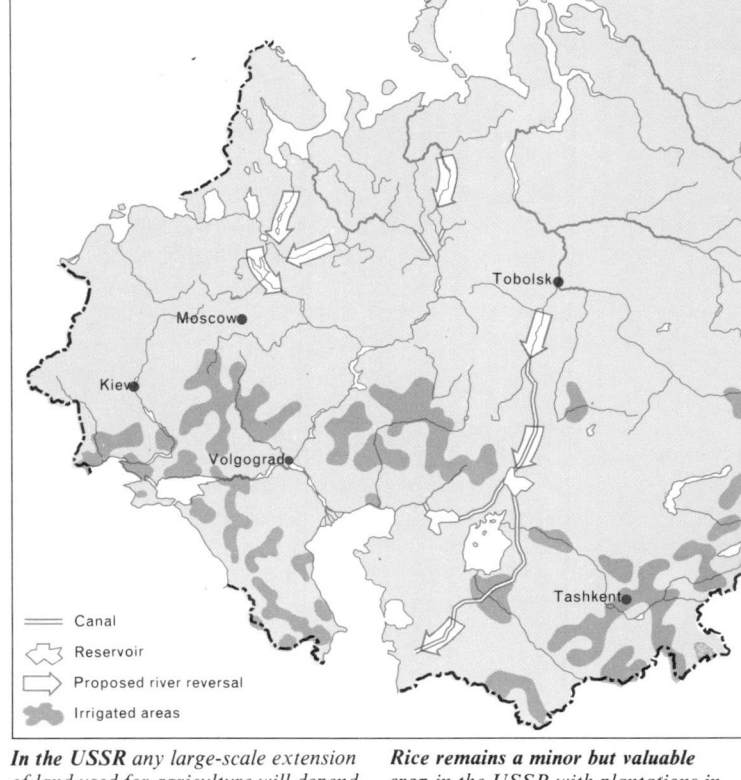

Rice remains a minor but valuable crop in the USSR with plantations in the northern Caucasus and here in southern Kazakhstan, where the land is being leveled and prepared for rice production. Irrigation canals were built to transport water from a reservoir on the Syr Darya River to the fields.

Forest
Grazing
Cropland
Marshland
Barren
Urban

that are seen as priority aims, with rapid, effective and large-scale results. The Soviet Union is now, for instance, the world's leading producer of coal, steel and cement. Frequently, individual projects have been on a huge scale, including, for example, many of the world's largest hydroelectric plants. The "pioneer" region of Siberia is growing rapidly on the basis of three large hydroelectric plants on the river Angara.

At the same time the system is inflexible. Individuals have, at best, limited opportunity to influence the decision-taking process. The planners themselves find it difficult to adjust plans speedily to changing circumstances and rapid industrialization has taken place without heed for the environment, with the result that there are serious pollution problems. Only in the last decade or so has attention been paid to them and to problems of wasteful use of resources.

New economic accounting

Since the mid-1960s efforts have been made to introduce flexibility into the system by the use of "economic accounting," a yardstick of profitability. This has undoubtedly led to considerable improvements, but to achieve maximum effect this system requires much devolution of decision-making to the managers of enterprises; so far there has been reluctance on the part of the central government to cede such powers.

The population of the Soviet Union also presents the planner with a major set of problems. In the first place, the bulk of the population is concentrated in the center and south of European Russia. Most of the central Asian desert and almost all Siberia except a narrow belt along the Trans-Siberian railway are exceptionally thinly inhabited, yet it is these empty lands of Siberia which contain much of the country's potential wealth, including the greater part of the energy and timber reserves. Similarly, a great part of the population, of industry and of industrial production lies south of an approximate line from Kiev to the Altai Mountains in a zone of water deficiency. This antithesis of population and natural resources is a major hindrance to the development of potentials; the largest fields of coal reserves, the Tunguska and Lena basins, are as yet totally unexploited. The difficulty has been compounded since about 1960 by the migration away from the areas of labor deficit in Siberia and the Urals and the labor shortage is now being exacerbated by the declining birthrate and the growing contingent of people over retirement age.

Given the imbalance of people and resources, together with the huge extent of the Soviet Union, the transport network acquires exceptional significance. The road network is underdeveloped but the railways, which carry the bulk of freight, are highly efficient. Rivers, although often of great size, suffer from the prolonged freeze-up and their use is relatively minor. Great distances have fostered a steady and rapid growth in air transport and Aeroflot is now the world's largest civil airline.

THE LIVING RESOURCE
USSR & EASTERN EUROPE

Despite its enormous size only a tenth of the Soviet Union is arable due to the severe constraints of climate. Of the three major zones, the largest, in the north and east, occupies nearly half the country's area and consists of barren tundra and extensive boreal forest. The shortness of the growing season and low average temperatures make agriculture almost impossible there—only reindeer herding is practiced. Farther south there is cattle rearing, and crops such as rye can be grown. The second zone, in central Asia and around the Caspian Sea, has a low rainfall and desert or semi-desert conditions. Temperatures are high in summer and along the rivers there is intensive cultivation. Cotton is overwhelmingly the dominant crop, although wheat and fruits are also grown for local consumption. Outside the oases, there is only nomadic pasturing.

Between the cold and arid zones lies the third zone, the so-called "fertile triangle," where most agriculture is concentrated. The northern half of the triangle has soils of low fertility, but in the south are the Black Earths, one of the world's most fertile soils. Up to four-fifths of the Black Earths are under the plow and sown to wheat, corn and other grains, together with sugar beet, potatoes and industrial crops such as hemp and tobacco. However, even the fertile triangle suffers from climatic difficulties: frosts curtail the growing season and damage crops: serious droughts occur, on average, up to one year in three. Bad seasons in this principal grain-producing region have in a number of recent years involved the Soviet Union in large purchases of grain from abroad. Moreover, overcropping and poor farming practices (at times a monoculture of wheat) have reduced the fertility of the soil.

Two types of farm

The problems imposed by hostile climatic conditions are compounded by difficulties arising from the Soviet systems of agricultural organization. The principal type of farm is the collective (kolkhoz), a cooperative unit with members, under an elected chairman, sharing the work and end-of-year profits. Originally there were 250,000 collectives, when they were first established after 1928, but a steady process of amalgamation has reduced their number to less than 30,000 huge units, each averaging 6,400 hectares (15,808 acres) and supporting about 470 families. The second type of farm is the state farm (sovkhoz), where the workers are wage-earning employees of the state, under a manager. The state farms are even larger than the collectives, averaging some 20,000 hectares (49,400 acres), and they have steadily increased their share of overall agricultural production. Both types of farm are involved in all aspects of agriculture, although there is a tendency for state farms to specialize in one particular activity and for collectives to engage in mixed farming.

Both types suffer from the centralized system. Central and regional authorities have determined cropping patterns and practices, and even the dates of farm operations, with little regard to local conditions. Incentives to high productivity are weak; in particular farm incomes are low compared with those of industrial workers. Consequently, workers tend to leave farming and Soviet agriculture is chronically short of skilled people. Although state farms in general are more mechanized and show higher returns per unit area and per worker than the collectives, on both productivity is low.

Most farm workers put their greatest effort into cultivating their small private plots, the produce of which is sold in the kolkhoz markets found in every town. These plots are intensively cultivated and although they occupy only one and a half percent of the total arable land, they yield a third to a half of the country's requirements of fruit, vegetables and meat, as well as providing a major supplementary income to the farmers.

The weaknesses of Soviet agriculture have caused successive governments to attempt improvements and there has been a marked improvement of productivity. New irrigation schemes have been put into operation in several areas such as the Crimea and the Kara Kum desert and techniques of strip-cropping, contour-plowing and tree-plantation are being used increasingly to combat soil erosion.

Eastern Europe

The eight countries of Eastern Europe (with a combined population of about 130 million) together cover 1,165,500 square kilometers (450,000 square miles). They may be divided into three major groups according to their degree of economic coordination with the Soviet Union. The largest consists of East Germany, Poland, Czechoslovakia and Hungary in the northern part of the region and Bulgaria in the south. The second group contains Yugoslavia and Romania and the third consists of a single country—Albania—which is the only one to have broken totally with Moscow.

Within the first group of countries the most critical question is one of energy supplies. Since World War II accelerated industrialization has been the core of economic development in Eastern Europe, with special attention given to heavy manufacturing and chemicals. This has been achieved at the expense of increasing importation of such key raw materials as petroleum, natural gas and iron ore, mainly from the Soviet Union. As a result of the energy crisis sharply increased prices for Soviet oil

In Hungary decentralization of the planning system has been in progress since 1968. Emphasis under the "new economic mechanism" is now on agro-industrial cooperatives.

Mechanized farming in the USSR is usually more evident on state farms than on collective farms. These hothouses are part of a highly mechanized farm complex growing fresh vegetables for Moscow, which is 30 km (18.6 miles) away. The hothouses cover an area of 54 hectares (133 acres) and produce tomatoes, cucumbers, onions, lettuce and other vegetables.

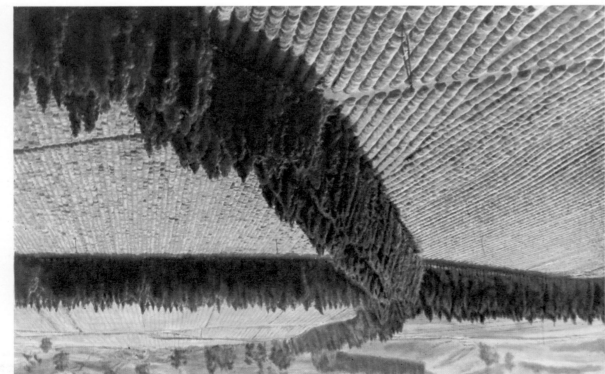

Windbreaks, using rows of conifers, are one of several measures designed to control erosion in the USSR. They are shown here protecting tea bushes. Windbreaks, which reduce the risk of wind erosion and soil disturbance by surface water, are particularly important in the Transcaucasus forests, where soil has been exposed by removal of vegetation and by overgrazing.

have caused budgetary disruption—forcing a re-assessment of many economic goals. In imposing an average 130 percent increase the Soviet Union boosted Eastern Europe's nominal import costs by about $4 billion (rouble equivalent) in 1975. Partly to compensate, the Soviet Union agreed to pay more for Eastern European machinery, manufactured goods and farm produce, but this still left deficits in the region of $2 billion. Natural gas consumption also will be facilitated by the completion of the 2,790 kilometers (1,733 miles) pipeline from Orenburg to Uzhgorod at an estimated cost of $1.5 billion. It will deliver 25–30 billion cubic meters (32.5–39 billion cubic yards) each year.

Population changes

A second feature of this group concerns problems related to its demography. World War II drastically changed the population size and structure of these countries (except Bulgaria), which in 1975 had a combined population of 85 million. Natural increase varies greatly within this area, from Poland, with the highest in both absolute and relative terms, to East Germany, with more deaths than births reported since 1969. However, even before that, natural increase was rather low—at its best, only six per thousand. Czechoslovakia reached its lowest

rate in 1968 (4.2/'000), but there was some improvement by 1976 (7.8/'000). Natural increase in Hungary during the 1960s amounted to about 0.3 percent, one of the lowest in the world; after recent improvement of fertility performances, the excess of births was more than 60,000 in 1974 (5.8/'000). Nevertheless, these latter three countries still portray some evidence of population stagnation. Already by the mid-1970s labor shortages existed in East Germany and Czechoslovakia, while deficiencies in specially trained manpower branches were also reported from Bulgaria and Hungary. Concurrent with these trends has been a greatly accelerated growth of urbanization. East Germany is the most highly urbanized country in Eastern Europe, with three-quarters of its population living in towns and cities.

Agriculture provides yet another problem area within this first group of countries. In all of them agriculture is marked by the coexistence of state, collective and private enterprises, clearly distinguished from one another in size and organization, and their reactions to national economic policy. Agricultural output in Poland, which de-collectivized its agriculture in the mid-1950s, has performed better than the other countries that have retained socialized methods. Only 15 percent of the

country's agricultural area is under state or collective farms; private farming with its small plots (2–10 hectares/5–25 acres) exhibits few differences from the socialized enterprises with regard to cropping, though the latter tend to grow more cereals and sugar beet and concentrate on livestock, whereas peasant farms emphasize potato production.

The second group of countries, Yugoslavia and Romania, in spite of less economic coordination with the Soviet Union, has distinct problems of its own. Perhaps most notable is that of the multinational state as evidenced by Yugoslavia. The 1971 census revealed 18 different ethnic groups living within the country, of which the most numerous were the Serbians (39.7 percent) and Croatians (22.1 percent). Antagonism between Serb and Croat has a long history. The Albanian minority presents a particularly difficult problem because it forms the poorest section of the country's population. The Albanians' feelings of relative deprivation have not been helped by the traditional hostility between themselves on the one hand and the Serbs and Montenegrins on the other.

Besides nationality, there are other problems. Given Romania's high rate of economic growth during the last decade (the highest in Eastern Europe in 1976 with 10.5 percent), a sudden natural disaster, like the floods of 1970 or the 1977 earthquake, can have long-term consequences. For example, the earthquake caused most devastation in the industrialized south and undoubtedly the economy has been retarded as a result. The fear of natural disaster is also common in Yugoslavia, well known as an earthquake zone. Yugoslavia also faces potential hazards arising from recent developments in oil imports. Rapid consumption of oil has forced the country to import increasing supplies from the Middle East, facilitated by the new Adria pipeline. This pipeline will ultimately have an annual crude oil flow capacity of 35 million tons, of which 24 million tons will be available to Yugoslavia. Should a tanker accident occur, then some of the country's most profitable tourist resorts would be heavily polluted.

High unemployment

Yet another economic problem facing Yugoslavia concerns labor supply. More than a million of its work force have gone abroad and at home more than 500,000 are unemployed. The situation has been further aggravated by a slow-down of the economy since 1974.

Albania has 2.5 million people who inhabit one of Europe's smallest, least developed, most physically rugged and by far its most ideologically isolated state. Ideological association with China since 1962 has led to elaborate planning methods based on the commune concept, and a deliberate policy of slowing down urban population growth. Cultivated land covers only 17 percent of the country's total area; forests 44 percent; pasture 25 percent; and more than 13 percent is unusable for any form of agriculture. To save agricultural land no new buildings of less than three storeys are allowed to be constructed. Strict controls are also enforced on internal migration to minimize permanent rural to urban movement; in turn, this is reflected in the much higher rural than urban birth and marriage rates.

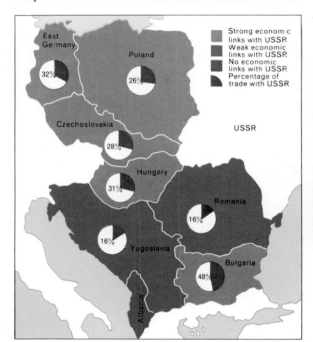

Soviet trade with Eastern Europe is still important, but links with the developing countries represent the fastest-growing sector of commerce in the Soviet Union.

Removal of Yugoslavia's extensive forest cover often leads to erosion. Strip cultivation, shown above, is practiced to stabilize the soil and prevent wind erosion.

Agriculture plays an important part in Bulgaria's economy: soils are fertile and 30 percent of the population work on the land. Increased mechanization continues, however.

which produce, process and market farm products. Output has increased considerably.

In Albania large areas of swamp have been transformed into usable land. Volunteers have tackled everything—ditch-digging to dam-building—so the regular workforce could continue its work.

Poland is still a leading agricultural nation—production rose by 27 percent between 1971 and 1975. Exports include many livestock products and the principal crops are grains and potatoes.

MINERALS

THE SUBSTANCE OF EARTH

There is hardly a single example of a mineral resource which forms during a man's lifetime, and there are few that have formed during the one and a half million years of human history. The deposits we exploit so extravagantly in a few years have taken tens or hundreds of millions of years to form in the Earth's continental and oceanic crusts.

Alteration — or metamorphism — of already formed rocks and minerals has been the result of earth pressures due to burial and to applied stress, to elevated temperatures and to the activity of solutions. The simplest examples are the hardening of and development of cleavage in clay rocks, which convert them into slates, and the recrystallization of limestone under elevated temperatures, which produces marble. Deep-seated metamorphism often leads to dehydration of the rocks and waters are released which may themselves become important agents of mineral concentration. Such metamorphic waters are augmented by buried seawater and by fresh water that has become increasingly saline as it has sunk through the rocks. Such saline solutions, when expelled from the depths, give rise to ores and other valuable mineral deposits introduced into faults and cavities, or formed by reaction with rocks such as limestone. Important nonmetallic minerals also accumulate under the influence of hydrothermal waters: asbestos, talc, fluorspar, barytes and kaolin are examples.

Life processes also influence mineral concentration. Sulfur bacteria promote the accumulation of this element in stagnant marine basins; the fossil remains of the calcareous parts of invertebrate creatures produce limestone. But most important of all is the preservation of carbohydrates from plants to form coal; and of hydrocarbons from marine organisms to form oil.

Continental and oceanic crusts

The continental crust—continents, continental shelves and most islands—is composed of a heterogeneous assemblage of rocks (predominantly granite) containing the lighter elements such as aluminum, calcium, sodium, potassium, with some magnesium and iron, mainly combined as silicates: with a large number of other elements in minor quantities. In contrast, the deep oceans, covering more than 70 percent of the Earth's surface, are floored at depths up to 10 kilometers (six miles) below water surface by oceanic crust, which is composed essentially of basalt and is more homogeneous than continental crust. Oceanic crust is continuously formed by eruption of basalt from the system of linked midocean fissures, from which the crust migrates at the rate of a few centimeters a year toward the continental margins. Oceanic crust is not only being created; it is also being destroyed where it plunges down beneath the continents along the ocean deeps, which at present form a belt around the Pacific. Adjacent to this belt, the rocks of the continental crust have been intensely folded

and injected with molten rock (magma), and mountain belts like the North and South American Cordillera have come into existence during the past 50 million years.

Many valuable mineral deposits have been formed in the continental crust. The slow migration of oceanic crust, the building of continental mountains, the volcanic eruptions at the surface and the intrusion of magma at depth all indicate that energy available inside the Earth is being dissipated. The main source of this energy must lie in the heat evolved from the spontaneous disintegration of radioactive elements such as potassium, uranium and thorium. These endogenous or "internal" processes may be contrasted with the superficial processes in which the chief energy source is solar radiation: weathering, erosion, glacial action, physical and chemical effects that may be classified as exogenous or "external."

Among internal igneous processes, settlement of early-formed crystals from basaltic magmas that have been static for extended periods in chambers far below the Earth's surface has produced concentrations of the platinum metals and of chromite, while sulfide-rich portions of the magma, not readily mixed with the silicates, have produced concentrations of nickel, copper, cobalt and iron sulfides. Significant examples of the first group occur in South Africa and of the latter in Canada. In granitic magmas, water and volatile elements such as fluorine and boron may become concentrated in residual fluids left after most of the silicates have crystallized. In residual hydrothermal fluids from granitic activity, metals such as tin and tungsten become concentrated as oxides, while copper, molybdenum, lead, zinc, antimony, bismuth and silver in sulfide form are also deposited. A spatial association between such deposits and granitic intrusions can be demonstrated for instance throughout the American Cordillera. But by no means all granitic bodies are accompanied by ore concentrations. The endogenous ore bodies are very small and expensive to locate. The most

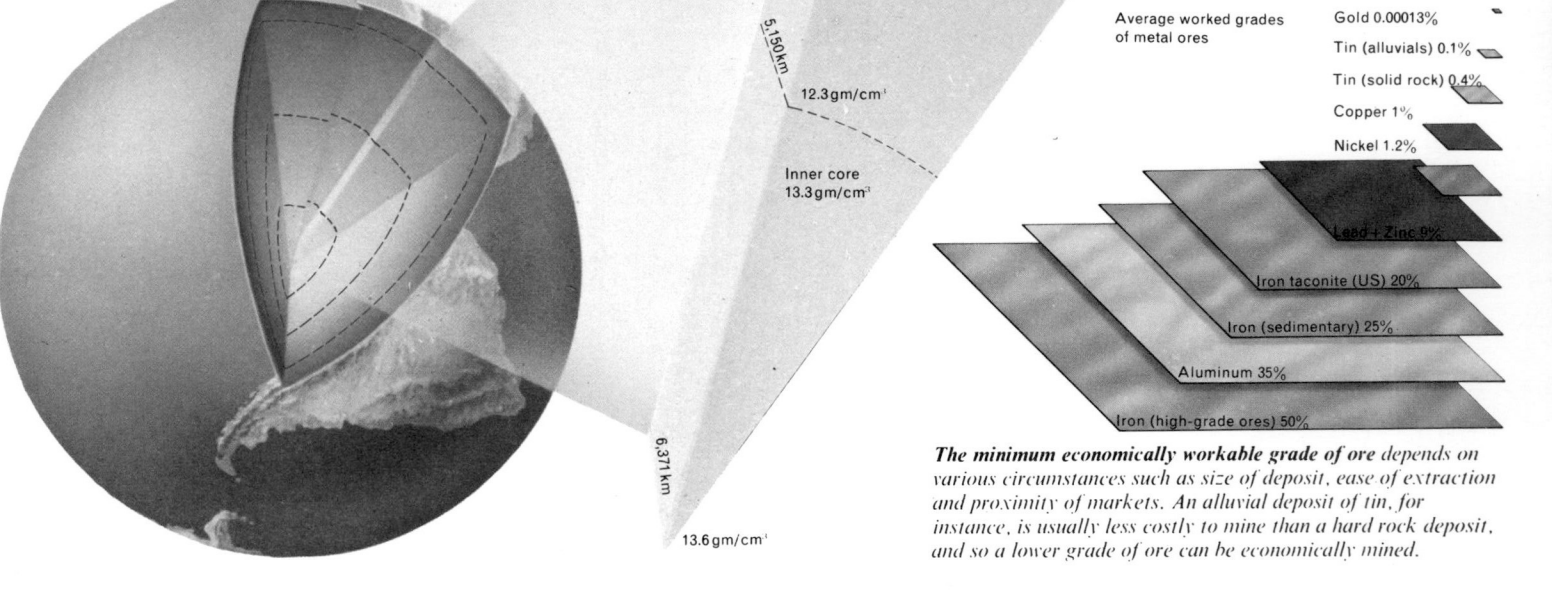

The Earth must have passed through a liquid stage during condensation in the course of which the material composing it became arranged roughly in layers increasing in density toward the center. Studies of earthquake waves which have passed through the planet reveal that it has a liquid core about 6,900 km (4,280 miles) in diameter surrounded by a thick mantle that is composed of viscous rock material with a temperature of about 1,000 C (1,832 F). Man is separated from this white-hot layer by a crust averaging only about 30 km (18.5 miles) thick made of cool rock. The core is thought to be molten iron, with some nickel, and the mantle is composed mainly of silicates of iron and magnesium, probably with some gas content.

Oceanic crust
Depth: 5 km

Silicon oxide 69%
Aluminum oxide 14%
Others 13%
Iron oxide 4%

700 km

Upper mantle
Density: 3.3 gm/cm³

Lower mantle
4.3 gm/cm³

Upper and lower mantle

Silicon oxide 43%
Magnesium oxide 37%
Iron oxide 12%
Calcium oxide 3%
Others 5%

2,900 km

5.5 gm/cm³

Outer core
10 gm/cm³

Outer and inner core

Iron oxide 90%
Nickel oxide 8%
Others 2%

5,150 km

12.3 gm/cm³

Inner core
13.3 gm/cm³

6,371 km

13.6 gm/cm³

Average worked grades
of metal ores

Gold 0.00013%
Tin (alluvials) 0.1%
Tin (solid rock) 0.4%
Copper 1%
Nickel 1.2%
Lead + Zinc 6%
Iron taconite (US) 20%
Iron (sedimentary) 25%
Aluminum 35%
Iron (high-grade ores) 50%

The minimum economically workable grade of ore depends on various circumstances such as size of deposit, ease of extraction and proximity of markets. An alluvial deposit of tin, for instance, is usually less costly to mine than a hard rock deposit, and so a lower grade of ore can be economically mined.

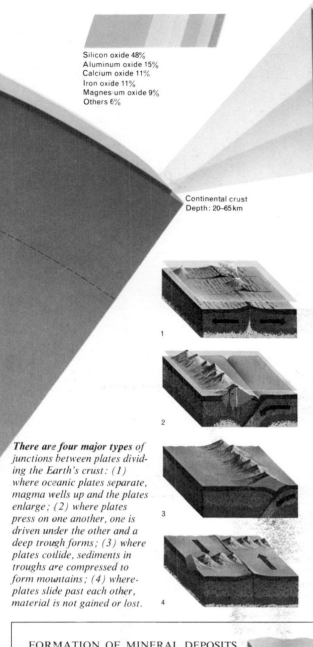

Silicon oxide 48%
Aluminum oxide 15%
Calcium oxide 11%
Iron oxide 11%
Magnesium oxide 9%
Others 6%

Continental crust
Depth: 20–65km

There are four major types of junctions between plates dividing the Earth's crust: (1) where oceanic plates separate, magma wells up and the plates enlarge; (2) where plates press on one another, one is driven under the other and a deep trough forms; (3) where plates collide, sediments in troughs are compressed to form mountains; (4) where plates slide past each other, material is not gained or lost.

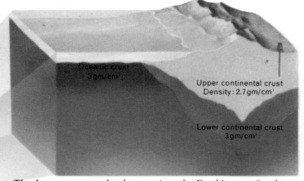

Oceanic crust 3gm/cm³

Upper continental crust Density: 2.7 gm/cm³

Lower continental crust 3gm/cm³

The deepest penetration by man into the Earth's crust for the purpose of extracting minerals is under a gas well in Oklahoma in the USA. After 503 days of drilling the distance reached was nearly 9.6 kilometers (5¾ miles).

Many metals occur in both the oceanic and continental crusts, but are only workable where nature has concentrated them. Average crust is not considered a potential source of supply.

Oceanic crust	Percentage	Continental crust	Percentage
Aluminum	8.4	Aluminum	8.3
Iron	7.5	Iron	4.8
Titanium	0.81	Titanium	0.53
Manganese	0.18	Phosphorus	0.12
Phosphorus	0.14	Manganese	0.1
Fluorine	0.042	Fluorine	0.047
Barium	0.037	Barium	0.04
Vanadium	0.017	Vanadium	0.012
Chromium	0.016	Zinc	0.0081
Nickel	0.014	Chromium	0.0077
Zinc	0.012	Nickel	0.0061
Copper	0.0085	Copper	0.005
Cobalt	0.0037	Lithium	0.0022
Lithium	0.002	Niobium	0.002
Niobium	0.0018	Cobalt	0.0018
Lead	0.001	Lead	0.0013
Thorium	0.0042	Thorium	0.00068
Tin	0.0019	Tantalum	0.00023
Molybdenum	0.0015	Uranium	0.00022
Uranium	0.0001	Tin	0.00016
Tungsten	0.00094	Beryllium	0.00015
Antimony	0.000091	Tungsten	0.00012
Beryllium	0.000083	Molybdenum	0.00011
Tantalum	0.000043	Antimony	0.000045
Mercury	0.000011	Mercury	0.00008
Selenium	0.00001	Silver	0.0000065
Silver	0.0000091	Selenium	0.0000059
Platinum	0.0000075	Platinum	0.0000028
Bismuth	0.00000066	Gold	0.00000035
Gold	0.00000035	Bismuth	0.00000029
Tellurium	0.000000088	Tellurium	0.000000036

consistent type is "porphyry" copper. Worked on a large tonnage basis at grades between 0.4 and 1.0 percent copper, these deposits supply about 60 percent of the world's demand for the metal.

External processes have been of equal or perhaps greater importance in concentrating minerals. Simple weathering of hard rocks, followed by transport and deposition by rivers, produces great spreads of alluvial sand and gravel; glacial erosion and subglacial stream transport have been even more effective in the Northern Hemisphere in leading to clean sand and gravel. Transport of sand eroded from the land surface by rivers or by seashore waves may produce conditions in which the heavier particles in the sand become deposited at low-energy points such as the bends in streams. Placer deposits result, yielding gold, and oxides of tin, titanium and iron-titanium. Gold placers were the objects of the gold rushes in the Klondike last century; the greatest gold deposits of the world, in the Witwatersrand, South Africa, are believed to be river placers, formed one billion years ago. The Florida and Australian beach sands are the chief

sources of titanium minerals and of large deposits of thorium, used in the generation of nuclear power. Weathering under humid tropical conditions causes residual concentration of iron and aluminum hydroxides; in areas where the latter predominate, valuable bauxite ores provide main raw materials for aluminum manufacture.

Important raw materials
At least five different types of mineral resource have been formed by deposition in the shelf seas: clays or shales suitable for brick-making; sedimentary iron ore deposits, apparently not forming at present, but formed in huge quantities in the geological past (the bulk of the world's iron ore comes from them); evaporite deposits yielding dolomite, anhydrite or gypsum, rock salt and potassium chlorides (all these are important raw materials for chemical and fertilizer manufacture); and phosphate deposits typically worked in Florida and along the coast of north Africa. Finally limestone, a common sedimentary rock, not only provides handsome building stone but is a source of lime for agriculture.

FORMATION OF MINERAL DEPOSITS

Man depends on relatively rare geological processes where the low amounts of metals in ordinary rock are concentrated to create a richer deposit which is economical to mine. There are two main types of processes, external and internal, that create a mineral deposit. Some of the external—those taking place near or at the Earth's surface—are shown in 1–3; those in 4–7 are the internal, taking place within the Earth. In practice many mineral deposits have been produced by more than one process, each taking place at a different stage in the deposit's formation. An ore deposit, for instance, may have been formed by hydrothermal processes but on reaching the surface it may have undergone further concentration by secondary enrichment. Internal processes are associated with earth movements and with molten rock welling up from the interior into the crust.

Mineral salts form when the Sun evaporates seawaters trapped in a barred basin. Deposits tend to settle in layers; the more insoluble are deposited first, the most soluble last.

Placer deposits occur where eroded particles of rock being carried by water are sorted by heavy mineral grains settling and lighter particles being carried away.

Residual deposits occur where minerals, concentrated in a rock, are left behind when other material within the rock is removed by mechanical or chemical weathering.

Main methods of magma separation: (a) minerals crystallize and settle to the bottom of the magma chamber; (b) the magma solidifies, forcing the molten minerals into fissures.

An ore deposit may result when gases and fluids, escaping from the magma, react with the rock face and alter the composition of the rocks by adding valuable elements.

Dissolved minerals are carried into fissures by (a) hot fluids left when magma crystallizes; (b) surface water heated by magma; (c) water from the hotter mantle.

In some cases mineral deposits are formed when an acidic water containing a metal reaches an alkaline environment, or where there are changes in oxygen content.

PROSPECTING & MINING

About 60 percent of the world's tin production is from alluvial deposits and most nowadays is mined mechanically. In Indonesia, Malaysia and Thailand (above) about 10 percent is produced by traditional methods such as panning. In an open-pit copper mine (right) huge amounts of rock need to be moved to win small amounts of copper.

Uranium, like most minerals, is mined by both surface and underground techniques, depending on the depth of the deposit. Veins located by a mine geologist with a geiger counter (left) are identified with paint before drilling.

The time and cost involved in setting up a mine are considerable and the complex preparations —from the exploration stage until production begins—can take as long as 10 years and rarely less than five. Moreover, although exploration work accounts for only a small part of the cost, it is a high-risk investment and the total risk involved in mining investment is normally much higher than in any manufacturing industry. One major mining company reports that out of 1,000 exploration efforts over a 30-year period, 78 warranted detailed drilling, 13 could be developed commercially, seven repaid their costs and one was extremely profitable.

Reflecting this high-risk situation, funds for exploration have traditionally come from the speculative investor in small exploration companies or, more important, from established mining companies reinvesting net revenue to sustain their operations. Other sources of exploration funds today include consumers anxious to secure a particular supply of their essential raw materials (steel works seeking their own iron ore sources for instance). These various funding sources are present in both the public and private sector. Specifically in the public sector, funds are available to the developing countries through bilateral aid programs and United Nations' agencies.

An exploration team will search for a deposit that can profitably supply the market—and for most metals this will be an international market. For the private corporation, the word "profitably" will have its conventional meaning; for a nation, however, and particularly a developing country, a mining venture may be worthwhile if foreign exchange earnings exceed foreign exchange costs.

For a domestic mining company, or perhaps a state exploration team supported by aid funds, the first exercise will be to select an appropriate area on the basis of the geological data available. For foreign or overseas mining companies there is a prior exercise, the selection of a particular country

for exploration. Geological considerations are again important, but there are also other factors, including, particularly, a government's attitude to foreign private sector development of its minerals. Some countries, for example, insist on majority local ownership, others on governmental control of marketing. Such factors, together with taxation levels, security of tenure, general stability and infrastructural development will all be important.

Meeting the targets
Apparent richness of the possible discovery is clearly a factor in selection, but more important is the degree of certainty with which the potential ore body might be proved. Taking an extreme situation, it is clearly possible to prove a low-grade ore body within 60 meters (200 feet) of the surface with much greater certainty than, say, a potentially high-grade ore body at 1,500 meters (5,000 feet) below the surface. For the companies, banks or governments financing a development, the prime concern is that the project will meet its targets—this is far more important than that the targets themselves should be especially rewarding. The proving operation can only be completed through detailed drilling, supplemented by pitting and trenching where practicable. Given knowledge of the ore body, the next stage will be a full study of the feasibility of development. This will include an assessment of mining methods and costs, the treatment systems and the possible recovery levels (clearly the value of an ore relates to the metals that can be recovered for sale, not the gross value of the metal in the ground), labor costs, the availability of power, and other supplies and transport facilities.

In the extreme, the largest mines today have an initial capital cost approaching a billion dollars. Such figures and even substantially smaller figures are beyond the capability of individual mining corporations and most major projects are joint ventures. The participants will normally include the

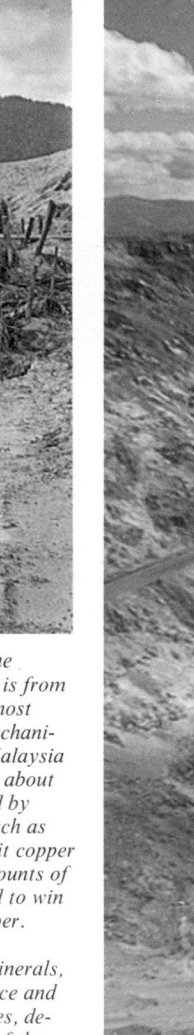

Size distribution of mines in Western World by annual ore production

■ >3 million tons
■ 1–3 million tons
■ 500,000–1 million tons
□ 300,000–500,000 tons
□ 150,000–300,000 tons

Underground mines
Open-pit mines

	0	100	200	300	400	500	mines
1969							
1971							
1973							
1975							
1977							

From 1969 to 1977 mine production rose by about 30 percent as demand increased and lower-grade ores were worked. No new mines opened, but more moved into the three-million-ton group.

mining companies (supplying the technical and managerial skills and the vital guarantee that the project will be brought to production); banks with long-term loan funds; industrial fabricators providing long-term purchasing contracts which may be used as collateral for the bank loans; and the equipment manufacturers who will assist with financing, perhaps through leasing.

Breakdown of costs

The mining industry's costs are essentially in three parts. First there is rock breaking (both the ore itself and frequently large tonnages of waste to give access to the ore), loading, in the open-pit mine or underground, and transport within the mine and to the treatment plant. Underground operations are generally labor-intensive and costs are higher per ton of ore produced; consequently it is necessary to operate on higher ore grades than with an open-pit operation. In contrast, open-pit operations are highly capital-intensive and a high tonnage output is needed if acceptable costs are to be maintained. The treatment plant is the second cost phase. The ore is normally ground to a powder and the mineral grains are separated from the unwanted rock grains by one of several systems that recognizes particular mineral characteristics—the mineral may be heavier, it may be magnetic, or, most frequently, its surface characteristics are such that valuable particles will attach themselves to bubbles in particular conditions and "float" to the surface. The product—concentrated mineral—is then shipped to the smelter and/or refinery, where the metal is isolated from the other chemical constituents of the mineral (usually sulfides of oxides). With large mines, the smelter may be at the mine site, but smaller operations usually ship their concentrates to a custom smelter.

The third major cost is transport, mainly the shipment of the product from the mine to the market, but the transport of supplies to the mine is also important. With operations in remote areas, roads and probably railways must be built for hundreds of miles and, initially at least, their function will be to serve the mines. The costs of transport facilities and other infrastructure items are very large in a mining development. For example, in the development of 11 major mines in Australia in the late 1960s it is estimated that some 65 percent of the total expenditure of $A800 million was for infrastructure items. However, infrastructure items have a value far beyond the mining operation itself; they can open up an entire area and this accounts for governments' enthusiasm for new developments.

Although the underground phase of mining operations is normally labor-intensive, the operation overall is capital-intensive and costs can only be minimized by maintaining high production levels. This is a contributory factor to the marked fluctuations that are commonly associated with the metal markets. In contrast to most industrial activities, where the costs from one manufacturer to another will be substantially similar and determined as much by management efficiency as the cost of raw materials, mining industry costs can vary over a wide range, reflecting the differing ore grades and mine locations. These variations in costs exacerbate the marketing problems, for there can be no general consensus among producers of price levels that could be considered adequate or rewarding. A surplus of supplies may cause a sharp downward pressure on prices before mines curtail production levels and, on occasion, lower prices can even prompt increased production from some operations anxious to limit unit costs. In contrast, although high market prices will encourage increased production from existing operators, the long lead time in developing new mining facilities means that new operations can have little impact on a short-term shortage situation.

Building limestone is soft enough to be cut by saw; harder stone is cut by flame jet. There is relatively little wastage in quarrying.

Mechanization is reducing the labor force in underground mines. This automatic machine is cutting potash in a Canadian mine.

Exploration costs like these, incurred in surveying difficult terrain in, for example, Greenland, may be 10 times those of surveying comprehensibly mapped and accessible regions.

Cost breakdown of mineral prospecting

- Minimum expenditure
- Maximum expenditure

5000 :1 Literature studies and visits £5,000–£10,000
Odds against commercial mining taking place

1000 :1 Initial investigations, geologists' samples, etc. £10,000–£20,000

Concentrated exploration with airborne surveys £500,000–£1,000,000 500 :1

Concentrated exploration without airborne surveys £200,000–£500,000 500 :1

Follow up investigation of prospects (preliminary drillings) £100,000–£200,000 20 :1

Detailed prospect evaluation £200,000–£1,000,000 4 :1

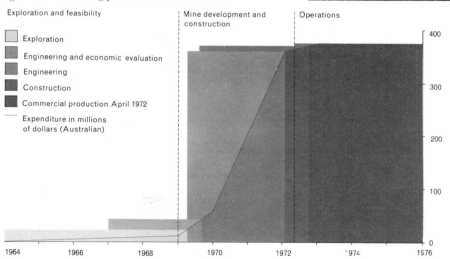

Exploration and feasibility

- Exploration
- Engineering and economic evaluation
- Engineering
- Construction
- Commercial production April 1972
- —— Expenditure in millions of dollars (Australian)

Mine development and construction

Operations

400
300
200
100
0

1964 1966 1968 1970 1972 1974 1976

The Ertsburg, a copper deposit believed to be one of the largest base metal outcrops in the world, rises to 3,600 m (11,800 ft) in the Carstenz Mountains of Indonesia and in 1977 produced more than one million tons of ore. Rich ores are often in difficult terrain, which increases costs.

The time and cost involved in establishing a mine and achieving production sets mining apart from other industries. Also, the siting of industry generally depends on the logistics of the market, but in mining the location of the ore body is the complete determinant.

IRON & STEEL

Iron ore is fed into blast furnaces to extract the crude metal, known as pig iron. Refining pig iron *for steel making was revolutionized by the advent of oxygen-injection furnaces in the 1960s.*

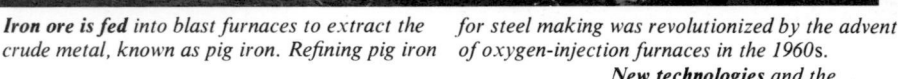

Oil/Gas	Sinter	Ore
	Electricity	Coal

1950 1955 1960 1965 1970 1974

New technologies and the changing pattern of production inputs (left) have greatly improved the efficiency of steel making. Sinter, an agglomerate prepared by heating pure ore with coke and a limestone flux, allows more effective smelting in larger furnaces. Most steel plants are only economically viable if they operate on the largest scale, with capacities of at least one million tons a year; but rising costs are making production in developed countries increasingly uncompetitive.

***Much valuable ferrous scrap** is wasted: 10 percent of household refuse is metal, mostly ferrous, but hardly any is recovered. The United States* *annually discards about 11 million automobiles each representing 1½ tons of scrap iron. Little of this is recovered because of the cost of*

Since the nineteenth century iron, the basic ingredient of steel, has been the dominant metal of industrial civilization. Current world production of steel is about 700 million tons a year, compared to 14 million tons for its nearest rival, aluminum. A single large steel plant may have a greater output than the entire world production of all other metals.

Iron, and the metals that can be combined with it, are collectively known as the ferrous metals (from the Latin word for iron, *ferrum*). Iron accounts for 95 percent of all metal mined, refined and used in the world today. Its importance stems from its strength, its readiness to alloy with other metals, its economy in use (because it can be recycled over and over again) and above all its cheapness.

Prices
Iron is the cheapest of all metals. A typical price for pig iron in 1978 was £98 per ton, compared with aluminum at £680 per ton and lead at £320. This low price can be attributed to iron's abundance, the fact that its ores are rich, and the comparative ease with which it is mined and processed.

Fluctuations in the economic climate affect steel consumption, but in the long term world consumption of steel, as with other metals, is growing exponentially and is expected to reach 1 billion tons a year by 1985.

The world's biggest steel producer is the USSR, followed by the United States and Japan. Of the top 10 steel companies in the world four are Japanese (Nippon Steel, with an output of 34 million tons in 1976, is the biggest) and three are American. Japan now produces around 14 percent of the world's steel, a fifth of it for export.

The growth of steel industries in developing countries has hit markets traditionally supplied by the United States and Europe. China has a target of 60 million tons by 1985. By the mid-1980s, countries such as Brazil and India are expected to rival some developed countries in steel production. This is one reason why the growth of steel production and consumption in the United States, for example, is slowing. Another factor is the increasing use in some industrialized countries of alternatives to steel, such as aluminum, and, in the construction industry, concrete.

New methods of steel making, which eliminate the need for blast furnaces and allow plants to be built on a smaller scale, have enabled some less-developed countries to develop their own steel industries. Conventional steel making involving blast furnaces and oxygen-blown converters is best suited to large-scale production. A typical plant would have a capacity of 7,000–10,000 tons a day and cost £140 million or more to build. The output necessary to justify such capital outlay far exceeds that which most developing countries can hope to achieve for many years.

A smaller plant employing a process known as direct reduction, with an annual output of up to 100,000 tons, can be built more cheaply (though the cost per ton of steel produced is still high). The direct reduction method was first tried in the 1870s but was not exploited because it calls for exceptionally high-grade ore. Only now, with new ways of processing the ore itself to make a synthetic "high-grade" ore, and methods of mass transportation, is this type of ore readily available.

The process, as its name suggests, extracts iron directly from the ore without employing a blast furnace. By the end of 1985 a total of 41 direct reduction plants are planned to be in operation worldwide, 18 of them in Latin America. Their combined capacity will be 24 million tons—about 2.5 percent of the anticipated world production.

Cuts in the labor force have been made in almost all steel industries in the developed world. In the United States numbers have been reduced from 500,000 in the mid-1960s to 370,000 in 1977.

Not until the advent of cheap steel could the first skyscrapers be built, masonry structures being limited to about 18 stories. Reinforced concrete is now increasingly used for high buildings.

removing unwanted material, such as plastics. For that reason, most scrap used for recycling is new metal from factory trimmings. In Britain, scrap accounts for half the steel output.

Corrosion-resistant stainless steel, widely used by the dairy industry, among others, is an alloy of steel, chromium and other metals. In Britain alone, corrosion costs £3,500 million a year.

European steel-makers were laying off workers at a rate of some 6,000 a month in 1977. Even Japan's steel industry had to reduce its work force.

These cuts were due in part to cheap steel flowing in from the growing industries of developing nations, where workers are not so highly organized and labor costs are lower. South Korea, where steel strikes are proscribed and steel workers earn about $100 a month, is now undercutting the Japanese steel industry, which itself has been undercutting steel makers in the United States and Europe.

The labor force in the steel industry is traditionally among the most powerful groups of workers in the West and union fears of unemployment have been instrumental in persuading governments to erect tariff barriers to imported steel. In an attempt to protect their interests the Common Market countries have formed a group called Eurofer, which aims at setting steel output targets in proportion to demand and has imposed compulsory minimum prices for imports.

On a wider scale the Organization for Economic Cooperation and Development is attempting to set up a committee to monitor international steel market trends and work out guidelines for individual governments. It would deal with all aspects of the steel industry's problems, including production costs, investment levels, and profitability. Members could also use it to voice complaints.

On another front the power of steel unions to secure big wage rises has contributed to the increasing uncompetitiveness of the steel industries of the United States, Europe and Britain. This in turn has discouraged private investment, leading to nationalization in Britain in 1967.

Reserves and resources

The primary resource, iron ore, occurs as concentrations of the oxide, silicate or carbonate produced mainly by ancient sedimentary processes. The most important deposits occur in precambrian rocks (2,000–1,000 million years old) forming the "shield" areas of continental crustal plates. The Ukraine, the Lake Superior region, Labrador, southern and northwestern Australia, Brazil, West Africa and India contain the main sources, all extracted by surface mining. The best of the deposits average more than 50 percent iron.

United States resources of ore, which gave that country world leadership in production 90 years ago, have now become depleted and 20 percent ores are now extracted and supplemented with imported high-grade ore. A few high-grade deposits of deep-seated origin are mined underground, for example the magnetite ore at Kirunavaara, Sweden, the largest deep mine in the world. The younger "minette" type of ore (150–100 million years old), self-fluxing owing to its calcium carbonate content, still provides substantial production in Lorraine, but Britain, which has reserves exceeding 3 billion tons of this general type, with 24 to 30 percent iron, has reduced annual production from more than 20 million tons a year during World War II to three million tons, finding imported high-grade ore cheaper to smelt. World trade in iron ore, to which the developing countries are significant contributors, amounted to 390 million tons in 1974, when the total mine output of ore was 904 million tons. Proved reserves of iron ore have been stated at 90 billion tons, while a United Nations team estimated the indicated total resources as 350 billion tons in 1970. Iron therefore has a long future, subject only to limitations placed on it by availability of coke and of energy generally.

The USSR leads in production of iron ore, with a production in 1974 of 225 million tons. It exported 43 million tons. The ranking order thereafter was Australia (97mt/79mt), USA (86mt/2mt), Brazil (75/59), China (70/–), France (54/19), Canada (47/37), Sweden (36/33), India (35/22), Venezuela (25/22), Liberia (25/25), and 11 African developing countries (excluding Liberia) (33/33).

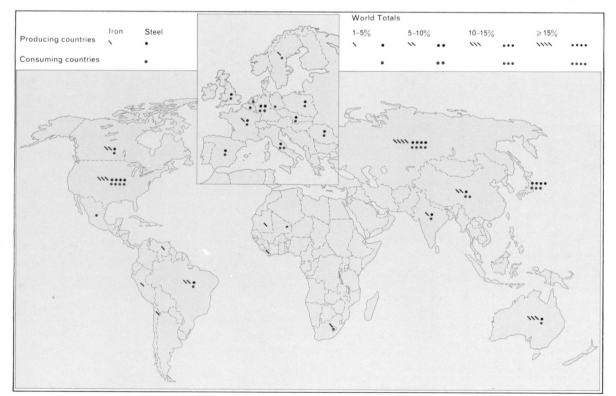

	Iron	Steel
Producing countries	\	•
Consuming countries		•

World Totals

1–5%	5–10%	10–15%	≥15%
\	•	••	••••
	•	•••	••••

Steel industry growth in developing countries has hit markets traditionally supplied by industrial nations. Production in most developed countries has declined since 1973–74.

Metallic input of US steel industry	
	Million tons
Iron	197.5
Manganese	1.123
Silicon	0.554
Chromium	0.296
Aluminum	0.2
Nickel	0.095
Vanadium	0.006
Columbium	0.002057
Molybdenum	0.0022
Tungsten	0.001438
Cobalt	0.005

Specialist alloys are the fastest-growing area of the steel industry. Most steels contain manganese for toughness and abrasion resistance. Chromium and silicon resist corrosion. Chromium also gives strength at high temperatures, as do cobalt and tungsten. Molybdenum reduces brittleness, and nickel is used when steel has to be deformed.

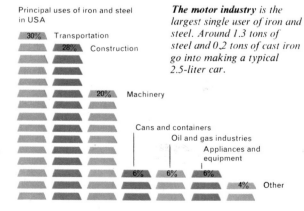

Principal uses of iron and steel in USA

30% Transportation
28% Construction
20% Machinery
Cans and containers
Oil and gas industries
Appliances and equipment
6% 6% 6%
4% Other

The motor industry is the largest single user of iron and steel. Around 1.3 tons of steel and 0.2 tons of cast iron go into making a typical 2.5-liter car.

COPPER, LEAD, ZINC & TIN

The four base metals are copper, zinc, lead and tin. Their importance to industry is indisputable, but even more significant is the role they play in international trade and ultimately the overall balance of economic power. Because much of the demand from the developed nations, for copper and tin especially, is met by exports from developing countries, base metals are among the commodities included in the North/South dialogue—the continuous discussions between rich and poor nations concerning the redistribution of wealth.

Predictions of supply and demand even over as short a term as five to 10 years are subject to many unforeseeable factors: price fluctuations, political events and others limiting supply. Forecasts, therefore, are tentative and experts inevitably disagree. Past trends for copper and zinc lead some experts to think that estimated demands will expand at rates of 4–4.5 percent a year. The growth rates for lead and tin are estimated to be considerably lower, three percent and 1.2 percent respectively. These figures take reasonably anticipated substitution into account, but not stockpiles, and they refer to demand for primary metal only, not recycled metal. About 50 percent of the lead needed now comes from new scrap as does 40 percent of the copper and 20 percent of the zinc. These figures may increase since recycling can be spurred on not only by economics but by environmental considerations. Even with tin there could be a dramatic change. Many experts have claimed that much of it cannot be recycled economically, but research is in progress at several plants. In England, an experimental plant in Newcastle upon Tyne magnetically sorts tin cans from local household waste; the recovered cans are then sent to a plant in South Wales where they are cleaned and the tin removed from the steel base.

Substitution could well affect future demand. Already France, India and the USSR prohibit the import of copper if aluminum can be used instead, and other countries may follow their lead. In Britain the national electrical system uses aluminum cables. In other areas, plastics have replaced many galvanized items in both industry and the household, and waxed paper, plastics, glass and aluminum are already replacing tin cans. In 1976 nearly 80 percent of the cans produced for the beverage industry in the United States were aluminum.

Political outlook

Though developing nations have some of the largest known deposits of important minerals (66 percent of known copper reserves, for instance), keys to them—capital and expertise—are often held by their customers, the industrialized nations. Traditionally, foreign mining concerns have invested in developing countries, a significant number of which (for example Zaire, Zambia, Chile) have consequently relied to a large extent on mineral exports as a source of foreign exchange. However, a World Bank survey shows that there is a trend toward imbalance in exploration. Between 1970 and 1973 more than 80 percent of total expenditure in the non-socialist world was concentrated in only four developed nations: Australia, Canada, South Africa and the United States. Even partially completed projects have sometimes been halted, the most notable being a mine in Zaire into which mainly foreign investors had put $250 million.

Some copper producers have much at stake. Zambia and Zaire among others have both strongly tied their economy to copper: in Zambia it makes

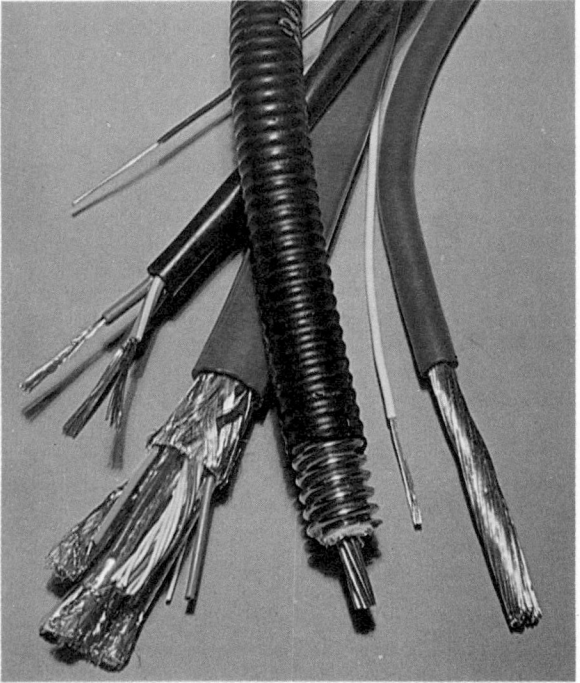

As a conductor, copper is second only to silver. Half the eight million tons used annually goes into electrical circuits—it is sufficiently ductile to be drawn into wires 0.32 mm thick.

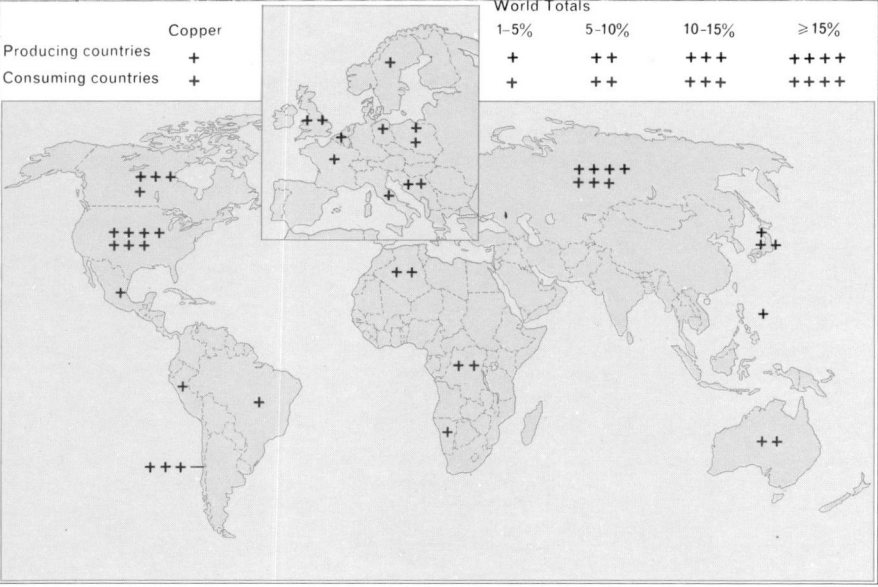

		World Totals			
	Copper	1–5%	5–10%	10–15%	≥15%
Producing countries	+	+	++	+++	++++
Consuming countries	+	+	++	+++	++++

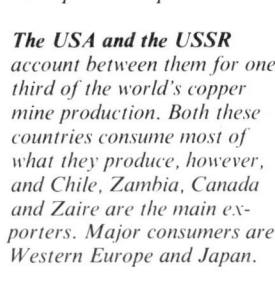

From Roman times till the end of WW II lead was the traditional metal used in the plumbing industry. It began to be superseded by copper principally because plumbers began to appreciate copper's properties: it is much lighter and thus easier to handle. Copper is also an excellent conductor of heat—a property that distilleries, such as this one producing aquavit, have been quick to exploit.

The USA and the USSR account between them for one-third of the world's copper mine production. Both these countries consume most of what they produce, however, and Chile, Zambia, Canada and Zaire are the main exporters. Major consumers are Western Europe and Japan.

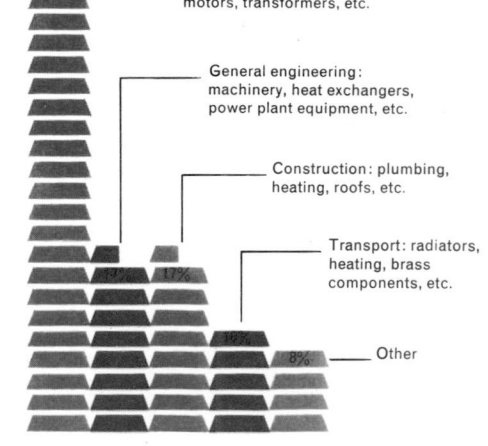

Principal uses of copper in developed countries

48% — Electrical: cables, motors, transformers, etc.

— General engineering: machinery, heat exchangers, power plant equipment, etc.

— Construction: plumbing, heating, roofs, etc.

17% — Transport: radiators, heating, brass components, etc.

8% — Other

more than 80 percent of the country's exports and fluctuating prices have put the government under increased domestic and international political pressure.

At present the key economic fact is that in the long run demand for most non-fuel minerals is insufficient to sustain price increases, though in the short term demand does not fall in proportion to price increases.

Consumers and producers of tin have long worked together under international agreements. A United Nations study group has been looking into similar arrangements for zinc and lead, while the United Nations Conference on Trade and Development (UNCTAD) in its proposed Integrated Commodity scheme includes suggestions for stabilizing commodity prices and for satisfying requests from developing countries for technology and capital to develop resources themselves. Copper producers of the developing nations have formed the council of copper exporting countries (CIPEC) to try to protect their interests, but it does not include all major exporters and there is disagreement among members about production limits.

Production and resources

Of the four metals, tin occurs as the stable oxide cassiterite, while copper, lead and zinc are mainly found combined with sulfur. More than 60 percent of the world's tin production comes from placer deposits in river and beach gravels; these include the important deposits in Malaysia, Thailand, Indonesia and Nigeria, some of which have already been processed several times over. The remaining sources are veins, like those of Cornwall, England, in preexisting rocks; Australia and Bolivia have significant amounts of these.

Copper deposits may be grouped into low-grade ores with 0.4 to 1.2 percent copper, found in the cracked-up tops of granitic intrusions, and higher-grade deposits, around four percent, found either in bedded form as in the Zambia–Zaire copper belt or the Kupferschiefer of East Germany and Poland, or as lenses and veins in ancient rocks. Important deposits of low-grade ores occur around the Pacific Ocean, for example in Canada (where production in 1974 was 800,000 tons of contained metal), the USA (1,400,000 tons), Mexico, Peru, Chile, Papua New Guinea and the Philippines. The Zambia–Zaire copper belt produced 1,180,000 tons, the USSR 1,200,000 tons and Australia 251,000 tons. The contribution of developing countries is significant in both tin and copper.

With few exceptions, lead and zinc occur in the same ore bodies. Producing countries with outputs in 1974 of more than 100,000 tons of contained metal of either lead or zinc included USA (606 lead/448 zinc), USSR (475/680), Australia (375/457), Canada (315/1,237), Peru (193/387), Mexico (218/262), Poland (64/200), Bulgaria (110/80), Yugoslavia (119/94), West Germany (30/112) and Greenland (37/168). Developing countries at present play a less significant role.

Indicated total resources in known deposits have been estimated as 20 million tons for tin, 310 mt for copper, 130 mt for lead and 235 mt for zinc. If sub-economic resources of zinc are taken into account, the figure may be as high as 1,510 mt.

The history of the tin can goes back to Napoleon Bonaparte, who wanted to find a way of keeping food fresh for his army, but it was in England that a process was eventually patented which involved plating iron with a layer of tin. Cans of 150 years ago were so thick that they had to be opened with a hammer and chisel. Today tin is electroplated onto steel and in recent years because of the constantly rising price of tin (more than £6,500 a ton in 1978) the emphasis has been on finding the minimum thickness of tin for plating—it can now be as thin as 0.002 of a millimeter. Despite this, and the fact that aluminum has largely replaced the tin can in the beverage section of the market, canning remains the biggest consumer of tin with 40 percent of all production going into the industry.

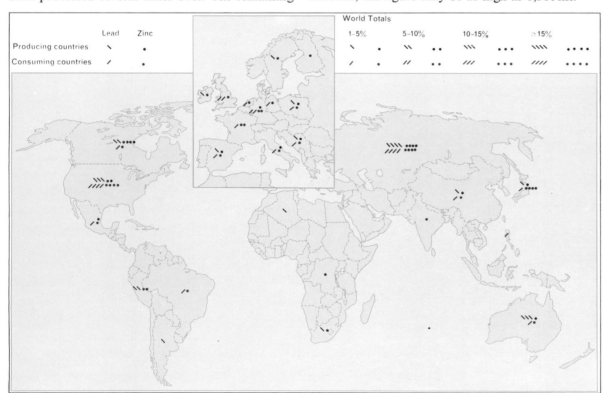

World Totals

Zinc's relatively low cost (£330 a ton in 1978), resistance to corrosion and ductility are assets the world has learned to use to advantage to the tune of six million tons a year, making its consumption second only, among the base metals, to copper. It is used mainly in galvanizing, when it not only protects steel physically against the elements but also inhibits rusting.

By far the greatest use of lead nowadays is in car batteries and as the antiknock component in gasoline. The cheapest of the base metals (£320 a ton in 1978) it is also used in a number of alloys, for instance in the printing industry, where its low melting point is exploited. Easily cast, it does not distort on cooling and takes detail well. Another property of lead is its density. It is effective in dulling noise and as a barrier against some types of radiation.

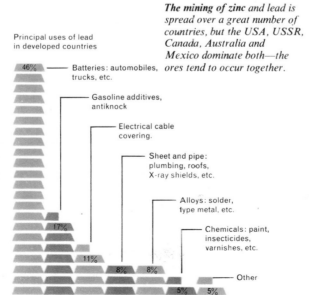

The mining of zinc and lead is spread over a great number of countries, but the USA, USSR, Canada, Australia and Mexico dominate both—the ores tend to occur together.

Principal uses of lead in developed countries

46% — Batteries: automobiles, trucks, etc.

— Gasoline additives, antiknock

— Electrical cable covering.

— Sheet and pipe: plumbing, roofs, X-ray shields, etc.

— Alloys: solder, type metal, etc.

— Chemicals: paint, insecticides, varnishes, etc.

17%

11%

8% 8%

— Other

5% 5%

Principal uses of zinc in developed countries

— Galvanizing

— Die-casting and alloys: components for automobiles, machinery, etc.

36%

— Brass and bronze: mainly brass for machinery, valves, etc.

30%

— Rolled zinc: flashlight batteries, roofs, guttering, etc.

18%

— Zinc oxide: rubber, paints, ceramic glazes.

6%

— Other

5% 5%

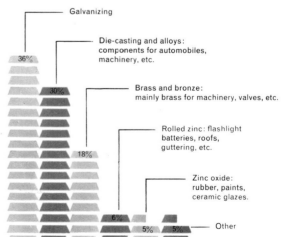

ALUMINUM, MAGNESIUM & TITANIUM

Aluminum is the most abundant metal on the planet's surface, accounting for 8.3 percent of the Earth's crust. Its existence was formerly doubted because it never occurs naturally in its native form and it was not until 1825 that the metal was isolated in the laboratory.

The other two light metals, magnesium and titanium, are also plentiful, but compared to aluminum they play a minor role in industry at present. All three are exceptionally light: aluminum is only 2.7 times heavier than water, magnesium 1.74 times and titanium 4.54 times. In contrast, iron and zinc are more than seven times heavier and lead is 11 times heavier.

Reserves and resources

The ore of aluminum is bauxite, a mixture of hydroxides of the metals, formed over a period of tens of thousands of years in tropical humid climates as a special variety of laterite soil. Three-quarters of world production comes from tropical countries, in particular northern Australia (20 million tons in 1974), Jamaica (15 mt), Surinam (7 mt) and Guyana (3 mt). Another 13 million tons was produced by Guinea and other African, Caribbean and Far Eastern countries. Bauxite is also found in older soils, notably at Les Baux in France, where it was first discovered, and in Greece, Hungary, Romania, the USSR and Yugoslavia.

Bauxite is a good example of a nonrenewable resource: when the power diggers have stripped off the soil, which may be several meters thick, the resource has gone and even in suitable climates it is unlikely to form again within the life span of the human race.

Neither the United States nor the USSR possesses major resources of bauxite and each imports large quantities. The USSR has attempted to use aluminous minerals concentrated from the igneous rock

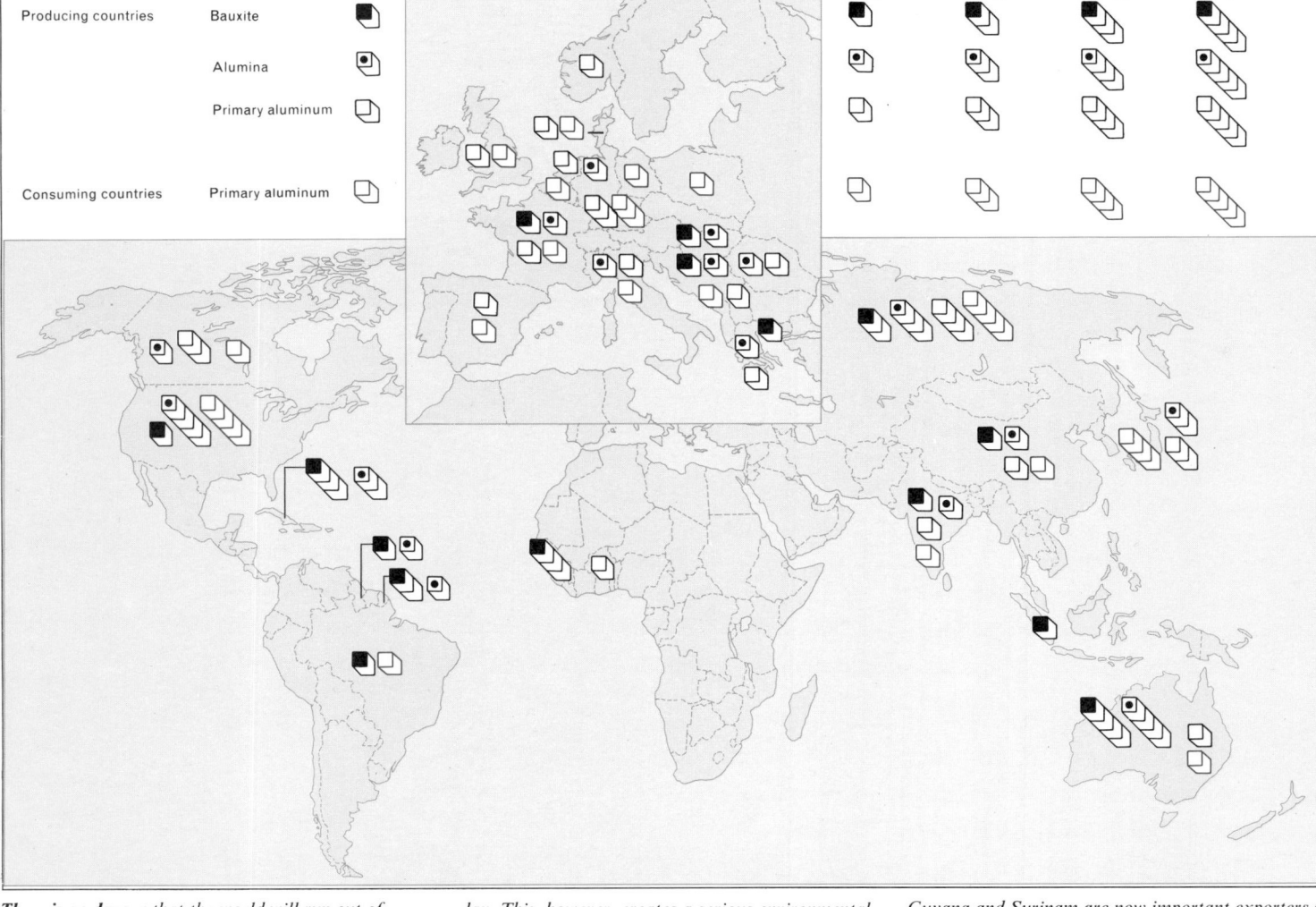

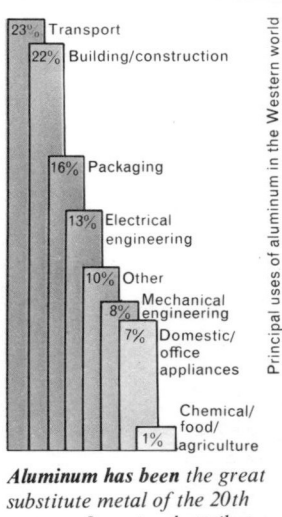

Aluminum has been the great substitute metal of the 20th century. Its natural attributes of lightness and resistance to corrosion have been supplemented by marketing tactics.

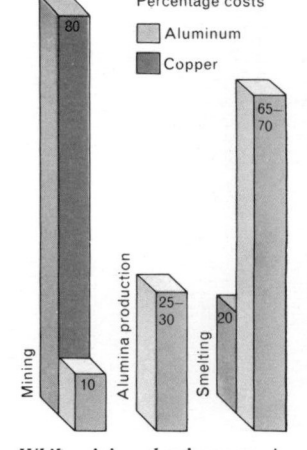

While mining aluminum ore is relatively cheap, refining costs are high compared to other metals such as copper. The ore has to be purified and the metal extracted by electrolysis, using a great deal of energy.

There is no danger that the world will run out of aluminum, with identified resources of three billion tons. At present 99 percent of all aluminum comes from bauxite, a soil found mainly in the tropics. The aluminum hydroxides form pealike concretions in the ore, and it is therefore possible to wash out the accompanying red iron oxide and clay. This, however, creates a serious environmental problem, especially in Jamaica. The next stage in refining is conversion of the hydroxides to the oxide alumina; this was formerly carried out in importing countries, but pressure from some developing countries has led to the setting up of dehydrating plants near the pits—thus Jamaica, Guinea, Guyana and Surinam are now important exporters of alumina. Conversion to the metal by electrolysis of aluminum fluoride, which makes high demands on energy, is mainly confined to industrialized countries able to supply cheap energy: the leaders are the United States, USSR, Canada, Japan, West Germany and Norway, none a major producer of ore.

Because copper is expensive, aluminum is being increasingly used in power lines. It is light, so its greater electrical resistance can be overcome by making the lines thicker; a central core of steel wire gives it strength. Copper cannot be used for domestic wiring, however, because it corrodes.

Designers of aircraft make extensive use of light metals. Concorde is 51 percent aluminum and titanium alloys are used in the engine nacelles. Titanium—light and resistant to stress and high temperatures—is increasingly important in the aerospace industry.

Disposal of the solid wastes (red muds) from bauxite is a major environmental problem. Solutions include using it as landfill material or as a neutralizer for chemical wastes.

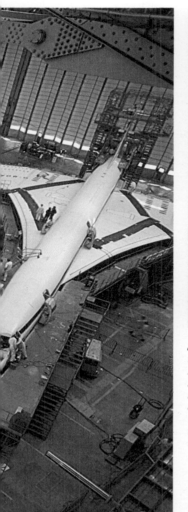

Bauxite is a soft, earthy material, dug out of the ground without drilling or blasting. The removal of impurities produces alumina, which must then be processed to extract the metal, aluminum.

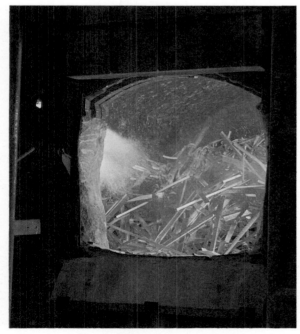

More than 3 million tons of aluminum are produced from scrap each year, a process which requires only five percent of the energy needed to make new metal. In the United States 2.3 billion old cans are recycled annually. But up to 80 percent of aluminum scrap is lost because it would be uneconomical to gather it up and sort it. Aluminum is highly reactive and impurities tend to combine with the metal in remelting.

nepheline syenite, but without commercial success. The principal substitute for bauxite is shale, but this contains only eight to 12 percent of the metal compared with more than 30 percent in bauxite; the use of shale would therefore more than double the energy costs in extraction, already more than five times higher than for iron. Identified resources of bauxite total (in terms of contained metal) three billion tons. Those of shale are unlimited, but are not economic to extract.

Extraction and marketing
Though the cost of mining bauxite is low, extraction of aluminum from its ore is expensive. The metal's bond with oxygen is stronger than iron's and conventional blast-furnace techniques cannot separate them.

In 1854 a Frenchman, Henri Sainte-Claire Deville, produced the world's first aluminum in commercial quantities by reacting aluminum chloride with potassium, but it proved prohibitively expensive. A kilogram (2.2 pounds) costs about $250. At that price any sizeable market was out of the question and use of the new metal was restricted to ornamental novelties, trinkets, jewelry and the like (visitors to the French court were especially honored if the imperial aluminum cutlery was brought out for banquets). Yet even in those early days aluminum's military potential was recognized. Napoleon III saw the possibility of producing lightweight equipment for his armies and encouraged research.

By 1885 the price had dropped to $15 a kilogram, but less than 50 tons of aluminum had been produced in the entire world. The following year saw patents granted to two inventors, Paul Héroult in France and Charles Martin Hall in the United States, for processes to extract aluminum by electrolysis. Their discoveries have formed the basis for virtually all production ever since.

A continuous tradition of aggressive marketing has given aluminum one of the highest sustained

growth rates of any major material. In 1905 world output of aluminum totalled less than 10,000 tons. Today, with annual world output at more than 14 million tons, it is second in importance as a metal only to steel.

The history of aluminum shows how demand can be increased not only in parallel with general rises in economic activity but through development of novel markets and through competition with other materials. For example, aluminum (rather than tin-plated steel) is now used for many soft drink and beer cans and it is being increasingly used as a substitute for iron and steel in the motor vehicle, aircraft and construction industries.

Its greater impact has been in transport. It was first used in ships and aircraft during World War I, when a German inventor, Alfred Wilm, produced an aluminum alloy called Duralumin, which contained small amounts of copper, manganese and magnesium. These gave the metal strength and the physical characteristics of structural steel. However, these light metal alloys are expensive to produce and it is only where weight is at a premium that they are preferred to steel.

In the motor vehicle industry, where weight means increased fuel consumption, aluminum is replacing cast iron in automobile engines, and as a casing for moving parts. Research is now being conducted into the use of aluminum as a production-line substitute for sheet steel in automobile bodies. It has also been found useful in the textile industry for machinery which has to move backward and forward very rapidly.

Aluminum is a good conductor of heat and electricity and so can be used as a substitute for such materials as copper in overhead power cables and for metal saucepans and other kitchen utensils. Another important quality is its resistance to corrosion, making it suitable for use in boatbuilding and in the construction industry.

While aluminum has replaced some existing materials, it has also proved important in new technology. A special aluminum alloy known as RR58 was developed to withstand aerodynamic heating and other unusual stresses in the Concorde supersonic aircraft. In the liner QE2 the four main decks are made of aluminum alloyed with 4.5 percent magnesium for strength.

Comparison to other metals by weight makes aluminum seem expensive. In March 1978 a ton cost around £700, against £650 for copper (an unusually low price), £270 for zinc and from less than £100 to more than £1,000 for iron and steel, depending on type. Comparison by volume, however, makes aluminum cheaper than the others.

Magnesium and titanium
The other two light metals are expensive from any standpoint, magnesium costing £1,350 per ton and crude titanium £1,120. Magnesium is the fourth most common metal in the Earth's crust. A cubic kilometer of seawater, for example, contains more than one million tons. But 15,000 kilowatts of electricity are needed to extract a single ton of metal. Magnesium is chiefly used in the production of aluminum and steel alloys and as a chemical in making cement, rayon, paper and rubber.

One of the main problems in extracting titanium is its high melting point—1,675°C (3,047°F), the highest of any metal. But this property, together with titanium's high strength and its excellent resistance to corrosion, makes the metal ideal for use in the manufacture of ships, aircraft and space vehicles. Another great advantage of titanium is that it can be alloyed with most metals. Major parts of some advanced aircraft are up to 85 percent titanium alloy. Titanium's most important outlet is in paints and varnishes, where titanium dioxide is used to impart whiteness, opacity and brightness. The dioxide costs much less to prepare than the pure metal. Both magnesium and titanium would be more widely used if they cost less to produce.

PRECIOUS METALS & RARER STONES

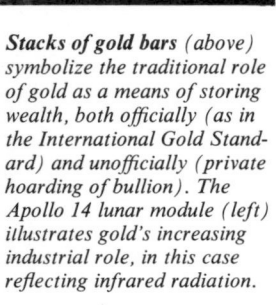

Stacks of gold bars (above) symbolize the traditional role of gold as a means of storing wealth, both officially (as in the International Gold Standard) and unofficially (private hoarding of bullion). The Apollo 14 lunar module (left) illustrates gold's increasing industrial role, in this case reflecting infrared radiation.

The manufacture of glass wool (right) is made possible by platinum. The platinum, with the addition of 10 percent rhodium, permits the free flowing of molten glass through the bushings and does not contaminate the mixture.

Gold, silver and the platinum group (palladium, rhodium, osmium and iridium) are defined as precious metals. The traditional value of gold lies in its role as a symbol or store of wealth, although small amounts are increasingly being used for industrial purposes. The major importance of silver, and especially of platinum, however, is in the industrial sphere.

The role of gold

Of the precious metals, gold takes pride of place. From the time of the ancient Egyptians it has been man's first choice as a store of value. And yet, surprisingly, the volume of all the gold ever produced remains comparatively minute. It is its scarcity and high costs of extraction that confer upon gold such a high unit value. Attributes that have ensured gold's lasting use as a monetary instrument include its effective immortality, divisibility and portability. It is the most malleable of metals and one of the most ductile, capable of being drawn to a wire 0.006 mm in diameter or beaten to a leaf 0.0001 mm thick, which is thin enough to be translucent.

Gold will readily retain an impression for official coinage, and it can be easily identified by its color, malleability and resistance to acid. And, more importantly, unlike fiat money, it is not vulnerable to overproduction. Apart from its usage in the fabrication of jewelry, gold is becoming more important as an industrial aid. It will not corrode or oxidize, hence its value in dentistry; and, as one of the most efficient conductors of electricity, is valuable to the electronics industry.

Two-thirds or more of all the gold ever extracted have been mined since 1900. In recent years, production has stabilized at about 1,500 tons a year, and outside the Communist world, the rate of mine production of gold is probably declining. The largest individual producer of gold is South Africa, which had a 1977 output of 700 tons. The USSR

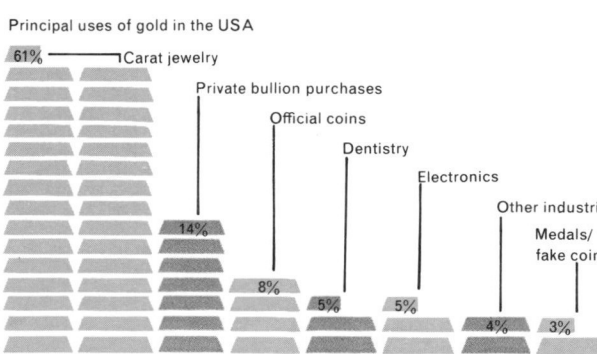

Principal uses of gold in the USA
61% — Carat jewelry
Private bullion purchases
Official coins
Dentistry
Electronics
Other industrial
Medals/fake coins
14%
8%
5%
5%
4%
3%

Principal uses of platinum in the USA
41% — Automotive exhaust fume control
Other
Chemical (catalysts)
Electrical and electronic
28%
16%
15%

The major uses of gold (above) and platinum (right) in the USA are noticeably different. Jewelry takes most of the gold, whereas platinum is used mainly in the motor industry.

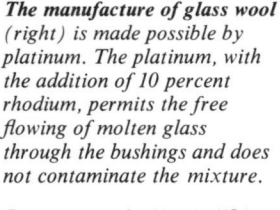

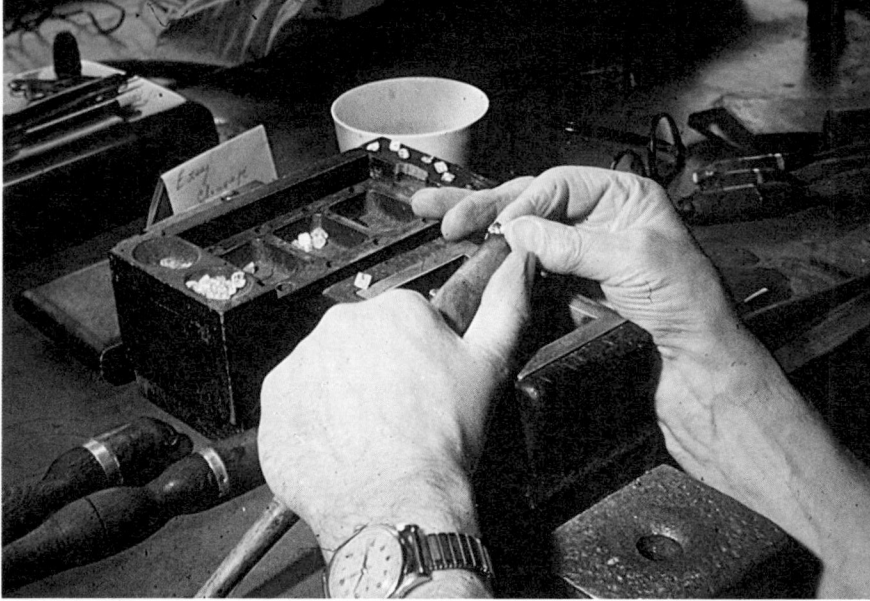

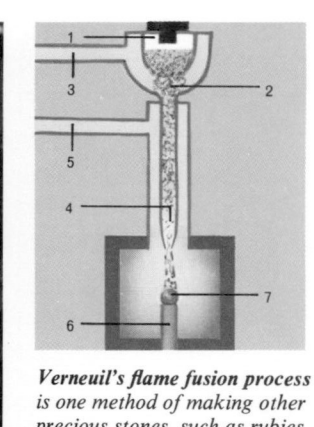

Gemstone diamonds, here being polished with diamond dust, fetch far more than the poorer quality industrial diamonds and, in many cases, pay for the mining of industrial stones. Yet the latter are more important. In 1977, nearly 80 percent of all diamonds produced were for industry. The total production of natural industrial diamonds, however, is far exceeded by the manufacture of synthetic ones for industrial use —more than 60 million carats.

Verneuil's flame fusion process is one method of making other precious stones, such as rubies and sapphires, synthetically. Pure alumina powder in the container (1) passes into the chamber (2). Oxygen (3) mixes with the alumina and carries it to the tip of the torch (4) where it burns with hydrogen from the tube (5). The intense heat fuses the fine alumina particles into gem droplets which fall onto a support (6) on which the body of the synthetic gemstone is being formed (7).

is in second place with an estimated 444 tons, followed by Canada, the USA and Papua New Guinea. Gold is mined in three ways. Best known and most spectacular is deep mining in South Africa at depths of nearly 4,000 meters (13,000 feet). The oldest method is panning of alluvial deposits. Most recently, gold has been recovered as a by-product from the smelting of copper. Though small in quantity, gold extracted in this way can make the mining of base metals economical when their prices are depressed on the world market.

World reserves of exploitable gold at the end of 1976 stood at about 34,830 tons. These reserves will be under extreme pressure within 20 years unless there are significant new discoveries or massive releases of this uniquely valuable metal from official monetary stocks.

The story of silver

The oldest of the precious metals, silver was mentioned as a possession of the Pharaohs in 360 BC. From that time on, the metal was increasingly used for coinage. Silver is harder than gold but softer than copper, and its malleability is second only to that of gold. Its high reflectivity has made it a natural choice for the jewelry industry, but it does tarnish in a polluted atmosphere. Its major use today (in the form of silver bromide) is in the photographic industry, which accounted for 35 percent in 1977. Jewelry and sterling accounted for 20 percent. Silver is also used in catalysts, brazing alloys and batteries, and in the linings of vats and other components in, for instance, the dairy industry, which requires a metal with a high resistance to corrosion from organic corrodents.

Native silver, which can be 99 percent pure, is occasionally found, but most of the metal comes from primary silver ore and as a byproduct from the refining of base metals. World mine production in 1978 was about 315 million troy ounces, of which

Mexico contributed 48 million, Canada 43 million and Peru 34 million. It is expected that in 1978 and 1979 there will be a deficit of supply over demand of some 25 million troy ounces each year, especially if inflation rises significantly.

Platinum precious to industry

Platinum has never enjoyed the status accorded to gold in jewelry, except in Japan. It has strong catalytic properties that are important in petroleum refining and in the chemical industry. In the USA, where there is increasing concern over car exhaust fumes, platinum is important in the car industry as an exhaust catalyst. The metal is completely free from oxidation and has a high melting point.

As with gold, the supply of platinum is limited largely to South Africa which, in 1977, produced 1.75 million troy ounces. The USSR was the second-largest producer with 575,000 troy ounces. In South Africa platinum is easily accessible at comparatively shallow depths of about 600 meters (1,970 feet), but the process of winning the metal is extremely complex and takes many weeks.

Consumption of platinum could soar to about 200,000 troy ounces a year in the early 1980s with the development of the naphtha fuel cell, which uses platinum as a catalyst.

Tungsten and mercury

Tungsten is used as a steel-hardening ingredient and is in demand for armor plating, metal-cutting and rock-drilling equipment. World reserves are estimated at 1.82 million tons, but new finds are regularly made. China, the USSR, Canada, the USA, Korea and Brazil have the largest resources.

Mercury is unique in that it is the only metal that is liquid at normal temperatures. The electrical industry uses about 40 percent of the world's mercury output, followed by the chemical industry (about 25 percent), which uses mercury principally as a catalyst and for its alloying properties. Mercury is marketed in flasks of 34.5 kilograms (76 pounds) each. Recent consumption has totalled about 250,000 flasks a year. Spain has the largest reserves—some two million flasks. The future role of mercury is doubtful, however. Its presence in chemical effluent has had detrimental effects on the environment and it is harmful to health.

Diamonds are not forever

The diamond is the hardest natural substance known and, as a gemstone, is the most concentrated store of wealth in the world. But only 20 percent of the world's 50 million carat output a year falls into that category: the remainder is made up of industrial diamonds whose hardness and resistance to wear is fully exploited for grinding, polishing, drilling and boring purposes. The diamond's high thermal conductivity, mechanical strength and chemical inertness make it invaluable for precision parts in the electronics industry. Another important use is as diestones for drawing fine wires.

Traditional deposits, in India and Brazil, have been more or less worked out, and today Zaire leads world production with 17 million carats a year, followed by the USSR with 12 million and South Africa with Namibia, 9.9 million.

Mining takes four forms: primitive panning, which is still significant in Sierra Leone; open-pit, where heavy earth-moving equipment carries the diamond-bearing rock to the crushing plant; deep mining, which is merely a continuation of open-pit, when the hole becomes too deep; and beach mining, as on the coast of Namibia, where diamonds are found on ancient beaches.

It is most likely that diamond resources are strictly limited, and official reports estimate that within the next 40 years or so all known deposits will have been worked out. Since 1954, however, when diamonds were first successfully synthesized, synthetic diamonds have come increasingly to replace natural ones for many industrial purposes.

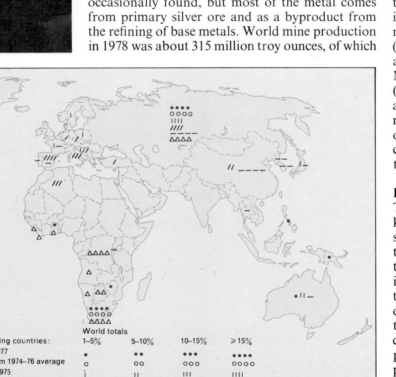

World totals

Producing countries:	1–5%	5–10%	10–15%	≥15%
Gold 1977	•	••	•••	••••
Platinum 1974–76 average	o	oo	ooo	oooo
Silver 1975	ι	ιι	ιιι	ιιιι
Mercury 1975	/	//	///	////
Tungsten 1975	—	——	———	————
Diamonds 1977	△	△△	△△△	△△△△

Large commercial deposits of gold, diamonds and platinum are concentrated in a few countries dominating world supply.

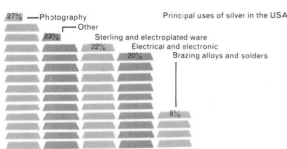

Principal uses of silver in the USA

27% — Photography
— Other
23% — Sterling and electroplated ware
22% — Electrical and electronic
20% — Brazing alloys and solders
8%

A pool of mercury in a reed relay for telephone exchange switching shows this liquid metal in use. When the glass tube is inverted, the mercury flows until it comes into contact with the electrode at the top of the glass, completing an electrical circuit. When the tube is reversed, the contact breaks.

MINERALS FOR INDUSTRY

The chemical industry derives its raw materials from the solid Earth's crust, from brines, from the atmosphere and from biological sources. In a very general way they may be grouped as follows: basic inorganic chemicals; fertilizers; petrochemi-cals; and pharmaceuticals.

Inorganic minerals

In the first group is common salt. A major re-source base is the great series of deposits incorpor-ated in the outer continental crust of the Earth as a result of long-continued evaporation of ocean basins in the geological past. When such a basin receives fresh water at a rate less than the loss by evaporation, salts are precipitated in a definite order. The upward sequence in natural deposits is often limestone, dolomite, gypsum or anhydrite, halite, potassium and magnesium salts, including especially sylvine and carnallite. A complete cycle

of evaporation may produce a sequence containing layers up to hundreds of meters in thickness. The basin (about 250 million years old) that extends from northern Germany under the North Sea to northeastern England was the site of four almost complete cycles of evaporation, and though huge thicknesses of very soluble salts were laid down, these were sufficiently sealed in with later clays to preserve them. These sedimentary deposits are vir-tually inexhaustible. Besides common salt, they provide limestone (for chemical processes) and dolomite (for magnesium compounds and refrac-tory brick manufacture). These are usually quarried at surface. They also provide gypsum and an-hydrite, which are mined, to provide sulfate for plaster and at present in England to provide sulfur for sulfuric acid making. The potassium salts are mainly recovered by mining, but solution recovery is beginning and may become more important.

Many processes in the inorganic chemicals in-dustry require sulfuric acid as the fundamental agent. Manufacture of this in 1974 demanded the production of 48.5 million tons of raw sulfur, or pyrite (iron sulfide), and in addition sulfur gases from the smelting of metallic sulfide ores were also employed. In 1974 world supply from sulfur de-posits was more than 10 million tons. This is now being rivalled by that recovered from petroleum. The close association of the source of supply with petroleum development and extraction makes it certain that it has only a limited future. Pyrite is at present less important, but may have to be sought more widely. If a satisfactory method for cleaning pyritic coal could be devised, the consequent ex-pansion of some coal industries such as that of eastern North America might provide large sup-plies of pyrite.

Total world requirements for potash amount to at least 25 million tons annually. This may be com-pared with 164 million tons of salt and 58 million tons of gypsum, but the evaporite deposits in the Earth's crust are adequate to maintain production at these rates for thousands of years, though there is a limit to deep mining.

Chemicals for industry

Among the fertilizers the most important is phos-phate. Phosphate deposits are of two types: a sedi-mentary variety produced by the accumulation of phosphate from organic sources; and the result of an igneous process, a concentration of the calcium phosphate mineral apatite. No shortage of re-sources is apparent—annual world production is 120 million tons—up to the next millennium, and an attempt by some north African producers to set up a cartel similar to OPEC was not successful. The ultimate exhaustion of the sedimentary deposits with more than 30 percent phosphate must never-theless be contemplated, and the figure of 20 billion tons as the ultimate resource of phosphate includes deposits of much lower grade than those at present being worked. **Phosphate recovered from the ocean bottom may ultimately contribute.** Further pros-

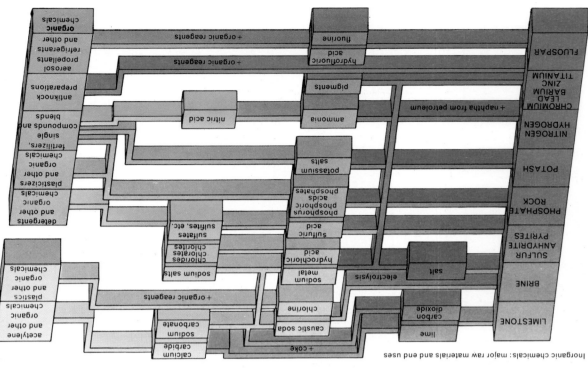

Inorganic chemicals: major raw materials and end uses

Sulfur production has exceeded demand in recent years because of the amount produced as a byproduct in the refining of metal ore, coal and particularly natural gas and petroleum. Shown here is a petroleum refining plant at Athabasca, Canada. Sulfur supply, however, is still dominated by deposits, particularly those around the Gulf Coast of the USA and Mexico.

Brine is first clarified before undergoing electrolysis to produce among other things chlorine (for solvents and PVC) and sodium hydroxide (used in the making of rayon and detergents).

*Guano was once an important source of phosphates until wide-*scale phosphate deposits were discovered in the 1950s. Deposits adequate for domestic needs occur in many countries.

8-9	What is a resource?	146-7	Prospecting and mining
10-11	Riches of the Earth	166-7	Conservation
24-5	Mapping minerals and energy	182-3	Minerals—are we running out?
70-1	Oil and gas—production and processing	184-5	Minerals—assessing future supplies
144-5	The substance of Earth		

CONNECTIONS

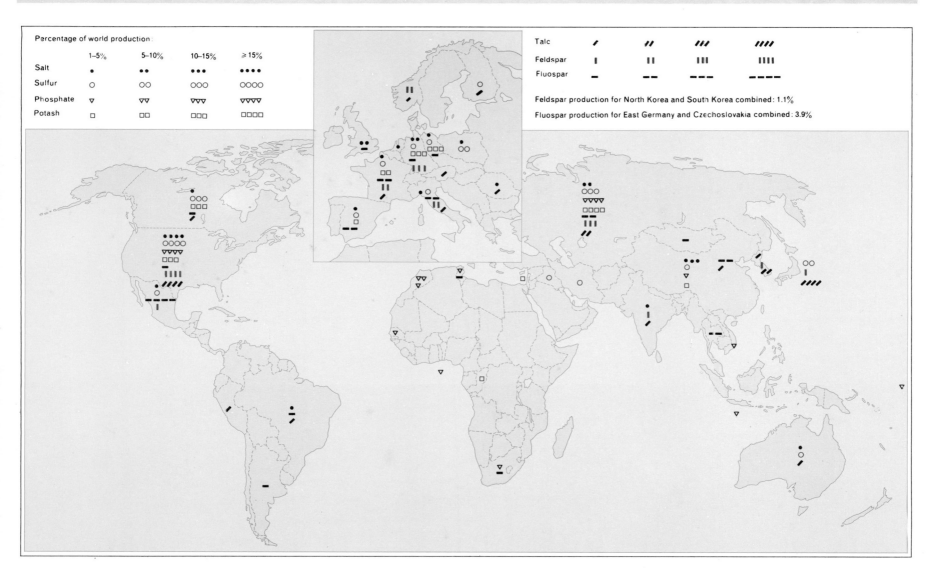

pecting may be expected to yield additional igneous deposits in which apatite is sufficiently concentrated to yield five to 10 percent phosphate rock that could be upgraded.

Chemical and allied industries also demand a range of mineral products that are associated in their occurrence with metalliferous ores. These include fluorspar, or fluorite, important both as the chief source of fluorine for hydrofluoric acid and fluorine chemicals, but also used as a flux, and barytes for barium chemicals, fillers and hydrogen peroxide manufacturing. Formerly fluorspar and barytes were thrown away as useless material, but now the world trade is five million tons and 4.4 million tons respectively. The indicated resource at 191 million tons may appear reassuring, but it is generally recognized that extensive prospecting will be necessary to maintain present production for more than a few years. Identified resources of

barytes have been placed at more than 300 million tons, but similar considerations apply.

All the preceding resources are solid materials from the Earth's crust; the petrochemicals industry, on the other hand, depends on gaseous or liquid fluids, forming byproducts of petroleum refining. The hydrocarbons are complex combinations of hydrogen and carbon atoms, particular fractions of which are used to carry out the fundamental chemical operation, to produce the lower olefins ethylene, propylene, butane and butadiene. After these have been isolated, they are used to produce a wide variety of industrial products, including plastics, synthetic fibers and chemicals for many other uses. Ethylene, for example, the production of which had reached more than four million tons in the United States and nearly two million tons in Europe by 1965, is used for making polyethylene for pipes, films and moldings.

In addition, feedstocks from petroleum refining can be used to produce hydrogen. From this the most important product is ammonia—production was 22.5 million tons from petroleum in 1965. The importance of this contribution to fertilizer manufacture can hardly be overemphasized. Thus although only a few percent of petroleum production goes into the petrochemical industry, the contribution is one of great significance. As available petroleum, and especially natural gas, since this accounts for two-thirds of the feedstocks used, become less, it will be necessary to turn to other sources, of which coal is the obvious one.

The pharmaceutical industry's raw materials necessarily include C-H compounds of many sorts, together with a wide variety of elements, ultimately derived from the Earth, and complex materials from living animals. Its future, from a resource point of view, is not in doubt.

The pharmaceutical industry uses a range of minerals directly and indirectly. Inert minerals include diatomite, a filter for antibiotics, and talc, used as a carrier for powders and tablets.

Because the quartz crystals used in electronics must be without imperfection there is an increasing use of synthetic crystals, grown from small pieces of quartz crystal.

US mineral demand by end-use in 1974

		Food products	Paper products	Chemicals products	Rubber products	Nonmetallic products	Primary metal industries	Electrical	Electrical Gas and Sanitary services	Construction	Oil and Gas industries
Chlorine	10³ tons		1,970	6,580				454		660	
Fluorine				224		9				317	69
Magnesium non metal				100		919					
Nitrogen compounds		200	70	10,830	80						
Nitrogen gas/liquid		1,460		4,800				590	600		
Sulfur			390	7,320				670			240
Titanium non metal			101	357	15	14					
Feldspar						707					
Lime				109		1,277	19,180			1,463	
Phosphate rock		2778		30,553							
Potash				6,086							
Salt		3,418	4,008	27,694		3,089	1,868			1,414	1,470
Soda ash			475	2,200		2,900				220	
Talc			89	240	25	253				46	
Petroleum	10⁶ tons			138						70	
Anthracite	10³ tons			355		122	870				
Bit coal lignite		5,160	9,430	13,090		8,100	95.902			390,068	
Natural gas	10⁹ m³	12	13	42		20	30			98	48
Peat	10³ tons			1,013							
Argon				15			20		5		
Helium	10⁶ m³							2		1	
Hydrogen	10³ m³			40			1				30
Oxygen	10³ tons			1,950		12,103					

BUILDING MATERIALS I

Sand and gravel pits are shallower than hard rock quarries but occupy far more land. In Britain their average yield is only about one-fifth the quantity of material extracted from rock quarries. Inland, sand and gravel pits tend to be located close to urban development; when worked out, wet pits may be rehabilitated for amenity purposes such as water-sports.

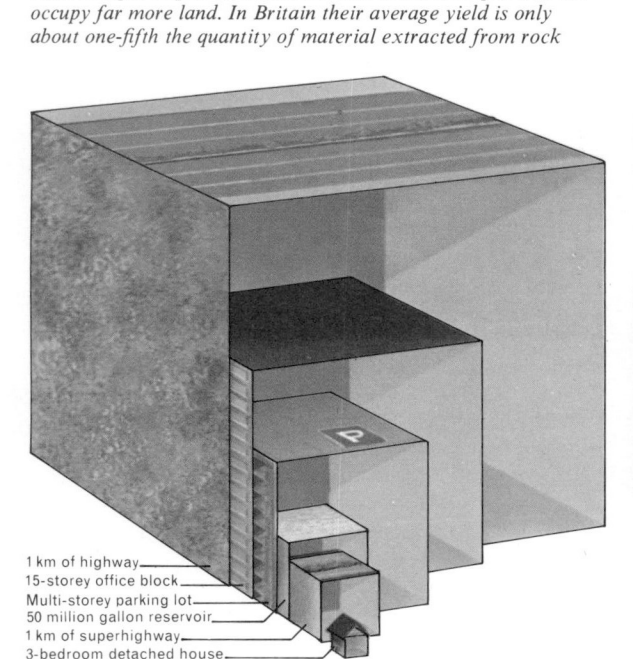

1 km of highway
15-storey office block
Multi-storey parking lot
50 million gallon reservoir
1 km of superhighway
3-bedroom detached house

Moraine, eroded rock material, is seen as dark stripes along an Alaskan glacier. Moraine deposited by the retreating glaciers of ice ages is a source of sand and gravel today.

Vast quantities of aggregate—cheapest of minerals to exploit— are used in construction work. Fifty tons are needed for a three-bedroom house, 62,500 tons for a kilometer of superhighway.

Extraction of high-value stone such as marble requires techniques other than blasting. As at this quarry in Tuscany, deep cuts are made in the rock face outlining the required size

Construction materials, the nonmetallic minerals which form the substance of all building development and roads, fall into two broad categories. In the first group are the aggregates—sand, gravel and other fragmented rock materials—and cut stone blocks, none of which require much in the way of processing before they can be used. Relatively ubiquitous, these minerals are bulky and generally of low value. This is why they rarely feature in world trade. Bracketed together in the second category are building commodities such as clays, cement, gypsum and asbestos, which are subjected to more sophisticated processing and which attain greater value as a result. So, while clays and limestone, for example, are relatively cheap and widespread as raw materials, it is their transformation into bricks and cement which secures them a place in a higher-value grouping.

Sand and gravel
Widespread throughout the world, sand and gravel originated as a result of the disintegrating effect of weathering on a wide variety of parent rocks, and are classified according to their origin or method of deposition. Deposits are known as glacial, those which are laid down by the massive ice sheets which cloaked much of the Northern Hemisphere during the ice ages; fluvial, carried by rivers and streams; lake and marine; or residual in the case of material found on top of a parent rock body. Sand and gravel production is sometimes associated with the foundry industry and with the manufacture of glass and various abrasive products, but the role of these minerals in the building industry is predominant. They are, in fact, some of the world's foremost construction materials, valued primarily as coarse and fine aggregates in the production of concrete. They are used extensively, too, in road-building and as fine aggregates in mortar and concrete blocks.

There is no comprehensive world survey of the available reserves of sand and gravel, but, on the basis of geological evidence, there is likely to be sufficient to meet demands for the foreseeable future. However, while the United States Bureau of Mines has described US reserves as inexhaustible, at the same time it admits that the geographical distribution and quality of land-based deposits often do not match market requirements. One answer has been, where possible, to develop ocean mining adjacent to areas of shortfall. Other countries, including the United Kingdom, which has by far the largest and most advanced offshore operations, have also begun dredging the waters of their continental shelves.

The bulky nature and low commercial value of sand and gravel dictate that supply should be located near to demand, to minimize transport costs. So, most permanent workings are sited close to urban development, to the annoyance of town-dwellers, who are increasingly reluctant to tolerate the environmental degradation which they entail.

Because of their abundance and ease of extraction—land workings are always open-pit—sand and gravel are usually low-cost materials. In the two decades up to the mid-1970s, their unit value generally declined in real terms. Here was a case where increases both in labor charges and land values were offset by increased mechanization. However, further improvements in operating efficiency are unlikely and, with more closely defined specifications by the construction industry, rising labor and property costs, the need to develop less favorable sites on land or deeper deposits at sea, and more stringent antipollution and rehabilitation regulations, sand and gravel prices are likely to show a slow but inexorable increase.

Stone as a resource
Stone quarried for the construction industry is of two kinds. First there are the building stones—blocks cut from a rock face such as limestone, granite, marble, sandstone, slate or basalt and shaped to requirement. Second, and vastly more

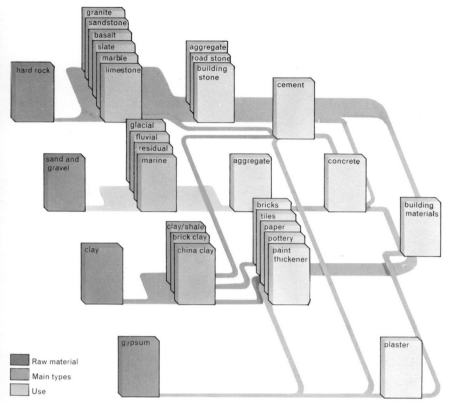

granite
sandstone
basalt
slate
marble
limestone

hard rock

aggregate
road stone
building stone

cement

glacial
fluvial
residual
marine

sand and gravel

aggregate

concrete

bricks
tiles
paper
pottery
paint thickener

building materials

clay/shale
brick clay
china clay

clay

gypsum

plaster

■ Raw material
■ Main types
□ Use

The materials used for building construction vary according to locality. For most purposes a specific rock composition is less important than particular physical properties—strength and resistance to abrasion, for instance, in the case of materials used for surfacing roads.

of block. Drills and wedges are then used to free the block from the surrounding rock.

Quarried in blocks, slate must be split and trimmed before it can be used in building. The splitting process has defied mechanization, and for this reason slate production remains labor intensive and is not competitive with roofing materials such as clay tiles.

With their processing plants, limestone quarries like this one in Derbyshire are often an eyesore in hilly countryside.

Little processing is required to convert low-value minerals to aggregates for construction. As at this quarry in Macao, hard rock is crushed and screened for separation into fragment size. Sand and gravel have also to be washed before they can be screened and graded.

Sand, gravel and stone production 1973	
Sand and gravel	Million tons
Europe	987
North America	1,087
Other	4,269
World total	6,343
Crushed stone	
Europe	1,784
North America	1,056
South America	222
Africa	181
Asia	1,179
Australasia	987
World total	4,620
Building stone	
Europe	25.827
North America	1.662
South America	0.218
Africa	0.340
Asia	5.896
World total	33.943

Recognized as an indicator of industrial growth, the quantity of building materials produced in any given country is directly related to home demand. The United States, with its renewal and development schemes, produced more than three times the quantity of crushed stone quarried by any other nation in 1973.

important, there are the fragmented rock materials which make up what is known commercially as the crushed stone category, primarily used for aggregates. Crushed stone dominates the building scene. In most countries, more than 80 percent of all stone produced is in this fragmented form, and of this limestone accounts for more than two-thirds. Stone suitable for crushing is widespread. The United States leads in production with more than 960 million tons a year.

Crushed stone can be used in many ways, chief of which is the role of limestone in the manufacture of cement. However, more than four-fifths of crushed stone is used directly for construction—roads are the chief consumer—and again most of this is limestone. In contrast with building stone, crushed stone prices are extremely low. In real terms, production costs have remained relatively stable, or in some cases actually shown a decline, in the 20 years up to 1976—mainly as a result of mechanization. Now, however, rising land prices, environmental controls during production and rehabilitation schemes for sites which are worked out are bound to have increasing impact.

An alternative to open-pit workings is underground extraction, which can eliminate most of the environmental problems and reduce land costs in urban areas where land is scarce. But underground methods can raise extraction costs per unit of saleable material by as much as half compared with open-pit techniques. Nevertheless, these methods can be made to pay where the site is adjacent to or even directly beneath centers of demand. In the United States, where underground production of crushed stone is furthest advanced, by 1976 some five percent of total output was coming from subterranean workings.

Building stone—stone quarried in blocks—is equally as widespread as crushed stone. In Europe output is dominated by three nations—Italy, Portugal and France. Although building stone accounts for a mere fraction of the total quantity of stone worked, about three-quarters of it, too, is used in the building industry, mostly in the form of exterior facing panels. However, low-cost substitute materials are available for most building stones, and these have made substantial inroads into the market.

By definition, stone resources as a whole may be reckoned to be virtually inexhaustible. The amount of stone available is so vast as to defy quantification. Occasional local shortages are not usually due to a lack of stone, but to urban encroachment on resource locations or to planning regulations which may prevent the development of quarrying operations, as in the case of some areas of outstanding natural beauty. However, it is possible to envisage a shortage of one specific stone or another, either nationally or regionally.

The importance of cement

In a sense, limestone is the link between the two groups of construction minerals; aggregates and stone on the one hand, and the higher-value, more intensively processed materials on the other. For limestone features prominently in the building trade, both as a crushed rock and as a major constituent of cement. Cements are made primarily from limestone together with shale or clays. Most cements are of the Portland type, which claims 99 percent of the market, though the rest are important for their specialized applications. Almost all Portland cement is consumed by the construction industry, where, mixed with water and aggregates, it goes to make concrete. It is the most widely used and versatile of all building materials, able to be poured on site for large projects such as buildings or dams or used in the form of heavy prestressed columns or beams, or as delicate precast panels or pipes. Also, builders use a small proportion of cement to make mortar. Cement is mostly produced in rotary kilns. The kiln discharge, known as clinker, is mixed with a small amount of gypsum.

BUILDING MATERIALS II

Steam from a Trinidad cement plant partly obscures dust-coated trees. Dust emission is a serious problem with cement works.

unless underground working can be developed instead. Environmental considerations, however, have had an even more profound impact on plants currently producing cement. The reaction in the United States by the producers to standards for air and water quality set by the Environmental Protection Agency has been marked. In particular the recent imposition of stringent regulations has led to many plant closures. Grinding mills have continued to operate using imports. Thus while of the total cement imports in 1961 only 10 percent was clinker, this had risen to 41 percent in 1973 (by which time the regulations had really begun to bite) but had eased to 33 percent by 1975. By 1980 the US cement industry is expected to have spent $254 million on the installation of filters and dust collectors in line with regulations.

Clays and shales
The prime use of common clays and shales—plentiful and indigenous to most countries—is in the manufacture of bricks, but these materials also feature in pipes, tiles and lightweight aggregates. In each process, value is added to what is otherwise a low-priced commodity. But, while the boost in value is more than that achieved in the washing and grading of aggregate, the finished product remains one of relatively low value.

The extraction and processing techniques used for clays and shales—the product of natural weathering of parent feldspar and mica—are quite simple. The raw material is worked by open-pit methods; blasting is not required. The material is either screened, crushed and dried, or extruded and cut into bricks, tiles or pipes before being fired in kilns. Increases in the size of individual workings have been accompanied by greater mechanization and consequent economies, but problems of rehabilitating worked-out sites have increased. While overall clay and shale reserves are enormous, some

In 1973 there were about 1,700 clinker-producing cement plants in 135 countries. Annual capacity was running at about 790 million tons, though actual production was about 11 percent less. The USSR was the largest producer with about 16 percent of total output, followed by the United States with 11 percent; and the European Cement Association, with 19 member countries, producing 30 percent. In a world market in which some cement and clinker shortages were evident, less than four percent of total output was traded internationally.

Recent shortfalls in cement production have arisen from two main factors: environmental pollution and fuel, the single most important cost determinant in the manufacturing process. Energy represents 40 percent of direct production expenses. When the oil crisis of 1973–74 brought about a fourfold increase in fuel bills some less-developed countries were faced with massive balance of payments problems. As a result a number curtailed or closed their clinker production facilities, making do with limited imports of clinker which were ground into cement. It seems likely that, in the long term, the trend in many countries will be toward the dry process of cement manufacture, which gives fuel savings of up to 50 percent.

Although there are no substitutes for cement in the production of concrete, there are, of course, alternatives to concrete in the construction industry. However, with such materials as wood becoming scarcer and the possibility of further inroads being made into the building stone market, it seems unlikely that the demand for cement will slacken. The raw materials from which cement is made appear in abundance on a worldwide basis and future demands can be met, though in specific areas the sterilization of resources as a result of urban development and the imposition of restrictions on the winning of limestone may have their effect

Clay bricks, once shaped by hand and left to dry in the Sun, are now mostly machine made (like those shown above) or extruded and dried in a kiln. The wet process of cement manufacture is illustrated on the right. Limestone is broken up in primary and secondary crushers (1). Clay and water are mixed in a wash-mill (1A) to produce a slurry. The crushed limestone and clay slurry are fed into a ball-mill (2) to be broken up and pounded together. This cement slurry is transferred to storage tanks (3), where it is continuously agitated. Next, passing through a kiln-feeder (4) into a rotary kiln (5), it is heated to drive off water. Escaping flue gases are filtered through an electrostatic precipitator (5A) to extract the dust. The dried mix is heated until the limestone content decomposes and carbon dioxide is given off with the moisture inherent in the raw materials (6), then further heated until the raw materials merge chemically to form clinker (7). The clinker passes into a rotary cooler (8) and is cooled by air streams. Hot air leaves the cooler (8A) and, mixed with coal (8B), is channeled into the main kiln tube to assist in the burning process (8C). The clinker moves from the rotary cooler and is installed in a clinker store (9). The clinker (10) with a five percent addition of gypsum (11) is then fed into a second ball-mill (12), where it is ground to a fine powder—Portland cement. This is pumped into storage silos (13) to await automatic sack fillers (14)

CONNECTIONS

distinction should be made concerning availability according to end use. Not all types, for instance, are suitable for use in cement manufacture or brick-making. However, these considerations are mostly of local rather than national significance. Most countries meet their own requirements for clay and shale, and world supply and demand is in balance. Total world consumption of these materials, for use in construction, was running at about 505 million tons in 1973.

Gypsum production

Deposits of gypsum are developed by both open-pit and underground mining, with open-pit workings fairly easy to rehabilitate. Modern extractive enterprises are capital as opposed to labor intensive, and designed to maximize economies of scale. Processing of gypsum depends on end use. When used in plaster products it is crushed, pulverized and then calcined. Plasterboard or wallboard is now the primary end product, and here the market is growing faster than that for any other building material. In the USA, more than 90 percent of the calcined gypsum output is used in this way. However, the use of plaster as a coating for walls and ceilings is likely to continue to decline since its application is labor intensive. Most crude gypsum goes to the cement industry for use as a retarder to prevent premature setting.

Production and consumption of gypsum are principally associated with urban development. Where imports occur—national consumption does sometimes exceed production—supplies are sought close at hand because of the low value and substantial bulk of the unprocessed product. For example, the United States, the largest producer and consumer of the mineral, works about 18 percent of world output, but consumes 28 percent; imports come from Canada. World production of gypsum amounted to 60.7 million tons in 1973.

World reserves, estimated at more than 1.8 billion tons, are regarded as more than adequate.

Asbestos

Asbestos is the name given to the fibrous forms of a number of minerals occurring in narrow veins in some types of rock. The most common source is chrysotile, 90 percent of the asbestos worked coming from this mineral. Much rarer than other building materials, asbestos is the subject of a substantial international trade. The two biggest producers are Canada (40 percent of the world output) and the USSR (an estimated 33 percent), although it is Canada which commands 67 percent of the free market. World production of asbestos in 1974 was estimated at between four and five million tons.

Asbestos extraction is generally open-pit, although African deposits are all mined underground and the USSR employs both techniques. A notorious problem of extraction, however, is that it creates considerable quantities of waste rock. In the early 1950s an average of 75 percent of the rock mined from the important Canadian sources passed on to the milling process, where the recovery of fibers ran at about 9.9 percent. In the 1970s the percentage of waste has risen markedly, with only 32.3 percent of rock mined going on to be milled and a fiber recovery rate of only 6.1 percent. The milling process is a complex one, chiefly involving the separation of the fiber from the rock and its classification according to length.

Open-pit excavations for asbestos are as much of an eyesore as many other open-pit mines, although the impact may be lessened by the remoteness of workings from urban centers. As for underground operations, waste can be back-filled, and, since processing on site is usually confined to basic milling, above-ground disturbance is limited. However, there is increasing recognition of the dangers of asbestos dust to health. Although safe limits for

levels of asbestos in the environment have yet to be determined, it is clear that pollution controls will prove an important additional cost factor.

At present about 70 percent of asbestos output goes to the construction industry, and most of this is the short-fibered type. Asbestos is mixed with Portland cement in the production of pipes and ducts, flooring and roofing materials and sheeting; small amounts of asbestos are used for thermal insulation in buildings. The rate of growth in the use of asbestos is relatively higher in the developing countries than elsewhere, although in terms of tons consumed the United States holds the lead. It looks as if demands for asbestos can be met until the end of the century from known reserves, even though these may become more costly to work because of a higher ratio of waste. Certainly a general downward trend in the viability of deposits worked seems inevitable as the better sources of supply become exhausted. There are a number of alternative materials available—ceramics, plastics, wood—which could fulfill the role of asbestos, but these will not necessarily remain competitive in price.

The future of building materials

What is universally true is that there is virtually no reliable way of estimating future demand for building materials, whether low or high in value, processed or not. For the fact is that the future of the extractive industries concerned is inextricably linked with that of their main consumer, the construction industry, which in turn is closely geared to national economies. Since the level of new building is not something which is fixed for all time, it will be factors such as the economic health of individual nations, their investment policies and population levels which will determine how much rock material—from humble sand and gravel to high-grade marble—is taken from the ground.

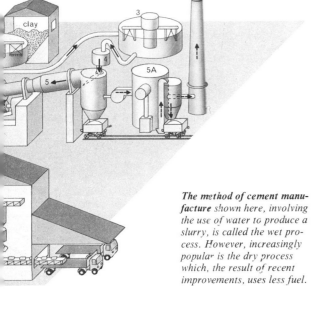

The method of cement manu-facture shown here, involving the use of water to produce a slurry, is called the wet process. However, increasingly popular is the dry process which, the result of recent improvements, uses less fuel.

From the furnace (left) molten glass is released into a float bath, to find its own level on a bed of molten tin. Sheets of float glass cooled in this way —molded to a smooth and level finish by the underlying tin—are used in building. It is the float bath molding technique which gives this glass— once known as plate glass—its up-to-date name. Fireproof clothing—aluminum-coated in the case of the fire-fighters seen on the right—is a vitally important use of long-fibered asbestos. Roughly 70 percent of the asbestos produced throughout the world is of the short-fibered type, most of it destined for the building industry. Remaining uses of long-fibered asbestos include electrical and marine insulation and packaging.

The predominant use of any one building material varies from country to country—depending on availability, building tradition and labor costs. Clay production is relatively low in the USA because brick is not widely used.

CLAY PRODUCTION *

	Thousand tons
Europe	231,207
North America	117,536
South America	17,191
Africa	17,890
Asia	89,334
Australasia	31,664
World total	**504,822**

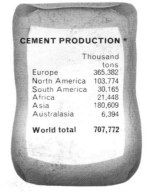

CEMENT PRODUCTION *

	Thousand tons
Europe	365,382
North America	103,774
South America	30,165
Africa	21,448
Asia	180,609
Australasia	6,394
World total	**707,772**

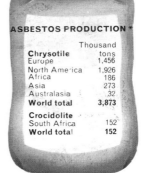

ASBESTOS PRODUCTION *

	Thousand tons
Chrysotile	
Europe	1,456
North America	1,926
Africa	186
Asia	273
Australasia	32
World total	**3,873**
Crocidolite	
South Africa	152
World total	**152**

GYPSUM PRODUCTION *

	Thousand tons
Europe	28,136
North America	22,026
South America	1,224
Africa	2,995
Asia	5,416
Australasia	978
World total	**60,775**

* 1973

MINERALS FROM THE SEA

No abrupt changes in the rocks or geological structures occur at most shorelines; the big change is at the continental margins, in most places some distance offshore. Rocks found on land are also present under the continental shelves, which are submerged extensions of the world's great landmasses. These should contain the same mineral deposits as are worked on land. Yet it is only fairly recently that attention has turned to the sea as an additional source of minerals. With the exception of salt (which has been recovered from seawater since about 2000 BC), marine minerals have had to wait for development of the relatively advanced technology needed to locate, evaluate and recover deposits on, or under, the seabed.

In addition to the problems posed by a hostile sea, progress was inhibited, too, by economic factors—until the cost of exploiting marine deposits could be brought into line with the rising price of extracting the same minerals on land. Now, with modern technology, marine mining is a growing branch of the world mineral industry. This has come about partly because of the rising costs of exploiting dwindling reserves of high-grade deposits on land, and partly because of the costs involved in transporting low-value minerals to their markets. So, just as the offshore petroleum industry progressed from shallow, sheltered water to the high-cost operations in the North Sea, and is now moving into very deep water indeed, so the recovery of other marine minerals has proceeded from the beach, to shallow and protected waters in estuaries and lagoons, to deeper water in the open sea.

Methods of recovery

Marine minerals can be classified on the basis of the methods used—or soon likely to be used—to recover them. First, there are the minerals recoverable from seawater: salt, magnesium and bromine. The cost of extracting salt, whether from underground salt deposits or from salt flats by using simple technology, is very low. Seawater therefore remains a prime source of salt in countries with a suitable climate and which are remote from other sources of supply. Seawater is the principal source of bromine and an important source, too, of magnesium—mostly used as magnesia.

Some minerals can be recovered by dredging unconsolidated deposits on the seabed. These include sand and gravel. It is the low cost of delivery, particularly to coastal towns, which has led to the growth of a marine sand and gravel industry. Production is concentrated on the shallow continental shelves of northwest Europe and Japan, and these two products—among the lowest-value minerals exploited anywhere in the world—earn more than all other marine minerals combined (except petroleum). In the United Kingdom more than 10 percent of all sand and gravel is dredged from the sea. The USA is reluctant to exploit sand and gravel deposits off the eastern seaboard to supply aggregates in coastal areas where shortages of deposits on land add to transport costs.

Iceland's cement industry is based on shell sand dredged from the continental shelf; some is also used as fertilizer and as an additive in animal foodstuffs. Small quantities of the calcareous algae *Lithothamnia* are dredged off the coast of Brittany for agricultural use, and elsewhere coral is won for both industrial and decorative purposes. Dredging

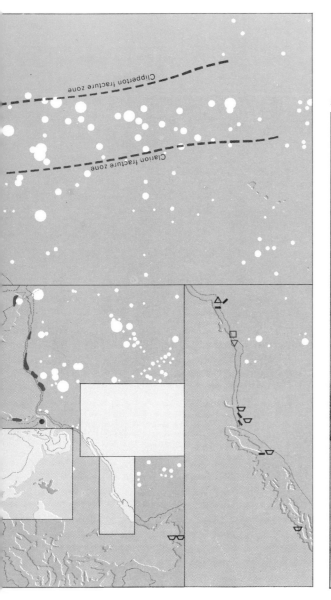

Nearly all marine mineral deposits that could feasibly be worked are on the continental shelves. Most are placer deposits—particles derived from the erosion of mineral-bearing rocks on land. At present, many marine deposits—including gold off Alaska and diamonds off Namibia—do not merit recovery (though diamonds are recovered from Namibia's beaches). Rising prices, brought about by scarcity of land-based deposits, could make the cost of marine mining worthwhile in the future.

The largest single offshore mining operation in the world is the recovery of aragonite sands, rich in calcium carbonate, from the Bahama Banks. The mining base is Ocean Cay, an artificial island created from dredged aragonite sand and large enough to provide harbor facilities and an aircraft landing strip. Mining began in 1968 and within four years' production was almost one million tons a year. Dredged from shallow waters, the sand is loaded by conveyor for shipment to the USA.

Of the 93 natural elements, 73 are found in the sea and 62 are trace elements only. There is 100 times more gold in the sea than on land, but, as with other elements, attempts to recover it have proved uneconomic. Exceptions are chlorine and sodium (combined in sodium chloride, salt), bromine and magnesium. Salt represents 75 percent of the dissolved mineral content of seawater and is extracted by evaporation in shallow coastal flats, shown here.

Chloride	55.04%
Sodium	30.61%
Sulfate	7.68%
Magnesium	3.69%
Calcium	1.16%
Potassium	1.1%
Bicarbonate	0.41%
Bromide	0.19%
Boric acid	0.07%
Strontium	0.04%
Fluoride	0.003%
Trace elements	0.01%

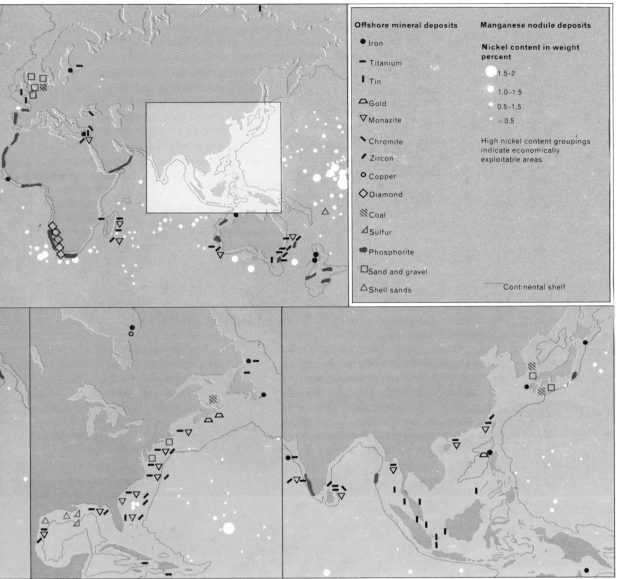

MANGANESE NODULES

Manganese nodules, which are abundant in certain parts of the ocean floor, could be of plant or animal origin.

Probably present over about 15 percent of the ocean floor, manganese nodules are laid down as concentric layered structures round a nucleus consisting of decomposed fragments of volcanic rock or of organic remains such as sharks' teeth. Varying in diameter up to five centimeters (two inches), they are polymetallic, sometimes containing as much as 1.5 percent each of copper and nickel, and 0.3 percent of cobalt in hydroxide form, as well as tiny amounts of other metals such as zinc, molybdenum, lead and vanadium. One of the technological problems in nodule mining is the need to establish efficient metallurgical processes for extracting metals from an ore unlike anything hitherto mined.

The presence in seafloor nodules of two commercially significant metals—nickel and copper—has been known for more than a century. But it was not until the mid-1960s, when it was realized that deposits being worked on land were falling off in grade, that interest arose in finding alternative sources. Already likely mine sites have been identified but not yet accurately sampled. Nodule deposits of potentially ore grade lie generally at depths of more than 4,000 meters (13,000 feet). Major consortia are evolving recovery techniques which involve pumping the nodules to the surface or trawling the seabed. Cost and returns of manganese nodule mining will only be known after a period of commercial production.

also secures chemical precipitates such as calcium carbonate—in the form of aragonite mud, silt and sand—phosphate deposits, manganese nodules and mineralized muds. The latter were first discovered in the Red Sea—beneath hot, concentrated and metal-rich brines—in 1965. Subsequent research has identified more such sites, in which the mud contains high enough concentrations of zinc and copper to be of commercial interest.

Recovered, too, by dredging are what are known as placer deposits, formed when mineral-bearing rocks on land are eroded and the particles are washed down by rivers into the sea, although here the valuable heavy minerals are only a minute part of the sediment. There has been quite extensive ex-

Marine mining does not feature significantly in overall production of minerals. But various factors, including growing scarcity of viable land deposits, indicate that marine exploitation may soon assume a key role in meeting demand. By 2000, seafloor nodules may yield 37.5 percent of world nickel and 21 percent of manganese.

Marine mining output 1970	
Commodity	Quantity (thousand tons)
Sand and gravel	55,000
Tin	12.5
Calcium carbonate	18,800
Sulfur	1000
Barytes	122
Iron sands	36

Percentage of total offshore production by value

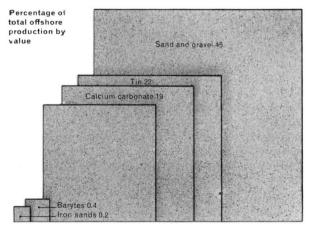

ploration of marine gold placer deposits—notably off Alaska—but exploitation has not been commercially feasible. Minerals such as platinum and chromite may be had from the seabed in future, but at present tin, diamonds and limited quantities of magnetite sands are the only examples of marine placer deposits.

Contained in cassiterite—probably the first mineral to be exploited on the seabed for its metal—tin in fact remains the only nonferrous metal produced by the marine mining industry. Production is restricted to Thailand and Indonesia, but there has been prospecting for tin off Malaysia, Tasmania, the UK and the USSR. Offshore prospecting, too, revealed that Namibia's valuable diamond deposits extend under the sea. Marine dredging began in 1962 but was found not to be profitable and was abandoned in 1971.

Although a low-value commodity, limestone is found in the alternative form of calcium carbonate (which forms its base) and is dredged from the seabed. In addition to Iceland's shell deposits (another form of calcium carbonate), the principal worked source is Ocean Cay in the Bahamas. Calcium carbonate is used in the manufacture of Portland cement; glass and animal feed supplements; in the regulation of the acidity of soils; and as fine aggregate in concrete.

Farther west, in the Gulf of Mexico, native sulfur, or brimstone, is associated with some of the salt domes in the continental shelf. Here is an example of minerals which can readily be converted to liquids or gases, to be pumped by way of boreholes. By far the most important is petroleum—crude oil or natural gas—but sulfur, too, can be pumped to the surface in molten form.

Otherwise there are those minerals which can only be had by tunneling into hard rock, an enterprise so far restricted to shafts starting on land and running beneath the seabed. The best-known example is coal, but tin and iron ores also come into

this category of working. An exception is an important barytes deposit—originally an island—off Alaska, where the mineral is drilled, blasted and then recovered by dredging. Technical and cost problems combined are likely to limit the recovery of minerals in this category.

Manganese nodule mining

Almost all recoverable marine minerals are associated with continental rocks. The principal exception—and it is a highly significant one economically—is manganese nodules, which form potentially workable thin layers spread out in ocean depths of three kilometers (1.8 miles) or more. These nodules in certain areas of the Pacific and Indian oceans contain cobalt, copper and nickel in addition to manganese. However, with land reserves of nickel decreasing and world demand rising at an average of six percent a year, it is this commodity above all which has aroused the interest of multinational companies geared to deep-sea exploitation. Already research and development programs are under way. Manganese nodule mining could make a significant contribution to the world mineral industry.

Meanwhile the main obstacles to progress are not so much technological as political and economic. For a start, nodule mining would almost certainly be carried out well beyond the limits of national jurisdiction, and here the problem is that the law of the sea is itself in turmoil. More than a decade ago the United Nations began considering the legal status of deep-sea mining operations, but the situation is notoriously complex and there is still no sign of international agreement. There is notably resistance from countries who see their conventionally mined exports threatened by a potentially rich haul from the sea. Until the law of the sea is decided in some way acceptable to all the nations concerned, manganese nodules must continue to languish on the ocean floor.

PLANNING FOR TOMORROW

CONSERVATION

PLANNING FOR TOMORROW

If resources continue to be misused and wasted by man, shortages and depletion are inevitable in the future. As this diagram shows, the effects of mismanaging a single resource can be widespread: unregulated burning of fossil fuels pollutes the environment, which may in turn affect forest growth and fish

population: large-scale felling of trees can cause soil erosion and the silting of rivers, so affecting agriculture and water supplies; and mining and smelting ever lower ore grades accelerates the depletion of our finite fossil fuel supplies. Almost all the raw materials and energy forms used by man today are in fact non-

renewable. To prevent depletion of these resources waste must be eliminated, materials recycled and substitution must take place wherever appropriate. But the renewable resources must be husbanded as well: forests must be replenished and the fertility of agricultural land preserved and extended.

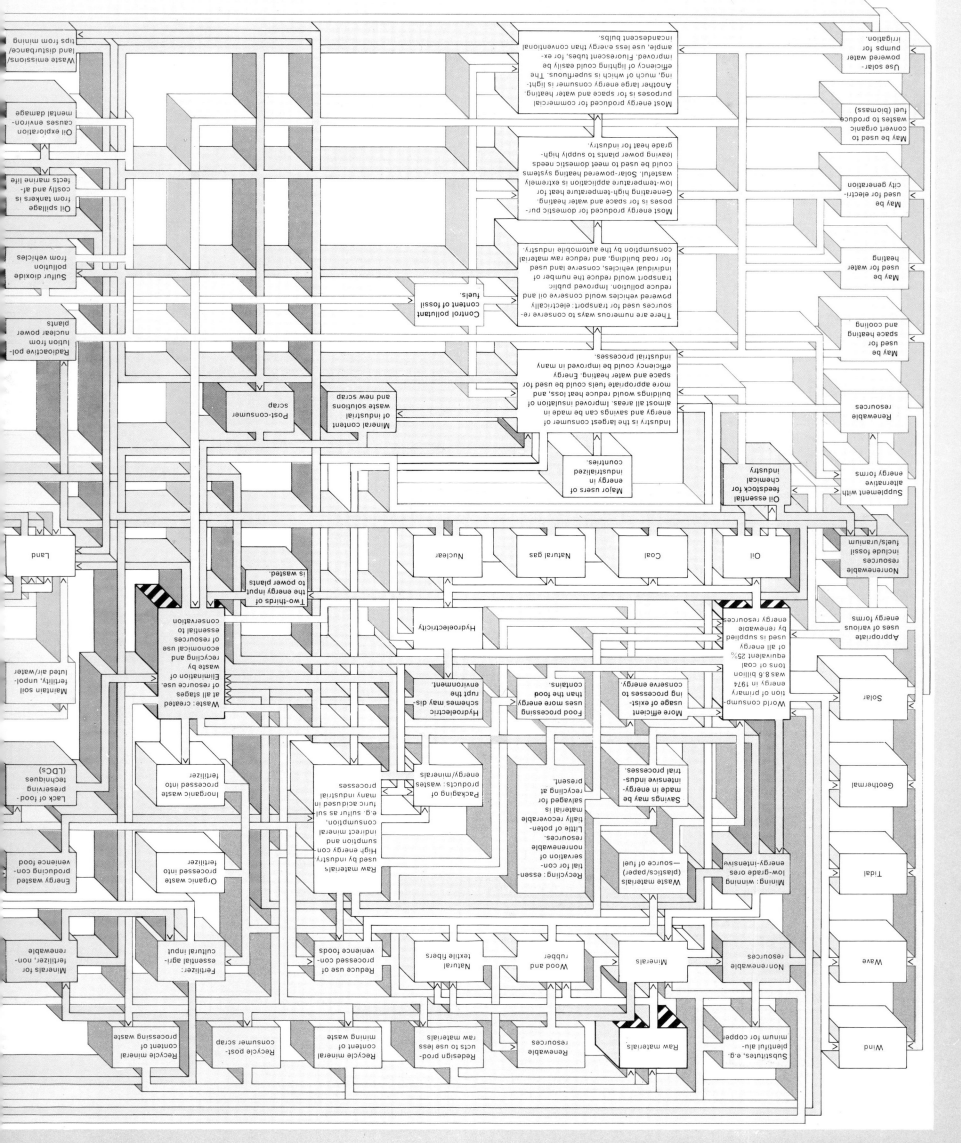

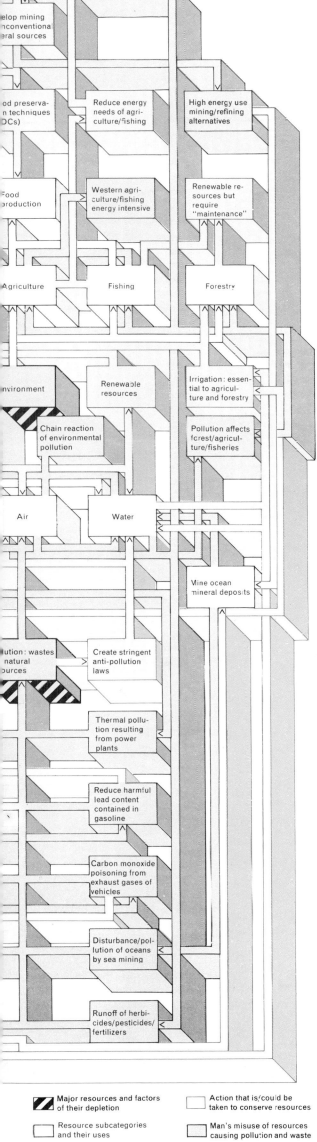

Too often in the modern world the mere word conservation is enough to conjure up visions of scarcity, hardship and frugality. It is an imagined regression to the bad old days, an admission of failure. Yet, properly understood, conservation is none of these things. It does not require that we beggar ourselves or revert back to some rough-hewn preindustrial age. Conservation is in no way a negative concept: it merely means producing more but using less. Seen in this light, it becomes a liberation—not an oppression. Conservation, the careful stewardship of all Earth resources, is safe and sane. It is a logical step forward.

The first step in any conservation strategy is the elimination of waste, and this is now a vital issue in the case of scarce fossil fuels. Conservative estimates of the energy savings which could be achieved by simple good housekeeping methods are in the range 10 to 15 percent (often a much higher figure would be possible). If economies of the order of 15 percent were to be applied to world energy consumption at present, the saving would be a prodigious 1½ billion tons of coal equivalent every year. This is an almost unimaginable figure, equivalent to three-quarters the present energy consumption of Western Europe or five times the amount used by the whole of Latin America. It is 10 times the present output of the world's nuclear industry. Applied to oil use, this figure of 15 percent savings would, at current rates of consumption, extend the life of world reserves by more than 50 years.

Savings in industry
The greatest scope for economies is in industry, where more energy is wasted—due to heat loss from buildings and uneconomic heating of water and space—than is actually used in the manufacturing process. In most existing buildings up to 30 percent of energy could be saved simply by better insulation, and in new buildings the savings could be as much as 50 percent. The use of waste heat from industrial installations to heat other buildings is now an economic proposition. One British estimate is that the cost of adapting a typical duplex house to this system could be recovered within two years. If all new houses were built to an energy-conscious design—at an additional cost of perhaps 10 percent—domestic consumption would fall dramatically with no loss of comfort.

On the subject of heating, there is much to be said for the appropriate use of fuels. For example, about a quarter of the world's fossil fuels go toward generating electricity, a very high-grade form of energy, with about two-thirds of their heat yield going to waste in the process. Yet a great deal of electricity is used to provide low-grade heat—for cooking or space heating—instead of the fossil fuels being put to this purpose direct. A prime example is the large-scale use of natural gas to generate electricity in the United States, when the gas could be used for low-grade heat purposes direct at two or even three times the efficiency. Sweden, however, manages to harness about a third of the heat lost from power plants.

Quite common in industry, combined heat and power plants, producing electricity and heat, could be used more widely to supply neighboring communities. The total efficiency of a well-balanced heat and power system (in which demand for both remains in fairly constant proportion throughout the year) can be 70 percent or more—twice the efficiency of a good modern power plant.

Most energy-using processes, from the boiling of a kitchen kettle to supersonic flight, could benefit from some modification to give more efficiency of use. Notoriously uneconomic, for instance, is the gasoline-driven car. At present 400 million tons of gasoline a year go into the tanks of a world fleet of 260 million cars, with the large American model consuming roughly twice the amount of the average European car. Refinements such as higher compression ratios and improved transmission systems could halve the consumption of the modest family car without any loss of performance. Worldwide this would give the same amount of mobility for about a third of the fuel.

Waste is a potential source of fuel. In the United States, where municipal authorities are running out of acceptable landfill sites for the disposal of waste, 125 million tons of household refuse were collected in 1971. Of this, 99.1 million tons were combustible material which, as fuel, could safely have contributed 24 percent to the US petroleum shortage of 730 million barrels a year. Typically US household waste contains two percent plastics and 10 percent each of metal (mostly ferrous) and glass—all materials which could be reused. One estimate is that 70 percent of the waste glass could be recycled to yield almost a third of the glass industry's raw material requirement. Used cans (99 percent steel) account for half the estimated 11 million tons of steel scrap found in American trash cans each year, yet here the recovery rate is a mere one percent. In addition, most of the 11 million cars discarded in the States each year—each representing 1½ tons of scrap iron—go to waste. Also lost is the metal content of waste industrial solutions.

While there are acknowledged problems of handling and sorting, waste in itself must be regarded as a resource, rather than something to be bulldozed into the ground. With waste metals, the case for recycling is strengthened by the fact that the energy needs for this are sometimes less than for producing the mineral from ore. Recycling of aluminum, for instance, only takes three to five percent of the energy required to extract this metal from bauxite.

Also keenly topical is the question of substitution as a way of conserving materials which are in short supply. The rapid postwar spread in the use of aluminum and plastics, for a great many applications previously served, say, by wood or steel, is a prominent example of substitution. But, originally at least, this was a trend prompted less by scarcities than by the superior qualities in some respects—strength-to-weight ratio, durability, ease of manufacture—of plastics and aluminum. Optimists insist that there are plentiful substitutes for threatened metals: aluminum, iron, magnesium and titanium are among the most abundant elements in the Earth's crust and these could replace scarce metals. However, in general it is true to say that so far substitution, like recycling, has been a product of market expediency rather than genuine need.

Threatened land
In land conservation there are three particularly intractable problems, all now issues of global concern. First, encroaching deserts, the result partly of climatic changes but mainly the result of abuse of the land, for example by overgrazing: one estimate is that, on the southern fringe of the Sahara alone, 650,000 square kilometers (250,900 square miles) of usable land have been forfeited in the past half-century. Second, soil erosion is largely due to mismanagement—misuse of agricultural land and the removal of vegetation. Third, deforestation is now occurring at an alarming rate, due to clearance for agriculture or building development and to overzealous felling of timber stock. In this latter context, it is worth recalling that one ton of recycled paper can save 17 trees—resources which may have taken more than a century to reach maturity.

Recognition of the need for conservation is most marked in respect of the fossil fuels, and this is reasonable enough, since it is on energy supplies that the future of society hinges. Similarly, there is growing environmental consciousness as more of the land comes under threat. But conservation is an attitude of mind, a habit which must be applied to all Earth resources—liquid or solid, organic or inorganic. If humanity neglects to meet the challenge of conservation it will not be due to any lack of technical ability or skill. It will simply be a failure of vision and purpose.

PROVIDING FOR PEOPLE

World population, which currently stands at 4.2 billion, has been growing at an unprecedented rate: each day the human race increases by 215,000, a figure exceeding the population of a city the size of Mobile, Alabama (208,100). True, everywhere except in Africa there has recently been a slowing down in the actual rate of growth (for the first time in three centuries), but, barring some global catastrophe, population must continue its inexorable increase for many decades. This is not to say that human beings will be standing shoulder to shoulder across the surface of the Earth. But, in a world where the highest density concentrations are already startling—Manhatten Island, New York, for instance, has 26,000 people per square kilometer (67,340 per square mile)—there will be considerable extra pressures.

World population seems certain to enlarge by 60 to 70 percent in the next quarter of a century and to double within the natural life span of those who are teenagers today. This projected increase will be an uneven one, with the burden of overpopulation falling more heavily than ever on the less-developed

countries. Already there are five people in the poor countries to every two in the rich, and within half a century the ratio will have widened to seven to two.

Reactions to the news that the growth rate in population—which peaked in the early 1970s—is in decline have been mixed. Traditionally there has always been an element of scepticism as to the validity of population statistics, which are acknowledged to be something of a minefield for the unwary. Figures for China alone (the current population is probably at least 900 million), compounded of guesswork plus some reliable corroboration, could alter world projections to an appreciable extent. But nobody can deny that birth planning has been operating in China for nearly two decades and that families are smaller as a result. It is clear that, in nearly 50 countries in which more than half the population of the developing world lives, there has been a fall of about 13 percent in birthrates since the 1960s.

Rival explanations for the decline range from the success of family planning initiatives to the trend toward increasing urbanization, the spread of education, and changed economic circumstances. It has even been suggested that here is a situation in which nature itself intervenes, applying its own corrective as happens, for example, following a major war, when the birthrate for males shows a slight increase). All that is certain is that a significant change is taking place in human fertility trends.

Enthusiasm for the decline is, however, tinged by the fact that it is a markedly uneven one, and that there are still pronounced regional differences in birthrate, especially within the developing world and even between different areas of the same country. India, for instance, has large discrepancies

between some parts of the north and the south of the country, where there has been a remarkable slowing down in rate. A heartening example is the southern Indian state of Kerala, where better social conditions—the spread of education and health care and an improvement in the status of women—have been identified as the main factors, together with extensive family planning services, contributing to a steep decline in fertility.

But if the omens are looking slightly better, it would be naive to assume that a decline in world birthrate means that the population problem is anywhere near solved. For, despite the statistical quibbles, the overall picture is clear: even if fertility were suddenly to take a tremendous plunge, we must soon witness the biggest additions to human numbers since history began. This is evident not least because about 41 percent of people in less-developed countries, where the population boom is already most pronounced, were under 15 years of age at the beginning of this decade. These young people will have families of their own by the turn of the century.

Dire planning problems

The whole question of population age structures is a dire one for the planners. At one extreme the world total of young adults needing homes, jobs and transport will increase from the 1975 level of 740 million to more than a billion by the end of the century. By far the greatest proportion will be in the developing countries, where these facilities are already in desperately short supply. Meanwhile, the West will bear the brunt of the problem at the other end of the scale: a surfeit of elderly, so-called unproductive people which will have far-reaching

	Population (millions)	Percentage population under 15/over 64	Dependent population factor	Percentage population urbanized	Per capita GNP ($US)	Percentage expenditure on defense	Percentage expenditure on education	Primary & secondary school enrollments	Tertiary education enrollments	Percentage adults literate	
United States	213.54	24/11	53	74	7,120	24.61	21.1	98	51.53	99	
Sweden	8.19	21/15	56	83	8,150	11.41	13.9	83	21.72	99	
West Germany	61.83	21/15	56	92	6,670	20.47	14.4	94	18.05	99	
Greece	9.05	24/12	56	65	2,340	17.85	6.9	91	13.56	84	
Hungary	10.54	20/13	49	50	2,150	3.48	6.1	85	11.06	98	
USSR	254.39	25/9	51	62	2,550	9.06	13.6	91	22.37	99	
Japan	111.56	24/8	47	76	4,450	6.39	21.4	96	18.52	98	
Australia	13.50	28/8	56	86	5,700	8.21	15.8	89	19.01	99	
Developed countries	1,131	24.9/10.4	54	n.a.	n.a.	n.a.	n.a.	n.a.	n.a.	n.a.	
World	3,967	36/6	72	37.5	1,650	n.a.	n.a.	n.a.	n.a.	n.a.	
Developing countries	2,836	40.3/3.8	78	n.a.	n.a.	n.a.	n.a.	n.a.	n.a.	n.a.	
Papua New Guinea	2.76	44/4	92	13	470	n.a.	15.3	44	n.a.	31	
Tanzania	15.31	47/2	96	7	170	12.39	15.0	26	0.22	15–20	
Chad	4.03	40/3	75	14	120	31.76	11.9	18	0.17	5–10	
Ghana	9.87	47/4	104	31	590	6.78	19.7	43	1.04	25	
China	838.80	33/6	63	24	380	n.a.	n.a.	n.a.	n.a.	73	
India	598.10	40/3	75	21	140	23.30	26.1	49	4.42	34	
Iran	33.02	47/3	100	47	1,160	33.77	12.2	56	4.40	23	
Saudi Arabia	8.97	45/3	92	21	4,010	15.49	11.7	29	2.04	15	
Mexico	60.15	46/3	96	64	1,050	4.61	13.1	74	8.53	74	
Brazil	10.23	42/3	81	60	1,030	9.53	21.1	61	8.40	67	
Jamaica	2.04	46/6	108	41	1,110	n.a.	20.2	80	6.68	82	

The countries listed above and on pages 178–181 have been selected to give a comparative profile of differing nation states and economies. Population totals are for 1975 and other data relate as closely as possible to that year.

Dependent factors represent the total number of people relying on 100 "active" members for support and represent a large drain on expenditure.

GNP figures reveal great income gaps between countries. Social expenditure, especially in LDCs, is often grossly outweighed by defense spending. For the cost of one Chieftain tank, 18,000 children can be fed for one year.

Correlations between illiteracy and birthrates have direct bearings on the progress of family planning. In many LDCs, especially Arab ones, female literacy rates are lower than male ones, reflecting the different status of women. Enrollments are shown as percentages of relevant age groups.

10–11 Riches of the Earth	**48–9** Feast or famine?	**178–9** Food—defining the problems
14–15 Keeping track	**50–1** Energy for the millions	**180–1** Are green revolutions the answer?
16–17 Awareness of crisis	**52–3** The worlds we live in	**186–7** World models
44–5 The mathematics of growth	**54–5** Population policies	
46–7 Searching for living space	**90–1** Feeding the world	

CONNECTIONS

implications for social policy. The likelihood is that the number of over-sixties will double to about 600 million in the next 20 years. Moreover, the number of people surviving into their eighties and beyond is also on the increase.

Meanwhile, the global dilemma is to determine how to provide for the six billion or so population projected for the year 2000, when to date we have failed conspicuously to provide needs as basic as food and shelter for many of the four billion who are already here. The gulf between rich and poor countries, which has widened steadily over the past two centuries, is particularly glaring in the case of the 40 or so countries categorized by the United Nations as being "most severely affected": those which have few marketable raw materials to depend upon and which are most vulnerable each time oil, food and fertilizer prices go up. This group of nations, which includes India, Pakistan, Bangladesh, Egypt and Ethiopia, between them account for nearly a quarter of the entire world population. The contrast between rich and poor is extreme and stark: in the West some children are overfed to the point of obesity; in the poorest countries of the world 13 million children a year die before the age of five— often from starvation. Equally it has to be said that the distribution of wealth within some of the poor countries is vastly more uneven than it is in the most blatantly capitalist democracies of the West. The inequalities are most noticeable in Latin America, the Middle East and Africa. In general it is true to say that in the less-developed countries the most needy 40 percent of the population receives only 10 to 15 percent of the total income.

For these under-privileged territories the issues of poverty and pressure of population seem to be inextricably linked, but what is significant is that the few (generally small) developing nations which have experienced a fall in birthrate are those which are furthest advanced in respect of literacy and education and the emancipation of women. It is, for example, a combination of social and economic development and effective birth control programs which seems to have yielded the recent sharp fall in fertility in countries such as Taiwan, Singapore, Hong Kong, Sri Lanka, Mauritius and Costa Rica.

This general principle was not lost on the United Nations World Population Conference in 1974. Here the view of most of the delegates was that rapid population growth is rooted deeply in conditions of severe deprivation: where there is real; grinding poverty, with poor nutrition, sanitation and health care, lack of educational provision and job prospects, and where the status of women is inferior. Negative circumstances such as these are in no way conducive to the introduction of planned, orderly concepts such as birth control. On the contrary, arguably the only positive life incentive is to have plenty of children—as a hedge against high infant mortality rates and to provide extra labor and some security for the parents in their old age.

Correcting inequalities
The developing nations argue that the new international economic order will be the ultimate answer to poverty. But at best this is still very much a tenuous concept, by no means wholly acceptable to the advanced economies which manifestly still have the upper hand. In any case, no redistribution of wealth at the international level is going to be of much benefit to the poor unless the developing countries deal effectively with their own internal inequalities, and this includes correcting the bias which too often favors the affluent urban element, along with big landowners, at the expense of the mass of the rural population. Until this happens, the exodus from the countryside to cities, which are already crammed beyond capacity, is bound to continue. Certainly the trend toward increasing urbanization is likely to create even more turmoil in the developing world than it has done in the West.

The only small sign of encouragement with regard to the population question is the success of some efforts to reduce birthrates by more direct means. In Indonesia, for instance, an all-out effort to spread family planning to every community, using traditional village groups, has produced quite striking results, with about 30 percent of women of childbearing age in Java and Bali practising contraception and a decline in fertility of 35 percent in Bali alone. However, in other countries such as Egypt, where only three percent of rural women have accepted family planning, efficient techniques for delivering the birth control message have yet to be tried. Meanwhile, what of the future quality of life in a country like India, where neither development nor birth control have made much headway, but which nonetheless contains nearly a sixth of the world's population, including a quarter of all women at risk of pregnancy?

In this context more than ever it can be seen that there is no room for complacency over the recent downward trend of the world growth curve. All this implies is that some measure of control over the global condition might be restored—eventually. Meanwhile, the dilemma for the planners is that population growth is an inexorable force imposing savage demands on resources of all kinds.

Percentage expenditure on health	Population per doctor	Per capita daily Calories	Life expectancy	Infant deaths per 1,000	Attitudes to family planning	Birthrate per 1,000	Death rate per 1,000	Percentage annual growth rate	Projected population 2000 (by variants)		
									Low	Medium	High
9.33	610	3,504	73	16.7	■	14.7	8.9	0.5	250.68	264.43	300.41
3.33	620	3,064	75	12.5	■	12.6	10.8	0.1	9.23	9.39	9.39
16.61	520	3,438	71	15.9	■	9.7	12.1	−0.2	61.52	66.24	67.67
8.03	490	3,288	72	23.9	▲	15.6	8.9	0.6	9.55	9.62	9.66
3.87	500	3,582	69	34.3	■	18.4	12.4	0.6	10.74	11.07	11.23
5.46	350	3,542	69	27.7	■	18.2	9.3	0.9	305.49	315.03	323.94
n.a.	860	2,835	74	10.8	●	18.6	6.5	1.2	131.15	132.93	134.21
8.06	720	3,310	72	16.5	■	18.4	8.7	0.9	18.35	20.25	25.92
n.a.	n.a.	n.a.	n.a.	n.a.		n.a.	n.a.		1,307.75	1,360.24	1,433.53
n.a.	n.a.	2,568	60	n.a.		32.0	13.0	1.9	5,839.68	6,254.37	6,638.22
n.a.	n.a.	n.a.	n.a.	n.a.		n.a.	n.a.		4,531.93	4,894.13	5,204.68
n.a.	n.a.	2,232*	48	106	●	40.6	17.1	2.3	4.65	5.04	5.32
7.27	18,490	2,002*	44	167	●	47.0	22.0	2.5	30.76	34.05	35.75
4.85	47,980	1,781*	38	160	▲	44.0	24.0	2.0	6.73	6.91	7.10
7.93	10,150	2,317	49	115	●	48.8	21.9	2.7	18.09	21.16	22.52
n.a.	n.a.	2,330*	65	65	●	26.9	10.3	1.6	1,072.81	1,147.98	1,208.52
1.44	4,100	1,971*	49	129	●	34.6	15.3	1.9	969.28	1,059.43	1,124.29
3.60	2,570	2,367*	57	104	●	45.3	15.6	2.9	63.53	66.60	70.05
4.02	2,480	2,476*	45	152	▲	49.5	20.2	2.9	17.49	18.60	19.47
4.89	1,840	2,725	65	52	●	42.0	8.6	3.3	123.12	132.24	140.96
8.46	1,660	2,515	61	109	●	37.1	8.8	2.8	190.53	212.50	232.38
10.04	3,510	2,663	68	26.3	●	30.8	7.2	2.3	2.55	2.73	3.05

Health spending affects the availability of family planning services, fertility, infant survival and life expectancy, and thereby population size.

inadequate intake. These inadequacies, as assessed by the FAO in 1974, range between those achieving almost sufficient nutrition (Iran) and those obtaining barely 75 percent of their Calorie requirements (Chad).

● official policy
■ official support
▲ neither

This 1973 UN assessment reveals the hazards of population forecasting. It failed to incorporate growth rate adjustments achieved by countries such as West Germany. Several 1978 projections proved more realistic.

ENERGY—THE SHORT TERM

S hort of a major war it is unlikely that there will be much change in the patterns of energy supply and use over the next 15 to 20 years. Any new energy project takes a long time to develop: a nuclear power plant takes a minimum of 10 years from initial planning to operation, and a large hydroelectric power plant may take 20 years; opening a large new coal mine or developing an offshore oil field takes at least 10 years.

Experience with the change from wood to coal and from coal to oil as the dominant fuels of the industrial world indicates that such a shift takes more than 50 years. This slow rate of change is a measure of the magnitude of investment locked up in the distribution systems and the appliances in which the energy is used. Any alteration to these

would take a great deal of time and money. Nuclear power illustrates the point well. With 20 years of development behind it and huge investments in the major industrial countries, it still provides only $1\frac{1}{2}$ percent of the world's energy requirements. Even by the turn of the century it cannot realistically be expected to be anything other than a useful supplement to the world's total energy supplies.

We are now heavily dependent on oil: it accounts for 45 percent of global power supplies. It is easy to store and transport, and easy to deliver. A gasoline pump delivering 50 liters (11 gallons) a minute is supplying energy at a rate of about 30 megawatts—a busy gas station has a peak energy delivery equivalent to that of a sizeable power plant. Compared with coal, oil is easier and cleaner both to handle and to distribute and until quite recently it has been remarkably cheap.

From the mid-1950s to 1973 the real price of oil was falling most of the time. This was the period of the most rapid change that human society has ever known: a worldwide rise in car ownership, spreading cities, high-rise property and residential development, and growing prosperity throughout the developed world. In the developing world, rising populations were fed from increased agricultural yields made possible by the application of fertilizers, pesticides and herbicides—all products of the petrochemical industry.

A vicious circle
With the abrupt increase in oil prices in 1973 economic growth was slowed everywhere: in many

countries it was replaced by recession. The world economy is now caught in a vicious circle. If the trade recession ends then it is almost certain that oil consumption will rise again; growing demand may meet with an unwillingness of the producers to increase output; and in this event prices will rise again, triggering a new recession.

The widespread belief that oil supplies are going to run out within the next generation or so is quite erroneous, but it is a fact that they will become increasingly restricted within the next 10 to 20 years. Limitations on oil supplies will cause major and fundamental adjustments; these constraints, coupled with inevitable rises in the price of oil, will have the effect of making other sources of energy economically competitive. Also, the belief is that, as ordinary crude-oil prices rise, alternative sources of oil (such as the Canadian Athabasca tar sands and the oil shales of Colorado, USA, and the production of oil from coal) will become much more economic to develop.

The problem is that it is the rise in the price of oil that has caused the economic recession and other difficulties. Introducing another source of energy which is just as expensive does not solve this problem. On a domestic level, if oil becomes too expensive to run a central heating boiler it is little consolation to know that it is then no more expensive to install a solar heating system.

When we start to plan future energy supplies we must therefore have in mind two points: the enormous resistance to change imposed on us by the magnitude of all previous investment in energy

	Uses	Renewable	Environmental impact	Capital intensive/ labor intensive	
Oil	Fuel for transport, electricity generation, heating. Used for lubricants and waxes. Feedstock for the petrochemical industry to produce plastics, rubber, solvents, etc.	No	Potential environmental pollutant	Capital intensive	At present, oil supplies 52 percent of all the primary energy the world uses. Such reliance, particularly in the industrialized countries, means that oil supplies constitute a politically sensitive issue. Efficiency: in heating 60 percent, in engines
Natural gas	Fuel for domestic heating and cooking, industrial plant, electricity generation, feedstock for the petrochemical industry.	No	Minor pollutant	Capital intensive	Oil and gas together provide the world with 71 percent of all the primary energy it uses, and natural gas provides 19 percent of world consumption of hydrocarbons. For heating, it is the most efficient fuel available. Gas was once thought of as
Coal	Fuel for electricity generation, source of coke for steel making, fuel for heating. Production of chemicals and synthesis of petroleum.	No	Major pollutant	Capital intensive	Coal production is regaining its former importance as a fossil fuel as oil becomes scarcer and prices rise. One technique being developed to improve the efficiency of coal-fired power plants is fluidized bed combustion. Research and development
Wood	Fuel for cooking and heating. Used as a building material. A source for paper and related products. New uses: feedstuff for animal consumption; methanol liquid fuel.	Yes	Nonpollutant	Labor intensive	There is a paradox encountered when considering wood as a resource. In some areas forestry occupies potential agricultural land, in others removal of forest cover can lead to desertification. Forests are vitally important to the Earth's
Uranium	Fuel for electricity generation and for nuclear-powered ships and submarines. Selected uses in industry and medicine, for example battery-operated heart pacemakers.	No	Potentially dangerous pollutant	Capital intensive	Uranium has become a major political issue both nationally and internationally. There are two main reasons for this: the first is the threat of nuclear proliferation; the second is concern over adequate safety measures in the disposal of radio-
Hydro-electricity	Fuel for electricity generation. Hydroelectric projects often include irrigation and flood control schemes.	Yes	Nonpollutant	Capital intensive	Hydroelectricity is potentially among the most desirable forms of power generation, with great untapped capacity, particularly in the less-developed countries. The disadvantages are that it involves loss of land and other environmental inter-
Geothermal	Fuel for electricity generation, industrial and domestic heating. Low-grade heat may be used for fish farming, deicing, space heating greenhouses, drying of foodstuffs, timber, etc.	No, but practically inexhaustible	Potential pollutant	Capital intensive	Geothermal energy supplies only 0.25 percent of the world's electricity needs at present. Further development depends on new technology to tap heat deep in the Earth's crust. Geothermal heat is also used directly as space and water heating
Solar	Fuel for electricity generation, space heating and cooling. Heating swimming pools. Chemical production by evaporation.	Yes	Nonpollutant	Capital intensive	The Sun's energy is, for practical purposes, inexhaustible. A free source of energy however does little to reduce the extremely costly technology required to produce electricity from solar-powered furnaces, collectors or photovoltaic cells.
Wind	Fuel for electricity generation. Traditional uses include pumping water and grinding corn.	Yes	Nonpollutant	Capital intensive	There has been a long tradition of using windmills to grind corn, pump water and generate household electricity. Before electricity-generating windmills can be used on a large scale, either on land or at sea (Offshore Wind Energy Clusters),
Waves	Electricity generation.	Yes	Nonpollutant	Capital intensive	Offshore wave power plants are still very much in the developmental stage and their potential contribution to electricity supplies is therefore difficult to assess. Wave power devices stretching some 500 km (300 miles) in the North
Tidal	Electricity generation.	Yes	Nonpollutant	Capital intensive	Tidal power plants are in operation, but cost and difficulty of finding suitable sites near major consumption areas has restricted development and may continue to do so. The only commercially viable plant is the La Rance tidal power scheme

distribution and utilization, and the vitally important role of oil in most of the developed economies. In addition, it must be remembered that future plans for the industrial world (and, indeed, for the developing countries) based on the continued use of oil will be dependent on the stability and goodwill of the members of the Organization of Petroleum Exporting Countries (OPEC).

To a certain extent, the world can be seen to be caught in a trap that it has made for itself and from which there is no easy escape. If we are to extricate ourselves from this situation we must do so by accepting the reality of this position and dealing with it as best we can. There are conceivable alternatives, but most of these can only be implemented over the long term. For the rest of this century we must lay the foundation of what will follow in the long term while solving the problems with which we are already confronted.

The first priority must be economy in use. By conserving energy the problem of finding substitutes for existing resources is reduced, and the time available in which to find them is extended. In addition, we must begin to study intensively the ways in which we consume energy at present and in which we may wish to use it in the future. Until now, energy supply systems have been planned mainly with special reference to the problems of supply and distribution rather than to end uses. In the past, trends in energy supply were taken as the model for future trends in demand. Governments and planners believed them and implemented them, and a kind of technological determinism took

over. We are now in a position where all of our ingenuity has gone into the design of our supply systems and little thought, if any, has been given to matching that supply to the aims and desires of the consumer.

Energy is not used just for the sake of consumption but to produce a certain result: to provide a hot meal, to print a book, or to plow a field. In the past we have allowed what has happened to govern what will happen. If the trend showed a shift away from coal toward oil it was assumed (perhaps rightly) that this was what the consumer wanted, and plans for the future were based on the assumption that the trend would continue. No one seriously examined whether the aggregate of such consumer choices made long-term sense or not. The trend was taken as law and by allowing freedom of choice we have ended up in a position where our prosperity depends on the attitudes of those who supply the oil.

Determining a path
For the future we can no longer casually assume that what has happened in the past was for the best. We need to examine carefully the way we intend to use energy, in what forms and in what quantity: this is demand analysis. Once we have determined the path that energy consumption should take, we will be in a position to match it with what our energy supplies are likely to be. Only then will we be in a position to formulate an energy plan: one that requires the collaboration of suppliers and users instead of hingeing solely on the unilateral decision

of the supplier. We have not yet reached the situation where any one of our major fuels is in imminent danger of running out; but we are becoming painfully, if gradually, aware of how little time there is left for maneuver. We may conclude that the steep increase in oil prices of 1973/74 was the best thing that could have happened. It was a reminder—a severe jolt to everyone's sense of well-being—of the heedless way in which we were proceeding. Reactions of those pessimists who saw in it an end to industrial society as we know it were as wide of the mark as were those of more complacent observers who assumed that, to solve our energy problems, we merely had to deploy a series of alternative energy sources, whether nuclear or solar, high or low technology.

Extricating ourselves from our present difficulties will surely be a slow and probably painful process. The transition to whatever comes after the oil age will not be easy. We will succeed only if we are brutally realistic about the constraints overshadowing our way of life and only if we are determined in our resolve to use all our resources as frugally and efficiently as we can.

It is in the next decades that the seeds will be sown for whatever energy future the world will enjoy in 50 years' time. Time—to understand the nature of our dependence upon energy in all its intricacies, and to devise alternative strategies for evaluation and choice—is perhaps the most precious of all our resources. We need to provide ourselves with as much of it as we can in order to plan for our longer-term energy future.

		Annual production	Annual consumption	Proven reserves	
25–35 percent. Tar sands and oil shales are being investigated to supplement dwindling oil supplies. Commercial production of tar sands may contribute 2 percent of world oil production by 2000. Exploitation of oil shales is less advanced.	Oil	3 billion tons	3 billion tons	88 billion tons	
an unavoidable byproduct of oil production and was either wasted or sold off cheaply. It has now become one of the most popular fuels available and efforts are being made to conserve supplies by reducing wastage.	Natural gas	1,394 billion cubic meters	1,362 billion cubic meters	72,359 billion cubic meters	
is also taking place to produce substitutes for oil and gas from coal. The most likely processes are gasification, liquefaction of coal and pyrolysis.	Coal	2.6 billion tons	2.5 billion tons	4,489 billion tons	
ecological system in maintaining oxygen supply. Wood is, of course, renewable but replacement takes at least 10 years.	Wood	1,199 million cubic meters	1,199 million cubic meters	Estimated to be sufficient to cope with fuel needs without affecting supply for industrial purposes.	
active wastes. As a fuel, one ton of uranium produces as much energy as 10,000 tons of oil or 20,000 tons of coal. Fast breeder reactors have the unique ability to produce as much fuel as they consume.	Uranium	29,000 tons (excludes China and the USSR)	23,000 tons (excludes China and the USSR)	1,650 million tons (excludes China and the USSR)	
ference. At present hydroelectricity contributes 6 percent of total world energy production.	Hydro-electricity	349,028 megawatts (installed capacity)		Very large resources available in selected countries	
for agricultural, industrial and residential purposes. At Ville-neuve la-Garenne, near Paris, a geothermal district heating scheme supplies 1,700 private dwellings with underfloor heating and constant hot water.	Geothermal	1,500 megawatts 7,128 megawatts thermal (installed capacity)		Unlimited	
Solar-powered devices are not at present used to generate electricity but they do provide heat which would otherwise be generated by burning fossil fuels. Many developing countries are climatically suited to exploiting solar power.	Solar	Not known	Annual production of electricity from these sources, including oil-, gas-, coal- and uranium-powered generating plants, is 6,438,900 million kilowatt hours. All electricity produced is used.	Unlimited	
storage problems must be resolved. One forecast estimates that wind power may contribute 10 percent of United States electricity needs by the year 2000.	Wind	Not known		Unlimited	
Atlantic may generate enough power to supply Britain with most of her energy needs. They may, however, be a menace to shipping and also adversely affect coastal sedimentation.	Waves	Nil		Unlimited	
in France, which generates 240MW of electricity. A handful of other potential sites exist around the world.	Tides	540 million kWh (estimated output)		Unlimited	

ENERGY—THE LONG TERM

Research initiated today will determine the range of energy alternatives when world oil supplies decline by the early decades of the next century. Because change is so slow it is important for us to begin now to examine all the possibilities and to determine which of them are desirable.

There are two opposing schools of thought about the long-term future of energy. They have widely differing beliefs about what is possible and what is desirable. These contrasting approaches have been called the "hard" and "soft" alternatives.

In the hard approach, nuclear power is generally assigned the key role. According to this view, the present generation of thermal reactors will gradually give way to breeder reactors, which convert the otherwise unusable isotope of uranium, U-238, into plutonium, and hence provide virtually unlimited fuel resources for the world to draw upon. Providing additional reserves of uranium are found, large-scale deployment of breeder reactors would mean that nuclear energy supplies were assured for centuries to come. In Britain alone the quantity of U-238 available, as waste, from the present nuclear power plants is equivalent to 20 billion tons of coal, or almost enough to supply our present energy needs for nearly 200 years.

The attraction of such a course of action is obvious. But there are many problems associated with the nuclear path to energy supply. Nuclear power provides its energy in the form of electricity. If, for instance, transport were to be electrically driven, we would need a network of battery replacement and charging centers in much the same way as

we now have filling stations. For industrial, domestic and commercial uses it would be necessary to replace the oil-fired machines with electric ones.

In other words, the electrification of society is a precondition for the widespread use of nuclear power. The present tendency, as oil prices rise, is for demand for electricity (much of which is generated in oil-fired power plants) to lessen. One of the most serious problems facing those who are planning for a nuclear future is that in the short term there is a strong tendency for the use of electricity to be curtailed, whereas in the longer term the reverse would be required.

Fears about fission
Nuclear power also brings problems and dangers associated with containing radioactivity and disposing of radioactive waste. Technical solutions seem to be available, but there remains an important residue of doubt among experts about their reliability. There is also the possibility of the proliferation of nuclear weapons. The breeder reactor produces large amounts of plutonium, which it then consumes as fuel: plutonium is the material from which nuclear bombs can be made. The idea of having a multitude of what amounts to plutonium factories all over the world is a frightening prospect for many people.

Beyond the breeder reactor, scientists are looking to what appears a much safer form of nuclear energy. This is fusion, in which isotopes of hydrogen and lithium are used to release energy in the same type of reaction that powers the Sun. Fuel

supplies for this reaction are readily available from seawater: the human race would never have to worry about fuel again. It would also be safer and cleaner than fission and there would be little waste to dump. However, at the moment no one knows whether we can actually achieve the aim of releasing usable energy from the fusion reaction.

The Earth has, of course, its own fusion reactor, the Sun, beaming a prodigious quantity of energy down upon it. This is difficult to capture and use for anything except low-grade heating. Solar heating is already economical in some areas and is likely to spread, easing the burden borne by conventional fuels, but it does not provide the high-grade energy needed for so many uses. Solar power plants, using large arrays of mirrors to focus the Sun's heat on to boilers perched on high towers, are already being designed in Europe and the USA. These will undoubtedly provide solar energy in the form of electricity; but their economic viability remains to be seen. For the cloudy, temperate countries, there is little prospect of such stations coming into general use without effective storage systems: various methods of storage are currently under investigation. However, there is no such problem in hot, sunny climates, and solar power plants could become common in the southern states of America and the Middle East.

Another possibility being given serious consideration is the solar space satellite. This would be placed in a synchronous orbit (orbiting at the same speed as the Earth is rotating and so remaining above a fixed point, like a communications

Reasonably assured resources	Total global resource		Future option: (a) Continue use at present rate for present purposes	Future option: (b) Restrict to transport fuel	
360 billion tons	448 billion tons	Oil	Proved reserves will last for only 30 years	This restriction would involve upgrading of heavy distillates by "cracking," which may increase costs. Supplies of oil to the petrochemical	industry would be reduced, affecting supplies of many essential products. This has to be balanced against benefit from extending petroleum supplies.
Difficult to estimate	Difficult to estimate	Natural gas	Proved reserves will last for 53 years	Not applicable	
Not available	Estimates vary from 7.6 trillion tons to 12 trillion tons	Coal	Proved reserves will last for 1,800 years	Not applicable	
Not applicable	Not applicable	Wood	Renewable resource	Not applicable	
540,000 tons	4,290 million tons	Uranium	Proved reserves will last until the end of the century	Uranium is used to power military-controlled submarines and ships. It may be possible at a future date for commercial application of this fuel for	shipping. The advantage of nuclear-powered ships is their ability to go for long periods without refueling.
Not applicable	Not applicable	Hydro-electricity	Resource will last indefinitely	Not applicable	
Not applicable	Not applicable	Geothermal	Potentially limitless	Not applicable	
Not applicable	Not applicable	Solar	Unlimited resources	Not applicable	
Not applicable	Not applicable	Wind	Unlimited resources	Not applicable	
Not applicable	Not applicable	Waves	Unlimited resources	Not applicable	
Not applicable	Not applicable	Tides	Unlimited resources	Not applicable	

satellite) and would have huge "wings" consisting of solar-cell panels to collect the Sun's energy, which would be beamed down to Earth in the form of microwaves, picked up by a receiving station, converted to electricity and sent out along the electricity grid. The vision is heroic, but not beyond the realms of technical possibility. The whole assembly, covering several square kilometers, would have to be built in space. And not everyone would feel confident that microwaves of the required intensity could be beamed to Earth with impunity.

There are other great technological dreams for supplying energy. Huge machines have been proposed which would tap the thermal difference between the ocean surface and the depths. Again there are many unknowns. Anything that might disrupt the equilibrium of the ocean currents needs to be considered with great care. It is possible that parts of Europe would become uninhabitable if the Gulf Stream were deflected from its course.

All these speculations form part of the "hard" approach to the future. They share a reliance on increasingly sophisticated and complicated technology to sustain human society in the long-term future. They are impatient of caution and optimistic about what can be achieved by technology. Looking at the astonishing achievements of the past, it is easy to understand this attitude, which leaves intact the values of modern industrial society.

A gentler society

The "soft" approach is just the opposite. The vision is of a much gentler and calmer society, one which consumes less, moves less, concentrates more on quality than quantity, on people and personal relations more than possessions. In such a society people would have more responsibility for their own lives and would as far as possible make their own decisions about energy and other matters. They would be liberated from the oppression of vast bureaucracies and state control of energy.

The energy used in such a society would be derived as far as possible from small-scale sources powered by the wind, the Sun, waves, or relying on the growth of energy-yielding plants. Needs would be carefully tailored to available supply. The concept owes much to the long tradition of Utopian thought, but it is not a harkening back to some lost golden age. The perceptive advocates of the soft energy option are well aware that life in the past was far from arcadian. Science has brought a great liberation from drudgery, oppression and disease. The soft path would strive to retain these gains but would try to channel the ingenuity of science toward the small-scale and renewable resources. In such a future the wants of society would be supplied by the subtle exploitation of all the energy flows available, avoidance of excessive consumption and the reduction of waste. Solar collectors, solar cells, heat pumps, fermenters and digesters of organic materials, efficient burners of wood and coal; all these would be used to supply energy how and where it was wanted, and with the minimum of waste and inefficiency.

The proponents of the soft energy path argue that not only does it lead to a more satisfying future but that it is also much safer than the hard path. They believe that to put our faith in large systems is dangerous and that if such systems do not succeed in every detail they are likely to involve the whole of society in their failure. In contrast, the decentralized soft path would not have the same kind of critical dependence on a single support system.

But if the hard alternative is technologically optimistic, then the soft path can be said to be socially optimistic to the same degree. It supposes that people will be content with enough and not seek more; that social responsibility and concern will begin to take precedence over individual acquisitiveness; that small will appear truly beautiful to people and to the politicians who make decisions on their behalf. The two options offer very different courses of action to prepare for them. Both are founded on deeply held beliefs about what is desirable and possible.

There is no doubt that great change must take place as the world moves from its large-scale dependence on oil toward a different energy future. The greatest danger is that we will fail to create a sense of direction for ourselves and merely drift into a future that is wasteful but unprovided for; and that rising energy prices will lead to increasing hardship and tension between nations and social classes. We face a problem which is as much one of the creative imagination as it is of resources and technology. The prospects for the first half of the next century depend on our ability to visualize an achievable and desirable energy future and to take the measures necessary for its realization.

Future option: (c) Restrict to chemical use only		Future option: (d) Restrict to use as electricity generating fuel	
Using oil as a feedstock for the petrochemical industries is, perhaps, more efficient than allowing it to be burned as a fuel. Much of the world has come to rely on the many	irreplaceable products that are petroleum based. However, substitute fuels, for example hydrogen, must be developed to replace the role of oil as a fuel for transport and power.	Trying to stretch our dwindling oil supplies by restricting usage in this way will make all internal combustion engines useless. Synthetic fuels such as hydrogen could be used	but this would require modification of existing engines and introduction of new distributive methods. The petrochemical industry would be seriously affected.
Gas, like oil, is a valuable ingredient in the petrochemical and fertilizer industries and is equally irreplaceable. The developed world relies heavily on oil and gas as heating fuels	in homes and industry and alternative fuels would have to be developed on a large enough scale to replace gas for this purpose.	Gas-fired power plants are used to a lesser extent than other fossil-fueled power plants as they are generally less efficient. Such a restriction, therefore, would not have any	benefits. Natural gas, like oil, is used in the manufacture of essential products of the petrochemical industry, which would therefore be seriously affected.
Coal is used to a lesser extent in the chemical industry than oil or gas. Such a restriction would stop production of coke, which can only be made from coal, and which is an	essential fuel in the iron and steel industries.	Using coal only to generate electricity would eliminate the small but valuable role it plays in the chemical industry and, most importantly, it would stop the production of coke,	which can only be made from coal and which is essential to the iron and steel industries.
New uses for wood are being found in the chemical industry as feedstuff for animal consumption. Production of methanol liquid fuel is also being investigated. These new	uses are not, perhaps, as important as the established uses of wood, such as manufacture of paper and related products, and as a fuel and building material.	Not applicable	
Not applicable		Until it was discovered that uranium atoms could be split, releasing enormous amounts of energy in the form of heat, the metal had little practical value. Our harnessing of this	heat to produce electricity is the principal use for it. Uranium is also used in industry and medicine but not in large enough quantities to affect fuel supplies.
Not applicable		The restriction of hydroelectric schemes to the generation of electricity would eliminate their role in regions where irrigation and flood control are equally important.	
Not applicable		Restricting geothermal energy to electricity generation would deprive it of its equally important use as direct heat to power homes, industry and agriculture. The many uses for	low-grade heat would also be wasted.
Solar power is used in photochemical reactions to produce electricity (photovoltaic cells). This process is established in space programs, but it is too expensive for com-	mercial use. Restricting the use of solar energy in this way would be neglecting its immediate potential for space heating and cooling, and water heating.	Research is continuing into methods of improving solar-powered devices such as photovoltaic cells and solar furnaces. Solar power plants orbiting the Earth may also contribute	to electricity supplies, but these are future possibilities. Restricting solar energy to electrical usage would neglect its potential for space and water heating and for cooling.
Not applicable		This option would eliminate two other important uses of windmills: pumping water and irrigation.	
Not applicable		The new technology evolving for harnessing wave power is intended solely for the generation of electricity.	
Not applicable		The main use of tidal power schemes is to generate electricity.	

ENERGY—NON-NUCLEAR OPTIONS

Current discussions of nonnuclear or renewable energy options in the Western industrialized countries tend to be colored by two basic assumptions: first, that renewable energy systems are at an early stage of development; and second, that such systems supply at present only a minute fraction of the world's energy needs. Nevertheless, before World War II many renewable energy technologies had been in widespread use or were being developed in various parts of the world.

In 1900, 100,000 small wind machines supplied Denmark with about 10 percent of its energy. Solar water heaters were used by about 30 percent of the houses in Pasadena, California, in 1897, and in 60,000 houses in Florida in 1940. Biomass alcohol, derived from wood, potatoes and other agricultural wastes, supplied 18 percent of Western Europe's transport fuel in 1937 and helped run four million vehicles. The world's first 100 percent active solar space-heating system, using seasonal heat storage, was installed in a building at Cambridge, Massachusetts, in 1939.

However, those renewable energy systems that were still in use during World War II were displaced in the industrialized countries as soon as cheap oil and gas came into widespread use. Consequently, most people do not realize that many renewable systems are not in fact new and that they are available again commercially or are likely to be so in the near future—and this time with some considerable improvements.

Information about current patterns of energy consumption almost always deals with commercial energy only—that is, energy bought by the consumer from the producer. This is an incomplete and misleading picture because a large amount of energy used today is noncommercial, and virtually all of it is renewable. Countries such as India rely on draft animals, wood and animal dung for much of their energy supplies. When these noncommercial sources are taken into account, it may be concluded that about one-quarter of the world's energy needs is met by renewable sources. Even in the USA, biomass fuels still make as great a contribution as nuclear power to energy supplies.

Much of the energy in less-developed countries is supplied by renewable resources, but it is often argued that as the populations of these countries multiply and their standards of living improve, nuclear power will become essential to meet the growing demand for energy. This suggestion overlooks one crucial factor—money. The capital costs of any central-electric system, whether nuclear or fossil fired, are extremely large, and in less-developed countries the associated transmission and distribution costs would be equally large since their electricity networks are barely developed.

Sunshine all year

Fortunately most developing countries are well placed to exploit diverse renewable energy sources, since many of them are in areas where the amount of solar energy falling upon the Earth is high and relatively constant throughout the year. Some renewable energy systems are therefore more competitive in the developing countries than in the developed ones. Such systems also have the potential to meet a much larger demand than currently exists, since a feature of today's pattern of noncommercial fuel dependence usually involves a high degree of thermal inefficiency.

The situation in the developed countries is more complicated. They have largely moved away from dependence on renewable resources to dependence on fossil fuels, and have become accustomed to large supplies of cheap energy. With forecasts of further large increases in energy demand, the conventional wisdom is that we need to build many nuclear and coal-fired power plants very soon in order to avoid a severe shortage of energy. However, this view is criticized on several grounds.

A feature of many Western European and North American official energy plans is that they assume that a large proportion of primary energy growth will be lost in conversion and distribution, in an increasingly elaborate and inefficient energy chain. This has happened in Britain since 1900, where primary energy production has doubled, while energy at the point of end use (the heating system, furnace or machine which it drives) has increased only 50 percent, although this is something less likely to be repeated in an era of rising fuel prices.

One of the fundamental problems of implementing strategy with regard to conventional energy is its sheer expense. Although the cost of energy from central-electric systems is lower in countries already industrialized, it is still many times greater than that of systems which burn fuel directly.

The indiscriminate substitution of nuclear- or

Future option: (e) Restrict to direct use in industrial plant (other than for electricity generation)	Future option: (f) Restrict to domestic heating and cooking (other than for electricity supply)		
This would eliminate domestic use, seriously affecting the developed world, which relies on oil to a large extent for heating.	This would eliminate use in industrial plant and in the petrochemical industry.	Oil	Option (a) is, in reality, unlikely, since energy consumption will be more inclined to increase rather than continue at present rate of consumption. If we do maintain present rates of consumption total recoverable reserves are probably four
This would eliminate domestic use, which would affect the developed world, where gas is becoming increasingly popular for heating and cooking.	This would eliminate use in industrial plant and in the petrochemical and fertilizer industries.	Natural gas	Option (a): if we continue to use natural gas at our present rate of consumption recoverable reserves, estimates of which vary considerably, are many times greater than proved reserves, which will last for another 50 years. Option (b): if
Coal is still used directly for domestic heating, which would therefore be affected, but to a lesser extent than oil.	This would eliminate industrial use of coal, which is particularly important in the iron and steel industries, where coke is used as a fuel.	Coal	Option (a): if we continue to use coal at the present rate proved reserves will last 1,800 years and total recoverable resources (on a medium-based estimate) will last 3,500 years. Options (b, c, d, e, f) are unlikely to be implemented since it
Theoretically there is enough wood available for industrial purposes without affecting domestic supplies.	Wood is estimated to be sufficient to cope with domestic fuel needs without affecting industrial supply. This restriction would therefore be unnecessary in the case of wood, providing adequate silvicultural methods were introduced.	Wood	Option (a): if the production of wood for domestic purposes continues at the present rate there may be a serious threat to the environment in the form of deforestation. This is particularly relevant in the less-developed countries. This may be
Not applicable	Not applicable	Uranium	Options (a, c) should be considered together as, in terms of energy, uranium is only used to produce electricity. If we continue to use uranium at present rates of consumption, proved reserves will last only until the end of the century. Option
Not applicable	Not applicable	Hydro-electricity	Option (a) suggests that the use of hydroelectric power will probably continue at present rates of consumption. This seems the most likely option since most of the prime sites for the exploitation of this extremely large resource have already been
This would eliminate the domestic use of geothermal energy, particularly in Iceland, where steaming water is pure enough to be pumped directly from deep wells to heat homes.	This would eliminate use in industrial plant.	Geothermal	Option (a): it is likely that we will continue to use geothermal energy at an increasing rate. Governmental and commercial interest is growing in the further development of geothermal energy for electrical and thermal heat. It shows particular
This would eliminate the important energy saving made by the use of solar energy to heat and cool homes and offices.	This restriction would eliminate the application of solar power to pump water and for irrigation purposes.	Solar	Option (a): it is likely that solar energy will continue to be used at an increasing rate. The use of this infinite resource could be expanded to make a significant contribution to future energy production, especially for powering relatively simple
Not applicable	Not applicable	Wind	Option (a): it is hoped by proponents of wind power that the use of windmills to generate electricity will expand rather than remain constant. Current production is limited since wind power research and development are, as yet, at an early stage.
Not applicable	Not applicable	Waves	Options (a, d) should be considered together as wave power is only used for the generation of electricity. It is hoped by proponents of wave power that generation of electricity from this source will expand. Presently it contributes nothing to
Not applicable	Not applicable	Tides	Options (a, d): it is hoped by proponents of tidal power, which is used mainly for the generation of electricity, that usage will expand rather than continue at present rates. There are economic and environmental constraints that will have to

coal-powered electricity for gas and oil (in a "hard" energy path) ignores the type or quality of energy required. The world's major energy need is for low-temperature heat, for heating space and water in buildings and for agriculture and industry. Much of this demand is currently met by the expensive and inefficient conversion of fuels to electricity. However, electricity is a high quality form of energy strictly only needed for a small range of tasks which between them account for only five percent of total energy demand. Inefficient use could, therefore, be eliminated by devising ways of matching energy resources to requirements—principally heat and portable liquid fuels.

One source of low-temperature heat is solar energy. Solar water heaters have been in widespread use in the USA at various times since the end of the last century, and are currently in use in Japan, Israel and Australia. Here, therefore, is a system that works and is already commercially available in many countries.

Solar energy also supplies about 20 percent of the space heating needs of British homes by incidental gains of sunshine through the windows—a fact that is often forgotten. By insulating buildings to the degree customary in new Swedish houses and designing them so as to capture and store midwinter sunshine, it is possible to have completely "passive" 100 percent solar heating. In addition, 100 percent "active" systems are being developed both for new and (more importantly) for existing buildings.

It appears that a combination of already developed active and passive systems is capable of meeting all our space- and water-heating needs. In the case of medium- and high-temperature process heat for industry, the alternative technologies are less well developed. Nevertheless, a number of commercially available systems appeared sufficiently promising for one recent study to conclude that by the year 2000 such systems could economically supply 30 percent of the process-heat requirements of all US industry.

The renewable energy systems described above (and many other wind, biomass and hydroelectric systems) have led researchers in the USA, Sweden, France, Britain and many other countries to conclude that 60 percent or more of those countries' energy needs could be met from renewable sources within the next 50 years—subject, that is, to competing pressures for land for food production. They will not do so, however, unless the numerous barriers—institutional, legal and economic—to implementing these technologies are removed.

A conserving future
An important factor in explaining why assessments of the potential of renewable energy differ so widely is that very different assumptions are made about the likely level of national or world energy consumption in 20 or 50 years' time. With a rigorous policy of conservation it is both technically and economically feasible to halve global consumption without lowering living standards. The contribution of renewable resources would obviously be greater in a conserving format than in one where consumption doubled by the end of the century. It is argued that there are a number of technical and social reasons why renewable energy systems are more likely to flourish than nuclear systems in a conserving future, and why the two are not likely to thrive together. A combination of energy-saving measures and renewable systems often has a self-reinforcing effect. For example, a well-insulated house reduces the heat load so that a seasonal store of solar heat can be smaller, less expensive, and still adequate to meet heating needs throughout the year, thereby doing away with the need for costly backup systems during the winter. Or the district heating network of a combined heat and power system could subsequently be coupled to a solar heat plant, reducing total costs.

The advocates of a nonnuclear future point out that if a vigorous conservation program were implemented the total amount of electricity needed might well decrease; on the other hand, nuclear power can be used only in the form of electricity. Thus it appears that the implied mutual exclusivity of the soft and hard energy paths stems from their cultural incompatibility; institutional antagonism (each requiring organization and policy action which inhibits the other); and logistical competition—each requiring money, materials, fuel, skills, political attention and time.

The industrialized countries of the world have only a few years to decide which of these paths to follow. Once they have made that decision, and have committed the resources necessary to that path, it will not be easy for them to turn back and follow an alternative course.

Suggested course of action

times proved reserves and, therefore, supplies could last for 120 years, but at a much higher cost of extraction. Option (b) would effectively mean that coal would have to be more extensively used in the chemical industry. Although coal is	more plentiful than oil it is still a finite resource. Options (c) and (d) are unlikely restrictions since they would be unacceptable from a political point of view.	Attempt to maintain current rates of consumption while trying to prove greater reserves, pursuing conversion of coal to oil and investigating other fuels for use in the internal combustion engine (hydrogen for example), so that one of oil's
we confine natural gas to use in the petrochemical industry only, considered by some proponents to be the wisest course of action, we might be making the best use of a valuable and irreplaceable resource. Substitutes would have to be found for	the traditional uses of gas and this would be subject to political and social constraints. Options (c, d, e, f) would be similarly bound and restricting gas to these uses would not be at all beneficial.	As resources of natural gas dwindle, we may have to concentrate on using gas in the petrochemical industry alone. We should therefore continue exploration to find new reserves, and at the same time try to find substitutes for the more
is improbable that coal will ever be restricted to one particular use. If anything, the uses of coal will become more diversified in an attempt to find substitutes for the less-plentiful fossil fuels—oil and gas.		Continue exploration to find additional sources of coal. Research into ways in which coal can be substituted for or can supplement the role of oil and gas in the petrochemical industry. Refine and make economic the production of oil
counterbalanced by the introduction of adequate silvicultural methods, but this may compete with agriculture for land. Option (d): using wood just for the chemical industry is unlikely as it has far more important uses. Options (e, f):	restricting the use of wood to industrial and domestic use, will be unnecessary if, as in option (a), adequate silvicultural methods are implemented.	The need for firewood is most strongly felt in the poorer nations, and this need will increase as the population increases. Fortunately wood is a renewable resource, but replacing it is a slow process. The need for firewood may well decrease as a
(b): it is unlikely that uranium will be used solely to power ships and submarines when its greatest potential is for the generation of electricity. Whether we continue to use uranium at the present rate or accelerate the growth of the	nuclear power industry by introducing fast breeder reactors, new supplies of uranium must be found in order to maintain the nuclear program in the next century.	The social and political ramifications of the future development of the nuclear power industry are greater, perhaps, than for any other energy source. The benefits to be gained from this potentially inexhaustible source of power
developed. The remaining sites lie mostly in the developing countries. It may not be possible or desirable to develop all potential sites: they may be situated too far away from the point of use, where transmission would prove uneconomic;	and development of some sites may severely disrupt local ecology. Option (d) is unlikely since few dams are built entirely for electricity supply. There is no benefit in restricting such a large resource to one use.	Continue to use hydroelectric power as at present, but concentrate any further development in less-developed countries, since, although initial capital costs are high, running costs are low. In addition to supplying electricity, hydroelectric schemes
promise in combined heat and power schemes. One site near Paris is exploiting semithermal heat to provide space and water heating for dwellings. A future geothermal goal is to tap heat deep in the Earth's crust. If current experiments	are successful the heat energy obtained would be at a higher temperature than can be produced in any nuclear reactor.	Continue research and development into the expansion of geothermal energy, including the direct use of heat for electricity generation and the possibility of extracting heat from "hot rocks" deep in the Earth's interior. If this could be
devices for space and water heating. Options (c, d) refer to the more sophisticated methods of solar power to produce electricity. It is unlikely that solar energy will be used for the generation of electricity only and there would be no benefit	gained from restricting such a limitless energy supply. This same basic premise applies to options (e, f).	Solar power has immense potential for electricity generation and for large-scale direct use in the heating and cooling of buildings as long as costs can be reduced enough to make commercial application economically viable.
Option (c): although current experiments involve the building of windmills solely for the purpose of generating electricity, windmills have equally important traditional uses in areas where pumped water and irrigation are needed. There is no	benefit to be gained from conserving or restricting so limitless a resource as wind.	Continue research and development into the use of wind power for electricity generation. Future application of wind power, however, should be integrated with other alternative technologies such as wave, tidal and solar power.
our supplies as most wave power devices are still in the experimental stage. Although this resource is limitless there are environmental constraints on its widespread application.		Continue research and development into the use of wave power devices for the generation of electricity. Wave power cannot be expected to be relied upon as the main source for power generation because of environmental constraints and
be satisfactorily overcome before this can be achieved.		Continue research and development into possible sites for the application of tidal power and investigate ways of reducing costs. Tidal power can make a valuable contribution to our future energy supplies if integrated with other renewable and

TABLE CONTINUED ON NEXT PAGE

ENERGY—FUTURE ALTERNATIVES

Nuclear fusion is the basic reaction in the stars and the source of nearly all the energy in the universe. The reaction takes place when two atomic nuclei combine to form one larger nucleus. It is the belief of some scientists that this process, with its almost unlimited fuel reserves, is the key to solving the world's energy problem.

The source of energy in nuclear fusion is the same as in nuclear fission: the transformation of mass into energy. Fission takes place through the splitting of heavy elements, and is the basis of present-day nuclear power plants—and the atom bomb. Fusion takes place through the coalescing of light elements, and is the basis of the hydrogen bomb.

The Sun is like a massive fusion reactor in which hydrogen nuclei fuse to form helium: the nuclei are thrown together with such force that their strong mutual repulsion is overcome, allowing the reaction to take place. Man's problem is to imitate this process in a controllable form.

Self-sustaining fusion reactions can occur only under conditions of extreme temperature and pressure. The reaction that seems most promising as a terrestrial source of energy is that between two isotopes of hydrogen—deuterium and tritium. A fusion reactor would be surrounded by a blanket of lithium one meter thick to act as a tritium breeder and to absorb the energy of the reaction. The absorbed heat could then be used to raise steam to generate electricity.

At the enormous temperatures required for fusion to occur, atoms exist as separate nuclei and electrons, in a form known as a plasma. A fusion reactor must meet certain basic conditions if it is to be a net energy producer. First, the plasma must be hot enough or the fusion reaction will not start. Second, the plasma must be held together for a long enough period: too short a reaction means that more energy is put into the system than is produced. The required containment time depends on the density of the plasma; the greater the density, the more reactions take place in a given containment period. A plasma is created in the first place at a temperature of 100,000 degrees centigrade, but it is not until the "break-even" point of 40 million degrees is reached that a self-sustaining fusion reaction is achieved in which as much energy is being produced as would be used to sustain the process. For a commercially viable reactor the plasma would have to be heated to 100 million degrees. In August 1978 a large step forward was made when a temperature of 60 million degrees was reached in the Princeton Large Torus reactor in the USA.

Finding the right reactor

One of the chief problems is to design a reactor that will contain and sustain plasmas at such temperatures. Two methods of containment have been attempted in the search for a suitable system. In the first, magnetic fields are used to confine the plasma long enough for fusion to occur. The second method uses lasers to compress the plasma to such an extent that the fusion reaction will take place before the particles can be blown apart.

Fusion scientists have devised several types of magnetic containment systems, the most promising being the Tokamak device, designed in 1969 at the Kurchatov Institute in the USSR. This reactor has a doughnut shape, which is the best shape for a magnetic field. The USSR plans to build the T-2 Tokamak to operate in the mid-1980s.

Laser-induced fusion has been less well studied than magnetic containment. The fact that a laser could trigger a fusion reaction was first demonstrated in 1968 in the USSR. The aim is to use a powerful combination of laser beams to blast a glass pellet containing a mixture of deuterium and tritium. In theory, a shock wave forces up the density of the material in the center of the pellet, producing the conditions necessary for fusion. As yet, the process has only been simulated by computer.

The only radioactive effluent from a fusion reactor would be tritium: the release of pollutants into the environment would be significantly less than for nuclear fission. Another important characteristic of the fusion process is that the reaction could not "run away" within the reactor to a sufficient degree to destroy the outer containment vessel. If an accident caused the loss of all power to a reactor, the worst that could happen would be the loss of the magnetic field holding the plasma together, and the reaction would then stop.

Enormous technical problems stand between us and the first commercially viable fusion reactor. If the programs under way do establish the feasibility of fusion as an energy source, a major research and development plan will be required to determine the reliability and economics of such a project. Even if the work is successful, fusion power will make

TABLE CONTINUED FROM PREVIOUS PAGE

			World energy consumption (million tons of coal equivalent)	World population	Per capita consumption (kilograms)
biggest uses, as a transport fuel, diminishes. Also pursue alternative technologies, such as the development of renewable resources, to take over part of oil's role in energy production.	Oil	1975	8,002,200 (source: United Nations Statistical Yearbook)	3,967,000,000	2,028
conventional uses of this fuel.	Natural gas				
		2000 zero growth	12,683,876,000	6,254,377,000	2,028
from coal. Any decision about the future use of coal or, in fact, any energy resource, will depend on political, economic and social decisions made now.	Coal				
nation becomes wealthier, and alternative methods of energy production are developed.	Wood	2000 assuming a 5 percent growth rate	42,948,806,859	6,254,377,000	6,867
should, therefore, be carefully weighed against the disadvantages of, for example, disposing of nuclear waste, as well as the advantages of the further development of other renewable energy sources.	Uranium				
may also solve other problems that often beset these countries by providing a means of irrigation and flood control.	Hydro-electricity				
achieved geothermal power could make a significant contribution to energy needs currently met by the fossil fuels.	Geothermal				
	Solar				
	Wind				
limited sites for application. It should, therefore, be integrated with other alternative technologies such as wind, tidal and solar power.	Waves				
conventional energy sources to help meet electricity needs at times of peak demand.	Tides				

In forecasting energy needs for the year 2000, we have based our assumptions on two criteria. The first figure is based on the assumption that per capita energy consumption will remain constant, while the second figure assumes a five percent annual growth rate (as currently achieved in the United States) compounded from the present day until 2000. Both estimates use a medium range forecast of population growth. The figures in each forecast for total consumption in 2000 differ widely and the true figure will probably fall somewhere between the two. If consumption were to increase at a rate of five percent, the total amount of energy used would double every 14 years. This is highly undesirable and, fortunately, unlikely. Many of the world's major energy resources are nonrenewable and must therefore be conserved in some way. Also, consuming energy at such a rate would result in even further damage to the environment. It is probably unlikely that energy consumption will remain static. Both these forecasts are inflexible in that they are based on one figure only with respect to future rates of consumption. Unfortunately this is a restriction common to most methods of prediction, since only one estimative figure can be used in any one permutation of the various factors. The pitfalls of forecasting are, therefore, obvious. The oil crisis of 1973–74 was a good example of forecasters and economists being caught out. They could not possibly have foreseen the political turmoil and the resulting rise in oil prices following years in which industrialized nations had enjoyed apparently limitless supplies very cheaply. This example illustrates well the fact that political, economic and social factors cannot be predicted easily, if at all. Nor, more significantly, can they be easily quantified in terms of mathematical formulae. Other problems of forecasting in this way include the fact that a figure for average per capita consumption does, by definition, ignore the large variations across the globe. Per capita energy consumption in the United States, for example, is at least seven times greater than in the rest of the world. We should also be wary of forecasts of consumption that are based on "demand." Projections of demand tend to assume that the processes that produced growth in the past will continue to do so in the future. Also, and this applies in particular to the less-developed countries, where demand is apparently less, low figures do not necessarily mean that demand is not there. And in industrialized nations, where the rate of increase in the growth of industry and commerce is slowing, we may well see a leveling off of energy consumption in the future. As energy supplies become scarce and prices rise, demand for energy is bound to decrease.

little difference to the patterns of world energy consumption in less than 50 years. However, the potential of fusion power is so great that it seems a worthwhile investment for those countries that can afford the high costs of the investigations.

The Sun's energy is absorbed by plants in the process of photosynthesis. The conversion of sunlight to energy in the form of wood has been a major source of power for the industrialized world. Energy can also be derived from waste and manure, and the term "biomass fuels" is applied to all renewable fuels coming from living things (as distinct from fossil fuels, which are not renewable). Certain plants, including sugarcane, cassava, sorghum, corn and soybeans, yield relatively high quantities of energy, and these could be grown on vast "energy cultivations" specifically for fuel. Biomass energy can be extracted by burning, by bacterial breakdown, or fermentation with yeast to produce alcohol or methane. Alcohol can be used in the production of fertilizers to improve the productivity of the soil, as a fuel in place of firewood, and in existing vehicle engines with relatively minor modifications. One drawback is the large area required to grow the crops, since there is already worldwide pressure on land for production of food.

Organic wastes can be converted in a number of ways. As well as producing fuel, the problem of disposal is also solved. Digestion of sewage sludge by microorganisms produces methane; in pyrolysis, the wastes are heated in the absence of air to produce gas, oil and a solid residue called char, which can also be used as a fuel; and hydrogenation is a process of conversion using carbon monoxide and steam to reduce organic wastes and produce crude oil. Studies in Brazil, the USA and Australia suggest that a significant proportion of their energy needs could be supplied by these biomass fuels.

Direct fuel and storage

Hydrogen can be used directly as a fuel and as a means of storing energy derived from other sources. The principle is that electricity generated from, say, a nuclear power plant would be used to break down water by electrolysis, whereby a current is passed through acidified water, splitting it into hydrogen and oxygen. Hydrogen can easily be stored and distributed in pipelines to consumers, in the same way as natural gas.

Hydrogen has many attractive properties as a fuel. It is "clean": it burns in air to produce water, and the only possible pollutants are the oxides of nitrogen, the levels of which would be very low. It can be used as a replacement for coal, oil and natural gas for most commercial purposes, and it can be used to manufacture other fuels. Prototype vehicles have been built that use hydrogen as a fuel. The main difficulty of hydrogen for transport uses is storage: a large volume has to be carried in order to produce a practical energy output.

Similar proposals have been put forward for the use of methanol (methyl or wood alcohol) as a fuel. It can be used in conventional gasoline engines with a simple conversion, and can be stored in gasoline tanks and transported in tankers and pipelines already in existence, and would cause less pollution than gasoline. Methanol can be manufactured from most other fuels, and, significantly, it can be made from organic waste and refuse by burning in a furnace with oxygen to produce carbon monoxide and hydrogen, which are then converted to methanol. One of the problems is the risk of contamination by water, for which methanol has a strong affinity.

Fuel cells provide a highly efficient potential for converting chemical energy to electricity, and could be used in association with hydrogen or methanol fuels. The principle is that two electrodes are immersed in an electrically conducting liquid; the gas or liquid fuel is introduced into one electrode and oxygen or another oxidant into the other. The fuel and oxidant combine, and an electric current is created. Fuel cells have been devised for a variety of fuels: they have been used in space capsules, and could be used domestically to generate electricity from hydrogen. They can also store energy: one application is the storage of wind power. A windmill generates electricity, which is then used to break down water into its components, hydrogen and oxygen; these are stored and can be used to regenerate electricity in a fuel cell when required. A major drawback at present is that the catalysts required to promote the reaction in a fuel cell are extremely expensive.

These are some of the many promising areas of research into alternatives for energy sources and supply. Although at a fairly early stage of research and development, they could all be of significance as supplies of fossil fuels are progressively depleted.

	Additional energy alternatives Fuel from wastes	Nuclear fusion	Ocean Thermal Energy Converters	Gasification	Fuel Cells
general comments	There is growing interest in utilizing solid organic wastes in the manufacture of synthetic fuels. This is a particularly attractive alternative as it helps alleviate the waste disposal problem as well as providing a renewable energy resource. There are three main methods proposed for conversion of these wastes: hydrogenation, pyrolysis and bioconversion. The first two have already reached pilot plant stage of development.	Since the early 1950s, attempts have been made to harness one of the most powerful energy sources known to man—nuclear fusion, the reaction that takes place when two atomic nuclei combine to form one larger nucleus, thus releasing energy. In fact, the Sun is like a fusion reactor, where forms of hydrogen are combining to produce helium. Man's problem is to try and imitate this process on Earth.	The principle behind OTECs lies in exploiting the temperature gradient between the warm upper layers of the ocean and the colder layers a few thousand feet down to generate power. The warm surface waters are used to evaporate low-boiling-point liquids such as ammonia, which vaporize and expand through the turbine to drive a generator. Cold seawater is used to cool the vapor so the process can be repeated.	The production of synthetic natural gas (SNG) is increasing as natural gas becomes scarcer. Gas is a preferred fuel for many reasons: it is one of the cheapest and most versatile of the fossil fuels. Increased demand has pushed many distributors to the limit of their capacity, particularly in the United States. This situation has spurred new developments, employing old and new techniques, for producing SNG.	Fuel cells have been widely used in space programs, but their high cost has precluded their application on the ground. Research is now being undertaken to develop this relatively simple concept, which consists of a fuel electrode (anode), an air electrode (cathode) and an electrolyte. Hydrogen-based fuel cells are the most efficient and the most highly developed. Numerous cells linked together could generate up to 100 megawatts.
advantages	The United States is a good example of a highly industrialized country producing vast quantities of waste. It has been estimated that the 100 million tons of combustible domestic refuse collected in 1971, used as a fuel, could have met almost a quarter of the US petroleum shortage. Hydrogenation is the most promising method of conversion, yielding about 1.25 barrels of oil per ton of dry waste. Commercial operation is envisaged by the year 2000.	The most promising fuel for magnetic containment or laser fusion consists of the hydrogen isotopes deuterium and tritium. Deuterium, found in seawater, is an extremely cheap and plentiful fuel. If all the deuterium in 1.5 km^3 of seawater could be burned in a fusion reactor, it would produce as much energy as the world's known recoverable resource of crude oil. Tritium is manufactured from lithium in much the same way that plutonium is manufactured from uranium.	The main advantage of OTECs is that they would use a constantly renewable resource, solar-heated water, as fuel. Additionally, the pumping of deep water to the surface would recycle nutrients lost from the ocean's photosynthetic layer, and these nutrients could be used in coastal or even open ocean mariculture farms. The greatest potential for these devices lies in areas of high temperature differential, but they would need to be no farther than 160 kilometers (100 miles) from the coast.	Gasification is the process whereby carbon from coal or oil is combined with water at a high temperature to form methane—the basic constituent of natural gas. Although oil gasification is simpler, there is competition for the raw material from the petrochemical industry, and this limits the amount available for gasification. However, reserves of coal are massive, and lower ranks of coal can be used for conversion to SNG.	Production of electricity by fuel cells as opposed to conventional power generation would result in less air pollution, as they do not emit harmful combustibles. Fuel cells also operate more efficiently at low power than steam or gas generators, and can maintain high efficiency when not on peak load. Thus they may be used to supplement conventional power plants at times of peak demand. On site generation of electricity may be the most effective use of fuel cells, reducing transmission losses.
disadvantages	The costs of all three processes—hydrogenation, pyrolysis and bioconversion in particular—will have to be reduced before such technologies can be widely introduced. They are all restricted by the amount of solid waste available, but they may be supplemented by phytoplankton, algae and other plants grown specifically for conversion to fuel. Investigations are currently being made into the possibility of direct combustion of wood from trees and fermentation of cereals to yield alcohol.	A major disadvantage at present is proving scientific feasibility. Today scientists can produce and control plasma at temperatures of about 60,000,000°C (the highest recorded temperature in a man-made experiment), but for a commercially viable reactor the plasma would have to be heated to a temperature of 100 million degrees. An experimental reactor is currently being built at Culham Laboratory in Oxfordshire, England.	Despite their large size, OTECs would generate only one-tenth the power of conventional power plants. Although no technological breakthrough is needed to build demonstration plants now, financial and economic incentives are required. Environmental damage from OTECs would be relatively insignificant. However, the marine environment could well be detrimental to the planned structures, causing corrosion and clogging of the machines.	Whichever process is used for gasification (commercial development has already begun in Europe) there are many engineering problems. General refinement of the process is needed to improve efficiency; there are structural and corrosion problems to be overcome; and further mechanical problems exist, especially in the case of coal gasification, in transporting the fuel through the system.	Central station generation of electricity with conventional fuel cells is presently impractical. Such cells are no more efficient than the best large turbines. In addition, the cost of fuel cells will have to be brought down before they are economically viable for commercial use.

FOOD—DEFINING THE PROBLEMS

Future world food prospects are the subject of widening controversy. At one extreme there are the prophets of doom (including the US World-watch Institute), who believe that the situation is getting desperate: that the Earth's carrying capacity is nearing exhaustion; that croplands cannot be extended much farther; and that land resources are becoming depleted. At the other extreme are those who claim that there is (or could be) enough food available, both now and for the foreseeable future: what is needed is more land for food production (only about 10 percent of the land surface is used for crops), increased productivity and a restructuring of world agricultural systems so that supplies become available to those least able to compete for food in the marketplace. At the center of the controversy is the simple fact that already—in advance of the population bulge forecast over the next generation or so—hunger and sometimes famine are harsh realities for millions of people throughout the world.

The UN estimates that one person in every eight is starving and that almost half the world's population is suffering from malnutrition to some degree. Obviously it is the poor of all nations who come off worst. There are pockets of real deprivation even in the advanced nations. In 1972 the US Bureau of Census reported that "at least 10 to 12 million Americans are starving or sick because they have too little to spend on food." But generally only a fraction of the population is affected to this degree. For the rest, the rich nations, with only a quarter of the world's population, consume fully half the world's food; their livestock alone consume a quarter of all the grain produced each year—the equivalent of the total human grain consumption of China and India combined. Nowhere in the developed nations are conditions so abject as they are in the three poor continents, Asia, Africa and Latin America, where the World Bank estimate is that 500 million people live in "absolute poverty."

Caught unawares
In a sense the food shortages of the 1970s have caught the world unawares. The previous decade had brought a relative bonanza—good harvests swollen by US-developed dwarf strains of rice and wheat. By the end of the 1960s the problem seemed to be one of overproduction, leading to glut and the threat of depressed prices. The United States took land out of production and, together with Canada, allowed grain stores to run down. But in 1972 bad weather reduced harvests in the USSR, Australia and parts of Africa, particularly the Sahel. The USSR, anticipating trouble ahead, started buying heavily on the international grain market (largely to feed farm animals rather than people direct). By mid-1974 world grain reserves were down to a few weeks' supply, and the price of wheat had nearly doubled. Attention was again focused on the problem—"the greatest crisis mankind has faced," according to the UN—at the World Food Conference held in Rome in November 1974.

Today the world continues to live beyond its means. In recent years we have been consuming more cereals than we produce. If there were two or three lean years in a row, with major producers like the USA badly hit, the global store cupboard would be completely bare. In this event the advanced nations would immediately buy up crops to feed themselves and their farm stock, but the less-developed countries would be unable to afford to import grain. So, until world stocks are fully replenished or some more equitable system is introduced to grow food or to make it available where it is needed, the threat of widespread famine in less-developed countries is very real.

What this crisis has shown is that, while the

	Population (millions)	Hectares per head of population	Total land area ('000 hectares)	Arable and permanent cropland as percentage of total land area	Forest and woodland as percentage of total land area	Patterns of production (comparison of 1961–65 and 1975 figures)	
United States	213.54	4.27	912,689	23.0	33.3	Land under farms declining, but production increasing, partly due to improved crop	varieties and strains of livestock. Corn production +54 percent, rice +88 percent.
Sweden	8.19	5.02	41,148	7.3	64.2	After reduction in agricultural self-sufficiency in the late 1960s, Sweden now aims at	producing an exportable surplus of farm goods. Wheat production +63 percent.
West Germany	61.83	0.39	24,403	33.0	29.3	Land reform was not considered seriously until the early 1970s. Recent reorganization	has improved crop production. Corn production +865 percent.
Greece	9.05	1.44	13,080	29.7	20.0	Despite a decline in the importance of the agricultural sector, production of wheat, corn	and rice has risen by 21 percent, 96 percent and 18 percent respectively.
Hungary	10.54	0.87	9,238	59.4	16.7	With more than 50 percent of the total land under cultivation, production of all	three major food crops has risen, corn particularly (+115 percent).
USSR	254.39	8.75	2,227,200	10.4	41.3	Large-scale drainage and land reclamation schemes have resulted in much new land	being put under rice. Production has risen by 415 percent.
Japan	111.56	0.33	37,103	15.0	67.5	Encouraged by the government to over-produce rice, farmers are now faced with a	decline in the production of other cereals. Wheat −82 percent, corn −88 percent.
Australia	13.50	56.42	761,793	6.0	18.1	Although Australia is primarily a wool and meat producer, the area under cultivation is	increasing as new areas are reclaimed. Wheat +46 percent, rice +185 percent.
Papua New Guinea	2.76	16.36	45,171	0.8	80.6	Production figures unavailable.	
Tanzania	15.31	5.78	88,604	6.8	35.1	Despite massive rural resettlement in recent years, production of the three staple grains	has improved. Wheat +154 percent, corn +143 percent, rice +258 percent.
Chad	4.03	31.24	125,920	5.5	13.1	More than 85 percent of the population is involved in subsistence farming, which has seen	little improvement in recent years. Only rice production has increased, by 27 percent.
Ghana	9.87	2.33	23,002	11.7	10.6	Efforts to expand the production base of the agricultural sector have resulted in a greater	variety of cultivated food crops. Rice +109 percent, corn +70 percent.
China	838.80	1.10	930,496	13.9	16.3	China remains a predominantly agricultural country, with efforts being made to expand	both cultivated area and crop yield. Wheat +84 percent, rice +35 percent.
India	598.10	0.49	296,608	56.4	22.7	Basic food crop production has increased, mainly due to the introduction of "green	revolution" techniques. Wheat +115 percent, corn +53 percent.
Iran	33.02	4.95	163,600	10.1	11.0	The output of the agricultural sector has improved recently with increases in the three	staple grains. Wheat +91 percent, rice +90 percent, corn +170 percent.
Saudi Arabia	8.97	23.96	214,969	0.4	0.7	With less than one percent of the land cultivated, oasis agriculture remains a vitally	important feature. Wheat production has increased +200 percent.
Mexico	60.15	3.27	197,255	14.2	36.3	Although there is little cultivatable land, production of the main food crop, corn, has	increased +67 percent. Rice production +62 percent.
Brazil	106.23	7.96	845,651	4.3	60.3	Agricultural output has risen recently through the implementation of state-aided schemes.	Double cropping of wheat has increased production by 211 percent.
Jamaica	2.04	0.52	1,080	24.1	45.5	The government is currently bringing more land under cultivation. Production of corn	in Jamaica has risen by 225 percent.

specter of mass starvation may be an emotive one, it is apparently not yet discomforting enough to force the reappraisal necessary to feed the world's existing 4 billion population adequately, let alone make a start on planning for the 6 billion or so projected for the year 2000. What is also clear is that radical changes are needed to replace past approaches which have largely left poor countries and poor people to fend for themselves. True, most of the continuing rapid population growth is in the less-developed countries, but in a survival situation the large family is seen as a social and economic necessity, and children—many of whom do not survive beyond the age of five—offer the only hope of security against destitution in old age.

The real dilemma is that much modern agriculture is more to do with making money than with supplying all the people who need food. The postwar trend has been to create a parallel between agriculture and industry, using higher and higher inputs—machinery, fuel, fertilizers, pesticides—to produce richer and richer yields for sale to buoyant market economies able to pay the price. Threequarters of the world grain trade consists of traffic from the United States, the biggest agricultural exporter of all, to Europe; England alone receives 12 times as much US wheat, per head of population, as India does. In the West (and in the United States in particular, where "agribusiness" is the backbone of the economy), the agricultural econ-omy is protected not least as a result of pressure to maintain the interests of the farmers concerned. There can be nor more conspicuous monument to protectionist policies than the EEC's Butter Mountain.

In the global context, one of the most disturbing aspects of Western agriculture is its heavy emphasis on the output of meat and dairy produce. A great deal of food of high nutritional value, especially cereals and grain, is given over to livestock, which means that about 90 percent of the original vegetable protein is lost. Britain alone feeds two-thirds of its home-grown cereals to animals (mostly pigs and poultry). Together the industrialized nations, including the USSR, allocate more grain to livestock than is consumed by all less-developed countries. This taste for meat seems not to have been dulled by the fact that a mere 10 percent of the grain fed to beef cattle alone in 1974 would have met the entire Asian shortfall. In a rational agriculture livestock would be more sensibly employed grazing ecological niches unsuited to crops.

Crops for cash

Historically the rich nations of the world have plundered the poorer ones for raw materials. Partly a legacy of the colonial period, this tradition survives as one of the most controversial features of agriculture in less-developed countries, involving as it does the loss of good land to cash crops which have little or no nutritional value. Greedy of space and of scarce agricultural inputs, cash crops such as cotton, rubber, tea, coffee and cocoa bring relatively little benefit to the bulk of the indigenous population: in Mali, for example, where a greater acreage is given over to currency-earning cotton and peanuts than to native food, export revenues do not even cover the cost of food imports. Whether the commodity happens to be peanuts from Nigeria, jute from Bangladesh or sisal from Tanzania, prices are governed by market fluctuations, and this means that export revenues for a country with a one- or two-crop economy can vary greatly from year to year. Worldwide, cash crops occupy some 647,500 square kilometers (250,000 square miles).

Wherever it is practiced, cash crop production is big business seeking big returns, not an essential service geared to feeding people—all people, regardless of purchasing power. It is this dichotomy which has to be resolved (and quickly) if the less-developed countries are not to see their development permanently stunted by a long-term deficit of food. This is not to say that the advanced nations should cease all imports from the developing world and abandon their own commercial agriculture overnight. But it does require some recognition of the fact that the Western agricultural model—energy intensive and in many ways profligate—is by no means the complete answer to global needs. For, in return for raw materials (and along with

Livestock per capita	Percentage of economically active population in agriculture	Nature of agricultural inputs		Per capita daily kilocalories (*less than total needs)	Percentage contribution of agriculture to GDP	Agricultural imports as percentage of total import trade	Agricultural exports as percentage of total export trade
0.9	2.8	Intensive farming, such as that in the United States, requires high-support energy inputs	and these in turn rely on the supply of nonrenewable fuel resources.	3,504	3	10.5	21.1
0.6	6.5	Very little of Sweden's land is cultivated and of this, only 1.7 percent is irrigated.		3,064	4	8.1	3.2
0.6	5.5	Germany is increasingly dependent on support energy inputs; between 1960 and 1975	the degree of mechanization rose by 287 percent and the use of fertilizer by 56 percent.	3,438	3	17.9	4.9
1.1	41.4	Cultivation in Greece is labor intensive rather than energy intensive. Some 22 per-	cent of the available cropland is irrigated.	3,288	18	11.7	36.2
1.7	19.9	Hungary, with fertile soil and a favorable climate, has only a small area needing	irrigation—2.8 percent of the total acreage of arable and cropland.	3,582	n.a.	11.2	23.6
1.3	20.5	Although a large area of the USSR is cultivated, farming remains relatively inefficient.	However, mechanization is increasing and large-scale irrigation schemes are in practice.	3,542	n.a.	25.1	7.2
0.1	14.8	The terrain and type of land holdings restrict the use of machinery, but yields are high due	to labor-intensive methods and other inputs such as irrigation and fertilizers.	2,835	5	19.2	0.6
14	6.8	Australia has a medium-support energy system with high mechanization but low	fertilizer input. Irrigation is used for fruit and grains and the extension of cultivated land.	3,310	7	4.9	44.7
n.a.	84.2	Figures unavailable.		2,232*	28	21.5	31.6
1.1	83.7	Only 0.9 percent of Tanzania's land is irrigated, although this area is likely to	increase as the country recovers from the recent resettlement program.	2,002*	45	20.0	77.7
1.5	87.2	Cultivation in Chad is labor intensive and a negligible amount of arable land is irrigated.		1,781*	52	15.3	94.0
0.3	54.6	Until recently agricultural inputs have been limited, but progress is now being made	with irrigation schemes in the southeastern coastal regions.	2,317	49	12.8	77.3
0.4	63.9	Agricultural methods have retained a traditional emphasis on labor and mechanization	has proceeded slowly. Irrigation is important.	2,330*	n.a.	n.a.	n.a.
0.4	66.6	In an attempt to keep food production ahead of population growth, the government has	been steadily promoting irrigation and the use of chemical fertilizers.	1,971*	47	25.1	39.7
1.2	42.2	Agriculture in Iran has recently shown an improvement with developments in irrigation	practices and some degree of mechanization.	2,367*	9	16.5	1.5
0.2	63.1	Oil revenue has enabled the Saudi Arabians to begin to combat their country's aridity.	Plans include increased irrigation and the construction of desalination plants.	2,476*	1	10.4	0.09
0.7	40.5	Mexico has a medium-support energy system with high fertilizer input but low mechaniza-	tion. The irrigated area covers 16 percent of the total extent of cultivated land.	2,725	10	15.0	33.2
1.4	42.0	In Brazil plans are going ahead for self-sufficiency in fertilizers and agrochemicals	to provide the country with the necessary inputs for improving agriculture.	2,515	8	6.6	56.4
0.2	24.8	Irrigation is reserved for the country's sugar plantations, although this may be extended	after current land reclamation projects.	2,663	8	17.5	27.0

ARE GREEN REVOLUTIONS THE ANSWER?

manufactured goods and services) the West has provided expertise which is gradually becoming recognized as often inappropriate to the needs of less-developed countries. The single most spectacular exercise was the "green revolution," the introduction of dwarf varieties—first of grain, later of rice—specially bred to give much increased yields. However, these high-yielding varieties (HYVs) only reach their optimum under ideal conditions, with plentiful water, good drainage, large amounts of fertilizer and chemical protection against disease. If only one of these requisites is lacking, HYVs may sometimes produce less of a yield than could be obtained with traditional varieties. The green revolution was pioneered with grain in Mexico in the closing years of World War II, and the results were astounding: corn output doubled, wheat trebled between 1944 and 1967. Mexico, hitherto hard up for grain, began exporting commercial surpluses.

The green revolution was extended to rice in the early 1960s, and this time the test-bed was in the Philippines. Here again the results were little short of miraculous and for a while it began to look as if no one ever need go hungry again. For not only did the miracle crops give more per hectare but they did so with a shorter growing cycle, thus allowing two or even three plantings a year. Besides Mexico, India, Pakistan and Turkey and, to a lesser extent, Afghanistan, Nepal and North Africa between them committed more than 17 million hectares

(41.99 million acres) to these new varieties of grain from the mid-1960s to the early 1970s; in the same period the area planted to the new rice strains—in the Philippines, Taiwan, Sri Lanka and India—rose to nearly 16 million hectares (39.52 million acres). Territories with particularly propitious climates reported increases in yields of up to 50 percent.

A costly formula

However, enthusiasm for the green revolution began to wane as it became obvious that here was a formula imposing severe and costly constraints on the recipient nation. Fertilizers alone have quadrupled in price since the oil price rises of 1973-74: and, besides proving a drain on foreign reserves—few less-developed countries have their own fertilizer plants—fertilizers are in short supply (although in the United States more fertilizer is expended on tennis courts, lawns and greens than India uses for all its cultivations). Then there is the cost of imported pesticides, high-pressure sprayers, crop-dryers and other mechanical equipment. In addition, as with all large-scale monoculture, the disease risk is far-reaching. True, a high degree of disease resistance has been bred into HYVs, but the occasional blight can obliterate vast areas of crops. The rice blight which hit the Philippines in 1971 was critical enough to force the country to import.

It is also argued that the green revolution has inflicted harmful effects on nature itself. According

to a study by the UN Research Institute for Social Development (UNRISD): ". . . many local varieties of food crops are in danger of becoming extinct, so that certain genetic characteristics could be lost forever. Parts of the Near East are being described as genetic disaster areas." Also, the HYV crops are rich in carbohydrates but fairly low in protein, and whereas poor countries have traditionally sought extra protein from crops like pulses—peanuts, lentils, peas, beans—these are now being eclipsed by the new varieties. Java, for example, where soybean production was once very profitable, has suffered badly in this respect. Says the UNRISD report: ". . . there seems to have been an unwarranted haste in committing the Javanese people to new world records of protein deficiency." Since much research in the less-developed countries has been green revolution orientated, there has been little work on high-protein crops and on alternate systems of cropping using nitrogen-fixing plants to minimize dependence on chemical inputs.

The biggest disillusionment of all is that the introduction of HYVs has done little to provide the mass of poor in the less-developed world with more to eat. In Mexico, where the green revolution started and where per capita wheat production has indeed been greatly increased, most of the profits go to the owners of large, mechanized farms and the produce itself goes for export. Elsewhere, too, the capital cost of the new technology has driven many

	Fish catches ('000 tons)	Production of nonfood crops	Roundwood production ('000 cubic meters)		
United States	2,798.7	Important producer of synthetic rubber, tobacco, cotton, linseed oil, hides.	302,033	Part of US agriculture has now developed as "agribusiness"—an interaction of agriculture	and industry, of which farming is only a small sector. As a major economic power the USA
Sweden	215.3	Of minor importance.	57,810	Most of Sweden's agriculture is concentrated in the south, although the country's most	important agricultural resource is its forests, which cover 50 percent of the total land
West Germany	441.7	Important producer of synthetic rubber.	27,503	Although West Germany still relies on food imports, the country's overall self-sufficiency	in foodstuffs (1974/75) stood at 82 percent. Fish catches are important but lumber
Greece	70.7	Of minor importance.	2,730	Recent agricultural developments have included rice-growing trials on land previously	considered unfit for cultivation. Also, Greece has applied for full membership of the EEC
Hungary	30.8	Producer of hides.	5,384	Although the cooperatives of the "new economic mechanism" have faced criticism	recently, farming retains its importance with agricultural products forming a large part
USSR	9,876.0	Important producer of tobacco, cotton, wool, silk, linseed oil, hides.	395,054	Soviet agriculture, based on the collective farm and the state farm, is part of the	country's centrally planned economy. Recent developments include the reclamation of
Japan	10,508.5	Important producer of synthetic rubber, silk.	38,385	Although agriculture is characterized by small farms and a largely part-time work	force, it is, however, highly efficient. Recent changes in national diet have encouraged the
Australia	103.3	Important producer of wool, sheep skins.	14,812	Agricultural production remains a key part of the Australian economy with farm goods	(mostly wool and meat) accounting for almost 50 percent of the export trade. A
Papua New Guinea	42.7	Of minor importance.	5,760	Since independence in 1975 the government has had a long-term policy of rural improve-	ment. Yet subsistence farming leaves the country's rich agricultural resources (coastal
Tanzania	n.a.	Producer of cotton, sisal, hides.	36,444	Contrary to most of Africa, where food production has failed to match the growth of	population, Tanzanian agriculture has improved since the mid-1970s. Recent efforts
Chad	115.0	Producer of cotton.	3,624	Landlocked Chad has an extremely underdeveloped agricultural sector, although some	cotton is grown in the south for export. The extent of the country's poverty is indicated by
Ghana	254.5	Producer of tobacco, cotton.	12,531	Primarily an agricultural country, Ghana is the world's largest producer of cocoa, which	forms the bulk of its exports. Future plans include self-sufficiency in cereal production
China	6,880.0	Important producer of silk, tobacco, cotton, tung oil, castor beans, skins.	195,131	Most of the land of China (another CPE) was reorganized in the late 1950s and expansion	of the cultivated area through land reclamation, soil improvement and irrigation is in-
India	2,328.0	Important producer of tobacco, cotton, castor beans, linseed oil, hides.	127,573	Despite improved food crop yields, wheat imports are still necessary and government plans	now include improved storage facilities to cut post-harvest losses. Agricultural income
Iran	n.a.	Of minor importance.	5,239	Although industry is increasingly important in Iran, agriculture still employs most of the	population. Fishing is important and the forest resource, once carelessly treated, is
Saudi Arabia	30.0	Of minor importance.	n.a.	The Saudi Arabian economy has been transformed by massive oil revenues which have	facilitated development of the agricultural sector. Desert reclamation and dune control
Mexico	499.4	Producer of sisal, hides.	14,783	Agricultural output is expanding, with increased livestock raising and a growing fruit	and vegetable export trade to the USA. Other sources of agricultural income are
Brazil	674.5	Important producer of tobacco, castor beans, hides.	163,995	Agricultural production provides a substantial proportion of Brazil's export earnings,	although the most important agricultural resource is probably forest, which covers
Jamaica	10.1	Of minor importance.	6	Sugar is presently the principal source of foreign exchange earnings. Fruit is also	cultivated. Although much of the country is wooded, it is necessary to import to meet

small farmers out of business. In many places land values have spiralled as wealthy landowners have sought to enlarge their holdings in order to capitalize on the profits to be made from the new methods. Too often the small farmer, who is and should continue to be a key agrarian resource in less-developed countries, has found himself overrun by a revolution in which there is no room for traditional husbandry. It is perhaps significant that one of the chapters in the UNRISD report is entitled "The Final Divorce of Agriculture and Nutrition through the Agency of the Green Revolution."

System tailored to need
This is not to say that the green revolution has been of no benefit at all to developing countries. At the very least it has made possible a marketable surplus useful for sale to urban consumers and as a currency-earner overseas. But many urge that it is not an acceptable alternative for what has long been needed: land reform; the improved exploitation of local resources, including traditional methods and crops; and the curtailment of privilege (including the concentration of land and capital in fewer and fewer hands). Arguably the role of the green revolution in the future should be a much restricted one—as part of a broadly based mixed agrarian system tailored according to local opportunities and above all to need.

The first essential is that the small farmer should

be positively encouraged to stay on the land—not least because it has been shown repeatedly that in the three poor continents small units produce proportionately more food in relation to their size than larger ones. In parts of Latin America modest family farms outdo the commercial giants by as much as 14 to one; and in India holdings of less than five hectares (12 acres) can sometimes turn out up to 40 percent more food than those of 50 hectares (124 acres) or more. Also a key figure in a diversified agricultural scene is the suburban market gardener: like other small farmers he succeeds in feeding his own family and, too, shows a small surplus to be traded close at hand.

To some extent, then, there must be a revival of traditional husbandry. But there must also be more effort to secure what is known as "appropriate" technology—aids ranging from the village well to the solar collector harnessing cheap energy—to help the small man to do his job more efficiently. It is the development of low-cost technology, in countries where up to 90 percent of the population may be rural, which will arm the poor against hunger.

To date the few developing countries which have really got to grips with the food problem have done so by means of central planning and the involvement of the people in their own fate. While there are instances in the free world—South Korea, Taiwan—the most conspicuous example is, of course, China. Here it is worth recalling that 30

years ago, at a time when the Chinese were accustomed to living with starvation as a fact of life, many observers believed the new revolutionary regime was bound to fail—because a population of about 400 million was simply too great. Today, China's population has more than doubled and mass famine is manifestly a thing of the past.

Elsewhere, too, there is a growing realization that national self-reliance provides a first defense against problems of shortage, and this is something which will require a rationalization of agriculture throughout the world. For their part the rich countries must come to rely more on home produce, less on imported cash crops; for the poor countries it means a shift from economic dependence on the West to policies designed to produce plentiful staple foods (albeit leaving the door open to vary the national diet by means of trade).

It is impossible to exaggerate the severity of the global food problem. If this planet is soon to accommodate a massive increase in population—and this seems to be the one incontrovertible fact in a sea of uncertainty—it will not do so with a system of housekeeping that permits half the world to remain undernourished while the other half makes wasteful use of food. Without some radical attempt to redress the balance, we are faced with the distressing prospect that, in the developing countries at least, population control in the future may be exercised by means of famine.

	International agriculture research Center, location and date founded	Research	Coverage	1975 budget (in '000 dollars)
has high fish catches, good timber yields and produces large amounts of nonfood crops.	IRRI (International Rice Research Institute) Los Banos, Philippines 1959	Multiple cropping systems, irrigated and upland rice.	Worldwide, but particular emphasis on Asia	8,520
area, providing about four percent of the annual world production of sawn softwood.	CIMMYT (International Centre for the Improvement of Corn and Wheat) El Batan, Mexico 1964	Wheat, triticale, barley, corn.	Worldwide	6,834
requirements have to be met by imports.				
together with Spain and Portugal.	IITA (International Institute of Tropical Agriculture) Ibadan, Nigeria 1965	Farming systems, grain legumes, root and tuber crops, cereals in conjunction with IRRI and CIMMYT.	Lowland tropics, but particular emphasis on Africa	7,746
of total exports. Fish catches, timber yields and nonfood crops are of minor value.				
lands in central Asia. Fish catches are an important source of income.	CIAT (International Centre for Tropical Agriculture) Palmira, Colombia 1968	Farming systems, field beans, livestock.	Lowland tropics, but particular emphasis on Latin America	5,828
growth of the livestock sector. Japan is the foremost fishing nation in the world.				
wider range of markets has been developed recently for traditional exports.	WARDA (West African Rice Development Association) Monrovia, Liberia 1971	Cooperative rice trials among West African nations with IITA and IRRI backing.	West Africa	575
fishing grounds and timber cover over 80 percent of the land) scarcely tapped.	CIP (International Potato Centre) Lima, Peru 1972	Potatoes, particularly problems of disease and storage.	Worldwide	2,403
include the establishment of a support price for grain and plans to create a food reserve.				
the average per capita annual income for 1975—a mere £33.	ICRISAT (International Crops Research Institute for Semi-Arid Tropics) Hyderabad, India 1972	Farming systems, cereal crops, pulses.	Worldwide, but particular emphasis on semiarid tropics and nonirrigated agriculture	10,250
and the cultivation of a wider range of both industrial and cash crops.				
creasing. Fish catches are important, both offshore and from communal fish farms.	IBPGR (International Board for Plant Genetic Resources) FAO, Rome, Italy 1973	Development of seed collections including links with national collections.	Worldwide	555
is also derived to some extent from the production of nonfood crops.	ILRAD (International Laboratory for Research on Animal Diseases) Nairobi, Kenya 1974	Trypanosomiasis, theileriasis.	Africa	2,170
now subject to elaborate management and reafforestation programs.				
are given high priority in these plans.	ILCA (International Livestock Centre for Africa) Addis Ababa, Ethiopia 1974	Livestock production systems.	Tropical Africa	1,885
coastal fishing and a considerable forest resource providing commercial lumber.				
more than half the land. Exploited in the past, the forests require careful conservation.	ICARDA (International Centre for Agricultural Research in Dry Areas) Beirut, Lebanon 1977	Crop and mixed farming systems, broad beans, barley, wheat, forage improvement.	Worldwide	n.a.
lumber requirements until new afforestation programs are fully under way.				

Definitions of land use categories such as arable and permanent cropland which are used in the main tabular material are based on FAO delineation.

MINERALS—ARE WE RUNNING OUT?

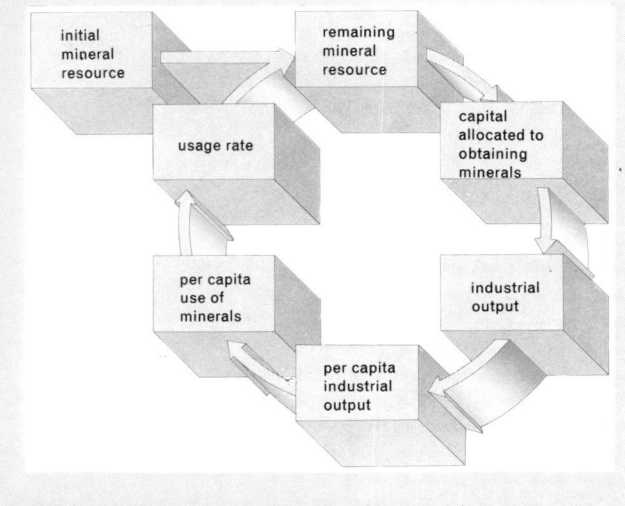

The controversy over the future of the Earth's great mineral resources has polarized at two extremes. On the one hand there are the ardent pessimists, convinced that world supplies cannot be indefinitely maintained. For ammunition they point to the continuing drain on known reserves and to the stupendous demand for minerals which is likely to be generated with full worldwide industrialization (which could materialize in less than a century from now). At best the pessimists predict an impending minerals famine; at worst a return to

an underresourced age in which a host of minerals which are familiar to us today will be reduced to being mere museum curiosities. The optimists on the other hand claim that this view is unduly alarmist, that there will still be plenty of minerals left in the Earth's crust for generations to come, and that, even though some materials may be in short supply, advancing techniques will keep pace with need.

Both sides, of course, concede that minerals can never run out in the literal sense. Even the most barren rock contains small amounts of most minerals, in what is known as the crustal abundance, and when only very small sections of the Earth's total crust are considered—say to a depth of one kilometer beneath the surface—the mineral tonnages involved are so vast as to be inexhaustible. But the problem is that profitable mining of the barren rock is unlikely ever to be possible where many of these minerals are concerned. Both sides, too, now recognize that reserves—defined as those identified resources which can be economically mined today using known technology—do not represent the total amount of mineral resources which will ever become available to us.

The significance of reserves is that they are known, and that their amount is dependent upon a specific price and upon a technology which is already developed. There are also some known

subeconomic resources, unprofitable at present but which could usefully be mined given some advance in prices or in extractive technology, and given adequate energy supplies and settled politics. In addition, it is reasonable, on the basis of geological evidence, to infer undiscovered resources. What, therefore, determines the mineral resources available at any given time is the level and extent of certain kinds of knowledge.

Price incentive

It is mineral demand which provides the incentive for increasing this pool of knowledge, and—in market economies at least—the size of the incentive is dictated by price. So, mineral flow (production and increases in reserves) and stocks (reserves/resources) are driven in the short term by prices and in the long term by a combination of prices and the advancing state of mineral knowledge. Since reserves are being depleted and added to simultaneously, the question of whether or not a particular mineral is running out is largely determined by the extent to which mineral technology can progress, and the question as to when hinges on both technology and price. The basic minerals race, then, is one between advancing technology—which adds to the usable mineral stock—and spiralling demand. Defending their position, the optimists point

	Major uses	Non-renewable resource		Annual global production (tons)	Annual global consumption (tons)	Global reserves [35] (tons)	Global resources [36] (tons)	Demand forecast for 2,000 [38] (tons)	Forecast base: 1973 production (tons)
Iron/steel	Transportation, building, machinery, cans and containers, oil and gas piping.	Yes, but relatively plentiful	95 percent of all metal mined is iron. Cheapest of metals. Essential to our civilization.	511,400,000 [1]	478,000,000 [2]	90,000 billion [3]	350,000 billion [3]	1.0 billion [39]	495,131,000
Copper	Electrical, general engineering, construction, transportation, alloys.	Yes	Three of four major exporters are UDCs. Efficient electrical/thermal conductor. Ductile.	7,296,000 [4]	7,493,500 [5]	409,500,000 [6]	1.8 billion [27]	20,202,000	7,872,000
Zinc	Galvanizing, diecasting, alloys and brass.	Yes	Resistant to corrosion. Ductile. Cheap metal.	5,892,400 [4]	5,035,400 [7]	235,000,000 [6]	1.5 billion [6]	11,238,500	6,106,100
Lead	Batteries, petroleum additives, electrical cable covering, sheet, piping, alloys.	Yes	Cheapest base metal. Pollution control reducing use in petroleum. Dense. Ductile.	3,556,100 [4]	3,904,300 [5]	150,150,000 [8]	303,300,000 [27]	6,888,700	3,712,800
Tin	Tinplate, solder, alloys, chemicals.	Yes	Most costly base metal. Soft metal with low melting point. Corrosion resistant.	205,500 [4]	211,500 [7]	3,720,004 [9]	20,776,392 [10]	340,464	239,112
Aluminum	Transportation, machinery, chemicals, nonferrous metal production, iron/steel.	Yes, but relatively plentiful	Light. Efficient electrical/thermal conductor. Smelting expensive.	79,441,900 [4]	11,600,900 [5]	12–15 billion [11]	Adequate [37]	60,387,600	16,098,810
Magnesium	Transportation, machinery, construction, packaging, electrical engineering.	Yes, but relatively plentiful	Major use is in aluminum alloys. Light, strong when alloyed. Smelting expensive.	276,400 [12]	227,400 [12]	2.5 billion [13]	Adequate [7]	10,392,200	5,123,300
Titanium	Paints, paper, transportation, rubber, plastics, ceramics, fabricated metals.	Yes, but relatively plentiful	More is used as nonmetal than metal. Light. Ductile. Strong. Corrosion resistant.	1,875,672 [15]	1,537,000 [16]	137,592,000 [17]	1.9 billion [18]	5,045,940	1,537,900
Gold	Official and private bullion holdings, coins, medallions, jewelry, dentistry, industrial.	Yes	Most malleable/ductile metal. Resists corrosion/oxidation.	1,429 [19]	1,448 [20]	41,056 [6]	59,096 [10]	1,810 [40]	945 [40]
Platinum	Car exhaust control (USA), chemical catalysts, electrical/electronic.	Yes	Superior to gold in resistance to corrosion/oxidation. Catalytic properties.	179 [21]	189 [22]	17,449 [23]	30–51,755 [24]	342 [40]	161 [40]
Silver	Photography, sterling/electroplated ware, electrical/electronic, solder, jewelry.	Yes	Efficient electrical/thermal conductor. Resists corrosion by organic acids. Ductile.	9,515 [25]	15,396 [26]	186,621 [27]	703,870 [28]	21,150 [40]	13,374 [40]
Mercury	Electrical apparatus, chlorine/caustic soda preparation, paint, industrial instruments.	Yes	Only metal liquid at normal temperatures. Efficient electrical conductor and catalyst.	9,145 [29]	7,790 [29]	170,479 [6]	590,000 [30]	9,302 [40]	7,349 [40]
Tungsten	Metal working, transportation, lamps/lighting, electrical, chemical.	Yes	Highest melting point of any metal. 2½ times heavier than iron. Hardens steel.	38,821 [31]	39,048 [32]	1,783,600 [33]	5,187,000 [34]	79,352	38,821 [40]

1 Iron content 1974, UN Statistics Yearbook
2 Iron content 1974 International Iron and Steel Institute
3 1969, UN Survey of Iron ore resources
4 Mine production 1975 Metal Statistics 1965–1975
5 Refined metal consumption 1975

Metal Statistics 1965–1975
6 1974, US Bureau of Mines
7 Metal consumption 1975 Metal Statistics 1965–1975
8 US Geological Survey professional paper 820
9 Measured + indicated reserves, US Geological Survey professional paper 820

10 Identified resources 1974, US Bureau of Mines
11 Total bauxite reserves, US Geological Survey professional paper 820
12 Primary magnesium 1975 Metal Statistics 1965–1975
13 Magnesite reserves, US Bureau of Mines (published 1976)
14 0.13 percent of weight of mineral

content of oceans is magnesium
15 Titanium content of ilmenite + rutile production 1973, US Bureau of Mines
16 Consumption in terms of titanium content 1973, US Bureau of Mines
17 Reserves of ilmenite + rutile in terms of titanium content, US Geological Survey professional paper 820

18 Identified resources, US Geological Survey professional paper 820
19 Mine production 1976 Consolidated Gold Fields Ltd
20 Gold purchases (private) 1976 Consolidated Gold Fields Ltd
21 Mine production of platinum group metals 1973 to nearest ton, US Bureau of Mines

22 Primary + secondary consumption of platinum group metals 1973 to nearest ton, US Bureau of Mines
23 Platinum group metals to nearest ton, US Bureau of Mines
24 Total resources (excluding undiscovered resources except USA and Africa) platinum group metals, US Bureau of Mines (published 1976)

to the century-long success of the mining industry in providing increased production from poorer and poorer ores—proof of its ability to advance technology in line with need. Examples cited include the fall of mineable copper grade from three percent in the 1870s to the present world average of 1.5 percent (in some places grades as low as 0.4 percent are now being profitably mined). Copper is a good example of the complexity surrounding this whole issue. The optimists, for example, quote Lasky's Rule in this context: that, as the mineable grade declines, the amount of reserves is increased (and moreover, in the case of copper, technology should be able to lower the mineable grade to 0.1 percent). In any case, if land ores become depleted, copper can be found in the nodules recovered from the deep seabed, and aluminum is already replacing copper for many applications.

Pessimists counter with the argument that Lasky's Rule only holds good for a narrow range of copper grades and for certain types of ores, yielding a much smaller value for potential copper resources. Besides scuttling the idea of winning copper from seafloor nodules, they predict an impending copper crisis with steeply rising prices fueled by runaway demand.

Less controversial examples of inexhaustible mineral resources which can be profitably exploited at today's rates include magnesium recovered from seawater and nitrogen separated out from the air. Within the Earth's crust, iron and aluminum both exist in such quantities as to be inexhaustible. In any case, the optimistic view is that the growth in demand for some minerals in the industrialized West is decelerating and that demand should finally level out. Or, in the event of depletion, there is great potential for the consumer to employ substitutes, to use less mineral content, to build in longer product life and to step up recycling of scrap.

A cautionary tale
Meanwhile, the most conspicuous weapon in the pessimists' armory is the cautionary tale of petroleum (which everyone seems to agree will sooner or later run out). They claim that, in the past, cheap mineral prices have been a reflection of cheap energy rather than a triumph of technical advance. Now we are faced with a situation where the sharp upswing in energy prices in recent years heralds endlessly rising mineral prices. In some areas, such as Canada and the United States, new reserves are becoming much more expensive to find, and this could be taken as a symptom of mineral depletion. Pessimists also point out that, while the growth in mineral demand may be slackening in the West, the clamor for minerals in less-developed countries will

intensify enormously as these emergent countries reach the take-off point in industrial development.

Midway between the two widely separated poles of the running-out controversy lies the distinct possibility that a few minerals will indeed become exhausted. But many more will pose serious problems of exploration and require considerable technological advance. Where depletion does occur, it will be a gradual process, allowing ample time for industries to look around for alternative materials. The world's economic sector has great potential for adjusting to the gradual disappearance of some raw materials without affecting the general supply of manufactured goods. But mineral supply problems will come more and more into the news. At national levels there will be increasing pressure to annex land now used for agriculture or other purposes for minerals exploitation. Internationally, mineral resources will no doubt come to feature more prominently in political power play. Our grandchildren may see a different combination of minerals in use: copper increasingly replaced by aluminum; the disappearance of gold and silver from jewelry and coin if their now vital industrial applications cannot be radically diminished; and further use of substitutes. But of the big three Earth minerals, iron and aluminum will remain in ample supply; only copper will have run out.

Assumed annual demand growth rate	Consequent depletion of present reserves by 2000	Future option: continue to use at present rate and in present manner	Future option: find substitute[42] materials or ways of reducing use of mineral	Disadvantages of substitutes	Future option: improve exploration/mining/processing techniques
2.8%	Insignificant	Reserves plentiful[41] but possible shortages of coking coal in near future.	Aluminum, plastics, fiberglass, prestressed concrete, paper/glass containers.	Plastics from oil, aluminum lacks strength, fiberglass lacks impact strength, glass/waxed paper containers fragile/will not preserve all foods.	Develop direct reduction and noncoking coals for smelting, recycle more scrap.
3.9%	84%	Present reserves could be 84 percent depleted by 2000.	Aluminum, plastics, steel, fiber optics, microprocessors, satellite communications.	Limited application of microprocessing, aluminum bulkier/lighter/less efficient conductor of heat/electricity, aluminum/steel less malleable.	Electrochemical processing, manganese nodule mining, recycle more scrap.
2.3%	100%	Present reserves could be exhausted by 2000.	Ceramic/plastic steel coatings, aluminum, electroplated steel, plastics, magnesium.	Coatings more limited applications than zinc galvanizing, cost of aluminum/magnesium in diecasting often prohibitive, aluminum/magnesium reducing agents limited.	Increase mining automation, direct reduction of ores, recycle more scrap.
2.3%	93%	Present reserves could be 93 percent depleted by 2000.	Mercury/calcium batteries, nickel in gasoline, polythene, metal/organic compounds.	Limited electrical properties of alternatives in batteries, nickel limited supply, polythene/organic and metal compound cable coverings do not resist corrosion well.	Electrochemical refining, recycle more scrap.
1.3%	100%	Present reserves could be exhausted by 2000.	Magnesium, titanium, tinplate, steel, PVC, wood, plastics, glass, waxed paper.	Aluminum containers lack strength, glass containers will not preserve all foods, plastic/aluminum piping using epoxy resins not as malleable as traditional copper piping using tin solder.	Improve mining methods, increase recovery from ore wastes, recycle more scrap.
5.0%	7%	Reserves plentiful[37] but high energy demands of smelting will raise price.	Aluminum, titanium, plastics, zinc, sodium, rare earth elements, calcium carbide.	Magnesium/titanium not economic substitutes at present, limited supplies of tin, steel heavy, plastics from oil, glass/paper fragile/not heat reflectors, wood not easily shaped.	Develop low-energy refining from bauxite/common clays, more recycling.
2.7%	100%	Present reserves[14] could be exhausted by 2000 but resources plentiful.	Plastic/ceramic coatings, intrinsic plastic colorants, clay paper coatings, tungsten.	Aluminum/titanium heavier, plastics from oil, aluminum/zinc less corrosion resistant for pipelines/lack strength. Rare earth elements for iron/steel manufacture scarcer.	Develop energy-efficient refining methods, recycle more scrap.
4.5%	58%	Present reserves could be 58 percent depleted by 2000.	Aluminum/glass containers, epoxy resin metal-joining, plastic/aluminum bearings.	Plastics from oil, tungsten in high-temperature machine parts adds unwanted weight to transportation.	Develop energy-efficient refining methods, recycle more scrap.
2.4%	61%	Present reserves could be 61 percent depleted by 2000.	Free floating/special drawing rights reserve currencies, mercury, silver, platinum.	Free-floating exchange rate creates instability for trade/investment. Limited supply of platinum/mercury (mercury amalgam dental fillings), silver less corrosion resistant.	Improve efficiency of small-scale mining, develop solution mining, deep-sea mining.
3.0%	36%	Present reserves could be 36 percent depleted by 2000.	Base metal exhaust/chemical catalysts, solid state electrical switches.	Base metal catalysts less efficient/more limited application/require development, limited supply of mercury.	Recycle more scrap.
1.7%	100%	Present reserves could be exhausted by 2000.	Light-sensitive polymers/electrostatic materials/copper, aluminum, stainless steel.	Photographic film with alternative light-sensitive materials still experimental, aluminum tubings requiring no silver solder for joining not as easily worked as traditional copper.	Improve efficiency of narrow vein mining, recycle more scrap.
0.7%	100%	Present reserves could be exhausted by 2000.	Lithium batteries, silver, glass silicate, electronic thermometers, diaphragm cells.	Shorter life of silver electrical contacts, diaphragm cells (manufacture of caustic soda/chlorine) less efficient than mercury cells, glass silicate dental fillings lack strength.	Electro-oxidation of mercury ores, recycle more scrap.
2.7%	85%	Present reserves could be 85 percent depleted by 2000.	Laser/maser metal cutting, titanium, fluorescent/wall panel lighting.	Laser/maser metal cutting requires further development, titanium does not resist stress as well at high temperatures if faults exist in the metal.	Recycle more scrap.

25 Estimate 1973, US Bureau of Mines
26 Primary + secondary consumption 1973 to nearest ton, US Bureau of Mines
27 Identified + speculative + hypothetical resources 1974, US Bureau of Mines
28 Identified resources 1974, US Bureau of Mines

29 1973, US Bureau of Mines
30 Identified resources (ore mineable at $1,000 per flask), US Geological Survey professional paper 820
31 Production in terms of tungsten content 1973, US Bureau of Mines
32 Consumption of primary + secondary tungsten 1973, US Bureau of Mines

33 In terms of tungsten content, US Bureau of Mines (published 1976)
34 Identified resources in terms of tungsten content, US Geological Survey professional paper 820
35 US Bureau of Mines reserve = portion of identified resource from which a usable mineral can be econ-

omically and legally extracted at time of determination
36 US Bureau of Mines Identified resources = specific bodies of mineral-bearing material whose location, quality and quantity are known from geological evidence supported by engineering measurement with respect to the demonstrated category, and

includes reserves and subeconomic reserves
37 Aluminum makes up 8 percent of the Earth's crust in weight
38 US Bureau of Mines Mineral Facts and Problems published 1976
39 Demand forecast probably too high
40 To nearest ton

41 Iron makes up 5 percent of the Earth's crust by weight
42 Only some of possible substitutes are included

MINERALS—ASSESSING FUTURE SUPPLIES

Earth minerals—metallic and nonmetallic, liquid and stone—represent a complex of resources which support and sustain all aspects of our existence, from the smallest coin to the largest ocean liner, from the trace elements in our diet to our buildings, industry, means of transport, communications and defense systems, even fertilizer for our land. All these things and many more depend on our ability to find concentrated mineral resources and to exploit them at prices we can afford. If the supply of minerals were ever seriously diminished, civilization itself would be threatened.

On the face of it, the threat is hardly a pressing one. The continental landmasses, the seas and the ocean beds contain enough of practically all the desired elements to keep humanity going for thousands of years to come. The question is whether this natural wealth can be exploited and how. The whole issue of mineral resources—involving political and strategic considerations as well as purely economic ones—is now so complex that governments are increasingly reluctant to leave the future of vital raw materials solely to free enterprise. To some extent control of mineral output has been an aspect of government activity for centuries. Close control of salt production by the Egyptian dynasties, by the Greek city-states, by medieval monarchs in Poland,

Austria and indeed throughout central Europe, and state supervision of the silver mines at Kongsberg in Norway and the Mines Royal in England all serve as examples of the long-standing interference of governments with individual enterprise. From the time of the Industrial Revolution many Western governments began to set up geological survey organizations to establish where valuable minerals existed beneath their lands.

Environmental controls

In many countries today minerals are regarded as state property, not as part of the estate of individual landowners. Even where this is not the case, planning restrictions tend to place mineral development under rigid control. In recent years the response of some governments to pressure from environmentalists has been to place considerable constraints on the activities of the extractive industries. In the United States, for example, where two decades ago 19 percent of federal lands were available for prospecting, environmental legislation has led to the closing of two-thirds of these areas.

If some of the less optimistic assessments are right—that we are in danger of exhausting some of the important workable minerals—then there would be a case for conservation and the limiting of consumption. The question is whether or not it

is essential to curtail the consumption of minerals drastically in the interest of future generations (even if this were politically feasible), and this is something which, on the basis of existing data, it is almost impossible to decide. Many mining enterprises have so far been able to maintain reserves equivalent in tonnage to 10 to 15 years' production at current rates. Most concerns, however, are unwilling to finance investigations beyond this point and any calculation of longer-term resource tonnage is therefore highly speculative.

However, the desire of many governments for a more complete picture of mineral resources is evidenced not least by the marked increase in state-sponsored geological survey activity during this century. The case of the USSR is perhaps the most striking. There, prior to 1917, was a land neglected by geologists and prospectors, with some of the few mines outside the Urals owned and operated by British companies. But the huge mineral potential of the Soviet landmass has been exposed by an All-Union survey project. This has enabled the USSR to take the lead in the production of many minerals, especially those essential to its heavy industry, including the manufacture of armaments. Similarly, if not quite on the same scale, other countries have stepped up their efforts substantially. Developing countries, for instance, recognize

	Major uses	Non-renewable resource		Annual global production (tons)	Annual global consumption (tons)	Global reserves[23] (tons)	Global resources[24] (tons)	Demand forecast for 2000 (tons)[21]	Forecast base: 1973 production (tons)
Salt	Chemicals, deicing, paper/food products, glass/ceramics, plastics, agriculture.	Yes, but plentiful	Major source of caustic soda and chlorine. Cheap to mine, win from sea and to process.	150,628,660[1]	150,954,440[1]	Adequate[2]	Adequate[2]	687,778,000	150,954,440
Sulfur	Manufacture of sulfuric acid and other chemicals, fertilizers.	Yes	Large amounts produced as byproduct of petroleum/coal/metal refining at present.	46,678,000[1]	42,312,000[1]	1.9 billion[3]	5.3 billion[4]	108,240,000	42,312,000
Phosphate rock	Fertilizers, detergents, animal feeds, food products.	Effectively	Most important mineral used by the fertilizer industry.	98,678,000[1]	101,498,670[1]	16.1 billion[5]	76.3 billion[3]	414,960,000	101,498,670
Potash	Fertilizers, chemicals.	Yes		21,708,050[6]	21,840,000[7]	10 billion[8]	79.2 billion[9]	54,600,000	21,840,000
Fluorspar	Chemicals, flux in iron/steel production, refining aluminum/magnesium, ceramics.	Yes	Most important source of fluorine for chemical industry (phosphate also used).	2,068,430[10]	2,068,430[10]	72,254,000[11]	342,706,000	6,679,400	2,068,430
Feldspar	Ceramics, glass.	Yes, but plentiful	One of the most abundant minerals in the Earth's crust.	2,542,540[1]	2,275,000[1]	910,000,000[3]	Adequate[3]	7,280,000	2,275,000
Crushed stone	Construction-roadstone/cement/concrete, soil improvers, metal smelting flux.	Yes, but plentiful	Deposits virtually ubiquitous. Intrinsic low value. Requires little processing.	4.6 billion[1]	34,165,950[1]	Adequate[13]	Adequate[13]	13.4 billion	4.6 billion
Building stone	Construction, cut stone products.	Yes, but plentiful	Deposits virtually ubiquitous. Higher value than crushed stone. Needs little processing.	34,052,200[1]	4.6 billion[1]	Adequate[13]	Adequate[13]	44,317,000	34,165,950
Sand and gravel	Road construction, heavy construction, general building, iron/steel casting, glass.	Yes, but plentiful	Deposits in almost all countries. More sand/gravel produced than other minerals.	6.3 billion[1]	6.3 billion[1]	Adequate[14]	Adequate[14]	15.7 billion[19]	6.3 billion
Clays	Construction-bricks/tiles/cement/aggregates, refractories, paper, ceramics glass.	Yes, but plentiful	Use subject to availability of deposits, building traditions, labor costs.	527,800,000[1]	527,800,000[1]	Adequate[14]	Adequate[14]	965,519,000	527,800,000
Gypsum	Construction-building plasters/cement retarders, soil conditioners.	Yes, but plentiful	Use of plaster board has grown faster than any other building material.	69,663,400[1]	67,400,100[1]	1.8 billion[1]	Adequate[14]	113,568,000	67,400,100
Asbestos	Construction-flooring/roofing/pipes/sheet, packing, gaskets, insulation, textiles.	Yes	Heat-insulating properties. Strength of fibers greater than steel. Resistance to acid.	4,184,160[1]	4,184,160[1]	145,000,000[18]	83.2 billion[4]	9,595,040	4,184,180
Industrial diamond	Drills, saws, tools, bores, wire drawing dies, grinding wheels, abrasives.	Yes, but can be synthesized	Industrial quality synthesized diamonds becoming increasingly important.	15[15]	15[15]	136[16]	Limited[17]	44[20]	15[15]

1 1973, US Bureau of Mines
2 The oceans are effectively a limitless supply
3 US Bureau of Mines (published 1976)
4 Identified resources. US Bureau of Mines (published 1976)
5 Estimated recoverable reserves at $27.66 per short ton, published

Phosphate Rock Export Association 70 BPL price f.o.b. Florida plant effective July 1st 1974 and competitively marketed at this selling price. US Bureau of Mines (published 1976)
6 Marketable potash K₂O equivalent 1973, US Bureau of Mines
7 K₂O equivalent 1973. US Bureau of Mines

8 At 1974. USA mine prices K₂O equivalent, US Bureau of Mines (published 1976)
9 Total resources in terms of K₂O. US Bureau of Mines (published 1976)
10 Fluorine content of fluorspar and phosphate 1973. US Bureau of Mines
11 Reserves of fluorine in fluorspar and phosphate 1974. US Bureau of

Mines
12 Identified resources of fluorine in fluorspar and phosphate 1974. US Bureau of Mines
13 Stone deposits ubiquitous
14 Lack of data but large deposits throughout the world
15 Natural diamond crushing bort + synthesized diamonds to nearest ton

1973. US Bureau of Mines
16 Natural diamond crushing bort to nearest ton 1973. US Bureau of Mines
17 Data not available
18 Based on average US price of asbestos in 1974 of $122 per ton. US Bureau of Mines
19 Forecast probably too high
20 To nearest ton

21 "Mineral Facts and Problems." US Bureau of Mines (published 1976)
22 Only some of possible substitutes are included
23 US Bureau of Mines reserve = portion of identified resource from which a usable mineral can be economically and legally extracted at time of determination

that it is greatly in their interest to know what resources their territories contain, and geological surveys have been undertaken. The Western democracies and Japan have had to expand their imports from developing nations as their own resources have proved inadequate

Mapping of mineral deposits can be done with varying degrees of confidence: satellite and aerial photography as a preliminary; ground survey followed by drilling for more specific determinations. Already a large proportion of the Earth's continents, together with some parts of the continental shelves, has been covered by geological mapping at scales between 1:100,000 and 1:250,000. At the larger scale (between 1:50,000 and 1:10,000) necessary for resource planning, only the Western European countries are at an advanced stage.

Estimates of potential
The United States has taken a leading role in bringing together estimates of global mineral potential. The 1952 Report of the Paley Commission, the US Bureau of Mines' data on reserves and the US Geological Survey's massive 1973 document (covering not only North America but other countries besides) constitute the best freely available summaries. Nevertheless, some US observers, anxious for firmer evidence as to how long mineral

resources will last, have advocated the drilling of a grid-pattern of boreholes right across the States to find out what deposits may lie beneath the surface. Such an expensive, all-embracing enterprise is probably not called for yet, but the technique is one which has already been applied in the United Kingdom, where the Institute of Geological Sciences is drilling boreholes at one kilometer intervals in an attempt to establish where sand and gravel resources exist.

In the USSR and other Eastern bloc countries, the favorable results of geological surveys are passed along to a state mineral development organization. Once workable deposits have been proved, the appropriate state industry undertakes the work of extraction. While some Western critics regard these state complexes as cumbersome and inefficient, it cannot be denied that they do achieve results. In many Western countries private enterprise undertakes prospecting, development and exploitation as independently as possible of government, but the whole operation is so highly speculative that a generous profit margin must be sought. Government surveys do, therefore, play some part in the exploratory stages of the work. For example, when members of the Geological Survey of Canada return from fieldwork in northern Canada to their base in Ottawa each September,

they immediately prepare summary reports on the new territory just examined, to be issued free to all interested parties. Would-be developers are usually waiting with helicopters to get on to the ground to stake their claims. While this Klondike-style speculation has at times achieved the status almost of a national pastime in countries like Canada and Australia, rising costs, statutory restrictions, currency variations and labor difficulties have all combined to make high profits more elusive, and in some places government intervention has occurred for both practical and doctrinaire reasons.

At present there are no grounds for an overconfident view as to our ability to maintain supplies of minerals, particularly with world energy prices continuing to rise. For energy cost is the factor most likely to determine the grades of ores which can be worked. At the same time, while obvious waste is to be avoided, a restrictive conservation policy with regard to minerals can hardly be justified on the basis of known facts. What is needed is further geological and geophysical exploration, coupled with more investigation of methods of processing and recycling, more studies of alternative materials and more attention to the reasonable preservation or restoration of the environment. Exhaustion of the world's vast mineral resources is not yet in sight, but clearly in this area knowledge is power.

Assumed annual demand growth rate	Consequent depletion of present reserves by 2000	Future option: continue to use at present rate and in present manner	Future option: find substitute materials or ways of reducing use of mineral	Disadvantages of substitutes	Future option: improve exploration mining processing techniques
5.8%	Insignificant	Salt content of oceans sufficient for any forseeable future demand.	Mineral cheap and plentiful. Substitution unnecessary.		Increase production from oceans.
3.5%	96%	Present reserves could be 96 percent depleted by 2000.	Fertilizers from phosphates/waste. Replace sulfuric with hydrochloric acid.	Phosphates nonrenewable resource. Waste collection/conversion requires further development. Hydrochloric acid limited substitute.	Increase production from "cleaning" metals/oil/coal. Sulfuric acid recycling.
5.4%	37.9%	Present reserves could be 37.9 percent depleted by 2000.	Fertilizers/animal feed from waste. Restrict use of phosphoric acid in soft drinks.	Waste collection/conversion requires development.	Develop mining from non-conventional phosphorus-containing rock sources.
3.5%	10%	Present reserves could be exhausted by 2000.	Substitution unnecessary.		Large-scale development of potash extraction from lakes/seawater/brines.
4.4%	100%	Present reserves would not be significantly depleted by 2000. Resources plentiful.	Liquid nitrogen/lithium chloride refrigerants. Reduce use of aerosol fluorocarbons.	Limited applications of alternative refrigerants.	
4.4%	13%	Present reserves would not be significantly depleted by 2000.	Substitution unnecessary.		Extract feldspar from granite.
4.0%	Insignificant	Environmental regulations/urban development may sterilize some future supplies.	Sintered heavy clay/shales, fly ash, slag. Magnesia for refractories.	Limited applications of alternative aggregate materials.	Develop underground mining. Rehabilitation of worked-out quarries.
1.0%	Insignificant	Environmental regulations/urban development may sterilize some future supplies.	Concrete, plaster/asbestos board, steel, aluminum, bricks, artificial stone.	May not be considered satisfactory for renovation of old/historic buildings.	Develop underground mining. Rehabilitation of worked-out quarries.
3.5%	Insignificant	Environmental regulations/urban development may sterilize some future supplies.	Lightweight aggregates. Brick facing panels. Ceramic iron casting molds.	Limited applications of lightweight aggregates.	Increase marine/beach mining. Rehabilitation of worked-out quarries.
2.3%	Insignificant	Environmental regulations/urban development may sterilize some future supplies.	Fly ash/waste glass bricks. Concrete, asbestos/plaster board, steel.		Rehabilitation of worked-out quarries.
2.0%	100%	Present reserves could be exhausted by 2000, but resources are plentiful.	Substitution unnecessary.		Rehabilitation of worked-out quarries.
3.2%	100%	Present reserves could be exhausted by 2000.	Ceramic/plastic roofing and floors. Cement pipes. Mineral wool/glass wool insulation.	Plastics from oil. Mineral wool/glass wool lack tensile strength of asbestos fiber. Not acid resistant.	Increase fiber recovery from rock. Automation/computer-controlled asbestos milling.
4.2%	Natural diamond 100%	Present natural diamond reserves could be exhausted by 2000.	Synthetically manufactured industrial diamonds.	High energy requirements of diamond synthesizing process.	Improve energy efficiency of synthesizing process.

24 US Bureau of Mines identified resources = specific bodies of mineral-bearing material whose location, quality and quantity are known from geological evidence supported by engineering measurement with respect to the demonstrated category, and includes reserves and subeconomic reserves

WORLD MODELS

One of the most striking uses to which modern computers have been put is producing forecasts of the world of tomorrow. World models were first brought to the attention of the public in 1972, with the publication of *The Limits to Growth*, which rapidly became a best-seller in many languages. This book was hailed as a remarkable confirmation of current fears about the exhaustion of natural resources and the threat of ecological imbalance—a confirmation backed by the authority of a computer. A team at the distinguished Massachusetts Institute of Technology had applied the study of system dynamics aided by the powerful capacities of modern electronic computers to build a computer model of the world—one which integrated forecasts of population growth, food supply, pollution, resource depletion and investment to present a holistic view of the future.

What provoked so much public attention was the ominous nature of the conclusions produced by what seemed to be an ultrascientific method of analysis. For the MIT analysis suggested in no uncertain terms that, without drastic and immediate steps to limit economic and population growth, industrial society in the twenty-first century would face a major crisis—a crisis that was promptly labeled doomsday. The problems of food shortage, pollution and exhausted resources were to lead inexorably to catastrophe unless the present pattern of growth was curbed.

The questions raised by this study are obviously important. But while the advent of powerful computers has made the building of world models possible, the mystique of these devices has meant that they are often accepted at face value or as producing results that are somehow beyond debate. We are most used to the term model being applied

to toys—to scale representations of trains, aircraft and the like. In addition, architects build models of their designs to demonstrate their appearance and structural properties, and aircraft designers test the aerodynamic properties of their designs by using models in wind tunnels. Full-scale models are also often used to test designs and in training exercises. For example, simulations of aircraft cockpits give would-be pilots experience in controlling airplanes. Simulations of this sort set out to reproduce the behavior of the thing being modeled. The trainee pilot is able to test, in safety, the effects of various actions, as the dials in the cockpit simulate responses to different movements of the control column, different speeds, and so on.

Many computer models are simulations, too. But computer models make no attempt to look like whatever is being modeled. Instead, they try to tell the operator about the behavior of the subject in the language that computers know best, numbers. A computer model is set up to give a numerical picture of how the world might be changing. It can give reports concerning trends in the world that can be expressed in numerical terms—for example, population levels, rates of economic growth, and the like. More precisely, the computer gives reports concerning the behavior of its simulation model of the world, and this is crucially different from reporting on the world itself. For, unlike a building or an aircraft, the world has not been designed by the modeler. The world model cannot hope to capture every aspect of world events: it only contains those features that the modeler considers to be relevant and so chooses to incorporate.

A computer modeler treats the world as a system. In building a model, the task is to specify the important variables and relationships between variables

that are to be taken into account. The variables and relationships may themselves be quite simple to talk about without using a computer. For example, we might argue that the relationship between investment in agriculture and food supply is a positive one, that more investment will lead to more food being produced. Computer models, however, have two advantages.

Numerical precision

First, computer models describe the relationships in mathematical, algebraic form. This means that they call for numerically precise specifications of the relationship: just what effect would a given increase in investment mean for food supply? In turn, they produce very precise results, expressed in figures rather than in more qualitative words. This, however, can be a disadvantage. It may be forgotten that the accuracy of a forecast depends primarily upon the validity of the assumptions used concerning the variables and the relationships between them, and only secondarily upon whether it is presented in numbers or not.

Second, the ability of the computer to handle many calculations simultaneously means that many more variables and relationships may be taken into account than is generally possible for the unaided human intellect. For example, we could also take into account the effects of industrial pollution and labor supply on food production, and relate these in turn to industrial investment, population growth and a host of other factors. Again, there is a disadvantage associated with the power of the computer. This time, the problem is that it may be difficult for even the modelers themselves to say which of a large number of relationships are the crucial ones in determining the model's behavior.

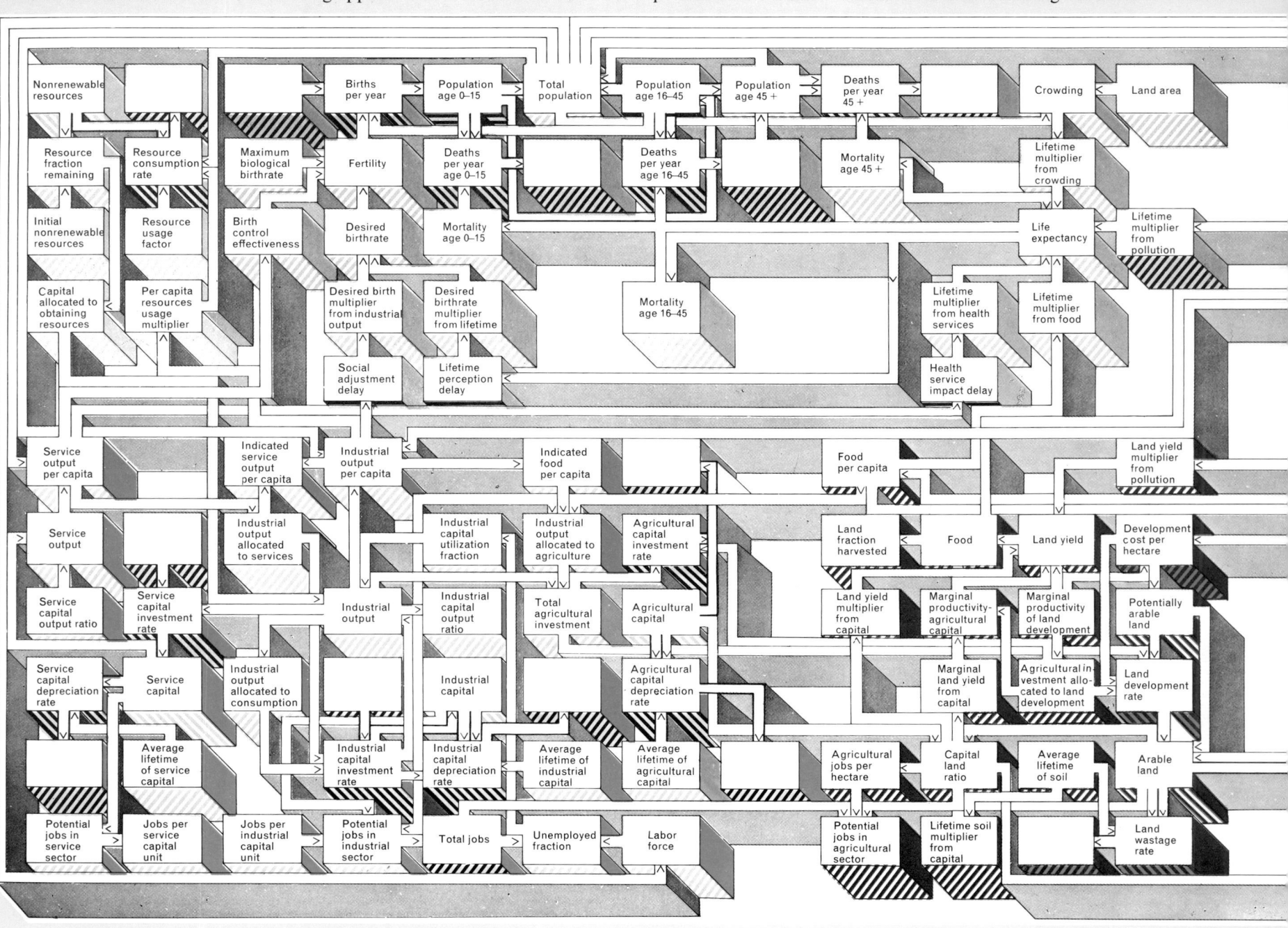

The computer, then, is a versatile and immensely useful tool but there are limitations on its use in the context of world models. It must be recognized that a computer model can only be as good as the assumptions upon which it is based. Much of the difference between the forecasts produced by different modelers is due to their being based on different assumptions. It should also be remembered that a world model must be calibrated—data has to be fed in concerning the state of the real world at present in terms of the variables involved. Again, the quality of these data is important; it can make a big difference if there are assumed to be 50, rather than 500 years' supply of oil in the Earth, for example. The computer has no power to correct errors that are built into a model. What it can do, however, is to perform immensely complex and rapid calculations which will tell us what would happen if the model does provide an adequate simulation of the real world.

How world models have evolved

The first generation of world models, like that used in *The Limits to Growth*, were very much a product of the environmental debate. They took the world as a single global system, rather than as a set of interacting regions. There was no consideration, for example, of how pollution levels or resource availability might vary from place to place. Food and resources were not broken down into different sorts of foodstuff and different raw materials.

Although some critics argued that the first world models in the early 1970s were already too complicated to be easily understood and evaluated, later modelers have, in the main, tried to go beyond global aggregations by taking into account more regions and variables. This means that the models

may become very detailed. The model used in *Mankind at the Turning Point*, which groups the world into ten regions, involves several hundred times the number of relationships which were featured in *The Limits to Growth*.

Probably the most striking feature of the more recent models is that none of them predicts the sort of ecological catastrophe forecast in *The Limits to Growth*. Much of the criticism of the early studies related to the pessimistic assumptions on which they were based concerning such things as resource availability, food supply and pollution, and particularly the possible development of technology to head off emerging problems.

While some of the more recent models point to continuing problems of food supply in certain regions (notably southern Asia) into the twenty-first century, they are generally much more optimistic about overall resource and environmental issues. Reflecting the course of the international debate, the recent studies have tended to focus much more on differences between regions, especially the rich industrial and the poor underdeveloped regions of the world. Modelers tend to agree that a projection of current trends into the future would lead to a widening or, at least, to constant and huge gaps in income between rich and poor countries.

Of these more recent studies, the United Nations Input-Output Model, *The Future of the World Economy*, is most concerned with demonstrating that there are no insurmountable physical limits to rapid growth in less-developed countries. It does so basically by calculating what pollution-abatement activities, resource availability, trade and investment would be needed for the levels of economic and population growth involved if the income gap between rich and poor nations is to be halved. Most

other studies have focused on the mainly economic changes they see necessary to produce a more equitable pattern of world development.

Perhaps the most distinctive model is that produced by the Latin-American Bariloche group, *Catastrophe or New Society?* This sets out to show that it would be possible to create a world in which everyone's basic needs (for food, housing, etc.) were met. The model does not predict that this is the future which faces the world. It simply argues that, if incomes were distributed more evenly within regions, and goods were produced according to social need rather than for private gain, this future could be realized.

Debating the future

With its picture of a radically transformed world, the Bariloche model may seem to be taking us far from scientific forecasting and into the world of politics. But it is important to remember that all world models necessarily involve assumptions about the world political system, if only by default. The shift of emphasis among modelers from concern with ecological matters to concern with international economics, involves a changing perception of political priorities. It also illustrates the central role played by conceptualization and selection of topics by the modeler.

As long as the mystique of the computer is not allowed to paralyze us, modeling can be a particularly useful way of thinking about the future precisely because it does call for assumptions to be made clearly and precisely. As long as the outputs from the computer are not taken as being somehow any better than the data and model that are put into it, they can be useful as guides for planning and debating the future course of world development.

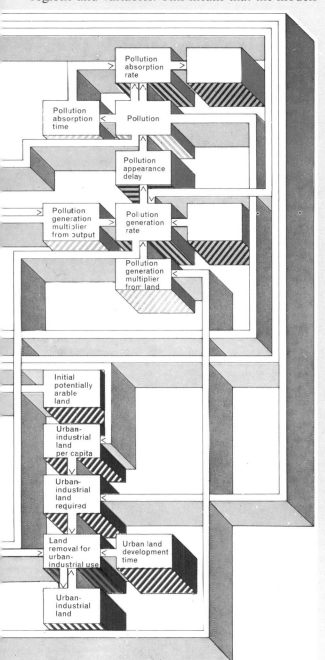

Name of model	Project leaders	Main Publications	Comments
World 2	J. Forrester (USA)	*World Dynamics* (MIT Press, 1971)	This was the first world model, commissioned by The Club of Rome as a trial run for *The Limits to Growth*. A relatively small model, using very little real-world data, the forecasts produced were as doom-laden as those of *Limits*.
World 3	D. Meadows (USA)	*The Limits to Growth* (Earth Island/Universe Books, 1972)	Also for the Club of Rome, the pessimistic forecast of this model first brought computer simulation to the awareness of the public. Again, the world was treated as a single region.
"A New Vision for Development"	Y. Kaya	(no popular publication)	This work carried out for the Japanese Club of Rome moved away from the ecological issues taken up in the first two studies and asked questions about the optimum global distribution of industry. Nine world regions were studied.
"Strategy for Survival"	M. Mesarovich, E. Pestel (USA West Germany)	*Mankind at the Turning Point* (Dutton, 1974)	A Club of Rome modeling study, this attempted to provide insight into many global problems. The study involves 10 regions, and can be used as an interactive "game" in which human participants can make decisions about policy issues arising as the model runs.
Sarum	P. Roberts (UK)	(no popular publication)	Following the publication of *Limits*, the UK Department of the Environment decided to construct its own world model. Three world regions (rich, middle, poor) were taken, the aim being to consider policy issues, e.g. energy.
Moira	H. Linneman (Netherlands)	(no popular publication)	This program focuses on world agriculture and on problems of food supply and distribution. One conclusion is that the maximum possible level of food production using present-day technology is 30 times higher than current production.
"Alternative World Model" (Bariloche)	A. Herrera (Argentina/Brazil)	*Catastrophe or New Society?* (IDRC, Ottawa, 1976)	Dividing the world into four and then 15 regions, this study set out to challenge the *Limits to Growth* thesis by demonstrating that basic human needs could be provided for with appropriate social and political changes. This model develops a vision of what could be from the point of view of the less-developed countries.
UN World Model	W. Leontief (USA)	*The Future of the World Economy* (OUP, 1977)	This study was commissioned by the UN to investigate raw material requirements and investment necessary for rapid development in less-developed countries up to the year 2000. Using 15 world regions, it is an "input-output" study rather than an orthodox simulation model: it explores the feasibility rather than the dynamics of patterns of world development.

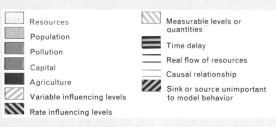

☐ Resources	▨ Measurable levels or quantities	
▤ Population	▬ Time delay	
▨ Pollution	── Real flow of resources	
▨ Capital	── Causal relationship	
▨ Agriculture	▨ Sink or source unimportant to model behavior	
▨ Variable influencing levels		
◥ Rate influencing levels		

The world model used in The Limits to Growth *(left) was divided into five interconnecting sections and analyzed global patterns of growth in order to predict the state of the world as it will appear if current trends continue.*

A simplified version (right) of three sectors of the world model from The Limits to Growth *shows the relationships between population growth and food per capita and demonstrates that the capital sector eventually affects agricultural capital and, therefore, the amount of food produced. Wastes from industrial output and the increased use of pesticides, however, create pollution which may contaminate food, thus increasing the mortality rate and, ultimately, affecting population growth.*

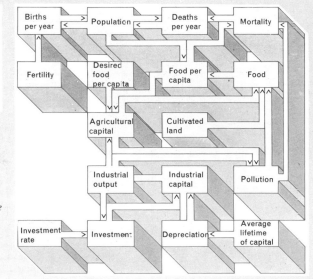

POWER POLITICS

I t is reasonable to assume that in the next 50 years the nations of the world will continue to practice power politics, in the sense that each will use power and influence to obtain what it wants; and many, if not most, will be prepared to risk war to safeguard vital territory and resources. The roots of this situation lie deep in history, economics and psychology. And, as a result, we must accept that the danger of armed conflict will continue, and that the likelihood of world government or of consensus between states is remote.

Wars and rumors of wars
This does not mean that war is inevitable, if by that we mean armed conflict between the major powers. Local fighting tends to flare up intermittently, such as that in 1978 between Ethiopia and Somalia, and between Vietnam and Kampuchea. These were essentially wars about frontiers arising from boundary changes in the past which had confined one ethnic group within the territory of another group. They were also wars fought with conventional weapons between states which in the military sense are relatively weak.

These are quite different from wars between great powers, especially between the superpowers because of their advanced nuclear arsenals. At first sight war between these might seem likely to break out at any time, if only because of the way they occasionally square up to each other. In Europe there is tension between the two Germanies and between the NATO and Warsaw Pact armies, which face each other equipped with the latest conventional and nuclear weapons, and are backed by navies and air forces of immense power. A similar situation exists along the Asian boundary between the Soviet Union and China.

War between the superpowers is unlikely to break out in the foreseeable future, not because the big powers are more virtuous than the smaller ones but because neither side is willing to commit suicide in order to destroy the other. There would seem to be only two ways in which the superpowers can contend for supremacy in the next 50 years or so. One is by peaceful competition; the other is by using smaller nations to fight proxy wars on their behalf. It is likely that both of these methods will be used.

The continuing Middle East conflict has many of the elements of a proxy struggle; so has the contest over the copper resources of Zaire. In Latin America and in parts of Asia and Africa, the United States and the Soviet Union compete with one another in terms of economic aid, markets for local products, investment and the provision of military training and equipment.

Carving up the world
Continued hostility between the United States and the Soviet Union is likely because both are strong and each sees its way of life as directly pitted against the other's, and is equally determined to restrict its rival's sphere of influence. China will also have to be regarded as a superpower before long, if not now, and the Chinese government seems likely to continue to pursue an independent line.

What kinds of blocs will be based on these three major states? It is tempting to think that they will divide the world between them, but experience suggests that this is an oversimplified view. In the 1950s there existed a Western bloc, a Soviet bloc and certain nonaligned states; but none of those groups is today as cohesive as it was and there are many newly independent states plowing a lonely furrow. The pattern now is one of a series of associations in terms of the economies of various states rather than their military strength or social systems.

At present there are three of these loosely bound associations: the so-called "group of 77," which now includes many more than 77 less-developed nations; the socialist states, especially those dependent on the Soviet Union; and the capitalist countries of the West, including Western Europe, North and South America (excluding Cuba), Australia and New Zealand, Japan and, in some respects, South Africa. So loose are these "blocs" that even the socialist countries of Eastern Europe are actively engaged in competing for trade and investment among the capitalist countries. Less-developed countries display various stages of development, with correspondingly different needs.

And the Western countries are divided, not only by economic competition but also by differences of outlook. The three so-called economic blocs exist partly because of contractual obligations within them and partly because some sort of organization is required when states take part in international negotiations on trade, tariffs and the like.

The utility of such groupings may not survive. They may be replaced in the foreseeable future by regional blocs, such as exist at present in Western Europe, Southeast Asia, the Caribbean and Africa, that is, groups of countries with similar economic needs, convinced that they will gain more from negotiating together rather than separately.

Given that the established superpowers may find it difficult to keep more than a nucleus of like-minded states in close association, and that most states will be able to maintain a variety of associations at regional and global levels, is it possible that more superpowers may arise, or are the United States and the Soviet Union already so powerful that they will forever maintain their lead? There is a sense in which power breeds power, as money is said to make money, and the two superpowers have already developed such a momentum in the technical development of weaponry that no other state could realistically hope to overtake them. Yet at the same time it should be recognized that a level of technology that produces unacceptable damage by nuclear weapons has already been reached, and that going beyond this into "overkill" may be a waste of time. Moreover, any other state that reaches this level can be as formidable a threat as the other nuclear powers provided it can deliver its deadly load on target.

Under these circumstances, China is the immediately obvious candidate for superpower status. Its acute hostility toward the Soviet Union, together with its deep suspicion of the United States,

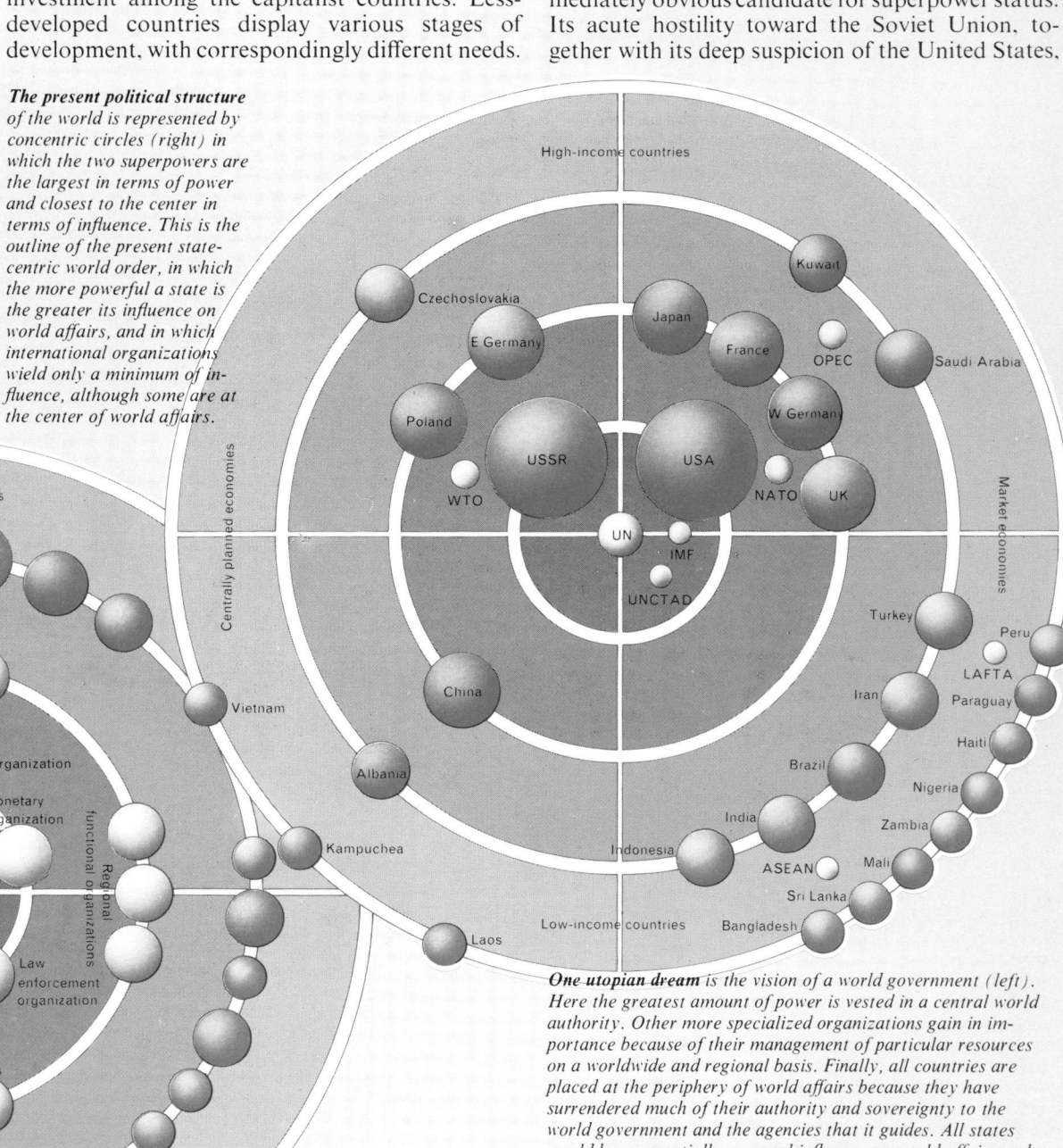

The present political structure of the world is represented by concentric circles (right) in which the two superpowers are the largest in terms of power and closest to the center in terms of influence. This is the outline of the present state-centric world order, in which the more powerful a state is the greater its influence on world affairs, and in which international organizations wield only a minimum of influence, although some are at the center of world affairs.

One utopian dream is the vision of a world government (left). Here the greatest amount of power is vested in a central world authority. Other more specialized organizations gain in importance because of their management of particular resources on a worldwide and regional basis. Finally, all countries are placed at the periphery of world affairs because they have surrendered much of their authority and sovereignty to the world government and the agencies that it guides. All states would have essentially an equal influence on world affairs under a world government.

has helped to accelerate its nuclear strike potential and it has all the requirements to assure itself of an independent bargaining position from strength. It seems unlikely that any other power will emerge with the same combination of hostility toward the superpower hegemony and determination to achieve complete independence. In the Latin American context it has sometimes been suggested that Brazil or Argentina might become a superpower one day. If superpower status were based simply on abundance of resources, this might be so. But there must also be the will to get on top, the social cohesiveness to make this possible, and the widespread conviction that the gains of the present will disappear in the future if the existing superpowers are not challenged. China meets these requirements; it is very hard to see either Brazil or Argentina doing the same.

The only other nation that might also qualify under different circumstances is Japan. Japan is constitutionally a nonnuclear state although it is often cited as an economic superpower, dependent on foreign sources for raw materials. For defence purposes, Japan has relied on the US nuclear umbrella. If the United States were to withdraw its guarantees, and if the Soviet Union appeared to threaten its supply lines, there might be strong pressure from within Japan to opt for superpower status by developing sophisticated nuclear weapons.

International organizations

So far it has been assumed that individual states are likely to continue the pursuit of their own interests largely unhindered by any influences other than fears for their own safety if they push those interests too far. It is important to inquire what influences are likely to be exerted in the next 50 years or so by international bodies, whether public or private. International organizations such as the United Nations, the World Health Organization, the International Monetary Fund and the World Bank have become increasingly active in the last few decades. Their greatest influence lies in the economic and technological fields, where their activities take on two different aspects: as operations by semiautonomous international officials, striving to achieve what the "international community" wants; and as operations that ultimately rest on the pursuit of national interests by the member states and which cannot be taken further than those states allow. The first sense represents a kind of common denominator of the second. Ultimately these organizations can do only what their members will allow, particularly what their richer members will finance. Can such a process continue?

There is no compelling reason to believe that it cannot. It is essentially a process attended by strain but it has aspects that are unlikely to change. For example, the markets of the Western capitalist countries appear to be indispensable to the great majority of the less-developed nations, and there is little indication that the Soviet Union or China could replace them, thereby reducing the influence of the West on the poorer states. In addition, there is scant willingness on the part of the less-developed nations to submit themselves, as suppliers of raw materials to the West, to the barter process which the socialist states substitute for market operations. On such a basis there is room for constructing the consensus required to keep international organizations in being.

Regional organizations are rather different from the universal organizations of the UN "family" because the member states are likely to have closer economic ties. ASEAN (Association of Southeast Asian Nations) and the OAU (Organization for African Unity) are both examples in which the member states see a limited but real community of interests when they confront the outside world. All international bodies have to cope with the problem of national sovereignty, in the sense that if a state is to derive continued advantages from the parent body, it must submit to a certain amount of discipline. If it opts out it will in the long run be working against its own interests.

It has sometimes been suggested that the increasingly interdependent nature of the world in the use of natural resources such as mineral wealth and those found in the seas, the atmosphere and the rivers will require new forms of international cooperation, indeed of world order. Some authorities even go so far as to prophesy that the sovereign state is doomed. Does this mean a real change in current power politics?

The answer is yes and no. It is in the affirmative to the extent that cooperation between states in such areas as exploitation of the seas and space will increase and require new international bodies to administer the resulting agreements. But the answer is in the negative to the extent that there are few signs as yet that, when it comes to the crunch, any nation really does regard an international body as superior to its own state machinery. Instead we see states extending their functions and authority more and more, in providing for their own citizens and in cooperation with other states. As a result, we can expect new forms of negotiation and agreement between countries, and perhaps a few more tightly drawn regional arrangements such as the EEC. But the EEC itself shows no sign of displacing the states that comprise it and there is unlikely to be any development of what might be called international loyalty. The individual states are the obvious focuses of loyalty through their appeal to national integrity and through the emotive effect of national symbols. Against this, the symbols of the world are still extremely pallid by comparison.

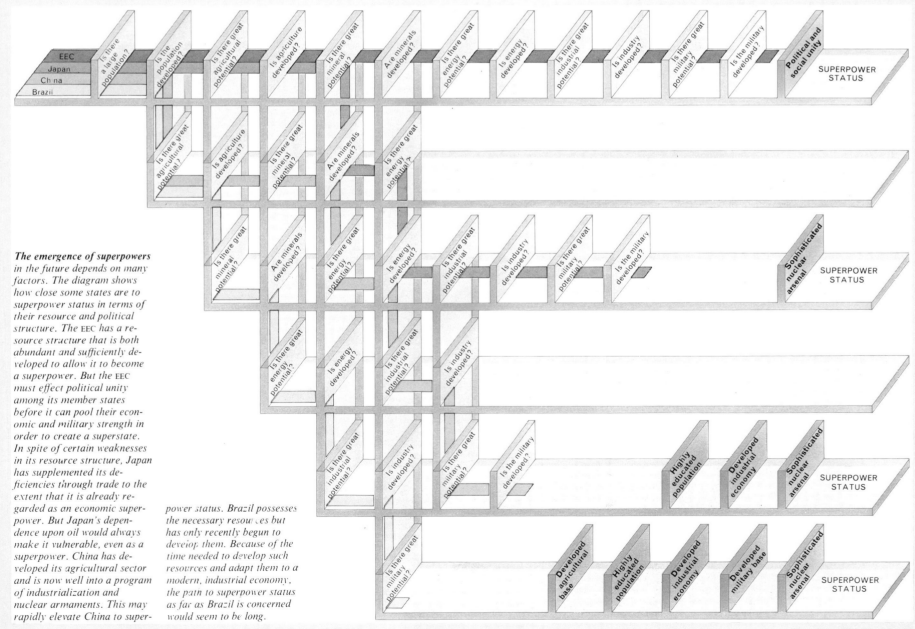

The emergence of superpowers in the future depends on many factors. The diagram shows how close some states are to superpower status in terms of their resource and political structure. The EEC has a resource structure that is both abundant and sufficiently developed to allow it to become a superpower. But the EEC must effect political unity among its member states before it can pool their economic and military strength in order to create a superstate. In spite of certain weaknesses in its resource structure, Japan has supplemented its deficiencies through trade to the extent that it is already regarded as an economic superpower. But Japan's dependence upon oil would always make it vulnerable, even as a superpower. China has developed its agricultural sector and is now well into a program of industrialization and nuclear armaments. This may rapidly elevate China to super- power status. Brazil possesses the necessary resources but has only recently begun to develop them. Because of the time needed to develop such resources and adapt them to a modern, industrial economy, the path to superpower status as far as Brazil is concerned would seem to be long.

WORLD ORGANIZATIONS

Until the beginning of the nineteenth century there had been little or no idea of formal multilateral organization beyond the nation state. The "Concert of Europe" formed at Vienna in the aftermath of the Napoleonic wars saw the first glimmerings of the idea. But it was not war as much as advancing technology in communications which gave the world its first international organizations.

The International Telecommunications (then Telegraphic) Union (ITU) was established in 1865, the General Postal Union (later the Universal Postal Union, or UPU) in 1875. They have worked smoothly and unobtrusively ever since, illustrating the fact that international organizations work best as organizers and managers of resources when they are narrowly restricted to practical, technical functions. Such organizations have become less effective as they have grown more ambitious and general in their aims, and thus closer to world politics.

But if technology has been the most effective path to organization among nations, the aftermath of wars has been the powerful propellant. The League of Nations created in Geneva after World War I was a grouping of independent powers dedicated to preserving world peace—although many still spoke for their colonial empires. Meanwhile, separate from the League, the International Labor Organization (ILO) was established in 1919. The ILO brought together trades union leaders, business managers and government to promote the wellbeing of workers in member states.

World War II killed the League of Nations (although the ILO survived it) only to spawn the United Nations "system." Founded in San Francisco in 1945, the United Nations was launched at once on an altogether more impressive scale than the League. The system, or family of institutions, has continued to grow. Today its 15 specialized agencies are concerned, like departments of a national government, the the movement and utilization of the world's resources.

The "other" UN
The overtly political part of the United Nations—its Security Council and peace-keeping forces—clearly demonstrates the fragile state of international resource management at its most vulnerable and political point. Peace and security are, after all, the supreme "commodities," because the use of all others depends on them. But these weak

yet visible UN activities absorbed only about five percent of the organization's total budget ($783.9 million) in 1977. At the same time, it must be remembered that the whole of this large and extended UN family of agencies, councils and institutions, which, excluding the World Bank and International Monetary Fund, spends about $1.5 billion a year, costs only about 25 cents per head of world population, an amount that is spent in a day by the world's governments on weapons and preparations for war.

Power of the purse strings
Small as these resources are in relation to the UN family's central task of correcting a gross top-heaviness in nations' enjoyment and control of the world's wealth, we must ask: how effective are these agencies in employing scarce resources?

The answer cannot be simple. Cooperation among governments in multilateral organization is still a very new development in human history. It is attended by many peculiar problems arising from political, social, linguistic and cultural differences within each organization which slow each one down and may divert its efforts. Problems arise, too, from the unplanned growth of these institutions. Almost all of the organic parts of the UN system were established at different times under different combinations of political pressure, which inevitably produced painful compromises.

The lesson of the ILO's survival of World War II weighed heavily with the UN's founders. This agency, and the ITU and UPU, survived, it was believed, because of their separate individual status and the practical nature of their work. They were "functional" rather than political bodies, so the

UN's founders followed this apparently proven pattern. Each of the specialized agencies, like the United Nations Educational, Scientific and Cultural Organization (UNESCO), the World Health Organization (WHO) or the Food and Agriculture Organization (FAO), was given sovereign independence, and a separate budget raised from "assessment" or progressive taxation of states. This independent power to tax made the agencies a little like medieval barons with their own lands, serfs and private armies. The Secretary-General of the UN could thus be little more than a feudal king: first—he hoped—among (almost) equals.

With the expansion of its active work in promoting economic and social development in the less-developed world, the independence of the UN's component agencies at once produced major struggles for primacy of place in the development programs of their member (and client) states. Unplanned growth of the system in response to new pressures and needs has exacerbated these inherent problems of direction and coordination.

A first move to improve coordination came with the establishment of a voluntary fund, known as the Expanded Program of Technical Assistance (EPTA), in 1949; the Special Fund was created in 1958. Later, EPTA and the Special Fund merged to become the UN Development Program (UNDP), which made its debut in November 1965. The UNDP has grown to be the main UN channel of technical assistance or "preinvestment" grants. Its projects, which range from mineral resource surveys or river-basin development studies to support for research and technical training, currently absorb more than $500 million a year. These projects have

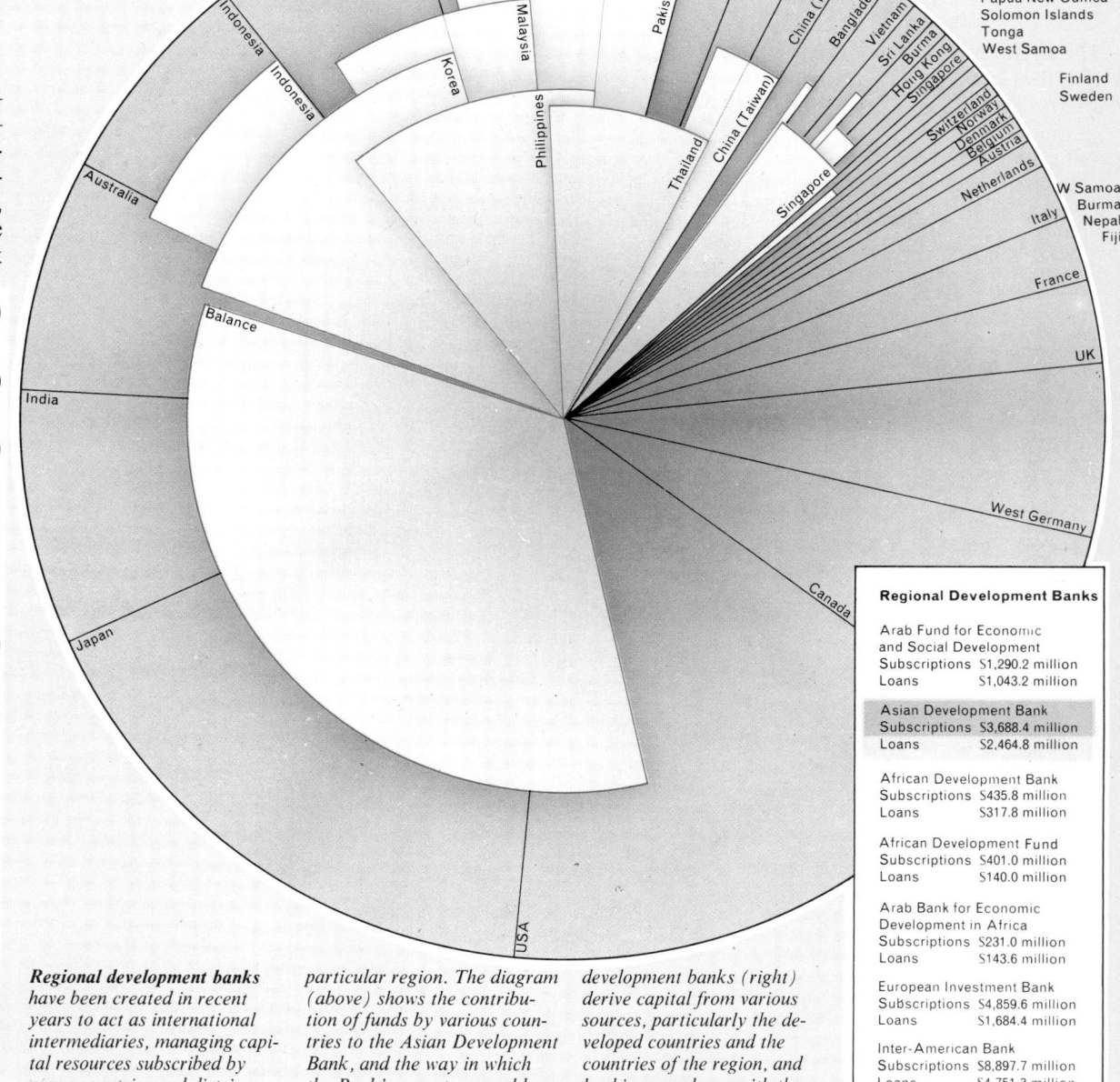

Like many other intergovernmental organizations, the Organization of Petroleum Exporting Countries (OPEC) depends for its power on unity of purpose between its member states. The power of OPEC in the future depends on the organization maintaining its solidarity, the ability of its members to diversify their economies, and the continued importance of oil as the source of energy for industrial society.

Legend for OPEC diagrams:
- No power | Minimal power | Medium power | Maximum power

Cohesion variables
- (−S) Collapse of solidarity
- (P1) Limited solidarity with some major exporters outside OPEC
- (P2) Limited solidarity including all major exporters
- (+S) Maintenance of complete solidarity

Economy composition variables
- (−D) Undiversified economy
- (−O) Oil reserves exhausted or without export value
- (+O) Oil reserves sufficient and with export value
- (+D) Diversified economy

Regional development banks have been created in recent years to act as international intermediaries, managing capital resources subscribed by many countries and distributing them to countries of a particular region. The diagram (above) shows the contribution of funds by various countries to the Asian Development Bank, and the way in which the Bank's monetary pool has been distributed. The regional development banks (right) derive capital from various sources, particularly the developed countries and the countries of the region, and lend in accordance with the capital needs of the region.

Regional Development Banks

Arab Fund for Economic and Social Development
Subscriptions $1,290.2 million
Loans $1,043.2 million

Asian Development Bank
Subscriptions $3,688.4 million
Loans $2,464.8 million

African Development Bank
Subscriptions $435.8 million
Loans $317.8 million

African Development Fund
Subscriptions $401.0 million
Loans $140.0 million

Arab Bank for Economic Development in Africa
Subscriptions $231.0 million
Loans $143.6 million

European Investment Bank
Subscriptions $4,859.6 million
Loans $1,684.4 million

Inter-American Bank
Subscriptions $8,897.7 million
Loans $4,751.3 million

produced resource survey findings and developed local expertise which has helped to attract an estimated $20 billion of public and private investment to less-developed nations.

UNDP projects are largely carried out by the UN's 15 specialized agencies. It was the hope of major contributing governments that the "power of the purse strings" and a centralized planning and management function, which had been wholly lacking in the UN, might evolve in the UNDP and produce a better coordination of the development aid effort in the UN system as a whole

Yet the problem of the specialized agencies as "feudal lords" has remained, and the system continues to be too subject to random specialist and political pressures for a generally favorable judgment to be made on its overall effectiveness. At the same time, the less political agencies like ITU, the World Meteorological Organization (WMO) and the International Civil Aviation Organization (ICAO) continue to perform their work with unobtrusive smoothness and efficiency.

Many further proposals to reform the UN system have occurred since the early 1970s. These have ranged from the creation of a new central office of Director-General for Development and Economic Cooperation at UN headquarters in New York, which took effect in 1977, to proposals for a complete review of the UN charter, designed to reform the UN's "feudal" structure along the lines of the central control now exercised in many national governments. So far, these more radical proposals have been stillborn: killed by fears that to open up such fundamental questions of control would produce far worse results than the present ramshackle and generally inefficient structure—especially if they would have to be voted on in the UN's General Assembly, where all of the 147 member states have a vote, although 83 of these states contribute only one percent of the total budget.

The Bretton Woods branch of the family
Parallel to the structure of the UN "family" has grown a group of large and powerful first cousins, technically part of the family, but springing from different political roots.

In 1944, at Bretton Woods, New Hampshire, USA, the allied powers, led by the United States and Britain, agreed on the creation of a pair of multilateral financial institutions which would be given major responsibility for financing postwar reconstruction and development. One was the International Monetary Fund (IMF), the other the International Bank for Reconstruction and Development (IBRD, or World Bank). They differ from other UN agencies in a way that clearly relates to the confidence placed in them by the USA and other Western industrial countries: unlike the rest of the UN, their Boards of Directors have voting powers formally related to their capital subscriptions.

The power and relative effectiveness of the Bank and Fund, when compared with other worldwide intergovernmental resource managing institutions, are not in question. What has been challenged is the degree of Western industrial, and particularly American, influence in their operations. Yet their attempt to be "nonpolitical," although strongly criticized, and their devotion to high standards of analysis and efficiency, have earned them a degree of influence and respect far beyond the impact of their substantial resources. This has given them a valuable leadership role in an intergovernmental community of agencies alarmingly weakened by internal politics, and by lack of the financial stature necessary to achieve its vast objectives.

There have been two further departures in the world of international organizations in their short history since World War II. First there has been the growth of organizations in all parts of the world, based either on geographical proximity or on shared geological features and common possession of vital raw materials such as (in the case of the OPEC countries) oil. The emergence of organizations such as these reflects several of the political realities already referred to: dissatisfaction with great power influence in some world organizations; the weakness and cumbersome operations of world bodies in which many contradictory interests always tend to clog the wheels; aspirations to protect regional resources for use within the region; or, as with OPEC, the desire to improve bargaining power on a worldwide basis.

The motives are generally the same worldwide—in East Africa as in Western Europe—but the effectiveness of their expression varies dramatically. This can be seen if we contrast the elaborate machinery and budgets of the regional and subregional development institutions of Asia, Latin America and Africa with the Paris-based Organization for Economic Cooperation and Development (OECD), often called "the rich man's club," or the nine-member European Economic Community, whose total budget in 1977 was $12 billion.

The other major recent evolution is the growth of nongovernmental international organizations. These should not be confused with the many and often immense world-spanning private companies, a number of which are household names and a few of which have a turnover larger than the total national incomes of three-quarters of the member states of the United Nations.

The resources of these nonbusiness, nongovernmental organizations are miniscule when compared with the UN and other intergovernmental organizations. But the International Planned Parenthood Federation, for example, or the World Wildlife Fund may have an influence on international policy far beyond what the scale of their staff and budgets might suggest. Simply because they are less politically and bureaucratically hidebound than their counterpart intergovernmental bodies (which often have responsibilities in precisely the same area), their numbers and the support that they generate among the citizens who finance and staff them may be expected to grow.

Future prospects
Another major initiative of the 1970s deserves a mention. It could, in fact, offer the basis for a more hopeful future for international organization. This was the series of major world conferences focusing on crisis issues of the decade. The series began with a world conference on the human environment which was held in Stockholm in 1972. This was followed by conferences on population (Bucharest, 1974); then on food (Rome, 1974); on human settlements (Vancouver, 1976); rights for women (Mexico City, 1976); the spread of deserts (Nairobi, 1977); and, on a very different basis—because it was concerned with specific issues of resource division—sessions of the United Nations Conference on the Law of the Sea, which have continued periodically but, sadly, with little progress, since 1970. There were earlier attempts at world conferences on critical issues in the 1950s and 1960s, but what distinguished the conferences of the 1970s was the urgency and popular appeal of the issues that brought governmental and nongovernmental organizations together into dual and "split-level," yet interacting, assemblies.

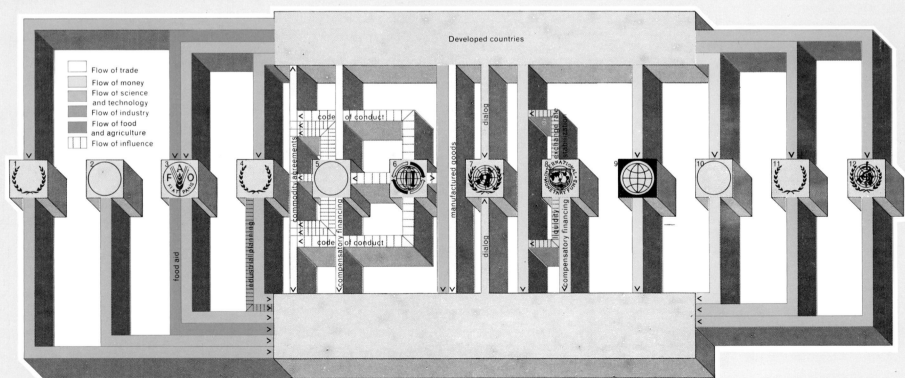

Flow of trade
Flow of money
Flow of science and technology
Flow of industry
Flow of food and agriculture
Flow of influence

Developed countries

International Organization in the New International Economic Order

1 World Intellectual Property Organization	6 UN Conference on Trade and Development
2 International Energy Institute (planned)	7 United Nations
3 Food and Agriculture Organization	8 International Monetary Fund
4 UN Industrial Development Organization	9 World Bank
5 Common Fund (planned)	10 Regional Development Banks
	11 UN Development: Program
	12 World Health Organization

In special sessions of the UN General Assembly in 1974 and 1975, guidelines for restructuring the international economic system were outlined. The key to the proposed New International Economic Order is a greater role for world organizations in the flow of trade and resources. The Food and Agriculture Organization, for example, would assume more control over the distribution of food aid. The UN Conference on Trade and Development, on the other hand, would set up guidelines to govern the flow of trade between developed and developing countries. The new order involves the transfer of considerable control over the management of resources from individual states to international organizations, and these states have yet to approve. The advantage would be greater coordination of resources on a global—and nonpolitical—basis.

GLOSSARY

aerodynamic heating: heating of a substance by passing air or other gas over its surface at high speeds.

afforestation: planting of trees with a view to the development or regeneration of forests.

aggregate: material, such as sand, gravel or crushed rock, which is mixed with cement or other adhesive to form mortar or concrete.

AGR: advanced gas-cooled reactor: nuclear reactor using a gas-cooled graphite moderator.

AL: Arab League.

alluvial: term describing material of a fine-grained texture deposited by flowing water.

anaerobic bacteria: bacteria capable of existing without air or free oxygen.

antiknock agent: substance added to gasoline in an internal-combustion engine to control its rate of burning.

ANZUS: defense pact signed in 1951 between Australia, New Zealand and the United States.

aquaculture: controlled production of aquatic organisms for food.

aquifer: layer of rock that collects and holds water.

arable: term referring to land suitable for plowing and tillage, as opposed to pasture or woodland.

ASEAN: Association of Southeast Asian Nations: an intergovernmental organization founded in 1967 and intended to foster cooperation between states in Southeast Asia.

autoclave: vessel, usually made of steel and resembling a large pressure cooker, used in the chemical industry for reactions at high pressures.

base load: minimum quantity of energy which is demanded of a power generator throughout a year.

bathymetric: term referring to the measurement of the depth of an ocean or lake.

bedrock: solid rock underlying alluvium or other surface deposits.

bilateral: term describing something which affects or pertains to two sides, usually with reference to arrangements between two countries.

bioluminescence: emission of light by living organisms, including bacteria, insects and marine animals.

biomass: total quantity of living organisms per unit area. Also, name given to organic materials and organic waste used as fuel in the production of unconventional sources of energy.

bituminous coal: most common variety of coal, used in the home and for the production of coke.

boreal forest: forest on the border of the northern subpolar regions, especially the coniferous forest ranging across North America.

BP: British Petroleum: British transnational oil company.

brazing: process whereby metallic parts are joined together by fusing them with alloys that have lower melting points.

brine: salt water; a major source of chlorine and caustic soda.

broad-based, or diversified, economy: economy based on a wide range of raw materials, industrial products and services.

BWR: boiling water reactor: nuclear reactor in which both moderator and coolant are light water.

calcareous: term describing a substance containing, or composed of, limestone or lime.

capital intensive: term referring to an economic activity that requires a large amount of capital, compared with other inputs such as labor, for its setting-up and operation.

caprock: an impermeable layer of rock covering or "capping" an oil or gas reservoir or a salt dome.

cartel: association of organizations or individuals formed to exert control, usually of a restrictive kind, on the marketing, price and/or production of a commodity.

cash crop: crop produced primarily for sale as opposed to one grown for consumption by the grower or his family.

catalyst: agent which, without undergoing any chemical change, facilitates a chemical reaction.

catchment area: region from which precipitation is drained into a stream or river.

cellulose: carbohydrate, forming the chief component of plant cell walls, and the most commonly occurring organic compound. Although eaten by herbivores, it is not digestible by man, but is used in the manufacture of plastics, paper, adhesives and food-thickening agents.

CENTO: Central Treaty Organization: mutual defense agreement established in 1955 between the United Kingdom, Turkey, Iran and Pakistan.

centrifuge: device which, by rapid rotation, separates substances of different densities.

CIA: Central Intelligence Agency: US government agency established in 1947 and charged with gathering and analyzing information from abroad on questions of national security and conducting various intelligence operations overseas.

CIPEC: Conseil Intergouvernemental des Pays Exportateurs de Cuivre: organization of copper-exporting countries, founded in 1967 with the intention of maximizing returns from the export of copper by means of increased international cooperation to regulate production.

climatology: scientific study of the Earth's climates.

clone: population of genetically identical organisms produced from a single individual by cell division.

CMEA: Council for Mutual Economic Assistance: *see* COMECON.

collateral: security given by a borrower as a guarantee of the repayment of a loan.

COMECON (CMEA): organization established in 1949 to assist the economic development of its member countries through the centralization of trading and credit arrangements. Members are the USSR, Bulgaria, Czechoslovakia, Hungary, Poland, Romania, the German Democratic Republic, the Mongolian People's Republic, Cuba and Vietnam.

convection cell: continuous system of convection, varying in size from one which may occur above a sun-heated field to the meridional atmospheric circulation within the tropics.

convection current: in geology, circulation within the core and mantle of the Earth that may effect structural changes at the Earth's surface, for example, continental drift.

CPE: centrally planned economy.

cracking: process used in the production of petroleum whereby heat is used to break up heavy hydrocarbon molecules into lighter, more volatile molecules.

curie: unit of radioactivity: that quantity of a radioactive nuclide which has 3.7×10^{10} disintegrations per second.

DAC: Development Assistance Committee: group of 17 aid-giving OECD countries.

DC: developed country.

degraded land: land where surface rock has been worn down, especially by rivers.

demographic transition: decrease in the rate of population growth achieved by a move away from high birth and death rates toward low ones.

demography: study of human populations, their distribution according to sex, age, etc., and their dynamic aspects, such as migration, birth and death.

denitrification: series of chemical changes within the nitrogen cycle which reduces nitrates to nitrites to elemental nitrogen or nitrogen compounds.

desalination: process whereby fresh water is produced from sea water by the removal of salt.

desiccation: process of drying out whereby land is largely deprived of moisture.

détente: easing of tension between parties, often used in reference to the attempts made in the late 1960s and early 1970s to improve relations between the USA and its allies and the USSR and its allies.

development program: plan designed broadly to effect a higher standard of living through a sustained increase in a region's production of goods and services.

devolution: the delegation of power to regional governments or authorities by a central government or authority.

diatomite: sedimentary rock composed of diatoms, the microscopic skeletons of algae and shells, and economically valuable for insulation, abrasives, etc.

die: tool used for shaping materials by cutting or stamping.

digital data: information in the form of collections of individual digits for assimilation by a computer.

distillate: product of a process whereby a substance is converted into a vapor and subsequently condensed into liquid form.

dry farming: method of raising crops, without the use of irrigation, in areas of low rainfall.

ecology: study of the relationships of organisms to each other and to their environment.

economic diversification: enlargement of a range of economic activities, spreading investment and returns among various economic sectors, such as mining, processing, manufacturing, services, etc. This tends to lessen dependence on any single economic activity or sector, thereby decreasing the risk inherent in such dependencies.

ecosystem: community of organisms, which interact with one another, together with the environment in which they live and with which they interact.

ECSC: European Coal and Steel Community: organization founded in 1952 by the six original members of the European Economic Community to promote cooperation in the production of steel and coal by providing a unified market for coal and steel products and a unified labor force.

EEC: European Economic Community, or Common Market: economic and political organization established in 1958 and dedicated to creating an economic union of common policies in areas such as agriculture, trade and employment, and promoting political cooperation. The founder members of the Community were Belgium, France, Italy, Luxembourg, the Netherlands and West Germany. They were joined by Denmark, Ireland and the United Kingdom in 1973.

EEZ: exclusive economic zone: region established by a country to control fishing and mining rights around its shores.

egalitarianism: doctrine asserting basic equality of opportunity and treatment for all men.

electrolysis: chemical reaction caused by passing an electric current through a substance: an important method of obtaining certain chemicals.

electron microscope: instrument which, instead of light, uses a beam of electrons in conjunction with magnetic lenses to illuminate an object.

electrostatic precipitator: device which removes impurities from gases by feeding an electrical discharge through them.

entrepôt: commercial center to which goods are brought for distribution.

enzyme: any of a group of proteins which act as catalysts in biochemical reactions.

evapotranspiration: loss of water to the atmosphere by evaporation from moist surfaces together with the exhalation, mainly from their leaves, of plants' water vapor, a process called transpiration.

exponential: term describing a continually increasing or decreasing growth rate, but one which changes geometrically rather than arithmetically.

FAO: United Nations Food and Agriculture Organization: oldest specialized agency of the United Nations, established in 1945 to improve world nutrition and provide technical aid.

FBR: fast breeder reactor: nuclear reactor that has no moderator to slow down the neutrons released by fission.

feedstock: raw material furnished to a process or machine.

ferrous metal: iron and the metalliferous elements used to form iron alloys.

fiat money: money established as legal tender by government decree.

fiber optics: system of communication using light signals transmitted along fine glass wires.

filler: fine mineral powder used to stiffen substances such as road tars, bitumens and paints.

flux: substance, used in the smelting of metal ores, that combines with impurities in metal ore which otherwise combine with the molten metal.

fossil fuel: any organic material in the Earth's crust that can be used as an energy source.

fumarole: vent in the Earth's crust through which volcanic vapors may issue.

galvanize: to coat a metal, commonly steel or iron, with a covering of zinc as protection against rusting.

gamma radiation: form of electromagnetic radiation of very short wavelength.

GATT: General Agreement on Tariffs and Trade: established in 1947 to promote principles of free trade between nations.

GDP: gross domestic product: figure derived from the computation of the total level of economic activity of all those resident in the territory of a country.

geochemistry: study of the chemical composition of the Earth and the chemical and physical processes that have produced it.

geometric, or exponential, progression: persistently accelerating growth rate by which numbers increase proportionately by ever greater increments, e.g. 2, 4, 8, 16, etc.

geomorphology: science of land forms that studies the biological, chemical and physical processes acting upon the surface features of the Earth.

geophysics: branch of geology which studies, among others, gravitational, magnetic, electrical, seismic and tectonic properties of the Earth, individually and as a whole system.

global tectonics: study of the Earth's crust in terms of the large moving plates which support the continents and float on the molten rock beneath.

GNP: gross national product: figure derived from the computation of the market value of a national economy's goods and services, whether at home or abroad, over a specified period, usually a year, which is a guide to that nation's level of economic activity.

GOSPLAN: state planning commission of the Soviet Union.

gravimeter: device used in mineral and oil prospecting for measuring variations in the gravitational field of the Earth.

hard copy: in computer terminology, readable material (e.g. printing) as opposed to digital data or codes.

head: height of a body of water supplying a mill, or kept back by a dam, etc.

HWR: heavy water-cooled reactor: nuclear reactor in which both moderator and coolant are heavy water.

hydrate: compound, most commonly a crystalline solid, which contains water chemically combined but retaining its identity.

hydrocarbon: organic compound composed of hydrogen and carbon only.

hydrology: study of the Earth's water, its source, circulation, distribution and chemical and physical composition.

hydroponics: science of artificially providing all a plant's needs within a protected and temperature-controlled environment, usually a water culture.

hydrostatic: term referring to the equilibrium of liquids and the pressure they exert when at rest.

hydrothermal: term referring to heated water, in particular its effects in the Earth's crust.

hydroxide: chemical compound containing the group OH.

IAEA: International Atomic Energy Agency: intergovernmental agency founded in 1956 to promote peaceful uses of atomic energy.

IBM: International Business Machines: British transnational corporation.

IBRD: International Bank for Reconstruction and Development (World Bank): organization founded in 1944 to make long-term loans to member governments to aid their economic development.

ICAO: International Civil Aviation Organization: agency of the United Nations, founded in 1944 to promote worldwide safety and growth of civil aviation.

IDA: International Development Association: established in 1960 as an affiliate of the World Bank to provide funds for development at low or deferred rates of interest.

igneous: term describing a rock produced from magma, as in volcanic activity.

ILO: International Labor Organization: international agency that became affiliated to the United Nations in 1946, its aim being to facilitate improved industrial relations and conditions of work.

IMCO: Intergovernmental Maritime Consultative Organization: specialized agency of the United Nations founded in 1948 and concerned with all international aspects of merchant shipping, especially safety at sea and control of pollution.

IMF: International Monetary Fund: specialized agency of the United Nations established in 1944 to secure international monetary cooperation and the stabilization of currency and exchange rates.

impervious rocks: rocks which do not allow fluids to pass through them freely.

import quota: limitation on the amount of a given imported product which may be received by those setting the limit, usually governments or cartels.

infrared radiation: form of electromagnetic radiation beyond the red or longer wavelength radiation, invisible to the eye but detectable as warmth.

infrastructure: structure of component parts: particularly of a country, the system of communications and services as a framework for social, economic or military operations.

insolation: the amount of radiation from the Sun received by a given area of the Earth's surface or by an object.

intervention buying: governmental buying of particular currencies or products as a way of intervening against market forces to gain economic advantage or prevent further weakening of national currency.

intrusion: in geology, the forceful entry of a mass of molten rock into the solid rocks of the Earth's crust.

ironsands: sands which contain iron ore particles.

irradiation: exposure to shortwave radiation.

isotope: element, the atom of which has the same number of protons in its nucleus as another atom of that element, but a different number of neutrons.

ITU: International Telecommunications Union: international organization that became affiliated to the United Nations in 1947, its aim being to encourage international cooperation in all matters relating to the telephone, telegraph, cable, radio and broadcasting.

IUD: intrauterine device: plastic or metal loop inserted in the mouth of the womb as a means of contraception.

IWC: International Whaling Commission: organization founded in 1946 to regulate the whaling industry, promote the conservation of whale stocks and encourage research.

labor intensive: term referring to any activity requiring a large amount of labor in relation to other inputs, such as capital, for its operation.

LAFTA: Latin American Free Trade Association: intergovernmental organization founded in 1960 and designed to promote regional economic integration among eleven member states.

laterite: red, porous soil rich in iron and aluminum hydroxides, formed by leaching in humid, tropical climates.

latex: viscous, white emulsion obtained from numerous flowering plants, notably rubber trees, and used in the manufacture of rubber, chicle, gutta-percha, etc.

LDC: less-developed country or, sometimes, least-developed country.

leaching: removal from a solid of soluble minerals by the prolonged action of percolating water.

lead time: amount of time between the planning of a project and the time of first returns.

legume: any plant which produces its seed in a pod.

lenticular: in geology, term describing a piece of rock in the shape of a lens.

lithology: study of rock and types.

LMFBR: liquid metal fast breeder reactor: nuclear reactor using liquid sodium as a coolant.

LNG: liquefied natural gas.

loess: soil deposit, composed of uniform, fine-grained material which was transported by wind from glaciated regions.

log interpreter: one who examines and explains the record of the types and vertical thicknesses of the rocks bored through by a well or bore-hole.

logistics: discipline concerned with the procurement, maintenance, transportation and supply of facilities or equipment.

LWR: light water-cooled reactor: nuclear reactor in which both moderator and coolant are light water.

magma: molten rock material formed at high temperatures within the Earth.

magnetometer: instrument which measures the strength of a magnetic field.

Magnox reactor: nuclear reactor using fuel clad in a special magnesium alloy called Magnox.

mantle: part of the Earth lying between the crust (30 kilometers/19 miles down) and the core (3,000 kilometers/1,900 miles).

marination: process whereby fish or meat is steeped in pickle or liquor prior to cooking.

marker bed: rock stratum discernable over a large horizontal distance.

mathematical ratio: ratio by which a number increases by an identical amount on each occasion, e.g. 2, 4, 6, 8, 10, 12, etc.

metalliferous: term describing any substance producing, containing or yielding metal.

meteorology: study of weather conditions.

microorganism: organism visible only with the aid of a microscope.

microwave: electromagnetic radiation, the wavelength of which ranges from short radio waves to the infrared region of the spectrum.

millirem: thousandth of a rem, a unit of ionizing radiation; that amount producing similar damage to humans as 1 roentgen of high-voltage X rays.

MIT: Massachusetts Institute of Technology.

monoculture: system of farming in which the cultivation of a single crop predominates.

monoproduction: production of a single article.

moratorium: temporary suspension of activity.

mulching: application of vegetable matter (shredded leaves, grass cuttings, etc.) to the soil surface to conserve moisture.

multilateral: term describing a situation or activity in which three or more parties are participating, usually with reference to agreements between states or intergovernmental organizations.

nacelle: streamlined housing of an airplane.

naphtha: any of numerous flammable, volatile, liquid hydrocarbons which are mainly used as solvents and as raw materials for conversion to gasoline.

NATO: North Atlantic Treaty Organization: postwar defense agreement between the United States, Canada and 13 European states to promote joint military aid and economic cooperation during peacetime.

NEA: Nuclear Energy Agency: agency of the OECD, including all European member countries of OECD plus Australia, Canada, the USA and Japan, founded in 1972 to promote cooperation between member governments with specific regard to safety, regulations and economics of nuclear power.

nonferrous metal: term referring to metals other than iron.

nova: faint star that undergoes unpredictable increases in brightness by several magnitudes and then slowly fades back to normal.

NPK: group of artificial fertilizers based on a ratio

of nitrogen, phosphorus and potassium, which varies according to soil requirements.

NPT: Non-Proliferation Treaty: agreement signed in 1968 by the USSR, the UK, the USA and many other countries to promote research and the use of nuclear energy for peaceful purposes.

OAS: Organization of American States: regional organization founded in 1948 and intended to strengthen collaboration among member states in the Western Hemisphere.

OAU: Organization for African Unity: founded in 1963 to foster development, independence and unity among African states.

oceanography: study of oceans, their origin, fauna and flora and chemical and physical properties.

octane number: indication of gasoline's ability to resist knocking when ignited in an internal combustion engine.

OECD: Organization for Economic Cooperation and Development: body of developed countries established in 1961 to promote economic and social welfare of member states.

oilseed: any of several seeds, including cottonseed, linseed and castor beans, grown for their oil.

olefin: an unsaturated hydrocarbon of the ethylene series.

oligopoly: situation in which there are few sellers and a small number of firms control the market.

OPEC: Organization of Petroleum Exporting Countries: established in 1960 by the world's major petroleum exporters to safeguard their interests.

open-pit mining: extraction of minerals by the removal of the surface layers of the Earth's crust.

osmosis: process whereby a solvent diffuses through an artificial or natural semipermeable membrane.

OTEC: ocean thermal energy conversion: offshore power plants generating energy by exploiting temperature gradients in the ocean.

outcrop: part of a rock stratum exposed to view by reason of its projection at the Earth's surface.

OWEC: offshore wind energy cluster: number of windmills in coastal waters, exploiting offshore winds for the generation of energy.

ozone: naturally occurring gaseous allotrope of oxygen, found in the stratosphere, where it absorbs harmful solar ultraviolet radiation.

paleontology: study of fossilized plants and animals.

pasteurization: process whereby controlled heat is used to kill bacteria, most commonly in milk.

pastoralism: use of land for grazing of livestock.

permafrost: permanently frozen subsoil.

petrochemical: chemical derived from petroleum and/or natural gas, used in the manufacture of plastics, detergents, insecticides, etc.

photo-cell: electron tube having an anode which collects the electrons emitted by a photosensitive cathode.

phytoplankton: free-drifting oceanic plant life.

phytotron: integrated group of facilities providing a controlled environment for the study of environmental effects on the growth, development and reproduction of plants.

placer deposits: concentrations of detrital heavy minerals in beach or stream gravels; the result of weathering processes.

polder: piece of low-lying reclaimed land.

polypropylene: organic substance prepared from olefins and used in the manufacture of hosiery, upholstery, etc.

precipitate (v): to separate a solid substance from solution or suspension.

precipitation: moisture that reaches the ground as a result of atmospheric condensation, such as rain, hail, snow, etc.

primary industry: term applied to all types of agriculture, forestry, fishing, mining and quarrying industries that provide food, fuel and raw materials.

primary metal: ingot metal, produced from newly smelted ore, not from recycled scrap.

private sector: that part of a national economy which is under private ownership.

procession: motion in which the axis of a spinning object "wobbles," or describes a right circular cone about the vertical.

profitability: ability of a product or program to yield profit.

pronatalist: term used to describe those people or countries opposed to family planning policies on political and/or religious grounds.

protectionist: term describing a policy restricting the inflow and competition of imported goods.

PSAC: United States President's Science Advisory Committee.

public ownership: majority ownership and control of commercial enterprises by government.

public sector: that part of a national economy which is under public ownership.

PVC: polyvinyl chloride: synthetic resin used in the manufacture of raincoats, packaging films, water pipes, etc.

PWR: pressurized water reactor: nuclear reactor that is cooled and moderated by water under high pressure.

radiometric dating: technique whereby the age of rocks can be determined from the known rates of decay of radioactive isotopes.

recession: a business slump, manifested by a decline in employment and production, leading to general unwillingness to invest.

reducing agent: substance capable of removing oxygen content or lowering the positive valence of another substance by supplying it with electrons.

reflectivity: ability of a substance to throw back rays or beams of heat, sound or light.

relief: variations in elevation of the land surface of a given area as demonstrated on a contour map.

roundwood: lumber before it is squared.

RTZ: Rio Tinto Zinc: British transnational mining corporation.

salinity: amount of salt contained in salt water, usually expressed in parts per thousand.

SALT: Strategic Arms Limitation Talks: discussions begun in 1972 between the USA and USSR with a view to limiting antiballistic missile systems and offensive missile launchers.

SASOL: South Africa Coal, Oil and Gas Corporation: state-owned corporation operating commercially to produce oil, gas and byproducts from coal.

scintillometer: device which detects and counts scintillations caused by ionizing radiation in a fluorescent material: used in prospecting for radioactive ores and in nuclear and medical research.

secondary industry: manufacturing and construction industries.

sedimentary rock: rock formed through the compacting of accumulated grains or fragments of minerals and rocks weathered from the Earth's surface.

seismic: resulting from, characteristic of, or subject to earthquakes.

self-fluxing: *see* flux.

silting: deposition of fine soil or mud from running water.

silviculture: care and cultivation of trees in a forest.

SLAR: side-looking airborne radar: means of topographical mapping.

SNG: synthetic "natural" gas manufactured from coal or heavy hydrocarbons.

solar radiation: energy reaching Earth from the Sun, including X rays, ultraviolet and infrared radiation, radio emissions and visible light.

sonar: underwater detection and navigation system which sends out a pulse and receives an echo from submerged objects.

spectral signature: characteristic appearance of an object when photographed on infrared-sensitive film.

spectrometry: branch of optics concerned with the measurement of the wavelength and intensity of lines in a spectrum.

spectrum: distribution of electromagnetic radiation according to wavelength.

stereoscopic: term referring to vision which involves two different perspectives of the viewed object being available to the viewer simultaneously.

subsistence agriculture: agricultural production which fails to attain a surplus beyond what is required for consumption by the immediate producer and his family.

supernova: star that undergoes a tremendous outburst of energy and matter that temporarily increases its absolute magnitude.

superphosphate: phosphate fertilizer, produced by treating ground phosphate rock with sulfuric acid.

superpower: nation of great political, economic and military power, able to influence the actions of all other countries in the international system.

support prices: prices which governments or, more specifically, departments of agriculture, are willing to pay for agricultural commodities, as part of their crop support programs.

symbiosis: partnership of two mutually dependent organisms, such as that between bacteria and the roots of leguminous plants.

tariff: tax on the importation, and sometimes on the exportation, of specific goods.

tillage: preparation of land for bearing crops.

TNC: transnational corporation: a business enterprise with operations or subsidiaries in several or more countries and characterized by a centrally coordinated corporate strategy.

topography: study of the surface features of a region.

trace elements: chemical elements occurring in minute amounts and required by living organisms.

tundra: treeless plain characteristic of arctic, subarctic and alpine regions.

UDI: unilateral declaration of independence.

ultrasonic: term describing frequencies beyond the range of human audibility.

ultraviolet: radiation of wavelengths between visible light waves and X rays in the electromagnetic spectrum.

UN: United Nations: international organization established in 1945 to enable countries to work together for peace and mutual development.

UNCTAD: United Nations Conference on Trade and Development: body within the United Nations General Assembly, established in 1964 to promote international trade.

UNDP: United Nations Development Program: established in 1965 from the merger of the Expanded Program of Technical Assistance and the Special Fund to promote technical cooperation and assist development.

UNESCO: United Nations Educational, Scientific and Cultural Organization: specialized agency of the United Nations established in 1945 to improve world standards or education and unite nations in cultural and scientific projects.

UPU: Universal Postal Union: international agency that became affiliated to the United Nations in 1947, its aim being to control and coordinate global postal services and rates.

VHF: very high frequency: range of radio waves.

VLCC: very large crude (oil) carrier.

volatile: description of any liquid or solid that will readily change to vapor at a low temperature.

WHO: World Health Organization: specialized agency of the United Nations established in 1948 to improve standards of world health.

WMO: World Meteorological Organization: specialized agency of the United Nations, created in 1947 to promote international cooperation in meteorology through a network of meteorological stations.

WTO: Warsaw Treaty Organization (Warsaw Pact): mutual organization for defense established in 1955 by the Soviet Union and its East European allies.

X-ray diffraction: technique whereby X rays are diffracted by the atoms of a crystal, producing a three-dimensional grating from which the internal structure of the crystal can be determined.

zooplankton: free-floating oceanic animal life.

In this Index page numbers in italics refer to illustrations and maps and/or their captions. Between pages 168 and 185 page numbers in italics also refer to tabular material.

BIBLIOGRAPHY
8-9 O'Riordan, T.: *Perspectives on Resource Management*; Pion, 1971. Open University: *The Earth's Physical Resources: Resources and Systems*; Open University Press, 1973. Paterson, J. H.: *Land Work and Resources: An Introduction to Economic Geography* (2nd Edn.); Arnold, 1976. US National Academy of Sciences: *Resources and Man: A Study and Recommendations*; Freeman, 1969. **10-11** Barnett, Harold J.: *Scarcity and Growth: The Economics of Natural Resource Availability*; Johns Hopkins University Press, 1966. Brown, Lester R.: *The Twenty-Ninth Day: Accommodating Human Needs and Numbers to the Earth's Resources*; Norton, 1978. Caldwell, Malcolm: *The Wealth of Some Nations*; Zed Press, 1976. Ehrlich, Paul R., *et al.: Ecoscience: Population, Resources, Environment*; Freeman, 1977. Lean, Geoffrey: *Rich World, Poor World*; Allen & Unwin, 1978. Mikdashi, Z.: *The International Politics of Natural Resources*; Cornell University Press, 1976. US National Academy of Sciences: *Resources and Man: A Study and Recommendations*; Freeman, 1976. Ward, Barbara, and Dubos, René: *Only One Earth: The Care and Maintenance of a Small Planet*; Penguin, 1972. **12-13** Buchanan, R. A.: *Technology and Social Progress*; Pergamon, 1965. Childe, V. Gordon: *What Happened in History*; Penguin, 1969. Derry, T. K., and Williams, Trevor I.: *A Short History of Technology from the Earliest Times to AD 1900*; O.U.P., 1960. Foley, Gerald: *The Energy Question*; Penguin, 1976. Mathias, Peter: *The First Industrial Nation: An Economic History of Britain, 1700–1914*; Methuen, 1969. Needham, Joseph: *The Shorter Science and Civilisation in China, Volume 1*; C.U.P., 1978. **14-15** Cottrell, Alan H.: *Environmental Economics*; Arnold, 1978. Goldsmith, E. R. D. (Ed.): *A Blueprint for Survival*; Penguin, 1972. Meadows, D. H., *et al.: The Limits to Growth: A Report for The Club of Rome's Project on the Predicament of Mankind*; Earth Island, 1973. Pirie, N. W.: *Food Resources: Conventional and Novel* (2nd Edn.); Penguin, 1976. **16-17** Borgström, Georg: *Too Many: A Study of the Earth's Biological Limitations*; Collier Macmillan, 1972. Borgström, Georg: *The Hungry Planet: The Modern World at the Edge of Famine*; Collier Macmillan, 1972. Camilleri, J. A.: *Civilization in Crisis*; C.U.P., 1977. Carson, Rachel: *Silent Spring*; Penguin, 1970. Malthus, Thomas Robert: *An Essay on the Principle of Population* (Ed. Antony Flew); Penguin, 1970. Meadows, D. H., *et al.: The Limits to Growth*; Earth Island, 1973. US National Academy of Sciences: *Resources and Man; A Study and Recommendations*; Freeman, 1969. Tudge, Colin: *The Famine Business*; Faber, 1977.

THE NATURE OF RESOURCES
20-21 Calder, Nigel: *The Weather Machine: How Our Weather Works and Why it is Changing*; British Broadcasting Corporation, 1974. Menzel, D. H.: *Our Sun*; Harvard University Press, 1959. Press, Frank (Ed.): *Planet Earth: Readings from Scientific*

American; Freeman, 1974. Schurr, Sam H. (Ed.): *Energy: Economic Growth and the Environment*; Johns Hopkins University Press, 1972. Scientific American: *The Biosphere*; Freeman, 1971. Scientific American: *Man and the Ecosphere*; Freeman, 1971. **22-27** Allum, J. A. E.: *Photogeology and Regional Mapping*; Pergamon, 1966. Barrett, E. C., and Curtis, Leonard F.: *An Introduction to Environmental Remote Sensing*; Chapman & Hall, 1976. Barrett, E. C., and Curtis, Leonard F.: *Environmental Remote Sensing: Applications and Achievements*; Arnold, 1974. Calder, Nigel: *Restless Earth: A Report on the New Geology*; British Broadcasting Corporation, 1972. Gass, I. G., *et al.* (Eds.): *Understanding the Earth: A Reader in the Earth Sciences*; Artemis Press, 1971. Gerster, Georg: *Grand Design: The Earth from Above*; Paddington Press, 1976. Lintz, Joseph, and Somonett, David S. (Eds.): *Remote Sensing of the Environment*; Addison-Wesley, 1976. Open University: *The Earth's Physical Resources: Mineral Deposits*; Open University Press, 1974. Porter, Richard W.: *The Versatile Satellite*; O.U.P., 1977. **28-33** Aron, Raymond: *Peace and War: A Theory of International Relations*; Weidenfeld, 1966. Bergsten, C. Fred, and Krause, Lawrence B. (Eds.): *World Politics and International Economics*; Brookings Institution, 1975. Bhagwati, J.: *The New International Order: The North–South Debate*; M.I.T. Press, 1977. Blake, David, and Walters, Robert: *The Politics of Global Economic Relations*; Prentice-Hall, 1976. Brookfield, Harold: *Interdependent Development*; Methuen, 1975. Bull, H.: *The Anarchical Society: A Study of Order in World Politics*; Macmillan, 1976. Caldwell, Malcolm: *The Wealth of Some Nations*; Zed Press, 1976. Calvocoressi, Peter: *World Politics Since 1945* (3rd Edn.); Longman, 1977. Connelly, Philip, and Perlman, Robert: *The Politics of Scarcity: Resource Conflicts in International Relations*; O.U.P., 1975. Dahrendorf, Ralf: *Class and Class Conflict in Industrial Society*; Stanford University Press, 1959. Haq, Mahbub ul: *The Poverty Curtain: Choices for the Third World*; Columbia University Press, 1976. Helleiner, G. K. (Ed.): *A World Divided*; C.U.P., 1976. Lean, Geoffrey: *Rich World, Poor World*; Allen & Unwin, 1978. McNamara, Robert S.: *One Hundred Countries, Two Billion People: The Dimensions of Development*; Pall Mall, 1973. Mikdashi, Z.: *The International Politics of Natural Resources*; Cornell University Press, 1976. Rhodes, Robert I. (Ed.): *Imperialism and Underdevelopment: A Reader*; Monthly Review Press, 1970. Sauvant, Karl, and Hasenpflug, Hajo (Eds.): *The New International Economic Order: Confrontation or Co-operation Between North and South?*; Westview Press, 1977. Singh, J. S.: *A New International Economic Order: Toward a Fair Redistribution of the World's Resources*; Praeger, 1977. Spero, Joan Edelman: *The Politics of International Economic Relations*; Allen & Unwin, 1977. United Nations: *A New UN Structure for Global Economic Cooperation*; UN Publications, 1975. **34-35** Anthony, V. S.: *Britain's Overseas Trade*; Heinemann, 1971. Cutajar, Michael Z., and Franks,

Alison: *The Less Developed Countries in World Trade: A Reference Handbook*; Overseas Development Institute, 1967. Katrak, Homi: *International Trade and the Balance of Payments*; Fontana, 1971. Stamp, L. Dudley: *Commercial Geography*; Longman, 1975. **36-37** Alderton, Patrick M.: *Sea Transport: Operation and Economics*; Reed, 1973. Barker, Theodore C., and Savage, Christopher I.: *An Economic History of Transport in Britain*; Hutchinson, 1975. Couper, A. D.: *The Geography of Sea Transport*; Hutchinson, 1972. Faulks, R. W.: *Principles of Transport*; Ian Allan, 1974. Hoyle, B. S.: *Transport and Development*; Macmillan, 1973. Munby, Denys L. (Ed.): *Transport: Selected Readings*; Penguin, 1978. **38-39** Clay, C. J. J., and Wheble, B. S. (Eds.): *Modern Merchant Banking*; Woodhead-Faulkner, 1976. Coombs, Charles A.: *The Arena of International Finance*; Wiley, 1976. Daniels, John, *et al.: International Business: Environments and Operations*; Addison-Wesley, 1976. Hirsch, F., *et al.: Alternatives to Monetary Disorder*; Council on Foreign Relations, 1977. Solomon, Robert: *The International Monetary System, 1945–1976*; Harper & Row, 1977. Strange, Susan: *International Monetary Relations, 1959–1971*; Royal Institute of International Affairs, 1976. Tew, Brian: *The Evolution of the International Monetary System, 1945–77*; Hutchinson, 1977. **40-41** Barnet, Richard, and Muller, Ronald: *Global Reach: The Power of the Multinational Corporations*; Simon & Schuster, 1974. Gilpin, Robert: *US Power and the Multinational Corporation*; Macmillan, 1976. Jacoby, Neil H.: *Multinational Oil*; Collier Macmillan, 1975. Madden, Carl (Ed.): *The Case for the Multinational Corporation: Six Scholarly Views*; Praeger, 1977. Radice, Hugo (Ed.): *International Firms and Modern Imperialism*; Penguin, 1975. Sampson, Anthony: *The Seven Sisters: The Great Oil Companies and the World They Made*; Hodder & Stoughton, 1975. Sampson, Anthony: *Sovereign State: The Secret History of International Telephone and Telegraph*; Hodder & Stoughton, 1973. Tugenhadt, Christopher: *The Multinationals*; Penguin, 1973.

RESOURCES AND PEOPLE
44-45 Brown, Lester, *et al.: Twenty-Two Dimensions of the Population Problem*; Worldwatch Institute, 1976. Ehrlich, Paul R.: *The Population Bomb*; Ballantine, 1971. Llewellyn-Jones, Derek: *People Populating*; Faber, 1974. Malthus, Thomas Robert: *An Essay on the Principle of Population* (Ed. Antony Flew); Penguin, 1970. McEvedy, Colin, and Jones, Richard: *Atlas of World Population History*; Penguin, 1978. McKeown, Thomas: *The Modern Rise of Population*; Arnold, 1976. **46-47** Brown, Lester R.: *The Twenty-Ninth Day: Accommodating Human Needs and Numbers to the Earth's Resources*; Norton, 1978. Ehrlich, Paul R., *et al.: Ecoscience: Population, Resources, Environment*; Freeman, 1977. Ward, Barbara: *The Home of Man*; Deutsch, 1976. Wilsher, Peter, and Righter, Rosemary: *The Exploding Cities*; Deutsch, 1975. **48-49** Berg, Alan, *et al.:*

Nutrition: National Development and Planning; M.I.T. Press, 1973. Clark, Colin: *Population Growth and Land Use* (2nd Edn.); Macmillan, 1977. Duckham, A. N., *et al.*: *Food Production and Consumption: the Efficiency of Human Food Chains and Nutrient Cycles*; North Holland, 1976. Eckholm, Erik P.: *Losing Ground: Environmental Stress and World Food Prospects*; Pergamon, 1976. George, Susan: *How the Other Half Dies—the Real Reasons for World Hunger*; Penguin, 1976. Lapedes, Daniel M. (Ed.): *The McGraw-Hill Encyclopedia of Food, Agriculture and Nutrition*; McGraw-Hill, 1977. Pirie, N. W.: *Food Resources: Conventional and Novel* (2nd Edn.): Penguin, 1976. Tudge, Colin: *The Famine Business*; Faber, 1977. **50-51** Brown, Lester R.: *The Twenty-Ninth Day: Accommodating Human Needs and Numbers to the Earth's Resources*; Norton, 1978. Cook, Earl: *Man, Energy, Society*; Freeman, 1976. Ehrlich, Paul R., *et al.*: *Ecoscience: Population, Resources, Environment*; Freeman, 1977. Foley, Gerald: *The Energy Question*; Penguin, 1976. Lovins, Amory B.: *Soft Energy Paths: Toward A Durable Peace*; Penguin, 1977. Makhijani, Arjun: *Energy Policy for the Rural Third World*; International Institute for Environment and Development, 1976. Odum, Howard T.: *Environment, Power and Society*; Wiley, 1971. **52-53** Brown, Lester R.: *The Twenty-Ninth Day: Accommodating Human Needs and Numbers to the Earth's Resources*; Norton, 1978. Clarke, John I.: *Population Geography* (2nd Edn.); Pergamon, 1972. Eckholm, Erik P.: *Losing Ground: Environmental Stress and World Food Prospects*; Pergamon, 1976. Ehrlich, Paul R., *et al.*: *Ecoscience: Population, Resources, Environment*; Freeman, 1977. **54-55** Brown, Lester R.: *World Population Trends: Signs of Hope, Signs of Stress*; Worldwatch Institute, 1976. Eckholm, Erik P., and Newland, Kathleen: *Health: The Family Planning Factor*; Worldwatch Institute, 1977. Sai, Fred T.: *Population and National Development: The Dilemma of Developing Countries*; International Planned Parenthood Federation, 1977.

ENERGY

58-59 Cook, Earl: *Man, Energy, Society*; Freeman, 1976. Feynman, R. P., *et al.*: *Lectures on Physics, Volume 1*; Addison-Wesley, 1963. Mitchell, Wilson: *Energy*; Time-Life, 1965. Resnick, Robert, and Holliday, David: *Physics for Students of Science and Engineering*; Wiley, 1962. **60-61** Central Electricity Generating Board: *Modern Power Station Practice*; Pergamon, 1971. Central Electricity Generating Board: *How Electricity is Made and Transmitted*; C.E.G.B., n.d. Skrotzki, Bernhardt G. A. (Ed.): *Electric Generation—Hydro, Diesel and Gas Turbine Stations, Electric Generation—Steam Stations, Electric System Operation & Electric Transmission and Distribution*; McGraw-Hill, 1954–56. **62-63** Francis, Wilfred: *Coal*; Arnold, 1961. Gilluly, James, *et al.*: *Principles of Geology*; Freeman, 1975. Holmes, Arthur: *Elements of Physical Geology*; Nelson, 1969. Trueman, A. E. (Ed.): *The Coalfields of Great Britain*; Arnold, 1954. US Bureau of Mines: *Mineral Facts and Problems*; US Bureau of Mines, 1976. Wills, Leonard J.: *Concealed Coalfields*; Blackie, 1956. **64-65** Bugler, Jeremy, *et al.*: *Coal—Technology for Britain's Future*; Macmillan, 1976. Ellington, Rex T. (Ed.): *Liquid Fuels from Coal*; Academic Press, 1977. Hottel, H. C., and Howard, J. B.: *New Energy Technology: Some Facts and Assessments*; M.I.T. Press, 1972. World Energy Conference: *World Energy Resources, 1985–2020*; I.P.C. Scientific and Technical Press, 1978. **66-73** British Petroleum: *Our Industry, Petroleum*; British Petroleum, 1977. Hodson, G. W., and Pohl, W. (Eds.): *Modern Petroleum Technology*; Applied Science Publishers, 1973. Ion, D. C.: *Availability of World Energy Resources*; Graham & Trotman, 1975; Supplements, 1976 & 1978. Tiratsoo, E. N.: *Oil-fields of the World* (2nd Edn.); Scientific Press, 1976. Campbell, R. W.: *The Economics of Soviet Oil and Gas*; Johns Hopkins University Press, 1969. Russell, Jeremy: *Energy as a Factor in Soviet Foreign Policy*; Saxon House, 1976. World Energy Conference: *World Energy Resources, 1985–2020*; I.P.C. Scientific & Technical Press, 1978. Tiratsoo, E. N.: *Natural Gas* (2nd Edn.); Scientific Press, 1972. Wardley-Smith, J. (Ed.): *The Control of Oil Pollution on the Sea and Inland Waters*; Graham & Trotman, 1976. Darmstadter, Joel: *Energy in the World Economy: A Statistical Review of Trends in Output, Trade and Consumption since 1925*; Johns Hopkins University Press, 1972. Hill, Peter, and Vielvoye, Roger: *Energy in Crisis: A Guide to World Oil Supply and Demand and Alternative Resources*; Robert Yeatman, 1974. Mangone, Gerard J. (Ed.): *Energy Policies of the World, Volumes I, II & III*; Elsevier, 1976–78. Workshop on Alternative Energy Strategies: *Energy: Global Prospects, 1985–2000*; McGraw-Hill, 1977. **74-75** Brown, John G.: *Hydroelectric Engineering Practice* (2nd Edn., 2 volumes); Blackie, Vol. I, 1958, Vol. II, 1970. Creager, William P., *et al.*: *Engineering for Dams* (3 volumes); Wiley, 1945. Creager, William P., and Justin, Joel D.: *Hydroelectric Handbook* (2nd Edn.); Wiley, 1950. Kyle, John H.: *The Building of TVA*; Louisiana State University Press, 1958. Paton, T. A. L., and Brown, J. G.: *Power from Water*; Leonard Hill, 1960. **76-77** Armstead, H. C. H.: *Geothermal Energy: Its Past, Present and Future Contributions to the Energy Needs of Man*; Spon, 1978. Armstead, H. C. H.: *Geothermal Energy: A Review of Research and Development*; UNESCO, 1973. Kenward, M.: *Potential Energy*; C.U.P., 1976. Larsen, E.: *New Sources of Energy and Power*, Muller, 1976. **78-83** Burn, D.: *Nuclear Power and the Energy Crisis: Politics and the Atomic Industry*; Macmillan, 1976. Cochran, T. B.: *The Liquid Metal Fast Breeder Reactor: An Environmental and Economic Critique*; Johns Hopkins University Press, 1974. Elliott, Mary (Ed.): *Ground for Concern: Australia's Uranium and Human Survival*; Penguin, 1977. Foley, Gerald: *The Energy Question*; Penguin, 1976. Kenward, M.: *Potential Energy: An Analysis of World Energy Technology*; C.U.P., 1976. Nuclear Energy Policy Study Group: *Nuclear Power Issues and Choices*; Ballinger, 1977. OECD Nuclear Energy Agency/International Atomic Energy Agency: *Uranium Resources, Production and Demand*; Organization for Economic Cooperation and Development, 1977. Patterson, W. C.: *The Fissile Society*; Earth Resources Research, 1977. Patterson, W. C.: *Nuclear Power*; Penguin, 1976. Royal Commission on Environmental Pollution: *Nuclear Power and the Environment*; HMSO, 1976. Willrich, M., and Taylor, T. B.: *Nuclear Theft: Risks and Safeguards*; Ballinger, 1974. **84-85** Anderson, Bruce: *The Solar Home Book*; Prism Press, 1977. Boyle, G.: *Living on the Sun*; Calder, 1975. Brinkworth, B. J.: *Solar Energy for Man*; Compton Press, 1972. Department of Energy: *Solar Energy: Its Potential Contribution within the UK*; HMSO, 1977. Halacy, Daniel S.: *Earth, Water, Wind and Sun*; Harper & Row, 1977. McLaughlin, Terence: *A House for the Future*; Independent Television Books, 1976. McVeigh, J. C.: *Sun Power: An Introduction to Applications of Solar Energy*; Pergamon, 1977. Portola Institute: *Energy Primer: Solar, Water, Wind and Biofuels*; Prism Press, 1977. Williams, J. R.: *Solar Energy: Technology and Applications*; Ann Arbor Scientific Publishers, 1974. **86-87** Golding, E. W.: *Generation of Electricity by Wind Power*; Spon, 1976. Halacy, Daniel S.: *Earth, Water, Wind and Sun*; Harper & Row, 1977. McLaughlin, Terence: *A House for the Future*; Independent Television Books, 1976. Portola Institute: *Energy Primer: Solar, Water, Wind and Biofuels*; Prism Press, 1975.

THE LIVING RESOURCE

90-91 Buringh, P., *et al.*: *Computation of the Absolute Maximum Food Production of the World*; Netherlands Agricultural University, 1975. Eckholm, Erik P.: *Losing Ground: Environmental Stress and World Food Prospects*; Pergamon, 1976. Freeman, Christopher, *et al.*: *Progress and Problems in Social Forecasting*; Social Science Research Council, 1976. George, Susan: *How the Other Half Dies—The Real Reasons for World Hunger*; Penguin, 1976. Griffin, Keith B.: *The Political Economy of Agrarian Change*; Macmillan, 1974. Pirie, N. W.: *Food Resources: Conventional and Novel* (2nd Edn.); Penguin, 1976. Tudge, Colin: *The Famine Business*; Faber, 1977. **92-93** Lapedes, Daniel M. (Ed.): *The McGraw-Hill Encyclopedia of Food, Agriculture and Nutrition*; McGraw-Hill, 1977. Leach, Gerald: *Energy and Food Production*; IPC Scientific and Technical Press, 1976. Makhijani, Arjun, and Poole, Alan: *Energy and Agriculture in the Third World*; Ballinger, 1975. Odum, Howard T.: *Environment, Power and Society*; Wiley, 1971. **94-95** Calder, Nigel: *The Weather Machine: How Our Weather Works and Why it is Changing*; British Broadcasting Corporation, 1974. Gribbin, John (Ed.): *Climatic Change*; C.U.P., 1978. Lamb, H. H.: *Climate: Present, Past and Future*, 2 vols.; Methuen, 1972 & 1978. Schneider, Stephen H.: *The Genesis Strategy: Climate and Global Survival*; Plenum Press, 1976. **96-97** Leopold, Luna B.: *Water—A Primer*; Freeman, 1974. Leopold, Luna B.: *Water*; Time-Life, 1966. Overman, M.: *Water—Solutions to a Problem of Supply and Demand*; Open University Press, 1976. Pereira, H. C.: *Land Use and Water Resources in Temperate and Tropical Climates*; C.U.P., 1973. Smith, Keith: *Water in Britain*; Macmillan, 1972. Van der Leeden, Frits: *Water Resources of the World—Selected Statistics*; Water Information Center Inc., 1975. Wiener, A.: *The Role of Water in Development*; McGraw-Hill, 1972. **98-99** Abelson, Philip H. (Ed.): *Food: Politics, Economics, Nutrition and Research: Readings from 'Science'*; Academic Press, 1975. Congdon, R. J. (Ed.): *An Introduction to Appropriate Technology*; Rodale Press, 1977. George, Susan: *How the Other Half Dies—the Real Reasons for World Hunger*; Penguin, 1976. Griffin, Keith B.: *The Political Economy of Agrarian Change*; Macmillan, 1974. Jacoby, Erich H.: *Man and Land—the Fundamental Issue in Development*; Deutsch, 1971. Scientific American: *Food and Agriculture*; Freeman, 1975. **100-1** Duckham, A. N., and Masefield, G. B.: *Farming Systems of the World*; Chatto & Windus, 1970. Mansard, Walther: *Tropical Agriculture*; Longman, 1975. Schuchart, Max: *The Netherlands*; Thames & Hudson, 1972. Wallwork, Kenneth L.: *Derelict Land*; David & Charles, 1974. **102-3** Earl, D. E.: *Forest Energy and Economic Development*; O.U.P., 1975. Edlin, H. L.: *The Natural History of Trees*; Weidenfeld, 1976. Madas, Andras: *World Consumption of Wood*; Akademiai Kiado, Budapest, 1975. **104-5** Bowman, J. C.: *Animals for Man*; Arnold, 1977. Edlin, H. L.: *Man and Plants*; Aldus, 1968. Hartley, C. W. S.: *The Oil Palm*; Longman, 1977. Janick, Jules, *et al.*: *Plant Science*; Freeman, 1974. **106-7** Beverton, R. J. H., and Holt, S. J.: *On the Dynamics of Exploited Fish Populations*; HMSO, 1957. Christy, Francis T., and Scott, Anthony: *The Common Wealth in Ocean Fisheries: Some Problems of Growth and Economic Allocation*; Johns Hopkins University Press, 1966. Cushing: David H.: *Fisheries Resources of the Sea and their Management*; O.U.P., 1975. Cushing, David H.: *Marine Ecology and Fisheries*; C.U.P., 1975. Food and Agriculture Organization: *Atlas of the Living Resources of the Seas*; UN, 1972. Gulland, J. A.: *Fish Population Dynamics*; Wiley, 1977. Hardy, Alister: *The Open Sea: Its Natural History* (2 vols.); Collins, 1970–71. Loftas, Tony: *The Last Resource: Man's Exploitation of the Sea*; Penguin, 1973. **108-9** Buringh, P.: *Computation of the Absolute Maximum Food Production of the World*; Netherlands Agricultural University, 1975. Chrispeels, M. J., and Sadava, D.: *Plants, Food and People*; Freeman, 1977. Hutchinson, J. B.: *Population and Food Supply*; C.U.P., 1969. Janick, Jules, *et al.*: *Plant Science*; Freeman, 1974. Pirie, N. W.: *Food Resources:*

Conventional and Novel (2nd Edn.); Penguin, 1976. **110-11** Bowman, J. C.: *Animals for Man*; Arnold, 1977. Cole, H. H., and Ronning, Magnar (Eds.); *Animal Agriculture*; Freeman, 1974. Hyams, Edward: *Animals in the Service of Man: 10,000 Years of Domestication*; Dent, 1972. **112-13** Bardach, John, *et al.*: *Aquaculture: The Farming and Husbandry of Freshwater and Marine Organisms*; Wiley, 1975. Gulland, J. A.: *The Management of Marine Fisheries*; Scientechnica, 1974. Huet, Marcel: *Textbook of Fish Culture*; Fishing News, 1972. Iversen, E. S.: *Farming the Edge of the Sea*; Fishing News, 1968. Koers, Albert W.: *International Regulation of Marine Fisheries*; Fishing News, 1973. Rounsefell, George A.: *Ecology, Utilization and Management of Marine Fisheries*; Mosby, 1975. **114-15** Bender, Arnold: *Facts of Food*; O.U.P., 1975. Birch, G. G. (Ed.): *Food from Waste*; Applied Science Publishers, 1976. Duckham, A. N., *et al.*: *Food Production and Consumption*; North Holland Publishing, 1976. Pirie, N. W.: *Food Resources: Conventional and Novel* (2nd Edn.); Penguin, 1976. Pyke, Magnus: *Food Science and Technology* (3rd Edn.); Murray, 1970. Pyke, Magnus: *Synthetic Food*; Murray, 1970. Yudkin, John: *Nutrition*; Hodder & Stoughton, 1977. **116-19** Carstensen, V. R. (Ed.): *The Public Lands*; University of Wisconsin Press, 1963. Clawson, Marion: *America's Land and Its Uses*; Johns Hopkins University Press, 1972. Conrat, M., and R.: *The American Farm*; Scolar Press, 1977. Frome, Michael: *National Forests of America*; White Lion, 1974. Higbee, Edward: *American Agriculture: Geography, Resources and Conservation*; Wiley, 1958. Paterson, J. H.: *North America: A Geography of Canada and the United States*; Pergamon, 1975. **120-23** Bailey, Richard: *The European Community in the World*; Hutchinson, 1973. Church, R. J. H.: *An Advanced Geography of Northern and Western Europe*; Hulton, 1968. Kerr, A. J. C.: *The Common Market and How It Works*; Pergamon, 1977. Monkhouse, F. J.: *A Regional Geography of Western Europe*; Longman, 1974. Robinson, Harry: *The Mediterranean Lands* (4th Edn); University Tutorial Press, 1975. Shackleton, M. R.: *Europe: A Regional Geography* (7th Edn.); Longman, 1965. Tracy, Michael: *Agriculture in Western Europe: Crisis and Adaptation since 1880*; Cape, 1964. **124-25** Alexander, G., and William, D. B. (Eds.): *The Pastoral Industries of Australia*; Sydney University Press, 1974. Hadfield, J. W.: *Arable Farm Crops of New Zealand*; A. H. Reed, 1973. Leeper, G. W. (Ed.): *The Australian Environment*; Melbourne University Press, 1971. Molnar, Imre (Ed.): *A Manual of Australian Agriculture*; Heinemann, 1962. OECD: *Agricultural Policy in Australia*; HMSO, 1974. OECD: *Agricultural Policy in New Zealand*; HMSO, 1974. **126-27** *Atlas of Israel*; Elsevier, 1970. Orni, E., and Efrat, E.: *A Geography of Israel*; Keter, 1976. Dore, R. P.: *Land Reform in Japan*; O.U.P., 1959. Fukutake, Tadishi: *Japanese Rural Society*; Cornell University Press, 1972. Trewartha, Glenn T., *Japan: A Physical, Cultural and Regional Geography*; Methuen, 1965. Cole, M. M.: *South Africa*; Methuen, 1961. Davenport, T. R. H.: *South Africa: A Modern History*; Macmillan, 1977. Houghton, D. H.: *The South African Economy* (4th Edn.); O.U.P., 1976. Liebenberg, E. C., *et al.*: *South African Landscape*; Butterworth, 1976. Schlemmer, Lawrence, and Webster, Eddie: *Change, Reform and Economic Growth in South Africa*; Raven Press, 1978. **128-29** Acland, J. D.: *East African Crops*; Longman, 1972. Brown, Leslie: *Africa: A Natural History*; Hamish Hamilton, 1965. Chambers, R. J. H.: *Settlement Schemes in Tropical Africa*; Routledge, 1969. Church, R. J. H.: *West Africa*; Longman, 1974. Jarrett, H. R.: *Africa* (4th Edn.); MacDonald & Evans (1974). Morgan, W. B., and Pugh, J. C.: *West Africa*; Methuen, 1969. Schwarz, Walter: *Nigeria*; Pall Mall, 1968. Williamson, Grahame, and Payne, W. J. A.: *An Introduction to Animal Husbandry in the Tropics*; Longman, 1969. **130-31** Blakemore, Harold, and Smith, C. T. (Eds.): *Latin America: Geographical Perspectives*; Methuen, 1974. Cole, J. P.: *Latin America: An Economic and Social Geography* (2nd Edn.); Butterworth, 1975. Farley, Rawle: *The Economics of Latin America: Development Problems in Perspective*; Harper & Row, 1973. Gilbert, Alan: *Latin American Development: A Geographical Perspective*; Penguin, 1974. Glade, William P.: *The Latin American Economies: A Study of their Institutional Evolution*; Van Nostrand Reinhold, 1969. Prebisch, Paul: *Change and Development: Latin America's Great Task*; Praeger, 1971. Robinson, H.: *Latin America*; MacDonald & Evans, 1977. **132-33** Beaumont, Peter, Blake, G. H., and Wagstaff, J. M.: *The Middle East: A Geographical Study*; Wiley, 1976. Clawson, Marion, *et al.*: *The Agricultural Potential of the Middle East*; Elsevier, 1971. Walton, K.: *The Arid Zone*; Hutchinson, 1969. **134-35** Fisher, C. A.: *South East Asia*; Methuen, 1966. Fryer, Donald W.: *Emerging South East Asia*; Philip, 1970. Johnson, B. L. C.: *Bangladesh*; Heinemann Educational, 1975. Johnson, B. L. C.: *South Asia*; Heinemann Educational, 1975. Spate, O. H. K., and Learmonth, Andrew: *India, Pakistan and Ceylon*; Methuen, 1972. **136-37** Buchanan, Keith: *The Transformation of the Chinese Earth*; Bell, 1970. Eckstein, Alexander: *China's Economic Revolution*; C.U.P., 1977. Howe, Christopher: *China's Economy: A Basic Guide*; Elek, 1978. **138-41** Dyker, David A.: *The Soviet Economy*; Crosby Lockwood, 1976. Hamilton, F. E. Ian: *Poland's Western and Northern Territories*; O.U.P., 1975. Hamilton, F. E. Ian: *Yugoslavia: Patterns of Economic Activity*; Bell, 1968. Hoffman, George W. (Ed.): *Eastern Europe: Essays in Geographical Problems*; Methuen, 1970. Kaser, Michael C. (Ed.): *Economic Development for Eastern Europe*; Macmillan, 1968. Lydolph, Paul E.: *Geography of the USSR*; Wiley, 1970. Mellor, Roy E. H.: *Comecon: Challenge to the West*; Van Nostrand Reinhold, 1971. Mellor, Roy E. H.: *Eastern Europe: A Geography of the Comecon Countries*; Macmillan, 1975. Pokshishevsky, V.: *Geography of the Soviet*

Union; Central Books, 1974. Shabad, Theodore: *Basic Industrial Resources of the USSR*; Columbia University Press, 1970. Sinanians, S., *et al.*: *Eastern Europe in the 1970s*; Praeger, 1973. Symons, Leslie: *Russian Agriculture: A Geographic Survey*; Bell, 1972. Turnock, David: *Eastern Europe: Studies in Industrial Geography*; Dawson, 1978.

MINERALS

144-45 Bott, M. H. P.: *The Interior of the Earth*; Arnold, 1971. Gass, I. G., *et al.*: *Understanding the Earth: A Reader in the Earth Sciences*; Open University Press, 1971. Holmes, Arthur: *Principles of Physical Geology* (2nd Edn.); Nelson, 1965. Jacobs, J. A.: *The Earth's Core*; Academic Press, 1975. Open University: *The Earth; Its Shape, Internal Structure and Composition*; Open University Press, 1971. Park, C. F., and MacDiarmid, R. A.: *Ore Deposits*; Freeman, 1964. Rankama, K., and Sahama, T. G.: *Geochemistry*; University of Chicago Press, 1960. US National Academy of Sciences: *Resources and Man: A Study and Recommendations*; Freeman, 1969. Windley, B. F.: *The Evolving Continents*; Wiley, 1977. **146-47** Bosson, Rex, and Varon, Benison: *The Mining Industry and the Developing Countries*; O.U.P., 1977. Bugler, Jeremy (Ed.): *Coal: Technology for Britain's Future*; Macmillan, 1976. McDivitt, J. F., and Manners, G.: *Minerals and Men*; Johns Hopkins University Press, 1974. Mikesell, R. F. (Ed.): *Foreign Investment in the Petroleum and Mineral Industries*; Johns Hopkins University Press, 1971. Open University: *The Earth's Physical Resources: Mineral Deposits*; Open University Press, 1974. Park, C. F., and MacDiarmid, R. A.: *Ore Deposits*; Freeman, 1964. Roberts, Willard, *et al.*: *Encyclopaedia of Minerals*; Van Nostrand Reinhold, 1975. Smith, David N., and Wells, Louis T.: *Negotiating Third World Minerals Agreements*; Ballinger, 1976. Warren, Kenneth: *Mineral Resources*; Penguin, 1973. **148-49** Alexander, William, and Street, Arthur: *Metals in the Service of Man* (6th Edn.); Penguin, 1976. Open University: *The Earth's Physical Resources: The Mineral Deposits*; Open University Press, 1974. Park, C. F., and MacDiarmid, R. A.: *Ore Deposits*; Freeman, 1964. US Bureau of Mines: *Mineral Facts and Problems*; US Bureau of Mines, 1976. **150-51** Alexander, William, and Street, Arthur: *Metals in the Service of Man* (6th Edn.); Penguin, 1976. Mikesell, R. F.: *Foreign Investment in Copper Mining*; Johns Hopkins University Press, 1976. Open University: *The Earth's Physical Resources: The Mineral Deposits*; Open University Press, 1974. Park, C. F., and MacDiarmid, R. A.: *Ore Deposits*; Freeman, 1964. Prain, Ronald: *Copper: The Anatomy of an Industry*; Mining Journal Books, 1975. Tucker, A.: *The Toxic Metals*; Pan/Ballantyne, 1972. US Bureau of Mines: *Mineral Facts and Problems*; US Bureau of Mines, 1976. Warren, Kenneth: *Mineral Resources*; Penguin, 1973. **152-53** Alexander, William, and Street, Arthur: *Metals in the Service of Man* (6th Edn.); Penguin, 1976. Open University: *The Earth's Physical Resources: Mineral Deposits*; Open University Press, 1974. US Bureau of Mines: *Mineral Facts and Problems*; US Bureau of Mines, 1976. **154-55** Bank, Hermann: *Precious Stones and Minerals*; Warne, 1970. Gawaine, John: *Diamond Seeker*; Macmillan, 1976. Green, Timothy: *The World of Gold Today*; White Lion, 1974. Hocking, Anthony: *Oppenheimer and Son*; McGraw-Hill, 1974. Metz, Rudolf: *Minerals and Precious Stones*; Collins, 1973. Roberts, Tucker, A.: *The Toxic Metals*; Pan/Ballantyne, 1972. **156-57** Borchert, Hermann, and Muir, R. O.: *Salt Deposits*; Van Nostrand Reinhold, 1964. Jones, W. R.: *Minerals in Industry*; Penguin, 1976. Skinner, B. J.: *Earth Resources*; Prentice-Hall, 1970. **158-61** Blunden, John R.: *Mineral Resources of Britain: A Study in Exploitation and Planning*; Hutchinson, 1975. Open University: *The Earth's Physical Resources: Constructional and Other Bulk Materials*; Open University Press, 1974. Taylor, G. D.: *Materials of Construction*; Longman, 1974. **162-63** Glasby, G. P. (Ed.): *Marine Manganese Deposits*; Elsevier, 1977. Loftas, Tony: *The Last Resource: Man's Exploitation of the Sea*; Penguin, 1973. Luard, Evan: *The Control of the Sea Bed: A New International Issue*; Heinemann, 1974. Mero, John L.: *The Mineral Resources of the Sea*; Elsevier, 1965. US National Academy of Sciences: *Resources and Man: A Study and Recommendations*; Freeman, 1969.

PLANNING FOR TOMORROW

166-67 Brown, Lester R.: *The Twenty-Ninth Day: Accommodating Human Needs and Numbers to the Earth's Resources*; Norton, 1978. Chisholm, Malcolm (Ed.): *Resources for Britain's Future*; Penguin, 1972. Ehrlich, Paul R., *et al.*: *Ecoscience: Population, Resources, Environment*; Freeman, 1977. *Energy Conservation: Ways and Means*; Future Shape of Technology Foundation, 1974. Hayes, Denis: *Energy: The Case for Conservation*; Worldwatch Institute, 1976. Leach, Gerald: *Conservation of Energy, Alternative Energy Sources and their Implications for Environmental Conservation and Future Ways of Life*; International Institute for Environment and Development, 1975. Schumacher, E. F.: *Small is Beautiful: A Study of Economics as if People Mattered*; Sphere, 1974. **168-69** Brown, Lester R.: *The Twenty-Ninth Day: Accommodating Human Needs and Numbers to the Earth's Resources*; Norton, 1978. Cole, John: *The Poor of the Earth*; Macmillan, 1976. Ehrlich, Paul R., *et al.*: *Ecoscience: Population, Resources, Environment*; Freeman, 1977. Lipton, Michael: *Why Poor People Stay Poor: Urban Bias in World Development*; Temple Smith, 1976. Power, Jonathan, and Holenstein, Anne-Marie: *World of Hunger*; Temple Smith, 1975. Ward, Barbara, and Dubos, René: *Only One Earth: The Care and Maintenance of a Small Planet*; Penguin, 1972. **170-77** Armstead, H. C. H.: *Geothermal Energy: Its Past, Present and Future Contributions to the Energy Needs of Man*; Spon, 1978. Carr, Donald E.: *Energy and the Earth Machine*; Norton, 1976. Chapman, Peter: *Fuel's Paradise: Energy Options for Britain*; Penguin, 1975. Foley, Gerald: *The Energy Question*; Penguin, 1976. Foley, Gerald, and Van Buren, E. A. (Eds.): *Nuclear or Not: Choices for Our Energy Future*; Heinemann Educational, 1978. Hammond, A., *et al.*: *Energy and the Future*; American Association for the Advancement of Science, 1973. Hill, Peter, and Vielvoye, Roger: *Energy in Crisis; A Guide to World Oil Supply and Demand and Alternative Resources*; Robert Yeatman, 1974. Hottel, H. C., and Howard, J. B.: *New Energy Technology*; M.I.T. Press, 1972. International Institute for Environment and Development: *An Energy Strategy for the United Kingdom, 1980–2025*; 1978. Ion, D. C.: *Availability of World Energy Resources*; Graham & Trotman, 1975; supplements, 1976 & 1978. Kent, Sir Peter (Ed.): *Energy in the 1980s*; Royal Society, 1974. Leach, Gerald, *et al.*: *A Low Energy Strategy for the UK*; International Institute for Environment and Development, 1978. Lovins, Amory B.: *Soft Energy Paths: Toward a Durable Peace*; Penguin, 1977. Lovins, Amory B.: *World Energy Strategies: Facts, Issues and Options*; Ballinger, 1975. Open University: *The Earth's Physical Resources: Energy Resources*; Open University Press, 1973. OECD Nuclear Energy Agency/International Atomic Energy Agency: *Uranium Resources, Production and Demand*; Organization for Economic Cooperation and Development, 1977. Royal Commission on Environmental Pollution: *Nuclear Power and the Environment*; HMSO, 1976. World Energy Conference: *World Energy Resources, 1985–2020*; IPC Scientific & Technical Press, 1978. Workshop on Alternative Energy Strategies: *Energy: Global Prospects, 1985–2000*; McGraw-Hill, 1977. **178-81** Abelson, Philip H. (Ed.): *Food: Politics, Economics, Nutrition and Research: Readings from 'Science'*; Academic Press, 1975. Allaby, Michael: *World Food Resources: Actual and Potential*; Applied Science, 1977. Buringh, P., *et al.*: *Computation of the Absolute Maximum Food Production of the World*; Netherlands Agricultural University, 1975. Chrispeels, M. J., and Sadava, D.: *Plants, Food and People*; Freeman, 1977. George, Susan: *How the Other Half Dies—The Real Reasons for World Hunger*; Penguin, 1976. McCalla, A. F.: *International Agricultural Research: Potential Impact on World Food Markets and UK Agricultural Strategy*; Centre for Agricultural Strategy, Reading University, 1978. Pirie, N. W.: *Food Resources: Conventional and Novel* (2nd Edn.); Penguin, 1976. Pyke, Magnus: *Synthetic Food*; Murray, 1970. Scientific American: *Food and Agriculture*; Freeman, 1976. Spedding, C. R. W.: *The Biology of Agricultural Systems*; Academic Press, 1975. **182-85** Barnett, Harold J.: *Scarcity and Growth: The Economics of Natural Resource Availability*; Johns Hopkins University Press, 1966. Maddox, John: *The Doomsday Syndrome: An Assault on Pessimism*; Macmillan, 1972. Meadows, D. L., *et al.*: *The Limits to Growth: A Report for the Club of Rome's Project on the Predicament of Mankind*; Earth Island, 1973. US Bureau of Mines: *Mineral Facts and Problems*; US Bureau of Mines, 1976. **186-87** Cole, H. S. D., *et al.*: *Thinking About the Future: A Critique of "The Limits to Growth"*; Chatto & Windus, 1973. Deutsch, Karl W., *et al.*: *Problems of World Modelling: Political and Social Implications*; Ballinger, 1977. Encel, Solomon, and Marstrand, P.: *The Art of Anticipation: Values and Methods in Forecasting*; Martin Robertson, 1975. Leontief, Wassily: *The Future of the World Economy*; United Nations Publications, 1977. Meadows, Donella, *et al.*: *The Limits to Growth: A Report for the Club of Rome's Project on the Predicament of Mankind*; Earth Island, 1973. Mesarovic, Mihajlo, and Pestel, Eduard: *Mankind at the Turning Point: The Second Report to the Club of Rome*; Hutchinson, 1975. **188-89** Burton, John: *World Society*; C.U.P., 1972. Dolman, Antony, and Van Ettinger, Jan (Eds.): *Partners in Tomorrow: Strategies for a New International Order*; Dutton, 1978. Kahn, Herman, *et al.*: *The Next 200 Years: A Scenario for America and the World*; Associated Business Programmes, 1977. Mendlovitz, Saul H.: *On the Creation of Just World Order*; North Holland, 1975. Sprout, Harold, and Margaret: *Towards a Politics of the Planet Earth*; Van Nostrand Reinhold, 1972. Sterling, R. W.: *Macropolitics: International Relations in a Global Society*; Knopf, 1974. **190-91** Claude, Inis: *Swords into Plowshares*; University of London Press, 1964. Goodrich, Leland M.: *The United Nations in a Changing World*; Columbia University Press, 1974. Gosivic, Branislav: *UNCTAD: Conflict and Compromise*; Sijthoff, 1972. Hinsley, F. H.: *Power and the Pursuit of Peace*; C.U.P., 1967. Luard, Evan: *International Agencies: The Emerging Framework of Interdependence*; Macmillan, 1977.

PICTURE CREDITS

Credits read from top to bottom, and from left to right on each page. Images which run over the left- and the right-hand page will be credited on the left-hand page only.

1 Dr Georg Gerster from John Hillelson. **2** Dr Georg Gerster from John Hillelson. **4** Dr Georg Gerster from John Hillelson. **6** Paolo Koch. **8** Dr Georg Gerster from John Hillelson. **10** George Hall/Susan Griggs. **12** Robert Harding Associates. **13** Alan Hutchison; Robert Harding Associates; Paul Brierley; Mary Fisher/Colorific!; Paolo Koch; Robert Harding Associates. **16** Keystone; Keystone; Camera Press; Camera Press; Keystone. **17** Keystone. **18** Dr Georg Gerster from John Hillelson. **22** NASA. **23** © Controller HMSO 1979. **24** IBM Corporation Federal Systems Division; Westinghouse; NASA; Plessey Radar Ltd/Hunting Surveys and Consultants Ltd; Plessey Radar Ltd/Hunting Surveys and Consultants Ltd. **25** Plessey Radar Ltd/Hunting Surveys and Consultants Ltd; Plessey Radar Ltd/Hunting Surveys and Consultants Ltd; Plessey Radar Ltd/Hunting Surveys and Consultants Ltd; Seismograph Service Ltd. **26** British Crown Copyright, Aerial Photography Unit, Agricultural Development and Advisory Service, Ministry of Agriculture, Fisheries and Food; NASA; NASA; NASA. **27** J. Douglas Heyland/Canadian Wildlife Service; NASA; NASA; NASA; US Geological Survey. **28** Camera Press. **30** Camera Press. **32** Alan Hutchison. **34** John Moss/Colorific! **36** Mary Fisher/Colorific! **38** Ray Witlin/World Bank. **42** Dr Georg Gerster from John Hillelson. **44** Alan Hutchison. **45** Paul Harrison; Paul Harrison; ZEFA. **46** Alan Hutchison; Alan Hutchison; ZEFA. **47** Adam Woolfitt/Susan Griggs. **48** Alan Hutchison; Alan Hutchison; WHO; Oxfam. **49** WHO; *The Sunday Times*, London. **50** Fairey Surveys Ltd; Carl Purcell/Colorific!; Agfa Infrared Systems; Horst Munzig/Susan Griggs; Alan Hutchison; **52** Picturepoint; Anthony Howarth/*Daily Telegraph* Colour Library; Carl Purcell/Colorific! **53** Robert Harding Associates; Paul Harrison. **54** Syntex Laboratories Inc; Mark Edwards/IPPF; Margaret Murray; Paul Harrison; Robert Harding Associates; Paul Harrison. **55** Paul Harrison; Richard and Sally Greenhill. **56** Ernst Haas/Magnum. **58** Terence Spencer/Colorific! **60** Adam Woolfitt/Susan Griggs; Roger Malloch/Magnum. **61** David Moore/Colorific!; CEGB; Topham. **62** British Steel Corporation; Mike Fear; Mike Fear; Mike Fear; Mike Fear; Mike Fear; Robert Harding Associates. **63** Australian News and Information Service. **64** National Coal Board; Combustion Systems Ltd. **65** Paolo Koch; Linda Bartlett/Colorific!; Mary Fisher/Colorific! **66** Picturepoint; Anthony Howarth/Susan Griggs; John Moss/Colorific! **67** Robert Harding Associates. **68** Tom Nebbia/Aspect; Eddie Adams/Colorific!; Robert Harding Associates; ZEFA. **70** Eddie Adams Colorific! **71** Paolo Koch; Shell Photo Service; British Petroleum. **72** Patrick Ward/*Daily Telegraph* Colour Library. **73** British Petroleum; Ormond Gieli/Camera Press. **74** ZEFA; Paolo Koch. **76** Paolo Koch; Mats Wibe Lund; G. R. Roberts. **78** Paolo Koch; Paolo Koch; UK Atomic Energy Authority; UK Atomic Energy Authority. **80-81** UK Atomic Energy Authority. **82** Y. Jeanmougin/Viva; Associated Press. **84** Reflejo/Susan Griggs; Paolo Koch. **85** Paolo Koch; Costis Stambolis. **86** ZEFA; Photothèque Electricité de France; © Pixfeatures/Stern. **87** G. R. Roberts. **88** Dr Georg Gerster from John Hillelson. **90** Alan Hutchison; Robert Harding Associates. **91** Alan Hutchison; Jerry Wachter/Colorific!; Robert Harding Associates. **92** George Hall/Susan Griggs; NOAA; NOAA. **93** Alan Hutchison; Sigurgeir Jonasson/Frank W. Lane. **94** Alan Hutchison; Robert Harding Associates; Richard and Sally Greenhill. **95** Peter Fraenkel; John Moss/Colorific!; Paolo Koch. **96** Alan Hutchison; ZEFA; Robert Harding Associates; Mireille Vautier; Alan Hutchison. **97** Mireille Vautier. **98** Paolo Koch; Robert Harding Associates; David Moore/Colorific! **99** Lee Battaglia/Colorific! **100** James Pickerell/Colorific!; Novosti; ZEFA; Robert Harding Associates. **101** Novosti. **102** Douglas Botting; Robert Harding Associates; Robert Harding Associates. **103** Robert Harding Associates. **104** Robert Harding Associates; ZEFA; ZEFA; Alan Hutchison; ZEFA. **105** ZEFA; Dunlop; ZEFA; Terence Le Goubin/Colorific! **106** Robert Harding Associates; Novosti; Robert Harding Associates; Novosti. **107** Robert Harding Associates; C. Wall/Behaviour-Controlling Chemicals Group, Rothamsted Experimental Station. **108** Robert Harding Associates; Alan Hutchison; Alan Hutchison; G. R. Roberts; Tony Carr/Colorific! **109** Paul Conklin/Colorific!; Robert Harding Associates. **110** Robert Harding Associates; ZEFA; Tony Morrison. **111** ZEFA; Photri; Robert Harding Associates. **112** Mireille Vautier; Richard and Sally Greenhill; ZEFA; Werner Braun. **113** NASA. **114** Mary Fisher/Colorific!; T. Lucas & Co Ltd; T. Lucas & Co Ltd. **115** ZEFA; ZEFA; Tropical Products Institute; Tropical Products Institute. **116** Photri. **117** G. R. Roberts. **118** Grant Heilman; G. R. Roberts; Grant Heilman; Mary Fisher/Colorific! **119** ZEFA; G. R. Roberts. **120** Topham. **121** Danish Agricultural Producers; Penny Tweedie/Colorific!; Picture-point; Robert Harding Associates; ZEFA. **122** Paolo Koch; G. R. Roberts; Paolo Koch. **123** Paolo Koch; Reflejo/Susan Griggs; Robert Harding Associates; Tor Eigeland/Susan Griggs. **124-25** G. R. Roberts. **126** Mireille Vautier. **127** René Burri/Magnum. **128** Alan Hutchison; Paul Harrison; Alan Hutchison. **129** Robert Harding Associates; Robert Harding Associates; Alan Hutchison. **130** Sullivan & Rogers/Bruce Coleman; Tony Morrison. **131** Mireille Vautier; Douglas Botting; John Moss/Colorific!; Abril Press. **132** Anthony Howarth/Susan Griggs; Tor Eigeland/Susan Griggs. **133** Tor Eigeland/Susan Griggs; Kay Muldoon/Colorific! **134** Robert Harding Associates. **135** ZEFA; Alain Compost/Bruce Coleman; Paul Harrison. **136** P. S. Ibbotson; Richard and Sally Greenhill; P. S. Ibbotson. **137** Colourviews; Richard and Sally Greenhill. **138** Novosti. **140** Novosti; Novosti; ZEFA. **141** Dr F. W. Carter; Bo Bojesen; Nick Birch; ZEFA. **142** Dr Georg Gerster from John Hillelson. **146** Paolo Koch; Paolo Koch; Paolo Koch; Linda Bartlett/Colorific! **147** Paolo Koch; Freeport Minerals Company. **148** British Steel Corporation; George

Hall/Susan Griggs; Farrell Grehan/Susan Griggs. **149** Topham. **150** Jon Wyand; Mike Fear. **151** David Moore/Colorific!; Photo RTZ; Mike Fear. **152** Ian Yeomans/Susan Griggs. **153** Mary Fisher/Colorific!; Penny Tweedie/Colorific!; Mike Fear; Paul Brierley. **154** Anthony Howarth/*Daily Telegraph* Colour Library; Terence Spencer/Colorific!; ZEFA/Photri; John Moss/Colorific! **155** Paul Brierley. **156** Paolo Koch; BP Chemicals Ltd; Tony Morrison. **157** Paolo Koch; Paul Brierley. **158** Amey Roadstone Corporation; Paolo Koch; P. Morris. **159** Mary Fisher/Colorific!; Stewart Galloway/Susan Griggs; Bob Gibbons/Ardea. **160** ZEFA; Redland. **161** Terence Spencer/Colorific!; Asbestos Information Centre. **162** Alan Archer; Robert Harding Associates. **163** Photo RTZ. **164** Dr Georg Gerster from John Hillelson.
Retouching by Sally Slight.

ILLUSTRATION CREDITS
12 Alan Suttie. **14** Mike Saunders. **15** Alun Jones; Studio Briggs. **20** Chris Forsey. **22** Chris Forsey. **23** Mike Saunders. **24** Chris Forsey. **25** Alan Suttie. **26** Alan Suttie. **28-29** Venner Artists. **30-31** Mike Saunders. **33** Arka Cartographics. **34** Tri Art; Studio Briggs. **35** Venner Artists. **36** Arka Cartographics; Ralph Stobart. **37** Arka Cartographics. **38-39** Venner Artists. **41** Alun Jones. **44** Arka Cartographics. **45** Mike Saunders; Arka Cartographics. **46** Arka Cartographics. **47** Mike Saunders. **48** Mike Saunders. **49** Chris Forsey; Mike Saunders. **50** Alan Suttie.

51 Arka Cartographics. **52** Arka Cartographics. **54** Arka Cartographics. **55** Mike Saunders. **59** Mike Saunders. **61** Mike Saunders; Arka Cartographics. **62** Chris Forsey. **63** Arka Cartographics. **64** Alan Suttie. **66-67** Mike Saunders. **68** Mike Saunders. **69** Mike Saunders; Mike Saunders; Arka Cartographics. **71** Arka Cartographics; Mike Saunders. **72** Mike Saunders. **73** Mike Saunders; Arka Cartographics. **74** Alan Suttie; Arka Cartographics. **75** Alan Suttie; Arka Cartographics. **76** Mike Saunders. **77** Chris Forsey; Arka Cartographics; Mike Saunders. **78** Chris Forsey. **79** Alan Suttie. **80** Mike Saunders; Alan Suttie. **81** Mike Saunders. **83** Arka Cartographics; Mike Saunders. **84** Mike Saunders. **85** Arka Cartographics; Mike Saunders. **86** Elaine Keenan/Aziz Khan. **87** Elaine Keenan/Aziz Khan; Mike Saunders. **90** Arka Cartographics; Alan Suttie. **91** Alan Suttie. **92** Arka Cartographics. **93** Arka Cartographics; Mike Saunders; Mike Saunders. **94** Chris Forsey. **97** Mike Saunders; Morgan Sendall. **98** Tri Art; Mike Saunders. **99** Arka Cartographics. **100** Arka Cartographics; Chris Forsey. **101** Mike Saunders. **102** Mike Saunders. **103** Arka Cartographics; Mike Saunders. **104** Arka Cartographics. **105** Mike Saunders. **106** Morgan Sendall. **107** Tri Art. **109** Arka Cartographics; Studio Briggs; Arka Cartographics. **110** Elaine Keenan/Aziz Khan; Mike Saunders. **111** Mike Saunders. **113** Mike Saunders; Chris Forsey. **114** Arka Cartographics. **115** Arka Cartographics. **116** Rand McNally/Arka Cartographics. **117** Mike Saunders. **118-19** Mike Saunders. **120** Rand McNally/Arka Cartographics, Mike Saunders.

122 Arka Cartographics; Alan Suttie; Alan Suttie. **124** Rand McNally/Arka Cartographics; Peter Hayman; Chris Forsey. **125** Rand McNally/Arka Cartographics. **126** Chris Forsey; Rand McNally/Arka Cartographics; Chris Forsey; Rand McNally/Arka Cartographics. **127** Chris Forsey; Rand McNally/Arka Cartographics. **128** Rand McNally/Arka Cartographics. **129** Mike Saunders; Mike Saunders; Arka Cartographics. **130** Rand McNally/Arka Cartographics. **131** Arka Cartographics; Mike Saunders. **132** Rand McNally/Arka Cartographics; Chris Forsey. **133** Arka Cartographics. **134** Rand McNally/Arka Cartographics. **135** Alan Suttie. **136** Rand McNally/Arka Cartographics; Mike Saunders. **137** Arka Cartographics. **138** Rand McNally/Arka Cartographics; Arka Cartographics. **141** Mike Saunders. **144** Mike Saunders; Alan Suttie. **145** Mike Saunders; Chris Forsey; Chris Forsey. **146** Alan Suttie. **147** Arka Cartographics; Alan Suttie. **148** Mike Saunders. **149** Arka Cartographics; Mike Saunders. **150** Arka Cartographics; Mike Saunders. **151** Arka Cartographics; Mike Saunders. **152** Arka Cartographics; Mike Saunders; Mike Saunders. **154** Mike Saunders. **155** Arka Cartographics; Mike Saunders. **156** Studio Briggs. **157** Arka Cartographics. **158** Ralph Stobart. **159** Ralph Stobart. **160-61** Tri Art. **162** Arka Cartographics; Mike Saunders. **163** Mike Saunders. **166** Studio Briggs. **168** Alun Jones. **170** Alun Jones. **178** Alun Jones. **182** Alun Jones. **186** Alan Suttie/Mike Saunders. **187** Studio Briggs. **188-89** Studio Briggs. **190-91** Studio Briggs.

ACKNOWLEDGMENTS
A great many individuals, organizations and institutions have given invaluable help and advice during the preparation of this book. A number of books, periodicals and technical journals have also been consulted. The publishers wish to extend their thanks to them all, and in particular the following:

Animal Agriculture by H. H. Cole and M. Ronning;
Annual of Direction of Trade Statistics compiled by the IMF;
Association of Light Alloy Refiners Limited;
Atlas of World Population History by Colin McEvedy and Richard Jones;
Availability of World Energy Resources by D. C. Ion;
Birds Eye Foods Limited;
Brazilian Embassy;
1978 Britannica Book of the Year Encyclopaedia Britannica, Inc.;
British Petroleum Chemicals International Limited;
British Petroleum Company Limited Public Affairs and Information Department;
British Steel Corporation;
Arthur Butterfield;
Central Electricity Generating Board Press and Publicity Office;
Ceres, the magazine of the FAO;
Geoffrey Chandler;
Changing Contraceptive Practices in the US, Married Couples, 1965 and 1975 compiled by the Population Reference Bureau;
Chemical Industries Association Limited;
Coal Conversion Processes for the Future by L. Grainger;
A Compact Geography of the Netherlands compiled by the Information and Documentation Centre for the Geography of the Netherlands;
Constructional and other Bulk Materials the Open University Press;
D. Dancy of the Public Relations Department, Culham Laboratory, Oxfordshire;
Department of Energy Press Office;
Dougal Dixon;
Tony Duncan;
The Economist;
Ecoscience: Population, Resources, Environment by Paul R. Ehrlich, Anne H. Ehrlich and John P. Holdren;
The Effect of Fuel Price Increases on Energy Intensiveness of Freight Transport by W. E. Mooz;
Anne-Marie Ehrlich;
Encyclopaedia Britannica (15th edn) Encyclopaedia Britannica, Inc.;
Energy Book 1: Natural Sources and Backyard Application edited by John Prenis;
The Energy Question by Gerald Foley;
Energy Resources the Open University Press;
The Europa Yearbook: A World Survey Europa Publications Ltd.;
Exploring: Remote Sensing by Stephen Pizzey;
FAO Production Yearbook;
FAO Trade Yearbook;
FAO Yearbook of Fishery Statistics;
Financial Times;
Financing the International Petroleum Industry by N. A. White et al.;
Food: Politics, Economics, Nutrition and Research edited by Philip H. Abelson;
French Embassy;
Dr. J. D. Garnish of the Energy Technology Support Unit, Oxfordshire;
Geographical Magazine;
Gold 77 by Christopher Glynn;
Goode's World Atlas Rand McNally and Company;
The Guardian;
Handbook of International Trade and Development Statistics Supplement compiled by UNCTAD;

Health and Safety Statistics 1975 Health and Safety Executive, Government Statistical Services;
Institute of Petroleum Information Service;
Institution of Mining and Metallurgy;
Intermediate Technology for Food Utilisation in the Developing Countries by J. T. Worgan in *Proceedings of the International Food Industries Congress* May 1975;
International Iron and Steel Institute, Brussels;
International Planned Parenthood Federation;
International Solar Energy Society UK Section;
Japanese Embassy;
Mr. D. Kovan of *Nuclear Engineering International*;
Lead Development Association;
The Limits to Growth A report for The Club of Rome's Project on the Predicament of Mankind, by Donella H. Meadows, Dennis L. Meadows, Jørgen Randers, William W. Behrens III, a Potomac Associates book published by Universe Books, New York, 1972;
David Macfadyen;
McGraw-Hill Encyclopaedia of Energy McGraw-Hill Book Company;
J. H. C. Maple of the Public Relations Department, Culham Laboratory, Oxfordshire;
Metal Content of Ferromanganese Deposits of the Oceans by D. R. Horn, B. M. Horn and M. N. Delach;
Metal Statistics Metallgesellschaft A. G.;
Methods for Estimating the Volume and Energy Demand of Freight Transport by D. P. Tihansky;
The Military Balance International Institute for Strategic Studies;
Minerals Facts and Problems US Bureau of Mines;
Mining Magazine;
Patricia Napier of the South Atlantic Fisheries Committee;
National Coal Board;
New Internationalist;
The Next 200 Years by Herman Kahn, William Board and Leon Martel;
Non-Fuel Minerals and Foreign Policy by Phillip Crowson;
Nuclear Engineering International;
Nuclear Power by Walter Patterson;
Ocean Energy;
Ocean Manganese Nodules: Metal Value and Mining Sites by D. R. Horn, B. M. Horn and M. N. Delach;
Oil and Gas Journal;
Only One Earth by Barbara Ward and René Dubos;
Open University;
Organization for Economic Cooperation and Development, Paris;
Christopher D. Parker;
People, the magazine of the International Planned Parenthood Federation;
People Populating by D. Llewellyn-Jones;
Petroleum Economist;
The Politics and Responsibility of the North American Bread Basket by Lester R. Brown;
The Politics of Scarcity: Resource Conflicts in International Relations by Philip Connelly and Robert Perlman;
Population and Affluence: Growing Pressures on World Food Resources by Lester R. Brown;
Population Reference Bureau;
Rio Tinto Zinc Corporation Limited;
The Role of Ruminants in Support of Man Winrock International Livestock Research and Training Center, Morrilton, Arkansas, USA;
Save The Children Fund;
Richard Shaw;
Shell International Petroleum Company Limited;
Shell Transport and Trading Company Limited;
South African Embassy;
The Statesman's Yearbook edited by John Paxton;
Steel HMSO;

Professor Susan Strange of the London School of Economics;
Swedish Embassy;
Dian Taylor;
Thinking About the Future: A Critique of "Limits to Growth" edited by H. S. D. Cole, Christopher Freeman et al.;
Time;
The Times;
The Times Atlas of the World Times Books in collaboration with John Bartholomew and Sons Limited;
Total Oil Great Britain Limited;
Jack Tresidder;
UN Demographic Yearbook;
UN Economic Bulletin of Europe;
UN Energy Yearbook;
UN Statistical Yearbook;
Uranium: Resources, Production and Demand Organization for Economic Cooperation and Development;
US Mineral Resources edited by D. A. Brobst and W. P. Pratt;
United Kingdom Atomic Energy Authority, Information Services Branch;
Frances M. Vale of the Rio Tinto Zinc Corporation Limited;
Westminister City Central Reference Library;
World Bank;
World Military Expenditure and Arms Transfers compiled by the United States Arms Control and Disarmament Agency;
World Subsea Mineral Resources by V. E. McKelvey and Frank F. M. Wang;
Worldwatch Institute;
Yearbook of World Armaments and Disarmaments compiled by the Stockholm International Peace Research Institute.

Diagrams on pages 26, 64 (centre) and 22 (bottom right) are based on information used with the permission of the Controller of Her Majesty's Stationery Office, London.

The map on page 63 is based on information which is British Crown Copyright and was used with the permission of the Director, Institute of Geological Sciences, London.

The publishers wish to extend their special thanks to *Scientific American* for the information contained in the following diagrams:
pages 20-1: from *The Water Cycle* by H. L. Penman, *The Carbon Cycle* by Bert Bolin and *The Nitrogen Cycle* by C. C. Delwiche. Copyright © (September 1970) by Scientific American, Inc. All rights reserved.
page 24: from *Side-looking Airborne Radar* by Homer Jensen et al. Copyright © (October 1977) by Scientific American, Inc. All rights reserved.
page 47 (bottom): from *The Migrations of Human Populations* by Kingsley Davis. Copyright © (September 1974) by Scientific American, Inc. All rights reserved.
page 48 (centre): from *Food and Agriculture* by Sterling Wortman. Copyright © (September 1976) by Scientific American, Inc. All rights reserved.
page 94 (bottom right): from *The Case of the Missing Sunspots* by John A. Eddy. Copyright © (May 1977) by Scientific American, Inc. All rights reserved.
page 96 (bottom): from *Underground Reservoirs to Control the Water Cycle* by Robert P. Ambroggi. Copyright © by Scientific American, Inc. All rights reserved.

The publishers would also like to thank *New Scientist*, London, the weekly review of science and technology, for the information contained in the diagram on page 81 (top right).

Mitchell Beazley Publishers has made every effort to trace the original sources of all the research cited in this book. Any source inadvertently omitted and subsequently brought to the publishers' attention will be acknowledged in all future editions.